BASEBALL:

THE GOLDEN AGE

BASEBALL:

BASEBALL

THE GOLDEN AGE • HAROLD SEYMOUR, Ph.D.

OXFORD UNIVERSITY PRESS
NEW YORK   OXFORD

Oxford University Press

Oxford   New York   Toronto
Delhi   Bombay   Calcutta   Madras   Karachi
Petaling Jaya   Singapore   Honk Kong   Tokyo
Nairobi   Dar es Salaam   Cape Town
Melbourne   Auckland

and associated companies in
Berlin   Ibadan

First published in 1971 by Oxford University Press, Inc.,
200 Madison Avenue, New York, New York 10016

First issued as an Oxford University Press paperback, 1989

Oxford is a registered trademark of Oxford University Press

Grateful acknowledgment is made for permission to reprint from the following:
You Can't Go Home Again by THOMAS WOLFE,
Harper & Row, Publishers, Inc.
The American League Story by LEE ALLEN,
Hill & Wang, Inc.

Library of Congress Cataloging-in-Publication Data

Seymour, Harold, 1910–
     Baseball / Harold Seymour.
       p.   cm.
     "First published in 1960[–1971] by Oxford University Press"—
V. 1–2, t.p. verso.
     Includes bibliographies and indexes.
     Contents: [1] The early years—[2] The golden age.
     1. Baseball—United States—History. I: Title.
     GV863.A1S48   1989   89–3406
     796.357'0973—dc20   CIP
ISBN 0–19–501403–0
ISBN 0–19–505913–1 (Pbk.)

10 9 8 7 6 5 4 3 2

Printed in the United States of America

PREFACE TO THE 1989 EDITION

The publication of this paperback edition of the second volume of my history of baseball will, I trust, reward the patience of those readers who have been trying to get a copy of it since the first edition sold out. Those who expected a long overdue third volume to have appeared by now and have written me asking about it will, I hope, continue to be patient.

On checking this book for the purpose of bringing it up to date, I find that for the most part the changes that were needed involved playing records, since old records have been broken or matched by contemporary players, and since by industrious checking statisticians have discovered discrepancies in old critical records and thus been able to alter them. I am glad to incorporate such changes in the paperback edition of this book and to acknowledge the work of statisticians and other researchers.

I am also grateful for the appreciative audience this book has found among journalists, historians, and fans, and for its having been widely recognized as the second volume of the premier work on the history of baseball, the basic reference in its field for librarians, speechmakers, and columnists.

Since the publication of this book sports historians, sociologists, and physical education specialists have explored the topics treated here in more detail. "On all great subjects much remains to be said," Macaulay remarked. But the new information these researchers have uncovered does not alter the basic description of a significant era in the development of America's national game.

As for those few who have cavilled at my work or used parts of it without crediting me, I can only say with Jonathan Swift, "I never wonder to see men wicked, but I often wonder to see them not ashamed."

Keene, N. H.   H.S.
October 1988

BASEBALL has long been a special game in America. Well before the turn of the century it was already known as the American National Game. Once a simple pastime for boys, it evolved in the nineteenth century into an amateur sport of gentlemen and then into a commercialized spectator amusement operated by promoters and played by professionals within a nationwide, monopolistic structure called Organized Baseball. Volume I of this history, *Baseball: The Early Years,* traced the evolution of baseball and its impact upon American society from its origin down to 1903, when the basic organizational structure of the professional leagues that was to prevail for half a century was established.

This second volume continues the story from 1903 through 1930. These first three decades of the twentieth century were in many respects a golden age for professional baseball. Despite a costly trade war, a World Series scandal, and other vicissitudes, the baseball industry in this spacious era consolidated its position, with the blessing of the United States Supreme Court; overall attendance and profits increased, new steel and concrete stadiums arose in place of the earlier wooden grandstands, the annual World Series became a national institution, and such new heroes as Christy Mathewson, Ty Cobb, and Babe Ruth won the acclaim of the public and press. Probably at no other time did baseball enjoy a stronger emotional grip upon Americans.

This volume places major emphasis upon the history of the professional structure. Certain other aspects of baseball that are dealt with incidentally will be treated more fully in a third book that will carry the story forward to the present. For example, after careful consideration I have deferred discussion of the important and long-neglected role of black Americans in baseball to the next volume, where it can be given the attention it deserves. Blacks had little impact upon Organized Baseball until after World War II. The present volume, like the first one, omits footnotes, since they inhibit the general reader, for whom the book is primarily intended. The chief sources of information are indicated, however, in a bibliographical note.

This book contains no foreword, testimony, or imprimatur either by a member of the baseball establishment untutored in history or by a professional historian unversed in baseball, and none has been sought. The work stands on its own, a product of a lifetime interest and experience in baseball combined with training as a professional historian. In the world of baseball I served as batboy for three summers at Ebbets Field in Brooklyn in the 1920's, played high school and college ball, coached amateur and semi-pro teams, umpired, and scouted unofficially ("bird-dogged") for two major-league clubs. I have talked with and seen in action most of the players mentioned in the text and interviewed many of them after their playing careers were over. In the academic world I did graduate work in history under the direction of Professor Paul W. Gates at Cornell University, where I prepared the first doctoral dissertation ever written on baseball, a study which I later revised as Volume I of this history and the first full-scale scholarly work on the subject.

No work of this scope is accomplished without assistance, and I gratefully acknowledge the help and kindness of many, particularly the American Council of Learned Societies for a grant-in-aid of research, and staff members of the New York, Boston, and Chicago Public Libraries, the Social Law Library of Boston, and the municipal Archives and Records Center of New York City. I am also grateful to my friend, the late Lee Allen, former historian of the National Baseball Hall of Fame and Museum at Cooperstown, New York, for giving me permission to examine the Herrmann Papers and his own notes; to George Toporcer, former major-league player and executive, for placing his manuscript material and scrapbooks at my disposal and for the lengthy discussions and correspondence with him about baseball; to Ben DeMott, who supplied me with much information about his experience in the major leagues; to J. G. Taylor Spink, former editor of *Sporting News*, baseball's trade paper, for providing the opportunity for research in his office and other courtesies during my visits to St. Louis; and to Laura Weber Haywood, one of my former students, for tabulating some statistical material and performing other chores. Finally, I express gratitude to my wife, Dorothy Zander Seymour, who not only contributed her knowledge and professional skills to all phases of the work but exercised such patience with the author as to make Job seem like a chronic complainer by comparison.

Bush League Farm   H.S.
West Newbury, Massachusetts

CONTENTS

PART FOUR · THE TARNISHED IMAGE

PART FIVE · THE CZARIST REGIME

PART ONE

THE RULE OF THE TRIUMVIRS

1

THE NATIONAL COMMISSION

A STRANGE help-wanted ad appeared in a New York newspaper in 1903. It asked for a boy who had never seen a baseball game and did not know the difference between first and third base. Struck by this unlikely request, the Washington *Post* commented that if such a youngster could be found, he would be fit only to "crawl off somewhere and die" and become a subject for some "bugologist's" experiment.

The reaction of the *Post* reflected the prominent place held by baseball in American life early in this century. It was taken for granted that every boy was acquainted with the game, because baseball was part of the heritage of American boys. They played it on city lots and open fields all over the country. Carl Sandburg's boyhood experience could have been that of any lad in the United States.

> On many a summer day I played base ball starting at eight in the morning running home at noon for a quick meal and again with fielding and batting till it was too dark to see the ball. These were times when my head seemed empty of everything but baseball names and figures. I could name the leading teams and the tail enders in the National League and the American Association. I could name the players who led in batting and fielding and the pitchers who had won the most games. And I had my opinions about who was better than anybody else in the national game.

As Zane Grey put it, "Every boy likes base-ball, and if he doesn't he's not a boy."

When these boys grew up they did not give up baseball. They clung to their early love and relived their boyhood days vicariously by watching the professionals at the ball parks, reading the sports pages, and discussing the game earnestly and often heatedly in barber shops and other places where men gathered. In other words,

American men were what James T. Farrell later called them, a nation of frustrated ball players. Even those who were less than rabidly interested in the game sometimes pretended to be because it was "the thing to do."

Thus baseball was more than a game for boys in America. It was part of adult society too. Its terminology infiltrated the language. It became the theme of a growing sub-literature, and songs were written about it. Newspapers, sporting-goods manufacturers, railroads, hotels, and other businesses found they had a stake in its success. It was equated with Americanism, democracy, and the health and well-being of the young and old. Morgan Bulkeley, onetime National League president, even recommended the game as an antidote to revolution:

> There is nothing which will help quicker and better to amalgamate the foreign born, and those born of foreign parents in this country, than to give them a little good bringing up in the good old-fashioned game of Base Ball. They don't have things of that kind on the other side of the ocean, and many spend their hours fussing around in conspiring and hatching up plots when they should be out in the open improving their lungs.

In short, baseball was ingrained in the American psyche. Its importance in the first decades of the twentieth century was astonishing. "Every city, town, and village in America has its ball team," observed the St. Louis *Globe and Commercial Advertiser* in 1905. "We have five seasons," remarked another observer, "spring, summer, autumn, winter, and the baseball season." Why did the game have such a strong grip on the public? Perhaps Zane Grey's explanation is as good as any: it fulfilled the American need for expression because it was open and manly, and full of risks, surprises, and glorious climaxes.

But it was the professional clubs that towered over the baseball scene and set its tone. It was they who determined the playing rules, exhibited the most artistic play, and received most of the newspaper space devoted to the game. Interest was particularly focused on the two major-league pennant races, climaxed with the annual World Series between the winners. Fans commonly got carried away by these baseball events at the expense of more serious affairs:

> Who cares which politician leads the bank?
> Who cares who'll be the coming White House tenant?

> We only know the season's open, and
> We know our club is going to win the pennant.

The professional clubs provided amusement mainly for the masses. In fact, among the wealthy and middle classes there still lurked the notion that baseball and baseball playing were lowbrow. Sensitive to this attitude, the baseball operators and sportswriters were at pains, almost to the point of protesting too much, to give assurance that people of all types, occupations, and classes patronized the game. They emphasized that not only laborers turned out but also merchants, members of the learned professions, the "hot-house social butterfly," and the "grave minister of the gospel." John T. Brush, owner of the New York Giants, boasted that among his season boxholders were members of the same class that purchased boxes at the Metropolitan Opera House, and *Spalding's Guide* noted increasing patronage among "that more conservative social element, which it has always been the effort of the higher class base ball club owners to reach."

A growing number of women were coming out to the ball parks as well. Anybody, said one of these female devotees, with "any real blood in her veins cannot help being a fan," because "being a true American and being a fan are synonymous." A magazine picture of a young couple at a ball park, with the husband carrying their child, was captioned, "Even if they have to take the baby." Many Negroes were reported becoming avid fans. Foreigners also attended. *Spalding's Guide for 1912* claimed that foreign-born spectators from seventeen different countries were observed at a game in New York. A number of well-known actors, including George M. Cohan, were regular patrons. Those who could not go to see the professionals followed their exploits in the sports pages. They might never have seen the professional stars, but they knew all about them.

However much the baseball people desired the approval of the wealthy and middle classes, they nevertheless were keen to maintain their association with the average man. People who sat in the bleachers—the lowest-priced section of the stands, unprotected from the sun—were traditionally celebrated as a special breed comprising the truest and best-informed fans of all. Sportswriters also liked to harp on the old democracy-in-action theme, describing the bank president or the stout prelate shedding his usually serious mien to enjoy the game with the crowd. The writers told of Supreme Court Justices and cabinet members rubbing elbows with government clerks at Washington games and discussing baseball with porters and bartenders. Sergeants-at-arms were said to hunt through the grandstand for Congressmen in order to fill a quorum in the House, or for Senators needed at a committee meeting. Presidents and Vice-Presidents, rejoiced one reporter, stripped to their shirtsleeves and drank pop with the multitude in the stands.

It is true that, beginning with William Howard Taft, Presidents have rarely missed the opportunity to become just "plain folks" by throwing out the first ball on opening day in Washington. Some of them even enjoyed baseball. Taft genuinely liked the game, having played it as an amateur in his youth, and during his presidency he attended a number of major-league games. Woodrow Wilson, as a boy in Augusta, Georgia, organized and played second base for the Light Foot Base Ball Club, and as President he was interested enough to travel to Philadelphia to see one of the 1915 World Series games. Warren G. Harding had not only played ball around his home town of Marion, Ohio, but later owned the minor-league franchise there. Oddly, Theodore Roosevelt, one President who might have been expected to be a baseball enthusiast, did not care about it. That Taft's successors have found it politic to signify some interest in baseball, if only by performing the opening-day ritual of throwing out the first ball, further attests to the depth of the game's penetration into American society.

At the apex of the nationwide professional structure that dominated the game after the turn of the century were two major leagues, the old National and the newly formed American. A host of minor leagues, classified according to quality, completed the structure. An intricate set of rules and agreements between and within the various leagues, known as "baseball law," regulated the entire industry, binding it together into a vertically integrated combine known as "Organized Baseball." At the core of these rules were a number of restrictive practices that shaped the government and economics of the business. Two of these in particular formed the bedrock of the entire edifice: the "reserve clause" and "territorial rights."

A singular part of the contract between the baseball clubs and their employees was the reserve clause. It gave the club an exclusive and perpetual option on the player's services. Furthermore, every club in Organized Baseball agreed not to employ or try to employ any player reserved by any other club. They also agreed not to play any team that employed a player who had broken the reserve clause, or even to allow their ball parks to be used by such a team. Their agreement not to compete with each other for players enabled the employers to exercise monopsony control—that is, a buyer's monopoly—over their men.

The reserve clause of this unique labor contract, which has since been modified, has been subjected to intermittent criticism ever since it was first instituted in 1879. Arguments in support of it have ranged from the plausible to the preposterous. The classic defense of the reserve * rests upon the assertion that it is necessary and reasonable to limit competition for players' services. Otherwise the wealthiest clubs would corral the best men and thereby destroy the industry by making a mockery of competition on the playing field. Evidence of what would happen, runs the argument, can be found in the large number of clubs that collapsed in the era prior to the inception of the reserve device.

Those who disagree with this view deny that without the reserve all the best players would necessarily gravitate to the wealthiest clubs. They reason that these clubs would reach a point of diminishing returns, when they would no longer find it desirable or profitable to hire additional star players. In fact, these critics maintain, a free market would bring about a better distribution of players among clubs, and the allotment of players would be at least as equitable without the reserve as with it. As for the instability among clubs during the early professional period, it was not the reserve but the balancing of consumer markets that brought greater equilibrium. In other words, it was only when big towns quit playing little ones and leagues were limited to cities of comparable size that a measure of stability was achieved.

This last point brings us to the second of Organized Baseball's two most important restrictive practices, the division of consumer markets among the clubs, which gave each a monopoly of the area in which it operated. "Territorial rights," as this market monopoly is called, were instituted on the assumption that consumer demand for professional baseball was limited, and that therefore if only one club exploited a given area, it would have a far better chance of prospering than if several competed for the same market. However, territorial rights did not solve the problem of the unequal size of markets among the clubs of a league. Even though minimum population requirements were set up for league membership, wide disparity in the size of metropolitan markets existed. For example, in 1900 the population of the New York-northeastern New Jersey area was 4,607,804, whereas that of St. Louis was 649,711 and Washington 305,684. In the long run such imbalance in consumer markets among the clubs produces inequality in economic strength, which sooner or later is reflected in inequality in playing strength. This disparity in turn lessens competition on the

* For other arguments see Harold Seymour, *Baseball: The Early Years* (New York: Oxford University Press, 1960), Chapter 10.

field, because, other things being equal, the teams enjoying the more lucrative markets have the wherewithal to acquire the better players. These more skilled teams attract still more customers, further increasing gate receipts and the power to compete in the player market.

The cycle also works in reverse. Teams faced with a static or shrinking market fall behind economically and lose out in the acquisition of good players. Attendance falls off and the ability to compete for players declines. In fact, the good players may have to be sold to make ends meet, thus further reducing the clubs' competitive ability on the field and their attractiveness to customers.

Appreciating the results of inequality of markets, the owners tried to compensate by sharing gate receipts, giving 50 per cent of the base admission price to visiting teams. Anything above that, taken in through the sale of seats that cost more than the base price, was kept by the home team as an incentive to improve its stands by adding more box and reserved seats. So long as most of the tickets available were for the base price, fifty cents in the early days, the plan for dividing gate receipts was helpful in overcoming the disparity in consumer markets. But as more and more higher-priced seats were made available, the percentage of the total gate receipts going to the visiting teams became lower. Thus in 1892 when there were few high-priced seats, visiting clubs received about 40 per cent of the total revenue, but by 1929 their share dropped to 21 per cent, and by 1950 to only 14 per cent. The progressive imbalance of consumer markets among the clubs was further exacerbated by the dramatic population shifts taking place in America, shifts to which the magnates, in clinging to the territorial rights of a bygone age, failed to adjust.

The reserve rule, territorial rights, and other restrictive practices established in the formative years of the industry continue in effect to this day. In fact, they have been extended to include leagues in Latin America, Canada, and Japan, thus in effect creating an international cartel. A measure of horizontal integration also exists in the industry. For example, a club owner may be engaged in another enterprise that produces a commodity, such as beer or chewing gum, which he can sell on an exclusive basis in his ball park, or he may be connected with television, through which he can sell baseball games.

Whenever outsiders tried to muscle into the business, Organized Baseball branded them "outlaws." Bitter trade wars for players and markets often resulted. One such war took place at the turn of the century when the newly organized American League claimed major status and challenged the monopoly of the old National. After a two-year struggle, the American forced the National to share the business. In their peace settlement in 1903, the owners in the two major leagues restored their monopsony control of players by agreeing to respect each other's reserve rights, and they allocated consumer markets by sharing New York, Philadelphia, Boston, Chicago, and St. Louis. The National League was given exclusive rights in Brooklyn, Pittsburgh, and Cincinnati, and the American in Washington, Cleveland, and Detroit. These territorial alignments remained intact for more than half a century.

To administer this realigned structure of Organized Baseball, in 1903 the two major leagues set up the National Commission, a three-man body composed of the two major-league presidents and a third member chosen by them to serve as chairman. This so-called Supreme Court of Baseball interpreted and carried out the National Agreement by arbitrating disputes between clubs in different major leagues or between major- and minor-league clubs, and was empowered to impose fines and suspensions for violation of the Agreement. Intra-league differences were handled by the particular league's board of directors.

The majors did not permit minor-league representation on the National Commission for fear that one major league might gain the support of the minors against the other. The players were also excluded from representation on the Commission. The Commission did, however, regard the protection of players as one of its duties, and there were instances in which it upheld their rights even to the point of fining a club. Nevertheless, the relationship was at best paternalistic: the players standing as individuals, the owners in combination.

The chief burden of the Commission's work fell upon the chairman, who received no salary but was provided with an office staff and expense account, generally $12,000 a year. The first and only chairman was August (Garry) Herrmann, president of the Cincinnati club, who held the post until the Commission fell apart in 1920. The genial, gregarious Herrmann was a political tool of George B. Cox, boss of Hamilton County, Ohio. Lincoln Steffens reported how Herrmann and Cox's other lieutenant, Rudolph Hynecke, once were talking to some outsiders when Cox broke in, " . . . when I whistle you dogs come out of your holes, don't you?" They were still. "Don't you, Garry?" he repeated. "That's right," said Garry. As Steffens revealed, Cincinnati was "one great graft," and Cox alone, or together with his two lieutenants, "controlled and cut the political graft which others received shares of as he directed."

Cox was also one of the owners of the Cincinnati club, along with the Fleischmann brothers, Max and Julius, producers of gin and yeast. Julius also served as mayor of Cincinnati for a time, but even then Cox ran the city by telephone. Herrmann owned a block of stock in the Cincinnati club, too, while the rest was spread out among minor politicians "to boom the club locally." However, a newspaper writer said that Cox and the Fleischmanns "know as much about baseball as a savage does about playing the violin," and Clark Griffith, the Washington owner, said later that the Fleischmanns "never belonged in the business."

Although Herrmann was a National League club president, he was a satisfactory choice for the chairmanship of the National Commission not only because he had been instrumental in bringing about peace between the warring leagues, but also because he was acceptable to the American League through his friendship with its president, Ban Johnson, since the latter's early days as a Cincinnati sportswriter.

Herrmann loved the prestige of his baseball job and worked hard at it, as his voluminous correspondence attests. But he relied on good fellowship and diplomacy as much as on administrative techniques. He was happiest when throwing parties for his fellow magnates and newspapermen, spreading *Gemütlichkeit* to the accompaniment of clinking glasses. Garry was partial to traditional German foods, particularly pigs' knuckles, sauerkraut, a sausage made from a special recipe—and, of course, beer. He cultivated good will for the club by presenting writers with gifts of his special sausage, being active in the Elks and the Turnverein, allowing the Cincinnati police and other organizations to use the ball park, and distributing passes copiously wherever they would do the most good.

The second member of the original Commission was Harry Pulliam, president of the National League, one of many newspapermen who became baseball executives. He had been city editor of the Louisville *Commercial* and then secretary to the local ball club, going with it to Pittsburgh when the owner, Barney Dreyfuss, bought the franchise and moved the club there in 1899. Pulliam, only thirty-two when he became president of the National League, was an honest, conscientious, sensitive man, who genuinely tried to enforce the rules, back his umpires, and cleanse National League games of rowdyism. At times he impetuously criticized owners publicly and appeared to be a little too punctilious, at least to the owners' taste, in carrying out his duties. He was also given to brooding over press criticism, said to be inspired by some of the magnates, and was upset by league problems that crowded in on him. Pulliam became ill in 1905 and suffered a breakdown early in 1909; he was given a leave of absence and returned to work apparently refreshed and restored to health, only to shoot himself to death a few weeks later in the New York Athletic Club.

The big man on the Commission was American League President

Byron Bancroft Johnson. He created the American League and led it successfully through its battle with the old National. Hard-driving, hard-drinking Ban dominated the American League and was accused by some critics of running the National Commission as well, by the force of his personality and his influence over Herrmann. But in the eyes of his admirers he could scarcely do wrong. To them, he was the Theodore Roosevelt of baseball at a time when T.R. was captivating American audiences with his bombastic speeches and moralistic effusions. Years later a sportswriter, in a nostalgic piece about that era, spoofed not only the Johnson image but those of his fellow commissioners in these words:

> Ban Johnson never missed an opportunity to make a speech. . . .
> No matter how often Ban made a speech it was always the same speech; all about how he, singlehanded and alone, had made baseball a gentleman's sport, and it must be kept forever clean because sportsmanship spoke from the heart of America and he would lay down his life to save our beloved nation, at which point he would begin to cry.
> Now, dear old Garry, this always made him very uncomfortable, because he was never quite sure what Ban meant. Harry Pulliam didn't care, being a very wise feller.
> [Ban was] the real baseball authority, for Garry never did know much about it. He had been chosen chairman, like it so often happens, because he was so delightfully what they call innocuous.

Like all caricatures, this description contains much truth. Johnson could be vindictive and even petty, and at times he seemed overly impressed with himself. Particularly in the later years of his presidency, he overstepped his prerogative and in the end had to face a revolt by his own club owners. But Johnson was a very able man, and the new American League under his strong leadership brought a fresh, healthy force into Organized Baseball, which had become stagnant during the National League's monopoly of the business all through the 1890's. Johnson continued as American League president until 1927, outlasting the life of the National Commission, whereas the National League had a succession of presidents after Pulliam's suicide and consequently was at a disadvantage because of the lack of continuity of its representation on the Commission.

The new National Commission was immediately confronted with quarrels between the two major leagues which were an outgrowth of the recent war between them. For even though peace prevailed on paper, a kind of cold war went on for the next year or two.

Much of the trouble involved ownership of players. The peace treaty supposedly settled conflicting titles to player contracts created by the wartime raids on each other's men, but some claims were still

disputed. One issue arose over William Bernhard and Napoleon Lajoie, former members of the Philadelphia National League team, who
during the war had jumped their contracts to play in the American
League and were now on its Cleveland club's roster. A court injunction obtained by the Phillies to prevent the two from playing in
Pennsylvania was still in force, and James Potter, new owner of the
Phillies, was demanding compensation from Cleveland in exchange
for quashing the injunction. This hassle was straightened out when
Herrmann persuaded Potter to give way.

A more serious wrangle started a few months later. George Davis
was another wartime contract-jumper who had left the New York
Giants to play for the Chicago American League club. According to
the peace settlement, he was supposed to stay with Chicago. Instead,
he was persuaded to report to the Giants for spring training in 1903.
President Pulliam first ruled that Davis would not be allowed to play
for the Giants, but complications set in when the Giants' local American League rival, the New York Highlanders, secured the well-known
shortstop Kid Elberfeld. He was another player whose status had
been in doubt because he had signed two contracts, one with the
Giants and one with Detroit of the American League. For the sake of
peace, the Giants' owner, John T. Brush, had relinquished his claim,
and Elberfeld had been assigned to Detroit. Little did Brush think
that this player would promptly bob up again in New York in the
uniform of his hated rival, the Highlanders. It was Ban Johnson who
was behind the move. Recognizing the importance to the American
League of having a good gate attraction in New York, he had arranged for Elberfeld to be transferred to the Highlanders.

Brush, a die-hard opponent of the American League who had re-
sisted making peace to the last, protested that the maneuver was a
breach of faith instigated for the purpose of stiffening his competition
in New York and draining off some of his gate receipts. He sought a
court injunction against Elberfeld, but the New York Supreme Court
refused his request on the ground that the Giants had waived any
claim to his services by signing the peace pact with the American
League. Brush also linked the Elberfeld deal with the fracas over
Davis and got Pulliam to reverse himself and declare that Davis
could stay with the Giants; whereupon the Chicago Americans obtained an injunction against Davis for breach of contract.

For a time it looked as though war between the leagues would
break out all over again. Johnson wired Herrmann that Pulliam's action was "unwarranted and absurd," and told Pulliam that the American League would have no further dealings with the National until
matters were settled. Once more Herrmann was the peacemaker, for

he persuaded the Giants to agree not to oppose Elberfeld's playing with the New York Americans and to keep Davis out of their own lineup that season. The following year Davis was returned to the Chicago Americans.

A similar issue cropped up the following year when the Boston Red Sox traded Pat Dougherty, a competent hitter, to the New York Yankees (as some were beginning to call the New York American League team) for Robert Unglaub, an untried utility infielder. National Leaguers took this apparently one-sided exchange as another deliberate American League effort to furnish stiffer competition for the Giants in the New York market. Pulliam publicly criticized Johnson for sanctioning the deal, although, as one writer pointed out, it was, strictly speaking, none of his business.

The question of harmonizing playing schedules caused continued strained relations between the former enemies. Instead of opening the season jointly, one league would try to start earlier than the other. They argued over how many games should be played and how long the season should last, and about equitable distribution of Sunday and holiday dates in the cities shared by both of them. If one league published its schedule early, the other might revamp its own to conflict with that of its rival. Or an owner might move up a game to create a Sunday doubleheader on a day when his opposite number in the other league was also playing at home.

The leagues finally settled on a 154-game schedule, which, with one or two exceptions, remained standard from 1904 until 1961. They set up a joint schedule committee and placed prime responsibility for scheduling in the hands of the two league presidents. But these decisions failed to suit some owners. Late in 1910 Charles Ebbets, Brooklyn owner, advocated an increase to 168 games as "a clean cut business proposition." Another National League owner, Charles Murphy, held that the "baseball business is not one that should be conducted on a sentimental basis, but it is purely a business proposition"; therefore scheduling problems should not be entrusted to the league presidents, who were merely employed by the owners and had not a cent invested in the game.

Other ideas were put forward for improving operations. Ebbets, after a careful comparison of weather in April and October, found that conditions for playing were better in October and suggested that the season be started later and extended into the fall—an idea still being proposed. Another suggestion advanced in those days and frequently revived was to play inter-league games as part of the official championship schedule, either during or after the regular season. But the only inter-league games played, aside from the World Series, have been "exhibition" games, and the owners were slow to adopt those. Only in St. Louis and Philadelphia did the two rival club owners in each city cooperate sufficiently to play a city series just after the war; in Boston, New York, and Chicago such cooperation was delayed until animosities died down.

The first real break in the cold war came when the two pennant winners of 1903, Pittsburgh in the National League and Boston in the American, agreed to meet for the championship of the baseball world at the end of the season in the so-called World Series, a spectacle that has become an American institution known all over the world. This first World Series of the modern era lasted the full nine games before Boston won the five requisite for victory.

This Series was played under a simple agreement worked out by the two club owners themselves. The text of their agreement was made public but not their plan for dividing the receipts. However, there is evidence that they agreed to split only the income from the basic admissions—75 per cent to the winner and 25 per cent to the loser—leaving each owner to retain whatever he collected over and above the base admission charge from the sale of grandstand and box seats in his own park. What the players were to get was up to the owners, and oddly, the losing players' shares exceeded the winners' because Dreyfuss, owner of the Pittsburgh club, added his personal share to his players' purse.

But bitterness between the leagues continued into 1904, and Dreyfuss observed, "Things are not going right and to me point to an early resumption of hostilities between the two Leagues." At the end of the season John T. Brush refused to allow his pennant-winning New York Giants to play Boston, again the American League victors, for the championship, dismissing the Red Sox as no more than winners in a minor league. Public outcry over missing the Series was widespread. Newspapers all over the country castigated Brush for his "smallness" and John McGraw, the Giants' manager, for his "malice" and denounced their refusal to participate as a "baby act" and "cowardice." [*] The Giant players themselves grumbled over losing the opportunity to make some extra money. President Pulliam could do nothing. He correctly pointed out that post-season games were left to the discretion of individual National League clubs.

However, relations between the two leagues definitely improved the following season. Brush, evidently affected by all the criticism directed at him the year before, relented on the World Series. The National League voted to make participation in such a series obligatory

[*] There is some evidence, however, that McGraw urged Brush to change his mind and play the Series.

for its pennant-winning team, and Brush even submitted a set of suggestions to Pulliam for conducting the Series. "Brush's rules," refined by the National Commission, have remained the core of World Series' rules ever since. So it was that after the 1905 season Brush sent his Giants, again National League champions, into the World Series against the Philadelphia Athletics. That was one of the memorable World Series in which the two famous managers, John J. McGraw and Connie Mack, opposed each other. McGraw's known flair for showmanship was apparent when the Giants appeared in brand-new black uniforms with white trim, while the Athletics showed up in the same old suits—"dirty, ragged, sweaty and torn."

The Brush plan provided for a seven-game Series to be ended as soon as one of the teams won four of them, and in that 1905 Series his Giants took the necessary four after playing only five games. The most remarkable feature of the Series was that all the games resulted in shutouts by the winning pitchers. Christy Mathewson, the Giants' star, won three of them, "Iron Man" Joe McGinnity the other Giant game, and the American Indian, Albert "Chief" Bender, the lone Athletic victory.

Fans have wondered ever since what might have happened had the Athletics not lost the services of their star left-hander, Rube Waddell. The eccentric pitcher was supposed to have injured his shoulder in a playful tussle with a teammate, Andy Coakley. Waddell tried to smash Coakley's straw hat because Andy was wearing it out of season. Sensational stories appeared charging that New York gamblers had bribed Waddell to stay out of the Series by feigning injury. Connie Mack denied them, and although the rumors were never substantiated, they persisted for years afterward.

After the Series, the Philadelphia fans feted the Athletics and Giants at a banquet. Ban Johnson and John T. ("Tooth") Brush, as some of the more irreverent writers were calling him, were at least civil to each other, and Brush actually proposed a toast: "Here's to the American and National Leagues! May they both live long and prosper!" From then on, inter-league relations were reasonably smooth, although some bickering continued and the hatred between McGraw and Johnson never abated.

The system of having the two major leagues share the business harmoniously was not enough for Frank Robison, president of the St. Louis National League club. He pressed for an even tighter monopoly through the consolidation of the two big leagues into a single organization of eight clubs in only eight cities, capitalized as one company. All players would be thrown into a common pool, parceled out among the clubs of the combine, and given high salaries to forestall any objections they might have. In short, this was a scheme to resurrect the much criticized "syndicate ball" of the 1890's, as the interlocking ownership was called that prevailed in the twelve-club National League at that time. Robison anticipated that "some people would probably say this was too much of a base ball trust"—as well he might at a time when Roosevelt's "trust-busting" program was in full swing and public opinion was especially alert to the abuses of monopolies. Nevertheless, Robison thought such objections could be mitigated by having each club remain a corporate entity. Rumor of the proposal led *Sporting News* to denounce the "plot against the people's pastime," saying it was "animated by greed." Harry Pulliam disapproved of the plan, too, and the American League squelched it by adopting a resolution affirming the "vital principle" of maintaining two major leagues.

Besides handling all the aforementioned problems, the National Commission had to carry on its routine duties. One of its major responsibilities was the supervision of the World Series and the distribution of the receipts from it, which soon became large sums. In 1912 gross receipts amounted to nearly half a million dollars—almost ten times what they were in 1905. Much of the Commission's time was spent deciding disputes between clubs and leagues over ownership of players, purchase and draft of players, and violations of "baseball law." The job was not always easy. As Harry Pulliam pointed out, it took "a Philadelphia lawyer to give anyone a correct interpretation of our rules and a Pinkerton detective to find the rules themselves."

The Commission also exercised its power to fine clubs for violations. It cost John T. Brush nearly $700 in 1907 for violating a contract with the minor-league New Orleans club, and in 1905 the Brooklyn club was fined $100 for playing an exhibition game against a team using a so-called ineligible player, but there is no evidence that Ebbets ever paid it. Once the St. Louis Cardinals played an exhibition game against a minor-league club that also used a blacklisted player. But in this case Ban Johnson privately advised Herrmann to proceed cautiously for fear of a lawsuit and to let the St. Louis owner off with a warning not to do it again.

The Commission also heard many appeals from players for redress of what they considered injustice or ill-treatment. In one case the Commission even compelled a player to pay up debts owed to other players on his former club. People wrote from all over the country asking the Commission to decide disputes and "knotty problems" regarding the playing rules, often merely for the purpose of deciding a bet.

The Commission summarized its work in annual reports, some of which still exist. In its first year it settled 110 cases, nearly all of them resulting in financial awards to minor-league clubs. The following year it disposed of 73 cases, sent out more than 2000 telegrams and letters, and spent $25,000. In 1912 it made 153 rulings, and in 1913 the number jumped to 3725. Salaries and office expenses amounted to $68,000 in 1915. The volume and scope of the Commission's activity are demonstrated by the more than seventy file boxes of letters, telegrams, and other papers accumulated during its existence. The Commission received financial support from the two major leagues, share and share alike, to cover the cost of performing its administrative duties, but its chief source of income soon became a 10 per cent portion of the World Series receipts. In 1915, for example, this percentage came to $25,000. The Commission also received a percentage for managing and supplying umpires for various city championship series, and derived additional income from fines and other assessments.

Despite the Commission's industry and solid accomplishments, it had its share of criticism. The commissioners frequently held their meetings at the Laughery Club, a hideaway a short distance down the Ohio River from Cincinnati, to which Johnson and Herrmann, drinking companions for many years, often repaired. Critics charged that they imbibed too much and neglected their duties. A reporter trying to cover one of their meetings told of following the trail of the empty glasses and lemon peel from the commissioners' meeting room at the Hotel Sinton down to the rathskeller, "and there, as was to be expected, I found the grave, sedate rulers of the national pastime, all agreed upon one important point: 'I'll take the same.'"

The commissioners were not alone among baseball men in such pleasures. *Sporting News* said that at the annual major-league gatherings of owners, the bar was the real meeting-place; the formal sessions in hotel parlors were a bluff for the newspapermen. Owner Barney Dreyfuss constantly sniped at the Commission, exclaiming at one point, "If I were to run my business in the manner of the National Commission I would consider myself a poor business man indeed."

More substantial objections were also raised. Charges were repeatedly made that Johnson dominated the more easy-going Herrmann. The fact that two members of the Commission were National Leaguers also occasioned criticism; if Herrmann and the president of the National League supported their own league in a case, they were called partial; if they did not, they were accused of disloyalty. Things were doubly difficult when Herrmann had to vote on issues involving his own Cincinnati club. Every so often the minors asked to have a representative on the Commission, and occasionally the players requested one as well. Eventually, many began to believe that what baseball needed was a single "czar," preferably an outsider without a financial interest. On the other hand, supporters of the National Commission maintained that it was doing a great deal for baseball and that the charges against it were unwarranted. An attorney who favored it compared the justice and integrity of the Commission to that of the Court of Chancery in fourteenth-century England.

What, then, is the verdict on the rule of the triumvirate? By and large, it did a creditable job, particularly during the first dozen years of its reign. Under the National Commission, Organized Baseball emerged from the slough of the 1890's into a period of universal prosperity. In the major leagues, attendance, profits, and confidence climbed to heretofore unprecedented heights, symbolized by the new ball parks most clubs built. The annual World Series intensified interest in the pennant races and climaxed each season with a splendid spectacle. The number of minor leagues grew from thirteen in 1903 to more than forty by 1913.

But the National Commission ran into a series of squalls after 1915. Leaks appeared that steadily worsened until eventually the Commission foundered and was abandoned in 1920.

2

POLITICS AND PARTISANS

CRITICS of modern baseball club owners complain of their dollar-chasing "What's-in-it-for-me?" attitude and contrast it with what they believe was a more sportsmanlike outlook on the part of owners of an earlier day. To be sure, the old-time owners were not engrossed in the intricacies of capital gains, tax deductions, and complex television contracts, but they were always intent on making money out of professional baseball. Perhaps, as is sometimes claimed, they had more affection for baseball than some of today's owners, but *Sporting News* stated in 1904 that their love of the game depended on the box office. "Don't for a minute think," the editor wrote, "there are any of the club owners in base ball for the sport."

The early owners themselves freely admitted they were running a business and made no bones about their interest in money-making. The venerated Connie Mack declared in his autobiography, "Baseball is strictly a competitive business that must be conducted on sound business principles." Charles Ebbets, in considering new grounds for the Brooklyn team, said, "The question is purely one of business; I am not in base ball for my health." In 1920 Colonel Jake Ruppert, owner of the New York Yankees, told a writer, "Baseball club owners are sensible business men. . . . You can bank on the fact that they will conduct their clubs as business men. They must do this to protect their investments." In fact, the purpose of the peace pact between the two major leagues in 1903, according to Garry Herrmann, was to create a "species of competition" that would put it "within the power of every club to make something on its capitalization."

In a more satirical vein, a poem printed in *Sporting News* in 1915 pointed up the gap between the attitude of professional owners and players and that of sandlotters.

What Constitutes the Game?

I asked a magnate great,
  In wealth and power and ease;
He said "In brief I'll state
  The game is mainly these—
My turnstile clicking around,
  My bankroll gaining heft,
While thousands leave my grounds
  With not a nickel left."

I asked a big league star,
  Of fame and great renown;
He stopped his motor car
  And looked benignly down.
"I take it that the game"
  He said with some hauteur,
"Is signing up your name
  For thirty thousand per."

I asked a ragged kid,
  He stared in blank surprise,
The wonder that he had
  Shown in contemptuous eyes;
"De game? A big lot—See?
  A gluv, a bat, a ball;
Yer gang, my gang and me,
  An' den—some scrap—dat's all."

There was so much talk of the business side of baseball in those days that National League President John K. Tener feared people's illusions would be destroyed, so in 1917 he cautioned the owners to remember in their public statements that the fans were interested in ball players, not the owners. "For after all," he said, "Base Ball to them is but a sport."

Modern owners frequently assert that professional baseball is a sport that belongs to the people, fosters democracy, and cures juvenile delinquency. They soft-pedal the fact that they are operating a commercialized amusement business. Owners of an earlier era did the same thing. In 1912 Charles W. Murphy, president of the Cubs, glorified baseball as a public benefactor, a friend of the anti-tuberculosis league since it brought people into the open air, and a beneficial influence on youth because of their emulation of big-league stars as models of conduct.

Actually, all club owners have been motivated by a mixture of economic and psychological incentives—profits or capital gains, together with the satisfactions of the prestige to be enjoyed, especially if they have a winning team—although the emphasis may vary with each individual owner. The psychological motivation in baseball ownership should not be overemphasized; executives in other businesses are also attracted by prestige and the supposed glamour of their positions. Old-time owners were simply more frank than the modern owners about admitting to the financial aspect of baseball. Far from denying they were businessmen, they strove to be so regarded, because in those days before the Great Depression businessmen were still the heroes of American society. It was a time when *Sporting News* could defend the baseball operators with the observation that making money was the greatest American game, and it was no crime to play it within certain bounds. Many of the early club owners affected the capitalist stereotype—cigars, heavy jowls, and aldermanic bellies— then regarded as signifying affluence.°

Old-time owners were also probably more closely involved with their teams. For many an early owner, baseball was his life. Men like Clark Griffith of Washington, Connie Mack of the Philadelphia Athletics, Charles Ebbets of Brooklyn, and Barney Dreyfuss of Pittsburgh grew up with the business, and many of them took a more direct interest in the operation of their clubs. As far as that goes, business in general displayed a sense of personal proprietorship often lacking now.

Baseball was also a smaller-scale business then and could be conducted on simpler lines. A few key men could virtually run the entire operation. Besides the owner, a club might have a treasurer, a road secretary, a business manager responsible for concessions and sale of advertising, and a team manager. To round out the organization it would have a scout or two, a couple of groundkeepers, some ushers, ticket-takers, usually a few special policemen, and a squad of boys to pick up papers, hawk scorecards, and operate turnstiles and the scoreboard. I can well remember a smiling Steve McKeever, part owner and vice-president of the Brooklyn club in the 1920's, with his high collar and gold-headed blackthorn cane, seated on a camp chair on the field in front of the grandstand, personally distributing bleacher passes written in longhand on strips of paper to a dozen or so eager boys. It was one of those bleacher passes for park cleanup that enabled me to see my first major-league ball game.

Of course, there are exceptions to the types of owner that prevailed in both eras. Although a majority of contemporary owners have basic business interests other than baseball, there are still some—for example, Horace Stoneham of the San Francisco Giants and Walter

° See picture of the National Commission after page 152.

O'Malley of the Los Angeles Dodgers—who give close personal direction to their ball clubs. Conversely, some early owners like Charles Somers of Cleveland and Jake Ruppert, who with Colonel T. L. Huston purchased the Yankees in 1915, operated other enterprises besides baseball and devoted only a portion of their time to their clubs.

But owners in every era were alike in keeping their operations as secret as possible. Newspapermen in the era before World War One repeatedly complained about the refusal of owners to supply solid news of what occurred in their meetings. One veteran reporter remarked that soon they probably would not even give out the official batting averages. League meetings were satirized by a New York *Sun* writer in 1913:

When the Magnates Meet

Ho, bartenders, set out your glasses,
    And waiters, quick burnish each plate,
For this week you have done with the masses
    And serve drink and food to the great.

The magnates have entered our city,
    So let there be popping of corks,
Wine livens the jests of the witty,
    And straightens some tongues that have forks.

Should you wish to have baseball expounded
    Just ask any owner his views,
And he'll answer all questions propounded
    That have no connection with news.

If you hear a loud noise like a boom or
    A crash don't be scared or upset,
It's just somebody chasing a rumor
    Though nobody's run one down yet.

For a rest from all brain stimulation,
    A cure for all mental fatigue,
Just quietly take up your station
    At this winter conclave of the league.

For relaxation many of the magnates, as well as the players, enjoyed hunting. Ban Johnson, his pal Charles Comiskey, owner of the Chicago White Sox, and other baseball executives, along with a squad of Chicago "sports," belonged to a hunting and drinking group called the Woodland Bards. The members took annual fall trips to a camp near Mercer in the wilds of upper Wisconsin. On one trip Garry Herrmann predicted he would be a failure at hunting, but a reporter wrote that he did all right, for within twenty-four hours he shot a "furious demi-john and laid a raging magnum lifeless on the plain." Another winter retreat was a 2400-acre tract in Glynn County, Georgia, used by the Dover Hall Club, whose members were owners, writers, a few managers, and a star player. Membership was limited to fifty, each of whom subscribed $1000 for one of the fifty shares of stock. The place offered a six-room dwelling with barns and outbuildings, and a chance to hunt turkey, wildcat, duck, coon, and possum.

Owners continually bickered and squabbled among themselves. Some of their spats were petty to the point of childishness; others were serious enough to have important repercussions on the industry. Most of them occurred in the National League, at least in the years before World War One. The American League's time of troubles came later; until then, it enjoyed comparative quiet under the firm hand of Ban Johnson. His forceful personality, combined with the fact that he, together with Comiskey, had been the architect of the American League, added up to a strong presidency. His term of office was to expire only with the end of the agreement under which the American League operated. When this came about in 1910, Johnson was promptly re-elected for a twenty-year term with a salary reported to be $25,000 and a liberal expense account. For a while at least, Johnson also held in his possession 51 per cent of the stock of each club, having required the owners to deposit it with him when the league was formed, as a precaution against the possibility of their deserting.

An exception to Johnson's generally smooth course was a falling-out between him and his old crony, Comiskey. Seemingly unimportant at first, their differences nevertheless rankled through the years until at last there was an irreparable breach, which was to play a signal part in larger events. Probably no one will ever know how it all began. One tale has it that on one of the hunting trips of the Woodland Bards someone, as a practical joke, removed the bullets from Johnson's new gun, replacing them with wadding. Johnson blazed away, hitting nothing. He blamed the gun, but Comiskey joshed him about being a poor shot. When Ban discovered the hoax, he accused Comiskey of being the culprit and for months would not speak to him.

Whether this occurred or not, it is clear there were tiffs between them before the incident usually cited as marking the beginning of their feud, the Ducky Holmes decision. Early in the 1905 season James "Ducky" Holmes, outfielder on Comiskey's White Sox, was suspended by Umpire "Silk" O'Laughlin for using abusive language—not the first time his tongue got him into trouble.° Johnson upheld the umpire, and Comiskey fumed, not so much at the penalty itself but at the way it was carried out. The news came by special messenger rather than through the usual channels, so the loss of Holmes took effect a day sooner than it otherwise would have and before the return of another suspended man. Left short-handed, the White Sox had to make shift with a pitcher in the outfield that day. They also lost the game.

Comiskey moved out of the office he shared with Johnson. After a time they patched up their differences only to split again over Johnson's suspension of Fielder Jones, White Sox player-manager, in the middle of the close 1907 pennant race. A frequently told fish story accompanied this episode, and like most fish stories it varies in the telling: Johnson was on a fishing trip and, as a gesture of good will, sent Comiskey a sample of his catch. It arrived just following the news of Jones's suspension. Comiskey exploded with something like: "Does Johnson expect me to play this fish in the outfield?"

Eventually the two again became reconciled, at least publicly, but the coolness continued until their final estrangement in 1918 over a disputed pitcher, Jack Quinn. He was with a Pacific Coast League team that year. When that league disbanded in July because of the World War, Comiskey, with permission of the National Commission, signed Quinn for the White Sox. Quinn won five games for them during the balance of the season. Meanwhile, the New York Yankees had purchased the player's contract from his former club. The National Commission, while recognizing the "peculiar and unfortunate" nature of the conflicting claims and the fact that both claimants were within their rights, nevertheless, with Johnson's acquiescence, awarded Quinn to New York. From then on, Comiskey was bitterly against Johnson, and in the dissentient years soon to rack the American League he was always a member of the anti-Johnson faction.

But the discord between Johnson and Comiskey was puny compared with the strife in the National League. There, the position of the league president differed. Unlike Johnson, who had practically invented the American League, the National's president headed a league that was already old and long accustomed to a weak executive. He was also restricted, at least in the early years, to a one-year term of office. His decisions could be appealed over his head to the league's board of directors, comprised of four owners and the president. Consequently his role was no more than that of a well-paid clerk. The real power rested with the club owners, or whatever combination among them was dominant. The contrast in presidential pre-

° See *Baseball: The Early Years*, page 298.

rogative between the two major leagues was evident even in such a small matter as the distribution of passes. Johnson had free rein to decide who got them, but when Pulliam asked for more leeway, Brush of the Giants asserted that no one had the right to give passes to his grounds, not even the league president.

Pulliam tried to curb the disorder and rowdyism during games which had plagued the National League for years. To do this, he had to stand behind his umpires and exercise his authority to crack down on disorderly players and managers with fines and suspension. League regulations gave him this power. The so-called Fleischmann Resolution of 1902 and the Brush amendment to it in 1904 made it mandatory for the league president to fine any player $10 who was removed from the game by the umpire. If on top of this the president suspended him, he was fined an additional $10 for every day he was out. But, in the final analysis, this paper authority turned on the support of the owners, and they often gave only lip service to their own rules and undercut their president by such tactics as paying the players' fines themselves, trying to get their players reinstated before their term of suspension was completed, and failing to restrain umpire-baiting managers.

Numerous instances testify to the extent of the problem of authority. One that exemplified it as well as any was the "Hey Barney!" affair. In May 1905 the Pittsburgh Pirates came to New York for a series with the Giants. In the second game, on May 19, John McGraw, the Giants' manager, had an altercation with the umpire, in the course of which he implied that the umpire was under the influence of Barney Dreyfuss, the Pittsburgh owner. Dreyfuss, seated in the stands, overheard him.

The next day McGraw, along with his star pitcher, Christy Mathewson, had another ruckus, this time with Fred Clarke, manager of the Pirates, and was put out of the game by Umpire Johnstone. On his way to the clubhouse he came upon Barney Dreyfuss talking with some friends. McGraw shouted "Hey Barney!" at the Pittsburgh owner and heckled him about owing money to a bookie and welching on bets. Dreyfuss, his dignity ruffled at McGraw's familiarity and resentful of his other remarks, replied in kind.

A few days later it was reported that Dreyfuss had filed formal charges with the league's board of directors against McGraw for using offensive language to him and for accusing him of controlling umpires, and that Pulliam had called a meeting of the board for June 1 to consider the part of Dreyfuss's complaint pertaining to his being accused of crookedness.

McGraw immediately denounced the whole move, denying that he had ever said Dreyfuss was crooked and insisting that he was entitled to a hearing to give his side of the story. He also got Pulliam on the telephone and abused him personally. Pulliam then notified McGraw that he was suspended for fifteen days and fined $150—$10 for each day's suspension—for using offensive language to Dreyfuss from the ball field on May 19, and an additional $10 for being removed from the field by the umpire on May 20. This part of the case was, in Pulliam's view, under his sole jurisdiction, according to the Fleischmann Resolution and the Brush corollary to it.

In dealing with the other prong of Dreyfuss's protest (the charge of crookedness), the board, after hearing the evidence and witnesses for McGraw, exonerated him and scolded Dreyfuss for "indulging in an open controversy with a ball player." * It also expressed the hope that "no other club owner, in a moment of excitement," will so far forget the "dignity" of being the president of a National League club.

But McGraw and the New York club were far from mollified. They and their supporters continued to rage that Pulliam's fine and suspension were overly severe and unjust because they were imposed without granting McGraw or Brush, the Giants' owner, an opportunity to present their case. The press took sides. As might be expected, out-of-town papers such as the Pittsburgh *Courier* called McGraw a "dangerous character," and *Sporting News* branded him a "rowdy." On the other hand, many New York writers rallied to McGraw with equal unrestraint, exemplified by James Montague's doggerel in the New York *Evening Journal:*

The Ballad of the Tyrant Pulliam

It was the mighty Pulliam who knit his tyrant brow
And said: "My morbid malcontents, attend this ukase now:
Who dares dispute the umpire's word, or says so much as 'Shucks!'
Whatever he may chance to think, gets set back just ten bucks!"

Louis Mann, a vaudeville comedian, circulated a petition on McGraw's behalf, and 100,000 signatures were claimed. But amidst all the clamor and despite a protest from Brush, Pulliam stuck by his contention that the quarrel had two facets and that he was within his rights in acting alone in pronouncing judgment on the portion of it having to do with McGraw's abusive language on the field and removal from the game.

So McGraw and the New York club went to court. The case was heard by Judge Sheldon in Boston, who ruled for the Giants. He granted an injunction restraining Pulliam from enforcing the fine and

* Manager McGraw was also still technically listed as a player and appeared in three games that season.

suspension and the umpires from keeping McGraw off the field, on the ground that the whole procedure was "un-American," since McGraw had not been given a hearing and an opportunity to present a defense before being penalized.

Pulliam salvaged as much as he could from this defeat. Declaring that "so long as I am President of the League there cannot be one law for John McGraw and another for Dan McGann" (Giants' first baseman, also fined about the same time), Pulliam remitted every fine levied against players that year above the $10 provided under the Fleischmann Resolution—a total of $490. This policy made little difference to the players themselves, since most of their fines had been paid by the clubs in the first place. As one of the players, Buck Weaver, admitted in 1917: "They want you to get out there and fight, don't they, and do you think that we pay for the privilege? Well, I guess the old club treasury looks after that, all right."

That winter at the National League meeting, Pulliam survived an effort to oust him and got the league to pass a resolution giving him "full power to discipline any player or manager for the violation of good order" with fines, suspensions, and any regulations he deemed necessary, except that the board of directors must ratify a decision to expel a man. But the fact remained that McGraw and the Giants had won. McGraw continued to uphold his reputation for aggressiveness, and many were the brawls that he participated in afterwards.

Pulliam's grip remained uncertain. For one thing, Brush, as might be expected, agitated against him and even tried to deprive the man he called a "narrow-minded incompetent" of his vote on the board of directors by raising the old cry that the league president had no financial interest in baseball and therefore should not have as much power as club presidents.

In 1908 Pulliam was again under heavy pressure. That was the year of the famous Merkle play, a dispute that tried him severely and will be discussed in another place. On top of this, a scandal over ticket-scalping in Chicago during the World Series that year caused him further difficulty. After investigating, the National Commission severely criticized the Chicago Cubs for their handling of the tickets, but uncovered no collusion with the scalpers. The aftermath brought a growing rift between Charles A. Murphy, president of the club, and Pulliam. Pulliam's growing irritableness and the increasing strain upon him were revealed in his abrupt dismissal of Dreyfuss and Ebbets from his New York office after a row with them.

No one can tell precisely how much all these vicissitudes had to do with Pulliam's suicide the following July, although undoubtedly they played their part. Pulliam revealed his discouraged frame of mind in a speech before the owners at a dinner that February, in which he re-proved their underhanded methods and added: "I expect that there are enough of the opposition to depose me as President, and, as a matter of fact, I would not regret such action on their part. The job is a thankless one for the most part, and the friction that one has to con-tend with is not worth the trouble."

The owners chose John A. Heydler to succeed Pulliam. As a youth, Heydler had worked in the Government Printing Office, where he be-came acquainted with Nick Young, National League president of the 1890's, who gave him a job as a substitute umpire. Heydler became a regular in 1898 but soon quit, deciding that there were better ways of earning a living than umpiring under the conditions that prevailed in those days. He returned to printing and worked for the Washington *Star,* where he later advanced to the sports desk. As a hobby, he liked to compile and print baseball averages. This interest led to a position under Pulliam as statistician in charge of the playing records when the latter became president of the league in 1902. Heydler soon be-came Pulliam's secretary and then in 1906 was elected secretary-treas-urer of the league. He also took charge when Pulliam was given leave of absence to recover his health.

Heydler was not a spectacular individual, but his solid competence in filling out Pulliam's term won him support from many writers and some owners. Other owners thought he was not a big enough man for the job, and they lost little time electioneering behind the scenes for their own candidates. One of the most surprising of these was John Montgomery Ward, former star shortstop and pitcher, who led the great player revolt against the magnates in 1890. Ward was now set-tled in his law practice, tamed and respectable after his fling as leader of the Players' Union. He had even taken up golf, then an up-per-class status symbol. But in view of his early union leadership, making him president of the National League was comparable to electing John L. Lewis or Walter Reuther as chairman of the board of a corporation.

Several National League owners would have none of him. And over in the American League Johnson butted his way into the controversy. He accused Ward of having advised Harry Davis to break his con-tract with the White Sox and sign with the Giants back in 1903. Ward was not the "clean" man the National League deserved, boomed Johnson, and if he were elected, Johnson would not recog-nize him or sit with him on the National Commission. Ward retal-iated by suing Johnson for libel on a number of counts, and was eventually awarded $1000 in damages.

The other leading candidate was Robert W. Brown, editor of the Louisville *Times.* He was sponsored by Garry Herrmann and was

more than anxious to get the job. Asking Herrmann to "land" the
presidency for him, he promised, "I'll never forget it." The voting that
winter brought a deadlock between Ward and Brown, four clubs
against four, which lasted nearly a week. Finally, John T. Brush resolved it by trotting out a dark horse, Thomas J. Lynch, a former National League umpire who was then managing a theatrical bureau in
Connecticut. Arguing that the chief function of the league president
was to supervise the umpires, Brush persuaded the others that no one
could do a better job in this respect than the former "King of Umpires," and Lynch was elected.

Ward returned to baseball briefly when he became part owner and
president of the Boston Braves at the end of 1911, and again as an executive with the Brooklyn club of the Federal League. Brown remained in the wings, a candidate favored during the next few years
by one faction of owners. Heydler returned to the secretary-treasurer
post at $5000 a year, content to wait.

Lynch soon gave the owners more than they bargained for, backing
his umpires by levying frequent fines and imposing suspensions on
players. Although rowdyism was perhaps not so rampant as in the
1890's when the notorious Baltimore Orioles and the Cleveland Spi-
ders rampaged through the league, nevertheless Lynch never lacked
candidates for discipline. Nor was he known for tact in meting it out.
He also refused to get rid of umpires displeasing to owners, although
he dismissed a few unsatisfactory to himself, and he failed to travel
around the league to check on umpires often enough to suit some of
the magnates. As sportswriter Ernie Lanigan, who was later historian
at the Baseball Hall of Fame, remarked at the time, Lynch and cowardice were strangers and he "read the riot act" more than once to
some owners for breaking their own rules.

Owners have always found ingenious ways to violate or skirt
around their own rules. In 1912 one of them admitted, "It seems to
me that no matter how our baseball laws are worded, some persons
can, when they feel disposed, find some way to drive a four-horse
team through them." They frequently tampered with players on other
teams. In contravention of reserve agreements, an owner or a manager would "feel out" an opposing player about playing for him. More
than once Garry Herrmann himself was charged with this tactic,
which "sowed discontent" among players by making them believe
they could do better on another team. Players, too, either personally
or through intermediaries, tried to find out if they could get themselves transferred to a preferred club.*

---

* The rules now provide for fines or forfeiture of games for tampering with
players under contract or reservation.

Another owner violation was "covering up"—collusion between a major- and minor-league club to keep a player off the market and in cold storage for possible future use. This practice had the double effect of depriving players of the full opportunity for advancement and of hurting the competitive position of rival clubs, which otherwise might have strengthened themselves by bidding successfully for such men.* Violation of the rule against covering up could bring a fine up to $1000.

President Lynch tried to uphold these rules, but when he fined Ebbets $500 for shipping a player to the minors without giving the other National League clubs a chance to waive on his services, Ebbets refused to pay, and the league directors let him get away with it, thus repudiating their own president. Lynch frequently fined Ebbets's manager, Bill Dahlen, as well, because of his many run-ins with umpires. So Ebbets, at odds with Lynch from the first over a difference about scheduling, speedily became disenchanted with him and agitated for his removal.

It was no secret that every year of Lynch's presidency a bloc of owners hunted for a replacement. Joined with Ebbets against Lynch were Garry Herrmann, still trying to put over his friend Robert Brown, Barney Dreyfuss, evidently dissatisfied with anyone sponsored by Brush, and Horace Fogel, figurehead president of Philadelphia. These four plotted Lynch's removal. In 1912 Fogel suggested that Herrmann arrange "a little caucus" among their group to decide on a successor for Lynch, who was "Brush's man." If they could achieve "a nice understanding all around" they could "spring a nice little surprise" at the league's annual meeting. In this way, "no newspaper fuss" would be made over it; it would "blow over" quickly, and even Lynch's friends would soon forget that he had ever been president of the league. Fogel's scheme failed. Dreyfuss believed that caucuses like the one proposed did no good, and refused to subscribe to Fogel's plan.

Ironically, Fogel was to be removed before Lynch was. Fogel, a former Philadelphia newspaperman and a National League secret agent who had been assigned to work among American League players during the war between the leagues, became president of the Philadelphia club in November 1909. Once in office, he lost no time in complaining about President Lynch and the umpires. His complaints were intensified after a fracas between his outfielder, Sherwood Magee, and Umpire William Finneran during a game in St. Louis. When Finneran removed Magee for disputing a decision, the player punched him in the face, and he had to be sent to the hospital. Lynch

* See below, chapter 9.

fined Magee and suspended him for the remainder of the season—
and for once was supported by the league board of directors. Later
Lynch relented and reinstated Magee on probation, because the Phillies, ridden with injuries, were short of men.

But Fogel was not satisfied. He wanted to know by what right
Lynch could reinstate a player "temporarily," and he continued his
agitation against umpires. The climax came in 1912 when Fogel publicly charged that Roger Bresnahan, manager of St. Louis and former
star catcher of the Giants, had helped his old team win the pennant
by having his present team "take it easy" against them. He also accused Lynch and the umpires of having connived to let the Giants
win the championship.

Lynch could take no more, and Fogel was charged before the
league on seven counts that winter. Julius Fleischmann acted as
judge, and seven other league owners formed a jury. The league condemned Fogel on five of the seven counts and banned him from ever
again sitting in league councils. It proclaimed its right to exclude anyone who fell short of the league's "high principles" and proved to be
"unfit to discharge the high duties devolving upon him in our deliber-
ations." In banishing him, the league owners were careful not to in-
fringe on any property rights Fogel had in the franchise, but he was
forced out anyway when the original backer of the club insisted that
Fogel honor his option to buy into the club, a move that was beyond
Fogel's financial capacity.

Many newspapermen questioned the justice of this verdict and
maintained that Fogel was made the goat for the real culprit, Charles
W. Murphy, owner of the Chicago Cubs. They knew that Charles P.
Taft, wealthy Cincinnatian and half-brother of the President of the
United States, had put up the money that enabled Murphy to take
control of the Chicago Cubs, and that both Taft and Murphy had financial fingers in the Philadelphia club, whose ball park was owned
by Mrs. Taft. And it was Taft and Murphy who had installed Fogel
as president of the Philadelphia club in a deal that provided for all
three to have equal shares of stock in the club and for Fogel to be
paid a salary and 10 per cent of the profits for running it. Fogel was
to pay 7 per cent interest on his shares of stock to Taft. Fogel's public
denial of outside financial backing at the time he assumed office,
made with Murphy looking over his shoulder, left him a laughing-
stock among the newspapermen. Some also suspected he was placed in
Philadelphia in exchange for promising not to vote for John A. Heydler as league president.

So when Fogel was ousted, newspapermen looked behind him to
Murphy, and the sports editor of the Chicago *Post*, G. F. Forman, re-

vealed that the article in his newspaper accusing Bresnahan and St. Louis of crookedness, and signed by Fogel, had in reality been written by Murphy. In short, the hapless Fogel, as many suspected, had fronted for Murphy, and had now paid the forfeit. Apropos of the affair is an excerpt from the "Book of Lynch" printed in *Sporting News* that December:

> And Lynch said unto Fogel, "Depart ye forever into darkness" but he said unto Murphy "Arise, thy sins are forgiven thee, be thou white as snow." But the multitude murmured and said among themselves, "why doth he make fish of the one and goat flesh of the other?" And none could make answer.

But Murphy's turn was to come shortly.

The interlocking control of clubs that was publicized in connection with the Fogel fiasco demonstrated only one aspect of the financial entanglement in the major leagues. It will be recalled that earlier proposals for one consolidated major league were rejected. Nevertheless, within each major league, ownership of clubs was highly interlocked. Cincinnati President Garry Herrmann was also an important stockholder in the Philadelphia club, held shares in St. Louis, and made loans to both St. Louis and Brooklyn to tide over Frank Robison and Charles Ebbets, their respective presidents, in periods of financial straits. Julius Fleischmann held stock in both Cincinnati and Philadelphia. Barney Dreyfuss, Pittsburgh owner, was another who had stock in the Phillies, and one year he shipped three players to them to help them out.

New York and Boston also had financial ties with each other. Arthur Soden, Boston owner, had long held stock in the New York Giants, and after he left baseball in 1906 these holdings remained in possession of his heirs until 1928. Later, the situation was reversed. It was commonly accepted, though never proved, that when the Boston club was sold in 1919 to a New York group headed by George W. Grant, a friend of John McGraw's, it was Charles A. Stoneham, then the Giants' owner, who advanced Grant $100,000 of the purchase price, thus bringing the Braves under the influence of the Giants. Ned Hanlon could even manage the Cincinnati team and at the same time continue to be a stockholder in Brooklyn; in addition, he was principal owner of the minor-league Baltimore club—a convenient setup for covering up players in Baltimore.

The American League, too, had some interlocking ownership. When it started, Charles Somers, wealthy Clevelander, supplied finances for several of its clubs. Even when it was more securely established, it still had some mingled ownership, though probably not to the extent that the National League had. The entire American League cooperated in running the Washington club for a while until Ban Johnson was able to find suitable owners. Johnson also had stock in the Boston club for a time and for years had a financial interest in the Cleveland club, as did Comiskey. The famous relationship between the New York Yankees and the Boston Red Sox is discussed later in a different context.

These interlocking ownerships reflected to some degree what the famous Pujo Committee of the United States Senate revealed in 1913 about the corporate structure of American business in general. The baseball owners were not proud of this situation. Certainly they did not publicize it, for syndicate baseball had long been in ill repute with fans and writers. When rumors or accusations cropped up in the press, they were met either with denials or weak justifications. "What the people want is good baseball," said Robison; "they don't care who owns the clubs." Although both major leagues gestured against the evil with weak resolutions in 1910, no rule prevented multiple ownership until the practice was banned in 1927.*

After the Fogel affair, the National League retained Lynch as president for a fourth term, but at the end of 1913 they decided to get rid of him and sought a more prestigious leader, who, as Dreyfuss said, could "bring together the petty factions that now exist in our ranks." They turned to John K. Tener, Governor of Pennsylvania. The movement for Tener was launched by W. F. Baker, onetime Police Commissioner of New York City, who became president and chief stockholder of the Philadelphia club after Fogel's departure. After a good deal of maneuvering—including convincing Ebbets, Dreyfuss, and Herrmann to abandon support of their perennial candidate, Bob Brown—the magnates sounded out Tener and, finding him willing, voted him a four-year contract reportedly for $25,000 a year, a great deal more than the $9000 Lynch had been getting. The greater job security provided by this long-term agreement promised to strengthen the National League presidency and consequently increase the stability of the National Commission.

Tener, like Lynch, had previous experience in professional ball, with Baltimore and Chicago in the 1880's. As a member of the Players' Union, he had pitched for the "outlaw" Pittsburgh Players' League team in 1890. He had also gone on the 1889 World Tour with the White Sox and All-Stars. After some experience in banking he entered Pennsylvania politics where he moved up through the Boise

---

* The American League owners, however, agreed in 1910 as part of a secret pact to prohibit syndicate ball "except as an emergency measure and only with the consent of the League's president and directors."

Penrose machine. Ebbets doubtless voiced the opinion of the other magnates when he said that Tener was an "ideal candidate" who "would go into office without one word of criticism from any quarter or any newspaper" and "would place the National League again before the world as the premier [baseball] organization." The league's official statement expressed the same theme: Tener would add "dignity and prestige to the office." The displaced Lynch replied sharply to the implied slur on him: "I hope you will inject some of that same dignity expected of him into yourselves and be a help instead of a hindrance to him." John A. Heydler continued to remain as league pack horse under the new president.

Like his predecessors, Tener had his problems. For one thing, Charles Murphy continued to act up until he became obnoxious to his colleagues. "Chubby Charlie," as reporters liked to call him, first entered baseball as a sort of press agent for the New York Giants; his job was to precede the team on its road trips and hand out information to boost the club. While going about his job in Chicago, he learned that the Cubs were up for sale. He moved quickly. Securing an option to buy from James Hart, president of the club, he rushed to Cincinnati where he succeeded in getting Charles P. Taft, whom he knew from his newspaper days there, to finance him, since he had only about $15,000 of his own. The price was reported by the Cincinnati *Enquirer* to be $105,000, $5000 of which was a bonus demanded by Hart for handling the deal.

Murphy turned out to be a growing trial to his fellow owners. His free-wheeling, often indiscreet comments to the press repeatedly irritated and embarrassed them. "He talks too much for his own good and the good of baseball," the usually genial Garry Herrmann once grumbled. "He is continually trying to stir up trouble and strife and to cause hard feelings between the club owners of the two leagues." Dreyfuss was even more scathing, publicly calling him a "rat" and a "sneak."

Murphy was in hot water with his colleagues from the first. The hassle over the World Series ticket scandal in 1908 has already been mentioned. In 1911 he stirred up the fuss that led to the Fogel trial by creating a scene in the lobby of the Waldorf-Astoria, shouting at St. Louis Manager Bresnahan, "You are a liar, I know the whole thing, and I've got something on you and will have you put out of the National League." This outburst was evidently touched off by Murphy's anger over Bresnahan's refusal to give waivers on a player Murphy was trying to slip into the minors. Bresnahan demanded an investigation by the National Commission, not because he himself needed the Commission's protection against "windbags" like Murphy, he said, but because baseball did. The Commission deliberated for a time over the question of its jurisdiction and finally decided that, since two National League people were involved, the issue should first come before that body. Nothing was done to Murphy at the time, but without doubt the incident inspired Murphy's accusations of crookedness against Bresnahan published in the Chicago *Post* under Fogel's name, which cost Fogel his career in baseball.

Murphy's own downfall resulted from his disposal of several high-salaried players who had been key figures in bringing three straight pennants to Chicago (1907–9) but who were showing signs of slowing down. Ignoring the fact that these men had helped him toward very considerable profits and heedless of the deep attachment Chicago fans felt for them, he shed all sentiment and rid himself of some of these favorites. He fired Frank Chance as his manager by unceremoniously sending him notice during the post-season Chicago city series of 1912. The New York Yankees wanted Chance for their manager, but Murphy, who still held property rights to him as a player, was unwilling to let him go without getting something for him. Garry Herrmann and other National League owners, recognizing that the "Peerless Leader" deserved the opportunity offered by the Yankees, cleared the path for him. Herrmann threw in an extra player in exchange for Chance as part of another player deal with Murphy; then, arranging for National League clubs to waive rights to him, he sold him to the Yankees for $1700.

Murphy also traded Big Ed Reulbach, a prominent member of his once fine pitching staff, to Brooklyn, and Joe Tinker, the famous shortstop, to Cincinnati. His most criticized action was the transfer of Mordecai "Three-Finger" Brown, one of the outstanding pitchers of his era and long the bellwether of the Chicago staff, to the ignominy of a minor league. However, Joe Tinker, who went to Cincinnati as player-manager, got Garry Herrmann to rescue Brown by bringing him to his own club.

After this housecleaning, Murphy appointed Johnny Evers, the sole remaining member of the legendary double-play combination of "Tinker to Evers to Chance," as playing manager for 1913. Most people thought that Evers did well to bring the team in third that season, but Murphy had plans for him too. Evers was working under a four-year contract at $10,000 a year but evidently thought he was in a position to demand a raise because the newly formed independent Federal League was dickering with him to join it. At any rate, he told Murphy that unless he received more money he would not play for the Cubs. Murphy, jumping at the opportunity of getting rid of Evers and his expensive contract, chose to interpret Evers's statement as a resignation and, without giving him the required ten days' notice, declared Evers was through.

But here the National League stepped in. The competing Federal League was pressing Organized Baseball and by this time had captured some of its "name players," including Tinker and Brown. Dismayed at the prospect of also losing Evers to the Federals and anxious to preserve as much public good will as possible in this trying time, President Tener insisted that Murphy respect Evers's contract.

Meanwhile, James Gaffney, owner of the Boston Braves, offered to trade for Evers, with a guarantee that he would pay him what he had been receiving from Chicago. Murphy agreed, but now Evers, realizing that the Federal League offer placed him in a strong bargaining position, balked and demanded that he be declared a free agent so he could make a deal for himself. The upshot was that he finally did go to Boston in exchange for Bill Sweeney, an infielder, and in addition to receiving the same salary, he collected a substantial bonus, probably paid by the league to keep him out of the hands of the Federal League.

The National League was now thoroughly fed up with Murphy and was determined to force him out, egged on by Ban Johnson who, Murphy said, tried to put him out of baseball "four or five times a year with a wave of the hand." Charles P. Taft bought Murphy's 53 per cent interest for more than $500,000. Taft's selection of William Hale Thompson as new club president brought further misgivings, since he had been Murphy's assistant. Thompson's appointment seemed to indicate that Murphy was not really out. Barney Dreyfuss protested that making a virtual office boy chief executive of a club was an insult to every club owner, and alleged that "the record and reputation of Mr. Thompson are not of the best and at this time we cannot afford to carry men of his character." Taft, however, reassured the owners that he had purchased all of Murphy's stock and convinced them to let things stand until new buyers could be procured.

As for Tener, he lasted the best part of five years as National League president, having signed a one-year contract for 1918 after his four-year agreement ran out. His first two years as a baseball leader overlapped his last two as Governor of Pennsylvania, thus presenting another of those "only in America" spectacles—a circumstance matched later by Baseball Commissioners Landis and Chandler, who for a time also continued in their respective jobs, the former as Federal Judge and the latter as United States Senator.

Tener, because of his prestige, perhaps commanded a greater measure of support from the owners than his predecessors did, although he himself recognized the limitations of his power when he asked,

"What can a president accomplish who is authorized by the laws of the league [only] to preside over the meetings and to supervise the umpires?"

If nothing else, he brought McGraw up short. Following a June 1917 game McGraw punched Umpire Bill Byron after the two had exchanged hard words. Tener suspended the Giants' manager for sixteen days and fined him $500. McGraw, when asked by Sid Mercer, a New York reporter, to comment, delivered an angry tirade against Tener. Mercer included it in his article and, since it was such a vehement attack, went so far as to submit his copy to McGraw for approval before sending it in and filing similar stories for three other New York writers.

When the story broke, the league board of directors summoned McGraw to explain himself. At the hearing McGraw repudiated the story, claiming he had never made such an outburst. Mercer and the other New York writers, aroused by this reflection on their veracity, demanded that the league investigate and find out who was lying. Tener agreed and convened a full-dress session, complete with attorneys and witnesses for all parties—the league, the writers, and McGraw. The writers were vindicated, and Tener levied an additional $1000 fine on McGraw and made it stick.

Nevertheless, in the end Tener, too, went the way of all National League presidents—the owners failed to uphold him when the chips were down. In August 1918 he called it quits because of their unwillingness to stand by him in a serious break with the American League over a disputed player, a break that was to play a significant part in the decline and eventual disappearance of the National Commission itself.

3

THE COMPONENTS OF PROFIT

Howrever MUCH baseball promoters may indulge in political maneuvering and factional rivalries, they have no choice in the final analysis but to cooperate. They are in the business of selling baseball games and, unlike operators of more conventional enterprises, they cannot create and market their product independently because a ball game can be staged only in conjunction with another team. In effect, a baseball game is, as the economist Simon Rottenberg has suggested, two companies producing one commodity. This situation makes the baseball owners at once competitors and partners.

It is also necessary that opposing teams match each other in skill as closely as possible if they are to arouse maximum consumer interest in their product—a fact that baseball promoters learned early. They also found that when teams from different cities were pitted against each other, the illusion could be created that each team symbolized the city in which it was located, and the local residents, identifying with "their team," would channel their civic pride and personal sentiment into the game. Carried away by fervid partisanship and imaginary ownership, the baseball fan would forget he paid money to watch professionals play for money in the interests of promoters.

Baseball operators soon discovered that these emotional drives and urban rivalries could be quickened and sustained, in season and out, with regularly scheduled games among a group of teams in the context of a pennant race for a league championship. Such a continuing series of games put on day after day fed and preserved interest by dangling the fans between hope and despair as their adopted heroes (few, if any, were of local origin) battled the hated rivals.

The mixture of competition and cooperation inherent in professional baseball subjects the club owners to conflicting urges: on the one hand, to strengthen their own clubs as much as they can; on the other, to keep all clubs of their league in reasonable equilibrium.

Otherwise, games would be one-sided, the pennant race would become lopsided, and interest would fade, to the detriment of attendance.

How did the owners work out their dual problem? A tempting method of guaranteeing close competition is establishment of the "syndicate ball" already mentioned: the clubs would be lumped together under common ownership; then all the players would be pooled and divided evenly among the clubs. The difficulty with such a system is that it casts doubt upon the genuineness of competition. Another extreme solution is to establish each club under completely independent ownership and permit no exchange of players among clubs. The disadvantage of this arrangement is that the wealthier and more skillfully managed clubs might outstrip the others, again to the detriment of real competition.

To avoid the drawbacks of both systems, pioneer baseball promoters gradually patched together a serviceable, albeit imperfect, solution. Declaring for honest competition, they rejected syndicate ball by confirming separate ownership of clubs, and in time specifically prohibited anyone from holding stock in more than one club in a league. On the other hand, to counteract the disadvantages of unbridled competition, they agreed to cooperate in a number of restrictive practices. Of these, the reserve rule, territorial rights, and the division of gate receipts have already been described. Others were the waiver and draft rules, designed to give all clubs an opportunity to acquire at least some players at non-competitive prices; ceilings on player salaries, particularly in the minor leagues; and a limit on the number of players each club could control.

These restraints on free competition, aimed at braking the financial power of the wealthier clubs, have fallen far short of their avowed objectives because owners either violated or circumvented some of them and clung to others too rigidly, with the result that most of the pennants and wealth have gone to a few clubs.

The partner-competitor relationship among baseball entrepreneurs is often cited to justify exemption of the industry and its restrictive practices, which the owners claim are essential to it, from the application of the anti-trust laws. However, the difference between conventional industry and baseball is not as great as might be supposed. Modern American corporations also work together closely. The various specialists employed by them meet in their own associations and exchange information on an extensive scale. Sometimes this cooperation becomes so cozy and collusive that the Federal Trade Commission finds it necessary to step in with penalties for restraint of trade. The difference between cooperation in American industry and in baseball is that in the former it is merely advantageous, while in the latter it is essential—which is still not to say that the anti-trust exemption is necessary, let alone desirable.

The chief income of the baseball industry derives from ticket sales. Practically all other sources of income are offshoots of attendance: the peddling of refreshments through direct or indirect operation of concessions, the sale of advertising on scorecards and ball-park fences, and, more recently, the income from radio, television, and parking lots. Rental of the park for other functions is another source of remuneration. Although gate receipts are still the life blood of the industry TV receipts have swelled steadily in recent years to the point of rivalling gate receipts in importance. There are even those who go so far as to predict that eventually television income will supplant gate receipts, and the teams will perform quietly among themselves in deserted stadiums for TV audiences.

Attendance in turn is determined by a host of variables. For purposes of simplicity, they may be separated into two broad groups: those extraneous to the business, which stem from the general economic, social, or cultural climate prevailing; and those inherent in the business, over which the owners, working individually and collectively, can exert a direct measure of control or influence. These two sets of factors are not sharply distinct; in fact, there is considerable interaction between them. For instance, the community determines whether Sunday ball is permissible, sometimes with an assist from baseball men; but the baseball operators decide upon the number of Sunday games and which clubs are to get how many. The same is true of night baseball. Technological advance makes it possible, but it is for the owners to say how many night games will be sold.

The outside forces that impinge on baseball attendance are more delayed in their effect and apply more to Organized Baseball as a whole than to clubs individually. Population growth belongs in this category, particularly if the increase is reflected in cities, since it is only there that a mass audience can be recruited for commercialized spectator amusements. The general level of prosperity, another factor, will sway the response of potential customers, for it involves wages, hours, disposable income, and the amount of leisure available. And war, of course, is bound to make itself felt in every corner of society.

Attendance is also affected by technological changes and improvements. As Professor John R. Betts has pointed out, those who have sought to explain the evolution of sports have usually emphasized the role of individuals while largely overlooking the influence of technology. The very concept of establishing professional baseball leagues among distant cities and playing a regular schedule of games would have been at best a dream were it not for the railroad networks of the nineteenth century and the airplane of the twentieth. A mere mention of the telegraph, electric light, airplane, automobile, and television is a reminder of the profound impact of technology on the business of selling baseball games. Or take rain, cold, or extreme heat, once fickle but unmistakable influences upon attendance; technology has increasingly reduced or eliminated their influence over the gate with such developments as improved methods of draining the playing fields, electric blankets and jackets for the players, artificial turf, and the domed stadium, making play possible in all weather, day or night. Now the computer is being introduced for such jobs as arranging league schedules and for handling ticket sales.

During the era of the National Commission, most of these attendance factors favored Organized Baseball. Generally good business conditions provided a sure foundation for the industry. Those were spacious, buoyant, and, on the whole, prosperous years for America. A prodigious $100 billion increase in national wealth brightened the first two decades of the twentieth century. Most classes shared in these gains, for although the cost of living rose, real wages edged slightly higher and the work week in non-agricultural industries declined sharply; most important, full and steady employment generally prevailed. Still, many workers, especially those unorganized, toiled under harsh conditions. In steel, for instance, about 30 per cent of them continued to work a seven-day week, and uncounted families still living in poverty further detracted from the overall economic advance. Then, too, short though severe depressions in 1907 and 1914 marred the era. But unless protracted, depressions do not seriously affect attendance at ball games. In fact, the unemployed may spend some of their enforced leisure watching this relatively inexpensive form of entertainment. World War One set attendance back temporarily, as did baseball's own economic war with the independent Federal League.

Other things being equal, the greater the population the larger the attendance at ball games. Moreover, population growth coincided with economic expansion in those years. By 1920 the total population in round numbers reached 105 million, as against 76 million in 1900. About 70 per cent of the people lived east of the Mississippi, a fact that gave some justification to the existing geographic location of major-league clubs. But would it always make sense? We can now see that the Pacific Coast's 73 per cent gain in those decades already promised a negative answer.

More significant for Organized Baseball was the unceasing movement of people from the country to the city. In 1900 approximately 40 per cent of Americans were city dwellers; by 1910 the proportion was nearly 46 per cent; and by 1920 America's urban and rural population were about equally divided. A craving for amusement and excitement accounted in part for the steady shift, and the baseball promoters, among others, capitalized on it.

Within the growing cities the elevated railway, the electric trolley car, and the subway transported the multitudes to the ball parks. The subway was just beginning to share the load. New York broke ground for one in 1900, and Boston, first to go underground, had already completed a short line. As the subway lines were steadily extended, they naturally carried more fans and got them there faster. They were to be of prime strategic importance to the less accessible parks, as they were to the Yankees when the subway opened a station at 168th Street, nearly at the doorstep of their old Hilltop grounds.

The trolley companies, too, reached farther and farther out, making suburban living feasible and extending the ball clubs' metropolitan markets along with the car tracks. In some areas, like Western Pennsylvania, Indiana, and Michigan, trolley lines hooked together strings of towns often as much as twenty-five miles apart. Such cheap and rapid transportation prompted the formation of trolley baseball leagues, with players and fans alike using the car lines to get from town to town. These leagues also provided a haven of sorts for professionals on the downgrade and a stimulus to youngsters to play ball.

In the large cities, the long-standing affinity between streetcar lines and professional ball clubs continued. Traction companies sometimes arranged for excursions to the games at special rates. Owners were aware of their dependence on the trolleys for bringing the fans to their gates. When Ban Johnson was trying to expand his new American League into New York, he sought backing from influential New Yorkers by presenting them with the financial statements of streetcar lines, showing their volume of business in taking fans to and from games. Barney Dreyfuss congratulated himself on locating his new park adjacent to sixteen car lines, which could add large cars and trailers on big days, although in a few years he complained that inadequate service was costing him money.

The customary cooperation between the railroads and professional ball increased. The roads were always eager for the major leagues' business, and in that era they realized an estimated $60,000 a year transporting teams. The railroads, like the trolley companies, offered cut-rate excursions to the ball games for fans from more distant areas. They advertised these package deals in newspapers that circulated in territories traversed by their lines or by means of fliers sent directly to the postmasters for display in towns lacking newspapers. The ball clubs obliged by supplying advance information about special attractions, such as a Sunday doubleheader with, say, the New York Giants, always a good crowd-puller. A sample ad in the Lexington (Kentucky) *Leader* in 1908 offered a round trip to Cincinnati for $1.50 on a special train leaving Lexington at 7:30 a.m. for a game between the Reds and Pittsburgh. Another railroad executive expected to bring from 1500 to 2000 people to Cincinnati on July 29, 1903, many of them making the trip just to see the ball game. That section of the country "is base ball crazy," he said, and he chose the July date knowing that the farmers would be through with their most urgent work at that time. The bumpkin character of the rural population in those days is attested to by the fact that the railroad prepared guides to help those "bewildered by city noises and streetcars" to find their way around the city.

The railroads and the professional clubs worked together in other ways. The roads offered special rates for teams and furnished passes to the baseball executives. And because the myth to the contrary is still perpetuated, it should be reiterated that as a rule the major-league teams traveled first class. Some magnates were known to abuse the pass privilege by requesting passes for the writers covering their teams and then using them for their own players. In the fledgling days of the American League, Ban Johnson even talked the Wabash railroad into providing his clubs' traveling accommodations on credit. The Wabash assigned a clerk named Will Harridge to Johnson's office in Chicago to handle the routing of the clubs. Harridge later accepted Ban Johnson's offer to be his secretary and eventually worked his way up to the presidency of the American League.

Railroads had long since been advertising on scorecards, and there were instances of their standing the cost of printing a ball club's tickets in exchange for permission to advertise on the back of them. On their part, ball clubs handed out season baseball passes to so many railroad executives that the National League finally passed a resolution curtailing their issuance. Sometimes executives in the two industries became quite chummy. At the time of the "Red Scare" after World War One, one railway executive expressed his hopes to a baseball owner that "your Bolsheviks"—meaning players holding out for more money—would "come to their senses and report."

A new technological contraption that increasingly influenced baseball was the automobile. At first it was hardly more than a toy of the rich. Fewer than 14,000 cars were registered in the entire United States in 1900, a time when some ten million Americans were still pedaling bicycles. Despite opposition from various quarters, churches among them, which rated automobiles with golf as threats to the traditional Sabbath, cars increased in number inexorably year after year, until mass production of an inexpensive machine turned a flood into a torrent. The social revolution perpetrated by the automobile touched baseball as it did practically every facet of American life.

The impact was not sharply felt until after World War One, when the automobile really came into its own. Nevertheless, professional baseball offered a foretaste of the future prominence of the automobile with the inauguration in 1910 of the Chalmers award—the presentation of an automobile of that long-forgotten make to the major-league batting champions of the season. A few baseball men also foresaw that if the ball clubs were to keep in step with the times they would soon be compelled to provide parking space for their patrons. Charles Ebbets arranged a special service for car owners: they could wait in a certain room after the game while an attendant brought their parked cars to them. Some minor leagues set up what might be called a drive-in system, marking off spaces along one side of the field which fans could rent on a seasonal basis for viewing the game from their cars—but with some risk of a broken windshield or dented body.

Bus, taxi, and trucking companies solicited clubs for the business of transporting players, baggage, and equipment between railroad stations and hotels and between the hotels and the ball parks. Ten cents for "grips" and twenty-five cents for trunks was the going rate.

The more affluent ball players were taking up "automobiling," purchasing cars as status symbols and outlets for conspicuous consumption. The new contraptions landed some players in difficulties. Two of them received thirty days in the workhouse for running down a trolley-car motorman. Others were injured in accidents. When the famous star Honus Wagner crashed into a railroad gate, a *Sporting News* editorial called upon club owners to "forbid this fad, a result of players' natural craving for speed and undue risk." In an era before credit buying became an acceptable part of the American way of life and when lack of thrift was frowned upon, ball players were sharply criticized for indulging in the "extravagance" of owning a "machine."

The more pertinent question for baseball, though unperceived at that juncture, was whether the deluge of cars, when it came, would be a help or a hindrance. It turned out to be both. The automobile was to make ball parks more accessible to fans, especially those from outlying districts, but it would also give them the mobility to escape from the cities and pursue leisure activities other than going to ball games.

Since Organized Baseball is a monopoly, it need fear no competition within its own sphere, except on those occasions when a rival league challenges its sway. But it does have to contend with other spectator amusements and commercialized entertainment, as well as with the varied and steadily expanding recreational activities of Americans. In the pre-1920 era, the baseball industry had relatively little outside competition. It maintained its enviable, long-held position as the most-watched and most-played game in America. "Unquestionably the premier position among American sports was held by baseball" is the rating given by a well-known social historian of the period; and Lord Bryce, that astute British observer of the American scene, judged the interest excited by baseball and football matches "greater than any other public event except the Presidential election." The language of a 1912 issue of *Sporting News* expressed the point vividly:

> There is only one sport that appeals to them all,
> When you size up the dope on the case,
> There is only one sport and its name is base ball,
> Others follow; it sets the pace.

Horse racing, America's first popular spectator sport, existed precariously, stained by association with touts and gamblers. Some states banned it outright, and in consequence it centered in Havana, where some of professional baseball's leading lights went to bet and invest until Commissioner Landis ordered them to stop. Boxing, too, was still associated with the underworld and, like horse racing, was illegal in many states.

Football, as Lord Bryce noticed, commanded a wide following, but it was still primarily a college game, stigmatized by its bone-crushing brutality. Injuries and deaths brought it to crisis around 1905. Harvard's President Eliot condemned it in his 1906 annual report and advised suspension of the game. Columbia College and many lesser schools eliminated it altogether. Immediately, under the urging of Theodore Roosevelt and some college authorities, the rules were reformed and the game restored. It was then ready to move forward to its peak collegiate years in the 1920's and to become big business under university and college operation. Basketball, about the only game indigenous to America, was just making its way into the colleges and cut no significant figure as yet.

Golf and tennis, long appropriated by the social elite, continued to be played largely by the few and scorned by the many, who regarded golf as a dude's game and who scoffed at tennis as an effeminate diversion fit only for tea-drinking fops and social celebrities. Popular antipathy toward these sports impelled Theodore Roosevelt to warn William Howard Taft of the political pitfalls in playing them: ". . . it would seem incredible that anyone would care one way or the other about your playing golf, but I have received literally hundreds of letters from the West protesting about it." Roosevelt further cautioned, "I myself play tennis, but that game is a little more familiar; besides, you never saw a photograph of me playing tennis, I am careful about that; photographs on horseback, yes; tennis, no. And golf is fatal."

Nevertheless, these games were showing evidence of democratization, a process undergone by baseball nearly half a century before. The cannonball service transformed tennis from its old pat-ball days and helped prove it worthy of more than sissies. Golf was on the way to becoming one of the fastest-growing sports in the country, aided by the mobility provided by the automobile and by the decreasing cost resulting from the spread of inexpensive municipal courses. Alarmed at the "growing charms" of golf, *Sporting News* called attention in 1914 to its "terrible threat" to the baseball owners.

Worse yet, the ancient Scottish game was seducing some of baseball's magnates and many of its outstanding players. Manager John McGraw, that epitome of the toughness and pugnacity then thought desirable in baseball, condemned golf as the worst game for players, not only bad physically and mentally but degrading morally. He would as soon have a player out to five o'clock tea or part his hair in the middle as play a game of golf, he said. Yet only two years later who should be found on the links in Havana, togged out in white flannels no less, but the same McGraw! "Who would have thought it of Muggsy," chided a reporter. "He at least was supposed to uphold some of the traditions of the old days. Well, baseball is getting to be one of the higher professions where to be right you have to change to evening clothes at 6 p.m. and be able to use three forks at meals without pulling a bone." Before long the ball players began bringing their golf clubs along with them to spring training camps.

One amusement that competed with professional baseball for the masses' entertainment before World War One was the new motion-picture industry. From the crude nickelodeons it graduated to regular full-length films with "The Great Train Robbery" in 1903. In 1910 the business enjoyed weekly admissions of ten million; by 1914 Marie Dressler and Charlie Chaplin were names even more widely known than those of outstanding baseball heroes. It is interesting, too, that the movie industry, like baseball and so many other American industries, developed a tendency to consolidate and formed a trust in 1908 for the purpose of pooling patent rights and injecting "discipline" into the business through a system of licensing.

The movie industry also lent itself to cooperation with baseball. Possibly the first moving pictures of players were taken in 1903 when

Napoleon Lajoie and Harry Bay were "immortalized" during a post-season series between Cleveland and Cincinnati. In 1910 a commercial film by the Essanay Company entitled "Take Me Out to the Ball Game" was a big hit.

The World Series was a natural for the new media. In St. Louis alone, pictures of the 1908 World Series packed two movie houses twice a day for a week. At first the National Commission regarded filming the World Series as just a novelty and failed to grasp its financial possibilities. But after observing public response, Harry Pulliam admitted that "American enterprise had caught the Commission napping." He declared that players, clubs, and the National Commission should share in the proceeds, since they furnished the attraction. So the Commission soon extracted a fee for World Series movie rights. It sold them for $500 in 1910. Ban Johnson, who disapproved of letting the movies in on the World Series, suggested raising the price to $5000 for the 1911 Series, with a view toward pricing the movie people out of the market. Johnson was not the first baseball man, nor would he be the last, to balk at innovations and to accept change only reluctantly or under pressure. National League President Tom Lynch, however, rejected Johnson's proposal, and $3500 was asked and received for the movie rights that year.

But the players were not cut in after all, as Pulliam had envisaged. Representatives of the Giants and Athletics protested to the Commission but were turned down. Players began to complain about posing and "pulling off stunts" for the cameras before games, as ordered by the National Commission, without getting any extra money for it. The issue of player cooperation for publicity purposes arose again on later occasions, with the result that the standard major-league contract now contains a proviso requiring players to lend themselves to a certain amount of public-relations projects.

Baseball began using the movies in another way—for instructional purposes. Taking movies of players in action so that they can study their faults and correct them is an accepted technique in modern baseball. The idea was conceived back in 1914 by Harry E. Aitken, president of the Mutual Film Corporation and an ardent Giants' fan, who got John McGraw to order movie "machines" for spring training to help the Giants improve their play.

All these external influences—the expanding economy, growing population and urbanization, technological innovation and improvement—provided a generally beneficial climate for professional baseball during the regime of the National Commission. They were conducive, or at least not obstructive, to good attendance. Although other games, commercial amusements, and signs of changing recreational habits stemming from more leisure pressed their claims for the consumer's dollars and time, with the exception of motion pictures they all appeared more as shadowy threats, portents of the future, than as serious contenders with baseball for major attention and emotional commitment.

But what of the second group of attendance factors, those over which the owners have some direct influence? Counted among these are the skill of the team and the crowd appeal of individual players, the continuity of the team's tenure in a particular city, and the permanence of its player personnel. Time helps to develop a team tradition, and to watch the same players year after year deepens the fans' sense of loyalty. On the other hand, introduction of some new faces from time to time also whets interest. A temporary stimulus to attendance is the sheer novelty of having major-league baseball in a town previously without it. Other factors are the price of admission and the type of park—its size, condition, comfort, and accessibility, and in recent years the safety of the neighborhood. As already explained, the size of the immediate market is of crucial importance. Because of modern transportation, the secondary market—that is, the territory within a radius of approximately a hundred miles of the city proper —has also become important.

Attendance can be strongly aided by intense city rivalries, such as the well-remembered fierce competition that prevailed between New York and Brooklyn, which the leaders of the Giants and Dodgers were at pains to exploit. Attendance is also stimulated by night and weekend games, since more people are free to go then. Even the starting time of the game can have a bearing. The quality and effectiveness of the team's publicity enter in as well. Innovation may play a part, but by and large it has been negligible in baseball because owners have been more prone to shun it than welcome it.

Among all the factors influencing attendance, however, the closeness of the pennant race stands paramount. A hard-fought, see-saw struggle for the championship is guaranteed to draw large crowds. And more than anything else it is financially beneficial not only to the clubs involved but to the entire league.

4

THE MAGNATES AT WORK

ALTHOUGH club owners indulged in petty politicking and circumvented their own rules, they often demonstrated enterprise in building up their businesses. During the era of the National Commission many of them were able to take advantage of the generally favorable social and economic conditions to construct new ball parks, renovate old ones, and make some gestures at promoting their product and thus contribute to increased attendance and profits. As some pointed out at the time, baseball was no longer a fly-by-night venture for shoestring operators, but a legitimate business stable enough to warrant long-term investment.

The most conspicuous example of enterprise was the construction of new ball parks. The old wooden structures of an earlier day were becoming ramshackle and unsightly. They could not accommodate even the crowds of that day, much less the larger ones anticipated. Fans were no longer content with uncomfortable, rickety stands, some of which were actually dangerous. The city of Cincinnati's building inspector in 1907 and again in 1908 presented a detailed bill of particulars about the unsafe condition of the park, including cracked girders and decayed supports, unsafe flooring, a fence in need of rebuilding, and a defective bleacher platform. The signboard on the roof was so loose it blew into the street. In St. Louis, too, the building commissioner was badgering the management. The Cardinals' grandstand, which dated back to the Union League of the 1880's, was in constant danger of collapse.

As owners embarked upon new construction, they often sought to secure their investments by lengthening their leases. It was even better, as some were quick to realize, to purchase the real estate on which the parks were built, as a long-term venture in the expanding cities of a growing country. The owners even toyed with a suggestion that each major league buy up all the ball-park sites of its member clubs, but they turned down the idea out of fear of being charged with syndicate baseball.

The building program also gave owners the chance to install more boxes and other high-priced seats as a means of increasing profits, since owners had to share only the base admission price with visiting teams and could keep all ticket money beyond that. Some owners realized that plowing back profits into larger, more elaborate plants might deter possible competitors, who would think twice before risking the big capital that would be necessary for crashing into the business with any hope of success.

The new parks, unlike the old, were massive concrete and steel structures. One day they, too, were to become shabby and outdated and in turn would be handed over to demolition crews who would ruthlessly tear them down to make way for apartment buildings. But once they were splendid stadiums in which generations of young boys, and old ones too, thrilled to unforgettable scenes.

The first of these "modern" parks was that of the Philadelphia National League club dating from the nineteenth century; however, the era of concrete and steel stadiums did not begin in earnest until 1909. The Phillies' opposite number in the American League, the Athletics, started the season that year in a new home, Shibe Park, named for the chief stockholder. The grandstand was a double-decker, all steel and concrete except for the brick walling. Even the bleachers were of concrete. The estimated cost of the park was half a million dollars. It could seat about 20,000, but the day it opened more than 30,000 fans were squeezed in. Water plugs were installed throughout the stands so that hoses could be attached for washing them down or for fighting fires. This improved apparatus can be appreciated in view of a contemporary assertion that probably not a third of the major-league grandstands were properly equipped for fire-fighting. Such apparatus as did exist was covered with the rust and dust of years, and the only water supply available was that used for sprinkling the diamond.

Building safer new parks also meant that insurance and maintenance costs were cut and the danger of collapse minimized. Nevertheless, a disaster in the Phillies' park in 1903 showed that even the newer parks were not entirely safe. In August that year several hundred fans, who had crowded against a rotted wooden railing to gape at a fight just outside the park, were hurled into the street twenty feet below when the railing gave way. As a result there were hundreds of injuries, twelve deaths, and a flock of lawsuits. Ironically, shortly before the tragedy the former owners had given assurances of the park's sound condition when they sold the property to a new syndicate, which included Garry Herrmann and Barney Dreyfuss. While repairs were being made, the park was closed down, so Ben Shibe of the local Athletics let the Phillies use his park.

Soon after Shibe Park opened, Barney Dreyfuss, with justifiable pride, opened his new "baseball palace" in Pittsburgh, which he named Forbes Field after a British general of frontier fame. Dreyfuss chose land in the best residential section of town opposite Schenley Park for his "most ornate" arena. The triple-decker stands had elevators, electric lights, telephones, and maids in the ladies' waiting rooms. Inclined-plane runways instead of stairs made the hike to the upper decks easier and also facilitated traffic. Dreyfuss cut down sharply on the number of cheap bleacher seats and devoted most of the space to the grandstand. Season boxes bearing removable brass name plates were available for a hundred dollars, although the box-holder still had to pay the seventy-five-cent general admission charge. Additional revenue came to Dreyfuss from rental of the park for horse shows, public gatherings, and other events. Barney's cup of joy ran over that season when his Pirates won the pennant and the world championship.

Two of baseball's most storied parks, New York's Polo Grounds and Brooklyn's Ebbets Field—alas, now only memories—opened in 1911 and 1913 respectively. Oddly, polo was never played at the Polo Grounds. In the 1880's James Gordon Bennett, the newspaperman, allowed the Giants to build a small park on part of the land at 110th Street and Fifth Avenue which he used for playing polo with his society friends, and when the Giants moved uptown to 155th Street a few years later they retained the name "Polo Grounds" for their new park.

That old hazard, fire, which had destroyed several wooden stands in the nineteenth century, struck the Chicago White Sox and Washington parks in 1909 and 1911. But when the wooden stands at the Polo Grounds burned down early in the 1911 season, the fire proved to be a long-term blessing for Brush and the Giants. With the season already under way and no place to play, Brush was in a quandary until Frank Farrell, president of his despised rival, the Yankees, let the Giants use his park temporarily. Brush quickly negotiated a new, long-term lease of the site of his old park with Mrs. Harriet Coogan, owner of the land, and without taking time to get competitive bids, he built anew at Coogan's Bluff on a cost-plus basis. By mid-season construction was well enough along for the Giants to return and for the job to be finished between games. Brush believed that the "interest in Base Ball has grown so great in this city that preparations to meet it justifies [sic] the erection of this mammoth structure," which he wanted to be "a model for all subsequent Base Ball structures."

Because the shape of the parks was determined by the contours of the real estate available in the inner city, playing fields varied in size and were often ill-proportioned. At the Polo Grounds, for instance, the right-field fence at the foul line was only 258 feet from home plate, whereas the center field fence was 425 feet away. The proximity of the right-field fence made for numerous "Chinese home runs"— homers on short pop flies that normally would be easily caught.

In Brooklyn, Ebbets correctly gauged the future growth and direction of the borough's population and acted to profit by it. He had already squeezed so many additional seats into his old Washington Park at Fourth Avenue and Third Street that boxes, only fifteen feet from home plate, encroached on the playing area, preventing catchers and infielders from demonstrating their skill in catching foul fly balls. Ebbets soon resolved to move farther out in the borough and over a period of several years quietly purchased bits and pieces of real estate in a depressed area called "Pigtown," where poor Italian immigrants lived in miserable shanties amidst goats and dandelions. Pigtown lay midway between the then fashionable Bedford section and suburban Flatbush. Upon completing his collection of real estate parcels from fifteen different owners, at a cost of $200,000, Ebbets began construction of his new park. He estimated it would cost about $423,000, which he planned to raise with a bond sale, a bank loan, and the club's $50,000 profit of 1912. But the cost turned out to be higher than his original estimate. Having seriously overreached himself financially, Ebbets sought loans from other magnates without success; so he welcomed the offer of the two Brooklyn contractors, Steve and Ed McKeever, to supply additional funds in exchange for a half-interest in the club.

The two-tiered grandstand of the new park seated about 22,000. The park's total capacity probably did not exceed 35,000 at most, including a section of wooden bleachers extending across left field, which was opened only on big days to handle the overflow from the regular bleachers, a small concrete section out along the left-field foul line adjacent to the grandstand. Sometimes Ebbets jammed the premises still more by selling standing room behind a rope stretched across left field in front of the extra bleacher section. Old Brooklyn fans will especially remember the marble rotunda that formed the main entrance at the corner of Sullivan Street and Cedar Place, ornate and impressive but an almost impossible bottleneck on busy days. Atop the outfield fences flew the flags of all the National League clubs, arranged from left to right each day in the order of the clubs' standings.

Although the new park was not in the heart of Brooklyn in 1913 when it opened for business, it was, as Ebbets pointed out, accessible to 90 per cent of the borough's population and within thirty to forty-five minutes' reach of three or four million people in the metropolitan area via trolley, subway, or elevated railway.° Nine direct trolley lines, which in turn transferred to thirty-two others, were handy for Brooklyn residents, and lower Manhattan's Wall Street and City Hall were only twenty minutes away by subway and the "el."

Those were the days of late-afternoon ball games. Choice of starting time was deliberate; owners were well aware of its relationship to attendance and strove to suit the preference of their customers. They eventually settled on 3 o'clock or 3:30 as the hour best calculated to send fans home in time for a 6 o'clock meal. After coming home later once or twice himself and finding his meal ruined, Charles Murphy, Chicago Cubs' president, concluded that 3 o'clock was just right, because "we must cater to the wives and cooks . . . and try to get our patrons home in time to keep peace in the family." Husbands would not even have to tell their wives that they were at the ball game, he added coyly.

The New York Giants, however, stuck to their customary 4 o'clock game time until 1912, when they changed to 3:30 after a steady hammering from fans and newspapermen. Brush was accused of starting late to suit Wall Street brokers without regard for other fans, including those from out of town, who liked to see a game but wanted to get away in time for dinner and a show. The Wall Streeters rallied to the status quo with a petition signed by four hundred of them. This pressure prompted one newspaper to headline its story "Wall Street Against the People Again." To settle the issue, Brush decided to poll the fans at the ball park, but he attached an attendance gimmick to this reckless essay into democracy by letting fans vote five times if they attended all five games of the series he chose for the balloting. He then accepted the verdict of the majority and switched to 3:30.

Probably Brush got the idea of polling the fans from Cleveland, where games had been moved up from 3:30 to 3 o'clock the year before in response to a fan vote of 12 to 1. In Washington, however, the trend veered for a time toward later games, owing to Theodore Roosevelt's enforcement of the 4:30 quitting time for government clerks, on whose patronage the club heavily relied.

Besides Dreyfuss and Ebbets, others with capital for new parks were American Leaguers Charles Somers in Cleveland and Charles Comiskey in Chicago, both of whom built parks shortly after Dreyfuss. National Leaguer James Gaffney opened a new park in Boston in 1915. But not all clubs built spanking new parks. Some, like the

° More important for me, it was only three blocks from my boyhood home.

Detroit Tigers and the St. Louis Browns, just renovated what they had, and others, like the St. Louis Cardinals, did not have the money to do even that.

A few owners dragged their feet, reluctant to spend until pressured into doing so. The previously mentioned report of the Cincinnati building inspector doubtless prodded that club into action. Besides, the management realized that it did not have enough high-priced seats in the old park. The New York Giants, it was pointed out, could count on $70,000 to $80,000 from the sale of box seats, even before the season started; Pittsburgh could figure on $20,000 in advance sales. Cincinnati, on the other hand, was limping along with the lowest per capita receipts of any club in the league because of the insufficiency of higher-priced seats for those willing to pay more. When the club did reconstruct in 1911, it went about the job in a businesslike way. A careful plan and a program for raising an estimated $225,000 to pay for it were prepared for the club's directors. Recommendations were made not to rush the work, as some others had done, because good results could not be had in a hurry. The concrete must be mixed properly and have time to set. And besides, a rush job cost more. The club added further improvements in the 1920's, remodeling and increasing the number of box seats.

Last to enter the ranks of the new builders were the New York Yankees. The club's original home, Hilltop Park, located in the vicinity of 168th Street, was as squalid as the reputation of its first owners. Ban Johnson accepted backers with strong Tammany Hall connections when he expanded his new American League into New York in 1903, in order to guard against the danger that Andrew Freedman, the New York Giants' owner at the time, might use his own Tammany political influence to have the city cut streets through any site Johnson might select for a ball park.

Chief among the new owners were Frank Farrell and Big Bill Devery. Farrell, an ex-saloonkeeper, had an interest in a number of operations. He was a bookie, "king" of a poolroom syndicate that controlled about 250 establishments, and part owner of a gambling house on West 33rd Street conveniently close to the Waldorf-Astoria Hotel. Devery was the subject of many trials and investigations for graft and corruption. He has been called "probably the most notorious police officer in New York City's history," an official who accumulated wealth and power by acting as "bag man" for Boss Sullivan, who in turn headed a syndicate that included Farrell. According to a New York *Times* estimate, the syndicate extracted about $3,095,000 annually from prostitution, gambling, and graft.

The Yankees played in Hilltop Park under the Farrell-Devery regime until 1913. By then the stands, never much to begin with, and the field, just dirt filling on rock, were completely inadequate, and the team, matching its surroundings, had sunk deep into the second division. Farrell's remedy was to sign a lease renting the newly built Polo Grounds from the Giants, with whom his relations had improved ever since he allowed them to use his park when the Polo Grounds burned. The team, however, showed no improvement. So Farrell and Devery, in financial straits and quarreling with each other, sold the club for about $460,000 to Colonel Jacob Ruppert, a brewer, and his friend Captain Tillinghast Huston, a self-made engineer-contractor.

Under the new owners, the Yankees continued to be tenants of the Giants with a new five-year lease, but in 1920 the Giants notified them that they were no longer wanted. The dispossess notice turned out to be a great boon to the Yankees. Ruppert arranged to stay on at the Polo Grounds for two more seasons, meanwhile picking up an option he had taken on land at 161st Street and completing construction of the present Yankee Stadium in time for the opening of the 1923 season. It was a cavernous three-decker ball park with a seating capacity of approximately 65,000, which made it the largest park in baseball.

At the very time the Yankees were being told to vacate the Polo Grounds, the National League's St. Louis Cardinals followed their precedent by becoming tenants of the St. Louis Browns. The Browns had not only adopted the name of Chris Von der Ahe's famous Browns of the 1880's but had taken over and renovated their plant, Sportsmen's Park. In 1920 the Cardinals, who had been scraping along in a run-down park used by the St. Louis Unions of 1884, persuaded the Browns to take them in. This arrangement enabled Sam Breadon, the Cardinals' owner, to sell the real estate on which his old park was situated and use the proceeds as working capital to improve the ball club.

By 1923 the fifteen stadiums that housed the sixteen major-league teams had seating capacities ranging from the 18,000 of the two St. Louis and the Philadelphia Nationals' parks to the 65,000 of the Yankees and the 54,000 of the Giants. The median seating capacity of the fifteen parks was 25,000, and the average came to about 30,000. If Americans are the Romans of the modern world, as is often said, the outdoor amphitheatres of Organized Baseball upheld such a comparison. They were a signature of American society, as their counterparts were of Roman life. And thirty years later a new splurge of stadium building would make this point even more striking.

Stadium construction brought Organized Baseball into contact with the protracted labor-management struggle then besetting American industry. A baseball owner might be exposed to attack from either side, depending upon whether the firms to which he awarded contracts hired union or non-union labor. The Cleveland club came under fire from the National Association of Manufacturers, which ever since 1903 had been directing the employers' attack on unionism through a widespread campaign to uphold "the American plan," meaning the open shop. The N.A.M. complained that the Cleveland club had allowed only firms hiring union labor to bid for the job of building its new park; when it questioned the club, the explanation was that the clubs in the American League had an agreement to deal only with unionized companies. The N.A.M., in a letter sent to all its members, sounded its pet theme: an agreement like that of the professional ball clubs, if there really was one, was "un-American and unjust discrimination against freedom of thought and action among builders . . . as well as against the independence of the working men themselves."

On the other hand, clubs that placed contracts with employers of non-union labor provoked threats of boycott by unions in several cities. In addition, owners who transported their teams by a struck railroad or patronized hotels whose employees were on strike risked secondary boycotts. The Cigar Makers' Union protested the sale of non-union-made cigars in ball parks. They reminded the owners that such cigars were made in tenements and sweat shops, often by child labor. However, bartenders and ushers employed in the parks were commonly unionized, and before the war generally received $2.50 for a single game and $3.75 for a doubleheader. Early in the 'twenties unionized private park police received $3.50 a game and $5.25 for a doubleheader.

Besides building and remodeling their parks, the owners took steps to tidy up their playing fields, which in those days were generally more cluttered than now. Bats were often laid out on the ground in front of the players' bench or carelessly left near home plate. Catchers were in the habit of dropping their chest protectors, mitts, and masks close to the plate too. National League umpires carried whisk brooms in their pockets for dusting off the plate, but in the American League they used brooms, which added to the litter on the field when not in use. One newspaper said it was a marvel that no accident had resulted from such untidiness. As if to underscore that remark, about ten days later Paddy Livingston, the Athletics' catcher, caught his spikes in a broom near the plate and hurt his ankle badly. After this mishap, Ban Johnson ordered that fields be kept free of all impediments. Even so, it was not until much later that all clubs cleared the field of bats. When I was batboy at Ebbets Field in the 1920's, racks had still not been installed, and part of my job was to keep the bats arranged in a neat row in front of the dugout.

Improved equipment for protecting the infield in case of rain was also adopted. Cincinnati spent $1800 for an army duck cover 160 feet square, with attached handles for twelve to fifteen men, but it proved leaky, so the manufacturer sent fifty gallons of waterproofing to caulk the seams. In 1915 the National League passed a rule requiring all clubs to have a canvas covering for the diamond so that games could continue after rainstorms. Prices quoted for such equipment in 1921 ranged around $3000, although a set of five smaller covers designed to protect only the key parts of the infield could be bought for less than $350. Sponge manufacturers claimed, however, that the best way to dry wet grounds was to scatter small, soft wool sponges over the diamond and then collect them. Other solutions were suggested. An inventor displayed a blueprint of a gadget rigged with an air cylinder and labeled TO CLEAN HOME PLATE—PUSH BUTTON, but umpires use whisk brooms to this day. Harry Pulliam's suggestion that a three-inch-wide piece of canvas or rubber be laid down for the foul lines was dismissed as impracticable, and lime continued to be used to mark them.°

As another means of stimulating attendance, some efforts were made to inform the audience about which players were in the lineup. But only reluctantly did the magnates begin supplying information that modern fans, accustomed to electric scoreboards and public-address systems, take for granted. Even a simple matter like putting numbers on the players' uniforms for easier identification took years to gain grudging acceptance. After all, did not real fans recognize the players by sight? And what would happen to the ego of a famous star if it were implied that fans would not know him without a number? Habitual fans, of course, did recognize the players on appearance, but many casual ones did not. The idea of numbering the players goes back at least to the 1890's. In the twentieth century, such sports-writers as Tom Rice and Fred Lieb pressed for adoption of numbers, and a few clubs actually tried using them, but it was not until 1931 that the American League made the practice official. The National League deliberated two more years before following suit. In 1960 that unsurpassed promoter, Bill Veeck, Jr., added the players' names to the uniforms of his Chicago White Sox.

In 1908 a fan, complaining about the lack of information at games, said that he was "nearly deafened" by the questions of people nearby: "Was that a hit?" "Who's playing third base?" and so on. He sug-

° A partial inventory of equipment used to operate a major-league park circa 1900 also conveys some of the flavor of the times. See appendix.

gested setting up a board listing the batting order and indicating when a hit was made and when a change in the lineup occurred. Tom Rice of the Brooklyn *Eagle* campaigned for this improvement too. The same year, George A. Baird of Chicago invented an electric scoreboard that instantly recorded balls, strikes, and outs. It was a simple, two-part contrivance: the display board itself and a little keyboard for running it that was set off to the side and behind the umpire. The section of the board showing the innings and score was still operated manually. Although players' names were not listed, numbers corresponding to the ones assigned to each man on the scorecard appeared on the board. The Boston clubs of each major league tried out the new electric board, and within a couple of years Shibe Park, in Philadelphia, had one that listed the names of the players in the batting order. Electric boards 50 by 24 feet could also be leased instead of purchased—at $2500 for the first year and $750 thereafter. Sale of advertising space on the scoreboard at a dollar a square foot might cover its rental cost and even bring a profit.

Having achieved the compromise of getting at least the players' numbers posted on the scoreboard, Rice and other reporters began to agitate to require that team captains and umpires announce changes in the lineup. In a short time league rules required this on pain of fines for failure to do so, and later a special announcer performed these chores. In my mind's eye I can still see the announcer at Ebbets Field in the 1920's standing in front of the stands behind home plate as the game was about to begin, impeccably dressed, head bared, megaphone raised toward the press box in the upper tier, as he began his familiar routine: "To the gentlemen of the daily press, the lineup and batteries for today's game—faw Noo Yawk, numbah one, Groh, third base; numbah two, Bancroft, shortstop. . . ." Then as the Brooklyn players trotted out to their positions and the Giants' leadoff man, Heinie Groh, swinging his famous "bottle bat," approached the plate, the announcer raced to the first- and then to the third-base sides of the stands, and finally to the bleachers, each time repeating the teams' batteries. As changes were made during the game, he announced them amidst the roaring of the crowd. All of this lent an air of excitement and expectation, particularly in the late innings of a close game with the hated Giants from across the bridge.

A prediction that electric scoreboards would soon be common in all parks proved premature. As late as the 1920's this author helped operate the old wooden relic at Ebbets Field, a crude contraption of ropes weighted with bricks for adjusting the ball and strike signs.

The unwillingness of the owners to provide the fans with free information stemmed from their fear of jeopardizing the revenue they secured from scorecard sales. A club official estimated that two out of every five fans purchased scorecards, although as the season progressed the proportion slackened to one out of three. Again, writers like Cy Sanborn supported fans who objected to paying an extra nickel on top of the admission price for a scorecard full of ads. They argued that theaters, burlesque houses, and nickelodeons supplied free programs; so why not baseball? While the owners never gave up selling scorecards, eventually they came around to putting numbers on players and listing their names on the scoreboard.

Paradoxically, one improvement eliminated a colorful feature of baseball—the custom of parading the players in uniform through the streets in horse-drawn carriages from hotel to ball park and back. Picturesque as the practice was, it nevertheless subjected visiting players to the jeers and missiles of fans thronged along their route, and to the discomforts of traveling in sweaty uniforms after the game. Charles Ebbets sounded the knell of these processions in 1906 when he got the National League to require that all parks install dressing rooms equipped with lockers and hot and cold running water for visiting players. In welcoming the end of what it called the "cheap circus act," *Sporting News* remarked, in the racially-bigoted terminology so freely employed in those days, that " 'coons' can do those things and feel proud of it [*sic*] but it is the most servile thing to compel gentlemanly players to do so." Comiskey, another opponent of player parades, said he was against them because he was not in show business—a delusion from which some owners still suffer.

But Charles W. Murphy again acted the maverick. He announced that he would defy any rule passed and stand upon his constitutional right to transport his team to and from the parks in any way he pleased. Furthermore, he vowed that in future his horse blankets would not only be more elaborate than usual, but would even have bells attached! He finally did make a gesture at providing a clubhouse for which he claimed an outlay of six or seven thousand dollars, but visiting teams constantly grumbled that it was unfit for use and that in the winter it served as a chicken coop. Murphy retorted that malicious Cincinnati players had twisted the doors from the lockers and thrown them outside. The owner wound up with a $25 fine from President Pulliam, and in 1909 the league passed a new rule, aimed squarely at the Chicago president, banning carriage parades.

Any loss of publicity resulting from the passing of the carriage parades was probably inconsequential. Professional baseball remained the most highly publicized business in the country, and the promoters continued to receive an amazing amount of free publicity the year round. This circumstance scarcely motivated owners to concern themselves about publicity or to exercise imagination in promoting their product, and public relations and promotion long remained murky concepts for baseball men, who slipped easily into the habit of thinking they needed to do little more than open the gates in order to have fans stream in.

Years ago, long before Madison Avenue exerted its influence, there were those who were urging the need for baseball to be advertised and sold like any other business. The editor of *Sporting News* was one who criticized the owners for being poor press agents. Nevertheless, they did undertake a certain amount of paid advertising and publicity. A routine device was the insertion of a simple announcement in the local paper:

NEW YORK
VS.
CINCINNATI

GAME CALLED 3:30

Charles Ebbets bought some trolley-car and elevated-railroad ads and gave away pictures of Brooklyn players for display in sporting hangouts. Traction companies were glad to put up baseball posters furnished by owners. In 1913 Schuyler Britton, upon taking over the presidency of the St. Louis Cardinals, actually gave away scorecards and presented flowers to the ladies. The device of having a "winning number" on a scorecard, used even in recent years, was introduced as early as 1917. Five fans holding winning numbers each received a prize—a ticket to another game. Aside from these expenditures, about the only public-relations cost borne by the owners was the relatively small outlay to cover the expenses of writers traveling with the team.

For many years it was the custom for owners to set aside certain days on which school children or orphanage youngsters were admitted free. The Brooklyn *Daily Eagle* held an Honor Roll Contest for Brooklyn public school children in 1914, with an anticipated 15,000 winners to be awarded free admission to Ebbets Field. In 1906 the Giants advertised with a parade from Union Square to the Battery, in which more than 2000 boys wearing their baseball uniforms marched, with the Giants and visiting Cincinnati players riding in front. One year more than two hundred amateur teams marched in review past the Giants and Pirates at the Polo Grounds. And on Amateur Day in Washington, Tom Noyes, president of the local American League club, offered cash prizes of $150, $100, and $50 for the three best-appearing teams.

Most active in this program for creating future fans were the Cardinals, who inaugurated their "knothole gang" in St. Louis in 1917. The program was originally conceived by a group of St. Louis businessmen as part of a scheme for bailing the club out of financial difficulty through a public offering of Cardinal stock. Purchase of two shares at $25 each entitled the buyer to a season pass for a St. Louis youngster. Much was made of the opportunity to combat juvenile delinquency, which the plan supposedly offered. Those who could afford to invest in baseball stock, however, were not acquainted with poor boys, so eventually the free admissions were handled by the club, which channeled them through such local organizations as the Boy Scouts, the Y.M.C.A., Protestant Sunday schools, Catholic churches, Jewish welfare, and a Negro boys' club. Under the program nearly 64,000 boys were admitted free in the 1920 season. League President Tener declared that the plan created a higher standard of sportsmanship among youthful fans, and he urged other National League teams to adopt the idea. So well did the youngsters learn their lessons in sportsmanship that they took up the cry of "Robber!" when the umpire called a decision against the home team, until Branch Rickey, club president, warned that further demonstrations would mean suspension of free passes. The problem was solved by having adults supervise the children at the park.

National League teams did not rush to adopt the "knothole gang" innovation. Certainly the Brooklyn club of the 1920's made no real effort to stimulate youthful interest. And in those days before the affluent society, few boys had fifty cents to spend for a bleacher seat. But there were ways to see games at Ebbets Field without paying. A boy could earn a pass to the bleachers by picking up trash in the stands the morning of a game, or he could work on a turnstile, for which he got fifty cents and a chance to see the game after the fifth inning. Such opportunities were available to a few interested youngsters at a time when operation of a ball club was far simpler and more informal than it later became. If a boy was not chosen for one of these jobs, he had other means of seeing a game free, provided he was resourceful and lucky. He might stand near the pass gate on Cedar Place on the chance that somebody would have an extra pass. He could pry up an unused side gate—one of those large metal doors that opened upward from the inside by pulling chains—and prop it up with a few bricks so that he could squirm underneath. Or he could slip into the park in the early morning when several gates were opened to take in supplies and then hide there until it was safe to mingle with the crowd. But hours of patient waiting in hiding might end in discovery by the special police and a rough ejection from the park.

Ladies' Day, a weekday on which women escorted by men were admitted free, was a promotion stunt about as old as baseball itself. But some owners had misgivings about the practice, believing that the ladies were getting too accustomed to free admission and, in any case, women had developed enough interest in baseball to be willing to pay their way, so why forego this source of income? The National League abolished Ladies' Day in 1909. However, there were sporadic attempts by a few clubs to revive it, and some American League teams kept it on. After 1917 the Ladies' Day idea regained momentum and became established in St. Louis, Chicago, and Cincinnati, even to the point where women were admitted without an escort.

In 1915 the Giants skillfully cooperated with New York suffragettes, to the benefit of both parties. By then women, who had already won the franchise in at least eleven states, were agitating militantly for a Constitutional amendment to give them the vote nationally. Announcing Women Suffrage Day, the Giants sold the local suffragette organization grandstand and box seats at substantial reductions and allowed the women to resell them at the regular price or, in the case of the boxes, for much more. This arrangement enabled the suffragettes to add more than $3000 to their war chest, and according to Harry Hempstead, then president of the Giants, the club took in an extra $2500, which it divided about evenly with the visiting Chicago club. With splendid impartiality, Organized Baseball also cooperated with an anti-suffragette group. The Cincinnati Reds made a similar arrangement with the Cinncinnati and Hamilton County Association Opposed to Woman Suffrage, from which the antis realized more than $500.

In recent years owners have capitalized heavily upon fan nostalgia by holding an annual Old-Timers' Day. Favorites of the past are introduced and usually go through the motions of playing one or two innings before the regularly scheduled game. Older fans can relive the past, and the old-time stars enjoy the renewed attention and the chance to reminisce among themselves. The added attendance more than makes up for the expense of bringing the veterans together. Old-Timers' Day is not an invention of modern owners, however; such days were staged from time to time in the early 1900's.

Another attendance gimmick was to set aside a special day to honor an individual player. The idea was so attractive to Charles Ebbets that he threatened to overdo a good thing by planning a whole series of player days, plus a day for manager Robinson and another for the league president—"bargain counter fads," one newspaper called them. If a team was out of the pennant race, owners tried to puff up flagging interest with a Field Day, during which players competed for prizes in hitting, throwing, and running contests of various kinds. In the 1920's two former players, Nick Altrock and Al Schacht, doubled as coaches and comedians for the Washington club. Their various baseball acts, all in pantomime, furnished comic relief for fans, particularly between games of doubleheaders. But there were some purists who complained about these shows, preferring to take their baseball straight.

After the long winter, the opening game of the season was like water in the desert to fans thirsting for baseball. To intensify their anticipation, glowing announcements were published and special ceremonies were planned. When the big day came, there was always the march of the two teams across the field to the flagpole in center field, where the opposing captains hoisted the flag, then the return march to the dugouts, followed by the throwing out of the first ball by some dignitary amidst shouts of "Play ball!" For the Detroit opener of 1903, the visiting club arrived dramatically by boat; there was a parade, swelled by five hundred Elks, who had purchased tickets in advance, and the mayor threw out the first ball. As a prelude to the Giants' opening day in 1905, the teams paraded around the city in automobiles lent by "prominent patrons of the game." At the next year's opener, the Giants had the advantage of being able to hoist the championship pennant won the previous season, and when it unfurled the crowd poured forth its enthusiasm "like the roar of Niagara Falls." The Catholic Protectory Band played, and the presence of many richly gowned women added to the splendor of the occasion.

The Giants' opening game of 1907, however, degenerated into a rowdy scene. New York's Police Commissioner had refused to let his men patrol the Polo Grounds because it was a private amusement park. In the ninth inning, with the Giants losing, some hoodlums in the crowd leaped onto the field, flinging cushions, bottles, and even snowballs. In the midst of this uproar the imperturbable Bill Klem, one of the best of umpires, waited the required time and then majestically declared the game forfeit to the visiting team.

The annual presentation of a gold season pass to the President of the United States created excellent publicity, but a shrewder public-relations stroke was to have the President throw out the first ball each year at the opening game in Washington, a ritual that in effect makes him a promoter of Organized Baseball and gives the appearance of conferring upon it the government stamp of approval. Theodore Roosevelt was the first President to receive a gold pass, and Taft inaugurated the throwing out of the first ball.

The dedication of a new ball park presented an obvious opportunity to stimulate fan interest. Comiskey celebrated the opening of his

new stadium in July 1910 by hiring five bands and bedecking the
grandstand with thousands of yards of colored bunting. His personal
box, built to look like a miniature Roman Coliseum, was filled with
flowers. The United States War Department assigned a detachment of
troops to conduct a flag-raising ceremony; the mayor presented a
banner to Comiskey, and "Hail to the Chief" was played in his honor!

Other activities of the owners, such as dealing with requests for
charitable contributions, fan complaints, and free passes, had a bearing on attendance. Club owners were solicited for contributions of all
kinds. Boys' teams wanted money to help buy uniforms. Schools, hospitals, and penitentiaries requested old baseball equipment. Organizations sponsoring junior baseball teams requested reduced admission
rates for the boys. Churches asked for outright donations; one
minister asked a club for ten dollars to help defray the cost of building a new church, larding his appeal with appropriate quotes from
the Scriptures.

Donations to organized charities naturally brought greater publicity. To read about them summons up the memory of events now
faded but once of lively interest to many Americans. Victims of the
great San Francisco Fire of 1906 received substantial financial help
from Organized Baseball. A number of clubs, both major and minor,
gave a day's gate receipts, and the National League office alone sent
$1000. The Giants and the Cincinnati Reds contributed more than
$9000 in gate receipts for the victims of the *Titanic* disaster. Clubs
also sent checks to help those who suffered in Russian pogroms.

The old public-relations problem of where to draw the line on distribution of free passes still bedeviled the owners. Hundreds who
could afford to pay tried to wangle passes, if only for the prestige of
being able to display them. People who did business with a club or
who could do a club some good (or harm), like railway executives,
hotel clerks, prominent city officials and their "heelers," usually expected passes. In 1913 every member of the Illinois legislature received a pass from the Chicago National League team to help ward
off passage of a bill authorizing the closing of any amusement park
that did not provide a seat for every ticket sold. Admitting that favored officials got free passes, *Spalding's Guide for 1910* pointed out
that few ball clubs were free from political interference. Brooklyn's
pass gate was overworked because owner Ebbets had to keep two sets
of politicians happy, those in Manhattan as well as those in Brooklyn.

In the American League, clubs customarily "took care of" the chief
clerks at leading hotels because, as the league president acknowledged, they could help "steer" hotel guests to the ball park. On some
days at the Polo Grounds, *Sporting News* claimed, as many as 2500

"deadheads" took up space, among them ward heelers, would-be comedians, broken-down actors, bartenders, and streetcar conductors.
In requesting a pass, a county assessor in Ohio reminded the management that he was a real friend of the ball club because he had assessed its property at a very low figure.

One of the best-represented groups among the "deadheads" was the
clergy. Owners believed that the presence of men of the cloth gave
tangible evidence of the respectability and honesty of the game. Of
approximately one hundred passes that one club distributed among
priests, ministers, and rabbis, about half went to Catholic priests because the owner thought they would bring wealthy people with them.
Clergymen were sometimes criticized for their interest in baseball.
Ministers were accused of joining the deadhead line on Saturday,
preaching against Sunday ball the next day, and then showing up at
the park for another free show on Monday. A good many were not
bashful about requesting season passes, and some made unreasonable
demands. When one club felt compelled to limit passes to local pas-
tors only, a minister from a neighboring state charged "discrimination" and threatened to boycott the club and let every clergyman in
his state know the reason. Sometimes individual fans applied for free
tickets, pleading lack of money. A woman who just wanted to see
"our boys" play said that if a pass was not forthcoming she would be
perfectly willing to sit on the bench with the players, or even in the
bleachers! Players, too, expected passes for wives, relatives, and
friends. In 1915 the American League inaugurated the policy of
supplying each player with two passes, good for any park in the
league.

Individual magnates soon began cutting down on their free lists,
and the National League adopted a rule limiting the total number of
passes to 6 per cent of the total season attendance. Barney Dreyfuss
of Pittsburgh questioned the wisdom of having Ladies' Day and knothole gangs. He cited figures showing that in a two-day series played
by his club in St. Louis, boys and women admitted free comprised 40
per cent of the total attendance, thus cutting down gate receipts. The
St. Louis owner defended the knothole program as an act of charity
for boys from the poor districts and good advertising for the National
League in St. Louis; he reminded Dreyfuss that the Cardinals had to
compete with the local Browns, one of the American League clubs
that held Ladies' Days, so he could not very well do less.

Ball clubs probably get more complaints than conventional businesses because their customers, the fans, entertain the illusion that
the team belongs to them, an illusion encouraged by the owners. Fans
have always assumed the right to criticize the players and the way

the team is managed. Typical complaints were: "They work on the field like a lot of broken down race horses"; the club has "for penurious reasons" sold almost all the good ball players to others and substituted a "kindergarten lot" at reduced salaries. One fan made the simple suggestion to "sell the Club for a Yellow Dog, then shoot the Dog." The magnate's mail always had a quota of letters from eccentrics who recommended player trades, volunteered to manage the team, or guaranteed the team's success by means of new gadgets or secret formulas for improving batting and instilling confidence. One fan offered to write encouraging letters to the home-club players "and a different kind" to those on opposing teams.

Modern fans may take some comfort in knowing that their complaints about long, boring games were just as common in the past. About the only difference was that in those days the time standard was more stringent. It was thought that games should be completed in one and a half or one and three-quarter hours. But every year there were complaints that many contests dragged on longer because players stalled, pitchers took too long between pitches, and umpires neglected to hustle things along sufficiently. When games take two and a half hours, said *Sporting News* in 1915, they tax the tolerance of even the most rabid fans. Yet try as they did, league officials were unable to satisfy the critics completely on this score.

Another irritant was the halting of a game abruptly in the late innings so that a team could catch a train, or calling one off unnecessarily after a few drops of rain in order to schedule a doubleheader later and get bigger gate receipts. Comiskey, however, was praised for making every effort to play after rain by spreading oil and burning it, and then applying sawdust to dry up his field.

It was not always necessary to depend on rain in order to schedule doubleheaders. Owners could arrange synthetic "bargain bills" by postponing weekday games and rescheduling them as part of a Saturday, Sunday, or holiday double bill, in spite of heavy criticism for using "Shylock" tactics and "cheapening the game." A gimmick that was better concealed from the public and press was the transfer of games. A game scheduled in the home city of a team drawing poorly would sometimes be quietly switched to the other team's park if the gate receipts promised to be greater. To cite one example, the Giants once persuaded another club to cancel a game between them and transfer it to New York by offering the other team $2500 in addition to its regular share of the gate receipts. Garry Herrmann himself was not averse to the practice when he thought it would enhance receipts.

Owners also had to deal with dissatisfaction unconnected with the contest itself. People complained about transportation to the park, undersized box seats, and the rudeness of park attendants. Fans sued for damages over alleged injuries, and one collected $750 as a result of rough handling and ejection from the park by the special police. Women demanded compensation for dresses torn on nails or concrete at the park. One wanted payment for a coat ruined "by having some-one expectorate tobacco juice all over" it. Someone else claimed his son fell and hurt his hand on a broken bottle in the park, necessitating five trips to a physician and ruining a suit; what was the club prepared to do about it? Then as now, there were many complaints about juvenile delinquents who hung around the parks, exacting tribute for "watching" automobiles, only to rifle them while their owners were at the game—something easily done in the days of open touring cars.

Most injuries sustained by spectators are caused by being struck by a batted ball, and considerable litigation resulted from such accidents during that period. But by 1920 the principle was established in law that it is sufficient for the owner to install a screen directly behind home plate to keep balls fouled in that direction from entering the grandstand; if a fan chooses to sit in an unprotected area, he is assuming a well-known risk, and if he gets hit, he is guilty of contributory negligence.

Balls fouled into the stands created another public-relations problem. Owners refused to allow fans to keep them as souvenirs. Consequently park police often made a nuisance of themselves by dashing in among fans to recover balls. Altercations resulted. Patrons were rudely searched and even ejected from the ball park for stealing club property. One conscience-stricken spectator actually sent a note to an owner asking him to accept "this one dollars [sic] for a base ball I stolen at the Ball Park," signing it "A. Fan." A New York alderman who objected to this "shortsighted and stingy" policy introduced a resolution to prevent clubs from recovering baseballs and to stop special police from molesting people. At Ebbets Field a boy lucky enough to grab a ball hit over the fence or fouled over the roof of the grandstand could exchange it at the gate for a seat. In 1916 Charles Weeghman, then owner of the Chicago Cubs, decided to allow fans to keep balls batted into the stands, but it was years before this policy was accepted in all parks. In 1923 a lad only eleven years old was arrested and kept in a house of detention overnight for keeping a ball that had been hit into the bleachers at the Phillies' ball park. However, the judge in the case ruled that "a boy who gets a baseball in the bleachers to take home as a souvenir is acting on the natural impulse of all boys and is not guilty of larceny." As late as 1937 a fan was severely beaten by ushers in Yankee Stadium while he and some others were trying to get hold of a ball lodged in the screen behind home plate. He sued and won a $7500 verdict against the corporation employed by the ball club to maintain and operate the park.

In the years following the peace settlement between the two major leagues in 1903, attendance increased substantially. Accurate information on attendance, however, does not exist. The owners refused to give out daily figures, so reporters resorted to guesses, which were usually inflated. The best statistics available, those compiled mostly from baseball guides by a congressional committee in 1951, reveal an almost unbroken rise in attendance from 1903 until 1914. Admissions climbed from nearly four and three-quarters million in 1903 to well above seven million in both 1908 and 1909, but these last two seasons had abnormally high sales because of unusually close pennant races in both leagues. In each of the following four years the figures fell off. Nevertheless, with the exception of 1912, they still remained higher than in any of the years prior to the 1908 and 1909 peaks.

Generally, the American League drew substantially more patrons than the National. In the period 1901–8 the American League averaged more than 2,750,000 people compared with the National's more than 2,500,000. The American widened its margin in the years 1909–13 by averaging more than 3,400,000 as against the National's more than three million.

Then in 1914 and 1915 a costly trade war cut major-league attendance sharply, and the 1914 depression did not help. With their monopoly re-established after the trade war, the two majors enjoyed another fat season in 1916, drawing more than six and a half million, only to have admissions slide in 1917 and then plunge in 1918 to a low of 3,080,126 because of World War One. Attendance then rebounded in 1919 to the level of 1916. The following year, 1920, it rocketed to well above nine million, heralding a new era of higher levels of attendance.

Viewing the National Commission era as a whole and taking into account its four poor seasons, we can conclude that attendance at major-league games kept pace with population increase in the United States, and that baseball succeeded in maintaining its position as a popular spectator amusement.

Prices charged by the owners in the early years of that period were 25 cents, 50 cents, 75 cents, and a dollar, depending on whether they were for bleacher, grandstand, pavilion, or box seats. A few seats cost $1.50. From 1909 to 1916 the average admission price was estimated to be 66 cents. One out of four admissions in 1910 was in the quarter class. But owners gradually reached the conclusion that 25-cent ball did not pay, and construction of new parks, coupled with renovation of old ones, gave them the opportunity to cut back gradually on the number of seats in this category. A few were still offered to maintain the impression that quarter ball was still available. The owners did not heed objections that the elimination of 25-cent admissions would end baseball's claim to being a poor man's game, and by 1920, 50 cents became the minimum charge.

Owners continued to supplement income from ticket sales by catering to the fans' need for refreshments, selling advertising on fences and scorecards, and renting the park for other functions. In the parks fans could buy cherry pie, cheese, chewing tobacco, tripe, chocolate, planked onions, and of course peanuts and hot dogs. Sportswriter **Charles Dryden complained that a sandwich with "translucent" ham cost five cents. Some fans objected to boys' running up and down the aisles shouting "Peanuts Cigars! Chewing gum!" and splashing them with soft drinks, but it was all part of the atmosphere.**

Sale of beer and liquor at the parks drew protests from the growing temperance movement, which by 1917 had collected two-thirds of the states under the prohibition banner. Ball clubs gained the plaudits of the drys by eliminating bars and hard liquor and selling beer more discreetly: "This is good news. . . . This is hallelujah news. . . . You do well to turn the rum devil out of the ball park," chortled one enthusiastic preacher. Soft-drink manufacturers showed that one group's loss could be another's gain when they advertised their products as "temperance drinks."

Except for a few random figures, information on concession profits for those years is non-existent. The sale of soda, ice cream, and the like was frequently farmed out by the ball club to concessionaires, doubtless to the profit of both. One club reported making more than $2000 in 1908. Another realized an estimated $1000 in a season as its share of Coca Cola sales alone, with a cut of forty cents on a case of twenty-four bottles selling at a nickel apiece. In fact, the desire of fans to indulge in baseball and Coke simultaneously impelled two promoters of the beverage to purchase bottling rights from Asa Candler, founder of the company. The story is that the idea of bottling Coke came to them while they were in Cuba serving in the army during the Spanish-American War, where they noticed Cubans enjoying a bottled drink called Piña Fria at ball games.

The leading concessionaire was still Harry Stevens, who from his start as a scorecard hawker in the 1880's continued to expand his business, branching out from ball parks into race tracks and Madison Square Garden. By 1910 he reputedly had a son in Yale Law School, rode around in a "swell" auto, sat in a box at the theater, smoked dollar cigars, dined at Sherry's, and lived in a "palace."

Fence and scorecard ads were purchased by a variety of companies, particularly those dealing in products for which baseball crowds were a conspicuous market. In 1908 one club took in more than $2500 from "advertising privileges." Purveyors of tobacco, ice cream, and chewing gum commonly purchased scorecard ads in exchange for exclusive rights to sell their brand to the captive market in the ball park. A fence ad at Ebbets Field cleverly linked the product with Brooklyn's well-known outfielder: "Zack Wheat caught 400 flies last season; Tanglefoot fly paper caught 10 Million."

A prime example of economic collaboration was the tie between the major leagues and Western Union Telegraph Company. After having contracted with Western Union for years, either club by club or on a league basis,* the club owners of the two major leagues agreed in 1913 to have the National Commission negotiate a single contract for them. It stipulated that Western Union was to pay each major league $17,000 annually for five years, plus $2000 for the same period to the National Commission. The individual major-league clubs, on their part, were to open accounts with local Western Union offices and channel all their telegraph business through the company. Two months later Western Union discovered that the contract was in violation of the interstate commerce regulations. The problem was resolved by having the company pay $18,000 to each league separately in quarterly installments of $4500, out of which the leagues would turn over $250 apiece to the National Commission. Substantially the same contracts have pertained ever since, giving Western Union wire rights to ball games in both major leagues; now, however, the only exclusive portion applies to the job of furnishing game reports to broadcasting stations.

Owners eked out their income by renting their parks for other functions, ranging from hippodromes to opera, track meets, boxing bouts, and industrial-league games, for which they received anywhere from $50 to $250. Sometimes these ventures seemed more trouble than they were worth. The playing field might be damaged or unexpected complaints be registered, such as when local movie operators objected to the ball club's competing with them by putting on five-cent picture shows in its park at night, pointedly reminding the owner of Organized Baseball's own territorial strictures against competition. In Cincinnati, where the park was rented for movies and dancing, the Juvenile Protective Association repeatedly complained in the 1920's about the "immoral dancing of the most extreme type" and the "vulgar conduct between girls and men in unlighted portions of the grandstand." The Cincinnati club finally decided to forego this source of income.

* See *Baseball: The Early Years,* page 200.

A club might make some extra money by playing a post-season series with another major-league club in the same city, or in the same state. The Cleveland Americans and Cincinnati Nationals grossed $18,512.76 in such a series in 1910. Out of this total, the players divided $8,565.62, the National Commission received $1,851.26, and the clubs realized $8,095.88.

Clubs fortunate enough to corral a player surplus could and did make money selling player contracts to other teams, often with considerable profit to themselves individually, but since money exchanged in such transactions remained within the major-league combine, it cannot be considered as income for the baseball business as a whole.

Few reliable profit-and-loss figures are available for the years prior to 1920, but it is clear from the attendance figures already cited that the major leagues as a whole prospered during that era, especially from 1903 to 1914. Year after year during that span, the leagues gave out glowing reports of financial success. Gross operating income for the majors in the years 1909–13 was $20,537,000, which, if divided among the sixteen clubs, averages out to more than $250,000 a year each. At the same time, operating costs were increasing. The fourth-place Philadelphia Nationals spent about $140,000 to run the club in 1908, including more than $5000 for park improvements and repairs, nearly $19,000 for traveling, almost $15,000 for rents, and just short of $70,000 in salaries. They claimed an attendance that year of 420,660, but with the help of some conservative bookkeeping, reported a profit of only $19,885.55. Charles Ebbets asserted in 1916 that it cost from $225,000 to $250,000 to operate a club, a sum, he said, that required an average daily attendance of 4000. However, if the reported league attendance figures are averaged out, it is plain that most clubs had better attendance than that.

But averages are deceiving and, as already suggested, the variables affecting individual club success are many. The New York Giants, with the advantage of a winning team and a good market, were probably the best money-making club in the National League, allegedly earning a profit of more than $500,000 from 1906 to 1910. In 1913 they were believed to be realizing an annual profit of anywhere from $150,000 to $300,000. Cincinnati earned nearly $151,000 in 1919, but that was a pennant-winning season. Comiskey reputedly admitted clearing more than $700,000 on his White Sox in the decade 1901–11, and in 1912 his annual profits were estimated to be in the neighborhood of $150,000.

On the other hand, the St. Louis Cardinals entered the era already saddled with a debt of nearly $60,000, which grew to almost $70,000 by the end of 1903. The club was saved by loans from Garry Herr-

mann and probably from the National League as well. They helped
out after repeated pleas and a scarcely veiled threat to sell out to the
American League, which would then be able to install a dummy club
alongside its own St. Louis Browns and thus wreck National League
attendance in that city. The ensuing seasons were an uphill climb for
the Cardinals as they gradually paid off the notes and interest, until
the universally good seasons of 1908 and 1909 lifted the club out of
the red for the time being.

It is also, of course, possible for a club's books to show little or no
profit while an owner and even his relatives make a comfortable living out of salaries and expenses, as in the case of the Griffith family
when it was running the Washington American League club.

Another indicator of prosperity was that by 1904 the National
League had finished paying off those clubs that were dropped when
its circuit was cut back from twelve clubs to eight in 1900. A few
years later it had also liquidated debts resulting from the war with
the American League.

The rising value of individual club franchises was a further sign of
success. Frank Farrell, who had invested $18,000 in the Yankees in
1903, sold them to Ruppert and Huston in 1915 for a figure between
$400,000 and $500,000. The Detroit Tigers, who had been purchased
by William H. Yawkey, son of the multimillionaire lumber baron, for
a sum variously estimated at $25,000 to $50,000, were valued at
$522,405 on a 1920 tax report and showed an average annual profit of
$48,006 through the years 1914–18. Other franchises, too, appreciated
spectacularly. John T. Brush secured the Giants for about $125,000 in
1903, but in 1919 Charles A. Stoneham had to pay a million dollars
for slightly more than half the corporate stock. The Boston Braves'
stock, worth $75,000 in 1907, jumped to more than $300,000 in six
years. The Cincinnati Reds were purchased for $125,000 in 1902; by
1913 the club placed a value of $450,000 on its franchise and players;
and in 1915 its land and building alone were assessed by the county
at $391,930.

The eagerness of outside capitalists to organize leagues in competition with Organized Baseball ° supplies another clue to the lucrative
possibilities of the business. The style of life enjoyed by the teams
traveling about on Pullmans and patronizing good hotels was also a
sign of baseball's general prosperity. And if further example is needed,
the decision of the National League in 1907 to hold its annual conclave at New York's famed Waldorf-Astoria should suffice. The press
joshed the magnates a good deal for meeting at a "swell" hotel and
bringing tuxedos so they would not look out of place after 6 p.m.
Nevertheless, the decision was symbolic of their growing affluence.

° See below, chapter 10.

PART TWO

HEROES AND HEROICS

5

THE MAKING OF A HERO

THE ADMINISTRATIVE and playing branches of professional baseball were not always separate and distinct. In baseball's amateur and early professional era the two functions blended, and the players for the most part ran the game themselves. But as the commercial factor thrust ever more insistently into the game, the promoters, imitating other business enterprises, effected a sharp separation by taking over control from the players. Albert G. Spalding, a giant among the pioneer entrepreneurs of professional baseball, explained that the change in policy was adopted by the National League in 1876 because the promoters believed that their success depended upon setting up two "interdependent divisions," the executive and the productive, with the former exerting absolute control over the latter. Henceforth, players became employees and the story of their relations with their employers, the club owners, forms a unique chapter in the history of American labor.

But the players also became something more. As members of the American pantheon of folk heroes, they tended to be regarded not simply as employees but as a special breed of men following a special way of life. In our time, a good deal of the romantic coating has washed off the players. They are said to act blasé on the field and to be engrossed in pension plans and stock-market quotations off it. In other words, they behave more like ordinary young men pursuing a commonplace career—"good gray ball players, playing a good gray game and reading the good gray *Wall Street Journal*," as Bill Veeck, Jr., has described them.

But caution should temper too easy generalizations about the attitudes and interests of contemporary players as compared with those of the old-timers, as it also should about their relative playing skill. Time nourishes nostalgia; as each generation of ball players recedes into the past, it gradually becomes enveloped in a fabric of fiction.

Back in 1910 *Sporting News* sounded the same lugubrious note heard today: players do nothing but talk money on and off the field. The paper fondly recollected a former time when sportsmanship and competition were uppermost. Current fans might be less dismayed at players' dabbling in the stock market if they knew that many of the titans of old also were interested in Wall Street quotations as well as batting averages, and that John McGraw asserted that players of those days were primarily businessmen trying to sell their wares. The truth is that from the beginning of baseball's professional era, as readers of the first volume of this history may recall, players were always keenly interested in such unheroic matters as salaries and working conditions, and on two occasions even formed a union. In the twentieth century, as subsequent chapters will show, they continued this preoccupation with bread-and-butter issues.

Yet the more prosaic, mundane side of the old-time player somehow was less prominent or perhaps not taken for granted by the unsophisticated fans of a less complicated era. A player who held out for a higher salary in those days was looked upon not so much as a dissatisfied employee but as a traitor who had put his own mercenary motives above his team and city. I well recall that when such a man reached an agreement and finally appeared in the lineup, he was often jeered with the cry "Holdout!"

Perhaps nostalgia blurs the recollection, but having read early baseball literature and spent summer days in a major-league park in the 1920's, I am left with a sense of the deeper emotional attachments and less inhibited loyalties of fans of those times. Parks were smaller and more intimate. Fans felt closer to the teams and players. Dyed-in-the-wool regulars knew the performers by sight. Players lived in the neighborhood adjacent to the park instead of in the suburbs, so they were often seen and recognized on the street or in some favorite saloon, such as the one on Tilden Avenue in Brooklyn.

During the season, Zack Wheat, possibly as great a baseball idol as Flatbush ever had, lived with his family just around the corner from me. Another Brooklyn star, Burleigh Grimes, sometimes passed by on his evening stroll with a great black cigar in his mouth while we youngsters were playing punch ball in the street. It was a thrill to be able to recognize him and say "Hiya, Burleigh!" and have him reply, "Having a workout, son?" This simple exchange imparted the feeling that we, too, belonged to the wonderful world of baseball, even though on a different level. Too much familiarity may not be conducive to hero worship, but too much distance breeds alienation. Some proximity helps people identify with the hero.

For adults, association with the ball players could be equally real and vivid. Devout fans organized themselves into the White Sox Rooters Association, the Cleveland Bards, the Pittsburgh Stove League, and similar rooters' clubs and attended games in a body. Civic organizations, like the Brooklyn Elks, sometimes did the same. The Chicago Board of Trade became so worked up over a forthcoming series between the Cubs and New York Giants in 1906 that it organized a rooting club and took off for the park en masse. Occasionally the boosters journeyed with the team to another city for a game or a short series.

John R. Tunis, who has written perceptively about American sports, remembers standing in line as a boy to see the World Series of 1903 when suddenly the sound of distant music signaled the approach of Boston's Royal (or Loyal) Rooters. At last the marching men came into sight, dressed in their best black suits and high white collars, blue rosettes pinned on their lapels. "Each man had his ticket stuck jauntily in the hatband of his derby," Tunis recalls, and "at their head was the leading spirit, 'Nuff Sed' McGreevy." Boston's famous mayor, "Honey Fitz" (John Fitzgerald), led similar parades when the Red Sox won in 1912 and 1916. Nearly half a century later his grandson, President John F. Kennedy, reportedly delayed an appointment with the Laotian Minister so that he could stay until the end of Washington's opening game in 1962.

Some of these booster groups became a nuisance. They harassed visiting players and teams and annoyed the more "sedate" spectators with their organized rooting, megaphones, fish horns, and "other nerve-racking and ear-splitting devices." The more orthodox among the faithful, who believed that rooting should be spontaneous, condemned "bidders for publicity" for turning "the sport of the people" into "a sideshow for rehearsed exhibitions." After the games, bands of city urchins waylaid the players as they left the parks and tried to get their autographs. As Thomas Wolfe so well described this characteristic scene, the hero "scrawled his name out rapidly on a dozen grimy bits of paper, skillfully working his way along through the yelling, pushing, jumping group, and all the time keeping up a rapid fire of banter, badinage, and good natured reproof."

Another custom already taking hold was for parties of fans to travel south or west on their spring vacations to watch their favorites in training. With the winter vacation becoming a part of the American way of life in recent years, this practice has accelerated. Many fans take the opportunity denied them in the impersonal atmosphere of the huge modern ball parks to view their heroes at closer range in the smaller parks of the training camps. In these surroundings the conditions of the past are recaptured. Fans can watch the players close up, see the expressions on their faces, hear their voices, talk to them, collect autographs, and snap pictures.

Hero worship includes bestowing offerings, and fans regularly brought presents to their idols. The usual gifts were gold watches, autos, and cash. In 1908 Pittsburgh fans made up a purse of $600 or $700 for their star shortstop, Honus Wagner. Two years later Walter Johnson received $500 from Washington fans for setting a season strikeout record. When a young Detroit outfielder named Ty Cobb drove out his hundredth hit of the season in the summer of 1910, his fans rushed onto the field and handed him a diamond-studded watch fob. Almost twenty years later he was given a civic banquet at which the ball club presented him with a check for $10,000 ° and the City of Detroit awarded him a $1,000 trophy.

Sometimes an owner would contribute the gate receipts to a player of long service on a day dedicated to him, as did President Taylor of the Red Sox on Cy Young Day in 1908. A grateful fan who won a bet on the World Series of 1910 shook hands with Jack Coombs and Jack Lapp, the victorious Athletics battery, and left a $50 bill in the palm of each. Connie Mack, the Athletics' manager, was given a two-ton live elephant to personify the team's nickname "White Elephants." The trainer walked the animal through the street to Connie's house and left it in his back yard "eating its head off." Other stars and teams also basked in civic recognition through banquets, parades, and legally proclaimed holidays. But official participation in those days was modest compared with the vast outlays of public funds in recent years for the purpose of building stadiums for privately owned baseball companies.

Similarly, personal tributes in those earlier days were paltry compared with the richness and variety of those lavished on player-heroes in our modern affluent society. Today's heroes are showered with a staggering assortment of sporting equipment, cars, motor boats, clothing, and all manner of household appliances and gadgets—as well as substantial amounts of cash, which they usually turn over to a charity or scholarship fund. The spectacle of ordinary working people giving presents to ball players who make far more money than they is indeed ironic.

To be sure, all the loot collected by the heroes is not furnished by individual fans alone. Manufacturers and merchants eager for advertising benefits have injected a strong commercial flavor, gladly donating their products in exchange for public mention. This practice is

° Cobb claimed later that the "gift" of $10,000 was a fake; it was really the balance of his salary, an amount agreed upon privately with owner Frank Navin, who, however, presented it publicly as though it were a gift.

not entirely new. In the first decades of the century the American Tobacco Company was awarding fifty-dollar checks to batters who hit
the company's Bull Durham sign displayed on the outfield fence in
practically every ball park in the country. A shoe company offered a
free pair to players who hit home runs, and for several years an automobile manufacturer presented one of its cars to the batting champion of each major league. Although this was small-scale largesse for
individual achievement compared with the special days now customary for players, some objections were raised out of fear that such
prizes and gifts would be detrimental to teamwork.

When their heroes were performing away from home, fans gathered
in the streets to watch simulated games, telegraphed play by play
and reproduced on an electrified scoreboard hung outside newspaper
offices. Those newspapers that had no mechanical board assigned a
man to report the game from their office windows by shouting each
play through a megaphone to the crowds below. Presaging the age of
television, boards were also set up in the theaters of many cities.

At World Series time especially, many thousands of fans filled the
streets opposite newspaper offices, causing streetcar and wagon traffic
tie-ups. In 1913 about 15,000 people jammed Times Square to "watch
a game" on the 18- by 24-foot board hanging from the Times Building.
Many more gaped at the boards furnished by other newspapers in
Herald Square and Park Row. The cheers or groans evoked by the
moving celluloid ball and the "white lozenges" representing the players testified to the fans' genuine interest and to their ability to visual-
ize the action through a remarkable projection of imagination, based
upon intimate knowledge of the game and the players. To a lesser extent, television viewers now do the same thing; only a part of the action is visible on the screen, the rest they see in their mind's eye.

Barnstorming, a custom of major-league teams now relegated to a
past age, provided dwellers in the more remote, rural areas of America a chance to glimpse the heroes they read or heard about. Each
spring after completing training in the towns of Florida, Texas, and
other warm states, big-league clubs, often traveling in pairs, undertook a long, meandering route home, stopping along the way at the
tank towns to play exhibition games. These tiring pre-season journeys, broken only for games on dangerously rough diamonds, were of
questionable benefit to the players, but they helped defray the cost of
spring training and gave people in the "bushes" a glimpse of big-
league heroes in action.

Fans in the provinces looked forward to these barnstorming stop-
overs. Posters announced the coming event, and when the great day
arrived people from even the smallest hamlets wended their way to

the game. Houses were decorated; automobiles carried American flags; shops closed; schools often declared a half-holiday and had the student band lead a player parade from the station through town, where fans filled the streets and shook hands with the heroes. If a local boy who had made it from the town team all the way to the majors happened to be with the cavalcade, so much the better. At the game, people packed the crude stands and spilled over onto the field. Youngsters climbed overhanging trees to watch free. Negroes gathered in their segregated section. What did it matter if the contest was only an exhibition or if it was interrupted or even terminated by eager droves of fans mobbing some particularly renowned star for his autograph? Such scenes were a measure of the depth and spread of baseball's roots, and over the years a rich store of baseball lore accumulated around these barnstorming experiences. Unfortunately, owners sometimes spoiled the show by palming off obscure rookie players on those who expected to see the regulars.

The reason for the idolization of ball players lies in man's urge to create heroes. This impulse springs primarily from his need to identify with some other person or group. For some people ball players satisfy this need, because in ball players they see living evidence that certain values and assumptions deep in the American psyche still have validity. Years ago, identification was easier, the bond between players and fans more plausible, because people retained a surer confidence in traditional American beliefs, and the players themselves more nearly personified them. According to the credo of that time, material success was the supreme goal. To reach it, one followed the path of individualism, self-reliance, and competition. Major signposts along the way read "hard work," "shrewdness," and "courage" (the last often spelled g-r-i-t or s-a-n-d). If one undertook this hard route, it would bring the added moral reward of strengthened "character."

The early settlers carried with them these Protestant-capitalist ethics, and in the decades after the Civil War a simplified version of that code, suited to the growing industrial character of America, was inculcated into generations of American youth by the Horatio Alger novels that flooded from the press and enjoyed sales second only to the Bible. Alger's heroes exemplified the poor boy's rise to success through willingness to learn, individual effort, and a bit of luck thrown in. Grownups read *The Short Line War* and *Calumet K,* whose heroes were adult counterparts of Alger's, acting out a similar theme of "every man for himself" in a no-holds-barred scramble for material success. The more literate could meditate on "The Gospel of Success" according to Andrew Carnegie, or ponder the economic dogmas of William Graham Sumner, which enunciated the same princi-

ples. The fact that so many actually did succeed in clawing their way
up the ladder of social and economic success lent credence to this
simple faith.

Profound changes, however, such as the growth of giant industrial
monopolies, combined with the transformation of a rural society to a
crowded urban one, were corroding this comfortable creed, which
could have meaning only so long as America remained an essentially
rural, small-town society. For increasing numbers, the avenues to material and social success were to all intents and purposes blocked.

Nevertheless, the gap between the rhetoric of traditional beliefs
and new realities had not yet become a chasm. People could still tell
themselves that the old formula worked, and they could find vivid expression of its validity in the career of a major-league ball player—
tangible evidence that their own long-bred beliefs and aspirations
were not, after all, unfounded. The successful ball player showed that
a man could still be self-made, that the individual could make the
grade on his own. Natural ability, persistent practice, courage, and
competitive drive were the requirements that brought reward in a
tough business where only about four hundred reached the top and
fewer still were outstanding. Here was one segment of American life
where merit and the storied American virtues actually paid off. As for
those who did not measure up, they went back to the minors or out of
baseball entirely, a solution satisfactory to the most exacting social
Darwinist of the time.

Implicit in the creed was the principle that a humble origin or lack
of formal education would not bar the way to the top. This ideal, too,
could be fulfilled in professional baseball. The single glaring exception was the American Negro, whose professional baseball aspirations
were restricted to the Negro-league ghettos. American Indians, immigrants, Cubans, and Jews, yes, but not black Americans. For them,
the years from the late nineties * down to 1946 were a blank as far as
playing in Organized Baseball was concerned.

The American Indian advance was led by Louis Sockalexis, a major-league outfielder who played before the turn of the century. Sockalexis, a full-blooded Penobscot, possessed great natural ability and
tremendous potential, but his addiction to alcohol cut short his major-league career. The sprinkling of other American Indians who
reached the major leagues included some outstanding performers.
One of the best was Albert "Chief" Bender, a Chippewa and a graduate of the Carlisle Indian School, famed for its fine athletes. He
pitched for fourteen seasons for Connie Mack's Athletics and appeared in five World Series. Bender had a reputation as a stout com-

* See *Baseball: The Early Years*, page 335.

petitor who was at his best when the stakes were highest. In October
1913 a band of Indians in blankets traveled 150 miles to join a crowd
watching the progress of one of the Series games on a scoreboard because Bender was pitching—a clear-cut case of identification. Another fine Indian player was John "Chief" Meyers, who provided John
McGraw with a solid catcher on some of his winning teams in the
second decade of the century. There were also pitchers Moses Yellow-
horse, a Pawnee who was with the Pittsburgh Pirates in the early
1920's, George Johnson, a Winnebago who played briefly for the Cincinnati Reds, and Ben Tincup, who spent several seasons in the National League.

The greatest all-around athlete of his day and, some believe, of all
time was also an American Indian, Jim Thorpe, a Sac and Fox. He
too attended Carlisle, where he was a sensational football player. He
reached his peak in the 1912 Olympics when he put on a one-man
show, winning a batch of prizes and leading the American team to
victory. Shortly after his triumph, it was discovered that he had once
violated the Olympics' amateur code by playing summer baseball for
money—a practice common among college athletes of the day. Nevertheless, the simon-pure authorities stripped Thorpe of his medals and
trophies, leaving him more famous than ever. Baseball magnates,
knowing he would be a sure-fire gate attraction, scrambled to sign
him. John McGraw succeeded in getting him for the Giants, and although Thorpe supposedly had difficulty hitting a curve ball, he managed to last for seven years as a part-time player.

Aside from English names, Irish and German ones were still the
most prominent on major-league rosters. Their forebears had
thronged to America in the 1840's, driven by hard times and political
turmoil in Europe. For them, as with other minorities, the most common way of gaining a foothold and moving upward in American society was through one's occupation, rather than through education, as
it is now. To earn a livelihood, the Irish and Germans commonly
toiled on farms or took unskilled jobs, which were more plentiful in
those days. For some of their sons, professional baseball provided a
more rapid and remunerative means of advancement. In the first decades of the twentieth century there were also signs that the "new immigration" from eastern and southern Europe, which got under way
in the 1880's, was beginning to affect baseball. The real influx of players of Italian and Slavic ancestry, however, did not come until the
1920's.

In the early part of the century, Jews were accepted although less
than joyously welcomed. According to Gerstein's study of anti-semitism in baseball, seven out of eight Cohens who played in the majors

thought it prudent to change their names. Johnny Kling of the Chicago Cubs, one of the best catchers of this early era, was generally called "the Jew" by his teammates, but recent information has shown that he was not Jewish after all. For years, humbug about Jews being "temperamentally unfit" for baseball was given countenance. The favorite canard was that they lacked the courage for rough-and-tumble physical competition. Those whose ability contradicted this assumption still had to endure the harassment and heckling characteristic of the more overt anti-semitism of the period.

The Giants, recognizing the financial advantage of having a player with whom New York's large Jewish population could identify, sought vainly for years to secure one of high ability. A much heralded outfielder named Benny Kauff, who was presumed to be Jewish, played with them for several seasons, but he did not come up to expectations, and then he got into trouble and was banned from Organized Baseball. Moses Solomon, another outfielder, had a very brief trial with them in 1923, and in 1927 they introduced infielder Andy Cohen with much ballyhoo, but he too fell short. While he lasted, however, every time he threw out a runner the play could be described with a phrase relished by everyone: "Cohen to Kelly." Ironically, the major-league teams of New York lost out on one of the greatest Jewish players, Henry Greenberg, who was elected to the Baseball Hall of Fame. Greenberg, a native-born New Yorker, who would have been a tremendous gate attraction for the Giants or Yankees, starred instead for Detroit.

Since World War Two, Latin Americans have firmly established themselves in Organized Baseball and now count among the foremost players of the game. Once they were a novelty, represented in the big leagues by a handful of Cubans. In 1904 sportswriter Revere Rodgers observed that Cuban players were "natural born artists" and accurately predicted that in the near future American managers would be recruiting them. In 1911 Rafael Almeida, a third baseman, and Armando Marsans, an outfielder, joined Cincinnati and stuck in the big leagues for three and eight seasons respectively. Clark Griffith, managing Cincinnati in 1911, pioneered in tapping the Cuban market, recognizing it as a source of inexpensive players. Upon transferring to the Washington club in 1912, he continued to seek Cuban talent and shortly introduced two more islanders to the majors, Jacinto Calvo and Balmadero Acosta.

Several more were soon signed up: Angel Aragon, Sr. with the Yankees, Emilio Palmero and José Rodriguez with the Giants, Eusebio Gonzalez with the Boston Red Sox, and Oscar Tuero with the St. Louis Cardinals. Rodriguez stayed with the Giants for three years and then became widely known in semi-pro baseball in the metropolitan New York area. Two front-rank Cuban players also made their debut in those years, Miguel Gonzalez and Adolfo Luque. Gonzalez, an expert catcher but weak hitter, played seventeen seasons in the majors and then stayed on as a coach. Baseball lore credits him with the most succinct scouting report in history. The Cuban, whose English left something to be desired, was asked to judge the prospects of a young rookie. After sizing him up, Gonzalez reported: "Good field, no hit." Luque was a clever pitcher with an unusually good curve ball. He had a twenty-year career with various National League teams and in 1923, his best season, was the number-one pitcher of the league, with a record of 27 games won as against only 8 lost. He also finished with the lowest earned-run average, 1.93.

The ugly face of bigotry grimaced at the Cubans too. Not only did they look "different," they might even be Negro or part-Negro. It may very well be true, as often claimed, that a few Negroes slipped into Organized Baseball by passing as Cubans or American Indians. Aware of this possibility, white racists among the fans were always suspiciously on guard against having a Negro "put over on them." This fear compounded the difficulties faced by Indians, Cubans, or any dark-skinned players. Many fans believed that Chief Meyers was really a Negro and let him know it by yelling "Nigger!" from the stands. Because of his dark complexion, Edmund "Bing" Miller, St. Louis Browns' outfielder, was always called "Booker T. Miller" by club manager Dan Howley. In 1908 the sports editor of the San Jose (California) *Mercury* sounded out the National Commission on the feasibility of signing "a couple of 'yellow' boys from Cuba" for the local team, asking whether there was any baseball law, "other than the natural objection of Irish and German players to playing on the same team with those off-colored boys," that would prevent their playing in Organized Baseball. Garry Herrmann passed the buck by telling the writer to take the matter up with John H. Farrell, secretary-treasurer of the minor leagues.

But three years later Herrmann had the opportunity to better his own club by adding the Cubans Marsans and Almeida. News of their coming to Cincinnati alarmed local lily-whites over the possibility that baseball's unwritten law against Negroes was being violated. Herrmann wanted to avoid the racial repercussions that had arisen when Marsans, Almeida, and two fellow Cubans, Alfredo Cabrera and Luis Padrone, opened their American careers with New Britain in the Connecticut League. That club's manager had even thought it necessary to make a special trip to Havana to verify that the Cubans were "genuine Caucasians." Herrmann realized that the Cubans would have strong box-office pull in Cincinnati and was eager, as one fan expressed it, to exploit their "freakiness." To cover himself, Herrmann made inquiries about the ancestry of the two players through connections he had in Cuba. Victor Muñoz, sports expert for the leading Cuban paper, *El Mundo*, accepted Herrmann's inquiry on its own terms, guaranteeing that the players had nothing but "pure caucasian blood in their veins."

A Cincinnati sportswriter made a clumsy effort to poke fun at the strenuous attempts to reassure patrons obsessed with race:

> Ladies and gentlemen, we have in our midst two descendants of a noble Spanish race, with no ignoble African blood to place a blot or a spot on their escutcheons. Permit me to introduce two of the purest bars of Castile soap that ever floated to these shores, Senors Alameda [*sic*] and Marsans. . . .

Cuban fans, proud of their countrymen's success in Las grandes ligas, quickly identified with them and followed their daily achievements through reports wired home by special Cuban correspondents traveling with the Cincinnati team. Although heroes in their native land, once they gained a place on an American team, Cubans, like Jewish players, were liable to brutal taunts from other players. There are those who still habor the suspicion that Latin American players do not have the sustained competitive spirit that others presumably possess.

Worse yet, Cubans with obviously Negroid features suffered exclusion under Organized Baseball's color ban. A flagrant example was the tragic case of José Mendez, a pitcher so expert that he was honored with the sobriquet "The Black Matty," after the Giants' star pitcher, Christy Mathewson. Mendez, a cigar-maker by trade, came to the attention of stateside baseball people by defeating major-league clubs in spring exhibition games in Cuba. In the opinion of a contemporary baseball writer, he would have been worth $50,000 to any major-league club if he could be "whitewashed." John McGraw wanted Cuba's "Black Diamond" for his Giants but, on the admission of baseball's trade paper, was "prevented by fellow National League excutives from importing the Cuban Negro star." So Mendez had to play out his career in the islands, leaving a record that has never been duplicated in Cuban baseball. Miguel Gonzalez, on the other hand, presented no problem with respect to the rampant racism of the time, for, as one writer bluntly expressed it, "His people were of pure Spanish blood, not of the mongrel Indian or negro mixture that has barred many a star of 'The Pearl of the Antilles' from major league company."

Most of the players still came from the northeast section of the country, with Pennsylvania still contributing the most of any state. The rank and file were products of modest background and rudimentary schooling—as so many Americans were before education became a big business and before high school and college were considered prerequisites to jobs and status. Joe Jackson, a superb player during the era of the triumvirate, is a striking example of Horatio Alger come true in baseball, as his very nickname "Shoeless Joe" implies. Jackson began as an illiterate millhand in the cotton factories near Greenville, South Carolina. He played ball for the local mill team and rose to the major leagues, where he was perhaps the greatest natural hitter in baseball. His lifetime batting average of .356, compiled over fourteen seasons, is the third highest ever attained, surpassed only by Ty Cobb (.367) and Rogers Hornsby (.358).

When Jackson first came to play in the big cities of the North, the manager had all he could do to keep him with the team because the simple countryman suffered from homesickness. Years after he was thrown out of baseball in disgrace for his part in a World Series scandal, I talked to him in his South Carolina liquor shop. In order to let him know that I recognized his skill as a ball player despite the opprobrium attached to his name, I asked him to autograph a baseball. To this day I believe that he still had not learned to write his own name, because he told me that if I would return the next day he would have a signed one ready for me; and he did.

Ty Cobb, considered by many the greatest baseball player who ever lived, was a product of rural Georgia. He began playing baseball at $65 a month, plus room and board, in Anniston, Georgia, and not only went on to acquit himself brilliantly for twenty-four years in the big leagues, but through profitable investment of his baseball earnings was one of the first ball players to become a millionaire. Baseball's most famous player, Babe Ruth, came from a squalid background—a juvenile delinquent in today's language or, to be more euphemistic, a deprived or underprivileged youth, rescued by St. Mary's Industrial Home for Boys in Baltimore, where he was given an opportunity to play baseball. For many another lad, professional baseball was a *deus ex machina* that rescued him from the drudgery and circumscription of the farms, coal fields, and mills. Such boys would have understood Larry Doyle, then an infielder on the New York Giants, when he said, "Gee, it's great to be young and a Giant." And for the sons of recent immigrants, baseball gave some substance to the much touted belief that America was a melting pot.

According to the American creed, the competitive struggle for success supposedly took place within a framework of rules (law), to insure not equal division of wealth but equal opportunity to obtain it. But again, there was the usual disparity between the ideal and the actual. Shrewdness in skirting the law, taking shortcuts to the goal, and, if need be, shoving others out of the way were all a part of the economic facts of life. In the business world such methods were not only tolerated but applauded, particularly if one emerged wealthy, and even more so if some of the wealth was handed back through philanthropy. Professional baseball reflected this mentality, as it did so many aspects of American society. Fans who understood what the business of making a living often entailed could again identify with baseball players who also tried to beat the rules or win advantage by cheating on them a little bit. In his book on baseball, ex-player Rogers Hornsby, outspoken as usual, has a chapter entitled "You've Got to Cheat to Win," which catalogs some of the time-honored ways of getting around the rules. A big-league player, he says, who does not like cutting corners or playing with "cheaters" is "as much out of place as a missionary in Russia." Those who gained an edge by such tactics were looked upon as smart ball players, whereas umpires charged with upholding the rules were the villains of the piece, just as those who exposed scandal in politics or, for that matter, in baseball were apt to be denounced as spoilsports.

Contrary to the pious adage intoned on ceremonial occasions, in professional baseball it is not how you play the game that counts, but whether you win or lose, because, other things being equal, the player's own personal success and the team's victory bring higher salaries and bigger profits. The premium placed on winning meant that tactics ordinarily considered unsportsmanlike went hand in glove with the professionalization of baseball. In 1920 the New York *Times* remarked: "Many baseball players believe that the recognized code of sportsmanship does not apply to baseball, and players will resort to all sorts of tactics when they believe that they will not be found out." Well-known sportswriter Hugh Fullerton pointed out that much that was fair in baseball would be "muckerish" in other sports.

It is easy to illustrate what Fullerton and others had in mind about the conduct of players. "Germany" Schaefer of Washington once threw his bat in front of the other club's catcher to hinder his pursuit of a foul ball. Arthur Devlin, Giants' third baseman, illegally attempted to hold back a runner to prevent him from scoring. A Boston catcher deliberately put his mask in the path of a Brooklyn player trying to score. It was routine to crash into the pivot man to break up a double play, or to "accidentally" bump a runner who was trying to advance to the next base.

The "beanball," or "duster," persisted in use. Pitchers threw at batters' heads to prevent them from taking a firm, confident stance at the plate. Under certain conditions, throwing at the batter was regarded as "entirely proper and ethical." If the hitter stood close and leaned over the plate, as many did, the pitcher's recourse was to drive him back by throwing at him, and it was considered good sportsmanship not to complain ir one got hit. The National Commission tried to legislate against the beanball in 1917, fixing a punishment of a five-year ban on a convicted pitcher. Baseball officials are still trying today, with equal lack of success. Pitchers are liable to fines, expulsion from the game, and even suspension, and batters are now required to wear plastic helmets. But the "headhunters" continue, except that pitchers no longer throw "beanballs"; they are called "brush-back" pitches.

A number of players' careers have been shortened as a result of being hit on the head. The most tragic case was that of Ray Chapman, Cleveland shortstop, who died after being struck by a ball thrown by Carl Mays in 1920. There were angry outcries and demands that Mays be banished from baseball, but it is unlikely that he deliberately tried to injure Chapman. Leaning over the plate was part of the victim's batting style; and Mays delivered the ball underhand, his knuckles almost scraping the ground, in throwing his famous "submarine ball," a pitch that sent the ball to the plate in a rising trajectory and made it difficult to gauge. Even so, Mays still had enough nerve after the accident to brush back batters if the occasion required. I sat on the bench as batboy for the visiting Cincinnati Reds during a game in the 1920's and saw Babe Herman, Brooklyn power hitter, get a lucky hit off Mays, who was pitching for the Reds that day. Enraged, Mays cursed Herman and promised to knock him down the next time he came to bat. Sure enough, when Herman came up again, Mays twice sent him sprawling in the dirt with two "dusters." Each time, Herman got up, brushed himself off, and renewed his position without complaint. It was all part of the game.

Some pitchers will throw at a batter's feet, "make him skip the rope," as it is called. This kind of pitch is more difficult to dodge and can cause a very painful blow, but it is not likely to cause mortal injury. Hardest to avoid is a ball thrown behind the batter. An experienced man can duck away from a close pitch or one coming directly at him, but he is apt to back into one coming from behind. Knowing this and realizing that such a pitch is almost certainly deliberate, the batter will usually come up fighting.

There were also numerous cases of spiking. President Pulliam once suspended Honus Wagner for three days for deliberately trying to spike a Cincinnati player. When Hans Lobert cut St. Louis catcher Roger Bresnahan (intentionally, in the opinion of the Cardinals) and left him bleeding in agony at the plate, Lobert's teammate, Sherwood Magee, took advantage of the confusion by shoving aside the Cardinal players gathered around Bresnahan and scoring a run. Once a minor-league player, spiked at Holyoke, Massachusetts, in 1914, went to court and won $1000 in damages. Some revived old demands that spiked shoes be barred, or at very least that spikes be covered or their length limited. Others pointed to the need for spikes on hard ground and slippery turf, while reminding critics that baseball was not meant to be "parlor tennis."

The ethic of the game filtered into some of the baseball books for boys. For instance, in *The Shortstop* by Zane Grey, one player jabbed another in the "hip" with a horseshoe nail in retaliation for being bumped while running the bases, and the fans "howled with all the might of fair-minded lovers of sport. . . . It was a play such as every ball player revelled in. It embodied the great spirit of the game." Grey went on to tell his readers: "ball playing is a fight all the time. . . . Every man for himself! Survival of the fittest! Dog eat dog!" As Richard Rovere observed a few years ago, although Americans think they have a sense of fair play, they also have a sneaking admiration for the "dirty player."

Some tactics merely involved trickery. The old "hidden ball" subterfuge was worked at least three times in the major leagues during the 1910 season alone. In this strategem, an infielder near the runner conceals the ball in his glove or under his arm; the runner, thinking the pitcher has it, steps off the base and is tagged out ignominiously by the wily infielder.° Sometimes a "phony" or "doped" ball was sneaked to the pitcher at a crucial point in the game, but the umpires became alert to this trick and learned to examine the ball more frequently. Once McGraw succeeded in a trick play that simply involved confusing another player. While coaching at third base, he stood on the bag beside one of his runners and shouted for the ball; Honus Wagner, thinking it was his own third baseman calling to him, threw the ball over, and of course the runner scored. Coach Miller Huggins pulled a similar stunt on a rookie pitcher. With the bases full, he demanded to see the ball; when the rookie tossed it to him, Huggins stepped aside, and all three Cardinal runners scored.

Every once in a while a ruckus was raised over decoding the signals ("signs," in baseball parlance) of the other team and then passing the information along via one's own code. A favorite method was to

° This trick is impossible to work if the runner remains on the base, as he should, until the pitcher steps on the pitching slab, because the pitcher must have the ball in his possession at that time; otherwise, he commits a balk, and the runner is permitted to advance a base.

station a man with binoculars in the clubhouse or behind the score-board to read the signs of the other team's catcher and then signal the batter what kind of pitch was coming. Sign "stealing" was looked upon as a "brazen" and "unsportsmanlike" procedure and, strangely, caused more objections than beanballing or rough tactics, although a distinction was made between "honest" and "dishonest" methods of stealing. To do it with skill and alertness or by taking advantage of the other team's carelessness was considered all right; recourse to me-chanical means was deemed reprehensible. At the annual American League meeting of 1909, a heated debate took place over the alleged sign stealing of the New York Highlanders (Yankees). After Ban John-son investigated, the accused club was exonerated. The following sea-son Big Ed Walsh, Chicago's star spitball pitcher, accused George Stallings, then managing the Highlanders, of using the same "second story methods" to win games. Owner Frank Farrell was said to be "hot under the collar" over this horrendous charge and asked Johnson to investigate again. Johnson went along with the drollery, offering $500 for proof, but nothing came of it. Connie Mack's Athletics had their turn in 1911 when they were charged with "working their signal bureau overtime" and playing "trick base ball."

Another questionable practice that is periodically engaged in is making a farce of a contest. Once Barney Dreyfuss became highly in-censed over the way the visiting Cincinnati players behaved in a game merely because the Pittsburgh grounds were "damp." The Reds smoked cigarettes at their positions, sent the pitcher in to catch, in-sulted the patrons, and burlesqued the game. What disturbed Drey-fuss most was that he felt obliged to refund every admission. Herr-mann mollified him by graciously returning his club's share of the gate receipts to the Pirates and giving his manager a talking-to.

In 1910 Roger Bresnahan, managing St. Louis, showed his pique over the decisions of an inexperienced umpire by stationing his men out of their regular positions. National League President Lynch repri-manded him in a letter. When Manager Frank Chance of the Chicago Cubs did the same thing in an exhibition game a few days later, the National Commission decided it was time to step in. They fined Chance $100 and two of his players $50 each.

In view of these tactics, to call professional baseball a sport and the players and owners sportsmen is to use language so loosely as to divest it of meaning. Games staged for money are not played for fun. Professional baseball is not cricket, where a team captain would sum-marily remove a man for behavior commonly accepted in baseball; nor is it tennis, in which a contestant will refuse a point if a ball is outside the line, even though the referee does not call it. On the other hand, baseball is a cut above sticking barbs into bulls, or having two men batter each other in a ring until one drops unconscious. These spectacles, too, have been called sports. But then even the word "warfare" is sometimes prefixed with the word "civilized."

Baseball should be seen for what it is—a boy's game played by grown men for a living and run by promoters for a profit. In professional baseball, therefore, winning is not just desirable; it is all-important. As a *Sporting News* editorial baldly stated in 1904, a victory gained by foul means is as much appreciated by owners and employees as any other. Hugh Fullerton once said with refreshing candor that in baseball almost anything short of maiming and injuring an opponent was permissible. Another sportswriter, W. O. McGeehan, observed that baseball is not a polite game, and, he reflected, come to think of it, that is why it is the national pastime. For good or bad, a consuming urge to win and a willingness to cut a few corners, if necessary to do so, have been a part of the American character since frontier days. These traits, which have contributed toward making the United States the kind of nation it is, were amply reflected by professional ball.

Organized Baseball could not tolerate unbridled violence, however. The promoters wanted baseball to appeal to the masses by being ruggedly competitive, but at the same time they were anxious that it be sufficiently respectable to attract the "better classes." If they permitted players to become overly competitive and allowed too much ruffianism and uncouth behavior, women and the more staid among the males might shun the games. On the other hand, if the boys were too well-behaved and agreeable, the spice and color would disappear, and the illusion of an all-out struggle for pennants would become increasingly unreal. Outright mayhem on the field had to be curbed, but so, too, did handshaking and fraternizing in public. Consequently, both extremes were officially ruled out.

In the formative years of the nineteenth century and the first decades of the twentieth, rowdyism among the players and attacks upon umpires were of chief concern. Severe measures to crack down on transgressors were taken in order to capture the approval and patronage of "respectable people." Disciplinary action, no doubt aided by an increasingly educated player personnel, gradually achieved a modicum of success.

It is precisely because ball players personified so many American traits that they were able to evoke strong responses from fans. If fans were not aware of this relationship, the press spelled it out for them. A 1909 editorial in *Baseball Magazine* asserted that the American boy's ambition was born of hero worship, and the lessons of athletics

were the same as those needed for success in life. These lessons
taught "perseverance, grit, and downright hard work." They developed the "do or die spirit, the primal factor in all the wonderful
things they do in America whether winning ball games or wars," and,
the editorial went on, "every American lad who ever amounted to
anything is willing to confess that at some time or other he used to
admire such and such a baseball player or athlete and made up his
mind that he was going to be one too." The place of ball players in
the lives of so many youngsters is captured by James T. Farrell in his
essay, "The Death of an Idol," in which he expresses his deep attachment to the famous second baseman, Eddie Collins.

Baseball was also said to promote alertness, resourcefulness, self-
control, self-confidence, abstemiousness, and readiness to sacrifice for
the glory of the team. No other game, said another writer, develops
traits requisite for a successful life and a successful nation as does
baseball. The St. Louis *Globe-Democrat* estimated in 1920 that nine
out of ten American boys played the game, and that since they took
their cues from professional baseball, there must be a close connection between its morality and American morality in general.

An increasing flow of detailed information in the press about the
personal lives and diamond exploits of the players added to their heroic stature. A study of the leading paper of a representative American town revealed that the relative amount of space given to organized sports jumped from 4 per cent of total news content in 1890 to
16 per cent in 1923. Sensitive to popular demand, newspapers brought
out a stream of editions in the afternoon to report on the progress of the games. After the turn of the century, the camera brought
the games visually to those who previously had little or no opportunity to see them. Newspapers employed photographers whose only
job was to take good baseball pictures, and write-ups of the game
were embellished with action shots. *Sporting News* was so pressed for
space that many of the minor leagues complained about lack of coverage. Alert editors, aware of the appetite of their readers for baseball
news, reminded their correspondents that the public's interest was not
confined to accounts of the games only. They encouraged them to
maintain fan interest with topics for "speculation, review or gossip"
and to heighten anticipation of baseball's annual spring revival with
off-season stories about the signing of players, rebuilding of teams,
rules changes, and trades.

By 1913 the Associated Press had wires strung across the continent
with loops running into every major-league park and into scores of afternoon newspaper offices. Reporters at the games flashed the batteries, umpires, and, at every half inning, the score, the way each run

was made, descriptions of key plays, and changes in the lineup. This service was later cut back somewhat. Sports reporter Ernie Lanigan claimed that newspapers were reducing the space given to baseball, and the editor of *Sporting News* warned the club owners of the danger, urging that the sooner they got "out of their shells and stopped being clams, the better."

A growing sub-literature supplemented the newspapers. Boys' books helped instill the lore of the game in the young. In the five-year span 1910–14 the *Reader's Guide to Periodical Literature* listed a peak total of 249 titles about baseball. Players were made larger than life in articles with such titles as "The Hard Job of a Baseball Star," "Clean Living and Quick Thinking," and "How the Ball Players of the Big League Live and Act When off the Diamond." Portrayals such as the following one of George Stovall were the style:

> . . . you cannot help admiring the man for his sterling honesty, his courage, and his fixity of purpose. He is one of the most picturesque characters in baseball, a man generous to a fault, free handed, democratic, without a possible trace of snobbishness in his make-up, a man who cares nothing for popular favor, who is impulsive to the point of rashness, but whose very faults have won him a strong popularity among his fellow athletes.
>
> There is a homely grace in his six feet-one of solid tendon and muscle. . . . There is an impressive power in his firm, protruding jaw, a seasoned endurance in his entire physical makeup. He has a keen brain, a ready wit, a blunt philosophy. But he is no man to trifle with. . . .

Thus were players presented as individuals of character, ordinary Joes despite their exalted positions: modest, yet tough, virile American males in keeping with the image glorified in Jack London's novels.

The press added another dimension to the hero by representing baseball as a game requiring a high degree of mental capacity and by emphasizing the role of "brainwork." Team managers were likened to military geniuses. Their "generalship" and "brain power" made them masters of baseball strategy. John McGraw became the "Mastermind" and the "Little Napoleon." Connie Mack was the "Tall Tactician," and Frank Chance the "Peerless Leader."

This was also the era of the new psychology, and its mysteries gripped the popular mind, particularly after Freud made his 1913 lecture tour in the United States. There was the psychology of this and the psychology of that, so why not the psychology of baseball? Not only did managerial masterminds know the intricacies of the game, but they were deemed experts in applied psychology as well, and baseball lore is full of stories about their use of it. McGraw (or Stallings—both have been credited), finding his team in a dismal batting slump, heard a player come into the clubhouse exuberantly announcing that he was bound to begin hitting that afternoon because on his way to the park he had seen that sure-fire omen of base hits, a load of empty barrels. The manager, ever alert to "psychology," forthwith hired a truckman to drive a load of empty barrels around the streets outside the park for the next few days. As each player spotted the good-luck omen, he broke out of his slump, and soon the team began to hit and to win. Players, too, reputedly waged psychological warfare, upsetting an opponent by heckling him on some personal sore point or harping on an embarrassing incident in his past.

Science was also becoming the fad, and, as with psychology, there was the "science" of almost everything, including, of course, the science of baseball. Articles appeared on the "science of fielding," the "science of batting," and so forth. Team play was equated with the precision of machinery, and teams themselves were referred to as "machines." This esoteric amalgam of psychology, science, and mental prowess bore the label "inside baseball," supposedly so complex as to be beyond the ken of most fans, however well-informed they were. Apparently, only a "knowing minority" who were "students of the game" could appreciate that much of the action on the field was the result of preconceived plans carried out in response to a complicated set of signals. Maybe the manager blew his nose or scratched his ear, and the third-base coach, catching this signal, called in a certain way to the batter, who in turn tapped his bat on the plate twice, signaling a runner who acknowledged it by touching his cap and then sped for second on the next pitch, knowing that the batter would cooperate by trying to hit the ball! It was revealed to fans that when pitcher Mathewson shook his head slowly it meant "yes," and when he shook it fast it meant "no," that when catcher Kling threw some dirt aside it meant he was going to throw to pick a runner off base. Chapters on "inside baseball" in books such as Christy Mathewson's *Pitching in a Pinch*, W. H. Claudy's *The Battle of Baseball* and *Touching Second* by Johnny Evers and Hugh Fullerton romanticized it in almost identical words.

So cloying did all this balderdash become that even *Spalding's Guide* said that more inside baseball existed "in the craniums of clever writers" than on the field, and Johnny Evers, regarded as one of the most occult practitioners of the art, acknowledged that there was no such thing as inside baseball and that most of it was played indoors with paper, pen, and ink.

If all this were not enough, fans could fall back on the growing accumulation of records. Americans have frequently been criticized for a lack of historical sense, but this generalization does not hold when it comes to baseball. The mass of statistics on players' performances allowed comparison of the current titans with former heroes, however much these comparisons became warped by changed conditions and rosy memories.

The question inevitably arises as to whether hero worship of ball players is desirable. Probably, most people believe that it is beneficial or at least harmless, particularly for youth, who, it is often said, need heroes to emulate. If so, the further question is whether ball players and, for that matter, athletes in general are suitable heroes. More than two thousand years ago the playwright Euripides expressed doubt:

> Of the myriad afflictions that beset Hellas none is worse than the breed of athletes. Never, first of all, do they understand the good life, nor could they. How can a man enslaved to his jaws, subject to his belly, increase his patrimony? . . . Shining in youth they stride about like statues in the square. But comes astringent age, they shrink in rags. Blameworthy is the custom of the Hellenes who for such men make great concourses to honor idle sports—for feasting's sake. What nimble wrestler, fleet runner, sinewy discus thrower, agile boxer, has benefited his city by his firsts? . . . 'Tis the wise and the good we should crown with bay, who best guide the state, the prudent and the just, whoso by discourse averts evil actions, banishes strife and contention. Prowess of such sort is to all the city a boon, to all Hellenes.

In our own day, we are from time to time told of the dangers of citizens' allowing themselves to be distracted from pressing problems by athletic contests and other entertainment. The horrible example of the Roman "bread and circuses" is usually held before us. We are further warned that hero worship leads to watching at the expense of participating. Ring Lardner put it this way: "hero-worship is the national disease that does most to keep the grandstands full and the playgrounds empty." A psychological study published in 1948 tells us that baseball is one of the games that profits from catering to "under-matured" people, those who retain "infantile" needs for "regressive" behavior. Another psychologist made the same point in 1969. He maintained that it is appropriate for an adolescent to look upon athletes as heroes, but for an adult to become overly serious about a man's ability to throw a "sphere" or to hit it with a piece of wood is a mark of regression. After all, the New York *Times* editorialized in 1904, these players were "merely Swiss mercenaries," and it suggested that the amount of local patriotism expended on them "if devoted to practical civic uses, would suffice to make and keep New York a model muncipality." The over-importance attached to the fortunes of the team has even led players to take the attitude that people somehow have a duty to support them and that the team is conferring a favor by winning the pennant. In 1909 Manager Fred Clarke criticized Pittsburgh fans for not encouraging the team sufficiently, and in recent years Duke Snider, Dodger outfielder, said that Brooklyn fans did not deserve a pennant.

On the other hand, it seems equally clear that spectator sports and hero worship fulfill important needs by supplying people in a high-pressure, complex society with an opportunity to let off steam by watching the players act out the spectators' aggressions. It all comes down to the desirability of keeping matters in proportion. So long as this form of diversion is not overdone, and people consciously realize that they are using baseball for escape, it may have actual value. Like it or not, baseball heroes and other athletic idols will probably retain their appeal, because for so many of us, in the words of Charles Merz,

. . . there is joy in the coming of a hero. There is a fine thrill in a new champion suddenly revealed. There is solid satisfaction in standing beside him when the drums roll and the cameras click, lining the streets to bid him welcome, packing the banquet-halls to hear him praised, basking in the aura of his sudden fame, breaking the humdrum routine of ordered living with a gala day, enjoying for a moment the thrill of self-identification with this fleeting bit of glory.

6

A HERO'S LIFE

BROADLY SPEAKING, there have been two main types of sportswriting about baseball and ball players; they are known as the "Gee whiz" and "Aw nuts" schools of journalism. In the first type, players are portrayed uncritically and romantically. Their less admirable qualities are played down or suppressed by sportswriters whose daily job, as Paul Gallico once said, was to "peddle treacle about the baseball heroes and soft-pedal the sour stuff." Accordingly, rowdies are called "fierce competitors" and "stormy petrels," and playboys and alcoholics simply "break training" or "like the bright lights" and "take a drink." Anecdotes that romanticize players of one generation are repeated and embellished for the next with new names substituted, and the lore of baseball grows apace.

In the second type of sportswriting, ball players are depicted more critically, often to their irritation and that of the professional baseball establishment, to whom whitewash is essential to the proper portrayal of the game.

During the early decades of this century the first school of sportswriting predominated. Newspapers, magazine articles, and books pushed the view that professional players were a fine group of clean-living young men who played the game for the love of it and whose leisure moments were spent in cultural self-improvement. Writers told of players reading and visiting museums when the team was traveling, and singing around the piano at their hotels. They admitted that players sometimes played cards, but only for low stakes set by the manager. There was some horseplay, of course, but as the season progressed the men, except for a few "irresponsibles," settled down to business under the nervous strain of the pennant race. "Gee whiz" writers also tried to endow the game with an intellectual complexion by describing the supposed intricacies of "inside baseball."

The first important writer to debunk the conventional concept of the ball player was Ring Lardner. He began his writing career as a reporter, covering the Chicago White Sox from about 1909 to 1913. Sardonic and irreverent in his attitude toward the players, and gifted with a remarkably keen ear for their language, Lardner contributed a new, refreshing interpretation. His typical player was an insensitive, oafish braggart, who rejected advice—"I don't think he can learn me nothing"—and possessed an inexhaustible supply of alibis for his failures on the diamond. Off the field he was a gluttonous, beer-guzzling penny pincher who sneaked off to cheap lunchrooms to save on his dollar-a-meal allowance and complained about tipping waiters ten cents. Lardner held no illusions about the character or intelligence of the average player; nevertheless, he satirized him with humor and compassion. Lardner's Jack Keefe and Alibi Ike were amusing antidotes to the stereotypes of his day. Yet his presentation of the ball player was, like that of the "Gee whiz" writers, incomplete, for his aim was to tell entertaining stories by gently lampooning the players.

What were ball players really like? As with any group, it is possible to find every kind of individual among them. As ex-player Davy Jones recalled, "We had stupid guys, smart guys, tough guys, mild guys, crazy guys, college men, slickers from the city and hicks from the country." All ball players were not Jack Keefes. For one thing, there were more college men among them than in earlier years, reflecting the increase in the percentage of college enrollment in the nation, which had nearly doubled between 1900 and 1914.

Some baseball men resented the collegians. Frank Frisch, who came to the Giants in 1919 directly from Fordham and became an outstanding second baseman, claimed that Manager McGraw had no use for "collegers" and persistently "rode" him as a "big thinker." But recollections of old ball players are often exaggerated. McGraw himself had attended college during the off season and was once recorded as favoring collegians as players because they had the equivalent of a two-year advantage in experience over the town-lot boys, "arrived" faster, and supposedly lasted longer.

Some thought the collegians' polish would rub off onto less cultured teammates, who would copy the college men's manners, speech, and dress. But the reverse might happen as well, and probably did, judging from the choice vocabularies of some college-educated ball players, especially when addressing umpires. However interesting these musings about "college-breds" were for sports-page readers, the notable fact was that professional ball was open to men from the campus if they had the ability, and more and more of them were proving that they did. One need only point to Connie Mack's championship teams of that era, which included such collegians as Jack

Coombs, Eddie Plank, and Eddie Collins. The two former were among the best pitchers in the game, and Collins, who played for twenty-five years, ranks among the best second basemen in the history of baseball. The Chicago Cubs was another team on which college men were well represented.

There is also reason to believe that baseball was affected by the increase in high-school graduates, whose numbers more than doubled between 1900 and 1914. Yet many players came from the South, where education still lagged and where 7½ per cent of the white population was still illiterate in 1910. Stories illustrating the ignorance of players were still popular, like the one about the player who was asked by a "literary gentleman" whether he admired great authors. "I surely do," he replied. "Good authors are my best pals, all the time." Pursuing the discussion, the gentleman asked, "Then do you not like Omar Khayyam?" The player answered, "For my part, this stuff I'm drinking is good enough for me." Another erudite teammate, jabbing his elbow into the first player's ribs, exclaimed, "You blamed chump, where's your etiquette? That name he's speaking ain't a drink. It's a cheese."

Ball players were also praised for their bearing and appearance in public. A 1912 observer marveled that there was so little to set them apart from others at hotels that they were often taken for a convention of salesmen. Some players could pass for college sophomores or actors. They dressed better than clerks; in fact, many wore clothes too "sporty" in cut and indulged in monogrammed linen, silk hose, and diamond garter buckles. Diamond rings were a mark of status, as they had been for years. Comments were also made about the players' familiarity with correct table manners and about the fact that the teams patronized the "swellest" hotels, as they had been doing ever since the 1880's. In fact, President Pulliam boasted that players were taken to the best hotels and comported themselves accordingly.

Fans working long hours day in and day out at humdrum jobs could easily envy the life of a ball player. He traveled first class; had his baggage hauled, checked, and placed in his room; was waited on by trainers who served as valets—in a word, he had the best of everything. One reporter deplored the "luxurious living" of players on the road and thought the magnates were too indulgent with the "petted darlings of the diamond." A writer for the New York *Tribune* told of players having dinner at the finest restaurants, dressing "modishly," attending theater parties, posing for photographers and film producers, reading stories published under their by-lines, and visiting manicurists, masseurs, and chiropodists. He pictured them as having one or two hours' healthful exercise a day and spending the rest of the time as they pleased—and on a salary of $150 a week. These accounts were truthful enough to be convincing, but were not the whole story.

The life of the ball player was actually not quite so idyllic. Spring training began about mid-February, but he received no pay other than his keep until the season began in mid-April, although for the sake of morale an owner might give him a few dollars for pocket money. Once the season started, the men usually had to report for morning practice when the club was at home. These workouts, which continued well into the season, are sometimes cited by old-timers as examples of how they labored to perfect themselves. Actually, they were of limited value, except insofar as they encouraged the men to retire at a decent hour so that they could be up in time to report for the morning workout.

After a game the players showered, changed, and left the clubhouse, home-team players going to their rented quarters, the visitors to their hotel, two men to a room. On "getaway day" when they had to travel to the next city, the trainer, who usually doubled as baggage master, helped the clubhouse boy pack and ship the equipment while the players took cabs or buses to the station. On the train, after invading the diner, the players smoked and enjoyed cards or checkers. Their favorite game was poker—the indoor national pastime, Lardner called it. A traveler with the Chicago White Sox reported that there was never a time when at least one game was not going. During their stay in a town players also bet on horses, played pool, and did a little dancing. Napoleon Lajoie enjoyed pool but would never play at night, possibly to save his eyes.

With justification, contemporary players grouse about the rigors of air travel, with its flights at irregular hours and across time zones, often interrupted by tedious waits in airports at unconscionable hours, but the train trips of former times were not exactly joyrides either. They entailed tiresome hours on coaches without air conditioning and fitful sleep in rattling Pullmans. A veteran player in Thomas Wolfe's novel, *You Can't Go Home Again*, tells of the monotony: "Boy, this may be a ride on the train to you, but to *me*—say!—I covered this stretch so often that I can tell you what telephone post we're passin' without even lookin' out the window. Why, hell yes!—I used to have 'em numbered—now I got 'em *named!*" Quirks of the playing schedule might add to the strain. Ford Frick remembered that once during his newspaper days the team he was covering played a Saturday afternoon game at Boston, then caught a train immediately afterward for Detroit, where it arrived the next morning;

after playing a doubleheader there, the team took another train back to Boston.

One problem of the team managers was the players' diets. Sometimes the men were given a daily "meal money" allowance, usually three dollars, and allowed to eat where they wanted. But this tempted them to skimp on food and save the money. On the other hand, if the players ate on the American plan, they might gorge themselves and "eat their way out of the big league." One rookie, who complained that his meal money was not enough to permit him to order raw meat for breakfast, was told by the manager that the bill of fare was for human beings, not animals. Ordinarily, players ate in the hotel dining room, where the manager sometimes required them to sit at one big table. After dinner they might indulge in another favorite pastime of ball players—lobby-sitting, which was taken up with talking, smoking, and looking over the baseball extras. Or they might go to a show, or relax by playing pool or cards. They were usually required to be in bed before midnight. Clubs tried to select hotels that were not too lively, preferably those without a "cabaret," to minimize the attractions of the local night life. Whenever possible, players slept late and then ate a heavy breakfast, either skipping lunch or limiting themselves to a light snack to avoid feeling logy during the game. Travel at first seemed glamorous, but after a while it became a chore, particularly for the married men, who missed their families.

Some managers disapproved of taking wives on road trips and would also bar them from spring training camps. On the other hand, there were managers who believed that wives could be a restraining and refining influence. Club policy aside, the extra expense to the player was a deterrent. Ralph Works was unhappy and worried at having to leave his bride behind for lack of money when he left for spring training in 1913. Roy Hitt delayed reporting in the spring of 1907 because his wife was expecting a child.

Baseball players, themselves in the limelight, sometimes met and married glamorous and talented women. One of the most celebrated matches was that of Mabel Hite, a well-known actress, and Mike Donlin, who had worked with her in vaudeville. She claimed she became interested in baseball after reading a startling line in a newspaper story describing how Donlin was put out sliding home: "Donlin got tired of life and suicided at the plate." A teammate of Donlin's, pitcher Rube Marquard, married actress Blossom Seeley, and Tommy Leach, outfielder for the Pittsburgh Pirates, married a dancer, Marie Trask. Another interesting pair was Benjamin Hunt and Edith Wolfe, a Vassar girl who appeared on the stage. Arthur Fletcher, Giants' infielder, married heiress Irene Dieu, and Eddie Collins wed Mabel Doan, daughter of a wealthy Philadelphia manufacturer.

Some players, as would be expected, found the matrimonial field rocky. The gifted but eccentric left-handed pitcher of the Athletics, Rube Waddell, whose first wife several times charged him with non-support, failed a second time. After only three weeks of marriage the former Margaret McGuire returned home, saying "Rube is too crazy for me." Later, his dallying with an actress subjected him to a $25,000 suit for alienation of a wife's affection. There were others who got into domestic difficulties and were sued for breach of promise, non-support, and abandonment.

Particularly unfortunate was the case of Shufflin' Phil Douglas, who was following a path to ultimate ruin. When his wife read that he had been fined $100, she asked the Cincinnati club if he had any money coming to him that she could claim. She said she could no longer put up with her way of living: he sent her no money, her board was never paid, she had only one decent dress to go out in, and there was no medicine for the children, who were suffering from colds. Actually, the club was trying to trade Douglas, who always seemed to have a problem—either his father or his wife was sick, or he was drunk. But other teams were hesitant to acquire him, capable though he was of pitching fine ball, because of his habits. Cincinnati finally did get rid of him, and it was not until he joined the Giants that final tragedy overtook him.°

A hazard the ball player sometimes faced was the woman who claimed to be his wife. There is reason to believe that a woman who asserted she was his pregnant wife hounded Chick Stahl, playing manager of the Boston Red Sox, into committing suicide. Athletics outfielder Rube Oldring was also harassed by a woman posing as his wife. Evidently she wanted his 1914 World Series money. Oldring maintained that the trouble "threw him off his game" in the Series. "What chance had I to play good ball," he asked, "when everyone in Boston was yelling that I deserted my wife?"

At spring training in 1911 Manager Clark Griffith exercised understanding and discretion upon learning that the woman with whom his pitcher, George McQuillan, was living was not legally married to him. Griffith kept the knowledge confidential because, he said, he had watched them and "they could not do better." "She keeps to herself and takes him out for a walk in the evening," he reported, "then they retire never later than 10. I don't think he would do as well without her." Moreover, the woman told Griffith tearfully that McQuillan had

° See below, chapter 19.

promised to marry her as soon as she got a divorce and that he was trying to stop drinking for her sake.

Ball players may be heroes but they certainly are not saints. Because they are human, they have shortcomings, without which they would be uninteresting. And failure to recognize their human weaknesses may result in disillusionment, especially among youth, should their heroes falter or go astray. A classic example is the pathetic tale of the youngster who pleaded with his hero, Joe Jackson, as the player left the courthouse after the sensational revelation that he and others had allegedly agreed to take money for losing the World Series. "Say it ain't so, Joe," the lad begged, and Jackson answered, "I'm afraid it is, son."

It may be that when play and work coincide, as they do in baseball, the performer's personality becomes arrested. As Thorstein Veblen said, the temperament that inclines men to sports is essentially a boyish temperament. Roy Campanella, the splendid Dodger catcher of the 1940's and '50's, had the same idea: "You have to have a lot of the little boy in you to play baseball for a living." This boyishness was noted by one of the early writers, who observed that when they won, players were apt to be full of pranks and ready for a "lark"; at other times, too, they were capable of behaving childishly, leaving their club in a sulk, going on a drunk, or even breaking a contract.

The era of the National Commission, like every other era in baseball history, had its quota of problem children. Connie Mack said of his 1912 team: "four or five of my boys had got bad cases of the swelled head, broke training, and I had to suspend them." One of his pitchers, Chief Bender, was "taken around," and soon his pitching suffered; but he straightened out in time and denied himself in "diet and pleasure." Once Cy Seymour went into a game under the influence of liquor—and, the reporter took care to mention, on a Sunday at that. Unable to "get out of his tracks," he let an easy fly ball drop in front of him, and when he came to bat he swung at every pitch. On another occasion drunken Brooklyn players ripped up their Pullman car on a road trip and had to pay damages and a fine as well.

Honus Wagner, generally considered the best of shortstops, liked his beer and, according to reporter Bozeman Bulger, when Pittsburgh came to New York he used to drop in at Sheehan's after the game and have six beers before going to his hotel, though he never "dissipated." In 1910, however, hints that he was drinking heavily appeared occasionally in the press. Wagner was about thirty-five then, and one manager thought that he could not last much longer if he kept it up. Actually, the Pittsburgh club tried to get him to sign a no-alcohol pledge at the end of that season, but he refused. He fooled them all by having seven more creditable playing years. A number of outstanding stars, including quite a few who made the Hall of Fame, were heavy drinkers, and the argument that they might have been even better players had they stayed on the water wagon is open to question. In view of the records they made, it is difficult to see how they could have been much better. So it is equally plausible to contend that without the relaxation that liquor evidently provided, they might not have done as well.

Nevertheless, drinking did seriously affect the work of some players. Once Rube Benton left his club to go on a spree, with the excuse that his sister was sick. When his suspicious manager wired Benton's home and found that everyone there was well, the club suspended the player and fined him $100. It also included a clause in his next contract under which he promised to abstain from the use of liquor and cigarettes during the season "to an extent that may be satisfactory" to the manager. He was promised a bonus if he kept the pledge.

When Pittsburgh pitcher Howard Camnitz claimed that he was short $1200 pay, his club admitted withholding it because it was intended to be a bonus for temperance. Asked if he had touched liquor during the season, Camnitz hesitated and then said he had not until his physician advised taking it. The physician, retorted owner Dreyfuss, was not running the club.

George "Chief" Johnson asked for an advance of $100 on his salary so he could "boil out" (take the baths) at Hot Springs. But after his arrival there he was fined $100 for being "in a disreputable house with a disreputable woman," for "drinking to excess," and for being away from his hotel the entire night.

Mike Donlin got into several scrapes. In 1902 he served a six-month jail sentence for striking a Baltimore actress. Four years later he was arrested for punching a conductor on the New York Central Railroad. Another time he reportedly "got a good nose full" and appeared on the stage very drunk. After his assault on the conductor, he was denounced in *Sporting News* as a "degenerate," "rowdy," and "woman-beater." Another player of this era pleaded guilty in Federal Court to violation of the Mann Act and was given four months.

Drink brought tragedy to Ed Delehanty. One night he became intoxicated on a train and created such a disturbance that he was ejected at the Canadian border. After an altercation with the watchman, who tried to prevent him from crossing the International Bridge, he continued on his way, falling through the open draw and drowning in the Niagara River.

Newspapers were full of gossipy stories about another unfortunate alcoholic, Larry McLean. One story that appeared in his home-town newspaper, where his wife and mother read it, had him missing a blackboard talk by the manager because he had a date with a flashy blond. The club tried everything in an effort to straighten him out. It inserted a special non-drinking clause in his contract, stipulating that if he fell from grace he could be suspended without salary for a year and there would be no redress to the National Commission. Nevertheless, his ways remained unchanged, and when he tried "resigning" from his contract the club suspended him. It later relented and signed him to another special contract providing for a fine every time he was away from the hotel after midnight. Finally, the club hired a detective to keep tabs on him. In one report the detective gave a run-down of McLean's activities on a certain evening: he started out drinking beer at Schubert's in Cincinnati and soon began shouting "To hell with Griffith!" (his manager); from there he made the rounds, moving from one saloon to another to elude his wife, who was trying to catch up with him and calm him down; when he woke up to the fact that he was being tailed, he tried to have the detective arrested. McLean's wages were repeatedly garnisheed to satisfy creditors, and the club arranged to have his wife or daughter pick up what was left of them. Violation of training rules, fights with the manager, fines and suspensions marked the rest of his short career. Several years later he was shot and killed in a saloon brawl in Boston.

Few players have inspired more anecdotes than Rube Waddell, a superb left-hander who could be just about as effective as he wanted to be and who, despite his eccentricities, is regarded as one of the best pitchers of all time. Again newspapers made much of his foibles and his weakness for drink; Timothy Sharp, a reporter, wrote that Waddell, tending bar in the winter of 1904, was the best consumer of the "wet goods" he was supposed to be selling. If he keeps throwing "high balls" at his back teeth, jibed Sharp, he "won't pitch any kind this summer." *Sporting News* dubbed him "the sousepaw" and the only "one ring circus now traveling with a ball club." Lee Allen, in his book *The American League Story,* catalogs the erratic pitcher's reported escapades in one year alone:

He began that year sleeping in a firehouse at Camden, New Jersey, and ended it tending bar in a saloon in Wheeling, West Virginia. In between those events he won twenty-two games for the Philadelphia Athletics, played left end for the Business Men's Rugby Football Club of Grand Rapids, Michigan, toured the nation in a melodrama called *The Stain of Guilt,* courted, married, and became separated from May

Wynne Skinner of Lynn, Massachusetts, saved a woman from drowning, accidentally shot a friend through the hand, and was bitten by a
lion.

Waddell's vagaries grew less and less amusing. In a row with his
wife's parents in 1905, he allegedly threw two flatirons at them. A few
years later he disappeared before a spring exhibition game in Texas
but showed up in the fourth inning with the imaginative explanation
that he had been invited by some cowboys to referee a boxing match,
and on his way back a freight car tied up the trolley line, making him
late for the game. That summer Connie Mack apparently lost whatever control he had over Waddell, and Philadelphia fans became disgusted at the way he "fooled away" two games after a week-long de-
bauch in Atlantic City. Mack finally sold him to the St. Louis Browns
in 1908, where he lasted three more seasons. He was only thirty-seven
when he died of tuberculosis in a Texas sanatorium.

References in baseball literature to players' drinking are usually
made in an indulgent, rather good-natured vein, somewhat as one
would describe mischievous boys climbing up to reach a forbidden
jam pot. But rarely is any mention made of players contracting the
"social diseases," as they were once euphemistically known. However,
unless one naïvely believed that ball teams were touring bands of as-
cetics, it might be surmised that some of the heroes succumbed to the
ills that many ordinary citizens contracted. When the press alluded to
maladies like syphilis and gonorrhea in those days, it frequently used
"malaria" or "rheumatism" as synonyms for what were considered
shameful diseases. John I. Taylor, a club owner, obviously had this
dodge in mind when he made the classic remark, "Beware Hot
Springs rheumatics." *Sporting News* came as close as any to forth-
rightness when it announced that George Barclay had fallen victim to
malaria, adding that it had reliable information that his condition
was due to an "indiscretion." What the papers did not report, or perhaps did not know, was that Barclay had a recurrence, or possibly a
continuation, of his "malaria" the following year. It is only through
sources other than the press that more straightforward terminology
can be discovered. A former player of that era told me in an interview that at one time there were five cases of gonorrhea on his club.
Not only was Cincinnati player George McQuillan an alcoholic, he
also contracted syphilis. His case and those of two others were substantiated by physicians' statements. Garry Herrmann sent McQuillan
to Hot Springs for treatment and provided him with generous financial aid, but eventually the Cincinnati club gave up on him. Newspapers reported certain other players, including some revered ones, as

having "malaria," but since it is not certain whether they really had that disease or another, they will remain unnamed.

No player is more worthy of membership in professional baseball's contingent of clay-footed heroes than Ty Cobb. His twenty-four-year career dazzles anyone who reads the playing records. It is studded with such achievements as attainment of the highest lifetime batting average (.367) and possession of the batting championship the most seasons (12). Until recently he also held the record for number of games played, number of lifetime hits, and number of bases stolen.

But impressive as these raw figures are, they do not reveal the intangibles of Cobb's play: his mastery of bunting and place hitting, an art that enabled him to do the unexpected at bat; his demoralization of opposing teams with his speed and daring to the point of recklessness on the bases; and his knack of being at his best before hostile crowds or when pressure on him was heaviest. He was the first player chosen for the Baseball Hall of Fame, and many still say he was the greatest of them all.

Nevertheless, Cobb was a tragic hero. Like those heroes of the Greek classics who were undone by *hubris*, the fatal flaw of excessive pride, Cobb, too, fell short as a human being. He was consumed by an unbridled urge to excel, an urge bordering on the abnormal. He did not so much play baseball as wage it, for to him it was a war. He was ruthless, even cruel, in his compulsion to be first. Opposing players were enemies to be cut down with his spikes if they got in his way on the bases. He fought his own teammates, too, and set his individual course as a "loner" among them. He battled the management, the fans, and everyone in the world who crossed him.

He was not always wrong in his conflicts, and he could courageously take punishment as well as inflict it. In his later life he anonymously aided many an indigent player, partly endowed a hospital, and established scholarships in his name. But in the end he was left with little but his records, his wealth, his loneliness, and an increasingly warped personality, respected for his skill but unloved, and alienated even from his family.

From the moment he joined the Detroit team in 1905 at the age of eighteen, Cobb was in hot water. Temperamental, humorless, and egocentric, he proved an inviting target for the torments of the hardboiled primitives on the team, who resented his sparkling intrusion and threat to supplant them either in job or in public attention. They took sadistic delight in hazing him, breaking his bats, and goading him into fights, particularly with Charles Schmidt, considered the strongest man on the club. He dined alone, traveled to the park by himself, and for years at a time was not even on speaking terms with some teammates. Stories in the Detroit *Times* had him admitting in

1907 that he had no friends on the club because his temper had estranged the other men. In an effort to end dissension on the team, Manager Hughie Jennings tried without success to trade Cobb in 1906—an example of the truth of the saying that the best trades are those never consummated. He finally coaxed Cobb into speaking to some of the others and also gave his prima donna as much leeway as possible. Cobb broke club rules, showed up late at the park, and once packed up and left the team because the hotel where they were staying was noisy.

Try as he did, Cobb never was able to live down his reputation as a dirty player who was willing to spike a man if it suited his purpose. His spiking of Frank Baker in 1909 contributed substantially to that reputation. He denied cutting Baker purposely, although at times he qualified his claim by stating that he spiked Baker intentionally but only because he had no other way of reaching the bag, since Baker was blocking it. Detroit writers defended Cobb at the time, and in fairness it can be said that Baker was not the most nimble in avoiding the spikes of an oncoming runner. The Athletics naturally scoffed at Cobb's denial, and their usually mild-mannered manager, Connie Mack, joined in the denunciations, declaring Cobb unfit for baseball and threatening to protest formally to the league. On Detroit's next trip to Philadelphia, Cobb received threatening letters, one of them warning that he would be shot from a nearby rooftop if he dared to play. A large police squad escorted him to and from the park and stood guard during the game. Meanwhile, attendance rose wherever Cobb played.

Shortly after Cobb's death, *Sporting News* editor J. G. Taylor Spink tried to counteract an article severely critical of Cobb; but it is interesting that at the time of the Baker controversy the paper joined the outcry against him with an editorial saying that complaints about his use of spikes to injure and intimidate infielders were so common that Cobb's denial would not relieve him of the "odium" attached to a player guilty of this "infamous" practice. "The list of his victims is too long to attribute the injury of all to accident or to the awkwardness of the victims."

Unlike the Baker incident, which occurred during a close pennant race, another well-known scrap, Cobb's run-in with Buck Herzog, started in a spring exhibition game when nothing was at stake other than Cobb's ego and, subsequently, Herzog's. The Giants and Tigers were traveling north together, playing exhibition games en route. One day when Cobb arrived just before the game after playing golf that morning, the Giants started to "ride" him hard on the general theme of being a privileged character. As usual, Cobb became angry. After reaching first base in the game, he dashed for second and tore into Herzog, who was covering the bag. The two grappled and other players joined in. Both principals were removed by the umpire, but that did not conclude matters. The teams were staying at the same hotel, and that evening Herzog came over to Cobb's table in the dining room and invited him to finish the argument in Cobb's room. Cobb obliged, and the two, each accompanied by his second, had another go. Versions of what happened vary, but evidently the 147-pound Herzog got the worst of it from a bigger and heavier Cobb, who then decided to leave the team for the rest of the trip and train with another club. At the conclusion of the tour, the Giants delivered a parting thrust with a telegram to Cobb reading something like this: "It's safe to rejoin your club now. We've left."

Cobb's apologists rationalize his conduct on the diamond as the manifestation of a singularly passionate competitive spirit; his conduct off it, which matched his baseball behavior, is not so easily explained away and reinforces the claims of those who say he was mentally disturbed. More than once baseball officials took notice of his deportment. After Cobb had altercations with fans in several cities, Ban Johnson notified the Detroit management that he would be punished if he did not curb his tongue. In 1913 the National Commission itself officially called attention to his public conduct "in many instances . . . too well known to the patrons of the game to require comment" and warned that continuation of it would in future be punished. No doubt the Commission had in mind instances such as the time he came into the Hotel Euclid in Cleveland about 1:20 one morning in 1909 and got into a fight with the hotel detective, Frank Stanfield, whom he cut with a penknife. Cobb denied that he was drunk but later pleaded guilty in Criminal Court and was fined $100 and costs for assault. In 1914 while driving to a train with his wife, Cobb was stopped and set upon by three hoodlums, one of whom slashed him severely with a knife. Cobb succeeded in driving them off but, not content with that, gave chase, caught up with one of them and beat him senseless with the pistol he habitually carried.

The same year an argument over twenty cents' worth of fish cost him a damaged hand and practically two months' layoff. Cobb's wife phoned a butcher to tell him that the fish delivered to her was spoiled when it came. The telephone argument that followed culminated with the butcher saying he did not care for the Cobb trade anyway. Cobb, taking this as an insult to his wife, went to the shop and, fingering his revolver, demanded that the merchant call Mrs. Cobb and apologize—which he did. The affair seemed settled until the butcher's young assistant appeared and dared Cobb to put the gun down and fight. He complied and was beating up the boy when the police arrived and took Cobb to the station house, where they released him after treating his hand, injured in the scrap. The butcher, however, later pressed charges against Cobb, who pleaded guilty. A newspaper reported that he settled out of court for $50, but much later another article stated that Cobb had smashed up the store and had paid $1500 in damages.

On more than one occasion Cobb's Georgia upbringing—his "Ben Tillmanism," as *Sporting News* called his racist attitude, after a famous Southern demagogue—betrayed itself. He had a mixup with a black groundkeeper at spring training in 1907 because the man did not address him suitably. When the man's wife joined in, Cobb clouted her and then nearly got into a fight with a teammate who chided him for hitting a woman. The next year he struck another Negro for "insulting" him as he left the ball park.

According to a leading Negro newspaper, the Chicago *Defender*, Cobb kicked a black chambermaid in the stomach and knocked her down the stairs in the Pontchartrain Hotel in Detroit because she objected to being called a "nigger." The *Defender* asserted that the white press and baseball officials suppressed the story because of Cobb's prominence and that the woman was quietly paid off in exchange for dropping her $10,000 damage suit. Another unpleasantness, this one widely publicized, was a baseball scandal, to be described farther on, which soiled Cobb's reputation and that of another hero just as they were approaching the end of their illustrious playing careers.

Throughout his life Cobb appears to have been obsessed by the dreadful circumstances surrounding the death of his revered father, a man of standing in the community. It was a tragedy that preyed on his mind and apparently exacerbated his disturbed personality. According to Al Stump, who helped write Cobb's autobiography, the reason Cobb gave for fighting so hard in baseball was: "I did it for my father, who was an exalted man. They killed him when he was still young. But I knew he was watching me and I never let him down." He went on, according to Stump, to say, "My father had his head blown off with a shotgun when I was 18 years old—by a member of my own family. I didn't get over that. I've never gotten over it." Stump later learned that it was Cobb's own mother who killed his father one night as he crept in the window of her bedroom to find out whether she was unfaithful to him, as he suspected. She was alone and, mistaking her husband for an intruder, she used the shotgun kept by her bedside. This shock, coming just as Cobb entered the major leagues and engendering in him, as it seems to have done, an irrational desire to vindicate his father, produced, in Stump's words, the "most violent, successful, thoroughly maladjusted personality ever to pass across American sports." Perhaps the best explanation of his turbulent career lies in Cobb's own words: "I had to fight all my life to survive. They were all against me . . . but I beat the bastards and left them in the ditch."

Cobb's emotional symptoms became increasingly pronounced with age. Stump, who moved in with him to collect information for Cobb's book, later wrote a magazine article vividly describing the last terrifying ten months of the former star's life. Cobb, racked with numerous serious diseases, subsisted on pills, medicines, and liquor, taking practically no food when he should have been dieting carefully. He alternately lived in two huge empty mansions, having driven away neighbors, servants, and former mistresses with his violent temper and gutter language. He would sit up nights with his pistol to catch "enemies," cut off his telephone because of "eavesdroppers," or set out at any hour of the night in any weather to drive to a gambling house.

The book that Cobb dictated to Stump during this pathetic period, aside from being a maze of contradictions, was filled with attempts at self-justification and denunciations of former associates, including Ban Johnson, Judge Landis, and the Detroit owner, whom he accused of cheating on gate receipts, among other things. It also reiterated a theme that he had always harped on—the inferiority of the modern game and its players as compared with baseball of the Cobb era. Finally, when death came at the age of seventy-four, only three people from all of major-league baseball attended his funeral, and the shrine dedicated to him in Royston, Georgia, remains only partly completed for lack of funds. Whatever one's judgment about Cobb as a person, it is fortunate for baseball that he was maladjusted; otherwise he would not have been the sensational player he was.

Lesser heroes had more prosaic weaknesses, like failing to pay their debts. Boarding-house landladies, tailors, jewelers, steam-bath proprietors, and sundry other creditors, including fellow players, turned to the National Commission for aid in collecting money owed them by players. The Commission adopted a policy of refusing to act as a collection agency for players' private debts, although it made exceptions in some instances.

It may surprise those who believe the old-timers were all hard-bitten individualists to find out that some of them were tied to the apron strings of overprotective parents. The Reverend Mr. J. Elmer Yingling, an Ohio pastor, constantly admonished the Cincinnati club to treat his boy Earl with kindness and tact. A mother, asking that her son be given a chance to play regularly with his team, pointed out that he wrote her every day and sent a telegram on Mother's Day. "He is my little wonder boy," she informed the manager. Her wonder boy eventually became an established major-leaguer.

Professional ball playing entails considerable physical exertion, more than is sometimes realized. Ed Walsh, the workhorse pitcher who came from coal-mining country, doubtless spoke for many players when he said, "This being regarded as a Star Pitcher is a harder job than being a coal miner." He had a good point. It took stamina to play 154 games, half of them on the road. On a hot afternoon pitchers could sweat off ten pounds or more, and I have seen them come back to the bench soaked with perspiration, and while being fanned with towels (in those days before air-conditioned dugouts), gasp for their teammates to "get some runs." Often overlooked, too, was the fact that before the regular schedule started, players put in weeks of spring practice and played thirty or forty exhibition games on their way north, so that toward the end of the season many came to detest the very sight of a baseball.

Mental and emotional stress could be even greater than the physical strain. If the team was contending for the pennant money in a tight race in which every game—nay, every play—counted, the pressure could be acute. If the team was hopelessly out of the running, floundering around and going no place, boredom could be equally intense. Fear of a slump and knowledge that if they failed others were eager to take their places dogged many of the players. Toward the end of the season reporters noticed worn, haggard faces and "jouncy nerves." If the team manager was a martinet, as some were, life for the player could be quite unpleasant.

The American propensity toward violence expressed through fan rowdyism constituted another burden of ball playing. Fickle fans might turn on their heroes at any time. Occasionally, overwrought crowds even surged on the field to attack them. As Mr. Dooley once said, "When ye build yer triumphal arch to yer conquerin' hero, Hennissey, build it out of bricks so the people will have somethin' convanient to throw at him as he passes through." Baseball fans bombarded players with anything from lemons to pop bottles. In Brooklyn, pop bottles were known as "Flatbush confetti." Once in 1907, when Brooklyn fans hurled pop bottles at Frank Chance, he picked up some and threw them back and badly injured a boy in the crowd. Later Chance admitted he had made a mistake, pleading that he had been provoked beyond human patience. In view of the circumstances and his good record, President Pulliam let him off easy. Brooklyn owner Ebbets stopped the sale of pop—for one day.

In 1922 Whitey Witt, Yankee center fielder, was hit by a bottle in

St. Louis and knocked unconscious. Ban Johnson offered $1000 reward for the arrest of the culprit, and after fans came forward with various versions, Johnson closed the incident by giving $100 cash, railroad fare, and a ticket to the World Series to a fan who made the extraordinary claim that Witt had stepped on the neck of a bottle and caused it to jump up and hit him on the head.

In response to criticism that they were not policing their parks properly and were putting profits from soft-drink sales before the safety of the players, owners moved to rectify the situation. Ban Johnson ruled that an owner would be fined $100 every time bottles were thrown in his park. Comiskey campaigned against bottle throwers and had several arrested. Occasionally arrests were made in other cities as well, and in 1920 New York's Chief Magistrate McGeehan sent letters to all his judges urging six-month jail penalties for all bottle throwers.

Paper-cup companies began soliciting business from ball clubs, with emphasis on the safety factor. The cups are "very light in weight," said one salesman, and although they can be thrown, "if they should hit anyone there would be no possibility of injury." "Why furnish excitable men dangerous weapons and expect them to behave?" another asked, offering paper cups as a solution.

In some respects taunts and personal abuse could be more damaging than pop bottles. The latter could inflict serious injury but had little chance of hitting the mark. Verbal missiles could wear a man down emotionally and even drive him out of baseball. A surprising number of professional ball players have committed suicide. What part occupational pressures contributed to such tragedies is difficult to say. A few experienced what used to be called a nervous breakdown. In no "sport," wrote the editor of *Sporting News,* is "vicious and vile objurgation" of a performer permitted as in baseball. Jibes like "You bum, you're all in" and "You're a has-been, you ought to be shining shoes or sweeping the streets" were mild compared with the profanities and obscenities frequently directed at players. A bank executive, complaining of these conditions, said that he would attend many more games if he did not have to listen to the epithets hurled at players. A traveling man who said he found conditions the same in all the ball parks objected particularly to such language being used in the presence of ladies. Jack Fournier threatened to quit baseball because of the harassment of Brooklyn fans who persisted in villifying him with "ugly epithets." His wife had already stopped attending the games because she could not stand the language directed at him.

Every so often an angry player climbed into the stands and attacked a heckler. Rube Waddell beat up one in 1903. Ban Johnson, who was present, realized Waddell had good cause but fined him anyway in the hope of stamping out rowdyism. Sherwood Magee knocked out a drunk who, after abusing him from the bleachers, followed him to the clubhouse to continue his insults. Once Nashville police escorted Detroit Manager Ed Barrow to jail for throwing a bucket of water over jeering fans during an exhibition game.

More serious repercussions resulted early in 1912 when Ty Cobb leaped into the stands in Hilltop Park, New York, and assaulted a spectator who had been heckling him. The umpires put Cobb out of the game, and Ban Johnson suspended him indefinitely, pending an investigation. The depth of player resentment of spectator abuse is indicated by the fact that, despite Cobb's unpopularity among them, all eighteen players on the Detroit team opposed Johnson's action. The team went on to Philadelphia where, after playing the next game without Cobb, the players wired Johnson that they would not play another game unless he reinstated Cobb. "If players cannot have protection," they stated, "we must protect ourselves." Johnson rejected their demands, declaring that they had no business taking the law into their own hands and that a player had only to appeal to the umpire in order to have ruffians ejected from the park. Consequently, the Detroit players carried out a sympathy strike by refusing to play the next day in Philadelphia.°

In order to avoid the $5000 penalty to which a club was liable under league rules for failure to play a scheduled game, the Detroit management hastily recruited a makeshift team of strikebreakers, made up of college players and the Detroit coaches, and sent them against the Athletics, who, as might be expected, drubbed them 24-2. Ban Johnson rushed to Philadelphia. The next scheduled game was called off, but Johnson threatened to expel any player who failed to report for the one following. Cobb, who had given out a bitter blast against Ban Johnson, now urged the players to forego the strike and return to work. This they did. Johnson imposed a $50 fine and ten-day suspension on Cobb and $100 fines on each of the other players. Although the strike was quickly broken, it was significant in that it exemplified a growing dissatisfaction among major-league players.

The fine line between the fan's right to jeer as well as cheer and abusive personal vilification was not always distinguishable. An Oregon judge, conscious of this problem, ruled in 1904 that fans had a right to hoot and fined a player $25 for assaulting one who did. And on another occasion park police in Philadelphia refused to eject a pa-

° This one-day strike, as it turned out to be, was not, however, the first player strike in professional baseball. See *Baseball: The Early Years*, page 128, and this volume, chapter 9.

tron who had merely shouted that the Chicago pitcher had a "yellow streak."

At times players could be at fault, too, by adopting a chip-on-the-shoulder attitude toward fans. Jimmy Archer once attacked a man he thought was flirting with his wife in the stands. Another time Carl Mays accused a spectator of pounding on the dugout, and when the man denied it and called him down, Mays hit him in the head with a baseball. The fan had a warrant sworn out, but the incident was settled when Mays indicated his willingness to apologize. In another instance Manager Bill Dahlen, overhearing a fan criticize one of his Brooklyn players, insulted him by prefacing the word "Jew" with a few profane adjectives and threatened to punch his head off.

Insulting gestures to the fans are nothing new. In a game between the Giants and Boston, Fred Snodgrass thumbed his nose at the home pitcher, so arousing the crowd that Mayor Curley went out on the field to quiet them down. Curley demanded that the umpires remove Snodgrass, and when they refused he registered a written complaint with the league president. Heinie Zimmerman was guilty of "offending public decency" with gestures so shocking that "even men were made to blush." He got off with a $100 fine.

Even a hero of Christy Mathewson's stature once overstepped the bounds in his relations with fans. The incident occurred at Philadelphia in 1905. It started with a fight between a New York and a Philly player. Others joined in, and during the fracas Mathewson punched a lemonade boy passing in front of the Giants' bench, supposedly for making a remark about a New York player. This "brutal blow," as a Philadelphia writer called it, struck in full view of the spectators by the "gentlemanly-appearing" Mathewson, split the boy's lip and loosened some of his teeth. After the game several thousand people mobbed the Giants in their carriages and pelted them with stones and other missiles before police could quell the mob.

This episode was not in keeping with the accepted stereotype of Mathewson and somehow got painted out during the process of portraying him as a paragon of virtue. His tremendous skill as a pitcher, his college background, the religious scruples that kept him from playing on Sundays, his appearance—tall, blond, and blue-eyed— and the happenstance that placed him in New York on a highly publicized team were among the raw materials that lent themselves to the molding of an American folk hero unsurpassed in that era.

Unlike Cobb, Mathewson was a hero who could be loved, and in those days if a boy with visions of becoming a pitcher were asked which player he would like to emulate, the chances were better than even that he would choose Christy Mathewson. He became such a symbol of clean living and sportsmanship that he was invited to address juvenile delinquents and boys' organizations. His prestige among adults was such that they gained confidence from his announced intention to buy stocks when the market dropped in 1914. In fact, so lauded were his virtues that there was danger of his being considered a prig; so assurances were given that he was also human enough to take a drink, play poker, and even utter an oath on occasion.

His tragic death in middle life added to his legend. He succumbed to pneumonia while trying to recuperate from tuberculosis, which evidently had been brought on by the gas he inhaled while serving in World War One. He died, said a printed eulogy, "with the sinking of the Western Sun"; his "message to Young America," it went on, was part of his "religion and mission in life": "to be truthful, to live, think and be clean." "He played the game of life as he did the game of baseball, fighting hard, but always fair and honorable [sic]." A memorial to him was erected at Bucknell University, and *Vanity Fair* selected him for its Hall of Fame because he was "a conspicuous standard bearer of honesty and the best sportsmanship" throughout his baseball career.

But in the early years of his career, before the canonization process began, some of his actions were less than saintly. When Mathewson came up to the majors, they were in the midst of a trade war and he, like a good many others, took advantage of the situation to break his contract—twice. There were those who said that he was disliked among the players for being a "four-flusher" and having a swelled head; perhaps his turkey-gobbler walk conveyed an impression of egotism. Some fans found him brusque and aloof, and he disillusioned one admirer by his ungraciousness with photographers. Nevertheless his name, together with that of John McGraw, symbolized the Giants and New York.

A traditional complaint among ball players was directed at Ren Mulford, Cincinnati reporter: he "don't care what he writes as long as he gets a story." But more often newspapers suppressed uncomplimentary stories and the more lurid escapades. If a man was removed from the game for carelessness or loafing, the paper might say he sprained a limb or had a sore arm. If he broke training or was involved in "a bad mixup," a reporter might omit mention of it entirely. A writer could also assist by acting as an intermediary, quietly tipping off a misbehaving player that the manager was onto him. This gave the transgressor a chance to straighten out, and the manager could avoid a direct showdown and the infliction of disciplinary measures. Ring Lardner performed this service for Chance's outfielder, Frank Schulte, and thus saved him a fine and suspension.

When the stresses and strains of the long season came to an end, many players went hunting. Others took various winter jobs, and there seemed to be less comment than there had been in the past about their spending the off-season as bartenders, and less criticism for lying around and becoming "corpulent." A sampling of their winter occupations would include streetcar conductor, glassblower, interpreter, newspaper writer, undertaker, snow remover, policeman, and printer. One spent a winter in jail—working as turnkey for his father-in-law, the jailer. Others engaged in more long-term enterprises in which they sometimes invested their own capital as well as their services. For example, Johnny Evers put his money into a shoe store in Chicago, and Miller Huggins invested in a roller-skating rink. Joe McGinnity was associated with his father in the management of the family ironworks in Indiana.

A good many players qualified as farmers: Fred Clarke had a wheat ranch in Kansas, Chance owned an orchard, Snodgrass had a California farm, and Lobert raised chickens. Louis Drucke was in the cotton business in Texas. Many other well-known players were also listed as "farmers."

It was observed that more players than ever were preparing for the professions, among them Richard Hoblitzel, a dentist, Ray Fisher, who taught school, and Dummy Taylor, a deaf-mute who taught others so afflicted. Other interests included fraternal organizations like the Elks, Masons, and Odd Fellows. One or two found pleasure in photography. Doc White, pitcher for the White Sox, wrote a "croon" song, "Little Puff of Smoke, Good Night," with words by Ring Lardner, which Stella Mayhew sang at the American Music Hall in 1910. They also wrote one called "Gee! It's a Wonderful Game." Outfielder Frank Schulte composed a "poem" about fans; to spare the reader, it shall remain unquoted. Then there was Rube Waddell who, a reporter claimed, did almost anything that no one else would think of doing.

One of the most publicized activities of players was acting. Since they were already in the public eye, an obvious place to exploit their names was on the stage. Few had real talent. Some simply did monologues, telling about "inside baseball" and exciting moments on the diamond. Others danced, did imitations, or took part in skits and plays, but most sang. Like so many in the days before radio and television, ball players liked to harmonize among themselves in the clubhouse or hotel for their own amusement or with vaudeville in mind.

Outstanding star players and members of pennant-winning clubs could make considerable money in show business. Ty Cobb, who later liked to tell how he and other old-timers spent the winters out-doors keeping in condition, once played the lead in *College Widow*, a play whose theme was changed from football to baseball to accommodate him. Charlie Dooin sang with Dumont's Minstrels in Philadelphia, and Larry Doyle was the villain in a melodrama. Johnny Kling put on a billiard exhibition. Doc White, the songwriter, who also sang "surprisingly well" formed a quartet with Artie Hofman, Addie Joss, and Jimmy Sheckard. In 1912 four teammates formed the Boston Red Sox Quartette.

Rube Marquard made his debut at Hammerstein's in 1911. The following year he did an act with his wife-to-be, actress Blossom Seeley, in which they danced something called the "Marquard glide." Joe Laurie, the famous vaudevillian, who saw Marquard's act, remembered that he sang very well. Another act featuring the two was called "The Suffragette Pitcher." The report on that was not so kind: *Sporting News* stated that as an actor Marquard was one of the greatest living left-handed pitchers.

Rabbit Maranville took to the stage too. A story has it that while he was regaling a theater audience with baseball stories he simulated a steal of second base; he was so realistic that he slid over the footlights, landed on top of the first violinist, and bounced into the snare drum, spraining his leg. Rube Waddell was paired with another zany pitcher, Bugs Raymond, in a play named "Stain of Guilt." Christy Mathewson and Chief Meyers made a big hit in 1910 with May Tully in a sketch called "Curves," written for them by the sportswriter Bozeman Bulger. They were booked for seventeen weeks, and Matty was said to have received nearly $1000 a week. His manager, John McGraw, reportedly was paid $2500 a week on the Keith Circuit in 1912 for a monologue called "Inside Baseball."

Joe Tinker surprised everyone by making quite a hit in vaudeville. The New York *Telegraph* called his skit "A Great Catch" a "clever little piece" that well deserved the applause it got. Tinker also received favorable notices, one of them in *Variety*, for other shows in which he appeared. The Chicago *Journal* called him a "refreshing change from most athletic champions who took to the stage—good-looking, bore himself like a gentleman, and neither clumsy nor obstreperous." Evidently impressed with his reviews, Tinker decided to quit baseball for 1913 and stay on the stage, but he changed his mind and became playing manager of the Cincinnati ball club.

Mike Donlin was even better than Tinker in show business. Joe Laurie thought "Stealing Home," in which Donlin appeared with

Mabel Hite in 1908, was "a great act," and comments in various newspapers agreed. The New York *World* said Donlin's dancing "brought down the house." According to the New York *Globe* it "created a small pandemonium of uproar." The New York *Sun* reported that he had "a very fine stage presence." Other papers were equally enthusiastic, but his biggest rave came from *Variety:* "If you haven't already attended the Big 42nd Street Ovation, by all means beg off from the office and do so without delay. Mike Donlin as a polite comedian is quite the most delightful vaudeville surprise you ever enjoyed, and if you miss him you do yourself an injustice."

The success of the act enabled Donlin & Hite to boost their price from $1000 a week to $1500 in New York and $2000 in other cities. So many offers flowed in that Donlin, like Tinker, began talking about not signing with his club the next season. "There is more money in being an actor than in being a ball player," he was quoted as saying. Donlin did interrupt his baseball career, refusing the Giants' offer for 1909, and stayed in vaudeville for the next two years, reportedly making five times the money he would have received as a ball player. Although he did not endear himself to New York baseball fans by his refusal to "help his team," he continued to receive praise as a "popular idol," whose picture appeared in *Vanity Fair* under the heading " 'Broadway Mike' Donlin, the Beau Brummel of Baseball." Donlin returned to baseball in 1912, this time with Pittsburgh, but gave it up again for vaudeville the following year, only to come back in 1914 for his last season. Meanwhile his first wife had died and he had married another actress, Rita Ross, and turned to the movies, where *Moving Picture World* said he became "something of an actor," although his obituary in the New York *Times* said he was never the actor he thought he was.

Regardless of how pleasant and rewarding the life of a big-leaguer might be pictured, his career was short. A man in his thirties was considered old, so it was not uncommon for players to misrepresent their ages. Estimates of the average career varied from five to seven years, but like all averages, they can be misleading. They are pulled down by the many who, after a very brief stay, fail to stick in the majors; they are lifted somewhat by a few who last twenty or more years. Only fifty-odd men have survived that long in the major leagues since the founding of the National League in 1876, and they are the ones pointed to by old-timers in trying to prove that the stars of their day had more endurance.

Thomas Wolfe in *You Can't Go Home Again* touchingly describes the thoughts and feelings of a veteran trying to hang on a little longer. In the sweltering July heat of St. Louis with the April grass long since burnt away, leaving the infield solid as concrete, the aging star makes a hit on which, in his younger days, he would easily have reached second base. He tells of his tired feet pounding the hard ground:

> An' when you git to first, them dogs is sayin', "Boy, Let's stay here!" But you gotta keep on goin'—you know the manager is watchin' you—you're gonna ketch hell if you don't take that extra base, it may mean the game. An' the boys up in the press box, they got their eyes glued on you, too—they've begun to say old Crane is playin' on a dime—an' you're thinkin' about next year an' maybe gittin in another Serious—an' you hope to god you don't git traded to St. Looie. So you take it on the lam, you slide into second like the Twentieth Century comin' into the Chicago yards—an' when you git up an' feel yourself all over to see if any of your parts is missin', you gotta listen to one of the second baseman's wisecracks: "What's the hurry, Bras? Afraid you'll be late fer the Veterans' Reunion?"

After their major-league playing days were ended, many veterans slipped down to the minor leagues, where they managed to prolong their careers for a few more years. The inglorious descent of a once mighty player to the necessity of scrounging a living in some obscure bush-league town or of picking up a few dollars playing semi-pro ball contained the ingredients of pathos. Jack Chesbro, the prominent spitball pitcher, underwent the ignominy of being discarded by the town team of little Whittinsville, Massachusetts. This theme is well depicted by John R. Tunis in his baseball novel *Young Razzle*, which portrays the humiliation of a onetime star knocking about in the minors.

Some were able to stay in baseball after their playing days were over by securing jobs as managers, coaches, umpires, or scouts. But the number of such openings was limited. College teams provided coaching opportunities for former professionals and some won reputations at this work—for example, Smokey Joe Wood at Yale, Jack Barry at Holy Cross, Jack Coombs at Duke, Andy Coakley at Columbia, Larry Gardner at Vermont, and Jeff Tesreau at Dartmouth. Occasionally there was a Jesse Burkett or Hugh Duffy who put his money into a minor-league club and helped run it. The sporting-goods business was a natural field for others.

But most of the men left baseball entirely when their careers closed. Their new occupations were at least as varied as the ones they pursued between seasons, including that of milkman, fur trapper, bowling-alley proprietor, cigar-store owner, real-estate investor, and salesman of anything from insurance to pianos. Others took up farming, and a few entered the professions: John Lavan, medicine; James

Casey, dentistry; and David Fultz, law. Fred Tenney wrote un-ghosted articles for a newspaper syndicate, and Al Demaree pub-lished a well-known sports cartoon about "inside baseball," which was syndicated for many years in several hundred newspapers. Men like Fred H. Brown, who became governor of New Hampshire, and Dr. Edward M. Lewis, president of two state universities, liked to point out that they had played professional baseball or at least had had "a cup of coffee in the big league"—the expression used to sig-nify a brief stay in the majors. Those ex-players who, for one reason or another, could not make a living outside of baseball and who did not or could not save money ended up in sore straits. Organized Baseball had no pension plan then, so down-and-out players were re-duced to a hunt for little jobs in baseball such as ticket-taker or watchman. Others solicited outright handouts from their former em-ployers or old baseball friends. John McGraw and Garry Herrmann, for instance, were known to respond quickly with fifty or a hundred dollars out of their own pockets whenever a needy old-timer ap-proached them. In a few instances the leagues voted small allotments to individuals or their widows in the form of charity or pensions.

Owners and managers were not immune from misfortune either. Chris Von der Ahe, once a power in major-league circles as owner of the St. Louis Browns of the 1880's, became destitute and was pre-sented with $4294 from a benefit game given for him in 1908. Even Nick Young, former National League president, required financial as-sistance. In 1911 friends of Fred Knowles, for many years secretary of the Giants, held a benefit at Wallach's Theatre to raise money to send him to Denver to be cured of tuberculosis. New York politicians and members of the Broadway theater and sporting set subscribed, among them Richard Croker, Jr., Andrew Freedman, Digby Bell, DeWolf Hopper, William Fleischman, Harry Stevens, and John M. Ward.

Sorry tales could be told of former players who became hopeless al-coholics and wound up on Skid Row, there to finish out their lives in squalor and indignity. Doubtless some who had devoted their early manhood to baseball and who knew nothing else were unable to ad-just to prosaic daily existence when they were removed from the focus of public attention. They tried to live on their clippings and past exploits, croaked about the good old days when "real" baseball was played, and became tiresome critics of present-day players. As Emerson once said, "Every hero becomes a bore at last."

7

A BALL IS A BALL IS A BALL

IN BASEBALL there is a constant struggle between offense and defense which seems to pass through cycles. For a time pitching and defense will dominate the game; then the pendulum swings in favor of batting and offense. Taken as a whole, the first two decades of this century favored the defense. In that era of the dead ball, as it is commonly called, pitchers could smother the attack. Batters used a shortened grip and, instead of swinging from the handle trying for long hits, they concentrated on meeting the ball and punching it safely past the fielders. Under these circumstances, home runs were rare and low-score games prevailed.

Since runs were so hard to come by, each one was precious. So team tactics aimed at scoring them one at a time, as peasants strive to save money—painstakingly, coin by coin. Therefore the attack stressed bunting and base stealing. Even in the first inning, if the leadoff man got on base, it was practically routine for the next batter to bunt, "sacrificing" himself in order to move the runner along into scoring position.° Teams scratched and scrounged, using every wile and strategem, to get a man on base, then tried all possible devices to get him home. Players and managers wrangled incessantly with umpires, since every decision might be crucial to the final result.

Those conditions applied especially to the first half of that twenty-year span. Pitching dominated and batting suffered. In 1907 National League teams made the fewest hits of any season, 9566. The next year American Leaguers reached their nadir with 9719. Scoring diminished, too. In 1908 a record low of 4136 runs were scored in the National League, and in 1909 the American reached bottom in this category with 4272. These figures mean that in those seasons the National

---

° In later decades of the lively ball and heavier scoring, the value of a single run was diminished, so teams seldom played for a single run until the late innings.

League averaged about 6.61 runs and the American League 7.03 runs
—not per *team*, but per *game*.

Low batting averages further showed the ascendancy of the defense. In 1908 the combined batting averages of the players in
each league were the lowest ever until American Leaguers reached a
new low in 1968. In 1905 just two men managed to average over .300
in batting in the American League, and in 1907 only four National
Leaguers achieved that distinction. In fact, Elmer Flick won the 1905
American League batting championship with a mark of .306, the lowest of any title winner until Carl Yzstremski's .301 in 1968. Only 126
National League home runs were hit in 1906 and a mere 101 American League ones in 1907—both record lows.

Why did pitchers have the upper hand? There were several reasons. Not only did the balls lack resilience, but owners doled them
out as sparingly as possible. Often only one or two were used for an
entire game. So as the innings wore on, batters were soon swinging at
a softened, discolored ball. If a new ball was tossed in, pitchers, in
spite of the rules and often with the connivance of teammates,
smeared it with dirt to darken it and make it easier to grip.° Pitchers
had also become adjusted to the lengthened pitching distance established after 1892. The foul-strike rule of 1901, which counted foul
balls as strikes except when the batter had two strikes on him, fortified pitchers further. Many of them added to their skill by developing
a variety of trick pitches through the application of such foreign sub-
stances as licorice, paraffin, or talcum powder to the ball.

Newest and deadliest was the spitball. To throw it, the pitcher wets
about a square inch of surface extending over the tips of the first two
fingers, thus eliminating friction at that point when the ball is thrown.
In this way the spin on the ball is diminished or removed, so it dips
or breaks sharply. Spitballers had their own peculiar style of delivery.
To prevent revealing which pitch was going to be a spitter, they
brought the ball up to the face before every delivery, whether they
intended to wet it or not, carefully concealing their intentions with
the glove. Most of them chewed slippery elm or some other substance
to ensure a steady supply of saliva.

The inventor of the spitball cannot be given with certainty. Once
the spitter became popular, many claimed they had originated it, and
of course old-timers, like Cap Anson, insisted that it was nothing new.
Elmer Stricklett used to be credited with its discovery. But more recently a former American League umpire, George Hildebrand, asserted he got the idea for the new pitch while playing catch with

° Nowadays the umpires remove the balls from sealed boxes before the game
and rub them with a special soil to remove gloss without ruining them.

pitcher Frank Corriden in 1902, when both were in the minor leagues. Noticing that the ball was behaving strangely after coming in contact with wet grass, he experimented by having Corriden spit on a dry ball and found that he could produce the same effect at will. Corriden did not exploit the discovery; he was under the mistaken impression that the spitball would be hard on the arm. Later, though, Hildebrand was transferred to Sacramento where, according to him, he taught Stricklett the trick.

The earliest masters of the spitball were American Leaguers Ed Walsh, who learned it from Stricklett when they were on the Chicago White Sox together, and Jack Chesbro of New York. Walsh was only a journeyman performer until 1906, when his effective use of the spitter brought him 17 victories, which helped Chicago win the pennant. That club has been known ever since as the Hitless Wonders because of its team batting average of .228, the puniest ever of any pennant winner and further testimony to the weak batting of the times. Walsh's biggest personal success, however, came in 1908 when he won 40 games and pitched an astounding total of 464 innings, still the modern record. As for Chesbro, his peak year was 1904 when he won 41 games for the New York Americans.

As the spitball vogue grew more widespread, objections arose that it was unsportsmanlike and practically unhittable, that it demoralized batters and made games actionless and dull. Some infielders claimed they had difficulty in throwing the moistened ball accurately. Many people were convinced that it was unsanitary. When pitcher Ad Brennan contracted diphtheria, the spitball was blamed. Philadelphia Manager Charlie Dooin's antidote for "using the ball as a cuspidor" was to put disinfectant on it. Umpire Lynch warned that a repetition would cost Dooin fifty dollars. Some praised Dooin for contributing to health and decency "in these days of individual drinking cups and anti-spitting campaigns" (1912). Others thought that his crusade, "like that of the prohibitionists, must fail."

A few pitchers used the shine ball: they made the ball "break" better by smoothing part of the ball's surface with talcum or paraffin so it would slip off the fingers more easily. Another interesting freak pitch of those days was the emery ball: pitchers roughened a portion of the ball's cover with a small piece of sandpaper, causing it to behave erratically in its flight to the batter. Russell Ford of the New York Highlanders, who was its most successful exponent, and other pitchers kept the trick secret by concealing the emery in their gloves. But one day in 1914 Jimmy Lavender of the Chicago Cubs made the mistake of fastening the sandpaper to his uniform. Opposing players soon wondered why he seemed to be constantly scratching himself.

They got the umpire to investigate, but upon his approach Lavender ran away. A ridiculous scene followed, with the umpire refusing to give chase and Lavender refusing to come to him for inspection, knowing that under the rule then in effect he faced a five-dollar fine if he was caught with the goods. Suddenly Hans Lobert of the Phillies, one of the fastest runners in the National League—so fast that he once raced a horse around the bases and lost by only a nose—dashed at Lavender and grabbed the evidence. Ban Johnson, who was against the pitch too, subsequently decreed that anyone who tried to turn "our good little American league into a sandpaper league" would be suspended for thirty days and fined $100. Eventually, the rules did strictly proscribe all freak pitches including the spitball.°

Meanwhile, the supremacy of the defense produced a constant flow of complaints and innumerable suggestions for weighting the balance more toward the attack. The theme of those calling for more hitting was that pitchers' battles and low-score contests relieved only by a few "punk hits" made games "monotonous" and "listless"; a ball game should be a contest between teams, not a duel between pitchers. Some of the proposed remedies will sound familiar to fans of the late 1960's. The catalog included reducing the strike zone; evening up balls and strikes, either by cutting the former to three required for a base on balls or by increasing the latter to four for a strikeout; placing the pitcher in the center of the diamond, thereby lengthening his throwing distance; eliminating pitchers, who were notoriously weak hitters, from the batting order; repealing the foul-strike rule; depriving fielders of their "cumbrous gloves" or at least modifying them; and even allowing runners left on base to return the next inning! Some suggested the simple expedient of livening the ball. On the other hand, supporters of the status quo relished the hard-fought 1–0 game as "the closest thing to perfect baseball." Writing on this issue for *American Magazine* in 1910, a leading sportswriter urged managers to employ "science and generalship" by having their men wait out the pitchers and bat "for the team" instead of swinging away at the ball.

When change did come it was accomplished not by the fans, rule makers, or players, but by baseball manufacturers, with the sanction of the National Commission. During the 1910 season, a ball with a cork center covered with a one-eighth of an inch layer of rubber was quietly introduced. It was also tried out in that year's World Series. The new ball was livelier and held its shape better. A decided increase in hitting resulted immediately, particularly in the American League, where there were more than thirty .300 hitters in 1911. Shoe-

° See below, chapter 21.

less Joe Jackson, then with Cleveland, batted a remarkable .408, but still missed the championship because Ty Cobb soared to .420, thirty-five points higher than his previous best. Home-run production jumped appreciably in both major leagues: 2433 in the National from 1911 through 1920 as against 1394 the decade before; and in the American, 1788 compared with 1571. *Sporting News* said the manufacturers and magnates had slipped something over on the public. But although some objected at first, players and fans in general liked the new deal, as a number of polls taken at the time bore out.

Judged by the yardstick of later seasons, the years 1911 through 1920 still belong to the so-called dead-ball era. But measured against the previous decade, they were not so dead as they have come to be considered. This matter of relativity is one of the considerations forgotten or ignored by those old-timers who lament, as Cobb did in 1952, that "they don't play baseball any more." Deploring the concentration on power hitting and home runs at the expense of "science" in batting, he boasted of how the players of his day would have hammered the modern lively ball. Perhaps he did not realize that he could be beaten with his own stick: after 1910 he and his generation of players also had the advantage of a livelier ball. Compared with the dead, rubber-centered one of the first decade of the century, it too possessed "jack-rabbit" qualities. A 1914 advertisement reflected the shifting balance of power from the pitcher to the batter. It gave assurance that, while the cork-centered ball had not "put the pitcher out of business," when the batter "leans up against it he is getting full value instead of dropping it dead."

The matter of relativity applies to other departments of the game as well. Take base stealing. The dead-ball era is generally thought of as an era of highway—or perhaps basepath—robbery, which it was as compared with the post-1920 decades and as the records of some notable base stealers bear out. In the American League, Eddie Collins stole 81 bases in 1910 and Clyde Milan 88 in 1912. Ty Cobb, who finished with a career total of 892, took 96 in 1915 alone. (He was also caught a record 38 times that year.) The National League had Bob Bescher who stole 80 in 1911. The career of Max Carey, another National Leaguer, stretched over into the 'twenties, and from the standpoint of sheer efficiency gauged by the number of successes in steals attempted, he was doubtless the most "scientific" of all; in 1922 he stole 51 bases in 53 tries! All told, major-league players stole 26,-734 bases from 1911 through 1920, nearly twice the 13,759 they were to accumulate from 1921 to 1930—a margin that was to grow even wider afterwards, when entire teams would not total as many steals in a season as single players achieved earlier. So from the standpoint of what happened later, the pre-1920 period was indeed one of base-stealing opulence.

Nevertheless, there were those who did not think of the decade preceding 1920 as an especially notable era for base stealing. Oldsters of that time harked back to the good old days of their youth, when "real" base stealers like Harry Stovey, who stole 156 in 1888, and Billy Hamilton, with 115 in 1891, made "moderns" such as Cobb and his base-stealing contemporaries look like petty thieves. And the old-timers had a point. It can be argued that base stealing never really recovered after 1892 because changes in rules and conditions made stealing more difficult.° Some sportswriters, too, were lamenting the decline of base stealing. As early as 1911 Hugh Fullerton decried the "death" of the stolen base, and in 1912, after two years of the "lively" cork-center ball, he detected a decrease in the one-run-at-a-time style of play with its premium on the sacrifice bunt and the steal. A later analysis of base-stealing figures bore him out. It showed that the art was already in decay, that with the exception of 1916 and 1919, when the overall downward trend was temporarily arrested, base-stealing totals dropped annually from 1914 to 1920.

Aside from the cork-center ball, possibly the most important new equipment was shin guards for catchers. Roger Bresnahan of the New York Giants introduced them to the majors in 1907 and immediately evoked both derision and protest. Fred Clarke complained to the league president when Bresnahan, wearing his "cricket shin guards," blocked off and tagged him out at the plate. The Pittsburgh player-manager asserted that the guards were a danger to runners and threatened to have his infielders wear them if Bresnahan was allowed to do so. New York writers promptly branded Clarke "yellow" and a "spiker." But before long, of course, all catchers adopted the new protection.

Bresnahan also experimented with the "pneumatic head protector" for batters advertised by the A. J. Reach Company in 1905. As a result of a blow on the head from a pitched ball, Bresnahan had "shaved eternity pretty close," so upon returning from the hospital he tried out the new device. It resembled a football helmet sliced in half and covered the side of the head exposed to the pitchers. Despite suggestions that every team should have two of them, one for right- and one for left-handed hitters, the protector did not catch on until much later, when demands for a similar device became more insistent. It was a forerunner of the plastic helmet required of all batters since the 1950's. Another improvement, credited to Fred Clarke, who played the outfield, was the pull-down sunglasses attached to the cap.

° See *Baseball: The Early Years*, page 282.

Uniforms remained essentially unchanged. In 1913 Goldsmith's Sons of Cincinnati offered shirts with sleeves that were detachable, elbow-length, three-quarter, or full-length. The earlier high collar gradually gave way to the more comfortable low-necked shirt. At the beginning of the century Rawlings & Company ordinarily sold uniforms with padded pants. But soon sliding pads, known since the 'eighties, were in general use, and by 1912 the Rawlings catalog was displaying them. The wearing of white suits at home and dark ones on the road contributed an aesthetic touch and helped fans distinguish between teams, but clubs were often careless about laundering them and slow to replace them. A poor organization like the St. Louis Cardinals might make the same set do for two seasons. Although gloves were still without webbing between the thumb and the first finger as late as 1909, diehards were objecting that "nothing has disgusted patrons of the game more than these hand coverings of inordinate size." Ed Reulbach, Chicago Cubs' pitcher, wore a rubber shirt in the World Series of 1911 to induce sweating—the same kind New York society women were wearing to take off weight, and it was said several baseball magnates wore them too for the same reason.

Playing rules underwent some refinement, as did those for scoring and conducting games. One instance was Charles Ebbets's recommendation for pre-game drill. Heretofore both teams practiced simultaneously in an unsystematic fashion, often batting in front of the stands to the peril of spectators. In 1906 the Brooklyn owner suggested allowing each team twenty minutes for separate batting practice and ten each for fielding, a procedure followed in the main ever since.

Superstition, both individual and collective, was another constant in the professional baseball equation. The "hoodoo" and "jinx" always lurked near the player and his club. Coming to bat, a man might take care to approach the plate from behind the umpire and catcher—or in front of or between them. Others felt compelled to step on third base—or first or second—while running on and off the field between innings. Fans enjoyed the "strike two!" call on one player in particular, knowing that whenever that happened he would transfer his chewing gum from the button on top of his cap to his mouth. Another star, convinced that a hat thrown on a bed meant a batting slump, would counteract the jinx by flinging the offending hat out the nearest window.

Left-handers, hunchbacks, and cross-eyed people were all considered something special. It had long been gospel in baseball that left-handed pitchers were not quite normal mentally—at best, eccentric. Touching a hunchback was popularly believed to bring good luck. With this idea in mind, the Philadelphia Athletics employed Louis

Van Zelt, a handicapped lad, as batboy in 1910. About the same time Brownie Burke, a midget to whom Garry Herrmann took a fancy, was in uniform daily with the Cincinnati Reds. He also appeared in a number of stage shows. Although the batboy stereotype of the era was supposed to be a tough, slangy little urchin who hated school, teased cats, and delighted in dogfights, there was at least one exception in Master John Connor of the Boston Braves, a "model of decorum," "grave and deliberate," and also "lucky," who even wore glasses—"and who ever heared of a mascot with glasses?"

The name of one "mascot," Charles Victor Faust, is actually listed in the records as having appeared in two games with the Giants as a "pitcher" in 1911. Faust, then thirty-one, was an unfortunate eccentric possessed by a delusion that he was a major-league pitcher. He made his way from his native Kansas and began hanging around the Giants. He convinced McGraw that he would bring the team good luck, and the Giants kept him with them as a "jinx dispenser." They even took him on the road with them and humored him in his fanciful pitching pretensions to the extent of letting him appear briefly toward the end of one season in two games that meant nothing, since the pennant was already safely won. His popularity brought a vaudeville contract at a hundred dollars a week, but he quit the stage because he firmly believed that the team needed him. After the novelty wore off, the Giants got rid of him. In 1914 Faust was declared insane and sent to an asylum, where he died a year later.

Movements on the field leaned more toward the known than the new. Teams polished and elaborated such nineteenth-century techniques and tactics as bunting, playing hit-and-run, and shifting fielders about according to the batter and the situation. For instance, contemporaries noticed a growing partiality for the squeeze play, a by-product of the bunt that required well-timed collaboration between base runner and batter. On this play the former dashes from third base for home plate as the ball is pitched, and the latter "squeezes" him safely across by bunting the ball. A few teams were learning to forego the sacrifice bunt routine when they fell several runs behind. Realizing that it made little sense to play for one run at a time when they needed a lot of runs to catch up, they "hit away" or tried the hit-and-run play instead—in other words, played "catch-up ball."

The intentional base on balls also became an integral part of strategy. Yankee Manager Bill Donovan attracted attention in 1915 when, with an opposing runner on third, he ordered two batters walked in succession, filling the bases and making a force play possible anywhere. When such strategy succeeded for the home team, its

manager and pitcher were applauded for smart baseball; when opposing pitchers avoided batters in this way, they were booed for cowardice. Recurrent talk of abolishing or limiting the practice has to
this day come to nothing.

Pinch hitters were being used more frequently. One of them, Harry
"Moose" McCormick of the Giants, is legendary because he became
the source of a stock story in baseball fiction about the batter who
wins the game with a home run only to be fined for disobeying orders
to bunt. McCormick hit a triple, but Manager McGraw supposedly
fined him because he had been ordered to bunt. Practically all teams
carried a man whose special job was pinch-hitting. Indeed, managers
soon employed them for a more occult form of strategy: having a
pinch hitter pinch-hit for a pinch hitter. One day in 1908 this maneuver provoked erudite debate among umpires, managers, and writers.
First the Phillies sent in a pinch hitter. Pittsburgh countered with a
new pitcher. Then the Phillies put in a pinch hitter to replace the first
one. So far so good. The argument started when the Phillies tried to
use the first pinch hitter again later. The Pirates protested that he
had already been in the game officially. The Phillies and some writers
vehemently disagreed because not even one ball had been thrown to
him, and just "posing near the plate" was not enough to constitute
being in the game. But the umpires sustained Pittsburgh, and the
playing rules have long since incorporated their view.

Managers were also in the habit of rushing in a relief pitcher whenever there was "a slight sign of wavering" on the part of the starter,
according to *Spalding's Guide for 1910*. Although this statement has a
modern ring, reliance on relief specialists in those far-off days was
picayune by recent standards. The increasing recourse to substitutes
fostered larger squads, and conversely the added manpower allowed
managers more scope for using substitutes. In 1907 writer I. E. Sanborn made an observation that has become a baseball truism: "The
strength of a modern major league team lies in its substitutes." Rosters generally fluctuated between 21 and 25, whereas once they varied from 14 to 16 men.° At first, though, there were objectors who
thought substitutes were undesirable except in emergencies. They believed it was bad psychologically for the regulars to see bench-warm-
ers waiting around to take their jobs. Others already recognized the
unwisdom of making it possible for rich, strong teams to hoard on the
bench men who could have bolstered the weaker clubs.

To care for their players, clubs hired a "trainer" or "rubber" whose
primary duty was to massage pitchers' arms and make himself generally useful. They began taking him on road trips too. For serious inju-

° However, clubs controlled many more players. See below, chapter 9.

ries or illnesses, men were sent to a physician designated by the club. The most popular healer among sore-armed players was John D. "Bonesetter" Reese. He was a Welshman who had migrated to Youngstown, Ohio, where he began working in the steel mills. He had no medical training and knew nothing about setting bones, but he did have a strong pair of hands and found he had a knack for relieving aches and pains with manipulation and massage. As his reputation spread, countless major leaguers sought his help.

The everlasting debate continued as to whether it was necessary for teams to go south every spring to get in condition. Skeptics questioned the expense and the risks: exposure to malaria in southern swamps; chance of colds and "charley horses" (pulled leg muscles) from sudden change of climate upon returning north; the possibility of going stale before the season began. No other business, said some, was so generous in letting the employees prepare themselves for work at the expense of the management. Even so, the spring rite was already too firmly entrenched to be affected by such carping. Annually the teams assembled in towns of North and South Carolina, Georgia, Alabama, Louisiana, or Texas. Florida was virtually ignored until baseball enthusiast Al Lang moved from Pittsburgh to St. Petersburg in 1911 and immediately set about coaxing teams to train there and persuading civic authorities to offer them inducements to come. California played host to Comiskey's White Sox. Nearly every year he led a large contingent of players, writers, and guests on a well-publicized expedition to the Coast via special train equipped with "every convenience and comfort known to modern travel"—observation, buffet, and sleeping cars, bath, barber shop, writing desks, library, and bulletin board for news and stock market reports. Whereas the ordinary Pullman cars used gaslight, the White Sox Special had electricity.

Under a 1909 headline "Nothing Too Good for Players," *Sporting News* boasted: "Millionaires receive no greater courtesies nor travel in more style than a base ball player." Civic and business groups in towns throughout the South competed eagerly every year for their business and sometimes offered subsidies to attract the clubs. Depending on the amount of local subsidy, if any, and the returns from exhibition games, spring training could cost anywhere from $2000 to $6000, but Barney Dreyfuss said one club cleared $12,000 in 1908, and others came out ahead too. More important was the free publicity given spring training by the press. Its value could not be estimated in dollars and cents.

Operations at the various training sites did not begin until late February, so clubs had a relatively brief stay before setting out on the long barnstorming tour homeward. Before reporting to camp some players went to Hot Springs, Arkansas, for a regimen of "boiling out," "taking the baths," "drinking the waters," and hiking. In the main, work at the camps consisted of limbering up through batting and fielding sessions and much running around the park. On some clubs an assortment of massage and "vibratory" equipment was available. After a week or so, intra-squad games were arranged between the regulars and "yannigans," as the second-string men and rookies used to be called.

Veteran players who harp on the refrain of "how tough it was when I broke in," aided and abetted by imaginative journalists, have created another pet of baseball lore—the training-camp rookie: the green, unsophisticated "busher" fresh from farm or small town, who shows up in an ill-fitting suit and carrying a cardboard valise. Regular players, fearful of losing their jobs, not only refuse to teach this greenhorn the fine points of the trade but obstruct him in every way through ostracism, practical jokes, or hazing, which could be quite vicious. To some extent this exaggerated portrayal was probably an offshoot of the changing concept of the American farmer from the respected, even romanticized symbol of a once rural America to the target for humor and the butt of jokes on the stage of an increasingly urban society.

Unquestionably the rookies of today are more sophisticated than the earlier generation. So is everyone. Thanks to modern technology and mass communication, the isolation that once separated city and country has been largely erased. Doubtless, too, the preparation of baseball neophytes is superior to what it was. Ben De Mott, a pitcher, assured me that he received no coaching from anyone during spring training with Cleveland in 1910. He did not even know enough to run over and cover the bag when a ball was hit to the first baseman and was "razzed" for neglecting to do so in a game. As late as 1916 *Sporting News* remarked that rookies got little chance to learn anything in spring training. This lack, combined with instances of rough treatment, sapped the spirit of many youngsters.

But the supposedly downtrodden position of rookies has been exaggerated. Veterans were not always hostile and unwilling to impart knowledge. First baseman Jake Daubert arrived at camp for the first time with great trepidation, but everyone treated him cordially and helped him. Newspaper sketches of pitcher Eddie Plank instructing young Rube Bressler and Herb Pennock at the Athletics' camp were captioned "The Schoolmaster and His Pupils." Manager Jimmy Callahan enlisted his White Sox veterans to work with rookies in the spring of 1912. A few years ago Chuck Jamieson told me that when he was with Cleveland, Tris Speaker asked him to instruct youngsters

in playing the outfield. Even though he realized it amounted to showing them how to take away his own job, he did it. George Toporcer
assured me that on his first trip to the St. Louis Cardinals' training
camp as a rookie second baseman, Rogers Hornsby, the star of the
team and a second baseman as well, gave him constant encourage-
ment.

Actually, the source of the rookie's predicament was probably not
so much hostility on the part of veterans as it was the want of system-
atic instruction and purposeful practice. As Jimmy Callahan expressed it, putting a bunch of young athletes through a course in
water drinking and hill climbing was a waste of time; what they
needed was schooling in the finer points of the game. He suggested
mustering them in the fall at a suitably warm spot, possibly Cuba, for
instruction under competent teachers—an idea adopted in modern
baseball.

There were other team leaders besides Callahan with progressive
training ideas. In 1910 Clark Griffith, managing Cincinnati, suspended disks on wires for his pitchers to throw at to improve their
control. Washington had one of the "new-fangled" batting cages 80
feet long, 14 feet high, and 37 feet wide installed at its 1911 camp.
John McGraw taught the Giants how to slide in 1907 and a few years
later experimented with a pitching machine. Another spring he had
his pitchers try tennis to limber up their arms. One of the most imaginative managers, already revealing his flair for innovation, was
Branch Rickey. Among his "theoretical absurdities," as a skeptic
termed them, were sliding pits, handball courts, and a series of batting cages. Not only did the latter permit a number of batters to hit
at the same time; they also relieved catchers from the drudgery of
catching during batting drill and gave them more opportunity to take
batting practice. Added to these portents of the future was the Carr
Base Ball School organized by Charles C. Carr, a former big-leaguer,
at San Antonio, Texas. In 1914 he advertised twenty diamonds and a
staff of big-league instructors available to youngsters wishing to en-
roll in his school.

Usually the clubs carried two coaches during the season. They
helped out in the pre-game practice hitting fungoes and feeding balls
to the batting practice pitchers. During the game they took up stations in the first- and third-base coaches' boxes, except when the manager himself liked to direct the attack from the coaching lines. Likely
as not, coaches were former players and cronies of the manager,
whose primary function was really to act as his traveling companions
and perhaps drinking partners. How much actual teaching of young
players they did is a moot question, but there were already indica-

tions of the specialization that was to characterize the job in the future. For example, some managers were assigning one of their coaches to take charge of the pitching staff and to advise who should pitch each day.

The manager's job and the authority he exerted varied from club to club. He might be a non-playing "bench manager," or a player-manager, as a good many were then. He might even act as player-manager and captain combined. And more rarely, he could be part-owner of the club as well. As the business manager or club secretary assumed more and more of the responsibilities formerly resting on the manager—such as making travel arrangements and checking gate receipts—the manager was free to concentrate on handling the team, arrogating to himself many of the functions that the captain used to perform. Consequently, the once important position of team captain continued to decline until it eventually became little more than honorific.

Aspirants for big-league managing jobs compete in a buyers' market. For half a century since 1900 there was a maximum of only sixteen possible openings in the major leagues in any given year, and there were not even that many available if positions such as those of John McGraw and Connie Mack, who were well-entrenched through part-ownership, are subtracted. There is never a dearth of ex-players or active stars scrambling for these few posts, which are highly prized despite the headaches and high attrition rate attached to them.

A big reason for the heavy turnover is that the manager provides a handy scapegoat when things go wrong, and replacing him is a ready means of assuaging disgruntled fans. To bring in a new face papers over inherent weaknesses in the team and creates the illusion of a fresh start. Some managers may get better results from players than others, but regardless of their ability they must have the material to work with. After all, without good players, Connie Mack, "the tall tactician," finished last seven seasons in a row, and Casey Stengel, "the old perfesser," did not achieve genius status until he managed the stars of the New York Yankees. A 1910 recipe for a winning team —nine cups of heavy batter, three or four good pitchers full of sand, one quart of ginger, mixed well and served hot—made no mention of the manager.

Disagreement over his prerogative often embroiled the manager with the owner and added to the precariousness of his tenure. For instance, who was to decide which players were to be retained and which disposed of? Understandably, managers wanted the right to hire and fire or trade players, or at least to have a strong voice in such decisions, since they were responsible for the showing of the team; whereas owners, with equal plausibility, believed that they should have the say when their property rights in players were involved.

An instructive case is the relationship between Garry Herrmann and Joe Tinker. When Herrmann sounded out the Chicago shortstop about managing Cincinnati, Tinker made it clear that he wanted "absolute control" without interference. But things did not work out as Tinker desired, for when he entered into negotiations for a new contract after managing the club in 1913, he made no bones about his dissatisfaction, enumerating all the player deals allegedly made without his knowledge. Herrmann agreed to let Tinker run the club and discipline the players but refused to allow him to release or purchase players without permission. Tinker seemed willing to go along with this, but Herrmann's plan to have a front-office man accompany the team to keep an eye on things, somewhat like a soviet commissar snooping on a field marshal, was too much for Tinker, who thought this new step indicated a lack of confidence in him. His objections brought his dismissal, and Herrmann issued a public statement charging Tinker with wanting to determine business and financial matters that properly belonged within the purview of the stockholders.

Installation of a new manager, Buck Herzog, did not resolve the question of prerogative for the Cincinnati club. No sooner did Herzog take over than the issue again arose, albeit in a different form. Some players attempted to bypass him and take their grievances directly to Garry Herrmann. However, Herrmann complied with Herzog's request that letters from the men be referred to him and promised to make it clear to players that they could not go over the head of the manager. Herrmann made good his promise. When Armando Marsans ran to the owner protesting a $100 fine imposed by Herzog, Herrmann refused to intervene. Marsans next threatened to go home to Cuba, but when Herzog stood firm the player paid up.

Even so, the club had gone ahead with the appointment of a man to keep tabs on the team manager, without untoward results at first. In fact, Herzog signed to manage again in 1915, only to run afoul of this emissary, one Harry Stephens, over the question of which players should be dropped. Stephens finally advised Herrmann that Herzog would have to be dismissed, "even though they do call it interferance [sic] with the manager. It is our property and we can not have it entirely destroyed." Early the following season Herzog was returned to the New York Giants in a deal that brought Christy Mathewson to Cincinnati as manager.

Policies and prerogative aside, there were naturally many instances where the sheer clash of personality disrupted owner-manager relationships. Not surprisingly, strong-willed Frank Chance was often at loggerheads with quixotic owner Charles Murphy. Murphy finally got rid of him in 1912. Were it not for the fact that Chance was part-owner as well as player-manager and captain, to say nothing of win-ner of four pennants for Chicago in five years, he might not have lasted as long as he did.

Player-manager Charles "Red" Dooin and Philadelphia president Horace Fogel repeatedly quarreled over player trades and discipline, and castigated each other with personal accusations of "swell-headed-ness" and even drunkenness. In this case Dooin outlasted the owner, for, as we have seen, the National League banished Fogel in 1912.

The managerial experience of Roger Bresnahan with the St. Louis Cardinals was somewhat different. Bresnahan worked under two suc-cessive owners. Under the first one, Stanley Robison, he demanded and obtained a free hand in directing the team, so much so that when another club tried to get Robison to waive claim to a player that Bresnahan wanted, the president refused, explaining that he had promised Bresnahan not to interfere with the handling of the men. Upon Robison's death in 1911, his niece, Mrs. Schuyler Britton, daughter of his brother Frank De Haas Robison, succeeded to the club ownership. Mrs. Britton, "the matron magnate," one of the rare female club owners and a suffragette into the bargain, was pleased with Bresnahan at first. After a highly successful season financially she rewarded her manager with a five-year contract, reputedly for $10,000 a year, and 10 per cent of the net earnings. The subsequent slump of the team, however, and certain misunderstandings brought bitter recriminations between the two, which ended with Bresnahan's being fired. Chicago signed him to a new three-year contract as a player, and he collected $20,000 from St. Louis in a suit settled out of court.

It is difficult to define what makes a successful major-league man-ager. Knowledge of the game and strategy are more or less taken for granted, at least nowadays, so it is commonly said that the chief re-quirement in running a team is the ability to handle men. Skill as a player is no guarantee that a man will have this knack; some who never made the major leagues as players, such as Frank Selee, Clar-ence "Pants" Rowland, and Joe McCarthy, were good leaders. Suc-cessful managers differ in style and methods for getting the most out of their men. There have been martinets who drove the players with tongue-lashings and fines, and coaxers who encouraged them with praise and back-slapping. The first type, like the traditional Prussian army officer, has all but vanished. But years ago he was more the rule than the exception. As a 1912 observer wrote, most managers were alike in "bullyragging" umpires and fining players who "pulled boners."

The vinegar versus the honey approach is epitomized in the personalities and methods of two of the outstanding managers in baseball history, Connie Mack and John McGraw. Both of these men left an indelible stamp upon the American scene. Yet they were quite unlike: McGraw pugnacious, tempestuous, given to brawling on and off the field, Mack serene, mild-mannered, seldom ruffled, eschewing rowdyism; McGraw the harsh disciplinarian, driving and haranguing his players with vitriolic tongue, Mack the stoically patient leader, rarely using profanity, talking quietly and privately to his men after the heat of conflict had cooled; McGraw taunting opposing players and crowds, Mack inspiring affection and regard, becoming venerable with the passing years; McGraw with decided friendships and enmities, evoking intense loyalties and hatreds, Mack less grudging and more forgiving; McGraw living life to the hilt, loving parties, frequenting the track, mixing with the Broadway crowd, and enjoying a highball, Mack tending to the quiet life, more sedate, unattracted by strong drink, a family man, judging by two marriages and eight children. Even in appearance they presented sharp contrasts: McGraw short, pot-bellied, at least in later years, with a hard-eyed, belligerent look that invited conflict, Mack tall and thin in the extreme, almost gaunt, with a more benign, disarming air.

McGraw and Mack personified the American success story in their climb from humble backgrounds to positions of importance in the baseball industry. Connie Mack, whose full name was Cornelius McGillicuddy, worked during boyhood in Massachusetts factories before escaping into baseball as a catcher. After the usual minor-league experience with various teams in New England, he made the big league in 1886. By 1894 he was player-manager for Pittsburgh. Ban Johnson, as president of the Western League, then a minor circuit, installed Mack as manager of its Milwaukee club in 1897. When Johnson converted the Western into a major league and expanded into the East in 1901, he awarded the managership of the Philadelphia Athletics and one quarter of the club's stock to Mack.

That opportunity launched him into the part of his career for which he is best remembered. He was to remain as manager of the Athletics for half a century and in due course acquired sole financial control of the club. In his unprecedentedly long managerial career he put together some of the most notable teams of major-league history and won nine pennants and five world championships. He also managed some of baseball's worst teams, finishing last no fewer than seventeen times. After dismantling his 1914 team he groped through seven consecutive last-place finishes, during which a horde of players were tried and found wanting as he attempted to rebuild. It was not until the 1920's, when he began going into the market and purchasing recognized minor-league stars, that he finally came up with another winner. Then as the depression closed in and the club got into debt, he broke up his combination once more, selling off his best men for cash. As a result, the club became a drag on the league, finishing last ten times out of Mack's last sixteen seasons of managing.

Despite his knowledge of baseball, his patience and tact in handling men, and his apparent bent for developing young, inexperienced players, especially collegians, into major leaguers, he scarcely could have lasted as long as he did and captured so many pennants were it not for the job security that partial and ultimately full ownership assured him. This circumstance enabled him to hang on as manager until 1950, his eighty-eighth year, even though, according to information given me by a sportswriter close to the scene, he had entered his dotage, calling out the names of his stars of bygone days to go in and pinch-hit, while the team was really being directed by the coaches.

To fans he had long since become an unforgettable figure, standing at the dugout steps in full view, wearing a dark suit, a tie, and a straw hat or fedora, waving his fielders into position with what became his trademark, a scorecard. His name and reputation spread far beyond the diamond, however, and as the years passed the honors bestowed on him accumulated. Perhaps the most signal of these came at the end of the 1929 season, namely the Bok Award, established by Edward Bok, the famous editor of the *Ladies Home Journal*. The prize, which included $10,000 and a gold medal, was presented annually to the individual who rendered the greatest service to Philadelphia and, up until Mack received it, had gone only to persons from the arts and professions.

But for all his excellent qualities, Mack was no plaster saint. At the time of the Brotherhood War he, like so many other players, jumped his contract. During the trade war between the new American League and the old National, he joined in the raids on the latter's players. He could scold his players when necessary but if, like Waddell, they tried his patience too hard, he simply got rid of them. Although anything but an umpire-baiter, Mack was so furious over a decision of Silk O'Loughlin's, which probably cost the Athletics the 1907 pennant, that for years he refused to speak to the umpire. Yet he was not vengeful or vindictive. After a run-in with another umpire, Mack, angry as he was, recoiled from a suggestion that he try to have the man fired. He also became reconciled with players who left him for the Federal League and later on employed some of them as coaches.

Mack was not above underhanded dealings either. He got Eddie Collins, then a student at Columbia University, to break collegiate rules against professionalism and play with the Athletics on their western trip toward the end of the 1906 season, using the name Sullivan to hide his identity. Another time Mack was caught shipping a player to the minors without giving other American League clubs a chance to waive on his services and was fined $250. In 1928 he violated baseball rules by collaborating in an illegal transfer of a player and was fined $500 by Commissioner Landis.

Like Mack, John McGraw was a small-town boy from a poor family. He was only twelve when he lost his mother and four siblings in a diphtheria epidemic. After a modicum of schooling and a variety of prosaic jobs, while playing ball with local teams on the side, he left his home town of Truxton, New York, to seek his fortune in baseball. He saw a good deal of the country and even had a glimpse of Cuba while playing with a number of bush-league teams before he reached the big league with Baltimore in 1891. There he starred for nine years, compiling the highest lifetime batting average, .334, ever made by a major-league third baseman, and earned an early reputation for rough, scrappy play. He became player-manager of the Orioles in 1899.

When the National League cut back from twelve to eight clubs that winter, Baltimore was one of those dropped. McGraw was sold to St. Louis but reported only reluctantly and with the proviso that the reserve clause be omitted from his contract, leaving him free to accept any opportunities that might present themselves the next season. At this juncture the hand of Ban Johnson touched his career, as it had Connie Mack's. Johnson chose McGraw to manage Baltimore, one of the clubs included at that point in the expansion eastward of Ban's Western League.

Hindsight reveals that two such domineering types as Johnson and McGraw sooner or later would clash. In their case, it was sooner. After only a year and a half at Baltimore, McGraw, soured by constant wrangling with Johnson, seized the opportunity in the summer of 1902 to assume the management of the New York Giants in the rival National League, there to glare across the Harlem River at the new American League club shortly installed by Johnson. Bitter recriminations followed. A lifetime enmity between Johnson and McGraw was born, and although Mrs. McGraw later claimed that the feud was a myth trumped up by newsmen, her assertion is unconvincing. For years pro-American Leaguers denounced McGraw as a deserter and a Benedict Arnold. On his part, McGraw always denied jumping his contract, maintaining that he left Baltimore legitimately.°

At New York he ruled supreme over the Giants for thirty years, winning ten pennants, a National League record (four of them in succession), but only three world championships. Mack and McGraw faced each other in three World Series, and Mack won two of them. McGraw also finished second in eleven National League pennant races and, in contrast with Mack, was last only twice.

Like Mack, McGraw had what amounted to carte blanche in managing the team, and no exchange of players could be made by owner John T. Brush without his approval. The security and leeway he enjoyed under Brush was jeopardized upon the latter's death in 1912 and the assumption of control by Brush's son-in-law, Harry Hempstead. Sensing that he was in an exposed position, McGraw cast about for some means of getting a financial stake in the club. With the help of Arnold Rothstein, the notorious gambler, he succeeded in 1919 by engineering the sale of controlling interest to Charles A. Stoneham, a Wall Street broker, with other shares going to Judge Francis X. McQuade and himself.

McGraw enjoyed an advantage over Connie Mack by the sheer fact of being located in New York, the foremost city of the country, where the National League, for the prosperity of all its clubs, needed a good gate attraction, a necessity that no one understood better than John T. Brush. A colorful team in contention for the pennant makes money and, although it is not the sole ingredient, money helps create teams capable of making money. Whereas Mack was often criticized for penny-pinching, McGraw had a reputation for loosening the purse strings to secure key men like Rube Marquard, Heinie Groh, and Dave Bancroft, to the extent that he was constantly charged with buying pennants. But he also developed promising youngsters such as Fred Snodgrass, Travis Jackson, Bill Terry, and Mel Ott.

The name "McGraw" came to symbolize strict discipline enforced by fines and scathing reprimands. Some players thrived on or at least were able to get along under his regimen, thrilled at being in the Big Town playing for the Giants and McGraw. Others who may have chafed under it at the time were inclined to romanticize their experience in later years and, like veteran soldiers who put aside the agonies of war and endow it with a certain nostalgic glow, remember only the glamour and excitement of their youthful playing days. There were some, however, like Edd Roush and Frank Frisch, who refused to take McGraw's abuse.

° See *Baseball: The Early Years,* page 322.

On the other hand, McGraw staunchly backed up his players and was quick to reward good performance. As already mentioned, he was also generous in handing out cash or providing jobs to old-timers in need. Nor is it true, as many believed, that his players were simply robots whose every move in the game was executed at his order; but at crucial points and in certain situations they did receive specific instructions, and many a time I saw his catcher look to the bench for a sign from McGraw on what pitch to call for in a tight spot.

Although the stern taskmaster type of manager personified by McGraw predominated, a commentator ventured to say in 1915 that the day of Simon Legree managers was waning, and even hardbitten Clark Griffith believed that players were becoming sensitive and resentful of being treated like "convicts." Despite the criticism of McGraw's tyrannical methods from some quarters, his teams possessed a cohesiveness and aggressiveness that not only reflected his leadership and spirit but impelled fans all over the circuit to come out in droves in hopes of seeing the hated New York Giants beaten.

By the early 1920's he had confined himself to directing the team from the bench, where he could be seen half an hour or so before game time dressed in civilian clothes, gray-haired, his Panama hat beside him. In his younger days he posted himself in full uniform in the third-base coach's box, urging on his men, badgering and insulting opposing players, and inciting the crowd. Let word get out that an owner contemplated trading one of his players, and the next day McGraw would be flinging "You're for sale!" at him.

Once the tables were turned. In a game early in July 1913, McGraw had carried on a bitter verbal exchange with the Phillies, centering his fire on Ad Brennan, one of their pitchers, with the object of upsetting him for the next day's game, which he was scheduled to pitch against the Giants. The burden of his jibes was that Brennan was "yellow" and that George Stallings, who had once managed the pitcher, had told McGraw as much. He kept up the abuse under the stands after the game, whereupon Brennan turned and smashed him in the face, knocking him out. League President Lynch suspended both for five days and fined Brennan $100.

Off the field, McGraw was part of the sporting set. He liked to bet on horses and sometimes wintered in Cuba, where for a while he and Stoneham had an investment in a Havana race track and casino. In his Baltimore days he and his teammate, Wilbert Robinson, ran the Diamond Cafe. In 1909 McGraw owned a poolroom alongside the old *Herald* building in New York, and Rothstein, who owned a piece of the business, came regularly to play pool for big stakes. In those days, according to a *Times* estimate, four hundred New York poolrooms were paying $300 a month, a total of $1,440,000 a year, in protection money for gambling.

McGraw also had close connections with the theatrical world, including membership in the Lambs' Club, headquarters for actors. The club was the scene of one of McGraw's worst scrapes. In the early hours of one August morning in 1920 he got into an argument there with actor William Boyd. In the fracas that followed McGraw was hit over the head with a water carafe. He left the club with John C. Slavin, another actor, and Winfield Leggett, a retired naval officer. The three took a cab to McGraw's apartment, and on their arrival Slavin somehow wound up on the sidewalk badly injured. Later, none of the others, including the cab driver, seemed to remember what had happened, but Slavin sued McGraw and obtained an out-of-court settlement. Another actor, Wilton Lackaye, joined the casualty list when he came to offer advice to McGraw some weeks later and was punched for his trouble.

Newspapers had a field day with that story, and rumors that McGraw had been drinking set federal agents on his track for violation of the Volstead Act. William Fallon, "the great mouthpiece," a well-known criminal lawyer acting as McGraw's chief counsel, demanded that, in justice to McGraw, his client be formally indicted on specific charges. Later in a federal court McGraw pleaded not guilty to the charge of possessing a bottle of whiskey and was promptly acquitted by a jury. He settled with Slavin out of court.

His many escapades notwithstanding, McGraw was not just a brawler. Ordinarily he was a gracious host, and it may surprise some that off the field his speech was refined. He also attended St. Bonaventure College and traveled widely on baseball exhibition tours and private trips. He was an international figure, acclaimed in many foreign countries and received by several American Presidents and the King of England. New York's Mayor Walker appointed a committee to arrange a celebration for McGraw's "silver jubilee" as manager of the Giants, and when he began his thirtieth season as manager, President Hoover sent a telegram praising him for doing so much "to uphold the traditions of clean sportsmanship."

Toward the end of his career ill health forced him to be away from the team for long intervals, and he finally resigned as manager during the season of 1932. He was called back in 1933, the year before he died, for one more honor—to manage the National Leaguers against the American League team headed by his old opponent, Connie Mack, in the first All-Star game.

STARS AND GALAXIES

THE BASEBALL ERA before 1920 glittered with famous teams and outstanding players whose names, though dimming with the passing of generations, are still vivid in the memories of old men who in their youth enjoyed sunny afternoons sitting in major-league ball parks. Fans of those days, like diners in a good restaurant, could select from an assortment of spicy, well-prepared entrees on the baseball menu. They could thrill at the expertness and color of John McGraw's Giants, of Frank Chance's Cubs, Connie Mack's Athletics, and Bill Carrigan's Boston Red Sox. They could be stirred by great players like Ty Cobb, Tris Speaker, Honus Wagner, Eddie Collins, Walter Johnson, Christy Mathewson, and Grover Cleveland Alexander, to mention only a handful—names that are still a source of wonderment even to modern fans who read of their exploits or come across their names in the record books. As Grantland Rice described it:

> Far off I hear the rolling, roaring cheers
> They come to me from many yesterdays,
> From record deeds that cross the fading years,
> And light the landscape with their brilliant plays,
> Great stars that knew their days in fame's bright sun,
> I hear tramping to oblivion.

But as with most menus, some dishes are better than others, and there are times when they are very much better than the others. So it was in the major leagues. The disparity in playing strength among the major-league clubs in the pre-1920 era continued to mock Organized Baseball's constant claim that its restrictive economic practices were essential "to provide and stimulate competition for the League pennants." That they have been ineffective is demonstrated by the fact that in the first half of the era, 1901–10, three teams monopolized all

National League pennants: Pittsburgh and Chicago four apiece, and New York two. In the second half, 1911–20, more teams were winners. In the American League's first decade, four clubs shared the pennants, Philadelphia and Detroit with three each, and Chicago and Boston with two each. In its second decade, again only four clubs tasted success, although Cleveland, picking up one championship, replaced Detroit among the victors. Three clubs shared the remaining nine flags. In short, seventeen of the National League pennants and nineteen of the American League ones went to only four teams in each circuit. In other words, only eight out of sixteen teams won thirty-six of the forty pennants. Washington and New York got none at all in the American League, although the Yankees had three second-place finishes between 1903 and 1910. St. Louis failed to win any in either league.

One of the first notable teams of the era was Pittsburgh, which won three straight National League championships. The Pirates' strength derived from a fusion of two teams. When the National League cut back from twelve to eight clubs in 1900, Barney Dreyfuss, then owner of Louisville (one of the clubs discarded by the league), purchased a half-interest in Pittsburgh, brought the best of his Louisville men along with him, and amalgamated them with the best of the Pirates. They immediately demonstrated their quality by finishing second, close behind Brooklyn, in 1900. The next season they took the first of their three pennants. In 1902 they further distinguished themselves by finishing an unprecedented 27½ games ahead of runner-up Brooklyn.

Leader of the Pirates was player-manager Fred Clarke, himself an excellent outfielder and hitter. Clarke had started managing for Dreyfuss at Louisville in 1897 and continued to direct the team at Pittsburgh through 1915. Like most winning teams, the Pirates had strong pitching. Charles "Deacon" Phillippe and Jack Chesbro, the spitballer, each won 20 or more games in each of the first two pennant-winning seasons. Keeping good pace with them were Jesse Tannehill, with 18 and 20 victories, Sam Leever, and Ed Doheny, a left-hander. Even when Chesbro and Tannehill jumped to the New York American League club, Pittsburgh still had sufficient pitching to win again in 1903.

The mainstay of these and later Pittsburgh teams was Honus Wagner. He is commonly rated the best of all shortstops, and some regard him as the greatest player of all time. One of those rare players who can do everything well—hit, field, run, and throw—Wagner could and did play almost any position on the team. Despite his bulky, ungainly build and lack of the grace usually associated with those who

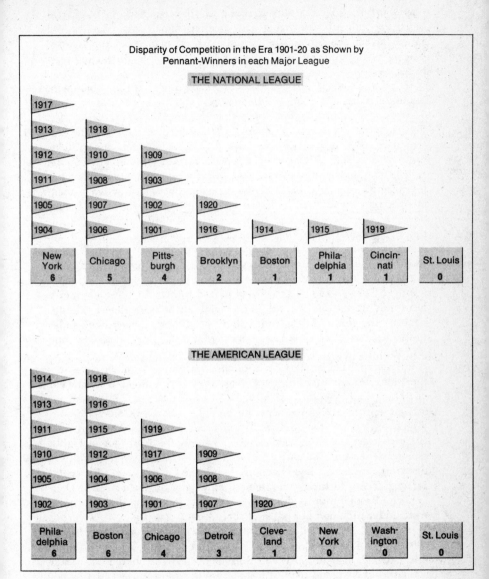

Disparity of Competition in the Era 1901-20 as Shown by
Pennant-Winners in each Major League

THE NATIONAL LEAGUE

New York 6	Chicago 5	Pitts-burgh 4	Brooklyn 2	Boston 1	Phila-delphia 1	Cincin-nati 1	St. Louis 0
1917	1918						
1913	1910	1909					
1912	1908	1903					
1911	1907	1902	1920				
1905	1906	1901	1916	1914	1915	1919	
1904							

THE AMERICAN LEAGUE

Phila-delphia 6	Boston 6	Chicago 4	Detroit 3	Cleve-land 1	New York 0	Wash-ington 0	St. Louis 0
1914	1918						
1913	1916						
1911	1915	1919					
1910	1912	1917	1909				
1905	1904	1906	1908				
1902	1903	1901	1907	1920			

play short, his speed, ability to make scoop-shovel pickups of ground balls, and powerful throwing arm enabled him to play deeper and range farther than other shortstops. He won eight National League batting championships—still a record—and led five times in stolen bases.

In addition to Wagner, the club had another batting champion, outfielder Clarence "Ginger" Beaumont, who won the title in 1902. That same season the team's little third baseman, Tommy Leach, led the league in home runs with only six! That paltry total and the fact that it resulted from inside-the-park drives hit between the outfielders, not into the stands or over fences, furnish another clue to the style of play in the days of the dead ball. Because outfielders played a lot closer then, a fast man who happened to hit a ball between them or over their heads had a chance to tear around all the bases before the ball was recovered and thrown home. For the same reason, another of baseball's exciting features, the three-base hit, used to be more frequent. Nowadays fans have less opportunity to thrill at the race between man and ball: the straining runner attempting to make it safely all the way from home to third base, while the outfielder frantically chases the ball, recovers it, and throws mightily, hoping to head him off; the runner and ball arriving at the base almost simultaneously; the cloud of dust and flash of the runner's spikes as he slides desperately to escape the baseman's tag; and the alert umpire leaning into the thick of it, the better to determine "safe" or "out."

Following hard on the heels of the 1903 Pittsburgh victors came the New York Giants. For some years they had foundered in or near last place, and even the arrival of McGraw as manager in the summer of 1902 and the reinforcements he brought with him from Baltimore —such as pitcher Joe McGinnity, first baseman Dan McGann, and Roger Bresnahan—were not enough to boost the team out of eighth place that season. But under McGraw's ministrations, dead wood was discarded and new players acquired, and the Giants soared to second in 1903. Then, further strengthened, especially by securing Bill Dahlen from Brooklyn through a one-sided trade, they won their first pennant under McGraw in 1904 and their second in 1905.

Dahlen, a very good though unsung shortstop, who by then had thirteen years of major-league experience behind him, admirably filled the short-field position. Bresnahan is remembered as a star catcher, but he could play just about any position. In fact, it was not he but Frank Bowerman, now nearly forgotten, who did the catching for the 1904 champions; Bresnahan played the outfield that season and settled into catching only the next year.

Joe McGinnity and Christy Mathewson shared most of the pitching load for the Giants. Between them they accounted for 68 (35 and 33 respectively) of the 1904 club's 106 victories. McGinnity, already famous for five times pitching both games of a doubleheader within two seasons and winning nine of the ten, was nicknamed "Iron Man"—not on that account, but because he often spoke of working winters in his father's iron foundry. To McGinnity also belongs the modern National League record for most games started, 48, and number of innings pitched in a single season, 438.

Mathewson was one of the master pitchers of baseball. His application of intelligence to mechanical skill elevated his pitching to artistry. He possessed the usual stock in trade of a good pitcher—speed and curves—but the pitch always associated with him was the "fadeaway," first called the "fallaway" and now the "screwball." * This pitch, when thrown by a right-handed pitcher, breaks the opposite way from conventional curve balls—in and down on a right-handed hitter, and down and away from a left-handed one. The reverse is true if a left-hander is doing the throwing.

Matty not only had the intelligence to study the hitters carefully to learn their strength and weakness; he also had remarkable control that permitted him to apply his knowledge by putting the ball where he wanted it. In one stretch he pitched 68 consecutive innings, the equivalent of seven and a half games, without allowing a base on balls. He also excelled at pacing himself—coasting a little when he was ahead and easing up somewhat on weaker hitters, in order to save something for a tight spot when the other team threatened to score. Today, as pitchers well know, almost any batter can at any time cause them sudden ruin by hitting a pitch out of the park, so they seldom risk letting up.

Mathewson spent practically his entire major-league career with the Giants. He finished with 373 victories, more than any other National League pitcher except Grover Alexander, with whom he shares the record, but he achieved his finest hour in defeating the Philadelphia Athletics three times in the 1905 World Series. Seven other pitchers have won three games in a single Series, but Matty's three were all shutouts.

The 1906 Giants and Pirates both had a winning percentage higher than .600, a figure ordinarily good enough to take the pennant. But not that year. Instead, the Chicago Cubs overwhelmed the National League with 116 victories (a total still unequaled), leaving the second-place Giants 20 games behind! The Cubs were to finish first four times in five seasons, missing out only in 1909 when Pittsburgh won its fourth and last pennant of the era.

* Pitchers who resort to it are known as "scroogies."

The architect of this splendid Chicago team was Frank Selee. Time has faded his name more than it should have, but in his day Selee had a reputation as a shrewd judge of player talent, and, before his appointment as Cub manager in 1902, he had molded and led the powerful Boston teams of the 'nineties to five pennants. Selee began reconstructing the Cubs by shifting a husky catcher, Frank Chance, to first base and moving Joe Tinker from third to shortstop. By late in 1902, when a scrawny little infielder named Johnny Evers joined the club as an emergency replacement, Selee had assembled what became baseball's most famous double-play combination, immortalized in Franklin P. Adams's poem:

> These are the saddest of possible words—
>   Tinker to Evers to Chance.
> Trio of Bear Cubs and fleeter than birds—
>   Tinker to Evers to Chance.
> Thoughtlessly pricking our gonfalon bubble,
> Making a Giant hit into a double,
> Words that are weighty with nothing but trouble—
>   Tinker to Evers to Chance.

The pen may or may not be mightier than the sword, but Adams's lines proved it mightier than the glove. Although all three were good ball players, their reputation for making double plays rests more on poetry than on performance. Statistics on double plays were not kept in those days, but according to sportswriter Warren Brown, who had the box scores checked, the famed trio made only 54 such plays in the four years from 1906 through 1909. This figure is inconsequential compared with the accomplishments of a modern double-play combination. Tinker did lead his league five times in fielding percentage; otherwise, none of the three names appears in the records under the categories that denote fielding supremacy. It is also significant that they were voted into the Hall of Fame as a unit, not individually; and, good as they doubtless were in their time, they are rarely mentioned when fans discuss the best players of those positions. Their personal relations also contradict the widespread notion that harmony among the players is essential to team success: Tinker and Evers were at odds with each other and spoke only when absolutely necessary. In fact Evers, a sour, humorless character, was nicknamed "The Crab."

Behind the bat Selee had Johnny Kling, and there was no better catcher in the league. Jimmy Archer, another first-rate Cub catcher, known for his powerful throwing arm, came up in 1909 in time to fill the opening created when Kling held out for the season. A third catcher, Pat Moran, acquired by the Cubs in 1906, shared the catching for four years and later became a pennant-winning manager himself.

Selee also obtained outfielders Jimmy Slagle, one of his old Boston boys, and Frank "Wildfire" Schulte, a power hitter who led the National League in home runs with 21 in 1911, the year of the new lively ball. Versatile Arthur "Circus Solly" Hofman provided excellent infield and outfield reserve strength. Carl Lundgren and Big Ed Reulbach, both collegians, and a third man with almost as many names as a Prince of Wales—Mordecai Peter Centennial "Three-Finger" Brown (actually he had four)—laid the foundation of an exceptional pitching staff. Brown got his nickname as the result of a childhood accident. He thrust his hand into a piece of farm machinery and lost the index finger below the second joint; his thumb and two of his other fingers were also badly damaged. He gripped the ball about the same as other pitchers except that he used his third and fourth fingers rather than the first two. He threw sidearm and possessed a curve ball that one writer said could be hit only with a shotgun. In the six seasons 1906–11 he averaged an impressive 24.5 victories, and the fact that he won 20 or more games in each of those years shows his remarkable consistency. Brown was one pitcher who could more than hold his own against Mathewson, and whenever the two opposed each other for the Cubs and Giants, who were bitter rivals, there was tense excitement among the fans.

Unfortunately, ill health forced Selee to quit before the 1905 season closed, just as his work was about to bear fruit. Chicago then got a new owner, Charles W. Murphy, as well as a new manager, Frank Chance. Finishing touches to Selee's handiwork were applied through a series of trades that brought in third baseman Harry Steinfeld to complete the infield, Jimmy Sheckard for the outfield, and two more pitchers, Orval Overall, a hulking right-hander, and Jack Pfiester, a left-hander whose penchant for beating New York won him the sobriquet "Jack the Giant Killer."

Of the four championships captured by these Cubs, the one of 1908 remains controversial to this day. McGraw and his players always maintained that the Giants were bilked out of that pennant because of the National League's ruling on the Merkle play. If one were to select the single most debated, most written-about play in baseball history, he would be hard put to top that bizarre episode. In a game between the Giants and Cubs at the Polo Grounds on September 23, 1908, the score was tied 1-1 with two out in the last of the ninth inning. The Giants had Moose McCormick representing the potential winning run on third and Fred Merkle, a nineteen-year-old substitute, on first. Shortstop Al Bridwell made an apparent safe hit to center field, and McCormick crossed the plate. Exultant at their assumed victory, the Giant players, Merkle included, raced across the field for the clubhouse in deep center field, as they had done countless times before, in order to escape the crowd surging out of the stands.

But had they really won the game? Precisely what followed will never be known. The alert Johnny Evers, realizing that Merkle had failed to touch second base before running off the field, supposedly ran over to second, shouting to the Cub outfielder to throw in the ball hit by Bridwell. Hofman returned the ball to the infield, but Joe McGinnity, perhaps sensing what Evers was up to, dashed from the coach's box, wrestled the ball away from some of the Cub players, and threw it into the stands. Evers is said either to have recovered the original ball (as the Cubs claimed) or to have got hold of another one somehow and touched second. Thus runs the traditional version that has come down to us.

The Cubs asserted that Merkle had been forced out, thus nullifying the run supposedly scored by McCormick and leaving the score tied. Base Umpire Bob Emslie, who did not actually see the play, asked Plate Umpire Hank O'Day if Merkle had touched second. When O'Day told him the player had not, Emslie ruled Merkle out. One wonders if O'Day saw the play either, since at no time did he state that Merkle was called out on the basis of a simple force-out. In his official report to the president after the game, O'Day stated that he did not order play resumed because it was too dark to continue. Furthermore, in the report he indicated only that Merkle had not touched second and that McGinnity had interfered with the play; he did not say precisely why Merkle was called out—it could have been for several reasons: because Evers actually touched the base with the ball in his possession, because of McGinnity's interference, or even because Merkle ran out of the base line. Six years later O'Day was quoted as saying that it was because of interference.

Chicago appealed to President Pulliam to declare the game forfeited to them because of the Giants' failure to clear the field and resume play. Pulliam rejected the claim of a forfeit but upheld the umpires' decision. He ruled the game a draw and directed that it be replayed at the end of the season should the two teams finish in a tie for the pennant. The Giants then appealed over Pulliam's head to the league board of directors, but the president was upheld.

In a novel it would have been unbelievable, but the two teams did finish in a tie and had to replay the disputed game to decide the championship. The excitement and tension can well be imagined; the Polo Grounds were packed, and thousands were turned away. The Cubs received threatening letters from fans before the game and required police protection after winning the game and thus the pennant.

Merkle was blamed for costing the Giants the pennant and vilified as "Bonehead" Merkle for the rest of his life. His mistake was dwelt upon out of all proportion and given an emphasis inconceivable today, when slips by players are taken less seriously. A modern owner would scarcely remark publicly, as the Cubs' Charles Murphy did, "We can't supply brains to the New York Club's dumb players."

In effect, Merkle's fate had been determined a few weeks before his "boner," in a game between Pittsburgh and Chicago. A Pittsburgh runner, Warren Gill, failed to touch second as the winning run scored in the ninth inning. Evers executed the same play, but the umpire, the same Hank O'Day, took no action on it, claiming he did not see it. The Cubs had protested this game to Pulliam, who disallowed it on the ground that he could not overrule umpires on the mere say-so of players. Upon reflection O'Day no doubt realized that Evers was technically correct, even though the letter of the rule had habitually been ignored, and made a mental note to watch for a recurrence of the situation. Since the incident was well reported on the sports pages, the question arises: why did not McGraw or some of the older men bring it to the attention of inexperienced players like Merkle? After the "boner," however, McGraw, to his credit, stood by Merkle and even raised his salary as a sign of confidence in a promising young player. Those who blamed Merkle for losing the pennant overlooked the fact that the Giants lost 55 other games that season and were overtaken by a losing streak at the end; a victory in any one of these games would have obviated the need for the replayed game and given them the pennant.

It is also unfair to lay the blame at O'Day's door, as the well-known umpire Bill Klem did years afterward. Calling it "the rottenest decision in the history of baseball," Klem criticized O'Day for basing the decision on a technicality rather than on the "intent" of the rules. All rules, like all laws, rest on technicalities, and the rule in this case is plain: when the third out of an inning is a force-out, no run can score. The fact that the rule had not hitherto been enforced is really immaterial, because an umpire cannot rule on plays involving oversights or omissions by players on one side unless those on the other side call his attention to them. Instead of damning Merkle, history should credit Evers as the first to grasp the implications of the habitual neglect of runners to touch the next base in such circumstances. Some credit should also go to the Chicago outfielder, Hofman, who was alert enough to return the ball to Evers, if he in fact did so, instead of following the common practice of letting it go and running to the clubhouse on the assumption that the game was over.

After the five years of Cub-Pirate dominance, the Giants resurged in 1911 with a practically new young team that stayed on top for three years. The replacements included Fred Merkle, who became the regular first baseman; the catcher Chief Meyers; and Otis Crandall, a relief pitching specialist. From the 1905 champions they still had Mathewson, who continued to win more than 20 games a season. Paired with him was a sensational young left-hander, Rube Marquard. McGraw had given a reported $11,000 for him in 1908—up to then the highest price paid for a minor-leaguer. His initial unsuccess brought him the tag "$11,000 Lemon," but after he found himself, he too contributed more than 20 victories toward each of the three pennants. He was the talk of baseball in 1912 for winning 19 straight games, a consecutive-win record equalled only by another Giants player, Tim Keefe, back in 1888. And under modern regulations for accrediting victories, Marquard would have been credited with 20 straight. Other than Mathewson and Marquard, the team had no outstanding stars, but it was a typical McGraw product—fast and aggressive.

After the Giants' three years of supremacy, a different team won each time in the National League's remaining seven seasons of the era. Some baseball men hold that the test of a true champion is the ability to repeat; judged by this standard, none of the winners from 1914 through 1920 qualify.

The first team to break the New York-Chicago-Pittsburgh pennant monopoly was the so-called "Miracle Braves" of Boston. The appellation "Miracle Braves" alludes to their dramatic climb to the top from last place, where they foundered as late in the season as July 18. In the course of the Braves' sensational drive to the top in that first year of World War One, Grantland Rice saluted them with the following lines:

> Wild Bill of Germany, they say,
>   Can beat the Frenchmen to a mush;
> J. Bull in any sort of play
>   Can batter back the Kaiser's rush;
> And Russia with a savage blow
>   Can drive the Austrians like slaves;
> But tell me this—before I go—
>   What clan can check those pop-eyed Braves?

The "miracle" of the Braves was due less to supernatural intervention than to a combination of fortuitous circumstances. The club had not won since 1898, and the franchise had decayed under a series of ineffectual owners. But in 1913 James E. Gaffney, a Tammany Hall politician-contractor and brother-in-law of Charles F. Murphy, Tammany

Grover Cleveland Alexander
Brown Bros.

Walter Johnson
Brown Bros.

A

B

C

D

A. Christy Mathewson   *Brown Bros.*
B. Two famous managers: John McGraw, Connie Mack.   *Culver*
C. The National Commission. LEFT to RIGHT: Ban Johnson, Tom Lynch, August
   Herrmann.   *Brown Bros.*
D. The Boston Royal Rooters   *Courtesy of the Print Dept., Boston Public Library*

A

B

C

COPYRIGHT 1906
BY FRED H. WAGNER

KID HERMAN

(1)PFIESTER (2)LUNDGREN (3)BROWN (4)SHECKARD (5)KLING (6)TAYLOR (7)SHULTE (8)HOFMAN (9)STEINFELD
(10)CHANCE (11)OVERALL (12)EVERS (13)SLAGLE (14)MORAN (15)GESSLER (16)WALSH (17)McCORMICK (18)

NATIONAL LEAGUE CHAMPIONS 1907

Chicago Cubs of 1907   *Courtesy of the Print Dept., Boston Public Library*

Philadelphia Athletics of 1911   *Brown Bros.*

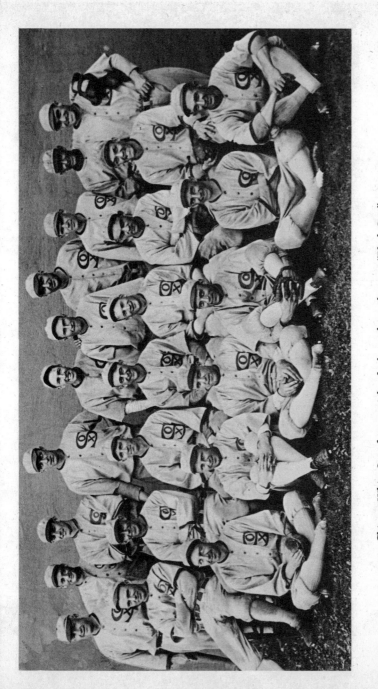

Chicago White Sox of 1919, eight of whose players became "Black Sox." TOP ROW, from LEFT: Kid Gleason, manager; John Sullivan, Roy Wilkinson, Grover Lowdermilk, Swede Risberg, Fred McMullin, Bill James, Eddie Murphy, Joe Jackson, Joe Jenkins. CENTER: Ray Schalk, John Collins, Red Faber, Dick Kerr, Happy Felsch, Chick Gandil, Buck Weaver. BOTTOM: Eddie Collins, Nemo Liebold, Eddie Cicotte, Erskine Mayer, Claude Williams, Byrd Lynn. *National Baseball Library, Coopers-town, N.Y.*

Boston Red Sox of 1912   *Courtesy of the Print Dept., Boston Public Library*

New York Highlanders (Yankees) of 1907   *Brown Bros.*

boss, secured control. Gaffney, inspired by his Tammany connections, changed the team's name to "Braves."

Gaffney also appointed George Stallings as manager. Stallings was something of a chameleon—away from the field, a gentleman of considerable schooling and owner of a 4000-acre plantation in his native Georgia; on the field, a superstition-ridden zealot with the vocabulary of a camel driver. He had previously shown his managing skill with a number of major- and minor-league clubs, and with the Braves he extracted every ounce of playing ability from an unevenly endowed crew.

Another happenstance was the coming of Johnny Evers to the club, as a result of Charles W. Murphy's attempt to fire him from the Chicago Cubs and the league's determination to keep this star out of the hands of the competing Federal League.° The acquisition of Evers assured the club of a first-class second-base combination, since it already had a fine defensive shortstop in the gnomelike "Rabbit" Maranville, whose unusual speed, sure hands, and quickness in releasing the ball made up for an ordinary throwing arm. His specialty was his "basket catch." He would scamper after pop flies and then, with a last-second flip of the hands, nonchalantly catch them below his belt-line. His escapades on and off the field are legend, and for twenty-three seasons, during which he appeared in more games and probably drank more than any other National League shortstop, the Rabbit entertained fans with his colorful pantomime, antics that would be dismissed today as "bush"—beneath the dignity of a more blasé generation of players.

The Braves also had three sturdy pitchers, Dick Rudolph, Bill James, and George Tyler, who accounted for 69 of the team's 94 victories. Hank Gowdy gave them competent catching. The rest of the team was a collection of undistinguished journeymen. It was strength in the key positions and Stallings's ability to make the players believe they were better than they were that furnish the temporal explanation for the miracle of 1914.

The late-season momentum of the Braves carried over into the World Series, and they defeated the much stronger Philadelphia Athletics team in four straight games. After this debacle Mack lost some of his stars to the Federal League and sold others to American League clubs. That winter Rabbit Maranville returned to the "miracle" theme, telling an audience at a church fair, presumably with a straight face, that Boston had won the Series because of prayer. He and seven teammates, he said, had agreed to attend holy communion each morning of the Series, and once in a "tough spot" they got to-

° See above, chapter 4, and below, chapter 10.

gether in the dugout and prayed silently that Evers would come through with a hit, and he did.

The Philadelphia team arrived at the pennant table in 1915 even hungrier than Boston. In all their years of National League membership they had never won, and they would not win again for thirty-five years. The principal player of this club was Grover Cleveland Alexander, who ranks close to the top in any reckoning of baseball's best pitchers. His easy, effortless style and pinpoint control gave maximum effectiveness to his speed, curve, and fine screwball. He wasted no time between pitches and concentrated on getting the ball over the plate, forcing batters to hit the kind of pitch he wanted them to. Often he would retire the side on five or six pitches in an inning, and fans could count on getting home early whenever he worked.

Alexander came up with the Phillies in 1911 and by 1915 had supplanted the fading Mathewson as the leading pitcher of the league. In that year he won 31 games and achieved both the highest winning percentage and lowest earned-run average while leading the Phillies to the pennant. His 1.22 average that year was a National League record surpassed only by Ferdie Schupp's 0.90 in 1916 and Bob Gibson's 1.12 in 1968. Alexander's 30 or more victories the following two seasons made him the only pitcher of the twentieth century besides Mathewson to win 30 or more games three years in a row, and they were all the more remarkable for having been accomplished in the Philadelphia ball park with its extremely close right-field fence that provided an easy target for batters. He also pitched 16 shutouts in one season (a major-league record) and 90 all told in his twenty-year career (a National League mark). He and Mathewson jointly hold the National League lead for most games won.

The Phillies also had a towering, quick-tempered Virginian, Eppa Rixey. Although he did not particularly shine in the 1915 season, he was to pitch a record twenty-one years in the National League, winning 266 games. Their right fielder, Gavvy Cravath, hit 24 home runs, an incredible number for those days.

Brooklyn's turn came in 1916. Two years before, they had secured a new manager, Wilbert Robinson, the old Baltimore Oriole catcher. He had been a Giants coach until an argument with McGraw caused his dismissal and a lasting estrangement between the two former teammates and friends. Robbie won with some newly acquired cast-offs, such as ex-Giants Marquard, Merkle, and Meyers, plus a few prominent players of their own, such as Jake Daubert and Zack Wheat. Daubert was a very good hitter and as smooth a fielding first baseman as any who ever played. Before a game Jake would smear Vaseline on the pocket of his glove and then sprinkle it with powdered resin.

Wheat was something special. He was a steady, quiet gentleman who daily did his job without fanfare or fisticuffs. In the outfield he was a sure catch of a fly ball and an accurate thrower. At bat he was a slashing, line-drive hitter, one of the few who could hit a low ball well. And in the 1920's when Rogers Hornsby, probably the best of all right-hand hitters, was in his prime, there were pitchers who said they feared Wheat in a crucial spot more than they did Hornsby. During his eighteen years with Brooklyn, Wheat appeared in more games and collected more of the club's batting records than any who ever played for Brooklyn.

Another member of that 1916 team was Charles Dillon "Casey" Stengel, a good ball player but one whose fame and fortune lay far in the future as a manager. "Charlie Stengel," said *Sporting News* in 1912, "has come into the league with a tremendous crash, and appears to be the real thing." It is ironic that by the time victory finally came to Brooklyn, their star pitcher, Nap Rucker, was past his peak, having expended his best years laboring at Ebbets Field for one mediocre team after another.

Despite the Giants' two amazing winning streaks in 1916, first 17 straight victories and then their record 26, they finished only fourth. However, they came on to win again in 1917. In 1918 the Chicago Cubs took the second wartime pennant.

Another newcomer to first-place honors, Cincinnati, captured its first National League pennant in 1919. The star of this club was Edd Roush, in his day probably the best defensive outfielder in the league. Not only was he fast but he was expert at anticipating where fly balls would go. An outstanding hitter as well, he regularly batted well over .300. He used a short, fat bat, the heaviest in the league, and punched his hits to all fields. He shifted his position in the batter's box before each pitch, but took care to move only after the pitcher had gone too far in his delivery to change his intention.

There was a widely believed story given out by the National League publicity bureau that after Roush's right arm had failed him in his early playing days, he learned to throw with his left. In view of his powerful throwing arm, this changeover would indeed have been remarkable. When I asked Roush about this at an old-timers' gathering, he told me that he was a natural left-hander but as a boy he learned to throw with the other arm because there was no glove available for his right hand; however, he found that he could not "get enough on the ball," so when he became a professional he merely went back to his natural style.

"Uncle Robbie" won his second and last pennant in 1920 with a Brooklyn team that was carried forward by a fine group of pitchers, including spitballers Burleigh Grimes and Clarence Mitchell. That year another of their pitchers, Leon Cadore, pitched in the longest major-league game ever played; he and his opponent, Joe Oeschger of Boston, went the entire 26 innings—only to have the game called on account of darkness with the score still tied, 1-1.

Although three National League clubs took 75 per cent of the pennants in the first twenty seasons of the century, every club except the St. Louis Cardinals had managed to take at least one. In the other league the maldistribution was, if anything, more accentuated. Three clubs took 70 per cent of the American League pennants in this era, and two shared the remaining 30 per cent, leaving three with none at all.

The first American League pennant went to the Chicago White Sox, a rather run-of-the-mill team. The fledgling American League was locked in a trade war with the National in 1901. Its teams were motley aggregations reinforced by a number of players acquired in raids on National League rosters. The White Sox, like their sister clubs, reflected these conditions. Their leading light was Clark Griffith, who jumped his contract with the Chicago Nationals to manage the White Sox and, as it turned out, to become their premier pitcher, winning 24 and losing only 7. Another pitcher, Jimmy Callahan, was also a jumper from the Cubs, and the Sox's leading batter, Fielder Jones, was an émigré outfielder from the Brooklyn National League champions of 1900. Both Callahan and Jones afterwards served as White Sox managers, the latter leading the champion "Hitless Wonders" of 1906.

Intensification of the trade war in 1902 brought more than the usual vicissitudes to that year's first-place team, Connie Mack's Philadelphia Athletics. A year before, Mack had executed a brilliant sortie against the Philly Nationals, coming off with a real prize—their second baseman, Napoleon Lajoie—and others, including two pitchers. The big infielder ranked with Honus Wagner as one of the foremost players in the game. He was a devastating hitter and an extraordinarily graceful fielder; he could, said one admirer, "pick the ball from off the ground with the ease of a sweet sixteen accepting a box of bon bons." But Mack's coup was short-lived. The Phillies secured a court order enjoining Lajoie and the two pitchers from playing with the Athletics, so in order to remove Lajoie from the jurisdiction of the Pennsylvania courts and yet preserve him for the American League, Ban Johnson switched him and one of the pitchers to the Cleveland Americans.[*]

Nevertheless Mack still had a good ball club, and in mid-season he offset the loss of Lajoie with the acquisition of Danny Murphy and

---

[*] The other pitcher rejoined the Phillies. See *Baseball: The Early Years*, pages 314–15, for details of the story.

Rube Waddell. Murphy filled the void at second base and added batting strength. Waddell proved to be the spearhead of the Athletics'
victory march. Mack, who had previous experience of the idiosyn-
cratic Waddell while managing him in Milwaukee, plucked him from
the Los Angeles club, which Waddell had joined after exhausting the
patience of several major-league owners. The left-hander with the
short attention span became distracted en route East, and it took
some Pinkerton detectives and a lot of persuasion by Mack to get him
safely in tow. Waddell, an overhand pitcher with tremendous speed
and a wicked curve ball, was well-nigh unbeatable when he chose to
concentrate on his work, and that season he stepped out of character
and, for once, did just that. Although he did not join the Athletics
until late June, he piled up an astonishing 23 victories and lost only 7
times. "Mechanically," said *Sporting News,* he was "the greatest of all
southpaws. Mentally he is a few chips shy."

Mack already had another left-handed pitcher, Eddie Plank, whom
he had signed right out of college a year before and who turned out
to be a better long-term investment than Waddell. He became one of
only eighteen pitchers to win 300 or more games in major-league history. Plank was known for his "cross fire"—a method of delivering the
ball so that it crossed the plate at an angle instead of directly. The
Athletics also boasted six .300 hitters—an unusual number in those
days—including Socks Seybold, who led in home runs with 16, an
American League record that stood until 1919 and the advent of Babe
Ruth.

Although Mack retained practically the same team for the next few
years and indeed bolstered it with fresh outfield and pitching
strength, such are the vagaries of baseball that his second championship did not come until 1905. Paradoxically, when that pennant did
come, the Athletics had not a single .300 hitter. They did, however,
have formidable pitchers—Plank and Waddell (when he was on his
good behavior), holdovers from 1902, and newer men like Chief
Bender, Jimmy Dygert, a spitballer, and Andy Coakley.

Actually, though, the Athletics' batting weakness was nothing unusual then. It was the era of the dead ball, and the reader will recall
that the 1906 American League victors, Chicago's "Hitless Wonders,"
were the most feeble batters ever to win a pennant. It was stalwart
pitchers like Ed Walsh, Nick Altrock, Doc White, and Frank Owen
who carried them through.

Sandwiched between the four pennants taken by the White Sox
and the Athletics were the Boston triumphs of 1903 and 1904. Boston
had been in contention for the pennant in the first two years of the
American League because of a nucleus of outstanding player talent

stolen from the Nationals during the trade war. It was that same nucleus, now awarded "legally" to Boston, that carried the club to the top in the first two peacetime years. Jimmy Collins, the foremost third baseman of his time, had simply crossed the street, so to speak, from the Boston National League club to the Boston Americans to become player-manager, just as Clark Griffith did when he crossed from the Chicago Nationals to the rival Chicago Americans. Three other intra-city jumpers had accompanied Collins: pitcher Bill Dineen, victor in more than 20 games for each of the two pennant-winning campaigns and later a famous umpire; Buck Freeman, a home-run-hitting outfielder; and Chick Stahl, another outfielder. Boston had also induced the star battery of Cy Young and his catcher Lou Criger to desert the St. Louis Nationals. Young, then already thirty-six and with thirteen years of big-league pitching experience, supplied 28 and 26 of Boston's victories in 1903 and 1904 respectively. In the latter year he pitched a "perfect game"—allowing the opposing team not a single hit or base on balls—a feat that has been accomplished by only six other pitchers. When he ended his career in 1911 he had accumulated the incredible total of 511 victories.

The year 1907 heralded the American League's first three-in-a-row dynasty, that of the Detroit Tigers. Their scintillating star was young Ty Cobb, who won the batting championship that year with .350, his first of nine in succession and twelve all told. Never was there a player quite like Cobb. From the moment he appeared on the field he conveyed a febrile excitement compounded of fear, hate, grudging admiration, and respect. A lean, sinewy six-footer, he combined the litheness of a greyhound with the temperament of a tiger. With hard work, practice, and craft he extracted the most from his speed and quick reflexes. These ingredients and his remorseless urge to excel made Cobb the superb competitor and player that he was.

Besides enjoying the normal advantages that all left-handed batters have in reaching first base more quickly (such as batting from the side of home plate nearer to first base and being launched toward it, rather than away from it, as they stride and swing), Cobb had the knack of making a fast start and the speed to beat out many bunts and "infield rollers." In short, he was basically what players call a "leg hitter." Those fans whose memories are still green will recall Ty coming up to hit swinging three bats, to make the one he intended to use feel lighter. In the batter's box he crouched slightly, feet fairly close together, and gripped the bat with hands apart, the better to control it. This posture permitted him to bunt or to hit to any field by shifting his feet and sliding his left hand up or down on the bat.

Those who saw him never will forget Cobb's taut, menacing figure waiting, confidently impatient, to have at the enemy.

On the bases no one could demoralize a team as he could. He ran wild to the point of foolhardiness, constantly doing the unexpected, often being caught, but creating such mental hazards in opposing players by intimidating and unnerving them with his artful, aggressive sliding that they fumbled the ball, threw it wild, or dropped throws. On a one-base hit to the outfield he would dash far around first base toward second. Let the fielder loaf, or delay ever so little in returning the ball, and Cobb would keep going. Many were the singles he stretched into doubles and the doubles into triples. Repeatedly he tore from first to third base on a bunt, scored from second on an infield out or on an outfield fly after the catch, or, having reached first, got home by stealing all the way round the bases.

Cobb was too individualistic, too egocentric to be a team player. He played more for himself and his personal records. With a teammate on base, he would bunt, not primarily to advance the runner while sacrificing himself but to try for a hit. If he succeeded, he improved his batting average; if not, he saved it by getting credit for a sacrifice. The taking of unnecessary chances on the bases in situations where the team had more to lose than to gain can also be cited as evidence of Cobb's self-centered play. The issue is debatable, but probably in the long run his team benefited more than it suffered.

Very likely the 1907 pennant would have flown over Philadelphia instead of Detroit were it not for an umpire's decision in a vital game between the two teams. Trailing the Athletics by only a few percentage points, the Tigers arrived in Philadelphia late in September for a crucial three-game series that doubtless would decide the pennant winner. Detroit took the opener, and with it, first place. Rain the next day, a Saturday, prevented the second game, and since baseball on Sundays in Philadelphia was still forbidden, a doubleheader was scheduled for Monday.

The first game that afternoon proved to be one of baseball's most memorable. The Athletics led 7-1 up to the seventh behind Rube Waddell, who was rushed in to replace their starting pitcher, Jimmy Dygert, when he faltered in the second inning. But in the seventh the Tigers clawed back with four runs, aided by Sam Crawford's two-base hit into the crowd with the bases loaded. The Athletics scored one more run in their half of the seventh, and the Tigers matched it in the eighth, so they were still two behind, 8-6, as they came to bat in the ninth inning.

Crawford, the Detroit outfielder who made 312 three-base hits in his career, more than any other major-leaguer, led off in the ninth. This time he came through with a single. Cobb then hit a home run over the fence, tying the score. Connie Mack immediately removed Waddell and brought in Eddie Plank. Meanwhile, Detroit's starting pitcher, Wild Bill Donovan, kept in by Manager Hughie Jennings despite the pounding given him, had settled down.

The contest stretched into extra innings. In the eleventh each side scored once more. In the fourteenth Harry Davis, the Athletics' captain and first baseman, made an apparent ground-rule double by driving a fly ball into the crowd that overflowed onto the outfield. Then the ruckus started. The Tigers argued that a policeman stationed in front of the throng had interfered with Sam Crawford as he tried to make the catch. Players of both teams swarmed onto the field. A fist-fight started, and Claude Rossman, Detroit's first baseman, was marched off by an officer.

Silk O'Loughlin, umpire-in-chief, hesitated, then consulted his colleague, Tom Connolly, and finally ruled that Davis was out. The decision was all the more galling for the Athletics because Danny Murphy followed with a hit that would have scored Davis with the winning run and put them back in first place. An enraged Connie Mack, asserting that O'Loughlin "had it in for him," charged the umpire with robbing the Athletics and refused for many years afterwards to speak to him. The game was finally called on account of darkness with the score still tied, 9-9, after seventeen innings. The second game was never played, so the Tigers left town still in first place and, with only a week to go, they clung there, winning Detroit's first pennant since 1887.

The Washington club finished last in 1907, but it came up with a nineteen-year-old right-hand pitcher of whom Clark Griffith, his manager, was to write in 1912: "[Walter] Johnson is my meal ticket, any time he pitches I can enjoy the game." Johnson threw with blinding speed, possibly faster than any other pitcher ever did. After a few years he added a curve ball and change of pace to his repertoire, but he was so extremely fast that for the most part he simply blazed the ball past the batters, something few pitchers can consistently do against major-leaguers. In his twenty-one-year career, Johnson set marks as phenomenal as any in the record book. He won 416 games, more than any pitcher save Cy Young and 43 more than the next highest winners, Mathewson and Alexander. No one is even close to him in total number of shutouts (110). Nor did anyone approach the 56 consecutive scoreless innings he pitched in 1913 until Don Drysdale of the Los Angeles Dodgers broke the record in 1968 with 58.

Another brilliant span of pitching equally demonstrated his mastery. On Labor Day weekend of 1908 Johnson shut out the Yankees three times in four days, and each time he did it he got better, allowing six, three, and two hits respectively. Then after loafing three whole days, he bested Eddie Plank 2-1 and the next day beat the Athletics again 5-4. In other words, Johnson pitched and won five ball games in nine days and allowed only five runs all told!

His tremendous speed has inspired stories that Johnson was haunted by fear of hitting a batter and killing him. That this did not happen has been attributed to Johnson's pin-point control and a gentle nature that kept him from throwing at batters. But as a matter of fact, Johnson hit more batters than any other pitcher—204. Maybe it was just a case of the batters' getting in the way!

The full luster of Johnson's records can be appreciated only if one bears in mind that they were made with a team that remained in the second division most of the time; other pitchers who rate among the best spent more years with better teams. The mediocrity of Washington teams inspired the description "first in war, first in peace, and last in the American League." It was not until 1924 that Washington won a pennant and Johnson, then nearly thirty-seven years old, played in a World Series. In his previous seventeen seasons with the team, they made the first division only seven times, and in the stretch from 1910 to 1919 Johnson won more than a third of all the games Washington took.

The stir over the Merkle play in the National League and the consequent Giants-Cubs playoff game in 1908 overshadowed the even closer pennant fight in the American League that year. Going into September, four clubs—Detroit, Chicago, Cleveland, and St. Louis (now that they had Waddell, Connie Mack's patience having run out) —were so tightly bunched at the top that only four games separated the first- from the fourth-place club. By the final week three clubs, the Tigers, White Sox, and the Naps (after Napoleon Lajoie, Cleveland manager), were still cheek by jowl. It was then that one of the notable pitching duels of baseball occurred, in a game between Chicago and Cleveland.

On the mound for Chicago that October day was Big Ed Walsh, the spitballer, whose right arm was mainly responsible for keeping the Sox in the race. Pitching for Cleveland was Addie Joss, one of the less remembered stars of that era. Walsh permitted only four hits but lost 1-0 because Joss pitched a perfect game. Joss was then in his fourth successive season of winning 20 or more games, but this career of such great promise would be terminated in less than three years by death.

The pennant race was not decided until the final day of the season in a game between Detroit and Chicago in which the Tigers, victorious, captured the pennant by only a half-game, and Cleveland was such a close second that this last defeat lowered Chicago to third.

In winning for the third straight time the following year, the Tigers were hard pressed by the Philadelphia Athletics. Connie Mack had gradually assembled a group of new young ball players, including more collegians. After considerable experimenting, he settled them in the positions for which they were best suited. Starting in 1910 these revitalized Athletics won four pennants in five years, as the Cubs had done in the other league.

Mack's prize performer was Eddie Collins, who came to him while still a student at Columbia. Once placed in his proper niche at second base, he became one of the standouts at the position. Collins had everything: he could hit, field, and run the bases with the best and was known for his intelligence and quick thinking. In his twenty-five years in the major leagues he compiled a lifetime batting average of .333 and stole 744 bases. He is also among the few players who made more than 3000 hits.

Alongside Collins was Jack Barry, a clever shortstop from Holy Cross. Home Run Baker covered third. Baker needed only twelve or fewer home runs to lead the league three times, but he got his nickname after hitting two in the 1911 World Series against the Giants, off Marquard and then Mathewson. When Mack decided to replace his veteran first baseman, Harry Davis, with another youngster, Stuffy McInnis, in 1911, the quartet that has ever since been famous as "the $100,000 infield" was completed. That price tag, astronomical for those days, had no relation to the players' cost to Mack; it was an estimate of their market value.

Mack secured additional pitchers to supplement the work of Bender and Plank, notably Colby Jack Coombs, who played a major role in the 1910 and 1911 victory campaigns. Illness sidelined Coombs for several seasons thereafter, but meanwhile Mack found other young pitchers to help take up the slack and put the team back on top in 1913 and 1914. One was Herb Pennock, a stylish left-hander; another was Bullet Joe Bush, who complemented his fast ball with an effective fork ball—a change of pace thrown by gripping the ball between the index and middle fingers. A third was Bob Shawkey. All three, however, were to have their best years with the Yankees in the 1920's. The Athletics also had a serviceable outfield, including Danny Murphy, who was shifted from second base to make room for Collins. A competent catching staff rounded off one of the best teams ever seen in baseball.

Again it was the Boston Red Sox who interrupted the Athletics' pennant string. In 1912 Boston's winning team featured one of the renowned outfields of baseball: Harry Hooper in right, Tris Speaker in center, and Duffy Lewis in left. All were first-rate fielders, but the two flank men were not in Speaker's class as hitters. When Speaker first came up, a Washington correspondent predicted he was a "cinch" to make good provided he could "stand the pace." He lasted twenty-two years. His .344 lifetime batting average included 793 two-base hits, the most ever made, and he is another of the select few to collect 3000 or more hits.

Speaker was a superb outfielder, so adept at racing back and catching balls hit over his head that he could afford to play closer to the infield than most outfielders. Hence he converted into an out many a short drive that otherwise might have dropped safely. This ability to play a "shallow field," together with his strong, accurate throwing arm, often enabled him to prevent runners from advancing an extra base or to throw them out if they tried. Speaker is still frequently used as the criterion whenever the great center fielders of the game are discussed.

The spectacular member of the Red Sox pitching staff was Smokey Joe Wood. He lost only 5 games that year and won 34, 16 of them consecutively—an American League record equalled the same year by Walter Johnson and since then only by Lefty Grove and Schoolboy Rowe. After that peak year he was never the same. The next spring he injured his arm, and although he tried for several years to make it back as a pitcher, he was finally able to continue in the big league only by becoming an outfielder.

It was the Red Sox who once again supplanted Connie Mack's Athletics as champions in 1915 and made it two in a row the following year. What is more, they succeeded in the latter year without their star, Speaker. Because of a salary dispute, the Boston owner, Joseph Lannin, traded him to Cleveland, where he immediately won the season's batting championship, ending Ty Cobb's nine-year reign. Despite Joe Wood's decline, the Red Sox could still boast a strong pitching staff, which included the combative submarine-ball pitcher, Carl Mays, and a rugged youngster named Babe Ruth. Their catcher was Bill Carrigan, who also managed the team.

In 1917 the White Sox unseated Boston by winning the first pennant for Chicago since that of the "Hitless Wonders" twelve years before. The team fairly glittered with talent. Moreover, the reader should mark their names well, for many of them would soon squander their fame and future in a squalid World Series sellout attempt.

In at least four positions the White Sox boasted men as good as or better than any in the business. At second base there was Eddie Collins; no more need be said. Buck Weaver at third was probably as expert as any who ever played there, and some consider him the ablest of all. He was such an agile fielder that it was said he was the only third baseman against whom Ty Cobb would not bunt. Peppery Ray Schalk caught most of the games. He excelled defensively and demonstrated that a small man could stand the wear and tear of the job.

Then there was Shoeless Joe Jackson in left field. Comiskey had seized the chance to buy him in 1915 when Cleveland owner Charles Somers, once the "angel" of the American League, got into a financial bind which, in the absence of aid from the league, soon compelled him to dispose of the franchise. Jackson was a formidable hitter. He belabored the ball with Black Betsy, his famous bat, so named because the top half of it was black. He said that once while he was in a slump he stuck the end of his bat in some tar; immediately he started doing well and, regarding the incident as an omen, he had all his bats made half black thereafter. Jackson's lifetime batting average came to .356, a mark exceeded by only two men, Cobb and Rogers Hornsby. Jackson was also a first-class outfielder endowed with speed and a powerful, accurate throwing arm.

The other White Sox players were also highly competent. In center field Happy Felsch ranged almost as far as Speaker, and he added a dangerous bat to the offense. Two good men alternated in right field according to the opposing pitcher: right-hand-hitting Shano Collins against left-handers, and left-hand-hitting Nemo Leibold against right-handers. Chick Gandil, a big, strong, sure fielder and "clutch" hitter, and Swede Risberg, tough, flashy, and hard-throwing, took good care of first base and shortstop. Fred McMullin, an infielder, and Eddie Murphy, an outfielder and pinch hitter, provided bench strength.

A corps of capable pitchers buttressed this impressive array, especially Eddie Cicotte, a 28-game winner, famed for his shine ball; Red Faber, a spitballer; and Lefty Williams, a crafty "control" pitcher. Furthermore, they won with a manager, "Pants" Rowland, who had never before been in a big-league uniform, and in spite of the dissension and cliques that wracked the squad.

The White Sox slid all the way to sixth in the abbreviated war season of 1918, while Boston came back to win again, making it four pennants and two second places for them in the seven years since 1912. Then with a new leader, Kid Gleason, but with virtually the same players, the White Sox won the fateful 1919 championship.

The last American League pennant of the era fell to the Cleveland Indians playing under their star center fielder, Tris Speaker. They went on to win the championship over Brooklyn in a World Series notable for the only unassisted triple play (Bill Wambsganss), the first home run with the bases full (Elmer Smith), and the first home run hit by a pitcher (Jim Bagby) in Series history.

But the Indians' success was anti-climactic. A few days before they clinched the 1920 pennant, long-smouldering rumor burst into searing fact as astounded fans learned that the 1919 World Series had been "fixed," and a shocked public discovered that its so-called National Game and vaunted heroes were, like the politics and business of the era, susceptible to dishonesty and corruption.

PART THREE

A TRYING TIME

9

THE SEEDS OF UNION

PROFESSIONAL baseball players are glamorized, publicized, and eulogized. The names of many of them are more familiar to Americans than those of any other people in the public eye save perhaps movie stars, radio and TV "personalities," and some athletes in other professional sports. Fans ordinarily think of ball players as heroes; seldom do they picture them as employees working for a living. But when players engage in salary disputes with their employers or form a union, fans become aware of a less romantic facet of the professionals' lives. And the fans are not always pleased at the spectacle. Even though they may be union members themselves, they are not keen to have ball players emulate them. A 1946 Gallup Poll revealed overwhelming opposition to unionization of ball players. Evidently the average citizen tied to a humdrum job entertains a wish to keep his sports heroes on a level above his own commonplaces. To him the prospect of a ball player manning a picket line seems out of character. To believe otherwise would shatter some of the illusions upon which professional baseball depends.

Historically, the players themselves have been unreceptive, if not actually hostile, to unionization. On those several occasions when they did band together, their organizations have been generally short-lived, largely ineffectual, and euphemistically named, apparently in the belief that by any other name a union smells sweeter.

What is the explanation for the players' attitude? The answer lies in the nature of their occupation. Their careers are short, seasonal, and uncertain. In a profession that counts men already old by the early thirties, players can at best bank on relatively few productive years, and even these are in danger of being abruptly shortened at any time by sudden injury. Workers in more conventional fields can better afford to sacrifice current income—by striking, for example— because their longer job expectancy promises an opportunity to make up temporary financial losses. For the ball player time is too short to take the long view. Consequently, he must "get it while the getting is good," but at the price of giving up one of the strongest incentives for unionization—the hope of long-term benefits.

Other conditions of work tend to vitiate that sense of solidarity required for concerted action. Ball players are shifted about from team to team and league to league. Come autumn, they disperse to homes scattered far from their work and from each other. A disposition toward individualism also dampens the desire to join forces: the highest-paid major-leaguers do not always appreciate the need for making common cause with marginal players, and both groups find it hard to unite with those in lowly minor leagues, where conditions in general have been less stable and where the forces inimical to unionization are therefore compounded.

The prospect of carrying a union card also runs counter to the ball player's self-image as reflected in public adulation. As historian Carl Becker once remarked, "If you keep telling a person he's a hero, he'll soon be telling himself, 'By God, I *am* a hero.'" Accepting as he does the heroic position and the psychological and material rewards accorded him by the public, the ball player flinches from unionism because its blue-collar connotations might detract from the public's and his own view of himself.

Unions that the players have formed were not organized "for light and transient reasons," to employ Jefferson's phrase. They arose when the players' grievances outweighed their inhibitions. The first union formed, the Brotherhood of Professional Base Ball Players, appeared in 1885. It gradually gained strength and eventually enlisted support from outside capitalists to establish a league of its own in 1890, only to be destroyed by Organized Baseball in the one-year trade war that followed.

It was ten years before the players attempted another union, the Protective Association of Professional Baseball Players.* Then in 1901 another trade war broke out as the new American League battled to share the business with the entrenched National League monopoly. During the conflict both leagues ignored each other's player contracts and raided each other's rosters, thus affording the men an opportunity to play one league against the other to their own advantage. But the Protective Association fizzled out when the two warring leagues made peace in 1903 and, among other things, agreed to respect each other's contracts and reserve rights in the players, thus re-establishing monopsony control over them.

* For the detailed story of these unions, see *Baseball: The Early Years,* pages 221–39, 309–24.

THE SEEDS OF UNION

Fortified once more in their property rights over the players, the owners were in a position to reduce their salaries, and in the years immediately following the settlement of the war there was a good deal of discussion about the necessity for doing so. Frank Robison, owner of the St. Louis Cardinals, strongly advocated cuts. Because he anticipated trouble in getting his players to take less pay and was not wholly convinced that the American League would really abide by the terms of the peace agreement, he asked Garry Herrmann to sound out Ban Johnson to make sure that the American League would not steal any of his men should they refuse to accept pay cuts. Two years later Robison was again planning a "not very excessive cut," just 20 per cent, but to sweeten the dose he offered a purse of $10,000 if the team finished first and $5000 if it came in second. Knowing the kind of team he had, he doubtless lost little sleep over the possibility of having to make good his promise. He then tried to have the league provide the salve for the cuts by supplying the bonuses from funds accumulated through its 5 per cent assessment on member clubs. The idea was a forerunner of the later division of World Series receipts among second-, third-, and fourth-place clubs as well as pennant winners in each league.

Clark Griffith, then managing the Yankees, had a novel definition of a cut: "a reduction of salary already contracted for." In other words, if a man had a two-year contract and his pay for the second year was reduced, that constituted a cut; but, according to Griffith, if the player was not yet under contract for the next year and could be persuaded to take less than the year before, that was not a cut, but just a simple business proposition. Ban Johnson implied that cuts were in order by saying that while the American League treated its players fairly, the men could not expect wartime salaries in peacetime.

Sporting News, which supported Robison's economy program and called for a wholesale one-third reduction in salaries, asserted that a big-league club's payroll should not exceed $35,000. In 1908 the same paper proposed a plan to keep salaries down by establishing a salary schedule for minor-leaguers entering the majors. For their first three years these men would become "wards" of the National Commission, which would handle their contracts during their apprenticeship. A player coming from a Class A minor league would start in the majors with a maximum of $1800 his first year and receive $300 increments in each of his two succeeding years. Class B players would start at $1500, and those below that at $1200; all would get the same increases. After the third year the salary would be up to the individual player and his club. The advantage of this plan, *Sporting News* pointed out, would be the practical elimination of high salaries, because few men lasted more than five years anyway. Nothing came of the suggestion, and for all the talk of cuts there was no concerted action to place limits on salaries, although one writer estimated that twelve of the sixteen clubs did institute reductions independently.

Figures on salaries before 1920 are as scarce as those on profits. With respect to finances, the baseball industry has traditionally operated behind what might be called a horsehide curtain of secrecy. The players of course have some idea about pay scales and doubtless discuss salaries among themselves; but if they knew precisely what each man was receiving, they would be more likely to make comparisons that might lead a good many of them to demand more money. In more recent times a great deal of publicity has been given the handful out of the entire industry who are in the hundred-thousand-dollar-or-higher bracket, so the public is left with the impression that ball players as a group are extremely well paid.

The historian can arrive at reasonably authentic data for the Commission era by putting together the few reliable figures that can be found and the many estimates scattered through newspapers, always taking into account that the latter are frequently inflated. A rookie starting out in the majors in that era could expect from $1500 to perhaps $2000. For example, pitcher Ray Fisher began with the Yankees in 1910 at $1500. Ty Cobb, in his first full season with Detroit, received the same. The Cincinnati Reds paid Al Bridwell $2100 in 1905 with a promise of $2400 if he made good, but when they offered him the same for 1906 he sent back the contract, so the club traded him to Boston. Rogers Hornsby has stated that he was paid only $1200 when he came up with the St. Louis Cardinals in 1915, but that was soon increased to $1500.

An established major-league regular made in the neighborhood of $3000 in those days. Outstanding players earned from $4000 to $5000. Johnny Kling signed for only $3500 with the Chicago Cubs in 1907, but he had the security of a three-year contract.

A handful of top-flight stars commanded still higher figures. After nine years in the National League, four of them on pennant winners, Three-Finger Brown's salary reached $7000 in 1912. Hal Chase, premier first baseman of his time, worked for $6000 in 1911, 1913, and 1914. Mathewson in his twelfth year with the Giants received $8000, and Walter Johnson, the best pitcher in the American League, drew $7000 in 1912 and 1913, and $10,000 in 1914. Cobb made $9000 for 1910 after winning the batting championship the two previous seasons. He was still being paid $9000 in 1912, although he had added two more batting crowns to his growing string.

The official itemized list of player salaries of the 1910 Cincinnati team reveals a total player payroll of $51,000 for nineteen men, which averages out to $2684. The salaries ranged from $1500 to $4200. The two highest salaries were $4200 and $4000; the two lowest, $1800 and $1500. Eight players made $3100 or more. (The manager himself received $10,000.) Less affluent clubs kept their payrolls considerably lower. Connie Mack, for instance, was highly praised for reportedly keeping his total at $36,000 for 1903. On the other hand, more prosperous teams, such as the New York Giants, were more generous. That is to say, a wide salary differential among players of comparable skill existed because of the disparity in club markets, congealed as they were in territorial rights—a disparity that increased as population in America shifted. Players fortunate enough to be on a pennant-winning team received extra money through sharing in the World Series gate receipts. Salaries in general showed improvements from 1910 onward, and talk of cuts diminished, at least until after another trade war had pushed salaries sharply up again.

On the face of it, these figures seem paltry compared with those of contemporary players, whose paychecks range from $12,500, the established major-league minimum, upward to more than $100,000 for a few stars. But the old-timer's dollar stretched a good deal farther. In 1913 one could order a steak dinner in a good New York restaurant for $1.25, plus a ten-cent tip. Good whiskey sold for $3.50 per gallon, and a fashionable five- to seven-room apartment rented for $50. Before World War One, the price of a Ford car fell as low as $360. No income tax ate into pay envelopes until 1913, and then it hardly nibbled at them, taking only one per cent on married persons' incomes in the $4000-to-$20,000 bracket.

Those who contended that ball players were overpaid liked to remind players of how much more they earned than they could have made in other occupations and that they worked shorter hours and only part of the year. Plainly, the gap between ball players and workers in general was wide. In the early years of the century the average earnings of American workers was roughly $525 a year. Steelworkers made about $700 annually in 1910, about $50 more than the average for all employees in manufacturing industries. Cotton-mill owners were paying their workers $251 a year.

But the comparison is largely irrelevant because ball players are a relatively scarce, highly skilled group. A more legitimate gauge is whether ball players have been rewarded in accordance with the earnings of the industry and its owners. Several recent economic studies of market conditions in Organized Baseball demonstrate that players have not been paid in proportion. By 1950 gross receipts of major-league clubs were eighty times what they were in 1883; yet the average major-leaguer's salary was only seven times as great. Furthermore, the percentage of major-league clubs' outlay that is spent for team salaries has steadily diminished. A nineteenth-century club could expect to devote more than 50 per cent to salaries; but by 1929 aggregate major-league team salaries amounted to only 35.3 per cent of total major-league expenses, and this share has continued to shrink, dropping to 32.4 per cent in 1939, 28.9 per cent in 1943, 24.8 per cent in 1946, and only 22.1 per cent by 1950.

The monopsony control that restricts the player's market for his services has in general had the effect of exploiting him, despite the owners' claim that players are paid the full value of their services. Owners who maintain that dissatisfied players are traded to other teams that will pay them more are evidently unaware that such an assertion undermines their basic defense of the reserve clause—that it is needed to prevent wealthy clubs that can afford higher salaries from snaring all the best players. Obviously, if dissatisfied players are really permitted to go where the high salaries are, then the restraint of the reserve is not needed.

In fact, the stereotyped argument that the reserve is necessary to keep players from gravitating to clubs able and willing to pay more is in itself a confession that some clubs are underpaying. Other things being equal, if all clubs were paying the players what they were worth, the reserve would not be needed to hold the men. A classic example, one of many such cases, is that of Walter Johnson, who would have made far more money had he not been tethered to a poor-paying club like Washington during his long career. *Sporting News* reported that when Johnson was having a salary dispute in 1911, there was a tacit understanding among American League magnates not to make an offer to Washington for him. While this agreement might seem like restraint of trade and coercion, the paper explained, the public would appreciate the advantages of baseball organization and this demonstration of "an element of fairness and consideration" toward the Washington club and its patrons.

Players dissatisfied with the pay offered them have sought redress by threatening to withhold their services. The resulting holdouts have sometimes been protracted and even bitter. A well-known pitcher, scorning a proffered $4000 salary representing an $800 raise, penciled a letter to his club owner in 1916 demanding $6000 and declaring that he wanted money, not the "glory" of pitching in the big leagues. He went on to express himself in terms worthy of a modern naturalistic novelist: "I see you want to give me a good fucking," but "I'll pick shit with the chickens before I'll play for any less. . . . I don't give a Dam [*sic*] to be in the big League unless I get something for my work."

He threatened to quit because "I won't stand to be fuck by no Jew S—B like . . . [the manager]." In his reply the owner reminded the player of the danger of sending such language through the mail. More restrained but nevertheless to the point was the approach of Edward Grant, infielder and practicing attorney: "You know . . . as well as I that baseball is a business proposition. We are in it for what we can get out of it. As far as a raise goes of course that is what I want." Another player argued that he needed more to make ends meet because of the increased cost of living in a big-league city.

Hall of Fame member Edd Roush was a repeated holdout and one of the most obstinate. Owner Garry Herrmann, appreciating his value to the Cincinnati team, confidentially enlisted the aid of emissaries to persuade Roush to sign in 1916. They pulled out all the stops in an effort to bring him in: he owed it to himself and his wife; he had a "brilliant future"; the team needed him, as the "large" offer ($4500) proved; he should consider "loyalty" to the team and the manager. In the end, Roush signed for $5000.

But the following spring the routine began all over again. In an interview not long ago, Roush told this author that the club tried to cut him back to $4500 and that Herrmann had admitted, "I know you're worth more but the directors don't want to pay it." Roush said he became angry and thought, "What the hell kind of a league is this?" Again Herrmann's emissaries went into action. One of them reported that Roush's talk about quitting baseball and buying a farm "is a Joke, This boy is to [sic] lazy to work on a farm, he prefers to sleep until noon, and then put on some old cloths [sic], and with a half dozen boys and three or four dogs lay around for the rest of the day." Herrmann's man soon gave up the assignment as a bad job: "I have handled several tough ones in my days, but he is the worst. The trouble with him is a lack of brains, if he had any gray matter in his head, he could be reasoned with, but he is as stubborn as a mule."

Another pet ploy of owners was to use spring training as leverage in dealing with holdouts: if the men did not sign they would lose their free trip to training camp. One story tells of an owner explaining to a holdout that, although his salary was cut $500, the club was paying for his training trip to California, and "just think of the grand scenery" he would see! The player supposedly replied, "I want my salary in money, not scenery. I appreciate the beautiful in nature and will take $50 worth of it, but I am not artistic enough to buy $500 worth of it all in one lump."

Owners also used the power of the reserve clause to pressure players who refused to sign their contracts. For example, John C. Lush was fined $200 for refusing to accept terms and for playing with an independent team. Another player, George Bell, held out the entire season against Brooklyn and was declared "ineligible" by the National Commission. He was reinstated for the next season but fined $200 for his temerity. The National Commission announced that "in future cases of a like character, the fine to be imposed will be increased from time to time, with a view of entirely breaking up this practice of players."

The most notorious case of this kind involved Ty Cobb and nearly resulted in a Congressional investigation of Organized Baseball. It presaged the holdout of the Los Angeles pitching pair, Sandy Koufax and Don Drysdale, in 1966.

Cobb and three other Detroit players joined forces after 1912, all refusing to sign until the club met their demands for pay raises. The holdout clique, as they were called, disintegrated by spring training time when three of them came to terms, leaving Cobb to carry on alone. Ty had just won his fifth straight American League batting title and was pressing owner Frank Navin for an increase to $15,000 from the $9000 he had received for each of the three previous seasons. Navin's answer was curt: "You will play for Detroit or you won't play for anybody and you will take what I offer."

Actually, both Cobb's and Sam Crawford's demands had been discussed informally at an American League meeting, evidently to weigh the impact that a firm stand by Navin would have on the public. It is also possible that the other owners were concerned lest the general level of salaries be forced upward should those two players succeed in winning salaries appreciably higher than the top ones being paid at the time.

The quarrel dragged on, both parties unyielding. When the season started and Cobb did not report, Navin suspended him. The National Commission, in accordance with the rules, placed him on the "ineligible" list for failure to sign a contract and thus ensured that no other team in Organized Baseball would employ him. The prominence accorded the dispute in the newspapers drove home to many people some of the less ennobling aspects of Organized Baseball. Senator Hoke Smith and Representative Thomas Hardwick of Georgia, Cobb's home state, requested a copy of his contract and called for a Congressional investigation.

With mutterings about the Sherman Anti-Trust Act sounding in Congress, Navin reached a compromise with Cobb, who signed for $11,332.55. The National Commission quickly reinstated him as of May 1. It imposed only a token $50 fine but reprimanded him severely both for his behavior in the recent holdout and for his public conduct in the more remote past as well.

Talk of the episode lingered in Congress. Representative Thomas Gallagher of Illinois introduced a resolution instructing the Speaker of the House to appoint a seven-man commission to investigate Organized Baseball as a "predacious and mendacious trust." Members of the National Commission and some club owners immediately issued separate statements expressing a common theme: there was no baseball trust, and an investigation would be welcomed. *Sporting News* hinted that Gallagher had political motives and suggested that an investigation of the baseball trust would show all the good it had done. The editor opined that Congress could find better things to do with its time:

> Thieving corporations may rob the public of its domain, hired thugs may shoot down poor working men who dare to ask a living wage, women may be forced to the dive and gutter by an industrial system that regards human bodies as only material to be ground into dividends, little children may be made to work 14 hours a day until hands bleed and bodies wilt . . . but these matters can wait.

Instead of looking into these abuses, Congress, scoffed the editor, proposed to devote its time to an investigation of "slaves" who worked two hours a day, traveled on Pullmans, and stopped at the best hotels. But a Cincinnati *Enquirer* headline read:

THE OLD ALIBI
Being Put Forward to Stall Off
Baseball Investigation

Nothing came of Gallagher's proposal. His resolution died in committee.

Another source of dispute between players and owners was a special contract sometimes used for rookies for the purpose of limiting their salaries. This "probationary" contract provided for a 45-day trial period during which the player was to be paid, at the discretion of the owner, up to 25 per cent more than his previous minor-league salary. If retained after the probationary period, such a player was supposed to be tendered a regular, uniform major-league contract. Sometimes magnates either neglected to offer a new contract or led a player to believe he was not entitled to one, and thus the man played out the balance of the season for less money than he should have received. On the other hand, the player sometimes was under the mistaken impression that the probationary contract entitled him to a full 25 per cent increase over his minor-league salary.

Salary disputes, no matter how vehement, remain essentially rearguard actions. But the player does have some defenses. The club

management can hardly beat down salaries to the extent of having a
squad of discontented ball players on its hands or to the point of losing a favorite player and alienating fans. Still, the bargaining positions of player and owner are unequal, for in the final analysis the
player must either sign with his club or leave the profession, since he
cannot sell his services to any other team in Organized Baseball.° An
early owner was painfully frank on this point: "He will report to this
club, or if there are any good peanut stands in the city where he
lives, perhaps he would prefer peddling peanuts."

Owners had long since engaged in selling and trading players, or,
more technically, transferring the exclusive right to employ a man, a
right rooted in the reserve clause. Consequently, a heavy traffic in
selling and trading player contracts is to this day an integral part of
the industry. There are many reasons for this brisk business. The most
common one is the hope of strengthening the team, and if the exchange of players turns out to be a fair one, all the clubs involved
benefit, as in any fair trade. A club may sell a player for cash, particularly if it is in financial straits; or it may want to get rid of high-salaried or obstreperous men. The practice is also a means of stimulating
interest by introducing new faces and holding the fans' attention, particularly in the off-season when even rumors of deals are fuel for the
so-called hot-stove league. Ethnic considerations may enter in. In
1907 an owner suggested that men with Irish names be sent to Boston, where they would be popular, and Germans to Cincinnati, for
the same reason. Players have also been swapped for a bird dog, a
turkey, and for use of a playing field in spring training—instances
that call to mind Shevchenko's painting of a Russian landowner ex-
changing his serfs for hunting dogs.

Personal animosity caused the trade of pitcher Jack Harper from
Cincinnati to Chicago. After Harper hit Frank Chance, Chicago manager, in the head with a pitched ball, Chance vowed to force Harper
out of baseball. He did it by persuading the Chicago owner, Charles
Murphy, to take Harper in a trade and then cut his salary from the
$4500 he had been getting with Cincinnati to $1500. Chance, a power
in the club as manager and stockholder, told Harper he could sign or
quit. Harper signed, but was kept on the bench. After staying on for a
while and appealing unsuccessfully to the National Commission, he
left baseball.

Under the contract he is obliged to sign, a player recognizes the
club's right to assign his services where it chooses,°° so the possibility

---

° The success of Curt Flood in breaking through the reserve restriction in
1970 may be heralding a change in this situation.
  °° For an exception, see below, chapter 11.

of being shipped almost any place at any time hangs over him. The club is not even bound to consult him on his destination. About the only protection he has against being sold, bartered, or released out-right is public sentiment, which sometimes makes it expedient for an owner to retain a popular hero long past his usefulness. Yet players have managed to live with the insecurity attendant upon their jobs. At any rate, few have declined, at least publicly, to go where they were sent. It is not the law of the land, however, that persuades them to keep their agreements; the courts have been reluctant to compel compliance because the Constitution of the United States prohibits involuntary servitude. Rather, it is the extra-legal threat of Organized Baseball's blacklist that induces players to accept the quasi-chattel or indentured status to which the industry reduces them.

Naturally the owners wanted to pay as little as possible for players. They might give out large figures for their publicity value and to cre-ate the impression that they were spending heavily to build a win-ning team for the fans. But their understandable desire as business-men to keep prices in check sometimes led to collusion: "Confidentially, at any time you and I are after the same player, I would be more than pleased to get in touch with you so we will not enter into any bidding match . . . as I do not think the prices minor league players are being held at are within reason at all." In a case with a different slant, one owner wrote another to say that he was planning to try out two minor-league pitchers in a forthcoming series against the other owner's club, and asked if his manager would ob-serve them in action and report confidentially whether the two were worth the prices asked. John T. Brush, hearing that a pitcher was up for trade, requested that the Giants be given a chance to obtain him because, he said, "I believe it is a good financial proposition to keep this club well to the front, for the money it will distribute to all club members of the League." Boston Braves' owner George B. Dovey went so far as to suggest a national clearinghouse to handle the sale of ball players at a fixed price scale; the National Commission could then distribute them among the clubs impartially. Nothing came of this proposal because it smacked too much of syndicate ball.

So did "loaning" players from one club to another in the same league. To give one example, in 1905 the Boston Nationals needed a catcher, and Cincinnati lent them Gabby Street. After catching three games, he returned to Cincinnati. There were even written loaning agreements that defined the terms of such transactions. Although the practice violated the rules and was often criticized in the newspapers, it persisted. In 1916 one major-league club was interested in securing a good minor-league prospect owned by Brooklyn. Ebbets refused to

sell him but offered to lend him to the other club for the balance of
the season, after which he would revert to Brooklyn. There was also
an instance of one minor-league team renting a player to another
team; the fifty-dollar "raise" the player received from his new club
went not to him but to the team that hired him out. The National
Commission called this incident "one of the pettiest and most perni-
cious acts of speculation in players" that ever came to its attention.

As a rule, players did not share in the sales price of their contracts.
There were exceptions, however, particularly if a man was advancing
to a team in a higher classification. Knowledge that he was bringing a
high price encouraged a player to demand a portion for himself, and
some were successful in this.

There were other practices that grated on the player. He might be
peddled to another team with a cut in salary or be forced to pay traveling expenses to his new employer; he might lose pay between assignments because of the stalling tactics of the new owner in offering
him a contract; he might have to stand the cost of new uniforms several times over, depending on how many times he was traded in a
season. A spray of cases illustrates some of these difficulties. Boston
immediately lowered infielder David Brain's salary after getting him
from Pittsburgh in 1906. Connie Mack offered Clarence Russell
$1800—less than he had been receiving in the minor leagues; Russell
held out all winter, and finally Mack raised him to $2400. James
Wiggs left Organized Baseball in 1905 because he was so disgusted
when Charles Ebbets offered him less to play with Brooklyn than he
was being paid in the minors. The National Commission, which later
removed Wiggs from the blacklist, vouchsafed that:

> While there is no rule on the subject, it has been and should be
> the custom that when a player advances from a minor league to a
> major league, he is to receive a reasonable increase in salary; and a
> major league club that does not conform to this custom is not deserv-
> ing of much recognition at the hands of the Commission.
>   . . . the player was forced into his position by the action of the
> Brooklyn Club.

But it was chiefly players demoted from a big-league club to the minors who were victimized by these in-season salary deductions. They
were often sent down without being told what their new salary would
be or even that a cut was in the offing. The fact that the minor-league
season generally terminated a month earlier than the major leagues
meant that the player was out that much more money in addition to
the cut he had taken. When Clark Griffith, the Reds' manager,
learned that one of his players, sent to an American Association club,

faced a sharp pay cut, he offered to take the player back if the minor-league team could not pay the same salary, because, he said, "I
don't think its [sic] fair to a ball player to be put out in the middle
of the season & then chopped. . . ." And there were instances of
other owners who felt as Griffith did and tried to rectify matters by
giving the demoted player a lump sum to help make up the salary
differential.

Referring to a similar case, that of W. J. Ingerton, Ban Johnson
stated, "It is plain to be seen that this man has been a victim of a
very bad practice, which we are now trying to eliminate from Professional Ball. We cannot permit such injustice to a player, and will, in
my judgment, be obliged to take some action to give him relief." The
Cleveland club, which controlled Ingerton, shifted him from one minor-league team to another in a lower classification in order to use
him as the pawn in a three-cornered trade, with the understanding
that Ingerton would continue to receive the same salary, $175 a
month. Meanwhile, the assignee club was shifted to another league
with a lower salary scale, which meant that Ingerton was offered less
money. His appeal, which elicited Johnson's statement, was successful, and he was returned to the higher minor-league club. These and
other similar rulings by the National Commission show that the players were not wholly without means of redress.

The case of Arthur Hofman is one of a number of instances in
which the Civil Courts refused to uphold so-called "baseball law" regarding assignment of players. Hofman contracted to play for the
Chicago Cubs for $5000 in 1912 and then was transferred during the
season to Pittsburgh, which club sent him to a minor league where he
received less money. He later sued for the difference and succeeded
in winning a judgment of $2944.47 from an Illinois Court of Appeals
in 1915.

With respect to the expense of traveling from one club to another
when a player was sold or traded, the National Commission's policy
was that the releasing club should pay the fare and then be reimbursed by the club the player joined. But clubs did not always comply, especially in minor leagues, where players sometimes had to foot
the bill of a long trip or even sit at home because they lacked the
money to join the club to which they were assigned. Special hardship
fell on players left in limbo between two or three clubs without salary
and without knowing who owned them or who was responsible for
paying them. This happened to Albert Kellogg. Connie Mack had
strings on this player, who was shuttled between two minor-league
teams. None of the three clubs involved accepted responsibility for
paying him, and despite the fact that he had a contract, he went

without salary after July 20. In his plea to the National Commission, Kellogg wrote: "I earn my living playing baseball and I have others depending on me I have lost you might as well say the whole summer which means a lot to me. You can see by the case that I have been used pretty rotten." Kellogg died four years later, and one wonders what became of those dependents of his in the days before comprehensive social legislation.

Players were not always scrupulous about money matters either. Boston sent Sam Frock to Atlanta and quite properly advanced him money for transportation, including berth and meals. Instead, Frock used the money to go to Baltimore, his home town, and stay there a while. Atlanta suspended him, and when he finally did report, he managed to collect from his new club the cost of traveling from Baltimore to Atlanta. When Boston sought reimbursement from the Atlanta club, the latter balked. The National Commission ruled that Atlanta had to refund Boston's money and then collect from the player the extra money it had paid him.

If the players are to realize the most from their careers, they must have a genuine opportunity to progress to the league of the highest classification in which they are capable of playing, and to receive salary increases commensurate with their progress. The National Agreement of 1903 recognized this principle and subscribed to the "promotion of the welfare of ball players as a class by developing and perfecting them in their profession and enabling them to secure adequate compensation for expertness." Yet the reserve clause, if applied in its logical extreme, without limitations or safeguards, would make it possible to confine a man to a low minor league for the duration of his playing days. Such total application of the reserve is, however, tempered by such measures as the draft and waiver rules. The former is a forced sale, by means of which a club in a higher classification can bring up a player from one in a lower league at a fixed price. The latter rule requires that before a club can send a man down, it must first get all the other clubs in its classification to "waive" claim to him. Ostensibly, the first rule facilitates a player's advance, and the second brakes his descent.

These slowly evolved measures were not instituted for the benefit of the players; they sprang from the desire of major-league owners to assure themselves an open market in which to secure talent. Benefits redounding to the players were by-products, which were important aids to them nonetheless and might have been more valuable had the owners always honored their own rules. The fact is that as fast as such regulations were established, major-league club owners figured out ways to evade them in order to engross as many players as possible, while the National Commission toiled to plug the loopholes that the owners so assiduously searched out.

To begin with, the National Agreement of 1903 stipulated a $500 fine on any club that "becomes a party to a conspiracy to prevent a player from advancing in his profession, or in any way abusing the privilege of selection." This threatened penalty did not deter the magnates, who employed more dodges to beat the rules than a sidewalk peddler without a license.

A minor-league owner who wanted to prevent higher-classification clubs from picking his players during the brief drafting period would "sell" his promising players to a big-league club, which would hold them until the drafting period was safely over; then the minor-league club "repurchased" them. For collaborating in keeping these players off the market—"covering up," as it was called—the major-league club received certain favors, such as the pick of the minor-league club's players the following season, or free use of its spring-training facilities, or even the sale of surplus baseballs to the minor-league ally. Some big-league owners simply collected a commission for the service rendered.

Or the process might be reversed, with the big-league owner drafting a bevy of minor-leaguers to keep other owners from getting them during the drafting period; the following spring, after taking his pick, he returned the rest of the players to the minor-league club. Some magnates drafted players not because they needed them or had any intention of using them, but just to sell them at a profit. One boasted of making a tidy $27,000 profit from peddling players in this manner. Either way, the player's progress was subordinated to the interests of the owners. The Commission tried to check this abuse by passing a rule in 1911 requiring a declaration of bona fide desire for the player on the part of the club president and threatening a fine equal to the draft price if the declaration proved false.

So pervasive was covering up that there is no lack of examples. The route between Brooklyn and Baltimore became familiar to many players when, in the first years of the century, Ned Hanlon combined management and a 10 per cent interest in the former club with the controlling interest in the latter. Unlike some other magnates who did not even go through the formalities, Hanlon took care to make these player journeys between the two cities appear bona fide by filing the appropriate documents and making out checks, although not a penny actually changed hands. One player victimized by this sort of juggling jumped to an "outlaw" club. Subsequently he applied for reinstatement and charged that he had been "the victim of a conspiracy" between the Baltimore and Brooklyn clubs in that Hanlon had "covered up" his Baltimore players with Brooklyn to prevent their being drafted by other major-league clubs. After twice rejecting his petition, the National Commission finally decided that an injustice might have been done and that the player had been punished sufficiently, adding, "We believe that it [is] far better for the Commission to make a dozen mistakes in the reinstatement of a player than to make one mistake by placing the ban on any player, when the facts in connection therewith do not fully warrant it."

Another well-worn trail connected Milwaukee and Comiskey's Chicago White Sox. Before the drafting season began, half a dozen of Milwaukee's best prospects would find their way to Chicago and would then make the return trip the following spring. Both Comiskey and another of his minor-league friends, the New Orleans club, were fined for one of these bogus transactions, and mention has previously been made of penalties imposed upon Connie Mack and Charles Ebbets for similar violations.

These shenanigans were doubly detrimental: they not only retarded the player's progress but also deprived clubs of the services of men they might have used. If, for example, a major-league team "drafted" a man from Class B, covered him up, and then returned him, it cheated the man out of a chance to advance in the profession and also deprived a Class A club that might have drafted him legitimately for its own use.

It was only to be expected that minor-league teams would endeavor to save their good prospects from forced sale in order to sell them at competitive prices, especially when one considers that players could be drafted from Class A, B, C, and D clubs for $750, $500, $300, and $200 respectively. An exception was that not more than two men could be selected from a Class A team in any one year. A modification of this rule in 1906 allowed only one man to be drafted from such clubs. This change forecast the whole future course of the draft —increasing exemptions, together with steadily rising prices—a trend that meant diminishing opportunities for players to advance via this channel.

The waiver rule, too, was conceived primarily in the owners' interest; its purpose was to aid the other clubs in a league by giving them first chance to acquire a surplus player from a fellow owner at a fixed price before letting him be sent to another league. Its effect could also be to ensure a player the opportunity of performing in the highest classification of which he was capable.

The chief invitation to abuse of the waiver rule in National Commission days lay in the fact that, during most seasons, major-league clubs could ask for and revoke waivers on a man as often as they liked. This left the way open for clubs to ask waivers on a man merely to test the market—to find out who wanted him and how badly. The request would then be withdrawn, and an attempt would be made to sell him for more than the waiver price to an owner whose refusal to waive claim to the player indicated that he was interested. The most common evil arose from the desire to hold onto a surplus player by slipping him out of the league to a friendly minor-league club. In this case a magnate who had refused to grant waivers was prevailed upon to let the player pass to a lower league in exchange for a promise to return the favor in the future. These "gentlemen's agreements," as one major-league official said, amounted to "I will kiss you today and you kiss me tomorrow," and made the waiver rule a joke.

Another misuse of the rule was to frighten a man into playing harder by putting him up for waivers. One hapless player whose work improved after this scare treatment was fined $100 on the ground that his improvement was evidence that previously he had not been giving his best! At times a player was not informed when waivers had been asked on him, or even when they had been secured. Or an owner might claim a man at the bargain waiver price, not to use him on his own club, but simply to sell him for more to another team. And there were instances in which an owner ignored the rule altogether and simply assigned a man to a lower league.

The waiver rule was also used for punishment. When Brooklyn players Mike Mowrey and Ollie O'Mara balked at sharp salary cuts, Ebbets determined to teach them a lesson by banishing them to the minors. He wrote all other National League club owners: "I particularly request that you promptly waive on these players in order that I may properly discipline them. Please keep this strictly confidential."

At first waivers were intra-league only; a big-league club therefore needed to obtain them only from the clubs in its own league before assigning a player elsewhere. Indeed it took several years, until the scars of their recent war had healed sufficiently, before the two major leagues felt inclined to deal with each other at all in players.

Then, in hopes of making the railroading of a player to the minor leagues through a gentleman's agreement more difficult, the National Commission broadened the rule in 1905 to require that all clubs of both major leagues and intermediate leagues be given an opportunity to claim players drafted or purchased the previous year before they could be sent to a lower league. This extension of the rule was incorporated into the National Agreement of 1912, and two years later a further extension covered all players assigned to minor leagues. But subversions of the waiver rule still did not cease.

"Farming" was another means of keeping players from reaching the top as rapidly as they might otherwise have done. This practice points up the conflicting motives that tugged at the club owners. On the one hand, it was to the owners' interest that all players capable of playing in the big leagues be made available through a free market and that they be spread among the different clubs by limiting the number each club could have. This policy would make for keen competition, close pennant races, and large attendance. On the other hand, the individual owner normally tried to make his club stronger than the others by collecting good ball players and storing them with some friendly or subsidiary minor-league club, to be held there against future need. The effect of this "farming" of men was to retard the advancement of players who were ready for the big leagues and who might have been useful to some other major-league team.

Because the evils of farming were so widespread, the authors of the National Agreement of 1903 explicitly banned it, and, by inference, the ownership of one club by another as well. But once again the ingenuity of the owners proved more than equal to the challenge. The New York Giants in 1905 obtained approval of a so-called working agreement, under which they sent their surplus players to a minor-league club in return for having the pick of its men at the end of the season. The breach was further widened by Charles Ebbets who, according to E. S. Barnard, one-time president of the American League, conceived the idea of skirting the no-farming rule by "selling" a player to a minor-league club with an "option" to "repurchase" him. So flagrant did this subterfuge become that the National Commission felt impelled to take steps to keep it at least within bounds. In 1907 it ordered that a player could be optioned out only once. The following year it added the requirement that a minimum of $300 must be paid for an optioned player who was repurchased, because major-league clubs were using the Commission's limited approval of options to sell and buy back players at nominal figures.

Again in 1911 the Commission made a further effort to hold the line by ordering that no more than eight players could be optioned out at one time. This ruling was in response to complaints from the minor leagues that option sales made it more difficult for them to acquire players not needed by major-league clubs. In fact, some minor leagues prohibited their clubs from accepting players on optional assignments, a prohibition overruled by the National Commission in 1912. Nevertheless, the Commission realized that some curbs were necessary to prevent major-league clubs from securing a player monopoly by means of the option loophole in the no-farming ban; hence the eight-man limit. But in a few years Jacob Ruppert of the Yankees wanted the number raised from eight to fifteen, with permission to option five of them for two years. And, like the waiver rule, the option rule was sometimes simply disregarded. Ebbets, for instance, sent outfielder "Hi" Myers down and recalled him three times in 1912.

Meanwhile, indefatigable major-league owners encroached deeper on the free market by acquiring outright ownership of minor-league clubs. For example, Ebbets, taking a leaf from Hanlon's earlier book, took over the Newark International League club, and Cleveland acquired Toledo of the American Association, these clubs to be used as supply depots and training centers for player reinforcements.

The result of these incursions on the free market showed up clearly in figures revealed in the National Commission's sixth annual report of 1909. Two clubs, Brooklyn and Cleveland, controlled 61 and 60 players respectively; six other clubs owned 50 or more men each; whereas the three lowest clubs averaged only half the top two—an imbalance that boded ill for player advancement as well as for competition.

Still endeavoring to halt this trend, the National Commission made two additional moves. It succeeded in convincing major-league clubs to follow the minor leagues and adopt player limits restricting the total number of men they could control and the number they could carry on their active rosters. Accordingly, the revised National Agreement of 1912 restricted major-league clubs to 35 players, except that between May 15 and August 20 they could have no more than 25 on their active lists. In addition, the National Commission in May 1913 circulated a confidential bulletin to all major-league clubs declaring that ownership of a minor-league club was "antagonistic of the rights of other major league clubs to recruit their teams and preventive of the promotion of players." It therefore directed major-league clubs to dispose of such holdings by January 1, 1914.

Minor leagues also helped clog the progress of players. In their own player transactions with lower leagues, high minor clubs mimicked the majors' methods of circumvention. To avoid the major-league draft, Class B, C, and D clubs, on their part, "sold" players to Class A clubs on option—but for future delivery, meanwhile retaining their services.

Thus it was that both major- and minor-league owners largely nullified the draft, waiver, player-limitation, and no-farming rules, modifications of the reserve clause which, if allowed to function freely, would have done much to ameliorate the restrictions that the clause imposed on the market and hence on the players. Moreover, this sidestepping of the rules was to increase as the National Commission's grip on baseball affairs loosened toward the end of its regime, and, as we shall see, owners of a new era extended and perfected methods of bypassing the rules.

Questions of salary and contracts are not the whole of labor-management relations in baseball any more than elsewhere. The nature of the player's work, emphasizing as it does physical fitness and the twin pressures of competition and constant exposure to the public, necessitates a certain amount of supervision and control on and off the field. Ball players are no worse and probably a lot better behaved than some other groups that could be mentioned, but few would mistake them for Salvation Army battalions disguised in knickers and flannels. Instances of fighting, rowdyism, and extra-curricular capers in National Commission days have already been described. Many more could be mentioned to underscore the need for disciplinary measures by the owners and their agents. One trouble was that players were not sure how far they could go. They were expected to be scrappy and aggressive on the field, but they were not always certain where to draw the line. The experience of one player serves to point up the dilemma. Instructed by his manager to "kick and kick hard," and assured that any fine that resulted would be remitted, he followed orders, only to learn that the club would not remit the fine after all. One owner, in a directive to his players in which he deplored rowdyism, tried to clarify the issue: "Rowdyism is not aggressiveness. The former will not be tolerated, while the latter is demanded."

Each club generally had its own rules regarding curfew, card- and dice-playing, drinking, and the like. The number of strictures and the rigidity with which they were enforced depended a good deal on the personality of the individual manager. However, in a kind of throwback to the paternalism of the nineteenth century, the National League adopted a uniform set of rules in 1917 governing all the players in the league. In addition to the usual requirements, this blanket code included the warning that players "guilty in public of gross misbehavior, including intoxication, fighting, quarreling, indecency, or any scandalous conduct" would be penalized with fines, suspension without pay, or both. Of course league presidents continued to inflict punishments for misconduct on the field, such as brawling or arguing with umpires.

The clubs dealt out the same kind of punishment. Players could be fined arbitrarily for any number of reasons—indifferent playing, dissipation, insubordination, or missing a train. George Stovall was suspended in 1907 for throwing a chair at his manager. The rub was that however necessary disciplinary measures were, abuses occurred. The editor of *Sporting News* charged that players were sometimes suspended to make room for more men on the club and thus circumvent

the player limit. Players felt abused when they were punished for re-
taliating against hostile fans, because they believed the owners were
lax in protecting them from their tormentors.

Teams hired detectives to keep tabs on the players in their hours of
leisure. The standard rate was five dollars a day for "shadows" and
six dollars for "investigators." A letter from a detective agency soliciting business read:

> In your employ you have a number of high-salaried players, whose
> efficiency means everything to your team, and who, when they are in
> a city like New York, find it hard to resist temptation, and conse-
> quently go out to see the sights which results in their not being in
> proper condition to do themselves justice when called upon to play.
>
> We can give you the best of service should you wish any member
> or members shadowed.

It went on to claim that banking, financial, and other institutions
used its services because "it pays them to know how their employees
comport themselves"—evidence that snooping and invasion of pri-
vacy are not new.

Though players could lose money in fines, it was also possible for
them to earn bonuses for unusually good work. A pitcher's contract
might stipulate an extra $1000 if he won 20 games. Bonuses for sign-
ing were also awarded. Ben De Mott, for instance, told me he was
paid $2500 for leaving college to sign with Cleveland. And, as al-
ready indicated, a player sold to another club might receive a bonus
to make him agreeable to the transfer. But special incentives came
under increasing criticism from managers. A pitcher striving to earn a
bonus might demand to pitch when he was not sufficiently rested,
and, conversely, there were cases in which pitchers on the verge of
qualifying for a bonus were kept from starting further games to prevent them from earning it. Bonuses also might breed jealousy and dissension, to the detriment of teamwork. So managers gradually came
to oppose these special deals.

Friction between the players and their clubs also developed out of
the players' efforts to make extra money. Famous players could pick
up additional income by endorsing various products. Posing for ciga-
rette cards dated from the nineteenth century, despite the fact that
some managers frowned upon cigarettes as a "batting-eye destroyer."
In the early 1900's an ad claimed that Ty Cobb kept a case of Coca
Cola in the dugout to prevent fatigue, and Larry Lajoie was quoted
in another Coke ad: "The other ball players can drink all the whiskey, beer, and wine they want, but none of that for me." Both these
stars also testified to the health-giving properties of Nuxated Iron,

and Dazzy Vance allowed his name to be used to sell "Dazzy Vance's Grandstand Green" paint. Judging from the advertisements, quipped *Sporting News*, Eddie Collins was quite an authority on a variety of products, including the best brand in baseball gloves, chewing gum, tobacco, and soft drinks.

Difficulties arose when players went in for activities of which owners disapproved, such as allowing ghostwritten stories to appear under their names, playing exhibition games on their own, or participating in other sports after the baseball season. From about 1911 on, it was quite common for famous players and some team managers to sell the use of their names over stories they had "written." One newspaper jibed that players must all be carrying pencils, and suggested that instead of writing "how I did this" and "how I did that" they stick to playing and leave the writing to the writers. Christy Mathewson should have heeded this advice. He and the other Giants pitcher, Marquard, "covered" the World Series of 1911, the one in which Home Run Baker got his nickname. After Baker helped beat the Giants with a home run off Marquard in the second game, there appeared in Matty's column an indiscreet censure of his teammate for pitching incorrectly to the Athletics' batter. The next day it was Matty's turn to face the Athletics. In the ninth inning Baker blasted a second home run that tied the game and returned the embarrassed Matty to mere mortality.

At length Ban Johnson, in response to the increasing complaints of sportswriters that the intrusion of players into their field belittled trained writers in the eyes of the public, asked the owners to put an end to the players' so-called journalism in syndicated dailies. The National Commission followed through by forbidding players eligible for the 1913 World Series or any city series that year to write or pretend to write any accounts of the games.

Complications arose from the fact that some of the players had already signed contracts with newspapers to "write" about the World Series. At first the National Commission threatened fines and even cancellation of the Series. Then it shifted its ground and decided to exempt players who could prove they had contracted with newspapers previous to the ban, announcing, however, that the players' Series money would be withheld until the whole matter was settled. In the end the players were paid their money, but the Commission prohibited them from working with ghost writers thenceforth. The custom persisted nevertheless; the Commission overlooked it and even the sportswriters relented in their opposition.

Owners tried to prevent their athletes from playing basketball and taking part in other sports in the winter, for fear of injuries. A contemporary cartoon exaggerated the lengths to which the owners might go in their prohibitions by showing one player caught in the dreadful act of playing croquet and another turning down membership in a pinochle club.

The magnates were also apprehensive over possible damage to their investments should their hired hands suffer injury on barnstorming expeditions. Nor did they relish the loss of face for the major leagues inflicted by motley groups of professionals advertising themselves as the world champion this or that, or masquerading under the name of a major-league club and then getting trounced by bush-league aggregations or, even more humiliating, by Cuban teams. "We want no makeshift Club calling themselves the Athletics," declared Ban Johnson, "to go to Cuba to be beaten by colored teams." Johnson and his compeers doubtless sensed that people might have second thoughts about Organized Baseball's segregation policy if dark-skinned Cuban clubs, many of them sprinkled with players from American Negro teams, could beat the vaunted white major-leaguers. Was it not enough that Jack Johnson was the heavyweight boxing champion of the world?

For a time, individual owners were left to cope with these extra-curricular activities as they saw fit, and some of them attempted to halt these junkets by writing prohibitions into their player contracts. In 1910 the owners tried a twelve-month contract, which had long been under discussion, to control their players' activities all year round. That fall the National Commission thrust itself into the problem to forestall a barnstorming project. A Cincinnati promoter, Daniel A. Fletcher, recruited a group of major-league players by offering them $500 to $1000 apiece in advance. He planned to split them into two teams and send them off to play each other that fall. The National Commission received the news with disquiet. How dare this interloper meddle with Organized Baseball's prime talent? All ball parks in Organized Baseball were ordered closed to Fletcher's troupe, and those players who had succumbed to his blandishments were persuaded to return his checks. The project was crushed before it got started, but Fletcher would be heard from again.

The Commission, having taken hold of this problem, incorporated into the uniform contract of 1914 a provision barring players from participating in exhibition baseball games, softball, basketball, or football without prior consent of the club. But the opportunity to cash in on name and fame proved too enticing, particularly to World Series teams. For example, the White Sox and the Giants, opponents in the 1917 Series, were all set to embark upon some exhibition games after the Series, but the National Commission gave them pause by announcing it would withhold $1000 of their Series shares as guarantee against such a violation. Only after they signed statements agreeing to forgo the planned exhibitions did the players receive their money. Nevertheless, the desire to supplement their salaries through baseball exhibitions and by participation in other sports was so strong that the problem continued to obtrude upon the magnates in the years ahead.

In those days ball players, as well as other workers, were without what are now called fringe benefits. As in the nineteenth century, there were still a good many players who could not last through the winter without advances on their next season's salary, let alone think about extras. They generally asked for anywhere from fifty to several hundred dollars to tide them over till spring. The St. Louis Browns advanced $1223.63 to Rube Waddell, most of it for alimony payments in his divorce suit. In fact, the sale of the club to Phil Ball later was complicated by the discovery that Robert Hedges, the former owner, had staked players to several thousand dollars. Officially, most clubs opposed the custom of advancing money, but they never quite succeeded in abolishing it. With the Giants, McGraw took care of the problem by advancing hundreds of dollars out of his own pocket. Joe Vila, the sportswriter, credited Ned Hanlon with equal generosity—at 10 per cent interest! In words dripping with bathos, *Sporting News* pictured a bleak winter scene in the home of a player denied an advance on his salary:

> Blackness reigns where once those beautiful pictures of Christmas felicity floated. The sprightliness and bonhomme [*sic*] of the man has disappeared and even the pet dog is afraid to go near him. The wife sings no longer the sweet carols of the happy Yuletide as she does her housework. . . . The baby on the kitchen floor feels the gloom that its infant mind can not comprehend.

The old question of whether or not to pay players forced out of the lineup by illness or injury remained unsettled. Contrary to popular belief, injuries are more common in baseball than they are in games of body contact. Serious injuries may not be frequent, although baseball has had its share of these; but the incidence of lesser injuries is much greater. The season is long, and few escape a sore arm, pulled muscle, sprained ankle, twisted knee, or split finger somewhere along the line. And since baseball is a game of finesse and fine timing, a slight injury, even a blister, is often enough to sideline a man.

In the days when the old common-law notion of personal responsibility for injuries still held, ball players who got hurt, particularly minor-leaguers, might find themselves suspended and removed from the payroll. The many appeals that flowed into the National Commission no doubt encouraged it to declare in 1912 that injury was no cause to suspend a player without pay and that the clubs should either pay injured men in full or release them outright. On the other hand, major-leaguers were often kept on the payroll even though sidelined for lengthy periods. A case in point was that of Arthur Fromme, a Cincinnati pitcher. The club granted his request at the end of July for a leave of absence for the remainder of the season because of illness and agreed to pay him $200 a month, provided that he worked himself back into condition. The arrangement turned out well for both player and club. Fromme came back the following season and pitched well for several years.

Spurred by the danger of injuries on the field and by several narrow escapes of teams in railroad wrecks, clubs began to purchase accident insurance. In 1909 Detroit took out a policy covering its players when they were off the diamond, including double-indemnity coverage when on public conveyances. The entire Brooklyn team and its owners were insured for more than $200,000 in 1913. Boston insured the whole team against accidents off the field and some of its players for accidents on the field as well. In 1921 Cincinnati took out a total of $150,000 in accident insurance on its players. By 1913, the Aetna Life Insurance Company claimed eight big-league clubs and one minor-league team among its customers, perhaps because its president was none other than Morgan G. Bulkeley, who had been the first president of the National League in 1876.

Few ball players made enough money to save for old age, and many of them were reduced in their declining years to dependence on handouts from old friends in baseball or on small jobs as gatekeepers or watchmen at ball parks. When Ezra Sutton, a veteran of eighteen years in the major leagues, died destitute in 1907, a sportswriter suggested that some kind of pension be set up for players. Ban Johnson more than once recommended that a relief fund for indigent players be established out of World Series receipts. Several other baseball men proposed a home for aged players. But these ideas went unfulfilled until a later day. Players also resented the inconsiderate treatment sometimes given veterans. After years of service they could be shunted unceremoniously to the minors, like rookies without any say-so in the matter, as was Three-Finger Brown.

This unfeeling attitude precipitated what amounted to a one-day strike by the Cleveland players in 1911. Their teammate, Addie Joss, had died just as they were about to open the season. Although they were scheduled to play Detroit on the day of the funeral, the Cleveland players petitioned for the day off so they could attend. But, anticipating that they would be turned down, the whole team took off for Cleveland without waiting for an answer. Ban Johnson denied that a strike had occurred and said that the game would be played later. During the season, however, the Cleveland club sponsored a highly successful benefit game for Joss's widow. In soliciting support for the game, Vice-President Barnard recognized that players like Joss "have been a very important factor in the general advancement of the game during the past ten years" and that "every major league owner profited indirectly" from his "gentlemanly deportment" and popularity. The club stood the expense of the game so that the total receipts of $12,931.60 could go to Mrs. Joss.

The abuses and discontents over which the players were brooding instigated and sustained another attempt, the third, to form a union. It was not the strike of the Detroit players in 1912 over Ty Cobb's suspension that precipitated the formation of the union, as is usually claimed. The reverse is nearer the truth: it is more likely that the existence of a player organization emboldened the men to strike, rather than that the strike led to the formation of the union. For union talk was simmering at least as early as 1910, and by September of that year the organization was far enough along for *Sporting News* to run an editorial listing purported demands of the players. In February 1912, months before the Cobb strike occurred, David Fultz replied in *Baseball Magazine* to a scathing attack by *Sporting Life*'s editor on the players and their organization. In November Fultz published another article reviewing the shortcomings of Organized Baseball from the point of view of the players.

Fultz was a former major-league ball player and a graduate of Brown University who had studied law at New York University and entered practice in 1905. By 1908 players were coming to him for advice about their contracts. They also sought his help in their dealings with the National Commission, which did not always reply to their letters of complaint, possibly, as Fultz suggested, because they were not always written clearly. Fultz was approached in 1910 to assume leadership of the players, and in September 1912 the organization was formally chartered as a New York State corporation under the name Base Ball Players' Fraternity, with Fultz as president, four players, two from each major league, as vice-presidents, and another as secretary. Fultz and the four vice-presidents made up an advisory board; later the Fraternity added a board of directors composed of one player representative from each team. Dues were $18 a year. By November 1912 the organization claimed nearly 300 members and at its peak more than 1200, including players in the high minor leagues.

In addition to the general goal of benefiting the players and the game, the stated objectives of the Fraternity were: to see to it that contracts were honored by both parties; to protect players from abusive spectators; to oppose rowdyism on the field; to provide financial help for deserving players and advice to those with financial grievances; and to instill pride in their profession among the men.

After the incorporation of the Fraternity, the players and the National Commission both acted cautiously, sparring, seeming to feel each other out. Ban Johnson and Garry Herrmann professed acceptance of the players' organization and even willingness to receive its representatives, provided no lawyers were among them—a proviso in keeping with the traditional distaste for negotiation with attorneys that still obtains today. On their part, the players confined themselves for a full year to sporadic requests and suggestions. It was not until September 1913 that they decided on a bolder, more aggressive course. For by that time a third force had intervened, one that posed a threat to Organized Baseball's monopoly. This new challenge arose from the formation of a rival organization that aspired to the status of a third major league.

Twice before, the fortuitous formation of a competing league had provided leverage for a players' organization in dealing with the magnates. Now, for the third time, the players were in a position to take a strong stand.

10

FEDERAL LEAGUE CHALLENGE

ORGANIZED BASEBALL has engaged in more than a dozen trade wars during its turbulent history. Six of them occurred before the National Commission was established.° The wars resulted from rival leagues' disregard for Organized Baseball's market monopoly, or its player monopsony, or both. The arsenal of weapons used against such "outlaws" has included boycotts, blacklists, salary duels for players' services, the use of conflicting schedules, price cuts, undercover agents, and the courts. The outcome has always been either the destruction of the competing league or its eventual absorption by the existing system.

Someone once said that history is the propaganda of the victors. This epigram fits Organized Baseball. The American League, for example, was once an outlaw itself. After a hard two-year fight, it succeeded in elbowing its way into major-league standing and the respectability that went with it. After years of basking in this respectability, the league took on a glow of legitimacy that belied its freebooting origins. When Clark Griffith, who jumped his National League contract to help found the American, was interviewed by a Congressional committee half a century later, he went so far as to deny that the American League had ever been outlaw "because we never broke faith." But the committee, breaking through Griffith's obscurantism, forced him to admit that the American had ignored the National League's reserve clause and invaded its territory. Furthermore, he acknowledged that his league never would have succeeded had it not taken such "direct action." And after the American League became established, Ban Johnson, its leader, said, "If we had waited for the National League to do something for us, we would have remained a minor league forever."

As one might expect, after the peace settlement of 1903 the Ameri-

° See *Baseball: The Early Years*, passim.

can League, now part of the baseball establishment, quickly showed that what was once good for the goose was not good for the gander. Having seized its share of the market, it proved just as tenacious in driving off intruders as that other old hand at dealing with competition, the National League, had ever been. Together, the two major leagues, along with the minors in the system, presented a united front against new competitors.

When the National Commission assumed office, a Pacific Coast League was already doing business outside of Organized Baseball. Ned Hanlon complained that several major-league clubs, including the one he managed, Brooklyn, were suffering severely from loss of players who had been lured to the Coast League by its long playing season, high salaries, and salubrious climate. Other players who did not actually join the Coast League were able to use it, another owner complained, "as a bluff to get unreasonable salaries from us." One reason Connie Mack put up with Rube Waddell's misbehavior was his fear of losing the pitcher permanently to the independent circuit.

To plug this leak, Ban Johnson, Ned Hanlon, and Jim Hart of the Chicago Cubs went to California and negotiated a settlement that brought the Pacific Coast League into Organized Baseball in February 1904, but at the price of acceding to certain Coast League demands, among them permission to keep whatever players they then had under contract.

A year later, a so-called Tri-State League, composed mostly of Pennsylvanian clubs, formed independently and grabbed some players from Organized Baseball. The National Commission responded by declaring that contract-jumpers would be "forever" ineligible to return, and reserve-jumpers would also be ineligible unless the Commission saw fit to reinstate them. But behind its public posture, the Commission was soon trying to persuade the Tri-State to come into the fold. Its president, Charles F. Carpenter, rejected Garry Herrmann's overtures, however, by saying that, while he personally saw financial advantages in aligning with Organized Baseball, it was not solely a question of money, since his league backers regarded their venture as a hobby and were prepared to do some spending to indulge it. Besides, the mere fact of "warring with the powers," as he put it, and securing one of their prominent players now and then stimulated interest and created sympathizers for his league. He was also unwilling to meet Herrmann's condition that players blacklisted for joining his organization remain ineligible: what "sportsman," having induced them to join his organization, would now "cast them adrift"? he asked. Harry Pulliam asked Herrmann to go more than half-way in order to remove the only remaining "menace" to Orga-

nized Baseball. But the Tri-State went its own way for a second season before the issue was resolved and it was admitted to the National
Agreement in January 1907, with permission to retain title to its
blacklisted players, although they remained ineligible to play anywhere else. Eventually these players were granted full reinstatement
into Organized Baseball.

No sooner was the Tri-State absorbed than another so-called outlaw, the California State League, appeared. It, too, harbored players
from Organized Baseball, some of them major-leaguers such as Hal
Chase and George Moriarty, drawn by the opportunity to pick up
extra money playing winter ball on the Coast. It also competed for
the Pacific Coast League's market in four cities. In fact, it was the Pacific Coast League, itself only a few years removed from outlawry,
that raised the hue and cry to have the California State League declared an outlaw. The National Commission complied in October
1907 and wielded both the blacklist and boycott to back up its ukase.
All players who had jumped contracts to play in the banned league
were to be permanently ineligible to play in Organized Baseball, and
those who had violated the reserve clause to do so were given thirty
days to return to the clubs that claimed them or suffer the same penalty. All other National Agreement players were forbidden to play at
any time with any club in the outlawed league or even with any club
playing against a Cal State club; a first offense would bring a $100
fine, and a second would mean permanent suspension. Seven players
who ignored the order were each fined the $100 upon their return to
their clubs; others obeyed at once. In March 1909 the National Commission issued a new directive, "to be rigidly enforced," setting May 1
as the deadline for the return without a fine of all players who had
left their clubs to join an outlaw organization; otherwise, a contract-
jumper was blacklisted for five years, a reserve-jumper for three.

In addition, the Commission let it be known that all clubs in Organized Baseball were free to take any players who were under contract
with the California State League, "the object being to break it up and
secure all of its players possible." The Commission also employed Bill
Lange, a major-league outfield star of the 1890's and native of San
Francisco, as its agent against the outlaws. Lange used his personal
influence with the sports editors of the local newspapers, and the
Commission paid him $600 for "a little entertaining" and other expen-
ses. The Pacific Coast League also delivered a hard blow to the Cal
State League by wrenching away its Sacramento club. Soon many of
its young players began deserting to National Agreement clubs. By
the end of the 1909 season a headline in the San Francisco *Examiner*
read, "California 'Outlaws' Now Under 'Organization' Flag." It was

not until 1912, however, that the National Commission relented on the players who had jumped to the banned league, and the last of them, Monte C. Pfyl, was not reinstated until 1913.

Those three leagues, the Pacific Coast, the Tri-State, and the California State, happened to be the most obnoxious to Organized Baseball, troublesome enough to require action. Numerous others, like the Tidewater, the Atlantic, and the Dixie leagues, also took a fling at operating beyond the pale. The National Commission narrowly watched all such potential competitors. It checked on their financial backing and ascertained what they were up to. But all those upstarts were extremely short-lived, some so weak that they never took the field. The United States League, launched in 1912 under the leadership of the mayor of Reading, Pennsylvania, lasted only about a month. It tried again in 1913, only to collapse in a few days. Daniel Fletcher, smarting from the National Commission's disruption of his All-Star project in the fall of 1910, immediately essayed a third major league. Offering $10,000 salary advances and long-term contracts, Fletcher succeeded in signing some National Agreement players. But his grandiose scheme collapsed almost as soon as it started, when he failed to raise sufficient capital and, according to *Sporting News,* had to "fly the coop" to escape a $200 suit for unpaid printing bills.

There were also some rumblings inside Organized Baseball from a restive American Association. For years rumors had been circulated that it was ambitious to become a major league. In 1911, after collecting more than 1,400,000 admissions, which was 40 per cent of what either one of the majors drew, it confronted the Commission with a set of demands which, if granted, would have given it quasi-major-league standing. But the National Commission flatly rejected them.

In 1913 a seemingly innocuous league was set up independent of Organized Baseball. The Federal League, as it was called, named as its president John T. Powers of Chicago, who had attempted to form an independent Columbian League the previous season. It established clubs in Chicago, St. Louis, Cleveland, Pittsburgh, Indianapolis, and Cincinnati, thus invading both major- and minor-league territories of National Agreement clubs. Its Cincinnati club played its games across the river in Covington, Kentucky, until mid-season, when it was transferred to Kansas City. At first none of Organized Baseball's players were molested. The Feds employed only "free agents," youngsters, and some ex-big-leaguers like Cy Young and Deacon Phillippe, who managed Fed teams in Cleveland and Pittsburgh respectively—cities where they had formerly starred.

With no reason to assume that the Federal League would do anything except disappear, like so many of its "mushroom league" prede-

cessors, Organized Baseball adopted a passive policy toward it.
Sporting News predicted it would "need a pulmotor" to survive until
the Fourth of July. But contrary to general expectation, it managed to
complete its season and inaugurate changes that made it a formidable
organization. By November, Powers was replaced by James A. Gilmore, a wealthy and dynamic Chicago stationer. Lloyd Rickart, an
experienced baseball man who had been secretary of the St. Louis
Browns, was installed as secretary of the Federal League. Not long
after, the Feds enlisted another able executive, Charles Williams,
treasurer and financial manager of the Chicago Cubs, known for his
mastery of railroad timetables and his use of "blind" (unscheduled)
mail trains to which Pullmans for the ball players could be attached.
The Feds also decided to expand from six to eight clubs for 1914 by
dropping Cleveland and moving east to take in Buffalo, Brooklyn,
and Baltimore. This lineup placed Federal League contingents in direct rivalry with four National League and two American League
clubs, as well as with four American Association and International
League teams. Competition promised to be especially stiff in Chicago
and St. Louis, which would now have three purportedly major-league
teams each.

Most important, Gilmore was able to entice fresh capital from
well-to-do friends in his circle. The recent prosperity of Organized
Baseball simplified Gilmore's selling job. Its unprecedented attendance and profits, the visual evidence of newly constructed concrete-
and-steel ball parks, and the enthusiasm for the annual World Series
all made baseball look like an attractive investment. Among those enlisted by Gilmore were Charles Weeghman, proprietor of a chain of
Chicago lunchrooms; Otto Steifel, millionaire St. Louis brewer and
director of banks and trusts; Philip De Catesby Ball, another St.
Louisan, who had made a fortune selling ice-manufacturing plants;
and the Ward brothers, owners of Ward's Bakery Company in Brooklyn, makers of Tip Top bread. The biggest financial catch was the oil
tycoon, Harry Sinclair, later one of the villains in the Teapot Dome
scandal. In 1915 Sinclair came in as the backer of the Feds' Newark
club, which replaced Indianapolis.

Unlike the clubs in Organized Baseball, those of the Federal
League were amalgamated into a single corporation, with the capital
stock divided among the owners of each franchise, ten shares apiece
at $100 a share. Each team posted a $25,000 guarantee and was required to hand over to the league the lease to its ball park. If it
owned its grounds, it gave the league sole rights to them. All these
measures were to guard against desertion of the member clubs. The

Feds also adopted an official Federal League ball, manufactured by Victor Sporting Goods Company of Springfield, Massachusetts.

The Federal League had a more liberal player-relations policy than the majors. Their player contract mitigated somewhat the force of the reserve clause. Under it the club owner possessed an option on the player's services for the ensuing season, provided he gave notice of his intention to exercise it before September 15. He was also required to increase the salary of his players each year by 5 per cent above the salary of the previous year, and men who had played any portion of ten different years in the Federal League could, upon demand, receive their unconditional release, thereby becoming free agents. A lampooning reporter divulged the terms of a Federal contract he pretended to have gotten hold of: the player was to receive $446,000, with only $8.89 in cash and the rest in "mess tickets" for Weeghman's Cafes; breakfast from Weeghman's Cafes would be served in bed to all players; and between innings of games, tea and bismarcks would be offered, courtesy of Weeghman's.

In conjunction with the Feds' reorganization plans, they gave notice that they would keep hands off players under contract to Organized Baseball, and at first they even required affidavits from players certifying that they were not already bound to such clubs. The Feds made it clear, however, that they would pay no attention to the reserve clause. They immediately underscored their statement by announcing the signing of George Stovall of the Browns as player-manager of their Kansas City team.

Although these moves were tantamount to a declaration of war, the hierarchs of Organized Baseball responded guardedly. Garry Herrmann, speaking before a minor-league convention in Columbus, Ohio, a few weeks later, addressed the delegates in double talk. He blandly stated that baseball was a game open to all, that anyone had a right to play it, and that there would be no interference with the Federals—except in "a retaliatory way when contractual obligations or vested rights are illegally interfered with." Since Organized Baseball had long since staked out the most lucrative markets and claimed the services of the best players, Herrmann's statement was the equivalent of barring access to pools larger than a bathtub, cutting the supply of water to a trickle, and then saying that anyone was free to go swimming.

Herrmann concluded his remarks with the threat that for those players who did not respect their contractual obligations "there will be no place in organized baseball, either now or in the future," but, he added, "There will be no blacklist"! A few months afterward Ban

Johnson was more plain-spoken: "I will not take a single man back who steps over the line dividing the American and Federal League. I hereby tell one and all of them that I will not even talk to them." Reinforcing these warnings was the legislation, passed during the fight against the California State League and still in force, which provided for the blacklisting of contract- and reserve-jumpers for five and three years respectively. But *Sporting Life* pooh-poohed these dire threats, reminding its readers that after previous trade wars players were always taken back.

The loss of Stovall to the Feds had caused little concern. At thirty-six he was past his peak, and his hard-bitten nature had involved him in a number of scrapes that culminated in a dispute with the owner and brought about his severance from the club. As player-manager of the St. Louis Browns in the 1913 season just past, Stovall failed to see eye to eye with Robert Hedges, the owner, who deposed him as manager in mid-summer. He was still under contract as a player, but was nevertheless told by Hedges that he could go home and that the balance of the salary due him as a first baseman would be forwarded to him. But Stovall, realizing that he was liable for reporting to work every day, demanded that Hedges put his permission and promise in writing. Hedges angrily refused, so the player doggedly reported daily, in order to safeguard his right to the rest of his salary. Hedges also refused Stovall an outright release, and Stovall on his part refused to be sold "like furniture" for Hedges's financial benefit. "No white man," he said, "ought to submit to be bartered like a broken-down plow horse." So when the opportunity came to join the Feds, Stovall took it, and was quoted as saying, in most unlikely grammar, "some one had to be first [to violate the reserve] and it might as well be I."

Whereas Stovall's departure had caused little excitement, in December Organized Baseball was dumbfounded to learn that Joe Tinker, the famous shortstop, had also cast his lot with the Federals. Tinker, long chafing under restrictions imposed upon him as player-manager of Cincinnati, had been sold to Brooklyn for $25,000 after the 1913 season with a promise from Garry Herrmann that he would be given $10,000 of the purchase price. The deal had been held up temporarily because the Fleischmann faction on the Cincinnati board of directors (which had been responsible for assigning a man to travel with the club as watchdog over Tinker) objected to giving the player part of the sales price. Ebbets kept after Herrmann and finally consummated the sale, paying Cincinnati $15,000 and agreeing to give Tinker $10,000, but Tinker never reported to Brooklyn. He balked at the $7500 salary proposed by Ebbets and, spurning the prospective

$10,000 bonus as well, signed a three-year contract to manage the Chicago Federal League team at a reported $12,000 a year plus stock in the club. Ebbets, out his $15,000, clamored for the return of his money, but Herrmann refused. Not until a year later did the two settle the matter privately. Tinker was quickly joined by Three-Finger Brown in the Federal camp as manager of their St. Louis team, and Johnny Evers doubtless would have followed suit as a result of his clash with owner Charles Murphy, had the National League not intervened.°

On top of Tinker's loss came the disclosure by Edward E. Gates, counsel for the Federal League, that an anti-trust action would be brought against Organized Baseball. This news goaded the National Commission into rejoinder. John K. Tener professed difficulty in taking seriously charges that baseball was a trust and declared that the Feds were out to make money without heed to the sport-loving public or the welfare of the national game.

Garry Herrmann repeated that rivalry would not be resented as long as "contractual and reservation rights" were respected, but "illegal and unsportsmanlike interference with and utter disregard of established privileges of national agreement clubs will justify the adoption of vigorous defensive methods." Attorney Gates replied that Herrmann should have been more explicit about "established privileges." "Is it possible," he asked, "that organized baseball, through its years of tyrannical rule and usurpation, has secured certain privileges and immunities which do not belong to other organizations in the country?"

Ban Johnson claimed to have seen it all coming, as a result of "evil practices and reckless extravagance" and a disposition in some quarters to ignore public opinion and in others to exercise "too drastically the power over players"—the latter doubtless a backhanded swipe at Charles Murphy. He went so far as to welcome the Feds as a cleansing agent that would rid baseball of "some of the undesirable elements which have attached themselves to the sport." Clark Griffith, now with Washington, also publicly adopted a sanguine view. He saw no reason to get excited over the Federal League; they needed baseball brains more than money, so let them run their course, he said, and they would soon realize that their visions of big gates and profit were illusory.

The pace of the war soon quickened. A rapid round-trip journey by Bill Killefer, catcher of the Philadelphia Nationals, to Weeghman's Chicago Feds and then back to Philadelphia within the space of twelve days in January 1914 extended the conflict to the courts. The

° See above, chapter 2.

Phillies, who had paid Killefer $3200 in 1913, notified him after the season that they wanted his services for 1914 and would increase his salary; on his part, Killefer promised verbally that he would play for them again. Instead, he signed a three-year Federal League contract totaling $17,500, with a $525 advance. But he was quickly induced to return to Philadelphia, the club that had reserved him, and to sign another three-year contract at $6500 a season. Killefer was chided for his tactics in this jingle:

> Weeghman Weeghman Federal man
> Make me a contract as fast as you can,
> Pad it and sign it and mark it O.K.
> And I'll go to the majors and ask for more pay.

Killefer's inconstancy impelled Federal owner Charles Weeghman of Chicago to seek an injunction to restrain him from playing with Philadelphia and to compel him to play with Chicago, on the grounds that Killefer had fulfilled his obligations to the Philadelphia club; that he had now broken a valid contract with the Chicago Federals; and that, because his services were unique, he would be difficult to replace. George Wharton Pepper, attorney for the defendant, argued that Chicago had "seduced" one of the Philadelphia club's employees and therefore was not entitled to relief in court.

The Federal District Court of Michigan upheld Pepper's argument that Chicago came before it with "unclean hands." It denied an injunction to the Chicago Feds and also rebuked Killefer for breaking his promise to play with Philadelphia "as a person upon whose pledged word little or no reliance can be placed, and who, for gain to himself, neither scruples nor hesitates to disregard and violate his express engagements and agreements." The Court of Appeals then upheld the decision, making the further point that, since the uniform contract stipulated that part of Killefer's 1913 pay ($750) was in consideration of his agreement to abide by the reserve clause, Killefer in return had a moral, if not legal, obligation to bargain in good faith with Philadelphia before signing with someone else.

The decision, however, was a pyrrhic victory for the National League. They had recovered Killefer on moral grounds only. During his trial, the courts, taking the same position laid down a quarter of a century before in the Brotherhood cases, declared the uniform contract to be "lacking in the necessary qualities of definiteness, certainty, and mutuality," leaving the clear implication that, had the issue been decided strictly on the question of contractual obligations, the judgment would have gone against Organized Baseball.

Meanwhile, James Gilmore and Ban Johnson had met secretly in

February in an unsuccessful effort to come to some agreement. Johnson rejected Gilmore's request for major-league recognition. He maintained that there was no room for a third league and thus chose to forget that in 1902, when the shoe was on the other foot and he himself was striving for major-league status, he had asserted that there was room for six more majors! The American and National Leagues also decided to act in concert against the Feds by making the National Commission the center of war strategy.

Then in March the Battle of the Dock took place. Agents of the Federals took up quarters in New York, where they began their "dock-watching" vigil, waiting to intercept major-leaguers returning from a world exhibition tour conducted by McGraw and Comiskey in hopes of winning the tourists over to the Federal League before they signed contracts with Organized Baseball clubs. But the Feds succeeded in signing only two, Mike Doolan of the Phillies and Steve Evans of the St. Louis Cardinals.

Organized Baseball's disregard of the Feds' contract in the Killefer incident gave player-raiding a different complexion. It served as a pretext for the Federals to terminate their self-imposed limitation of not tampering with players under contract. Now they could say, "Since you don't respect our contracts, we need not respect yours." They acted accordingly. Tinker, as manager of the Chicago Feds, wired players all over the country: "You are invited to come to the Federal League quarters in Chicago and discuss terms. Even if you decide not to sign a contract, all your expenses will be paid by the Federal League." And come spring, agents of the Feds, armed with attractive offers, prowled the training camps of Georgia, Florida, and Hot Springs, Arkansas. Assuredly, the long-nursed grievances of major-leaguers (which even some of Organized Baseball's staunchest supporters recognized needed correcting) did nothing to hamper the approach of the Feds nor to diminish the susceptibility of the players to their enticements:

> Sing a song of dollars:
> A pocket full of kale;
> See the players jumping,
> Hear the magnates rail.
>
> Soon the season opens
> Salary coming due
> If it's not forthcoming,
> Jumpers will be blue.

Major-league clubs endeavored to stop tampering by means of court injunctions, but with little effect. Federal League poachers succeeded in taking a mixed bag of players—221 all told in the course of the two-year struggle that ensued, 81 of them major-leaguers and 140 minor-leaguers. In joining the Federals, 18 players jumped major-league contracts; 25 broke minor-league contracts; 63 disregarded reserve claims of major-league clubs; and 115 ignored the minor-league reserve. The balance of the 264-man total employed by the Federals comprised free agents who had previous professional experience and 18 who had none.

Additional players—there is no telling how many—were discouraged from responding to Federal League cash by fear of the blacklist and the doubts raised in their minds by major-league propagandists about the Feds' ability to make good on their contracts. For these reasons the players who did jump generally insisted on long-term contracts, frequently for three years, and on guarantees that their salaries would be paid, thereby making raiding very costly to the Feds. But the scramble to secure men cut the other way. This was one of the few times the players could reap the advantage of a free market. To retain them, Organized Baseball had to pay more. And certainly the exodus from its ranks would have been even greater had not the owners "purchased the loyalty," as one of them expressed it, of many of their men by hiking salaries, offering bonuses, and tendering long-term contracts. That such rewards were necessary was ample proof to the editor of *Sporting News* that the widely held idea that players performed out of love of the game and only secondarily for money was an illusion.

A sample comparison of prewar salary figures with those under wartime conditions tells the costly tale. In 1913 twenty important players attached to clubs in both major leagues received a total of $76,350, an average of $3,817.50 apiece. But in 1915 they were paid $146,550, an average of $7,327.50—an increase of about 92 per cent. Ty Cobb advanced from $12,000 to $20,000, Rabbit Maranville of the Boston Nationals from $1800 to $6000, and Brooklyn's Jake Daubert from $5000 to $9000 with a five-year contract. Even when it is taken into account that in the normal course of events these men might have received some increases anyhow, the comparison between peacetime and wartime salaries is still striking.

Of the twenty players in the sample, four were double jumpers—"rubber legs"—who, after having skipped their reserves and signed with the Feds, "did a Killefer"—broke their new contracts and returned to Organized Baseball. The fickle ones, besides Bill Killefer already mentioned, were Ivy Wingo, Ray Caldwell, and Walter Johnson. Wingo, paid $2600 in 1913, ended up with $6500 in 1915. Caldwell moved from $2400 in 1913 to $8000 and a four-year contract in 1915. Earl Hamilton, a double jumper not listed among the twenty, accepted a Federal offer of more than twice what he was getting with the St. Louis Browns—putting money before honor, in the view of the *Sporting News* editor. He quickly changed his mind and returned to the Browns as a result of "moral suasion" (and a matching salary), purging himself with a "manly" confession of his "mistake."

Most unsettling to the owners and their sympathizers was the defection of Walter Johnson, already regarded as one of the white knights among the professionals. After he won 36 games in 1913, Washington paid him $10,000 for 1914. That winter Griffith turned down Johnson's terms for 1915, and the player signed a three-year contract with the Chicago Feds at a fat salary and also was given a putative bonus of $6000. Washington fans were shocked on discovering that their idol was interested in money. Even before the news broke there had been rumors that the Feds were dickering with him. In a story headlined "Almighty Dollar Johnson's Ideal," the Feds were reported to have "taken him up into the mountain" where he was seriously considering "yielding to temptation."

As soon as Clark Griffith learned the worst, he hastened to Johnson's home in Kansas and persuaded the star to break his contract with the Federals and return to Washington at a salary of $12,500. The $6000 bonus was returned to the Chicago Feds, possibly paid by Comiskey after a nudge from Griffith, who impressed on the Chicago American League owner that it would be a cheap way for him to avoid having to compete with a Chicago Federal team featuring such a crowd-puller as Walter Johnson. A few months later Johnson acknowledged in *Baseball Magazine* that he had wronged the Feds by jumping their contract but said that to stay with them would have been a greater wrong to the Washington club, so he had acted for the best, upon which a Pittsburgh sportswriter advised him to stop talking about his "double flop."

It was not always as easy as Griffith had found it to "bring 'em back alive." Cincinnati salvaged one player only at the risk of physical violence to the scout who rescued him. In May 1914 the Chicago Feds wired $1000 to Tim O'Rourke, their Seattle agent; of this, $500 plus $71 for transportation to Chicago was to be given to Pete Schneider, a promising young pitcher, to jump his Seattle contract. Schneider accepted the money. Concurrently, Cincinnati was conducting intensive negotiations to purchase him from Seattle and finally got him for $7500, whereupon Schneider was persuaded to switch from Feds to Reds. He tried to return the Feds' money but their representative refused it, so he left it with the president of the Seattle club.

Meanwhile O'Rourke learned that Cincinnati scout John J. McCloskey was about to leave with Schneider in tow. Bilked out of the player, O'Rourke, who ran a "dive saloon" where a colony of old-time ball players hung out, paid some of them to track down McCloskey and his "kidnapped" rookie before they could board the train for Cincinnati. Fortunately for McCloskey, they failed to catch him in time. One "rummy," Jack O'Brien, had a gun, and McCloskey said later, "I came very near getting my head shot off in Seattle when I escaped that night with Schneider." The harassed McCloskey was still not out of the woods, however. No sooner had he settled himself and his captive in the Great Northern train than he received a wire from President Dugdale of the Seattle club warning him that other Federal League agents might attempt to intercept him at Kansas City or St. Louis. But nothing untoward happened, and the pair reached Cincinnati safely. At the end of the season, Dugdale, hearing that Schneider was again flirting with the Feds, told him:

> You have a grand future ahead of you and, for your own good, you want to stay in an organization where you will be the most good to yourself and organized ball is the only place for a promising player with a future. . . . I don't want to see you leave a ship that has been floating successfully for many years and go into a row boat which the waves will surely get, and if the row boat sinks you would have to sink with it.

Schneider stayed with the ship.

Rube Marquard also had dealings with the Feds. When he was refused an advance of $1500 on his two-year contract with the Giants, he went to Robert B. Ward and told him he was free to sign with the Brookfeds. Before giving Marquard the $1500 and signing him to a two-year Brookfed contract at $10,000 a year, Ward had him make an affidavit that he was not legally bound to the Giants. Ward soon found out that Marquard's representations were not correct. The player was returned to the Giants, and McGraw promised to "square" Marquard's debt with Ward if he would not prosecute for fraud.

Aside from having to pay more competitive salaries, owners on both sides had to contend with laxity in discipline among players and a tendency toward less exertion on the field. According to *Sporting Life,* there was "overt and covert insubordination" among the players. The "fever of defiance is endemic," it said. The Negro newspaper, the Chicago *Defender,* hoped that the same scarcity of talent that caused the players to act so independent would also be the means of giving "darker players" an opportunity in Organized Baseball, along with Indians and Cubans, some of whom were "darker than our men."

Organized Baseball, in an effort to shore up its legal defenses, re-

cast the 1914 contract. It was this change that had led Garry Herrmann to discount the judgment in the Killefer case that the baseball
contract was inequitable. Pointing out that the Killefer decision applied to the 1913 contract, Herrmann had voiced confidence that the
revised 1914 form would stand up if tested in the courts. The old
form had stipulated that 25 per cent of the player's salary was in consideration of his granting the club the right to reserve him, whereas
the new version named a specific sum to be given him in exchange
for an "option" on his services for the next year. That sum, ostensibly
in addition to the player's salary, was in reality part of it and would
be paid him whether the club actually exercised the option or not.
The idea was to make the contract seem more equitable by having it
appear that the player was being paid for giving the club a claim on
his future services.

This seemingly binding option clause stood Clark Griffith in good
stead in convincing Walter Johnson to renege on his agreement with
the Federals and return to Washington. In fact, it was part of the formula Griffith urged on other owners for recovering runaway major-
leaguers: first persuade them that the option clause was valid, then
wield the "big club"—a good offer, together with a two- or three-year
contract. "All of there [sic] players get scared after they have signed
with the 'Feds' and are easy to do business with if you show them
something."

Despite the studied changes of wording in the new contract, it still
contained the one-sided provision permitting the club to release a
player any time during the season on ten days' notice. In other words,
the club committed itself to only ten days at a time, whereas the
player in effect bound himself for his entire career. Aware of this imbalance, some owners struck the ten-day clause from the contracts of
their best players (since they would have little occasion to fire such
men anyhow) in a further effort to tidy things up legally.

Nevertheless, all this tinkering with the contract was to little avail.
When pitcher George "Chief" Johnson violated his contract and
signed with the Kansas City Feds, Cincinnati secured a permanent
injunction against his playing for the independents. Judge Foell of
the Superior Court in Chicago ruled that the ten-day clause did not
invalidate the standard contract. He anchored his decision to the
rather far-fetched position that for twenty years virtually all contracts
had contained this proviso and that he could not believe players
would repeatedly sign unfair contracts. However, Foell was overruled
by an appellate court, thus bearing out Mr. Dooley's definition of an
appeal as "where ye ask wan coort to show its contimpt f'r another
coort."

In June 1914 Hal Chase, the foremost first baseman of the era, turned the tables on the Chicago White Sox by giving them ten days' written notice of his resignation from his $6000 contract ($4500 salary and $1500 for option). He shortly appeared in the uniform of the Buffalo Feds—just in time to be handed a court order temporarily enjoining him from playing in New York State. Judge Herbert Bissell soon vacated the injunction to the accompaniment of a blistering opinion. He gauged the validity of the contract as it functioned within the context of the entire baseball structure. This structure, he said, was an "ingeniously devised" monopoly of the baseball business. Although that monopoly was not in violation of the Sherman Anti-Trust Act, it produced "a species of quasi peonage unlawfully controlling and interfering with the personal freedom of the men employed."

> It seems [said Bissell] that the promotion of the ballplayer is also hedged about with such limitations as to make the property in him absolute whether he will accept terms or not, and to make those terms when arrived at only liberal enough to prevent the player from seeking other means of earning his livelihood. . . .

Consequently, Bissell went on, the player's "only alternative" is "to abandon his vocation. . . . The absolute lack of mutuality, both of obligations and of remedy, in this contract, would prevent a court of equity from making it the basis of equitable relief by injunctions or otherwise." Continuing his barrage, Bissell pronounced Organized Baseball to be "in contravention of the common law" by its invasion of "the right of labor as a property right" and "the right to contract as a property right," and because "it is a combination to restrain and control the exercise of a profession or calling." This quasi-peonage of baseball players, he concluded, "is contrary to the spirit of American institutions" and "to the spirit of the Constitution of the United States."

Organized Baseball did, however, extract some temporary balm from the Marsans Case. The same month that Chase left the White Sox, Armando Marsans, Cincinnati's Cuban outfielder, likewise served his club ten days' notice and skipped to the St. Louis Feds. A friend of the Cincinnati club, Ben Hirschler of the Hirschler Optical Company, in a letter to Marsans used every appeal he could think of to influence the Cuban to change his mind:

> I hope you will show true Spanish chivalry. . . . Cincinnati wants you—the Cincinnati Club needs you—Henry Straus needs you to help sell Fabrica Tobacos de A. Marsans y Ca. . . . If you do not return . . . the name of Marsans will suffer. . . . You will not sell any cigars —you will have no friends in organized Base-Ball. Organized Base-

Ball will not visit Cuba and Cuba will have lost some of its prestage [*sic*] in base-ball. By all means show true sportsmanship. . . .

When these appeals to Marsans's chivalry failed, the Cincinnati club took the more mundane legal course and succeeded in obtaining a permanent injunction barring the player from performing for the Federals. Judge Walter Sanborn ruled that Marsans's contract, with its ten-day clause, was binding, especially since he had entered on its performance and had received compensation. Moreover, Sanborn by implication also adhered to the doctrine laid down in the Lajoie Case of 1902 by observing that "it is a settled rule of law that when a person agrees to render services that are unique and extraordinary" and promises not to render them to others, a court may issue an injunction to keep him from violating the "negative convenant." °

In its legal efforts to recover players, Organized Baseball was seeking redress only where players breached their contracts during the term of such agreements. Doubtless because of previous unfavorable legal experience in both the Brotherhood and American League wars, no effort was made to enjoin reserve violators. Indeed, Organized Baseball's attorney, George Wharton Pepper, adopted the view that, whereas jumping a club while under contract was actionable, ignoring the right of reservation was not. The reserve clause, he reasoned, was just an internal safeguard to protect clubs and leagues within Organized Baseball from depredations on each other's players. As far as the players themselves were concerned, the reserve clause was an "honorary" rather than a legal obligation.

Garry Herrmann took the same line. Testifying under cross-examination after the war, he made no pretense that the reserve could legally prevent a man from joining an outside organization:

Q. Why should not the Federal League bid for their services if they wanted to?

A. I was under the impression that when a minor league club paid a player a certain stipulated sum for the right of reserve, from then on they had a right to retain the player's service.

Q. How long?

A. Until he signed another contract.

Q. Suppose he did not want to sign another contract, could not agree on terms?

A. That was up to the player.

Q. Then what happened to him?

A. That would end it.

Q. If that were the case, why would not the Federal League be at perfect liberty to come and employ that same player?

° The injunction was dismissed after one year.

A. I would say that they would be, and have a perfect right, and did have.

Yet the legal strategy followed in the Federal war failed. Neither Marsans nor any of the other players brought to court returned to their clubs, and Organized Baseball was as unsuccessful as it had been in the past in retaining its players through legal action—or, for that matter, extra-legal measures, as the figures on desertions already given show. And just as it chose to make no effort to enforce the reserve clause during the Federal League war, Organized Baseball henceforth was to forgo any effort to enforce even the players' contracts in the courts but was to rely instead on extra-legal means of coercion.

The most potentially explosive wartime litigation was the suit brought against Organized Baseball by the Federal League in January 1915 in United States District Court of Northern Illinois, Judge Kenesaw Mountain Landis presiding. The Feds charged Organized Baseball with being a combination, conspiracy, and monopoly, in contravention of the anti-trust laws, and named as defendants the sixteen major-league club presidents and the three members of the National Commission, Herrmann, Johnson, and Tener. Included in the evidence filed by the Federal League were the affidavits of a number of former players and managers citing alleged mistreatment and malpractices in Organized Baseball, such as farming and covering up. Garry Herrmann submitted a 47-page affidavit in defense.

With anti-trust proceedings dangling over them, the magnates presented their usual bold front, issuing statements the tenor of which was that they welcomed the suit and had nothing to hide. Privately, however, they fretted, anxious and fearful.

They need not have. The Feds doubtless chose Landis's court mindful of his reputation as a trust-buster; they did not know, or chose to ignore, that Landis was also a baseball fan. He soon disabused them. At the hearings he expressed "shock" that the Feds should call playing professional ball "labor," and he asked the Feds' attorney: "Do you realize that a decision in this case may tear down the very foundations of this game, so loved by thousands, and do you realize that the decision must also seriously affect both parties?" He informed both sides that "any blows at the thing called baseball would be regarded by this court as a blow to a national institution."

Never one to permit judicial impartiality to interfere with his personal biases and leanings, Landis then proceeded to take the case under advisement and stall it a full year, during which time the Feds abjured legal reprisals against some half dozen of their own contract-jumpers. By then the war was ended and the need for a court ruling obviated. No doubt his delaying tactics demonstrated Landis's "love, faith, and belief in baseball," as one of his biographers has stated. They had the practical effect of preventing the possible disruption of the business as well. But from a purely legal point of view, the judge's conduct fell short of that disinterestedness in interpreting the law that is to be expected from the bench.

In the final accounting, however, the turnstiles, not litigation, were to determine the outcome of the war and the fate of the Federal League.

11

PEACE RESTORED

NOTWITHSTANDING their success in assembling an imposing array of players and in winning early legal victories, the Feds faced a formidable task in trying to found a third major league and to compel recognition of it. True, they commanded considerable capital and could anticipate a brisk market, judging from 1913 major-league attendance totals. They also could take heart from the example of the thriving American League, which had pushed and shoved its way into major-league status only a dozen years before. In addition, the Feds could take courage from the knowledge that there were now those who thought a third major league desirable and feasible. Finally, the Feds could count on a certain amount of sympathy owing to their position as underdogs and as would-be emancipators of major-league players.

But what of the other side of the ledger? In the first place, the majority of major-league players, among them the most renowned, remained with Organized Baseball. Furthermore, the Feds were dealing with a different situation from that of the American League at the turn of the century. Ban Johnson and his colleagues had to contend with only one major league, and a weakened one at that. The National League monopoly of those days was racked with internal dissension and had just lopped off four franchises from its former unwieldy twelve-club circuit, leaving their cities exposed to American League invasion. The Feds, on the other hand, faced two major-league opponents, and, although the National League was still faction-ridden and suffering from the embarrassment of "Murphyism," it nevertheless was much stronger than it had been in 1900 when the American League was challenging it. Another point of difference was that Ban Johnson started with a lusty minor league, and by gradually expanding it, he constructed a circuit resting on strong foundations before he took on the National League; whereas the Feds started practically from scratch and entered the field with a circuit that was doubly disadvantaged by the inclusion of three minor-league cities and the omission of New York. Moreover, the Feds launched themselves under operators who were newcomers to professional baseball and untutored in its ways. Lastly, Gilmore, for all his qualities of leadership and executive ability, was no Ban Johnson.

Novelty, freshness, and a sprinkling of well-known major-league names bore the Feds forward at the outset, and during the first weeks their games in many instances vastly outdrew those of the National and American Leagues. The Feds began the season by staggering their opening-day schedule, staging each of their four openers on successive days. They also used the old conflicting-schedule maneuver—arranging to have their clubs play on the same day as those of Organized Baseball in those cities where they confronted each other directly.

The Feds had succeeded in making eight new or renovated parks sufficiently ready in time for the opening of the 1914 season—testimony to the exertions and enterprise of Gilmore and his associates. One of their new parks was built by Weeghman's group on Chicago's populous North Side; it eventually became Wrigley Field, and for years was widely regarded as the prettiest park in the majors. Weeghman also showed baseball operators a better way to sell refreshments. Appreciating the fans' annoyance at having vendors block their view and yell in their ears, he set up stalls in back of the stands and manned them with trained people.

In Baltimore work had begun on a new park February 1 and was completed in time for the season. The cost of the park came to more than $82,000 and included construction of the stands; grading, sodding, and drainage of the grounds; and installation of seats, furniture, turnstiles, and other equipment. The park seated approximately 15,000 and was constructed of "wood above concrete" rather than entirely of concrete, as were Organized Baseball's new ones. The Baltimore structure was cooler but the risk of fire was greater. The Pittsburgh Feds took over the former Pirates' Exposition Park in Allegheny, and the Brooklyn Feds built a new park on the site of the old Washington Park. Construction of the latter was delayed somewhat because of the Ward brothers' reputation as employers of non-union workers in their bakeries. Union men refused to work on the ball park and called on union members in all Fed cities to boycott Ward's team.

Whether Fed teams were of major-league caliber is doubtful. The Feds were able to sign enough men to give their clubs a nucleus of major-league performers and to hurt their opponents but not enough of them to reach the level of the two older circuits. On balance, they were probably no better than equal to teams in the top minor leagues. We can be sure, however, that their teams were superior to some of the names they went under: horrors like Sloufeds (St. Louis), Chifeds (Chicago), Buffeds (Buffalo) excited ridicule, not imagery. In Brooklyn, the Wards tried to foist "Tip-Tops" on the fans to advertise their bread, but the outcry was such that they dropped it for Brookfeds, scarcely an improvement. The only catchy nickname was "Whales," adopted by the Chicago Feds in 1915 as the result of a contest that Weeghman held among fans. Partisan reporters had other names for the Feds: "outlaws," "anarchists," and "traitors to the game." They declared that the men who instigated the Federal movement should be "cast into the outer darkness" and that players who joined them were "ingrates." Inspired by Weeghman's lunchroom chain, Joe Vila, correspondent for *Sporting News,* habitually called them "the flapjack league" and "the lunchroom circuit."

Each of the three leading baseball publications took a different position toward the belligerents. *Baseball Magazine* claimed neutrality. *Sporting News* editor Charles C. Spink, as one of those who believed that the times were ripe for a third major league, was sympathetic to the Feds. His son, J. G. Taylor Spink, an admirer of Ban Johnson, disagreed. Charles Spink died shortly after attending the Federal League opening game at St. Louis in 1914. His son assumed control of the paper and swung its support to Organized Baseball. *Sporting Life,* while it professed being "the friend and champion of Organized Ball" in this "war of capitalists," nevertheless refrained from calling the Feds outlaws, gave them full coverage, and more and more came to advocate some kind of compromise settlement. The Associated Press carried Federal League box scores despite the amount of space then being taken up by news of the trouble between the United States and Mexico.

After its first flush of success, the Federal League suffered a falling-off in attendance. By midsummer 1914 several of its clubs cut admission prices. Fans could see its games for as little as twenty-five cents and, in some cases, even ten cents. The Wards of Brooklyn explained their decision to play quarter ball by pointing to the economic depression and calling attention to the motion pictures as an example of public demand for popular-priced entertainment. These belt-tightening measures delighted Federal League critics. The Feds were as dead as Coney Island in mid-winter as far as Brooklyn was concerned, wrote one, and the rest of their clubs were ready for cremation. President Gilmore "is as quiet as a chloroformed bow-wow these days." A cartoon in the Cincinnati *Enquirer* showed a gate man snoring at a Federal League turnstile, with the caption "Our idea of a soft job." *Sporting News* quipped that the Feds might eventually do away with turnstiles altogether and serve freshly baked cherry pie from Ward's Tip Top Bakery.

These outpourings proved premature. Organized Baseball was also hurting. To meet price competition, some major-league clubs increased the number of their cheap seats. This generally meant an admission price of fifty cents, although a few parks offered some quarter admissions. The big leagues also suspended the player limitation rule, so that clubs were left free to engage as many men as they wanted in hopes of keeping the Feds from getting them. Because of the "great annoyance" caused by the Feds, the National Commission found it necessary to suspend some provisions of the "organic laws of the game" to help National Agreement clubs protect their rights to players. For example, the Commission permitted Washington, which was over the player limit, to cover up two extra men with the Los Angeles club.

Organized Baseball's minor-league flank felt the pinch most. The American Association and the International League, the minors challenged directly by the Feds, were severely mauled. Anticipating serious trouble, these Class AA leagues requested the National Commission to drop the draft rule so that they could retain their best players, the better to compete with the Feds. The National Commission refused to comply because to drop the draft would prevent players from advancing according to their ability, but it did concede to the extent of letting those leagues keep any drafted men until the close of their season.

In 1914 the International League's Baltimore club was hardest hit. The Baltfeds not only built a better, more modern park than the one operated by Baltimore International League owner Jack Dunn, but also boldly chose to locate it across the street from his. The Baltfed stock was widely held. About six hundred citizens, ranging from bankers to men of little means, had put up a total of $164,400. An additional $36,000 to $38,000 was raised through loans. Ironically, one of the leading sponsors was Harry Goldman, an insurance man and baseball enthusiast who, back in 1902, had unsuccessfully striven to keep Baltimore in Ban Johnson's new American League. The largest shareholder was none other than Ned Hanlon. Several years before, he had sold the Baltimore International League club, which he then owned, to Dunn, who took possession of the park, leasing the land from Hanlon, who also owned the land across the street. Several times Hanlon offered Dunn a chance to lease this land for $1500 a year, but Dunn, hoping the Feds would locate in some other part of the city, did not consider the offer. The Feds, however, did lease the site from Hanlon and set up in business there, leaving Dunn fuming in frustration across the way.

From the very opening of the season the skids were well greased for Dunn's Orioles. They outclassed the other International League clubs in the pennant race, and thus caused fans to lose interest in their games. They were also a minor-league club playing other minor-league clubs, whereas their Fed competitors could not only pose as major-leaguers but could also bring in teams with big-city names—Chicago, Brooklyn, Pittsburgh, and St. Louis—all studded with well-known players from National and American League clubs. The notion of being "big league" cast a warming glow over Baltimore fans, and they crowded into the Feds' park. Dunn was soon in sore financial difficulty. Loans from Joe Lannin, Boston Red Sox owner, and Connie Mack were not enough to save him. Another resort remained. Hanlon's purchase of Baltfed stock had been conditioned on the Feds' promise to keep hands off Dunn's players. The agreement was kept, so Dunn had an opportunity to dispose of his players for badly needed funds. By summer he began unloading them for cash to various big-league teams. One of those sold to the Red Sox was a strapping nineteen-year-old left-handed pitcher playing his first year in professional ball, Babe Ruth.

After the season was over, the Orioles and the International League abandoned Baltimore altogether and moved the franchise to Richmond, Virginia. This shift constituted an invasion of the Virginia League's territorial rights, for which $12,500 compensation had to be paid, $10,000 of it by the International and the rest by the hard-pressed Dunn. After the war, Garry Herrmann revealed that approximately $30,000 had been loaned and contributed to the International League by the majors in 1914 to help keep it in the fight. Ban Johnson personally loaned $3200 to Ed Barrow, its president, to aid the Buffalo club. With the German invasion of Belgium vivid in everyone's mind that year, the suffering International became the "Belgium of Baseball" on the sports pages and its harassed president "King Albert." The American Association, the other minor league in the direct line of Federal fire, also came off badly. Its president, Tom Chivington, reported at the end of the season that only three of its teams had made any money.

The trade war also caused tremors in the rest of the minor-league structure. The lower leagues, to whom player sales often made the difference between finishing the season in red ink or in black, complained strenuously that major-league economy measures meant diminished player purchases. Conversely, the supply of players from the majors, so the minors claimed, was reduced, both because of scarcity

and because it was more difficult for the majors to deliver surplus
men to the minors while the Feds were standing by ready to waylay
them. That these protests may have been exaggerated is indicated by
National Commission figures showing that money paid to the minors
for players drafted and purchased dropped from $264,000 in 1913 to
$231,000 in 1914, a difference of only $33,000. Yet in spite of widespread hardship throughout the minor leagues, some twenty of them
unanimously adopted a loyalty pledge to Organized Baseball at their
fourteenth annual convention in Omaha in November.

The collective dollar losses provide the most telltale evidence of
the war damage on both sides in 1914. The New York *Times* estimated the overall loss to the five leagues directly concerned at $1,-
250,000. While it credited the National League with a net gain of
$115,000 and the American League with $58,000, it stated that only
eight of the sixteen major-league clubs made money. The *Times*
placed Federal League losses at $176,000, the International League's
at close to $150,000, and the American Association's at $90,000. The
surprise pennant victory of the so-called Miracle (Boston) Braves undoubtedly furnished a lift to National League attendance. Sensible of
the financial shambles wrought by the trade war, *Sporting News*
lashed out at the Feds:

> Isn't it a crime to see base ball, once a prosperous institution provid-
> ing high class sport for the great army of fans, torn in shreds because
> the Lunch Room League still believes that there is room for it? Why,
> boys, the Gilmores and Weeghmans are doing their best to kill your
> favorite pastime.

From August on, a good deal of peace talk was bandied about, and
the following month Weeghman and Herrmann met secretly amidst
rumors that Weeghman might be given a chance to purchase the Chicago Cubs. However, Herrmann, at a National League meeting afterwards, reported there was little hope of coming to any satisfactory
terms with the Feds because they wanted too much.

The failure of the fragile peace negotiations was signaled by a
Sporting Life headline in December: "Feds Terminate All Peace Negotiations." Federal player raids resumed, this time with especially
dire results for Connie Mack's Athletics. Even before the 1914 season
was over Mack realized that two of his outstanding pitchers, Eddie
Plank and Chief Bender, were all set to join the Feds for the coming
year, and that other players, among them his star second baseman,
Eddie Collins, were listening to tempting Fed propositions. The rout
of the powerful Athletics in four straight games by the inferior Boston
Braves in the World Series that fall was attributed by Mack to the

fact that so many of his players were hearkening to the siren call of the Feds. Unwilling or unable to meet Fed salary competition, Mack decided to dismantle the famous team that had won four pennants in five years. The dispersion started with the sale of Collins to the Chicago White Sox for a figure reported to be anywhere from $20,000 to $50,000. Ban Johnson, who was on friendly terms with Comiskey at the time, arranged the sale for the twofold purpose of keeping Collins out of the hands of the Feds and providing the American League with a gate attraction in Chicago to offset Walter Johnson, who had just been acquired—temporarily, as it proved—by the Chifeds. Not all American League owners rejoiced at Johnson's strategic stroke. Jake Ruppert and Colonel Huston, the new owners of the New York Yankees, resented being denied an opportunity to bid for Collins. They had just purchased the decrepit Yankee franchise that winter and had been promised five good players to help strengthen their team.

Mack had tried to sell Plank to the Yankees, but he jumped to the Feds first. Most of Mack's other stars, however, were quickly sold. As a result, in 1915 his Athletics plummeted to last place, where they remained for seven dismal seasons. Mack preferred to peddle his men and collect a tidy sum, estimated at $180,000, rather than pay competitive salaries. In contrast, Ebbets, who had a reputation in Brooklyn as a skinflint, was determined to hold on to his best players. That winter he traveled 4500 miles to sign them personally, and he succeeded because he was willing to outbid the Feds in order to keep such stars as Jake Daubert, Zack Wheat, and Nap Rucker.

To gird themselves further for 1915, the Feds planned to switch their Kansas City team to Newark, under the aegis of Harry Sinclair, their wealthy new magnate. But when Kansas City stockholders tried to block the transfer through the courts, the Feds gave way and permitted the club to stay. Instead, Sinclair took over Indianapolis, which had done poorly at the gate even though it had won the Federal League pennant, and shifted it to Newark. However, in a step that was to create complications, they detached the star Indianapolis outfielder, Benny Kauff, from the team and assigned him to Ward's Brookfeds.

Kauff, with only brief major-league experience as a member of the Yankees, had jumped from Organized Baseball and batted .366 with Indianapolis in 1914. Heralded as "the Ty Cobb of the Feds," Kauff promised to be a sure counter-attraction to the Brooklyn Nationals. But he spoiled the plan, temporarily at least. After signing a three-year contract with the Brookfeds, Kauff slipped over to the Polo Grounds and signed with the Giants, having assured them that he was not under contract with the Feds. As soon as President Gaffney of the Braves heard about the acquisition, he complained to President Tener that the Giants had signed a contract-jumper. Tener advised him not to pit his club against the Giants if Kauff appeared in their lineup. So when the two teams came up against each other, with Kauff playing for New York, the Braves refused to take the field. But Umpire-in-Chief Ernie Quigley declared the game forfeit to the Giants before his umpiring partner arrived with Tener's instructions to award the game to the Braves.

When Tener heard of Quigley's decision, he set aside the forfeit and ordered the game played, with Kauff on the bench. Kauff then applied for reinstatement, but the National Commission refused by invoking the rule against contract-jumpers, and the Giants relinquished claim to Benny, who was now a man without a team. The flamboyant Kauff, a colorful character on the field and a fancy dresser off it, threatened lawsuits all around, avowing "I'll make Cobb look like a bush leaguer if I can play for the Giants," a boast that inspired the following lines by a sportswriter:

> Though I hate to pull the chatter,
> I admit that I'm some batter;
>   If I play I'll make a sucker out of Cobb:
> I'm a one-man batting rally,
> And I knock 'em down the alley,
>   I'm modest little Benny-on-the-job.

The upshot of the fiasco was that Benny was on the job with the Brookfeds after all during 1915. But this was not to be the last of him.

The Feds started their third season, and second as a "major" league, with much fanfare—automobile parades, band concerts, lavish advertising, and free tickets and souvenirs without stint. Their Newark club hired usherettes and draped them in red, white, and blue sashes. Nevertheless, attendance began to flag early. Mid-summer brought general price cuts in Fed parks and more ten-cent admissions—disparaged as "jitney ball." In one July game the Brookfeds simply opened the gates and let fans in free, to prove, so they said, that there was still interest in baseball. Weeghman introduced a lottery in his restaurant chain: every patron who bought a meal (beans, flapjacks, or "sinkers," said Joe Vila) received a ticket that gave him a chance to win a season baseball pass.

Ban Johnson predicted a poor year in Organized Baseball and warned that it behooved all clubs to "hew to the line." To reduce costs, the majors restored the player-limitation rule and restricted each team to twenty-one men. To coax fans into their parks the mag-

nates held special days—Boosters' Day, Flag Day, Newsboys' Day,
and School Children's Day. One club eliminated salaried scouts and
instead paid only for players actually discovered, on a commission
basis. A press bureau was set up in Shibe Park, and special days were
set aside to honor a player on each visiting team. *Sporting News* denigrated these public-relations gestures as being made only because
owners were forced to recognize that fans were no longer so willing
to stand in jam-packed trolleys or cling to overhead straps in subways
just to see a ball game.

In 1914 Organized Baseball had ignored a Federal League challenge to a "world championship" contest between Indianapolis, the
Federal champions, and whoever won the World Series. In 1915 the
Feds called for a three-cornered World Series and again were ignored. They also advocated a three-way Chicago city series among
the Cubs, White Sox, and Whales. Fed fans were given pamphlets addressed to Chicago's mayor which asked him to use his influence to
bring about such a series. Failing in these attempts, the Feds decided
to award medals inscribed "Champions of the World" to the Whales,
the second-year champions of the Federal League.

Attendance picked up appreciably for the National and American
Leagues in 1915, but the American Association and particularly the
International League again fared badly. Ed Barrow, the International's tough, courageous chief, expecting to bear the brunt of the fight
again in 1915, pursued a policy of "strict retrenchment." He also set
up an $80,000 war chest by assessing each club $10,000. He overrode
the objections of the clubs that had lost money in 1914 with the argument that establishing the fund was the only means of assuring the
league's survival.

Nevertheless, the Newark Internationals quickly fell behind Sinclair's Newark Feds, whose attendance was stimulated by combining
bike races with ball games. Barrow stubbornly refused to dilute baseball with such side shows—the same stern policy he continued many
years later as general manager of the Yankees; and by mid-season his
Newark club, like Baltimore the year before, had to vacate its territory, moving to Harrisburg, Pennsylvania. In the American Association, Kansas City, badgered by Fed raiders, secured a temporary injunction that prevented the Feds from tampering with its players, but
within a month the court order was dismissed.

The Feds had minor-league difficulties of their own in 1915, but of
a different sort. Lacking minor-league connections, they had no outlets for their surplus players and were compelled to carry approximately thirty men per team, at considerable expense. To relieve this
player jam, they infiltrated the Colonial League of New England,

with the help of subsidies from the Ward brothers. When the National Board, which governed the minor leagues, realized what had happened, it withdrew protection from the Colonial League, but in the several months before that was done, there existed the ludicrous situation of a league full of contract-jumpers with Federal strings attached to them operating under the shield of Organized Baseball.

During all this time the Players' Fraternity was still alive. It had been rather quiescent during the year following its incorporation in September 1912. However, the National Commission kept an eye fixed on its activities. An informer posted Garry Herrmann regularly on its doings: "none of the players will tell me what action they are taking but Fultz is framing up something. . . ."

The Fraternity did, however, back Bert Hageman in his quarrel with the Boston Red Sox. Hageman's experience illustrates some of the abuses that the Fraternity would soon seek to rectify. The Boston club had contracted with the pitcher to play for $400 a month in 1912, but in May it optioned him to Jersey City, with assurances that he would soon be back in Boston. In Jersey City Hageman signed another contract for the same pay, so in effect his Boston contract followed him. In a month or so, Jersey City informed Boston that it had no further need for Hageman, so the Red Sox assigned him to Denver and said he would have to arrange his own salary terms with that club. Denver wanted to pay him only $250 a month, but Hageman insisted that he receive the $400 stipulated in his original contract with Boston. When Denver refused, Hageman went to Boston and told President McAleer he would not go to Denver unless Boston made up the salary difference. After McAleer declined, Hageman said that there was a manager in the International League who was willing to pay him the $400 per month. McAleer replied, "I do not care, that is the hard luck of base ball, you must go to Denver, or wherever I send you. . . ." McAleer added, however, that he would give Hageman his release if the player could get some club to pay $1500 for it. Hageman did, but then McAleer refused to go through with the deal.

Hageman next appealed to the National Commission, but at the same time he reported daily to the Boston team. The Commission, ruling that Hageman had to go to Denver, wired him, ". . . the Denver club has a right to regulate your salary, you cannot expect a major league salary in class A co [mpany]." When Hageman again wrote the Commission, it merely endorsed its earlier decision. So Hageman took his case to the Players' Fraternity, which brought suit on his behalf against the Boston club for breach of contract and recovery of $1480 in back salary. Fultz's law firm represented him. The New York Supreme Court ruled against Hageman, on the ground that the player, by signing with Jersey City, had "disabled" himself from performing services for Boston. This judgment was overruled by an appellate court, however, which decided that Hageman was entitled to a new trial. The case dragged on for five years, at the end of which Hageman finally won his point and was awarded $2348.56 in back salary, interest, and costs. Then when the Red Sox did not pay up, and Harry Frazee, their new owner, failed to appear before the court for examination, he was ordered to show cause why he should not be punished for contempt, whereupon he satisfied the debt.

Aside from its pursuit of the Hageman case, the Fraternity's activities during most of 1913 consisted of communiqués from Fultz to the National Commission requesting various reforms and improvements, such as prevention of spectator abuse of players; assurance that players put out of a game by an umpire would have a hearing before being suspended, or at least an opportunity to file an affidavit explaining their side of the case; and a guarantee that players transferred from one team to another should not suffer a salary decrease.

These efforts were largely ineffectual. On one occasion, when Fultz accompanied player Ad Brennan to the Commission to ask for remission of a $100 fine imposed for assaulting McGraw, Fultz was told his presence was an "intrusion," and the player's fine was not remitted. The Commission repeatedly sought to deflect attention from issues raised by the Fraternity and at the same time to alienate Fultz from the players by questioning his fitness to represent them: he was an "outsider"; he was not in "active" touch with baseball; he was a lawyer, not a player. Finally, the Commission became so piqued by his frequent importunings that it declared it would have no further dealings with him.

The skittishness of the baseball employers about the player organization and their aversion to Fultz coincided with the prevailing attitude toward organized labor expressed by people of property and position. If anything, the note sounded by the baseball owners was less rasping than that struck by many of their contemporaries. When President Theodore Roosevelt summoned mine operators and union leader John Mitchell to Washington to arbitrate the great anthracite strike in 1902, George Baer, head of the Reading Railroad, haughtily exclaimed, "We object to being called here to meet a criminal, even by the President of the United States." Nor did the National Commission appear any less enlightened than President Eliot of Harvard, who praised the strikebreaker as the true American hero. And Woodrow Wilson, for all his reputation as a liberal, once declared, "I am a fierce partisan of the open shop and everything that makes for individual liberty."

Despite the Commission's attitude, the Players' Fraternity was able to venture a more aggressive policy in the fall of 1913. The revitalization of the Federal League at that time strengthened the bargaining position of the Fraternity. On November 8 the players presented the National Commission and the minors' governing board with a petition listing seventeen demands endorsed by nearly five hundred ball players, who were pledged not to sign their 1914 contracts unless the list was acted upon.

These demands were, in effect, an index to the grievances that had piled up among the players over the years: violations of draft and waiver rules, arbitrary fines and suspensions, pay cuts for men transferred to different teams, failure to provide copies of contracts and to live up to agreements, relegation of veterans to bush leagues, and so forth. By demanding the correction of these and other abuses, the players indicated that, unlike industrial unionists, they were not so much concerned with direct bread-and-butter benefits as with the practices and treatment that affected their earning power; nor were they so much interested in new rules as with the observance of existing ones.

Garry Herrmann responded to the Fraternity's petition at the November minor-league convention in Columbus, Ohio, in the same artful language in which he spoke about the Federal League on the same occasion. Concerted action by players, he said, would be of benefit to baseball provided it was taken "with due regard to all other interests." The Commission would be glad to receive representatives of the Fraternity but thought it best that it be represented by its own committee rather than by someone like Fultz, who was not directly connected with baseball and who, Herrmann hinted, was trying to create "strife and dissension." Besides, Fultz had criticized rulings of the Commission and had cast aspersions on some players. Nevertheless, the Commission would be "broad-minded" enough to receive Fultz if a committee of the players was also present. Herrmann concluded on another divisive note by suggesting that the membership of the Fraternity really comprised three groups: those players in the process of development, those who had made good and were still in their prime, and those whose careers were on the wane. Care had to be taken, therefore, that legislation would not be passed for the benefit of one of these groups at the expense of the other members of the Fraternity or to the injury of the National Agreement, the ball clubs, or the game itself.

Fultz, exasperated by this latest effort to drive a wedge between him and the players, replied that it was time Organized Baseball dropped the petty "quibble" about his being an outsider who was engaged in "this fight for private ends." The question was one of principles, not personalities, he said, but if Herrmann wanted a committee of players included, the Fraternity would accommodate him.

And that is what happened. Early in January 1914 Fultz and a five-man player committee met with the National Commission in Cincinnati. The meeting began as an open one, and from two to three hundred baseball men were on hand. Joe Tinker's defection to the Feds the previous month and the realization that the Federal League represented a genuine threat certainly did nothing to impede either the calling of the meeting or the compromise agreement reached at it.

The National Commission conceded a majority of the Fraternity's requests. Thereafter, a released major-league player could negotiate immediately for a new job, although he still had to work out the ten-day notification period; previously he had to wait until the expiration of the ten days before he could negotiate. Class AA and A minor leagues were to give five days' notice of release with pay, but lower leagues were still not required to give any notice. They could even fire a man between innings.

A player released or transferred was to receive written notice. If transferred, he was to be notified of the conditions in writing—that is, whether he was sold outright, sent out on option, or whatever. Every player had to be given a duplicate copy of his contract. A probationary player had to be tendered a regular contract at the end of the trial period if the club decided to keep him; otherwise he was to be considered a free agent.

The Commission also agreed that a veteran who had served any portion of ten different seasons in the majors and had been waived on by the other clubs in his league was entitled to his release, free to make a deal for himself with any team. The purpose of this proviso was the elimination, in the words of the Fraternity, of any "such contemptible agreement" as the one that had enabled Charles Murphy to discard Three-Finger Brown in 1913. This exception to the rule that players had to go wherever they were sent represented a further limitation on the application of the reserve clause. The Fraternity wanted the same protection extended to players who had a total of twelve years' combined service in the majors and Class AA minor leagues; however, they compromised on fifteen years instead.

A player fined or suspended by the team manager or club (not the umpire) was to be served written notice of the reasons. The ball clubs agreed to pay traveling expenses to spring training and also the cost of uniforms, except for shoes. (Most major-league teams were already supplying uniforms.) All major- and high minor-league ball parks were required to have a dark-green background in center field to make it easier for batters to see pitched balls. Some major-league owners had already met this condition, and a few even went so far as to keep fences free of advertising for aesthetic reasons. The dark-green background requirement was left optional in the lower minor leagues because many of them had no fence or stand in center field. Lastly, no player was to be discriminated against in any way because of membership in the Fraternity.

Other requests were rejected. The Commission refused to require that a player's contract follow him when he was transferred, but it did agree to give a fair hearing in all complaints of unreasonable salary reductions attendant upon a man's assignment to a lower league. After much argument, the request that all "side" agreements be honored just as if they were written into the contract was also denied, on the ground that such under-the-table agreements had no validity in any event and were intended to deceive somebody. Clubs found guilty of making such agreements, however, were liable to a $500 fine. Also refused was the request that players be notified in writing whenever waivers were asked on them; Herrmann convinced the men that such a rule would do them no good and might adversely affect their work.

Upon the conclusion of the conference Herrmann asked Fultz privately, "What are you going to do for us?" Fultz said he knew of nothing the Fraternity could do except lift the ban the players had placed on signing their contracts. Herrmann then asked if the Fraternity would expel contract-jumpers, to which Fultz replied that they were not going to enter the fight between Organized Baseball and the Feds. Fultz and the Commission publicly issued statements expressing general satisfaction with the conference. But the ink was scarcely dry on the Cincinnati agreement when sniping and recriminations resumed. Only a few days after reaching agreement, Ban Johnson charged Fultz with inventing the grievances to justify his salary. Before the month was over, Fultz directed minor-league players not to sign their contracts because the $500 penalty for making side agreements was not being enforced. The threat brought quick results. The minors gave assurances that they would comply. In March Fultz accused the National Commission of planning to violate the agreement by allowing players drafted from a Class A club to be returned to it without giving AA leagues a chance to secure them. This point was cleared up through correspondence with Herrmann.

The players' president was also criticized for not ranging the Fraternity more unequivocally on the side of Organized Baseball against the Feds and specifically for not coming out in support of the reserve clause. The somewhat specious reason Fultz gave at the time for not urging the players to adhere to the reserve was his fear that he might be urging them to do something they were not bound to do, should the courts later decide the reserve was unenforceable. Fultz did, however, advise players against jumping their contracts, and the Fraternity decided to expel members who did so without first submitting their grievances to its advisory board. Those who went ahead and jumped even after the board decided against them were also to be expelled.

The name-calling continued. To the editor of *Sporting News,* Fultz was still "an outlaw and a baseball anarchist." M. H. Sexton, president of the National Association, belabored him as an "agitator" who created "an impression that the professional ball player was a much-abused individual who needed the constant care and assistance of an aggressive lawyer-president to prevent him from becoming an absolute slave tied in bondage." John H. Farrell, secretary of the minors, chimed in with the opinion that Fultz was a "professional" agitator.

Then in mid-summer the Clarence Kraft episode provoked a crisis. The argument centered upon the old sore point of a player's right to play in a league as high as his qualifications would allow. Brooklyn had drafted Kraft from the New Orleans club after the 1913 season. At the same time, Nashville of the Class A Southern Association filed official notice that, should the player fail to make good with Brooklyn and be sent back to the minors, Nashville wanted first chance at him. Kraft lasted only briefly in the big leagues. Brooklyn sent him early in 1914 to the Class AA Newark club, which Ebbets controlled; whereupon Nashville, exercising its prior claim, insisted that Kraft should play there and was upheld by the National Commission. But Kraft demurred at going to a lower league for less money. In the words of *Sporting News,* he was not going to give up work thirty minutes from Broadway for "biscuits and chickory land."

The Fraternity went to bat for Kraft, charging violation of the Cincinnati agreement, which stated that a player must pass through all intermediate leagues before he could be sent to a league of a lower classification. Ban Johnson argued that Nashville had recorded its claim before the Cincinnati agreement was made and that its provisions were not retroactive. But Fultz wrote the Commission to demand that the Kraft decision be reversed: "Inasmuch as organized ball sees fit to continue its violation of . . . the Cincinnati agreement which . . . is a part of every player's contract," the Fraternity's board of directors had authorized him to inform the Commission that "on and after Wednesday July 22 the members of the organization will no longer consider themselves under contract."

Indignation greeted this strike threat. Never before had entire leagues threatened to walk out. Single teams had struck—Cleveland and Detroit in the Joss and Cobb episodes—as had individual players. In 1903, for example, Mathewson refused to pitch for the Giants against Pittsburgh after only two days' rest and was joined by his catcher, Frank Bowerman. Now entire leagues of players were threatening to strike. The New York *Times* gave the Fraternity strike-threat story page-one coverage in the best position, the right-hand column, with a three-deck headline and five different subheads. *Sporting Life* characterized Fultz's letter as "an insolent ultimatum" and called him an "impractical, non-producing lawyer" and an "irresponsible professional organizer" who did not have one dollar invested in baseball. Ban Johnson, understandably annoyed at the prospect of the American League's being interfered with because of a National League club's dispute with a player, branded Fultz "a menace to the game" and blustered that regardless of the National League's attitude, if the players struck, his league would close all its parks, cut off salaries, and fine offenders heavily. It was later disclosed that Johnson was working with Ira Thomas, part-time catcher and "lieutenant" of Connie Mack, to organize a kind of company union among American League players as a counterpoise to the Fraternity. President Tener of the National League declared that ball players were professionals, "not miners or hod-carriers or ditchdiggers"—and "professional men do not strike."

A strike was averted when Ebbets paid $2500 compensation to Nashville, and Kraft remained with Newark. *Sporting News* congratulated the players, although it refused to endorse Fultz's methods. It blamed the whole thing on the "bumbling, obstinate" Ebbets. *Sporting Life* reported that the American League was not pleased with Ebbets's "single-handed" settlement, and it charged that the National League was "afraid" and had "quit cold" in the face of intimidation by the Fraternity. Ban Johnson, according to a New York *Times* reporter, seemed disappointed that a showdown had been avoided. Fultz, helped by the victory, was re-elected president of the Fraternity for a three-year term in October.

Toward the end of the year the Fraternity submitted nine additional demands, most of them variations or extensions of those put forward at the time of the Cincinnati agreement. With one exception they were rejected, either outright or with the assertion that they were already in force or that they pertained exclusively to the minor leagues.

After this setback, nothing as newsworthy as the Hageman Case, the Cincinnati agreement, the strike threat, or the victory in the Kraft Case stamped the activities of the Fraternity in 1915. But the union conducted a good deal of routine business and quiet constructive work on behalf of the players. Its annual report listed 22 meetings held, 2800 letters sent, 32 articles written, eight bulletins issued, a yearbook published, and eight cases taken to the National Commission, of which seven were decided in favor of the player and one against. Of four other cases appealed from the National Board of the minors to the Commission, two were reversed and two affirmed. In addition, 20 claims were taken up with the National Board, ten of them decided in favor of the player and eight against; two were pending. Six more cases were brought up with individual clubs, and in each one the Fraternity succeeded in recovering money for the player. All told, it collected $3184.35 from owners.

Meanwhile, the war with the Federal League dragged on, although rumors of peace revived early in 1915. One evening in April, only a few months after the Herrmann-Weeghman talks fell through, Ban Johnson and Phil Ball, owner of the St. Louis Feds, met for dinner at McTeague's, a popular St. Louis café. Their meeting was arranged by Taylor Spink, the new young editor of *Sporting News*. The story of the meeting leaked out and brought fresh speculation about the possibility of peace. A few weeks afterward the two were spotted watching a game together in Comiskey's ball park. During the game, Ball supposedly was heard to say that it was too bad baseball was not fought on the field instead of in stuffy courtrooms, a remark with which Johnson reportedly agreed. Soon after, Gilmore was quoted as saying that it was a shame the lawyers and the players were getting all the money and the promoters little but experience for their pains. At about this same time the major leagues were giving serious thought to the idea of ending the war by expanding the majors into two ten-club leagues to make room for some of the Fed clubs.

In October, talks were held between members of the National Commission and Federal leaders Gilmore, Sinclair, and Ball at Philadelphia, where everybody who was anybody in baseball was on hand for the World Series. The death of Robert Ward that same month may have added impetus to the desire of the Feds to parley, since he was one of their wealthiest and most enthusiastic backers. As a report to the Baltimore stockholders said, his loss removed from the Federal League "its most courageous and determined spirit in the most critical period of its history."

All these signals and overtures, especially the talks at Philadelphia, laid the groundwork for the successful peace plan outlined in New York that winter. National League owners, gathered in New York preparatory to their annual meeting, met with Gilmore and Sinclair in President Tener's office December 13. That evening they had dinner together at the Republican Club. The result was a rough, tentative peace agreement outlined in the form of a memo. But nothing more could be done until they found out whether the American Leaguers would go along with it. So Barney Dreyfuss, who had good rapport with them, was selected to go at once to Chicago, where the American Leaguers were meeting, and lay the plan before them.

Dreyfuss succeeded in his mission, and the American League immediately dispatched a committee, headed by Johnson, to New York. "Principles will prevail . . . rather than mere money or personal consideration," intoned Ban solemnly upon arrival. First the two major-league committees met on the afternoon of December 17 to discuss the matter. Then in the evening they sat down at the Waldorf with the Fed representatives, together with Ed Barrow, Thomas Chivington, and John Farrell acting for the International League, the American Association, and the National Association respectively. President Tener and attorneys for the National League and the Feds were also present.

An immediate stumbling block to peace was the anti-trust suit still on Judge Landis's docket. Some club owners feared that they would be held in contempt of court if they proceeded to a settlement while the case was pending. Benjamin Minor of Washington urged clearing with Landis first in view "of the character of the man we are dealing with, the Judge I mean—he is very jealous of his powers and prerogatives." J. Conway Toole, counsel for the National League, had also measured Landis: "This particular court is very jealous of its prerogative and has decided notions on what ought to be done." The Feds' suit, Toole reminded the owners, charged criminal conspiracy, and now while the case was still before the court the plaintiffs were in effect negotiating to join that conspiracy. "It is the most absurd proposition I ever heard of." To be on the safe side, it was decided to sound out Landis before going ahead and meanwhile to turn the whole matter over to the National Commission and a new committee of the Feds. The two new committees were to reconvene at Cincinnati in several days. This pause would allow time for the National Commission's Chicago attorneys, who were handling the case, to advise them regarding the suit before Landis.

All went well. Landis issued an order dismissing the suit with the consent of both parties, and on December 22 a peace pact was signed in Cincinnati that ended the two-year fight. "Mere money" may not have talked at the peace table, but it certainly made some loud noises. To begin with, Organized Baseball paid $600,000 in exchange for the dissolution of the Federal League and the amalgamation of two of its clubs into the major leagues, in a deal similar to the large-scale business compromises of those days, such as the one between the Morgan-Hill and the Harriman railroad interests. Of the total sum, the Wards received $400,000 in twenty annual payments of $20,000 each; $100,000 went to Sinclair in ten annual payments; and $50,000 went to Edward Gwinner of the Pittsburgh Feds in five annual installments. Weeghman and his Chifed associates were permitted to buy the Chicago Nationals, with the National League putting in $50,000 toward the purchase price; and Phil Ball and his Sloufed group bought the St. Louis Americans.

The advent of Weeghman into Chicago with fresh money and a new ball park meant that the National League had finally eliminated the troublesome Charles W. Murphy. The sale of St. Louis enabled Robert Hedges, the former American League owner, to dispose of a franchise that was beginning to show signs of deterioration. Nevertheless, he left baseball with a bonanza: all told, he was believed to have realized $765,000, counting salaries and dividends over thirteen years, on an original investment of $30,000.

Organized Baseball took over the Federal ball parks in Pittsburgh, Newark, and Brooklyn. Kansas City and Buffalo, two of the weaklings of the Federal League, got short shrift. Other Fed clubs had had to make loans to Kansas City in 1915 and finally its franchise was declared forfeit. Buffalo was in similar shape. Baltimore, also in debt, was offered a $50,000 settlement, which it rejected; so in order not to hold up the settlement a committee was appointed to decide the fate of Baltimore later—a postponement that was to haunt Organized Baseball for seven years.

In spite of all its rules and fulminations against "deserters," Organized Baseball under the peace terms recognized the Federal League's right to the players it had signed and its full authority to dispose of them whether they had violated contracts or had ignored the reserve clause. Organized Baseball also agreed not to ban such players from playing with any of its clubs that wanted them. These provisions cleared the way for Sinclair to take over the contracts of all Fed players, except those held by Weeghman and Ball, as a speculation and sell them to the highest bidders. In this way the Feds had a chance to get out from under the long-term contracts they had with numerous players and at the same time apply the proceeds from any sales toward outstanding debts. By thus acting as a clearinghouse, Sinclair became a broker in player contracts in a deal that made him the greatest trader in human merchandise since slavery was abolished. The Feds succeeded in selling seventeen players for $129,150. In short, Organized Baseball not only abrogated its ban on the Federal jumpers but paid for the return of some of them. Players not pur-

chased reverted to their former clubs in Organized Baseball. Those
not claimed by their former owners faced the problem of trying to
find jobs with whatever team would have them, and there were some
who instituted suits to collect on their contracts with Federal League
clubs. Lastly, all lawsuits pending between clubs and leagues were to
be dropped, but it is interesting that Garry Herrmann agreed to pay
$2500 damages to Phil Ball for keeping Marsans from playing with
the Sloufeds during the war.

Total losses from the war have been estimated as high as ten million dollars, a figure that seems exaggerated. For the Feds, investments and operating losses reached $2,500,000 by the end of 1915.
The Brookfeds alone had deficits considerably over $800,000.

Upon the conclusion of peace, the National Commission announced
that the National Agreement was once more in full force. The magnates of Organized Baseball and their adherents also made valiant efforts to save face. Weeghman and Ball underwent a rapid metamor-
phosis in some newspapers, changing from villains to "sportsmen"
who were in baseball not for money but out of love for the game.
Sporting News also urged that a place be found in baseball for Sinclair, a "real sportsman" who would make an ideal magnate. At the
same time, the compromise peace was made to appear a victory for
Organized Baseball, and the myth that the Feds had "thrown in the
sponge" and sued for peace has been carefully nourished ever since.
To be sure, the Federal League disappeared. But the terms of the settlement show that it was far from a total victory for Organized Baseball. And while the struggle inflicted severe losses on both sides,
there is reason to believe that it was Organized Baseball that first
sought peace, particularly the National League, four of whose cities
were in direct competition with Federal League invaders, against
only two that the American League had to contend with. Peace may
also have been hastened by a "gigantic bluff"—the threat that Sinclair was on the verge of invading New York. As Gilmore later testified, when the Feds decided they were no longer able to continue,
they took an option on grounds at 144th Street and Lenox Avenue
and a two-year lease on elaborate offices in New York. They went so
far as to apply to the city authorities to close off the necessary streets
and to have an architect's plan for a 40,000-seat stadium prominently
displayed in a store window on 42nd Street. The majors "fell" for this
strategem, Gilmore claimed, and began the negotiations that ended
the war.

Another misconception passed along by a succession of writers is
that the depression in 1914 and the onset of World War One caused
attendance to diminish drastically and thus hastened the end of the

baseball war. Major-league attendance did decline sharply in 1914, dropping off 1,902,817 from the previous year. However, some of this slack no doubt was taken up by attendance at Federal League games. Besides, in 1915 major-league attendance started to recover, increasing by 409,838. Actually, the depression of 1914 was too brief to affect baseball attendance. And the outbreak of war in Europe soon brought a flood of Allied orders for munitions that pulled the United States out of its economic doldrums. The big 1914 decline in attendance was already apparent in May, whereas the World War did not break out until August, by which time the baseball season was two-thirds over. The only clubs that conceivably felt the impact of the war before 1917 were Canadian minor-league teams like Montreal and Toronto. The World War had no more bearing on major-league attendance than did the 1914 depression until the United States became involved in Europe in 1917, and by then the Federal war was long since over.

The end of the two-year trade war with the Federal League marked the last attempt within the United States for half a century to break through Organized Baseball's monopoly. Although the Fed challenge was met successfully, in the next several years Organized Baseball was to suffer from the effects of World War One and to be shaken to its very foundations by internal strife and scandal.

12

FROM OLD WAR TO NEW

The DEAR-BOUGHT peace with the Federal League did not bring tranquility to Organized Baseball. To begin with, the usual wholesale postwar salary cuts were delayed because many players either had signed for 1916 before peace was declared or had a year or two to go on long-term war contracts. The players' union still had some life left in it and, though deprived of much of its bargaining power as a result of the Feds' disappearance, it nevertheless remained a cause of anxiety to the owners. An anti-trust suit instituted by the Baltimore Feds because of their dissatisfaction with the peace pact was another legacy of the Fed war. And soon fresh and even more pressing problems were to arise.

With peace restored in the business, major-league attendance rebounded strongly in 1916. It increased by more than 600,000 in the National League and by more than a million in the American over that of the year before. Nevertheless, the owners wielded their cleavers on payrolls in 1917. If something were not done to increase revenue by cutting expenses, said Ebbets, baseball would become a losing proposition. As they used to say in the boys' books of the time, he suited the action to the word, and even though Brooklyn won the 1916 pennant, he cut the salaries of eleven of his players whose wartime contracts of Federal League days had expired. If they hold out, said Ebbets, "we'll fill their places with ambitious youngsters." In Jimmy Johnston's case, Ebbets did not even wait for his contract to expire. Johnston, one of the players auctioned off by Sinclair after the peace pact, had signed a two-year contract with the Feds at $4000 a year, but Ebbets declined to honor it and offered the player only $3400. Half a dozen Chicago Cubs whose wartime contracts had run out were slashed a thousand dollars or more by Weeghman, that former champion of downtrodden players. Connie Mack also cut some of his men.

And so it went. The Pittsburgh Pirates offered Honus Wagner a cut of nearly 50 per cent, from $10,000 to $5400. He held out until mid-season and then accepted payment on a monthly basis at the rate of $6000 a year. In a similar case, the Boston Red Sox halved Tris Speaker's salary from the $18,000 that they had paid him to keep him from the Feds. The star outfielder refused to accept his prewar pay of $9000, held out all spring for $15,000, and agreed to come to spring training on a daily-fee basis only. When the club reached New York on the trip north, Lannin told Speaker that his terms were acceptable and he could sign the contract when the club arrived in Boston the next day. That evening while he was packing in his hotel room, Speaker was stunned to receive a phone call from Cleveland informing him that he had been sold to that club for $55,000 and two players. Speaker did not relish being shunted from the champion Red Sox to seventh-place Cleveland but finally consented to go on condition that he be paid $10,000 of the selling price. Lannin agreed to this but stalled on paying it, and Ban Johnson had to order him to send the money. Things turned out well for Speaker in Cleveland despite his aversion to the idea of going there. Eventually he became player-manager and led the Indians to the 1920 world championship.

Salary questions like these were still considered by the Players' Fraternity to be outside its province. Its conservatism was further shown by its endorsement of the professional baseball system. Fultz himself declared in 1915 that dissolution of the National Commission would have the undesirable effect of leaving the players free to sell their services to the highest bidder. "Professional baseball without proper organization and control," he went on to say, "would result in complete disruption of playing and business standards. Such conditions would be the forerunner of chaos." The extent of the Fraternity's interest in changing baseball's organizational setup was occasionally to voice desire for a player representative on the Commission. But even A. G. Spalding, who had been as zealous as any in looking out for entrepreneurial interests, had recommended representation for players—and umpires too—on the so-called supreme court of baseball. And once when the Fraternity broached the idea of having a player representative, Ban Johnson answered that he had no objection to it so long as the player did not come as a delegate of the Fraternity. Fultz was left to wonder how one man representing the players "in the abstract only" would be able to cope with the National Commission.

Even on the reserve clause Fultz was ambivalent. About all that can be concluded from a number of rather fuzzy statements he made is that he saw it as a necessary evil that probably needed some modification. It did not even seem to occur to the Fraternity to establish a pension system. It did grant a monthly allowance to Cal McVey, a member of the first openly professional team, the Cincinnati Red Stockings of 1869, but this charitable act toward a single needy old-timer did not kindle the thought of setting up a broad pension system for all old-timers in need.

Books about baseball have accorded the Fraternity less than justice, however. A recent one, for example, allotted only two sentences to it, both inaccurate. None of these books tells anything about the Fraternity's activities after the Federal League war. The Fraternity is simply dismissed with the usual oversimplified statement that the government's "work-or-fight" order of World War One caused it to disintegrate.

Actually, the Fraternity continued to register some gains after the Federal League war, despite its enfeebled position caused by the elimination of the rival league. Before the war's end and as the likelihood of peace became increasingly apparent, Fultz spoke out several times in behalf of players who had joined the Feds to urge that they should be granted full reinstatement into Organized Baseball. Any other solution, he proclaimed, would be "grossly illogical" and "unfair." He also called upon owners to fulfill any long-term contracts they might have with players, and he threw his support to Jimmy Johnston and others who were having salary controversies. He also made it clear that peace would automatically restore returning players to full membership in the Fraternity. This policy helped to nourish the Fraternity's membership, which, according to its annual report, numbered 1215 at the end of 1916. The report further indicated that during the year the Fraternity had recovered $7,521.98 from club owners for players and in addition had established the validity of certain contracts, saving $2775 for the players involved.

The Fraternity also tangled with the major-league owners in 1916 over the injury clause in the player contract. Under its terms owners were obligated to pay injured men for only fifteen days. As a general rule, however, the clubs, particularly major-league ones, went beyond that and continued on full pay men injured in service. Nevertheless, the right to suspend them without pay after the fifteen-day period existed, until the Fraternity succeeded in having the clause changed to require clubs to pay injured players in full for the duration of their contracts.

But the Fraternity focused most of its postwar reform efforts on the minor leagues. Whatever abuses players were subjected to in the majors were compounded in the minors, especially in the lower ones. The minors were more loosely organized and less stable, because their often precarious financial circumstances caused frequent turn-over in clubs and leagues. They were also more lax in enforcing the rules governing player relations. Consequently, the National Commis-sion was kept busy with player complaints and appeals from adverse decisions rendered by the National Board of the minor leagues. Among the large variety of abuses, the Fraternity chose four on which to concentrate in its drive to better the lot of minor-leaguers. First, it demanded that clubs stop suspending injured players without pay, and either give them full salary while they were incapacitated or else release them. In other words, the Fraternity believed that if a club held an injured man on its reserve list he was entitled to full pay. Secondly, Class AA and A players should be free to sign with another club immediately upon receiving five days' notice of release, instead of being forced to wait and see if the release was going to be withdrawn. Thirdly, the Fraternity insisted that ball clubs should pay traveling expenses, including ticket, berth, and meal money, from the player's home to spring training. This expense was not of the player's own making, Fultz argued, and should not be borne by him. Lastly, when a player's claim was heard by the National Board and its deci-sion was unfavorable to him, a copy of the club's defense against him should be sent to the Fraternity. "Not even the most depraved crimi-nal is convicted without being given a chance to defend himself," Fultz gibed.

Members of the National Commission were cognizant of the many injustices perpetrated in the bush leagues, and they were often sym-pathetic toward the victims. In 1910 Tom Lynch told Herrmann, "There is too much ignoring of players' rights going on in National Agreement clubs." Herrmann himself suggested that the Commission give some thought to the predicament of many injured players. "Surely if a player is injured in the service of the club," he said, "it would not be fair to not allow him any compensation for any time after such injury is received." In 1912 Ban Johnson called attention to complaints that had come before the Commission in the past two or three years from minor-league players who, after signing a contract, were left fretting at home without either instructions or release, com-pletely ignored—a practice, he said, that "works a great injustice on the player." Johnson also declared that club owners "must not impose a hardship on players in the matter of transportation. When a player is obliged to travel half way across the continent to fulfill his contract . . . the heavy expense must be fully considered." This attitude was at variance with that of a minor-league club owner who advised one of his players: "Of course, it is no fault of ours that you live so far away from your job, and we cannot establish a precedent by paying railroad fares." Once when a minor-league club tried to settle the salary claims of a number of its players on a discount basis, Johnson recorded his disapproval in no uncertain terms: "The salary obligation of a club is worth one hundred cents on the dollar and there can be no discounting of claims. The Commission must handle this subject without gloves. The salary debts of all Clubs must be paid at their face value." And in referring to another case, Johnson put the entire problem of employee relations in a nutshell: "All clubs must deal justly with players."

Manifestly there was room for improving working conditions in the minors. The Fraternity had a case. *Sporting News* believed that its demands were fair and contained nothing minor-league owners could not well grant; they should not have to be "prompted" by Fultz. Nevertheless, both the National Board, which had long been hostile to the union, and the National Commission, which had appeared to believe the demands had some merit, rejected the Fraternity's four proposals. The minors' governing board gave their reasons in a letter signed by their secretary, J. H. Farrell, and other officials. They said the demand concerning pay for injured players was already covered by the rules. On the second one, that which pertained to the release of AA and A players, they claimed that the Fraternity had misinterpreted the rule. Regarding traveling expenses, they maintained that most clubs paid them, but poor ones could not be compelled to. As for the last demand, the letter stated tartly that copies of the evidence and decisions arrived at in deciding player claims against clubs were always sent to "interested parties." Doubtless the underlying reason for turning down the four demands was the hierarchy's inability to stomach the idea of being put straight by the union or of conceding anything to it, particularly since the players had practically no source of baseball employment outside of Organized Baseball now that the Feds were gone.

The Fraternity reacted vigorously to the rebuff of its demands. Terming the attitude of the National Board "dictatorial in the extreme," the union's advisory board canvassed the players in December on whether to call a strike. It pointed out that the issue was of concern to major- as well as to minor-leaguers and urged the players to stand together; ". . . the time has come," it told them, "to show whether or not we have the grit." Two weeks later Fultz announced that unless the demands were met, the players would strike. The tactic to be used was the same as that employed in the Kraft case of 1915—that is, the players would refuse to sign their contracts for the coming 1917 season. Between six and seven hundred of them actually pledged to withhold their services. Fultz accompanied his announcement in words reminiscent of those enunciated nearly a generation before by the first players' union, the Brotherhood: °

> For over two years we have, through petition, argument and appeal to public sentiment, and to the sense of fairness of the [minor league] Board . . . attempted to get not sweeping reforms but only those ordinary considerations which were well recognized to be the just portion of the players, things which the National Commission long ago granted us on behalf of the major leagues and which they have gone on record as approving for the minors. . . . This Board does not comprehend these methods and has, in addition, violated its agreement with us.

News of the threatened walkout came to the owners like a "thunderclap." All through the winter a tedious verbal barrage fell upon the Fraternity. Functionaries of Organized Baseball and their spokesmen marshaled all their pet clichés and familiar denunciations. To John K. Tener the proposed sympathy strike of the major-leaguers seemed "to border almost on conspiracy," and he asserted that the minor leagues were in no financial position to grant concessions. Ban Johnson vowed that Fultz would be driven out of baseball and the Fraternity crushed. He promised to "lay a strong hand on" John Henry, the Fraternity's Washington representative, whose union activities annoyed him. Johnson later announced that American League owners would propose ordering the Washington club to fire Henry immediately, and would pay the club a sum of money as compensation. "Such persons are undesirable in our league," he said. Later, when Henry was "waived" out of the American League, it was widely believed that he had been "railroaded out." Ed Barrow warned that if a strike occurred the International League would lock out the players. President Baker of the Phillies pointed out that "Baseball is a sport, and the same conditions cannot be applied as are resorted to by labor unions in other lines."

The owners were further alarmed by a front-page story in the New York *Times* saying that the Fraternity had applied to the American Federation of Labor for a charter and that Sam Gompers favored their strike decision. This report touched off another volley of words from baseball leaders. While he was in favor of union labor, said Tener, he did not think union men should sympathize with the labor movement "where a principle involved was wrong." Gompers was a fair man, assured Garry Herrmann, and when he heard the evidence he would know that Fultz and the Fraternity did not have much to stand on. John B. Foster, the same writer who had said that the players' first union, the Brotherhood of the 1880's, was "a bolshevik move-

° See *Baseball: The Early Years*, page 230.

ment," now railed that a secret player organization was "foreign, hostile and injurious to sport. . . . Secret societies," he added, "have no place in honest sport." But Colonel Huston, one of the Yankee partners, proclaimed, "We cannot stand for the players taking such action as they contemplate. We must stabilize our business, just like any other business." (He evidently neglected to compare notes with Foster and Baker beforehand.) Secretary Farrell charged that Fultz was miffed because in many minor-league cases the National Board dealt directly with the player, not with Fultz, whose efforts, Farrell sneered, were "schoolboy, Fourth of July oratory." Ban Johnson feigned disbelief, but if the story were true, he added, it would mean the end of Fultz and the Fraternity, because "Organized Ball cannot and will not tolerate any such action by the players." Then, warming to his own words, he predicted darkly that a baseball union would result in the adoption of a wage scale and the end of the star system.

Fultz then had his inning. Labeling Johnson's statements "bombastic," he explained that where wage scales existed, employees, not employers, had instituted them. The club owners had long since unionized, said Fultz, and now had one of the strongest organizations in the country. Would it not be logical for the players to fight fire with fire? Fultz asserted that unionized ball players would continue to bargain individually, just as members of Actors' Equity did; then, in a final sally: "We have not heard of De Wolf Hopper working for a chorus girl's salary."

Nothing came of the proposed affiliation with the A. F. of L. Had the players obtained a charter, however, they would probably have been under the jurisdiction of the vaudeville union, the "White Rats," and the rumor was that they did not fancy being lumped in with matinee idols. During the winter the Fraternity tried to maintain its position. Several meetings were held, and at one of them in January nineteen big-league players showed up and at least two more, Tris Speaker and Al Demaree, sent telegrams. They were supporting the minor-leaguers, as one stated, "because we don't know when we will have to go back to the minors ourselves." Some players, including a number of major-leaguers, broke their pledges, though, and signed their contracts, so the Fraternity expelled them. The fact that any major-leaguers at all would openly express solidarity with minor-league players came as a surprise to many, for all during the winter the owners reported that major-leaguers were disregarding their pledge and signing their contracts. Fultz countered with repeated denials, but the truth was that more and more players were capitulating.

The folly of the Fraternity's unrealistic expectation that major-leaguers would risk their necks in the interests of "bushers" became increasingly plain. Added to this handicap was the harsh reality that owners were in no mood and had no need to bandy with the union. The situation was different from that which obtained while the Federal League was operating. In mid-January the magnates discarded all pretense: Johnson and Tener announced that the major leagues had severed relations with the Fraternity and thereafter would refuse to recognize it.

In a rather pathetic last-ditch effort in early February, the Fraternity sent a conciliatory note to the Class AA and A minor-league owners but got no satisfaction. It was reported later that month that Fultz had reached a compromise with McGraw, who acted as emissary for the National League. But before they had a chance to present it, the league "turned its back" and officially abrogated the 1914 Cincinnati agreement because the Fraternity had "violated the letter and spirit" of it. Herrmann acknowledged that the National Association (the minors) "may have erred in the manner of hearing some of their cases" but "not as badly" as Fultz. The American League immediately followed suit, and the National Commission "ratified and approved" the action of the two major leagues. Others moved in for the kill. Tener warned that striking players would "automatically suspend themselves" and their places would be filled by others. Dreyfuss held that the Fraternity had "caused altogether too much handshaking among players"; more fighting spirit was needed, he said.

Fultz finally had no choice but to call off the abortive strike. He requested that none of the men be discriminated against for union membership, released the players from their pledge not to sign contracts, and in a face-saving gesture announced that the Fraternity would not disband but would continue to work for the players, in the hope that baseball's leaders would some day see the merits of the organization in a different light. But the Fraternity, to all intents and purposes, was dead—and contrary to accepted belief, it died more than a year before the "work-or-fight" order of World War One.

Another important legacy of the Federal League war was the problem that grew out of failure to conclude a settlement with its Baltimore club. The peace agreement had left the Baltfeds high, dry, and angry at what they regarded as betrayal. Gilmore, along with the big money men of the Feds—Sinclair, Weeghman, and the Wards—had negotiated the peace. Baltimore officials stoutly insisted that they had had no inkling of what was going on until the last minute, when a wire from Gilmore summoned Baltimore club president Carroll Rasin and Ned Hanlon to meet him in New York at the Biltmore the morning of December 17, 1915. Upon arrival they were dismayed to learn that the Feds were through and that no arrangement had been made for Baltimore, because Gilmore and Sinclair claimed that they had no authority to act for the club.

Even before the arrangement that left them out of the peace settlement was made, Baltimore officials had been suspicious of the intentions of their colleagues, and some Baltimore leaders had made a special trip to Chicago toward the end of 1914 to satisfy themselves about Weeghman's and Gilmore's intentions. Although they received assurances that there was nothing to rumors of flirtations with Organized Baseball, they left with their suspicions unallayed. At the New York parley at the end of 1915 their worst fears were proved well founded. They arrived to find the broad outlines of settlement already agreed upon and Baltimore's fate left to be worked out among other details later. Baltimore was out of business, its assets largely wiped out, and its player contracts a liability. As the saying went, Baltimore had been given the "dinky-dink."

At the Waldorf peace meeting, the evening of the seventeenth [*] with representatives of the majors and the affected minors present, Baltimore tried desperately to salvage something. Its officers contended that the city was deserving of major-league status, and they asked permission to buy the franchise of the St. Louis Nationals, which Garry Herrmann had previously indicated might be available. Baltimore's population in 1910 was not only greater than that of St. Louis, which was already proving incapable of supporting two major-league clubs adequately, but larger than that of four other major-league cities —Washington, Detroit, Cincinnati, and Cleveland. Nevertheless, the strong appeal of the Baltimore representatives was met with ridicule. Comiskey threw up to them the city's failure to support the franchise Baltimore had once held in the American League. When the Baltfeds' attorney said they were willing to pay $250,000 for a franchise, Comiskey replied, to the amusement of the fifty-odd men present, that it was just the right price for a minor-league franchise. "Baltimore is a minor league city and not a hell of a good one at that," he mocked. Ebbets seconded Comiskey. Baltimore was a minor-league city, he said, "positively and absolutely," and "will never be anything else." Furthermore, Ebbets exclaimed, it is one of the worst minor-league towns in the country: "you have too many colored population to start with. They are a cheap population when it gets down to paying their money at the gate." It did not occur to Ebbets and the others that the chance to see a few Negro stars on the lily-white teams might have opened their wallets.

The following week Gilmore telephoned the Baltimore leaders from Cincinnati, where the peace pact was being completed, and said that

[*] See above, chapter 11.

the best he could get for Baltimore was $50,000. Baltimore spokesmen flatly rejected the offer and refused to withdraw from the suit, which had been dismissed in Landis's court "without prejudice" to the Baltimore club. The peacemakers at Cincinnati then put the matter in the hands of a committee, which was to meet early in January. However, the Baltimore men declined to have their future decided by a committee heavily weighted against them. When the Feds finally met in Chicago on February 19, 1916, to wind up their affairs, Baltimore refused to attend or to have anything more to do with them. The club recouped $25,000 through the sale of its ball park to Jack Dunn, and the stockholders raised $50,000 to finance legal action.

On March 29, 1916, Baltimore sued Organized Baseball and former Fed leaders Sinclair, Gilmore, and Weeghman for treble damages under the Sherman Act. The action was withdrawn in June 1917, not because an out-of-court agreement had been made but because the parties expected to reach one. When that hope failed, Baltimore reinstated the suit in September in the District Court of Columbia. After a two-week trial in 1919, Judge Stafford found that the activities of Organized Baseball constituted an attempt to monopolize the business of baseball exhibitions within the meaning of the Sherman Act. The jury fixed damages at $80,000, and the court entered judgment for $240,000 plus $24,000 in attorneys' fees. When the defendants appealed, Chief Justice Smyth reversed the decision on the grounds that a baseball exhibition was not in the category of trade or commerce since it "affects no exchange of things," and that the restrictions of the reserve clause related merely to the conservation of personnel and did not directly affect the interstate aspects of the plaintiff's business. Baltimore in turn appealed Smyth's decision to the United States Supreme Court. Each side had won one round. The question now was, Who would take the third and last one? As we shall see, it was to be several years before the final outcome would be known.

Meanwhile, trials of a different nature beset Organized Baseball. Up until 1917 World War One had had practically no impact on the industry, although baseball scores were no longer cabled to Great Britain and space allotted to ball games was reduced in the American press. The National League did hold a Red Cross Day in 1914 and donated a percentage of gate receipts. In the American League fans responded to Ban Johnson's appeal to contribute toward sending baseball equipment to Canadian troops in Europe—gifts that would be more welcome, remarked *Sporting News*, than tracts or Bibles. An interesting reflection of public sentiment in some quarters of the United States early in 1915, just before the sinking of the *Lusitania* helped change many minds, was a chain letter sent to Garry Herrmann requesting relief money for suffering Germans. The covering note was signed "Deutschland über Alles." That such a request could be made is a graphic reminder that American opinion moved only gradually from the neutrality advocated by President Wilson at the outset to intervention on the Allied side.

But the severance of diplomatic relations between the United States and Germany following Germany's resumption of unrestricted submarine warfare on February 1, 1917, made war imminent and aroused speculation about professional baseball's future. Should the "graver apprehensions of these days be realized," editorialized the New York *Times* obliquely, the American public would have little interest in baseball, and if attempts were made to continue it, there might be "manifestations of disapproval." Nevertheless the owners exerted strenuous efforts to stay in business.

A few days after the *Times* statement, Ban Johnson announced that the American League would not suspend operations should war come. After all, he said, the National League had not done so during the Spanish-American War. Both major leagues passed resolutions calling for the players to put in one hour of military drill daily. Army sergeants were secured to conduct the drills. They began in spring training, and most American League clubs continued them into the season. Fans were treated to the spectacle of ball players substituting bats for rifles and going through what passed for military exercises. Ban Johnson offered a $500 prize for the best-drilled team. The St. Louis Browns, who seldom won anything, were awarded the prize. Some minor-league teams joined the drill act, but the Brooklyn players, with refreshing good sense, voted against participation and declared that though they were patriotic they could scarcely master the rudiments of warfare in the time allotted. *Spalding's Guide* stated, perhaps with some slight exaggeration, that the drills "anticipated" and "nullified" any charges of "slackerism" that might be directed toward Organized Baseball. Eventually the program was abandoned.

Formal American entry into the war unleashed a flurry of activities and projects on the part of Organized Baseball, some of them worthy contributions, others, like the player drills, more showy than helpful. The "national game" should lead in "patriotic movements," club owners were told in a notice from the National Commission. It suggested that one or more Sunday exhibition games be played in eastern cities, with the receipts, less expenses, to be turned over to Army and Navy dependents. It is just possible that in staging Sunday games for a patriotic purpose, the Commission had in mind conditioning public opinion in the East to demand Sunday ball as a regular diet in the future.

In April Ban Johnson proclaimed that on "Wake Up America! Day" announcements urging enlistment in the armed forces would be made before the game in all parks. In October he stated that he himself had volunteered for military service in France but declined to say in what capacity. Memories of the Civil War draft riots had been revived in the minds of some government officials, so they welcomed the opportunity offered by the ball clubs to have contingents of troops parade in the parks before games in order to stimulate martial spirit and make conscription more palatable to the public. Soldiers and sailors were admitted to games free on certain days. The purchase of Liberty Bonds by baseball personnel was encouraged, and contributions were made to the Red Cross by clubs and leagues. Garry Herrmann, for example, sent Secretary of War Newton D. Baker a check for $16,-034.32, a sum taken out of the 1918 World Series receipts.

Clark Griffith was very active soliciting funds for the purchase of baseball equipment for the armed forces. In the three years from 1917 through 1919 he raised thousands of dollars for baseball paraphernalia. A total of 3100 kits was sent, each containing a catcher's mask, mitt, and chest protector; a first baseman's mitt; three bats; three bases; a dozen balls; a dozen scorecards; and a rule book. Each set cost about thirty dollars. General Pershing wrote Griffith saying that the equipment was welcome and expressing his thanks, and he and other officers were reported as claiming that playing baseball made the soldiers more proficient at throwing grenades! Griffith's fund also allocated money for *Baseball Magazine* subscriptions and for copies of *Sporting News*. When the latter's circulation dropped to only 5000 at one point during the war, the paper was rescued by the American League's purchase of 150,000 copies for the troops overseas.

These early wartime activities were accompanied by efforts to persuade public opinion of the desirability of continuing Organized Baseball in operation. In May, John K. Tener asserted:

> This is a war of democracy against bureaucracy. And I tell you that baseball is the very watchword of democracy. There is no other sport or business or anything under heaven which exerts the leveling influence that baseball does. Neither the public school nor the church can approach it. Baseball is unique. England is a democratic country, but it lacks the finishing touch of baseball.

The July issue of *Baseball Magazine* devoted much of its space to "the baseball business and the war," including a reprint of, and editorial comment on, President Wilson's recommendation that "sports" go on as usual. The magazine, one of the editors informed Garry Herrmann, "is circulating to the newspapers printed propaganda to

help keep sports as usual—and baseball in particular." This propaganda, he added, may deter the continuation of that "pessimistic
stuff" by "a few [sportswriters] who fail to realize that they might
write themselves out of a job."

The swing of the country to a war footing left Organized Baseball
relatively unscathed in 1917. The draft required all men between
twenty-one and thirty inclusive to register on June 5, and the first
drawings were made July 20, but few ball players were called up and
few volunteered. The greatest immediate cause for concern was the
slackening off of major-league attendance by more than 1,283,000. In
November Ban Johnson suggested asking the government to exempt
eighteen men on each major-league team from the draft; however,
John K. Tener immediately assailed the idea as "preposterous" and
"unpatriotic." At a joint session in December the major leagues decided that it would be time enough to retrench when circumstances
forced them to do so. They therefore went ahead to adopt a full playing schedule and to maintain their player limits for 1918.

The decision provoked sharp criticism from the New York *Times:*
"With an astonishing disregard for the new proprieties and new de-
cencies . . . the so-called 'magnates' of baseball have proclaimed in
both 'leagues' their unswerving adherence to the wretched fallacy of
'business as usual.'" That policy, continued the editorial, "is not calculated to make us proud of baseball as an American institution." The
criticism was somewhat softened when it was shortly made known
that the National League, in a direct rebuff to Johnson, had formally
resolved to ask its players to offer their services to the military. This
information led the *Times* to comment that the "indifference" of most
players to enlistment had put baseball in a bad light and that many
of them, realizing this, had volunteered in the past few weeks.

The magnates soon modified their December decisions. They cut
the number of games for 1918 to 140, and they abolished player limits
to offset losses from the draft. The spring-training period was shortened, and to reduce railway travel training sites closer to home were
selected—although some teams disregarded this curb. The playing
schedule was also juggled for the same reason. Except on the most
prosperous clubs, there was a general reduction in players' salaries
throughout both major leagues, with war conditions given as the reason. In announcing cuts all along the line for his Athletics, Connie
Mack asked the players to take a chance on their salaries. He promised that if the club made money the profits would be distributed
among the men: "If we make ten thousand we will gladly share it
with them."

By this time the government had levied a 10 per cent tax on entertainment admissions. The Internal Revenue Bureau also applied the tax to those who rented space on rooftops or in trees adjoining ball parks. Herrmann said bluntly that the war tax "must be paid for by the patrons." It was, and then some. The tax was three, eight, or thirteen cents, depending on the type of ticket, but to avoid the inconvenience of handling pennies in making change, the magnates raised 25-cent seats to 30 cents, 75-cent ones to 85 cents, and $1.25 tickets to $1.40. They therefore not only passed the charge along to the consumer but had extra pennies left over on each ticket. A proposal that all clubs donate the extra change to charity was rejected, and the individual club owner could decide whether to give the money to the Red Cross or "pocket it." The new plan also marked the end of what was left of quarter ball. By 1920 the price of admission, including the 10 per cent Federal "war tax" still in effect, ranged from 55 cents in the bleachers to $1.10 in the grandstand and $1.65 for a box. Throughout the 1920's these same prices were retained, even after the excise was removed.

The real crunch for professional baseball came May 23, 1918, when the government issued the so-called work-or-fight order, setting July 1 as the deadline for men to get into essential work or face induction into the armed forces. Provost Marshal Crowder's edict, endangering as it did the continued operation of the baseball business, induced a flow of rationalizations for its continuance from the baseball owners. The claim that during World War One they sought no special favors or consideration is a part of baseball mythology.

At first Tener and Johnson stood on high ground awaiting interpretation of the directive from Crowder's office. If baseball came within the scope of the order, said Tener, it would do its part, but it might have to close the parks if replacements for drafted men could not be found. Johnson was reported as saying that if he had his way he would "close every theatre, ball park, and place of recreation in the country and make people realize that they were in the most terrible war in the history of the world." Apparently he had second thoughts a month later. Expressing surprise that baseball and other "sports" were classified as non-essential, he said, "I cannot understand the statement [that] the game is non-productive when the two major leagues will deliver to the government a war tax in the neighborhood of $300,000." Claiming that players, umpires, and stockholders had bought more than eight million dollars' worth of Liberty Bonds and had subscribed to the Red Cross and other charities, Johnson asked, "Where is there another class of men earning so much for the government?" Tener was also adopting a different line. He called baseball a "moral and spiritual production" and added: "Simply because what baseball produces is intangible I do not think it can be called non-essential or not productive."

Another source of resentment within Organized Baseball was the exemption of theatrical performers because they supposedly did so much to preserve morale. Theatres were open only six months in winter; why should not baseball parks be kept open in summer? *Sporting News* surmised that the reason ball players were being called up while actors and tenors escaped was not only that baseball was a daytime function and so drew men from useful employment, but that players had been "inclined to shirk their duties and their country in its war crisis." But the impression that ball playing was "a profession of slackers" was not true, said the editorial, claiming that as of the first of May 560 players were in military service. A sportswriter rushing to the defense said, "any one who takes [it] upon himself . . . to cast odium on baseball and drag it to the level of discredited occupations is taking an awful and an undeserved slam at a national institution and . . . is committing nothing less than sacrilege."

Clarification of the work-or-fight order came before the end of July. Washington owner Clark Griffith had an appeal prepared on behalf of his drafted catcher, Eddie Ainsmith. The appeal in this test case rested on three arguments. First, baseball was a business with large investments and valuable property which would be made temporarily worthless because it could not be used for other purposes. Second, ball players did not have the necessary skill to enter new occupations that would permit them to maintain the living standard to which they and their families had become accustomed through their baseball earnings. Third, baseball was accepted as the national sport and, because it provided almost the only opportunity to many workers and businessmen for outdoor recreation, to end it would inflict social and industrial harm far out of proportion to the military loss of the limited number of players in question.

Secretary of War Newton D. Baker swept these pleas aside and not only refused to change the regulations but called for their extension to other occupations.° He reminded the petitioners that times were not normal and all must make sacrifices, and he expressed confidence that the American people were resourceful enough to find other means of recreation and relaxation.

The New York *Times* heartily endorsed Baker's decision. It was "perfectly evident to everybody whose common sense is not distorted by self-interest," stated the editorial coldly, that professional ball has no claim to be considered essential. The *Times* recognized that "the game as played by professionals" held a "mysteriously large place in

° Later, theatrical performers were included.

the hearts of many Americans," but although it was an excellent game intrinsically, it "degrades its practitioners and votaries as soon as it is changed from a sport to a trade." *Stars and Stripes* likewise took a sour view of the owners' effort to obtain special dispensation, and a little later on, when some baseball men proposed sending a couple of teams to play exhibitions for the troops overseas, it opposed the idea. American soldiers had plenty of talent and could do without visiting stars, said the Army paper, and as a parting shot it added that the AEF recalled the "recent difficulty" between the big-league magnates and the Secretary of War "and rejoices in the prompt and righteous settlement thereof."

After Baker's pronouncement, the exodus of ball players, already under way, became a rush. Major-league teams were decimated as the men left for war jobs or the service. Altogether, 124 American and 103 National Leaguers entered the armed forces. The first to enlist was Hank Gowdy, Boston Braves catcher, who joined up almost at the outset and saw considerable action. At least three professionals were killed, including Captain Eddie Grant of the Giants, who is usually the only fatality remembered, perhaps because of the tablet erected to his memory at the Polo Grounds after the Armistice.

Many of the professionals, like other American soldiers and sailors, played ball in the training camps and in England, France, and the occupied zones of Germany. The yeoman branch of the Navy became a snug harbor for ball players. Some of the naval stations went so far as to advertise sinecures for players in order to get them to enlist. At the Boston Navy Yard a select team of major-league ball-player yeomen, headed by Jack Barry, had arranged a "pretty program" of exhibition games that would have taken up the greater part of the summer of 1918, but Admiral Wood, the commandant, ordered the schedule canceled and the former players to work as ordinary seamen. Some of the stars who went abroad endeavored to teach the game to foreigners. One of the instructors, Johnny Evers, the star second baseman, sent home a clipping about his tutorial efforts with the French headlined, "Célèbre Professeur du Sport Américain," which also referred to him as the "maître de géographie de la deuxième base." But in the long run their converts, like the "rice Christians" of China, were not permanently impressed.

To avoid the draft, a number of players chose to go into airplane, nitrate, and electrical plants. Some did farm work. Favorite havens were steel mills and shipyards. These industries were so anxious to have a fast brand of baseball in their leagues that they offered well-paid "soft" jobs to professional ball players and even sent out "scouts" to bring them in. Consequently, much criticism was leveled at these industries and their "camouflaged" ball players. Calvin Page, a member of the Massachusetts legislature, toured East-Coast shipyards and reported that ball-player "painters" in some of them carried two pails of paint a day to the real painters and then spent the rest of the time on the diamond at $500 a week. At Cramp's Ship Yard, Philadelphia, 2000 striking workers charged that ball players and actors in the role of foremen came to work well dressed, and in cars, and then did nothing but talk baseball and give foolish orders. The government's Emergency Ship Corporation investigated and reported that the accusations were exaggerated and that not all the "slackers" were ball players; another investigator found that the number of ball-player "painters" was negligible. Nevertheless, the yards began passing rules limiting the number of professionals on their teams to anywhere from two to five each. An eventual crackdown by the government was headlined by the *Sporting News*, "Players Must Be Able To Use Brush; Shipyards Threaten To Can All Who Can't Paint."

The flight of players to industrial teams met with objections from the club owners. There was even some talk of blacklisting those who got into war work while the getting was good. "There is no room on my club for players who wish to evade the army draft by entering the employ of ship owners," declared Comiskey, ignoring the fact that the players had a perfect right to choose between war work and the Army, and also forgetting that those who left had given up their "room" on the team anyway. What really irked Comiskey and other owners was the opportunity afforded players to use their talent to find other employment in spite of the reserve clause. A statement by Ban Johnson revealed what was annoying them. It was unjust, he said, to "draft" players into factories and shipyards "for their ball playing ability, and leave their clubs holding the sack." A particular culprit, in the eyes of the owners, was Bethlehem Steel, whose agents invaded the ranks of players under contract and offered them jobs in the "Schwab League." Ban Johnson finally presented the problem directly to Charles M. Schwab himself, who pledged not to induce any more players to break their contracts.

Another false impression that has gained currency with the passage of time is that the government forced the baseball owners to shut down. There was nothing in either the work-or-fight order or in Secretary Baker's interpretation of it which compelled them to close shop. Indeed, a letter from the White House dated July 27, 1918, stated that the President saw "no necessity at all for stopping or curtailing the baseball schedule." The choice rested with the owners. They could either quit or carry on as best they could by scraping together makeshift teams of minor-leaguers and superannuated veterans, as they were to do in World War Two. In fact, they were already filling gaps by "exhuming" (as sportswriter Fred Lieb termed it) over-age players. Minor-leaguers were also becoming increasingly available because their clubs were disbanding; out of the nine lower leagues that started the 1918 season, only one finished it. The truth is that the big-league owners chose to shut down early because of dwindling gate receipts.

What actually happened was that the day after Secretary Baker's decision was handed down Ban Johnson announced that the American League would close for the duration of the war after that day's games. But American League owners flouted his edict and continued playing—an ominous portent that his tight grip upon them was finally loosening. To add to the confusion, the National League was reported in favor of going ahead with players under and over draft age, only to reverse itself shortly. The upshot was that the owners again sought and obtained special dispensation from the government. In answer to their request that ball players be exempt from the draft until October 15, the end of the playing season, Secretary Baker gave them until September 1 to find essential jobs—in short, a two-month extension of Crowder's original deadline.

Still the owners could not make up their minds. They were in accord on shortening the season but differed on the closing date and on whether to squeeze in a World Series before September 1 or try to play one after it. At last they decided to continue through Labor Day, one day past the government deadline, in order to reap the holiday gate receipts, and to play the World Series afterwards. But the Chicago players, likely winners in the National League, were not going to risk being drafted during the Series, so they demanded that explicit government permission be secured beforehand, else they would not play. Again baseball leaders met with War Department officials, who granted a two-week extension to those players participating in the World Series but refused to extend the September 1 season deadline the extra day. The players would have to take their chances with their draft boards, Crowder commented.

The teams did play the extra day anyhow, except for Cleveland. Its players had been given to understand by owner Jim Dunn that the team would not play beyond Sunday, September 1, so many of them had lined up war jobs and were scheduled to go to work early Tuesday morning. Consequently, they refused to go to St. Louis for the final two games on Sunday and Monday (Labor Day). The Browns demanded that the games be forfeited and that Cleveland pay the $1000 penalty for each, but Ban Johnson declined to take any action on the matter.

Not only did the owners cut short the season; but they also managed to avoid paying the players the balance of their salaries. This purpose was accomplished by the simple subterfuge of "releasing" all of them with ten days' notice, as provided in their contracts. This act would normally have made them free agents, but the magnates entered into a gentlemen's agreement not to tamper with each other's men. Thus the owners had it both ways: they saved an estimated $200,000 in payrolls and at the same time retained their monopsony control over their players, pending the reopening of business. As Connie Mack later admitted, "It was only natural that we should enter into an agreement to protect our interests."

Some players sued to recover the balance of their salaries. Jake Daubert, Brooklyn first baseman, who was completing the last year of a five-year contract at $9000 a season, claimed $2150 as the balance of his 1918 salary. The suit was finally settled out of court, with Daubert obtaining most of his money. Ebbets, highly displeased with him, traded the star to Cincinnati. Burt Shotton was another "not willing to accept the fortunes of war." Because he sued the Washington club for $1400, one reporter said that "something or other turned him Bolsheviki." Owner Clark Griffith put him on the block; he was "waived" out of the American League but was able to sign with a National League club.

What with the war and the abbreviated season, major-league attendance plunged to only 3,080,126, a decline of well over two million from the previous year and the worst showing of the century. On the other hand, the owners saved about six weeks' of payroll, their crocodile tears shed over the players and their families in the Ainsmith draft appeal having quickly dried. The poor seasonal attendance carried over into the World Series and helped touch off a near-strike by the players. They objected to receiving a much lower sum for playing in the Series than what they had been led to expect.

One reason for their skimpy portions was the introduction of a new method of dividing receipts that year. Originally, when the National Commission took charge of the Series and instituted the Brush Plan in 1905, 60 per cent of the gate receipts from the first four games went to the players, to be divided 75 per cent to the winning and 25 per cent to the losing team; the remainder of the receipts was split equally between the clubs. (The reason for limiting the players to a share in only the first four of the seven games was to remove any temptation for them to extend the Series purposely in order to increase their take.) However, the 75-25 ratio between the winning and losing shares was so out of proportion that most of the players "hedged their bets" and made private deals among themselves to split the money 50-50, regardless of which team won—a practice employed even as early as the Temple Cup Series of the 1890's.° To overcome this difficulty, the split was soon changed to 60-40 and still remains the same today. Thereafter, about the only complaint the players made was that the owners were not reporting the receipts honestly.

Then in 1918 President Tener put over his plan to permit the teams finishing second, third, and fourth in each league to share in the Series receipts along with the pennant winners. The players were not consulted about the change. When Series time came, the magnates, anticipating a falling-off of interest, charged only the regular season prices instead of the higher ones customary for the Series. Besides, the players had pledged 10 per cent of their Series money to the Red Cross. The National Commission had indicated that the winning and losing shares for players on the contending teams, the Boston Americans and the Chicago Nationals, would be at least $2000 and $1400 respectively. But small crowds at the first three games in Chicago, the low admission prices, and the new plan for eight teams, instead of two as formerly, to share the players' pool were obviously going to necessitate cutting a small pie into little pieces. So the National Commission decided to reduce the Series shares of the Red Sox and Cubs to $1200 and $800,°° in order to leave something for the other six clubs.

After talking things over on the train from Chicago, the World Series players concluded that these reductions were unreasonable and appointed a four-man committee, two from each team, to take up the question with the Commission. The player committee finally tracked down the Commission the morning of the fifth game, but their meeting was inconclusive. The players wanted the new plan for cutting in the other first-division clubs postponed until after the war, or else their original shares restored. The Commission said the receipts were only half what had been expected and tried to put off a decision until after the Series. Later Herrmann telephoned Leslie Mann, one of the player delegates, to say the Commission could not change the rule for apportioning the players' shares; it was up to the leagues to do that.

Figuring that the Commission was stalling, the players decided not to play the rest of the games. The Commission arrived just before game time to find the stands full of people and the field empty of players. Extra police were called in case of trouble, and the game was delayed an hour while the Commission met with the player representatives in the umpires' room under the stands. Johnson was inebriated and made a maudlin appeal to the men. The players, realiz-

° See *Baseball: The Early Years*, page 289.
°° Figures at issue vary.

ing that he was in no shape for serious discussion, elected to go ahead, not because ordered by the Commission, they said, but for the sake of the game, the public, and the wounded soldiers in the stands. They also agreed to play only on condition that there be no penalties for their strike action. The Commission exuberantly assured them that nothing would happen. But that winter the players received letters informing them that because of their threatened strike they were fined their championship emblems. And they never have received them. The winning share was $1,102.51, the smallest ever, and the losing share was $671.09, next to the lowest on record.

After the Armistice in Europe, baseball officials appealed once more to the War Department, this time for the release of players in the service in time for the 1919 season—acting, as the New York *Times* observed, in the same way as large corporations and business houses, which wanted their key men back in a hurry. Other measures adopted by the owners for 1919 reflected their eagerness to recoup financially from the poor previous season and their uncertainty about the coming one. They agreed secretly to place a limit on club payrolls—which meant salary cuts. As Colonel Huston, a Yankees partner, said, "the players can sign at the salaries offered or not at all"; the New York club will now be placed "on a strictly business basis." The owners also reduced the number of players per club from 25 to 21, and they shortened the spring-training period by delaying its start until late March. Finally, the magnates decided to maintain the short 140-game season.

The decision to stand pat on the short schedule and to "wait and see" proved costly to the major-league owners. As it was, they drew 6,532,439 fans, a signal improvement over the previous year. Had they ventured to return to the 154-game season, they would have drawn approximately 650,000 more—assuming, of course, that the average rate of attendance continued for the additional fourteen playing dates. In that case, the total attendance would have surpassed seven million, matching the best years before World War One. But it was not given to the owners to peer into the future and foresee that a prosperous new era was about to burst upon professional ball, as indeed it was to burst on most of the nation. If they had been more aware of the history of their business, they would have known that baseball prospered after the Civil War and the Spanish-American War. But before entering upon a new phase of its history, the industry was to undergo further travail.

PART FOUR

THE TARNISHED IMAGE

13

DOWNFALL OF THE NATIONAL COMMISSION

CONCURRENTLY with the problems created by the last thrust of the Players' Fraternity, the anti-trust action of the Baltimore Feds, and the entrance of the United States into the World War, there erupted among major-league executives a series of unpleasant disputes that were largely responsible for the ultimate downfall of the National Commission and the near disruption of the entire structure of Organized Baseball.

Four quarrels over rights to ball players lay at the root of the dissension. The first one, involving George Sisler, really started as far back as 1911, when Sisler, not yet eighteen years old, signed a contract with the Akron club of the Central League, then changed his mind and enrolled at the University of Michigan, where, as an all-round player—pitcher, first baseman, and outfielder—he progressed brilliantly. Meanwhile, Akron had transferred the contract to its parent club, Columbus, which in turn sold it to Pittsburgh. Sisler had never played a game for any of these clubs and had accepted no money. When he persisted in not reporting, Barney Dreyfuss placed him on the Pirates' suspended list.

The case first came to the National Commission's attention in August 1912, at which time Detroit Judge George B. Codd, who was to handle Sisler's interests throughout the controversy, pointed out that the annual reservation of Sisler by a professional club jeopardized his eligibility as a college player. About the same time, Sisler himself wrote the National Commission to repudiate the contract, because he was a minor when he signed it and did not "in any way understand the nature of the contract" he signed. He asked the Commission to certify that he did not belong to any club. Sisler's father also wrote the Commission along similar lines and attested that he had not given George his consent to sign. The guiding hand behind all this strategy was Branch Rickey, who had studied law at Michigan and was base-

ball coach there when Sisler arrived. Apprised of the lad's predicament, Rickey, as his biographer described it, "took protective steps
in the boy's behalf."

While Sisler was in college the case simmered along inconclusively.
The National Commission delayed and equivocated. On the one
hand, it realized, as Ban Johnson put it, that neither Columbus nor
Pittsburgh had "a moral or legal claim" to the player, who had signed
with Akron "through misrepresentation by an obscure umpire." On
the other hand, it felt that Dreyfuss deserved consideration because
of the money he had spent on Sisler's contract. Therefore Herrmann
finally suggested to Codd that Sisler should be made a free agent but
that when he decided to play professional ball Pittsburgh "should be
given every opportunity to secure his services." Codd, however, was
unyielding: his client must be made a free agent with no strings attached. Meanwhile Sisler became the outstanding college player of
the country, and his value as a baseball property appreciated accordingly.

At last in October 1914, with Sisler in his senior year, Codd forced
the issue to a head. He wrote Herrmann that "the time is at hand
when this young man should be allowed to make a profit out of his
own ability and every day's delay is adding to the damage which he
is sustaining by your deprivation of his legal rights." Sisler was preparing to sue for triple damages unless the matter was brought to a
satisfactory conclusion. At this juncture an unnamed major-league
owner suggested "that the Commission declare the player a free agent
[but] that no major league clubs negotiate with him . . . other than
the Pittsburgh club, thus affording that club the sole right to contract
with him." But Dreyfuss thought that this scheme would only make
matters worse because of the danger of charges of conspiracy. He
suggested that Herrmann seek legal advice. The Commission's attorneys told Herrmann categorically that the contract was invalid and
that trying to force a man to play with Pittsburgh, which had no
legal claim whatever to his services, would lay the Commission and
the clubs involved open to damages for conspiracy. This advice, together with the fact that the National Commission had its hands full
with the Federal League litigation, settled the matter, and the Commission unanimously agreed to declare Sisler a free agent.

In June 1915 Sisler, having finished college, wrote Herrmann that,
while he would give Pittsburgh every chance to sign him, he had also
been in touch with other teams and furthermore had received large
offers from teams outside of Organized Baseball (the Feds). Dreyfuss
in fact offered him $700 a month for the balance of the 1915 season
plus a $1000 bonus, which, by prorating the salary over a six-month

period, made a total of $5200. But in mid-June Sisler wired Dreyfuss, "Have decided to join the St. Louis American League team." The Browns paid him $400 a month and gave him $5000 for signing, bringing his total to $7400. The club also agreed to eliminate the ten-day clause from his contract and to give him a substantial raise the following year if he made good. The manager of the Browns? Branch Rickey.

Dreyfuss immediately filed a complaint with the Commission against the St. Louis club in which he claimed that he had proof of tampering and interference by Rickey. He charged a breach of faith by St. Louis and asserted that Pittsburgh had unquestioned right to the player under baseball law. But Ban Johnson was unwilling to suspend Sisler unless Herrmann took the responsibility. "I am not courting damage suits," he wrote. So, "pending further investigation," Sisler was allowed to continue playing with the Browns. Because the case involved a dispute between a National League and an American League club, it was up to Herrmann to decide it. It was not until June 1916, a year later, that Herrmann dismissed the complaint of the Pittsburgh club for lack of evidence—a decision, he added, with which the other members of the Commission "fully concurred."

Dreyfuss was outraged, and his wrath was fed constantly by the sight of Sisler developing into a great first baseman and one of the best players ever. The Pittsburgh owner became the implacable foe of Garry Herrmann and thenceforward bent every effort to unseat him as chairman of the National Commission. That winter Dreyfuss introduced a resolution at a National League meeting calling for Herrmann's replacement by a neutral chairman. The measure failed, but Dreyfuss never let up. And his was never an entirely lone voice against Herrmann in National League councils. During the costly Federal League war some other owners had entertained the idea of saving money by doing away with the Commission entirely. They estimated that to date it had cost them in the neighborhood of $400,000, most of it, in their view, spent on petty minor-league squabbles or held by the Commission. They saw this as money which had come out of their pockets and which they could have used to help offset the cost of the war.

After the Federal peace, sentiment for change persisted. Some American League owners were dissatisfied because two of the three members of the Commission were National Leaguers. On the other hand, some National Leaguers felt that Herrmann was too much under Ban Johnson's thumb. Many believed the remedy lay in selecting an outsider as chairman, someone without a financial interest in baseball, and the names of William Howard Taft and Judge Landis, "a firm friend of the established order of things in the National pastime," were mentioned from time to time. There was even thought of democratizing the Commission by broadening its base to include a suitable player representative, someone like Sam Crawford, the Detroit outfielder. The minor leagues were also interested in representation and at one point named a committee to consider the idea.

All this talk of revamping the Commission remained largely in the realm of speculation until in June 1918, two years almost to the day after the Sisler decision, more serious trouble broke out because of another disputed player, a pitcher named Scott Perry. The Boston Nationals had acquired Perry from the Atlanta club for $2500 the year before on a thirty-day trial basis, with $500 put down, the balance to be paid if they kept him. After seventeen days with the Braves, Perry jumped the club and joined an independent team, and so the deal between Boston and Atlanta was left uncompleted. The National Commission ruled that if Perry should return to Organized Baseball, Boston could have him if it paid the $2000 balance. This arrangement gave Boston a kind of equity in the player. Meanwhile, he was kept on Atlanta's ineligible list.

Some months later Atlanta sold Perry to Connie Mack, the "Tall Tutor" or the "Slim Schemer," depending upon which writer one read. Perry, hitherto an indifferent performer who had bounced around with a number of clubs, began winning games for the Athletics, including one over Walter Johnson. Noticing this, Boston decided to exercise its claim to Perry and appealed to the National Commission to verify its right to him. Since the dispute involved clubs in each major league and a minor league, the decision rested with the National Commission, the secretary of the National Association, and the president of the minor league to which Atlanta belonged.

By a 3-2 vote, Perry was awarded to Boston on the grounds that Atlanta had no right to sell him to Mack, who in effect was dealing with a contract-jumper, and that no agreement between Atlanta and the Athletics had ever been promulgated with the Commission. Mack, however, refused to accept either the decision or Boston's offer to compromise by accepting another player from the Athletics. With at least the tacit approval of Ban Johnson, who had cast one of the minority votes, Mack ignored Organized Baseball's custom of settling its own disputes. He went into the civil courts and secured an injunction preventing the Braves from getting Perry. Those who supported Mack argued that, while technically Boston may have had a claim to Perry, Mack had a moral right to him.

But National League owners fumed. After all, they had abided by the decision in the Sisler case, but now when the tables were turned and the decision went against an American League club, it refused to accept the verdict and ran to court. President Tener was so angry that he refused to sit on the National Commission again unless Connie Mack handed over the player to Boston. Relations between Tener and Ban Johnson had already been strained. Johnson had favored a tougher policy toward the Feds than Tener, Herrmann, and the National Leaguers had taken. Another reason was Johnson's resentment when Tener criticized his suggestion earlier in the year that the major leagues should ask draft exemption for players. The Scott Perry case not only made the break between the two league presidents an open one; it came close to ending the National Agreement and starting a war between the two leagues. The National League president even recommended cancelling the World Series unless the American League complied with the decision. When his owners refused to back him to that extent, Tener resigned from the presidency. However, under John A. Heydler, who took over Tener's duties and was officially elected president of the National League that winter, a compromise was reached. The Athletics kept Scott Perry but withdrew the injunction and paid Boston $2500 as compensation for his services. Incidentally, Perry, reverting to form, later jumped the Athletics and went into the tailoring business; then, reportedly "tiring of sewing on buttons," he returned to the Philadelphia club.

After the Scott Perry affair, matters went from bad to worse. The Commission's prestige suffered further from its undignified handling of the threatened players' strike during the World Series that fall. Heydler came out of the experience convinced that there had to be a change at the top. Then in November two owners, with the blessing of several of their colleagues, took it upon themselves to ascertain if William Howard Taft would be willing to take over as the commissioner. One of those who approached Taft was Harry Frazee, owner of the Boston Red Sox. Frazee and some other American League owners, growing more resentful of Johnson's high-handed rule, saw the possible appointment of Taft as a way to scuttle Johnson as well as Herrmann. But Taft declined the offer.

That winter National Leaguers again evinced strong opposition to Herrmann. But at a joint meeting of the majors it was Ban Johnson, paradoxically, who defended Herrmann against his own league and saved him as chairman of the National Commission. Nevertheless, time was running out on Garry. The magnates appointed a committee to search for a neutral chairman, and Johnson himself was soon beset with difficulties in his own league more grave than those that hounded Herrmann in the National.

First in the train of events that were to erode Johnson's power was his decision early in 1919 in the case of Jack Quinn, the pitcher who was claimed by both the Chicago White Sox and the New York Yankees.° Since this was an issue between two clubs within the American League, it was up to Johnson to settle it, and he decided in favor of the Yankees. Just as Herrmann's decision in the Sisler case brought him the enmity of Dreyfuss, so now Johnson's in the Quinn case won for him the lasting antagonism of Comiskey. The long-standing differences between them, patched up periodically, now reached the point of no return. Johnson was also feuding with Harry Frazee, the Boston owner. Frazee objected to what he considered Johnson's interference in his business, and Johnson charged Frazee with permitting gambling in Fenway Park and threatened to drive him out of baseball.

The fruit of these personal fights would not be long in ripening. In the middle of the 1919 season the Carl Mays incident precipitated within the American League a prolonged, acrimonious struggle which warrants full discussion because its impact on the league and Organized Baseball was to be felt for years to come. It pried loose Johnson's hold on the American League, it was instrumental in ending the Commission's rule, and it temporarily ripped the American League apart in the process.

On July 13 Mays, pitching for Boston in Chicago, stalked out of the game after two innings, went to the clubhouse, dressed, and departed for the East. Mays was an excellent pitcher but a temperamental character who, as someone once said, had the disposition of a person with a permanent toothache. He had already got into trouble earlier in the season for throwing a ball at a spectator who was heckling him. Why Mays left the team in Chicago is not entirely clear. The accepted story is that he became angered at the poor support of his teammates and, upon quitting the game, vowed that he would never pitch for the Red Sox again. But there may have been extenuating circumstances that are never mentioned in popular accounts. For one thing, during the game Mays was hit in the back of the head with a ball by his catcher, Wally Schang, who was throwing to second to retire a Chicago runner. For another, Boston sportswriter James C. O'Leary claimed that he had seen a note, written by Mays just before he left Chicago, which indicated that the pitcher was despondent over some real or imaginary personal troubles. O'Leary also reported that a messenger sent to look for Mays when he left the bench had found him weeping in the clubhouse.

These points are confirmed in an affidavit submitted by Mays later on, which stated that he left the team on account of "injury" and difficulties in his personal affairs. Other affidavits made it appear that

° See above, chapter 2.

Mays's explanation was satisfactory to the Boston management, which therefore saw no reason to take disciplinary measures. On the other hand, it is conceivable that the story of injury and personal problems was fabricated afterward to disprove Ban Johnson's argument that Mays should have been penalized.

In any event, when other clubs showed interest in dealing for Mays, Ban Johnson let it be known that he wanted no trade made until Mays returned to the Boston team in good standing, presumably after appropriate disciplinary measures had been taken. However, after Mays had absented himself for more than two weeks, Frazee traded him to the New York Yankees. This move was not only contrary to Johnson's wishes but further strengthened a team that already had a good chance to win the pennant, and in effect rewarded Mays into the bargain.

Johnson, enraged at this unprecedented defiance, immediately suspended Mays indefinitely and ordered umpires not to allow the pitcher to play for New York. Colonel Ruppert of the Yankees wired Johnson to ask that he lift the suspension. Ruppert questioned Johnson's right to interfere in a matter between Boston and one of its players but asserted that if Johnson were going to take disciplinary action, he should have suspended Mays during the time he was away from his club and not wait until the Yankees had him.

Johnson refused to raise the suspension, expressed surprise that any owner would dicker for a player who acted as Mays had done, and declared that since the Boston club had not suspended the pitcher, it became his duty to do so. He gave ground to the extent of proposing that a special American League meeting be held in New York to iron out the problem. The Yankees' owners refused to attend, for they figured that with Johnson in control the outcome was foreordained. They did, however, have a stormy interview with Johnson in which they unburdened themselves of all their stored-up vexations, past and present. They charged that it was Johnson's stockholding interest in the Cleveland club that had motivated him to keep Mays from playing for New York after Cleveland, which was also in the running for the pennant, failed to get him. Johnson, added the Yankees' owners, had for the same reason seen to it that Cleveland obtained Tris Speaker from the Red Sox in 1916. On his part, Johnson ignored the financial-interest accusations and stoutly maintained that Mays was a contract-breaker and that to allow him to be traded under those circumstances would be to encourage insubordination by dissatisfied players—a view, Johnson said, in which a majority of American League owners concurred.

Having reached this impasse, Ruppert and Huston, following

Mack's precedent in the Scott Perry fracas, turned to the courts and secured a temporary injunction restraining Johnson and American League clubs from interfering with Mays's playing for New York. The mere fact of going to court put another dent in the Commission's, as well as in Johnson's, authority and prestige. The New York owners quickly obtained a second injunction preventing Johnson from using American League funds to fight the first one. Then, in a last effort to settle the matter in a friendly way (Ruppert told the press), the New York colonels invited the other owners to meet at the Biltmore, where it could be made "abundantly clear" to them that "our [court] action was essential for the protection of our respective interests in our several club organizations." They also invited Johnson to "hear what is said and also to be heard if you so desire"—assuredly a new role for the "czar" of the American League!

Only Comiskey and Frazee attended. The others, including of course Johnson, either ignored or declined the invitation. Phil Ball wired: ". . . your business sagacity and acumen in Mays matter does not appeal to us. Your sportsmanship smells to heaven. We decline your invitation." To which Ruppert replied: "Refusal not unacceptable in view of your gratuitous insult in reply to polite invitation."

The Johnson and anti-Johnson supporters were lining up. On one side were the "insurrectionists," Ruppert and Huston, owners of the Yankees, Comiskey, and Frazee; on the other, besides Ball of the Browns, were Clark Griffith of Washington, Mack and the Shibes of Philadelphia, Frank Navin of Detroit, and Jim Dunn of Cleveland— the so-called "loyal five." The complexion of American League operations was indeed changing. For years the league had prided itself on being a smooth, disciplined organization, while it gazed with a certain hauteur upon the National League, which had been repeatedly convulsed with factional fights. Now the American League was about to equal, if not surpass, anything the older circuit had achieved in undignified behavior.

Ruppert's next gambit after the failure of his attempted league meeting was to summon the league's board of directors. The five-member board, comprised of Johnson and four owners, was controlled by the Insurrectionists, since Ruppert, Comiskey, and Frazee were on it. Jim Dunn resigned and Johnson refused to attend, explaining that he did not recognize the authority of the board to act, since it was contrary to the league's constitution for clubs to sit on a matter in which they were involved. The three-man rump board, proceeding without Johnson and Dunn, reinstated Mays to good standing with New York. Afterwards Colonel Huston called for a curb on Johnson's power and for the elimination of "czarism." "Such arbitrary rule . . . is un-American," he declared.

With the coming of the World Series Frank Navin injected a new issue into the mess. That year only the first three teams shared in the players' pool. The Yankees finished third, only a half game, five percentage points, in front of Navin's Detroit Tigers. Navin objected to the Yankees' receiving third-place money, which totalled a little more than $13,000. He argued that games won by New York with Mays pitching were illegal because he was under suspension. Those victories should be thrown out and Detroit awarded third place. Ruppert replied, "This protest from Mr. Navin verifies my opinion of the gentleman's sporting caliber, and it is my belief, based upon his well-known timorousness, that without the suggestion of support from the self-constituted powers in baseball he would not have the temerity to champion his untenable position so boldly." The National Commission withheld the third-place American League shares until such time as the whole controversy should be settled.

Meanwhile the New York club was seeking to have the temporary injunctions granted against Johnson made permanent. During preliminary examinations Johnson underwent a two-hour grilling in which he admitted holding $50,000 worth of Cleveland stock. It was revealed that when Cleveland bankers took over the club after Charles Somers went bankrupt, Johnson had loaned Jim Dunn, the new owner, $100,000 to help rescue the club from receivership. Half the loan had been repaid at four per cent, but Johnson still held $50,000 in Cleveland stock. In fact, the previous November (1918) he had advanced an additional $8500 to Dunn. Johnson had also held stock in the Boston Red Sox in 1912 and another time had loaned $30,000 to Washington out of American League funds without permission of the owners. It was further disclosed that Comiskey, too, put up $100,000 when Dunn assumed ownership of Cleveland and had been repaid $50,000 to date.* Comiskey, like Johnson, had also put money into Boston. In addition, Johnson admitted under examination that he had suspended Mays two days after the Yankees got him and that he had sent telegrams to all American League owners except Frazee to tell them not to dicker for Mays. The reason he had omitted the Boston owner, Johnson said, was that he was waiting for Frazee to suspend the pitcher and discipline him.

Joseph Auerbach, attorney for New York, called the American League president "a czar" and an "unmolested despot." Referring to the Cleveland tie-up, he flailed Johnson with the old syndicate-ball

* In February 1920 Comiskey stated that he had sold his Cleveland stock.

stick while conveniently passing over Comiskey. He also accused Johnson of having been "curiously slothful" in meting out discipline to other players and clubs in the past.

In answer, Johnson's attorney said the legal action of Ruppert and Huston was prompted by "commercial reasons only." He eulogized Johnson for making baseball so clean that state lawmakers had approved it as suitable Sunday sport. Others defended Johnson's connections with the Cleveland club on the ground that he was merely Dunn's creditor and held the stock only as collateral against the balance of the loan. The other owners, Ruppert and Huston included, already knew about the Cleveland-Johnson relationship, his supporters claimed, and most of them did not believe it prejudicial to Johnson's governing the league. In fact, more than one writer lauded Johnson (and Comiskey) for having come forward with financial aid while the other owners hung back. "Time was when these methods of bracing up weak points in the league were praised," wrote one; "Now they seem to be regarded as high crimes." Syndicate baseball was not good, he admitted, "Yet sometimes it is a necessity."

The legal fight ended in victory for the New York club and a check to the power of the league president. Late in October Justice Robert Wagner of the New York Supreme Court (later a United States Senator) granted a permanent injunction restraining Ban Johnson from interfering with Mays's performing with the Yankees. The essence of the court's ruling was that clubs had the right to regulate their own affairs and that the president of the league had no right to interfere. Wagner's reasoning stemmed from his view of professional baseball. "The commercialization of baseball," he said, "is a highly-profitable undertaking, rendering lucrative returns to the member clubs, to their stockholders, and to their players." The "large capital" invested in it consisted principally of contracts with individual players. Therefore, the court reasoned, the suspension of a player not only interferes with his individual contract; it may also interfere with the reputation and collective ability of the club. The court refused to accept Johnson's contention that, even though the power to suspend a player was not delegated to him, nevertheless the exercise of similar powers in the past gave him such a right. In rejecting this argument, Wagner ruled that Johnson could not "prescriptively acquire power of continual usurpation."

The triumphant Ruppert and Huston declared, "Our fight has not been for Mays alone, but to safeguard the vested and property rights of the individual club owner against the continual encroachments on club rights by the president, who has never been clothed with the powers that he has taken unto himself." Nor did they believe, "as Mr.

Johnson's baseball organ [*Sporting News*] would have us believe, that without Mr. Johnson's guiding hand the game could not long endure. . . ." Comiskey followed up with a slashing attack on Johnson with the avowed purpose of driving him out of baseball. The White Sox owner excoriated his former friend for "endangering not only the value of our properties but the integrity of baseball." The league's directors were going to inquire into Johnson's "perpetual franchise" as president and intended to rid Organized Baseball of this "impediment"—mild invective by comparison with Huston's designation of Johnson as "a carbuncle on the league organization." The directors of the league, Comiskey went on, "are the owners of properties worth at least several million dollars." Johnson owned nothing in baseball, added Comiskey, disregarding the league president's recently exposed financial tie with Cleveland.

A faint and what proved to be brief glimmer of peace lighted the bleak American League scene early in December. A New York newspaper described the setting: "Two and a half leagues meet here this week and half a league in Chicago." The headline referred to the simultaneous foregathering of the National League, the International League, and the American League's Insurrectionists in New York, plus the preparations of Johnson and the Loyal Five for a meeting in Chicago. At the last minute Johnson and his supporters decided to comply with the summons from the three Insurrectionists who, acting in the capacity of the board of directors, had called the American Leaguers to meet in New York. Frank Navin, as the "peacemaker," asserted, "I have no ax to grind and I would like to see the property rights of the club owners protected." Through Navin's good offices the Insurrectionists withdrew an injunction application against the proposed meeting of the Loyal Five, and in return the latter honored the summons of the rump board to meet in New York.

But the flickering hope for peace expired almost as quickly as a candle in a wind storm. The night before the full body of the American League was to convene, Comiskey learned from Navin that Johnson and the Loyal Five intended to vote the Insurrectionist members of the board out of office and install a brand new one. Hearing this, Huston cried, "Nothing but the vanity of one man [Johnson] stands in the way of peace in baseball."

The meeting that took place was "the most torrid session the American League has held in the nineteen years of its existence." There "probably has never been a baseball conclave in which there was such a violent display of bitterness," wrote a *Times* reporter. Although the meeting was held behind closed doors, the shouts of the sportsmen came through. Ruppert was heard to "thunder" at one point, "You can't drive us out of baseball." Johnson and his supporters of course held the balance of voting power and exerted it every time ballots were cast. As a result, the Loyal Five deposed Comiskey as vice president and elected Navin in his stead. Ruppert, Comiskey, and Frazee were ousted from the board of directors and replaced with Ball, Shibe, Navin, and Minor of Washington. The Insurrectionists had been questioning the existence of a contract Johnson professed to have signed in 1910 making him president for twenty years at $30,000 a year. Now in the meeting Johnson stood on his claim, and no election for president was held. After it was over, Huston described what had happened: "They rode over us with a steam roller and we are going to send the steam roller right back at them."

Thereafter, as Comiskey remarked, the American League was in a state of "armed truce." Beaten at every turn on the parliamentary front, the Insurrectionists resumed their attack in the sector in which they had triumphed earlier—the courts. In a cascade of legal actions they sought to remove Johnson from office and to hold up his salary. They tried to force him to open his books for examination; to produce the presidential contract he supposedly signed in 1910; and to disclose details of the league's contract with Western Union as well as his disposition of the money from it. The Insurrectionists also moved to have the league's funds impounded and, lastly, to prevent the loyal clubs from aiding Johnson.

In early February 1920 the Yankees' owners capped all the litigation with a suit against Johnson for $500,000 on the ground that he instigated the move to drive Ruppert and Huston from baseball. There is little doubt that Johnson wished to get rid of the two colonels. That scheme was related to the departure of the Yankees from the Polo Grounds into their own stadium. The usual explanation for their leaving was that the Giants' management became increasingly jealous of the Yankees' growing popularity and refused to renew their lease. According to Fred Lieb, a reliable sports journalist, the notion that the Giants ordered the Yankees to leave is incorrect; the version once given him by Ruppert was that the colonel felt uncomfortable with his year-to-year lease and did not wish to be in a position in which the Giants could raise the Yankees' rent to some prohibitive figure. Ruppert told Lieb that the Yankees offered to take over half interest in the Polo Grounds, but when the Giants were not responsive, he went ahead with plans to build the new Yankee Stadium.

Actually, the Yankees had been under pressure from the American League to secure more suitable grounds ever since 1915 when Ruppert acquired the club, although at that time the other owners agreed that New York would not be ousted for failure to secure new grounds after reasonable effort. More recent evidence has been found by Bill Veeck, Jr., in a diary discovered in a hole in the wall under the stands of Comiskey Park. The diary indicates that Johnson personally persuaded the Giants' owner to cancel the Yankees' lease and tried to get control of the lease himself, in the name of the American League, so he could force out Ruppert and Huston. In exchange Johnson was willing to allow the Giants to select the new Yankee ownership if they wished and even to pick the third member of a new National Commission.

Whatever the precise truth is with respect to the departure of the Yankees, the damage suit brought by the Yankees' owners against Johnson was never concluded; nor were any of the others. Both factions must have realized that to prolong the conflict would hurt all concerned. League affairs were at a standstill, with a new season rapidly approaching. Besides, there were rumors that the Insurrectionists were toying with the idea of breaking away and either starting a third major league or joining forces with the National Leaguers, most of whom were fed up with Herrmann and the National Commission, to form a twelve-club circuit. So once more Frank Navin succeeded in getting the warring American League factions to meet, this time in Chicago on February 10.

Another tumultuous scene ensued. "There were many times," said one writer, "when all were talking at once." At one point in the meeting Ball and Ruppert got up, faced each other, and "seemed to be all set for a passage at fisticuffs," but "cooler heads prevailed." After sitting through three grueling sessions throughout the day and into the night, the weary owners plodded from the room at two in the morning with a settlement pounded out. It represented an unmitigated defeat for Ban Johnson. Shorn of much of his power, he came out of the meeting "drawn and pale" and walked away without saying a word.

The Insurrectionists had their way, and the Yankees gained practically all they sought. Carl Mays was reinstated in good standing without penalty and remained with the New York club, and the Yankees were awarded third place in the league standings plus the money that went with it. A two-man board of review was created to serve for two years, with Ruppert and Griffith as its members. The board had "final and binding powers" to review penalties or fines in excess of $100 and suspensions of more than ten days. It could also review any "act" that any member felt affected his constitutional rights as a member of the league. In case of a tie vote by the board, a federal judge in Chicago was to decide the issue. The broad powers conferred on the board hobbled Johnson and reduced him almost to a figurehead similar to the National League's president. On their part, the Yankees and Insurrectionists agreed to call off all lawsuits. The New York owners claimed that the seven-months-long fight had cost them $60,000, but Huston thought the results justified the expense. A tenuous peace was achieved; the bitterness remained.

The unity of Organized Baseball and the position of the National Commission were further weakened by the withdrawal of the minor leagues from the National Agreement. Meeting in New York in January 1919, the National Association announced its opposition to the continuation of the draft and the optional assignments of players. Herrmann signed a pact permitting the minors to pull out of the National Agreement, but majors and minors tacitly agreed to respect each other's territorial and reservation rights. In his report to the majors on this arrangement Herrmann raised the ghost of the Federal League. He recommended that any new agreement be deferred until the Baltimore Fed case was finally adjudicated: "I am not keen for a new agreement until the Baltimore Federal League case . . . has been finally disposed of, because as matters now stand . . . the national agreement as well as the commission itself is illegal."

Meanwhile, the converging streams of opposition welled up against Herrmann and swept him from office. Herrmann's hope of holding on to his post depended upon Ban Johnson, who, as previously mentioned, had already rescued him once. But Johnson's power depended upon the support of a solid phalanx of American League owners, which the Mays case broke. At the same time dissatisfaction with Herrmann remained strong in the National League, fed as it was by Dreyfuss's grudge against him over the Sisler issue, the rancor caused by the Scott Perry affair, and the disillusionment of Heydler after the undignified handling of the abortive 1918 World Series strike.

So in a September 1919 meeting in Heydler's New York office the National League owners again voiced their wish for a neutral chairman. Nearly a year before, a committee had been appointed to find a candidate, and the owners now signified their willingness to accept the committee's choice. Then at their annual meeting the National Leaguers once more showed that they were resolute for change, and when it came time for the two league presidents to meet for what used to be the formality of choosing Herrmann for chairman, Heydler refused to vote for him for 1920. This time Johnson, hamstrung by a deeply disunited American League, was powerless to save his old friend, and Herrmann resigned January 8, the resignation to become effective after the joint meeting of the major leagues February 11.

Johnson, who had refused to meet with the selection committee so long as Ruppert was on it, continued to block the appointment of a new chairman. With no progress, let alone agreement, on naming a neutral chairman, Organized Baseball drifted in disarray through 1920 and was without coherent leadership or direction when the most severe storm in its history struck. In September 1920 the shocking news hit the country: the 1919 World Series had been crooked.

14

WARNING SHADOWS

THE BELIEF that baseball was honest and upright constituted an article of secular faith in the America of those far-off, less complicated decades early in the century. That dogma was embraced by the public, from chief executive to newsboy. President William Howard Taft himself offered his testimonial in 1910: "The game of base ball . . . is a clean, straight game, and it summons to its presence everybody who enjoys clean, straight athletics." Theodore Roosevelt also praised the "rugged honesty" of professional ball players. Boys' fiction indoctrinated youth in the same outlook; the hero of *Won in the Ninth* (1910) loved baseball, as did "all good healthy boys in this country . . . for its squareness and thrills." Americans might tolerate corruption in government and business and indeed take a certain amount of it for granted, but baseball to them occupied a loftier sphere. As *The Nation* expressed it in 1920,

> . . . we do not trust cashiers half as much, or diplomats, or policemen, or physicians, as we trust an outfielder or a shortstop. . . . There is something about the very nature of the game, played in the bright sunlight with nerves at the very edge of tension, that produces the illusion of a cleanness in the characters of the performers more or less comparable to the sharp, clean movements and instinctive responses of their bodies. Bribery is something to be hatched in furtive rooms, by lamplight.

In short, Americans regarded baseball as no mere commercialized amusement. It was set apart as the "national pastime," an institution occupying a niche just below belief in God and respect for motherhood.

Not surprisingly, baseball's leaders and its publicists promoted and helped mold the public's reverential attitude toward their enterprise. If there was one theme descanted upon by baseball men and their spokesmen it was the purity and honesty of the game. John Heydler proclaimed that "the entire superstructure is founded upon absolute integrity." Whether professional or amateur, said *Baseball Magazine*, baseball was "played on the square, first, last and all the time"—the only professional sport left on "the top shelf of honor." Boosters of baseball dwelled on the theme that its aura was cleaner and sweeter than that emanating from other commercialized sports, like boxing, racing, and wrestling. Allen Johnson in *Sporting News* reinforced this theme with unmistakable pride and conviction:

> In this day of great temptation,
> In this time of graft and get,
> There's a bit of consolation
> For the fans to cherish yet—
>
> Although boxing is a gamble,
> And some people think it is,
> Saying gold's the real scramble
> In the festive fighting biz—
>
> Although racing's retrograding,
> And is placed beneath the ban
> Of those people masquerading
> As deliverers of man—
>
> Although wrestling has been shackled,
> And expressed up Crooked Creek,
> Since a man named Bartl tackled
> And o'erthrew a mighty Greek—
>
> Although all of this is rumored,
> In this day of graft and get,
> Still, we've cause to be good-humored—
> There's some consolation yet—
>
> For the base ball game is soaring
> High above it all, serene,
> Unaffected by the roaring—
> For the Grand Old Game is clean!
>
> There is consolation oozing
> From each thread upon the pill—
> What's it matter if we're losing?—
> For the Game is sootless still!

Sour skeptics so perverse as to wonder "Could it happen here?" were told that it was impossible. Connie Mack simply could not believe there was "a possibility of crookedness" in baseball. A sports-writer asked, "How can you fix eighteen men?" Those who pointed out that only the pitcher need be corrupted (since he was the key man) were countered with the confident statement that the moment a pitcher fell down on his work the manager would yank him out of the game.°

Especially unthinkable was the idea that a player would stoop so low as to "throw" a World Series, or that anyone would even try to tamper with one. The Series was an important annual event in the lives of Americans. It furnished the glamorous culmination of the baseball season, with the entire nation preoccupied with the heroes of the diamond as they vied for the highest prize, the so-called world championship. At such times newspaper circulation increased. Fans congregated in city streets to watch the play-by-play progress of the games as they were simulated on boards displayed in front of news-paper offices. Throughout the country factory hands and farmers cen-tered their interest on the outcome of the Series. In view of this deep absorption of the fans in the World Series, underpinned as it was with their belief in the integrity of baseball, the enormity of the 1919 Series sellout and the shock its disclosure gave the country can be ap-preciated.

When the startling news finally burst into the open, stories of the Red Scare that was then raging in the United States were relegated to the back pages of the newspapers. The Series scandal created a greater stir than the charges of corruption that were leveled against members of President Harding's cabinet a few years later. Cartoonists were quick to reflect the mood of the hour. The New York *Times* printed a drawing showing a figure called "the great American game" being hit on the head by a ball labeled "baseball scandal," and the Chicago *Tribune* had one depicting baseball joining pugilism, poli-tics, high finance, and horse racing in the "Black Eye Club." Editori-als enlarged upon the event. The Philadelphia *Bulletin* declared that the player who succumbed to a bribe was in a class with "the soldier or sailor who would sell out his country and its flag in time of war." "When cheap leeches strike at this sport of sports," trumpeted the Grand Rapids *Herald*, "they strike at one of the institutions of the Re-public." The Chicago *Defender* said that the world was "aghast." Harvey Woodruff, sports editor of the Chicago *Tribune*, mourned that the news "almost destroys our faith in human nature," and one reporter claimed that hundreds of men had vowed to abandon base-ball. A poem in the *Tribune* about Eddie Cicotte, one of the stars who confessed his guilt, captured the disillusionment of local fans:

° Actually, the man in the best position to "throw" a game is the catcher.

Reaction to the Black Sox Scandal. Reprinted, courtesy of the Chicago *Tribune*.

I remember, I remember, just back in '17,
The Sox and Giants battled in the days the game was clean;
And Cicotte—smiling Eddie—stopped them Giants with his hook,
And now our good old Eddie confesses he's a crook.

O, somewhere in this favored land the sun is shining bright,
But the south side's sorely stricken by an overwhelming blight.
We can stand for honest errors, bonehead plays we somehow brook,
But heavy are our hearts today—for Eddie is a crook.

Emotional reaction to the scandal spilled over into violence at Joliet,
Illinois. An overwrought fan accused Buck Herzog of being "one of
those crooked Chicago ball players," and in the fight that ensued
Herzog was stabbed. Herzog was a member of the Chicago Cubs, not
the White Sox, but "Chicago" on his uniform was enough to arouse
the fan.

Many a lad of those days took the sad tidings deeply to heart. The
Boston newsboys' club passed a resolution condemning this "murder-
ous blow at the kids' game" struck by the "Benedict Arnolds of baseball." The writer Nelson Algren, then a boy on Chicago's South Side,
had fixed upon Swede Risberg as his "fayvrut," and when the story
broke and Risberg was implicated as one of the tainted players, the
other boys considered Algren guilty by association. Algren finally had
to fight it out with one of them, and took a drubbing. He later expressed his disillusion when he said that "everybody's out for The
Buck, even big leaguers."

Yet the shock need not have been so great or so sudden. Warning
shadows were there to be seen or to be pointed out. One of them was
the prevalence of gambling. Wagering on athletic contests is as old as
the contests themselves, and certainly baseball was no exception to
the practice. Betting was associated with the game from its inception
as a polite amateur pastime. As the sport evolved into a commercialized amusement, gambling kept pace with it. During the era of the
National Commission baseball's relation to gambling was essentially a
recapitulation of the experience of the early years but on a larger and
therefore more dangerous scale. Open betting in the ball parks was
rife, particularly in Pittsburgh and Boston, and a section of the
Braves' park near third base was known as "gamblers' reservation." In
Cincinnati fans complained about "loud and obstreperous" professional gamblers who gathered in the stands opposite third base,
where they exchanged bets freely.

Although the owners deplored the evil, their vigilance in suppress-
ing it was sporadic and lacking in zeal. Resolutions were passed, and
at times clubs barred or expelled known gamblers from their parks.

City authorities cracked down spasmodically. They were particularly active after a reform administration had been elected. Policemen would swarm into the park, flash badges, wave billy clubs, and hustle people off in patrol wagons. Often as not, those arrested were fans guilty only of betting a dollar or two with each other. At times the energy of the authorities inadvertently added to the problem of ball-park gambling, for whenever they clamped down on the race tracks, they simply diverted the betting to baseball; and when the tracks were shut down entirely, as they were during World War One, the gamblers devoted even more attention to ball games. So despite these intermittent and often half-hearted measures, betting was not eliminated from the ball parks, and in 1919 the New York *Times* reported that there was more of it than ever before.

For that matter, baseball men themselves were not averse to betting. Some liked to play the horses, and there were those who wagered on ball games. Some even consorted with professional gamblers. McGraw, labeled "an inveterate gamester" by one writer, was arrested and jailed at Hot Springs in January 1904 for gambling and resisting an officer. Ban Johnson himself once mailed a check for $50 to Garry Herrmann to cover a bet they had on a ball game. At another time Weeghman, president of the Chicago Cubs, sent Herrmann a $75 check "as per our little wager on our opening game." More open to question was Garry Herrmann's foolish revelation in 1906 that he had bet $6000 against $2000 with three well-known gamblers that Pittsburgh would not win the pennant. When he realized his mistake he asked to be released from the wager and vowed that he would never bet again. But there were repercussions when he traded Cy Seymour to the Giants, because fans suspected that he did it to strengthen New York's chances of beating Pittsburgh for the pennant. Ball players, too, bet both on their own clubs and on games in which they had no part. Innocent and harmless enough, perhaps, but what if they should bet against their own team and then contrive to accomplish the desired result?

Gambling inside the parks was trifling compared with that outside them. Before a New York-Detroit game some Yankee players walked into a Detroit cigar shop and saw a big slate on which were posted the odds for that day's game, depending upon which pitcher was selected to work for New York. There was plenty of opportunity for action in saloons, billiard halls, and other gambling centers that subscribed to the play-by-play accounts telegraphed from the parks by Western Union, which had purchased a monopoly of the wire service from Organized Baseball. As the result of an investigation of pool-room gambling and of Western Union's alliance with it in the

early 1900's, the company ostensibly cut off service to gambling outlets. But according to Alvin F. Harlow's book on Western Union, it
secretly went back to supplying this service.

Outside the ball parks, the most popular form of baseball gambling
was the baseball pool, which for as little as ten cents sold tickets that
gave the purchaser a chance to win cash for picking the team that
scored the most or fewest runs or won the most games, and so forth,
in the week. Fans holding pool tickets crowded around bulletin
boards to root for the teams they held in the pool.

These pools honeycombed the country, and one could try his luck
with any team in any league, major or minor, anywhere. Not only
were the pools widespread, often they were large-scale operations
employing hundreds of agents. One in Pittsburgh, called Fort Erie,
ranged over the East and Canada, offering prizes of $1000 a week.
Another big one was the Keystone of Pennsylvania, which earned anywhere from $30,000 to $50,000 a week under the protection of some
leading Pittsburgh politicians. The extent of pool-selling is further
measured by an estimate in 1911 that some 40,000 New Haven factory
men and boys held pool tickets costing $10,000, and that a Philadel-
phia pool sold 20,000 tickets on the World Series alone that year. By
1920 the Chicago *Tribune* was estimating that Chicagoans bought
more than 400,000 pool tickets every week, at a cost of $150,000. Ex-
tensive as the pools were, they were the betting medium for small fry
only. The important money was wagered by the professional gamblers and through them by the big bettors, particularly at World Series time. Newspapers assisted pools by printing weekly "total runs"
tables. They also published betting odds and offers such as the following, which appeared in the Cincinnati *Enquirer* in 1912: "$1,000
to $7,000 St. Louis beats Brooklyn." Another example of the open-
ness of betting was a large sign spread across the houses opposite
Shibe Park: "Make your bets."

Baseball owners inveighed against the pools, sometimes for the
wrong reason—for instance, that people were spending their twenty-
five or fifty cents on the lotteries instead of on baseball tickets. But
some owners thought pools stimulated interest in baseball. Newspapers periodically exposed pool operators, and at times the authorities
prosecuted. But the big pools plied their business sheltered by powerful politicians, and police raids on them, like those on prostitution,
were often faked. Consequently, baseball owners were not really keen
about attacking the pools. Henry Chafetz, an authority on gambling
in the United States, summarized the problem during the era: "The
National pastime of betting on games was immune to the economic
ups and downs, and it took the 1919 World's Series scandal to break

A

B

C

A. Judge Landis signs as Commissioner in presence of major-league owners
New York Public Library
B. Branch Rickey *Culver*
C. Edward G. Barrow *Culver*

The New York Yankees of 1927 *Brown Bros.*

Yankee Stadium *U.P.I.*

Lefty Grove
Wide World

Burleigh Grimes
Wide World

A

A bunch of Yankees were whooping it up at an old Joliet brewery...

B

C

D

A. Manager Wilbert Robinson *Wide World*
B. New York Yankees break training. *New York Public Library*
C. First fruits of Branch Rickey's farm system: the St. Louis Cardinals of 1926.
   Acme
D. New York Giants of 1922 *Brown Bros.*

Fans "watch" the World Series in Times Square before the era of television. *Photoworld*

Rogers Hornsby
Brown Bros.

Babe Ruth
Brown Bros.

A   B   C   D

E

A. Armando Marsans   *New York Public Library*
B. Morris Berg   *Brown Bros.*
C. Ping Bodie   *Brown Bros.*
D. Stanley Coveleskie   *Culver*
E. John "Chief" Meyer and Charles Albert "Chief" Bender   *Culver*

the public faith that major team sports were incorruptible and you could at least bet on them with no danger of being cheated."

That was the whole point. The peril lay not so much in the betting itself, provided the games were honest. It lay in the fact that, wherever gambling flourished, its insidious offspring, "the fix," lurked nearby. That fact was borne out in the early years of baseball when the throwing of games was widespread, as in two notorious incidents in which players were expelled for accepting bribes from gamblers to lose games intentionally.*

By the time of the Commission era the owners should have realized that the price of honesty in baseball games, like the price of liberty, is eternal vigilance. The National Commission did pass a rule forbidding players from receiving any World Series money if they were traded away during the season by a club that eventually won the pennant. This rule resulted from a demand by players and the public after Pittsburgh traded two players to St. Louis in 1909 and then announced that both would get a share if the Pirates won the pennant. Everyone watched to see if this conflict of interest would affect the two players' performances when St. Louis played Pittsburgh. But on the whole, in the years before the 1919 scandal exploded publicly, the owners were remiss about taking stern measures when they were called for. More often they hushed up and concealed wrongdoing "for the good of the game," assuming the attitude that what the public did not know would not hurt it. The usual excuse for not acting summarily was lack of evidence, without which the owners would expose themselves to lawsuits. In some too flagrant cases, crooked players were quietly banished, and occasionally some of the facts did penetrate the fog of rumor surrounding the secrecy and mystery of the magnates. But much of what is now known dribbled out only later, and without doubt there is more that still lies hidden.

The gingerly manner in which Organized Baseball treated alleged instances of dishonesty is reflected in the case of John W. Taylor, which was heard before the National Commission in the winter of 1904–5. The dispute grew out of public charges made by James Hart, president of the Chicago Cubs, that his club's post-season series with the White Sox in 1903 for the championship of Chicago had not been on the level because Taylor, who had pitched for the Cubs, had been "bought." Hart told newspapermen that when the St. Louis club, to which he had sold Taylor after the series, came to Chicago in early 1904, Taylor, chided about losing games in the city series, said, "Why should I have won? I got one hundred dollars from Hart for winning and I got five hundred dollars for losing." Taylor denied the allega-

* See *Baseball: The Early Years*, pages 53–54, 87–88.

tions before the Commission, which dismissed the case for want of evidence. Herrmann and Johnson signed the report, but Pulliam was dissatisfied. He viewed the charges as so serious that "the most searching inquiry" should be made.

Throughout the hearing there were overtones of the prickly relations between the majors. Pro-American Leaguers had from the outset denigrated Hart's charges against Taylor—based on hearsay evidence, they pointed out—as no more than pique over having lost the city series—an attitude that fueled the ill feeling between the leagues. The cycle of charge and countercharge was extended when Comiskey accused Hart of casting reflections on baseball and on his character and asked the Commission to rewrite its report on the case to include censure of Hart. Herrmann chose to let the matter rest, no doubt hoping to break the cycle. He succeeded only in calling forth a basic criticism of the Commission itself—namely, that it was incapable of dispensing justice so long as two of its members were National Leaguers, and that from the first its chairman should have been a disinterested outsider such as "a high-class lawyer or supreme court justice."

Taylor's indictment entered its second phase almost immediately. After his acquittal by the Commission he was called on the carpet again, this time by the National League's board of directors, on a fresh charge that he had thrown a game between St. Louis and Pittsburgh in July 1904. While he admitted that he had been drinking heavily the night before (and even that he had once used loaded dice to even the score against teammates who had cheated him with marked cards), Taylor denied having thrown the game. "I am not a saint," he assured any who might have doubts, and "at times have dissipated," but "that don't make me a baseball crook." Wary of a lawsuit, the board delivered a Scotch verdict, exonerating Taylor from throwing the game but fining him $300 for conduct prejudicial to the St. Louis club.

Few, least of all the magnates, were convinced. Everyone he talked with agreed, wrote reporter I. E. Sanborn, that the decision was "the weakest effort ever produced." It left the impression, he said, that the only way out was to "whitewash" and "hush" the whole thing. Indeed, a club official wrote confidentially that his boss believed Taylor was guilty and it was unfortunate that "we could not make out a stronger case." The public was of the same mind, he added, but the newspapers were willing to drop the matter and "allow the people to forget it as they surely will" if baseball men refuse to talk about it. But the rub was that Taylor might continue to talk; he was already refusing to pay the fine, confident that the board had no case against him.

Barney Dreyfuss thought it would be good for the league if Taylor and his drinking companion, Jake Beckley, who was also under a cloud, could be fired without, however, weakening the St. Louis team. There is also evidence that some entertained the idea of the St. Louis club's paying Taylor's fine in exchange for his promise not to talk. The manager of the St. Louis team was willing to take the "desperate" chance, but others feared Taylor could not be relied upon to keep his word and would put the league in a bad light if it became known that the board's punishment was "a bluff." In whatever way the matter was finally resolved, Taylor pitched in the National League four more years.

Another example of the owners' policy of concealment or at best grudging disclosure, which foreshadowed their handling of the 1919 World Series scandal, occurred after the playoff game between New York and Chicago for the National League pennant of 1908. Right after that crucial game rumors began circulating that the Giants had several times tried to bribe their way to the pennant. Near the end of that 1908 season, after the famous tie game with Chicago, the one in which Merkle forgot to touch second, the Giants had eight games left with Philadelphia and three final games with Boston. It was around these that some of the post-season rumors revolved. One story was that McGraw tried to get Philadelphia pitchers to throw games to the Giants. Another was that Boston, managed by Joe Kelly, an old Baltimore Orioles teammate of McGraw's, "laid down," allowing the Giants to win the three games they needed in order to tie with Chicago and meet them in the playoff. Kelly vigorously denied these calumnies, and little attention was paid to them. A third rumor did not evaporate so readily—that someone connected with the New York club had tried to bribe umpires Bill Klem and Johnny Johnstone to assure a Giants victory in the playoff game itself. Still, there was nothing definite until the National League meeting in December. Then it was learned that the umpires had actually reported such an attempt and had submitted sworn statements. These were read at the meeting, and a committee was appointed to investigate. Heading the committee was John T. Brush, president of the club whose employee was implicated.

Nothing more was given out. Whenever the magnates were asked the name of the alleged culprit, they "put fingers to lips." The newspapers kept after them, and finally, when Brush submitted a report in February, more information was doled out to the press: Klem had alleged that "a masseur" on the Giants, acting for three members of the New York club, had offered him first $2500 and then $3000 to assure a victory for the Giants in the game that would decide the pennant.

The National Commission, which reviewed the case, contented itself with commending the umpires and telling reporters that the offender's name would be given to all the owners and he would be banned from all parks in Organized Baseball. It was not until the end of April that Harvey Woodruff of the Chicago *Tribune* ferreted out the name of the mysterious "masseur"—a Dr. Joseph M. Creamer, the team physician of the Giants. It also developed that Creamer was a friend of McGraw's, hired by the Giants' manager without Brush's knowledge. Creamer, a practicing physician interested in and well-known to the professional sports crowd, vehemently denied having anything to do with Klem or bribery.

Newspapers, particularly the New York *Evening Journal*, tried to uncover who was back of Creamer. Some urged him to seek vindication in court, in the hope of forcing open the whole story. That Creamer did not do so leaves his innocence in question and the names of those behind him unrevealed to this day.

The Commission cited lack of evidence as its reason for doing so little. New information shows that it took this course on advice from Brush. After consulting an attorney, he advised Herrmann: "While the individual mentioned is unquestionably a S.O.B. it would be hazardous for any one financially responsible . . . to publicly charge him with having committed the offense." Brush sought to turn the case to advantage by using it to show the public "how next to impossible it is to corrupt the game, even if anyone was disposed to do so." If as little as possible was said, the press and the public would turn their attention to the coming pennant race, he added.

One of the stories about the Giants stooping to conquer in 1908 had an unsavory postscript. After the 1919 World Series scandal blew wide open, a good deal of dirty baseball linen was washed in public. At that time the former nominal owner of the Phillies, Horace Fogel, bobbed up in the news again. He corroborated the rumors of 1908 by claiming that an emissary from the New York Giants had attempted to fix games with Philadelphia at the end of the season. The reader may remember that Fogel had been banished from baseball in 1912 for charging that Roger Bresnahan, McGraw's former catcher, had, as manager of St. Louis, helped the Giants win by fielding a weak team against them. It would be easy to discount Fogel's latest charges as the act of an irresponsible, discredited baseball exile seizing an opportunity to retaliate. But Fogel's story was supported by first baseman Kitty Bransfield and catcher (later player-manager) Charles "Red" Dooin of the 1908 Phillies. Dooin claimed that he, Bransfield, Mike Doolan, Otto Knabe, Sherwood Magee, and other Philly players were offered even more cash to throw their 1908 series to the Giants than the White Sox were promised to throw the 1919 World Series. "I have never said anything about this before now," Dooin stated, "because the other players and myself believed it would be in the best interests of baseball not to say anything, as none of us accepted any of the bribes." And so the dark rumors circulated about the attempted fix of the Philly-Giants games in 1908 were confirmed twelve years later. Not only that, but when a member of the Giants admitted trying to fix another Series with the Phillies late in 1924,* Dooin reiterated his experience of 1908.

Next on the list of sordid events was the 1910 batting-award scandal, which was not without its absurd aspects. Batting awards had been given before. In 1907 a St. Louis jewelry company presented a "beautiful and valuable" medal to the batting champions of each major league, Honus Wagner and Ty Cobb. In March 1910 the Commission announced that the Chalmers Motor Company would present an automobile to the leading batsman of each major league that year. Cobb and Napoleon Lajoie were the leading contenders in the American League. At the end of the season Cobb, who appeared to have the prize safely won, stayed out of Detroit's final two games, but Lajoie, undaunted, made the amazing total of eight hits in eight official times at bat against the Browns in a final Sunday doubleheader at St. Louis. These hits apparently put him ahead of Cobb for the championship by a tiny margin. One of Lajoie's hits was a clean triple smashed over the center fielder's head. Of the other seven, six were made on bunts toward third base, and one was scored as a hit after the St. Louis shortstop threw wild to first. In a ninth turn at bat, Lajoie again dropped a bunt toward third, but this time it was scored as a sacrifice and error.

It did not require a sleuth to detect that there was something rotten in St. Louis. There in full view of fans and sportswriters alike was Lajoie, a veteran of thirteen campaigns in the American League and never particularly fast anyhow, outracing all those bunts, while the Browns' third baseman, John "Red" Corriden, a twenty-two-year-old rookie in his first major-league season, played back on the left-field grass, utterly ineffective against Lajoie's rollers. Besides, it was no secret that most of the other players in the league preferred Lajoie to win the car over Cobb, who was about as popular among them as a mosquito in a bedroom. The shabby scheme to cheat Cobb out of the championship and the car was a "disgraceful proceeding," said *Sporting News*. If the pitching was honest, it was "mighty poor"; if the fielding was honest, it was "execrable."

Ban Johnson dutifully investigated, and the explanations given

* See below, chapter 19.

would have taxed the credulity of even Candide. The Browns' manager, "Peach Pie" Jack O'Connor, who also caught the second game, attributed Lajoie's success to his shrewdness in springing the unexpected on Corriden by switching to bunting. At least "Peach Pie" sportingly credited an opponent's alertness, when he could have blamed Corriden's negligence or stupidity—or even his own as manager! Corriden was equally resourceful. He said that he was afraid to play his normal position for fear one of Lajoie's line drives would hurt him.

In the end O'Connor was fired and so was Harry Howell, a Browns' scout who, the inquiry brought out, had repeatedly visited the press box during the games in question to try to influence the official scorer to record hits for Lajoie and who probably was the one who had sent the scorer an unsigned note offering him a forty-dollar suit of clothes as a bribe. These men were cleared of any dishonesty by Ban Johnson, *Sporting News* reported, but President Hedges of St. Louis was so chagrined over public talk of scandal that he thought it best to get rid of them in order to be "above suspicion." Howell returned to baseball as a minor-league umpire, no less, but O'Connor never did. He had a two-year contract with the Browns with one year to go; he sued and eventually won the $5000 in salary for 1911.

There was a happy ending for everybody else. None of the players was penalized. Corriden was exonerated because he had merely followed O'Connor's orders. The Browns' pitchers Albert Nelson and Alexander Malloy also went scot free. Lajoie emerged not only unblemished but rewarded. Although the final official averages showed Cobb the champion by an eyelash, the Chalmers people graciously awarded cars to both Cobb and Lajoie. Lastly, the award was abolished in favor of one for the most valuable player in each major league, to be selected by a trophy committee composed of newspapermen, one from each major-league city. The first and last stanzas of a poem printed in the Chicago *Tribune* captured the essence of the whole distasteful affair:

> When Larry [Lajoie] faced the St. Louis' fire
> He'd eight to go to be secure.
> And what they thought he might require
> They slipped it to him, that's pretty sure.
>
> What must a meek outsider think
> When tricks like that they put across?
> When at one frameup they will wink
> How do we know what games they toss?

In 1916 the Giants again fell under suspicion, this time aspersed by their own manager, McGraw. The team went to Ebbets Field for two games with Brooklyn to wind up the season. The Robins (so nicknamed now that Wilbert Robinson was managing them) needed to win both games to clinch the pennant over Philadelphia. They had won the first game and the next day were leading in the second when in the middle of it McGraw suddenly left the bench in anger, calling his players quitters. Sensational headlines immediately had McGraw accusing his team of helping Brooklyn to the pennant.

Some speculated that the Giants may have taken it easy in deference to former teammates Chief Meyers, Rube Marquard, and Fred Merkle, who were now playing for the Robins. The New York *Times* had a different theory. It asserted that there had been hard feeling between New York and Philadelphia ever since 1908 when the latter's pitcher, Harry Covaleskie, spoiled the Giants' chance to win the pennant in the regular season (he beat them three times in that late-season series). The *Times* concluded, "It would take no mind reader to understand that when it came to a question of the pennant going to Philadelphia or Brooklyn, just where the New York players would rest." In view of the statements made five years later by Fogel, Bransfield, and Dooin, the *Times* was probably correct.

McGraw later backed down somewhat, telling reporters it was not that his players were not trying to win but that they had refused to obey orders and disregarded his signals—most assuredly an unprecedented experience for the famed martinet of the dugout!

Cries of outrage could be heard all the way from Philadelphia, where Pat Moran, the Phillies' manager, was demanding an investigation. In Brooklyn a fan leaving the game said, "It smelled like a cheese factory." When Robinson learned of McGraw's comments, he indelicately accused him of "piddling on my pennant." The pastor of Grace Methodist Episcopal Church saw fit to preach a sermon calling upon McGraw to retract his foul charges. Ban Johnson, never overlooking a chance to sting McGraw, purportedly called him "cowardly." President Tener, though no lover of McGraw, bristled at Johnson's comment and inferred that if Johnson wanted trouble he could find it in his own bailiwick. There was a good deal of talk about having the whole thing aired at the winter meeting of the league, but when the time came the matter was quietly dropped.

Henceforward, until 1928, baseball scandals and rumors of scandals, like birth pangs, became more frequent and more intense. In 1917 the St. Louis Browns' owner, the former Federal Leaguer Philip de Catesby Ball, raked over his own players in a newspaper interview for "laying down" in a September game with the Chicago White Sox.

The Browns' second-base combination, John "Doc" Lavan and Derrill Pratt, went to Ball and demanded an apology for his aspersions on their characters. Failing in their demand, they brought suit for $50,000 damages for slander. Pratt's attorney said he was prepared to call up every player of note in the American League to testify. What might have been an embarrassing lawsuit was avoided through the intercession of Ban Johnson and Clark Griffith, who persuaded the two players to accept an out-of-court settlement. Pratt was then traded to the New York Yankees and Lavan to Washington, although the latter returned to the Browns, "the Siberia of baseball," the following year.

That skirmish was only a surface irritation. Most of the villainy of 1917 festered under the surface, for a time undiscovered and for a longer space unrevealed to the public. At the core of it was that malignant genius, Hal Chase. Until somebody worse can be found, he will serve as the archetype of all crooked ball players. Chase was a superb first baseman whose sparkling play long remained the yardstick by which others who played the position were measured. Only George Sisler, Lou Gehrig, and sometimes Bill Terry are mentioned in the same breath with him when talk turns to the greatest first basemen in baseball history. But unfortunately his defects of character more than matched his playing skill. Yet despite those defects Chase played fifteen years in the big time, counting his fling with the Feds, and served with four major-league teams, two in each major, in a squalid passage through baseball, bespattered throughout by discord and dishonesty. He came up first with the New York Americans in 1905. At twenty-two he was already a finished ball player, as this early description of him attests:

> I took a look at Hal Chase the . . . new first baseman, today, and was impressed with his style. He is a natural ball player, fast as greased lightning, easy, confident, and brainy. He is the counterpart of Fred Tenney in the way he goes after grounders, widely thrown balls and bunts. Better still he seems to know what is meant by inside ball. [He will] always be a star.

But the twisted, flawed personality of Chase soon emerged. He worked at and succeeded in undermining a succession of managers. In 1908 he was publicly criticized for not giving his best, pouting because Kid Elberfeld and not he had been made manager to succeed Clark Griffith, in whose departure Chase had already been instrumental. In September of that year he climaxed his clash with Elberfeld by jumping the club and playing "outlaw" ball in California but was reinstated the next year after a nominal fine of $200. Soon teammates and New York newspapers accused him of lying down and throwing games in order to drive yet another manager, George Stallings, out of his job. When Stallings himself complained that Chase was not giving his best, Frank Farrell fired Stallings and for some unaccountable reason made Chase manager. Ban Johnson upheld Farrell: "Stallings has utterly failed in his accusation against Chase. He tried to besmirch the character of a sterling player. Anybody who knows Hal Chase knows that he is not guilty of the accusations made against him."

As manager in 1911 Chase succeeded in leading to sixth place a team that had finished second in 1910. After the season Chase was admitted to the growing troop of ex-managers of the Yankees, but he remained at first base, where he incurred renewed charges of not putting forth his "best licks."

In his ninth year with New York (1913), Chase's obnoxious behavior scraped against the new manager, Frank Chance, the rugged old Chicago Cubs leader. A showdown was not long in coming. Sportswriter Fred Lieb, in his admirable book *The Baseball Story*, tells what occurred. One day after the Yankees had lost, Chance stormed over to the press box where Lieb and Heywood Broun were finishing their work and asked, "Did you fellows see what was going on out there? Chase has been throwing games on me." Lieb's editor advised against printing the remark, but Broun inserted it as a note in the New York *Tribune*. The next day Broun was upbraided by Frank Farrell, who maintained that Chance had never said such a thing. Farrell's own disreputable pursuits would hardly entitle him to be fastidious about Chase's conduct. Nevertheless, a few days later Chase was traded to the Chicago White Sox for two run-of-the-mill players, Babe Borton and Rollie Zeider. Borton was not in the same class as Chase, either as a first baseman or as an extra-curricular operator. He was banished in 1921 for crookedness in the minor leagues.

After Chase's period with the Feds and his legal victory over the White Sox in their suit for breach of contract, it was plain that Chase was through in the American League, where he had as much chance of acceptance, said *Sporting News*, "as a nihilist in Russia." The paper also recalled the firing of Stallings on Chase's account as "a lasting disgrace to American League politics." But his quality as a player was such that he returned to the majors with Cincinnati in 1916.

In the National League Chase allowed full rein to his talents. Not only did he throw games himself; he corrupted or tried to corrupt other players. He became a full-fledged fixer and gambler, collecting commissions on money he induced others to bet on games he himself fixed. Thus did he function with Cincinnati until August 9, 1918. On that day, after weeks of urging by players on the team, manager Christy Mathewson suspended Chase without pay for the rest of the season for "indifferent playing." Garry Herrmann, the owner, would not divulge the real reason, but Chase airily admitted that he was accused of betting on games and attempting to get a pitcher (Pol Perritt of the Giants, it was soon learned) to throw a game for money—all of which he denied. Late in August he started suit for $1650 in back salary.

Five months passed without further action against Chase. The reason given for the delay was that the National League had no president; Tener had resigned just before the suspension of Chase, and Heydler, who filled in, was not officially elected president until that winter. However, there were newsmen who predicted from the beginning that the magnates would never make public the truth about Chase because it would be too injurious to baseball. At last on January 30, 1919, Heydler held a five-hour secret hearing in his office. Chase arrived with three character witnesses and an equal number of lawyers. Testifying against him were three Cincinnati teammates— Greasy Neale, Mike Regan, and Jimmy Ring—as well as Pol Perritt and McGraw himself. Christy Mathewson, star witness against Chase, was still serving with the army in France, but his affidavit was read. The pith of the players' testimony was that Chase had offered them money to throw games.

On February 5 Heydler cleared Chase. In a calculated announcement he said, "it is nowhere established that the accused was interested in any pool or wager that caused any game of ball to result otherwise than on its merits, and that Player Chase is not guilty of the charges brought against him." Many things that Chase said in a joking spirit were construed otherwise, Heydler explained. On the other hand, said the league president, Cincinnati was justified in bringing the charges even if unsubstantiated, and the investigation was necessary because of so much gossip in Cincinnati; there had been "much careless talk" by Chase and others, and "an atmosphere of distrust" had been created among his teammates. Heydler also promised that "any player who during my term as president of the National League is shown to have any interest in a wager . . . whether he bets on his club or against it . . ." would promptly be expelled from the league. Thus in one stroke he exonerated Chase, shielded Cincinnati from a possible slander suit, and threw a sop to the public.

Chase was not even reprimanded. To the contrary, he was immediately signed for the Giants by McGraw, who supposedly had just been testifying against him. Chase dropped his suit for back salary but was probably recompensed by the Giants. Mathewson returned to the Giants as coach, so the accuser and accused became teammates once more. With the Giants, Chase resumed his reprehensible habit of attempting to fix games and persuading other players to collaborate with him. In September McGraw quietly removed both him and infielder Heinie Zimmerman from the lineup. Queried by newsmen, McGraw said, "I cannot talk of the matter." Evidently this time Heydler had sufficient evidence against the two and had alerted the Giants' owners, because Chase went without fuss and neither he nor Zimmerman ever played in Organized Baseball again.

That winter the Chicago Cubs also released a player, Lee Magee (Leopold Hoernschemeyer), although he still had another year to go on a two-year contract. Had he left without demur, that probably would have been the end of it. Instead, he fought back. Declaring that he was not going to be made the "goat" while others equally guilty went untouched, he threatened to "show up some people for tricks turned ever since 1906" and to name four other players who had connived with gamblers. His suit against the Chicago club for breach of contract, recovery of salary, and expected World Series share for 1920, which came before United States District Court in Cincinnati in June 1920, revealed what the owners had hoped would remain hidden and confirmed beyond doubt Magee's guilt and that of Chase as well.

The story of Magee began in 1918 when he was second baseman for Cincinnati and teammate of Hal Chase. He was also a confederate of Chase's in throwing games. According to the testimony of a Boston gambler, Jim Costello, at the trial, Chase and Magee came to Costello's poolroom at the Oxford Hotel, Boston, on the morning of July 25, 1918, and told him they were prepared to throw the first game of that afternoon's doubleheader with Boston if Costello offered the right proposition. Costello pointed out to them that gamblers would not bet unless Magee and Chase put up some of their own money, so they each gave him a $500 check, and in return he agreed that if they lost the game he would return their checks plus an equivalent sum and, in addition, one third of whatever the gamblers won.

They did not succeed in losing the game. Cincinnati's pitcher, Pete Schneider, who they claimed was "fixed," did not pitch it. Schneider later issued a denial and said that when he was alerted by a teammate that something strange was going on, he refused to work in the first game. He did pitch and win the second game, 5–0. But there was some surprise when he was waived out of the National League at the end of the season. Ironically, it was Magee who scored the winning run in the first game. With two out in the thirteenth inning, Magee was safe on a ground ball that "took a bad hop" and broke shortstop

Johnny Rawlings's nose. Edd Roush followed with a home run, which scored Magee ahead of him with the winning run. Chase let his $500 check go through, but Magee stopped payment on his.

At the trial, Magee denied any intent to fix the game. His alibi was that he had planned to bet the $500 on his own team but that Chase had double-crossed him and put the money on Boston. Christy Mathewson testified that he had been suspicious of Magee's playing, particularly in the July 25 game. His club had traded Magee to Brooklyn at the beginning of the 1919 season when he failed to come to terms; then after a few months Brooklyn had passed him on to Chicago. Probably Herrmann and Ebbets, his two former owners, felt an obligation to Chicago for having shipped them damaged goods, for they had each agreed to compensate the Cubs $2500 when Chicago released him. Heydler and Veeck further testified that when Magee began registering his objections and making threats over being released, they confronted him with evidence of crookedness and extracted a confession in which he blamed Chase for leading him astray.

The end came for both Chase and Magee not so much because of Heydler's diligent efforts, as is usually claimed, but because Magee and Chase made the mistake of doing business by check, and thus provided Costello with evidence that he was able to use in retaliation for Magee's welching on payment of the $500. When Magee lost his suit against the Chicago club, not only was his fate determined but any remaining shadow of doubt about Chase's guilt was also removed.

Chase was not cured, however. He returned to California, where he was born and where he had played "outlaw" ball, and resumed his old ways. He turned up in 1920 as player and part owner of San Jose in the independent, semi-pro Mission League, where he was shortly accused of corrupting players in his own league as well as in the Pacific Coast League, which was already shot through with dishonesty.

The fact that the contagion of gambling and game-fixing had spread to some of the minor leagues has rarely been mentioned. But the minors were not immune. By 1919 corrosion in the Coast League was well advanced. In October 1920 the deputy district attorney of Los Angeles County charged before a grand jury that at least five of the eight clubs in the league were controlled by a powerful gambling ring, which cleaned up enormous sums and distributed thousands of dollars to ball players who did their bidding. He asserted that at least six players on the clubs in question had received instructions to lose deliberately. One of the witnesses, the same Babe Borton who had figured in the trade that sent Chase to the Chicago White Sox in 1913, admitted to a $2000 "slush fund" to be distributed to Portland and Salt Lake City players to ensure that the Vernon club would win the 1919 Coast League pennant. The grand jury dismissed indictments against three players and Nathan Raymond, who gambled with Arnold Rothstein and was later a suspect in his murder. However, the three players (and one other, who had disappeared), all former big-leaguers, were expelled by the minor leagues' governing body. Others were released by their teams, and the Mission League barred Hal Chase. Coast League president William H. McCarthy carried on the cleanup drive, at times in the face of the objections of some owners that their clubs were being picked on. The wrangling at one meeting ended in a fist fight, during which the club secretary of Salt Lake City was "knocked out cold." McCarthy also barred certain known gamblers from the ball parks of the league and continued to have players watched.

The foregoing catalog of distasteful events omits reports of teams "going easy" against a favored opponent to help it win the pennant, or against one contender to lessen the chances of another; of certain World Series or pennant races being fixed; of gamblers' boasts of controlling certain players and keeping them on their payrolls. The evidence is abundantly clear, without considering every hint, rumor, and veiled accusation, that the groundwork for the crooked 1919 World Series, like most striking events in history, was long prepared. The scandal was not an aberration brought about solely by a handful of villainous players. It was a culmination of corruption and attempts at corruption that reached back nearly twenty years.

Nevertheless, when the scandal of 1919 became public knowledge, the men who controlled Organized Baseball acted as though it were a freakish exception, a sort of unholy mutation. Hypocritical as their reaction was, it was also understandable. They could hardly admit to imperfections in their business after having painted themselves into a corner, so to speak, with years of concealing misconduct, influencing sportswriters to soft-pedal or suppress what was going on, and issuing pious pronouncements of the game's purity, all the while abetted by the honest majority of players who had become accessories to the fact by remaining silent.

15

BASEBALL'S DARKEST HOUR

PAINFUL consequences resulted from Organized Baseball's failure to deal with crooked behavior and the magnates' refusal to admit that there were any "so despicable" as to "betray the national sport." The success of Hal Chase in escaping punishment and being allowed to play again in 1919 emboldened him, as well as gamblers and other ball players, to continue scheming in the coming season. As *Sporting News* ruefully remarked in the afterlight of the 1919 World Series scandal, "We know now what a mistaken policy it was." By the time Chase, Zimmerman, and Magee were quietly dropped at the end of the 1919 season, plans were already afoot leading to the most sensational scandal in the history of American professional sports. After half a century the enormity of the 1919 World Series scandal still excites interest, as shown, for instance, by the publication of Eliot Asinof's *Eight Men Out* in 1963 and Victor Luhrs's *The Great Baseball Mystery* in 1966.

Nevertheless, in spite of all that has been written, precisely what happened remains uncertain or unknown. Before the case came to trial important evidence disappeared from the Illinois district attorney's office. Most of the gamblers never even testified at the trial, and not a single one of them was ever brought to book. And from that day to this the players, "honest" as well as accused, have maintained an almost unbroken silence.

Suspicions that something was wrong were widespread even before a ball was thrown in the Series. The Chicago White Sox, as befitted one of the strongest teams ever put together, were at first heavy favorites in the betting, the more so because their star, Eddie Cicotte, winner of 29 games in 1919, was to pitch the first game. Then just before the game the odds suddenly shifted in favor of Cincinnati, from 7-10 to 5-6, and in some cases to even money. The lobby of Cincinnati's leading hotel, the Sinton, where the White Sox were staying, was jammed with gamblers, and there was a rush to place bets on the underdog Reds. In other cities the trend was the same. Jack Doyle, whose Billiard Academy was an important betting center in New York City, estimated that the night before the first game more than two million dollars had been bet. "You couldn't miss it. . . . The thing had an odor," said Doyle. "I saw smart guys take even money on the Sox who should have been asking five to one."

But this was recalled later. Doubts voiced at the time were shrugged off: There are always wild rumors about a World Series, aren't there? Besides, didn't you hear? Cicotte has a sore arm! (This last remark was probably circulated by gamblers as a blind.)

In the first game of the Series, Cincinnati defeated Cicotte and the powerful Chicago team 9-1. The Reds then continued on to win the Series, five games to three.

How had it happened? Was it just another of those upsets that occur in the unpredictable game of baseball? Some writers suggested that it was because the White Sox were "too careless" or "out of condition" and "stale," or because their star pitchers, Cicotte and Lefty Williams, who between them lost all five games, were "tired." Highly placed baseball officials knew better. Hugh Fullerton was one of the sportswriters who did too.

Fullerton, who was deeply interested in the welfare of baseball, had long been something of a gadfly to the owners. Once in reply to Garry Herrmann's complaints about him, he said, "If you owners and officials would supply straight facts I do not think there would be any occasion to accuse many writers of untruthfulness." The day after the 1919 Series ended, Fullerton hinted broadly that it had not been above board. He predicted that when spring training started seven men on the White Sox would be missing.

Charles A. Comiskey issued an immediate disclaimer:

> There is always some scandal of some kind following a big sporting event like the world's series. These yarns are manufactured out of whole cloth and grow out of bitterness due to losing wagers. I believe my boys fought the battles of the recent world's series on the level, as they have always done.

The White Sox owner offered $20,000 (later reported as $10,000) for "a single clue" leading to evidence that any of his players had deliberately attempted to throw any of the games. Subsequently it was learned that he was conducting an investigation.

The immediate response of *Sporting News* to "the peddlers of scandal" was a vicious editorial:

Because a lot of dirty, long-nosed, thick-lipped, and strong-smelling gamblers butted into the World Series . . . and some of said gamblers got crossed, stories were peddled that there was something wrong with the games. . . . Comiskey has met that by offering $10,-000 for any sort of a clue that will bear out such a charge. . . . [but] there will be no takers, because there is no such evidence, except in the mucky minds of the stinkers who—because they are crooked— think all the rest of the world can't play straight.

Writing in the same issue, Joe Vila spoke of "Fools . . . , not baseball men, who tried to create the impression that there was something 'screwy' about the Series." There were always some who were skeptical about its honesty, he remarked, but baseball's integrity was never questioned by any who knew it from the inside.

Baseball Magazine, a mouthpiece of Organized Baseball, opened a vitriolic personal attack on Fullerton in its November issue, in which it declared: "If a man really knows so little about baseball that he believes the game is or can be fixed, he should keep his mouth shut when in the presence of intelligent people." The editorial proceeded to "look dispassionately at the recent Series" to see "wherein there was any evidence of crookedness." Then, having demonstrated to its own satisfaction that there was nothing to the charges, it concluded that the possibility of fixing a ball game was "practically nil."

This feinting between accusers and disclaimants, with nothing to show for it, continued on and off into the winter. Fullerton reiterated his suspicions in the New York *World* while the magnates were gathered at New York for their December meetings. Again he achieved little other than to evoke more denials from Comiskey, who claimed that his investigation had not turned up anything and that certain "St. Louis parties" who had come to Chicago at his request could give only hearsay evidence. Comiskey renewed his offer of $10,000 to anyone who would come forward with information and promised: "If I land the goods on any of my ball players I will see that there is no place in organized ball for them."

Herrmann, at this time still chairman of the tottering National Commission, took cognizance of the charges too. He claimed that the Commission had "made inquiries" and had discovered nothing. He also said that when the rumors persisted they were referred to Comiskey, since he was "responsible for the conduct of his players." Thus Herrmann overlooked past claims that the National Commission's presence ensured the integrity of the Series. The Commission did adopt a lame statement early in January in which it resolved to make every effort to stop gambling "in view of the many insinuations and complaints" about the last World Series. Later on it was announced that Ban Johnson had asked a private detective agency to take over supervision of private police in American League parks and to get evidence against gamblers.

One other interesting development was a December interview given by Ray Schalk, the White Sox catcher. He was quoted as saying that seven Sox players would not be with the team in 1920. Thus he echoed what Fullerton had written right after the Series. *Sporting News* called on Schalk to tell more if he knew anything; instead, he shortly denied his statement and said he saw nothing wrong with the Series.

In March, *Sporting News*, which had toned down its view considerably since its October tirade, acknowledged, "It is not denied that there is a certain amount of evidence against quite a number of players," who would be watched closely in 1920. But *Baseball Magazine* still lambasted Fullerton and called him a "visionary and erratic writer." Meanwhile, there was enough other off-season news to divert the fans: the continual wrangle among American League owners over the Carl Mays incident; the resignation of Garry Herrmann from the National Commission; and finally the Lee Magee trial with its evidence against him and Chase, the first public revelation of crookedness on the part of ball players since 1877.

Soon a new season was under way. All the White Sox players were back with the team again in 1920 after all, except for Chick Gandil, the first baseman, who did not report. There had been some severe holdout trouble with half a dozen or so of the players, and Comiskey himself had gone to the coast to negotiate personally with Gandil and Swede Risberg, the shortstop, but then it was not unusual for players, especially on a pennant-winning team, to want more money. As the season moved into late summer, close pennant races developed in both major leagues, and Babe Ruth, playing his first year in New York, was on his way to hitting a phenomenal 54 home runs. Unpleasant talk about the 1919 Series had subsided, and the whole thing bid fair to be forgotten, as other unsavory episodes of the past had been.

Then on September 4 news broke that a National League game at Chicago on August 31 had been fixed for last-place Philadelphia to win over the Cubs. Bill Veeck, Sr., Chicago president, explained to reporters that shortly before the game he had received telephone calls and telegrams of warning, so at the last minute he had directed his team manager, Fred Mitchell, to start Grover Alexander out of turn, instead of Claude Hendrix, who was scheduled to pitch. Alexander had even been promised a $500 bonus if he won, but the Cubs lost 3-0 anyway. With the story now public, Veeck also revealed that he had hired the Burns Detective Agency to investigate and had invited the Chicago chapter of the Baseball Writers Association to do like-wise. Any expenses entailed would be paid by the Chicago club. "Our unfortunate experience of last year [with Magee]," said Veeck, "made us feel doubly responsible to the great baseball loving public." Hendrix denied any knowledge of a fix, but he never played in Organized Baseball again. The Cubs released him in February 1921 with the explanation that they were rebuilding their pitching staff, and no other clubs signed him.

On September 7, three days after the story of the Philly-Cubs game, it was announced that a special Cook County grand jury with Judge Charles MacDonald presiding would investigate not only the game in question but baseball gambling in general. District Attorney MacClay Hoyne, in charge of the probe, promised to use every resource of his office to "bring to justice the ring of gamblers whose operations threaten to besmirch" baseball.

Announcement of the investigation rekindled suspicions about the 1919 World Series, and it suddenly came to light that Comiskey had held up the World Series bonus checks of eight White Sox players but had finally mailed them out. Soon demands were made for the grand jury to extend its investigation to the 1919 Series. So by the time the hearings commenced on September 22 their scope was broadened to encompass the Series as well. It was also decided that the hearings would be closed, thus limiting the public to second-hand information and statements handed out by the various parties concerned.

The grand jury summoned a mixed cast of baseball officials, players, and sportswriters to testify at the hearings. Ban Johnson and Charles Comiskey were among the first witnesses. Johnson seized the opportunity to strike indirectly at Comiskey. He revealed that he knew about the White Sox checks being held up because Gandil, Cicotte, and McMullin had asked his help in obtaining their money from Comiskey. Reporters also quoted Johnson as saying that Chicago would not dare win the 1920 pennant because gamblers, who had certain Sox players in their power, had forbidden it! This remark caused a sensation, especially since it came at a time when Chicago and Cleveland were locked in a close struggle for first place. Comiskey retaliated. He assailed Johnson for impugning the White Sox just as they were about to start an important series with Cleveland, "a team in which this man is [financially] interested."

Comiskey shortly issued a statement that amounted to a personal white paper with respect to the 1919 World Series. In it the White Sox owner admitted that he had been convinced after the first game that someone had fixed some of his players. He claimed that he had gone to John Heydler and told him of his fears, whereupon Heydler had apprised Johnson of the situation the next day while the two were together in a box watching the game, but Johnson had dismissed the information with a sneering remark.* After the second game, Comiskey stated, he was more convinced than ever of skulduggery and had gone to Heydler again. At no time, averred Comiskey, had he received any cooperation from Johnson or the National Commission "in ferreting out this charge of crookedness." Comiskey went on to tell of his own investigation aimed at unearthing any irregularities, and he ended with a ringing avowal to fire any dishonest players, no matter who they were, and to close his park if he could not replace them with honest ones.

The reason Comiskey communicated his suspicions to the president of the National League rather than to his own chief, as ordinarily would have been the case, was the frigidity between him and Johnson, sealed by the Jack Quinn decision and the Carl Mays affair. Nor could Comiskey very well approach Garry Herrmann, at that time still chairman of the National Commission, since Herrmann was also owner of the Cincinnati club: how could Comiskey have told him that the Reds had won only because the Sox had let them?

No one seemed aware of the anomalous position in which Comiskey's statement had placed him. He was now admitting what for a year he had repeatedly denied—that from the very beginning of the Series he had believed some of his players were dishonest; and at the same time he was upbraiding Johnson for casting aspersions on his team which, except for the missing Gandil, included those selfsame players.

The most arresting early testimony came on the second day of the hearings when Giant pitcher Rube Benton supplied the first concrete evidence of crookedness in the 1919 Series by admitting that he had known beforehand that it was fixed. It took some doing, however, to get Benton to tell what he knew about the Series. At first he told only of being offered $800 in September 1919 by his teammates, Hal Chase and Heinie Zimmerman, to lose a game to the Chicago Cubs, and he

---

* The usual version of what happened portrays Comiskey in his bathrobe in the dead of night tiptoeing from his hotel room down the corridor to awaken Heydler, and Heydler then arousing Johnson, who had just gone to bed after celbrating; Johnson's response to the information supposedly was: "that's the yelp of a beaten cur!" It makes a good story, but recent information from the diary of Harry Grabiner, White Sox secretary, states that it was he who alerted Heydler, by telephone, after the second game, but Heydler refused to believe the games were dishonest. After a second phone call from Grabiner, however, Heydler proposed speaking to Ban Johnson. In an entry inserted in the diary afterwards, Grabiner stated that although Heydler promised to get in touch with him again, he heard nothing more from the National League president.

claimed that Chicago infielder Buck Herzog was in on the deal. Benton stated that he had refused the bribe, reported it to manager McGraw, and then won the game.

It was Benton's allegation against Herzog that forced the former's admissions about the World Series. Herzog turned the tables by testifying that his alleged complicity in the bribe attempt had already been discussed the previous June (1920) in John Heydler's office. Herzog described how he had confronted Benton before the league president and had produced affidavits from friends of his on the Boston Braves, Tony Boeckel and Art Wilson, certifying that Benton had boasted to them of winning $3200 on the World Series, thanks to a tip from Hal Chase. According to Herzog, Heydler had given him a letter of clearance and told everybody to keep quiet about the matter. Herzog attributed Benton's effort to blacken him to a grudge that traced back several years to when he was Benton's manager at Cincinnati.

Herzog's testimony, backed by the Boeckel and Wilson affidavits, obliged Benton to submit to further questioning at the hearings and to admit that he knew beforehand that the first two games and the entire Series as well were fixed for Cincinnati to win; that he had learned of the fix from Hal Chase, who, he believed, had won $40,000 in bets; and that he had also seen a telegram to Jean Dubuc, another Giant pitcher, from Sleepy Bill Burns, a one-time obscure major-league pitcher who, Benton indicated, had acted for gambling interests during the Series. Thus Herzog, Boeckel, Wilson, and Heydler himself had evidence, by June 1920 at least, that the Series was tainted.

Heydler substantiated Herzog's story and contributed to the evidence against Chase and Zimmerman by stating that in 1919 the two had offered Benny Kauff $500 to throw a game to St. Louis. Kauff, whom the Giants had bought from the Feds, had refused and told McGraw. Heydler extolled McGraw for firing Chase and Zimmerman at the risk of losing the pennant, although it was not clear just what risk McGraw was taking in ridding himself of the players who were jeopardizing his chances of winning it.

The first phase of the hearings produced an interesting revelation from restaurateur Charles Weeghman, who had purchased the Chicago Cubs after the Federal League war but had since divested himself of his baseball interests. He testified that his friend Monte Tennes, a leading Chicago gambler, had told him as early as August 1919 (while the pennant races were still on!) that the coming World Series was fixed. He stated that Tennes had given him the information at The Brook, a luxurious Saratoga gambling place owned by Arnold Rothstein, New York's notorious gambler—"the Big Bankroll"—whose name was beginning to filter into the hearings. Weeghman said he knew Rothstein well and doubted that a man of his standing would be "mixed up in a thing like this." Tennes promptly denied having had any conversation with Weeghman about the Series.

Other names were soon in print: Abe Attell, ex-featherweight boxing champion and henchman of Rothstein, for instance, and a number of White Sox players—McMullin, Cicotte, Williams, Gandil, Felsch, Weaver, Risberg, and Jackson. As early as the end of the first day's hearing, Assistant District Attorney Hartley Replogle categorically asserted, "The last World Series between the Chicago White Sox and Cincinnati Reds was not on the square. From five to seven players on the White Sox team are involved." The next day Henry H. Brigham, foreman of the grand jury, told the press, "Chicago, New York, Cincinnati, and St. Louis gamblers are bleeding baseball and corrupting players. . . . I am shocked at the rottenness so far revealed." Nevertheless, the first several days' hearings meandered along without much progress. And what of the Philadelphia-Chicago game, which had triggered the investigation? All that was turned up was a letter from a sports editor, which Ban Johnson put in evidence. It claimed that on August 31 a gambler named Frog Thompson received a wire, believed to be from Claude Hendrix, who was scheduled to pitch that day, in which the sender placed a bet of $5000 against his own team, the Cubs. The letter also claimed that Chase had wired Thompson that the game was crooked. Thompson denied everything, and from then on the grand jury simply ignored the question of crookedness in the Philadelphia-Chicago game.

Then on September 27 came a major breakthrough. The Philadelphia *North American* published a page-one story headlined "Gamblers Promised White Sox $100,000 To Lose." The story was written by reporter James Isaminger as the result of an interview with a small-time gambler named Billy Maharg, who was also a former boxer and semi-pro ball player, at that time working in a Philadelphia auto plant.

According to Maharg, the White Sox deliberately lost the first and second games of the 1919 Series for a bribe, and Abe Attell and Arnold Rothstein were implicated. It all began when Eddie Cicotte came to Sleepy Bill Burns in Maharg's presence at the Ansonia Hotel, New York, and offered to lose the World Series for $100,000, payable on the morning of the first game. Maharg endeavored to get Philadelphia gamblers to put up the necessary money, but they said it was "too big a proposition" for them and suggested he try Rothstein. Rothstein, however, turned down Burns and Maharg because he did

not believe such a "frame-up" was possible. They thought the deal
was off, and Maharg returned to Philadelphia. Meanwhile, Abe Attell, who had heard of it, told Burns that Rothstein had changed his
mind and agreed to put up the bribe money after all. So Burns wired
Maharg: ARNOLD R. HAS GONE THRU WITH EVERYTHING. GOT EIGHT IN.
LEAVING FOR CINCINNATI AT 4:30. Maharg joined Burns in Cincinnati,
where Attell was handling the betting at the Hotel Sinton. But Attell
stalled on handing over the $100,000 Burns had promised the players,
with the excuse he needed the money for betting. He proposed instead to pay them $20,000 after each thrown game.

After the first game, according to Maharg, Attell continued to hold
back on paying any money. To allay the players' suspicions and reassure them that Rothstein was supporting the fix, he showed a faked
telegram signed with Rothstein's initials: HAVE WIRED YOU TWENTY
GRAND AND WAIVED IDENTIFICATION. When at the end of the second
game Attell handed over only $10,000, the Sox players decided to do
a little double-crossing themselves and win the third game. Attell suspected what they were up to. But Maharg and Burns had been assured by the players that after losing behind Cicotte and Williams,
they were not about to win behind the "busher" Dickie Kerr, starting
pitcher in the third game. So the two gamblers had bet every dollar
they had on Cincinnati and consequently were left broke in Chicago.
Maharg added that later on he heard that some St. Louis gamblers
had made a new deal with the Chicago players to lose the last game
and that a member of the St. Louis Browns had acted as go-between.
After telling his story to Isaminger, Maharg wired Comiskey to claim
the $10,000 reward for evidence. He never received an answer.

Maharg's account, which Sleepy Bill Burns corroborated at the trial
later, was doubtless true as far as it went, but he (and Burns) had
only a mole's eye view of what had happened. He saw the fix only
from his own vantage point. Besides, whatever firsthand knowledge
he had did not extend beyond the third game. The importance of Maharg's statement was that it unplugged information either dammed up
in the jury room or only seeping out from it. The resulting open flow
pressured others into admissions, denials, or dodges. In fact, Maharg's
revelations flushed out confessions from four White Sox players. All
were made without advice of counsel, and at least three of the men
waived immunity.

Cicotte and Jackson, the first to crack, confessed the day after Maharg's story broke. The newspapers printed different versions of their
confessions, none of them complete. The essence of Cicotte's tearful
admissions was that he had thrown the first and fourth games by various artifices: putting nothing on his pitches, making a wild throw,

and purposely intercepting a throw from the outfield that might have cut off a run. He had sold out for $10,000, which had been placed under his pillow before (or after) the first game. He did it for the wife and kids, he said, and he used part of the money to pay off the mortgage on his farm. Later in the hearings the "mystery woman," Mrs. Henrietta Kelly, Cicotte's landlady, testified that she had overheard him tell his brother after the Series, "I got mine." The only gamblers Cicotte mentioned were Burns and Maharg.

Jackson followed hard on the heels of Cicotte. He told of moving slowly after balls hit to him, making throws that fell short, and deliberately striking out with runners in scoring position. Although promised $20,000, he said he had received only $5000—"I never got that $15,000 that was coming to me," he reportedly complained. According to the Chicago *Tribune,* Jackson asserted that he and the others had done their best to lose the third game but that Dickie Kerr, the Sox pitcher, won it anyhow; the gamblers, however, thinking they had been double-crossed by the players, then reneged on the promised money. It was as Jackson was leaving the courthouse that the well-known "Say it ain't so, Joe" incident supposedly occurred.

Cicotte and Jackson implicated six other teammates: Chick Gandil, whom Cicotte named the "master of ceremonies" of the plot, Swede Risberg, Fred McMullin, Buck Weaver, Happy Felsch, and Claude Williams. The grand jury indicted all eight. Comiskey immediately sent telegrams suspending them indefinitely because of information "which has just come to me, directly involving you . . . in the base-ball scandal now being investigated. . . ." If they were innocent, he told them, they would be reinstated; if guilty, they would be retired from Organized Baseball for life if he had any say in the matter. It was because of the public that he was taking this action, he said, "even though it costs Chicago the pennant."

Williams was next to lay bare his connection with the frame-up. He unburdened himself naïvely to Alfred Austrian, Comiskey's attorney, and the question-and-answer text was printed in full. It added new facets to the plot, some of which Maharg and Burns were apparently unaware. Williams said that he was first sounded out by Gandil at the Ansonia; he then attended a meeting at the Warner Hotel, Chicago, with several of the players and two men introduced as Brown and Sullivan (in reality, Nat Evans and Sport Sullivan), emissaries of New York gamblers. Williams was supposed to get $10,000 after pitching and losing the second game; therefore Brown and Sullivan had apparently promised a total of $80,000 to eight players. Williams stated that Gandil had told him Bill Burns and Abe Attell were fixing the games, too, and would pay the players an additional $100,000.

However, Williams said he received only $5000, and that not until after the fourth game. He stated that the players were supposed to throw the first two games, but he never knew whether they were to win or lose the third, the one that Kerr pitched. Austrian asked him nothing about the eighth and last game, and Williams, who pitched and lost that one too, volunteered nothing.°

The fourth player to talk was Happy Felsch, who divulged his tale to a newspaper reporter. He was quoted as saying, "I'm as guilty as the rest. . . . Looks like the joke's on us, doesn't it?" Felsch admitted receiving $5000. However, he claimed that while he had not intended to double-cross the gamblers, he had done nothing to lose the Series on purpose because it so happened that no opportunities were presented.

The confessions, indictments, and suspensions that tumbled forth following Isaminger's scoop on Maharg were devastating. They dissipated whatever hope there was left within Organized Baseball of concealing or glossing over the machinations within its ranks. Shocked and disgusted,°° the press and public branded the eight White Sox players "Black Sox" and convicted them collectively long before they were tried. The obloquy attached to their names has never been expunged.

On the other hand, some of the immediate responses to the somber disclosures were not without unintentional humor. Colonel Ruppert publicly expressed admiration and sympathy for Comiskey in his "terrible sacrifice to preserve the integrity of the game" and placed the entire Yankee roster at his disposal for the remainder of the schedule and, if necessary, for the World Series! Harry Frazee, the third member of the "insurrectionist" troika which the Carl Mays incident had suborned, thought each club in the American League should contribute a player toward replacing the guilty Sox players. However, they were saved from such singular selflessness by the rule banning from the World Series any players acquired after August 31.

To commemorate the indictment of their accused teammates, the so-called "Square Sox" † had dinner together in downtown Chicago. "No one will ever know what we put up with all this summer," one of the diners was quoted as saying. "Hardly any of us have talked with any of those fellows, except on the ball field, since the season opened. . . . We went along and gritted our teeth and played ball . . . and all the time felt that they had thrown us down. It was tough. Now the

° Maharg intimated that Williams had been threatened with foul play if he did not lose the eighth game, and many years later his wife confirmed this.

°° See above, chapter 14.

† "Square" in slang used to mean "honest" and usually was preceded by "fair and." They were also called "Opposite Sox" and "Clean Sox."

load has been lifted. No wonder we feel like celebrating." Captain
Eddie Collins acknowledged, "We've known something was wrong
for a long time, but we felt we had to keep silent because we were
fighting for the pennant." And a few days later two of the Square Sox
testified that some of the players purposely tossed away a three-game
series at Boston on Chicago's last eastern trip of the 1920 season.
They claimed that the betrayers played with their eyes on the scoreboard: if it showed that the other pennant contender, Cleveland, was
winning, they played to win (and the other way round), so as to keep
the pennant race close in order to maintain betting interest.

Therefore, the "honest" players had known or strongly suspected
the perfidy of their teammates all along but, like the owners, had adhered to the code of silence and done nothing about it.° With the
scandal exposed, they now hastened to disassociate themselves from
the Black Sox under cover of smug, self-righteous, and self-pitying
statements.

The Square Sox reaped their reward. Comiskey presented each
with a $1500 check, ostensibly "the difference between the winning
and losing players' shares" of the 1919 Series, together with a letter
released to the press that declared they had been deprived of the
winner's share through no fault of their own. With equal gallantry ten
of the players signed and released a letter addressed to the fans of
Chicago: "We the undersigned players of the Chicago White Sox,
want the world to know the generosity of our employer who of his
own free will, has reimbursed each and every member of our team
the difference between the winning and losing share of last year's
World Series, amounting approximately to $1500." The word "approx-
imately" was used somewhat loosely. The actual difference was $1,-
952.71.

Right after these chivalrous ceremonies, crusty old Cap Anson,
titan of the Chicago White Stockings of the 1880's, was so gauche as
to tell the press that Johnson and Heydler were "weak-kneed" in not
finding out what was going on and cleaning up the game themselves
instead of waiting for a grand jury to do it. And Horace Fogel and
Charlie Dooin were inconsiderate enough to choose this time to tell a
Philadelphia reporter about the attempted bribe of Philly players by
a member of the New York Giants toward the end of the 1908 season.°° But after a brief rattling, that skeleton was left undisturbed in
its closet.

° Eddie Collins did, however, go to Comiskey when the team returned from
Boston and complained that the series with the Red Sox had been thrown. Comiskey thanked him but took no action.

°° See above chapter 14. Fogel also charged that Rube Waddell was bribed to
stay out of the 1905 World Series. See above chapter 1.

The possibility of cashing in on the front-page news created by Maharg's story and the ensuing confessions and indictments did not go unnoticed by publicity-conscious officeholders. Attorney General MacClay Hoyne, who had become a lame duck after losing the Democratic primary before the hearings started, had gone to New York on vacation and had left his assistant Hartley Replogle to conduct the investigation. When he discovered that his assistant was, as the *Times* put it, "getting all the glory," he announced from New York that the indictments would not stand up because they had to be returned in a court of law, and he ordered that the investigation not be concluded until he returned with additional information he was gathering. He also expressed doubt that any crime within the jurisdiction of the Cook County courts had been committed. Judge MacDonald fired back that the law certainly did cover the crime. The *Times* said that Hoyne ought to know the law, but if the sellout was not a crime it ought to be. Within a few days Hoyne decided there was a law after all. Replogle went him one better by calling for passage of a federal statute making the throwing of ball games a felony—a panacea already offered by Ban Johnson. The *Times* could not resist commenting on this suggestion, tongue in cheek: "Such an offense, striking, as it does, at the very heart of this nation, should be made capital, and it should be defined and have its penalty fixed, not in a Federal law, but in the Constitution of the United States."

Similar noises were coming from Washington. Congressman Sydney E. Mudd, an old ball player, was ready to come to the rescue with federal legislation, declaring that it would be criminal to allow professional baseball to be ruined by crooked players. "It means too much to the nation; it means too much to the youth; it meant too much to our soldiers during the war." Another Congressman, Nicholas Longworth, with whom Garry Herrmann was on "Dear Nick" terms, announced that he was in favor of anti-gambling legislation and was looking into what Congress might do to protect baseball.

Brooklyn District Attorney Harry E. Lewis snatched some headlines by summoning Brooklyn players, who were about to play Cleveland in the World Series, to question them about gamblers. He took his cue from Hoyne's sensational statement that a bigger scandal was threatening because there was evidence that the approaching Series was fixed. But Lewis found that there was nothing to the rumor.

Meanwhile, the grand jury hearings maundered through most of October. A lugubrious procession of baseball people filed in and out of the jury room. Among those called were Garry Herrmann, John McGraw, and several former teammates of Chase and Zimmerman, all of whom expatiated on the misconduct of the two proscribed players. McGraw also acknowledged that he knew about Sleepy Bill Burns's telegram to Dubuc, and Dubuc himself admitted receiving the wire and passing on to Rube Benton the betting tip contained in it.

Another witness was Joe Gedeon, infielder for the St. Louis Browns, who told the grand jury that he had bet on Cincinnati at the suggestion of Swede Risberg, but that he did not realize, at least at first, that the Series was to be thrown. Gedeon also implicated another group of gamblers, including Carl Zork, a St. Louis blouse manufacturer and former manager of Abe Attell, and admitted having sat in on a meeting with them. Zork was also named by Harry Redmon, a St. Louis theater operator, who claimed he had overheard Zork say that the Series was fixed and that he had been invited to a conference where he learned of the plot. A few weeks after the Series, said Redmon, he had told Kid Gleason, White Sox manager, about the fix, and was then asked to go to Chicago, where he repeated his story to Comiskey, Alfred Austrian, and Harry Grabiner, secretary of the Chicago club.° Redmon said pointedly that the White Sox officials did not seem anxious to do anything about the fix and that Comiskey had remarked that his players had "cost him a lot of money." Thus the public learned, said *Sporting News*, that Comiskey had suppressed news of the players' "rottenness" because they "cost him a lot of money"; he had protected his investment "at the expense of the public."

The Yankee colonels, Ruppert and Huston, immediately requested Comiskey to counteract the impression harbored in some quarters that he had been delinquent in his duty not only by failing to act promptly but also by hushing up information. Comiskey complied. He issued another statement to the effect that he had brought Redmon to Chicago at his own expense after learning that he was willing to talk if he was reimbursed for the $5500 he lost betting on the rigged Series. But the evidence he gave, Comiskey added, was only "hearsay" and "no one would have been justified in taking affirmative action such as would destroy the character and reputation of men even though they were ball players." Ban Johnson had also interviewed Redmon at about the same time, said Comiskey defensively, and had taken no action either, so he must have reached the same conclusion. Comiskey meant, of course, that Johnson did not put much stock in Redmon's story either, for he evidently did not consider that Johnson's inaction could also have meant that he, too, wanted to keep the story quiet, at least for the time being. Comiskey repeated that he had told Heydler of his suspicions before the Series was over, that

---

° Gedeon and Redmon were the "St. Louis parties" referred to by Comiskey in his earlier white paper.

Heydler had informed Ban Johnson, and that furthermore he, Comiskey, had conducted an investigation, at a cost of about $10,000, that did not end until May 20, 1920. It was his investigation, maintained Comiskey, that enabled his attorney to obtain the ball players' confessions that "ruined my ball team, possibly cost me a pennant and certainly destroyed property [in players] of a value of many hundreds of thousands of dollars." Comiskey thus chose to overlook the fact that it was Maharg's disclosures that prompted the confessions, not his investigation. He also tended to bear out Redmon's observation that he seemed primarily concerned over losing players of high market value.

The public bickering and sniping of the baseball men was matched at first by that of the gamblers. When Abe Attell heard in New York that Maharg had put the onus on him, he was furious. Dismissing Maharg's story as "a lie" and his tale of faked telegrams as "all bunk," Attell blamed Rothstein: "It looks to me that Rothstein is behind these stories. I am surprised because I have been a good friend of his. He is simply trying to pass the buck to me. It won't go. . . . Rothstein is trying to whitewash himself. . . . in a day or two I will shoot the lid sky high."

Gambler Sport Sullivan, named by Claude Williams in his confession, threatened to tell the grand jury, which had already indicted him, "the whole inside story of the frameup. . . . They have . . . made me a goat and I'm not going to stand for it. . . . I know the big man whose money it was that paid off the Sox players—and I'm going to name him."

Such open recriminations would never do. To behave like the baseball men would endanger all the gamblers. Arnold Rothstein decided to take action, and he had the means of doing it.

Rothstein was the "financial genius of the underworld plutocracy." He bet on horses, ball games, elections, and prize fights. As one writer put it, he was ready to gamble on anything except the weather, because "there was no way of fixing that." He was involved in a vast illegal drug trade and was a fence for expensive stolen goods as well as a banker for racketeers. He operated a number of plush gambling houses, and among his clientele were some baseball owners. Charles Stoneham, owner of the Giants, had business connections with him and, as already mentioned, John McGraw was Rothstein's partner in a poolroom for a time.

In this vexatious situation Rothstein called on the well-known criminal lawyer William A. Fallon to extricate him. Fallon, as counsel for various underworld figures, was known as "The Great Mouthpiece." He was a brilliant attorney, master of criminal law, and an eloquent pleader, notorious for bribing jurors. He, too, mingled with baseball men and had friends on various clubs, particularly the Giants.

Fallon's strategy was to take the offensive and have Rothstein appear voluntarily before the grand jury in an attitude of injured innocence. Fallon set the stage by alerting Chicago newspapers so that Rothstein could pretend indignation at being treated like a criminal when the reporters and photographers arrived. The plan worked. Upon his arrival Rothstein was met by a crowd of photographers and writers, to whom he issued a statement claiming that "Attell and some other cheap gamblers" had framed the Series, that when he was "asked in on the deal" he "turned them down flat." In his speech before the grand jury Rothstein, playing the role planned for him by Fallon, was quoted as saying:

> Gentlemen, what kind of courtesy is this? What kind of a city is this? I came here voluntarily, and what happens? A gang of thugs bars my path, with cameras, as though I was a notorious person—a criminal even! I'm entitled to an apology. I demand one! Such a thing couldn't happen in New York. I'm surprised at you!

He denied having bet on the Series and spoke of his love of baseball and his friendship for McGraw. Evidently the grand jury was taken in, for District Attorney Hoyne stated publicly that he did not believe Rothstein was involved. Equally interesting was the clearance given by Comiskey's attorney, Alfred Austrian, who declared that Rothstein "had proved himself guiltless." These vindications had already been preceded by one from Ban Johnson, who earlier had gone to New York, interviewed Rothstein, and concluded that he knew about the fix but had not participated in it.

In curious contrast with Rothstein's eloquent riposte at Chicago was the sudden silence of the other gamblers and their equally sudden urge to travel. Attell, on Fallon's advice, took off for Montreal to escape the New York District Attorney's subpoena. Sport Sullivan left the country too. Maharg decided he did not want Comiskey's $10,000 after all, even if the offer was genuine. The wily Hal Chase, whose name threaded all through the hearings as the "real fixer," the one who had approached Attell and Sport Sullivan, needed no urging to sit tight in California and keep his mouth shut.

The grand jury terminated the hearings October 22 and by the end of the month had handed down indictments. In addition to the eight Chicago players—Cicotte, Williams, Gandil, Risberg, Weaver, Jackson, Felsch, and McMullin—they named gamblers Hal Chase, Abe Attell, Sport Sullivan, Sleepy Bill Burns, Nat Evans (Brown), and one

Rachael Brown, "steerer" for Rothstein. Indicted later were Carl Zork and Ben Franklin, the St. Louis gamblers implicated in the scheme; David Zelser (Bennett), Attell's aide; and the Levi brothers, associates of Zelser. Rothstein was not indicted.

The foregoing is the pith of what the public knew up to the close of the hearings. Many months would pass before the accused were arraigned and tried. But Organized Baseball dared not wait. Even as the squalid disclosures unrolled, the owners in their consternation rushed to restore public confidence in their blighted business. Basic structural changes in Organized Baseball were to result.

16

AN ELECTED CZAR

THERE IS still widespread belief that the Black Sox scandal brought about the overthrow of the National Commission and its replacement by a new form of baseball government under Judge Kenesaw Mountain Landis. That was not quite the case. The National Commission was wobbling many months before the scandal occurred, and it collapsed altogether before the Series sellout came to public knowledge. It had been stumbling along for several years under mounting difficulties and criticism before, under pressure from dissentient owners, it fell apart with the resignation of August Herrmann in February 1920. Efforts to replace him with someone financially disinterested in professional baseball had reached a standstill, particularly since Ban Johnson had dragged his feet over selection of a new chairman.

Furthermore, a blueprint for a new type of baseball government was in existence before the scandal ever came into the open. In the midst of the fierce row over Carl Mays, roughly a year before exposure of the Series scandal, Albert D. Lasker had formulated a plan for a new regime in Organized Baseball. Lasker was a prominent Chicago businessman and a power in the Republican Party. He was also the largest stockholder in the Chicago Cubs after William Wrigley, the chewing-gum manufacturer. His plan, albeit considerably modified, became the foundation of a new governmental structure in Organized Baseball.

The basic premise of Lasker's plan was that the club owners were incapable of governing their own business, in view of their interminable politicking, their public squabbles, and the growing whisperings about game throwing. In effect, Lasker was saying that professional baseball was too important in America to be left to baseball men to run. His plan provided for another triumvirate to rule Organized Baseball, a body to be comprised of eminent persons without finan-

cial connection with the business who would be invested with "unre-
viewable authority," including power to reprimand or fine owners as
well as players and even to declare a franchise forfeited. Among those
mentioned as possible chairman of the proposed tribunal were Gener-
als John J. Pershing and Leonard Wood, Senator Hiram Johnson,
William McAdoo, former Secretary of the Treasury, and Judge Landis, whose name had bobbed up repeatedly for a baseball post, particularly after the beneficence he showed toward Organized Baseball
when he avoided a decision on the Federal League's anti-trust suit
against it.

Lasker's prescription for the ills of Organized Baseball scarcely
pleased the magnates, and for a time they did not pay it much attention, although Dreyfuss and Wrigley discussed the plan with Lasker
and intended to take it up with the other owners after the 1920
World Series. The Black Sox exposé intervened, however, and badly
frightened the magnates. Their plight permitted no further delay; restoration of public confidence required a prompt, dramatic move. In
their anxiety the owners turned to the Lasker plan, even while the
grand jury hearings were still in progress. Thus the Black Sox scandal
precipitated and accelerated a structural change already contemplated and which very likely would have come about in some form
anyway.

Most of the groundwork for the new order was laid in a series of
conferences in Alfred Austrian's office. Austrian was attorney for the
Chicago Cubs as well as for the White Sox, and his office was a convenient rendezvous, since many of the owners avid for the plan or
whose backing was needed to effectuate it were either located in Chicago or were due there for the hearings.

These owners marched in and out of Austrian's quarters in different
combinations for informal talks over a period of more than a week, so
that by September 29 the Lasker plan had a nucleus of influential
baseball men from both major leagues committed to its support. The
National Leaguers were Wrigley and Veeck, Sr., of Chicago, Stoneham and McGraw of New York, and Dreyfuss of Pittsburgh. Aligned
with them were the old American League Insurrectionists of Carl
Mays days: Comiskey of Chicago, Ruppert and Huston of New York,
and Frazee of Boston. Significantly, Ban Johnson had not been consulted.

The National League cadre had even gone so far as to pledge that
its circuit would deny recognition to any American League clubs that
refused to accept the new form of government. Thus a shift in the balance of power was taking shape. Formation of a phalanx composed of
eight National League clubs and the three renegade American

League clubs that were prepared to sever connections with their league and throw in their lot with the National would pit eleven clubs against five. Besides, the four clubs in the two biggest money-making cities, New York and Chicago, would be in the Lasker camp.

To further its plans, on October 1 members of the junta sent a letter to all major- and minor-league owners. In it they pointed out what they regarded as the weaknesses of the old Commission: the financial interest of its members in the cases they had to adjudicate and the fact (rather belatedly discovered) that it did not directly represent the minor-league owners or the ball players. The signers of the letter believed that "the present deplorable condition in baseball has been brought about by the lack of complete supervisory control." They recommended Lasker's idea as a solution and promised that only men of the "highest standing" would be considered for the new commission, men against whom there could never be "a breath of suspicion." The same day the letter was sent, National League President Heydler also advocated that a new body of financially disinterested men should supplant the National Commission.

Less than a week later (October 7) the National League owners met in Heydler's New York office, unanimously endorsed the Lasker plan, and invited the American League owners to a joint meeting at the Congress Hotel in Chicago on October 18 to map out the reorganization of Organized Baseball. The three anti-Johnson American League clubs—Chicago, New York, and Boston—accepted the invitation. Soon after, fifty minor-league officials were reported having endorsed the plan.

But as might be expected, Ban Johnson opposed the meeting. The time was inopportune, he argued. To meet before the grand jury completed its work and handed down indictments would be a mistake; to discuss a new tribunal before "we know Who's Who in Baseball" would be premature: "I believe in a thorough housecleaning before starting to remodel the house." Further results of the grand jury investigation, he suggested, would be even more surprising to the public than those already revealed. With this mingling of objections and enigmatic comments, Johnson announced his refusal to summon his club owners to the meeting. His Loyal Five—Philadelphia, Washington, Detroit, Cleveland, and St. Louis—joined him in the boycott. The legacy of the Mays affair had taken full effect. The American League was again openly split. Heydler insisted, however, that the joint meeting must be held because public opinion would brook no delay; accordingly, the eight National League clubs and the three anti-Johnson American League clubs went ahead as planned.

After a twelve-hour session on the eighteenth, the reformers scrapped the National Agreement and, in keeping with Lasker's idea, outlined a plan for a new three-man board of control composed of men without financial interest in professional baseball. They set the salary of the chairman at $25,000 and of the two associates at $10,000 each. They also appointed a six-man committee to draft a new agreement that would cover all major and minor leagues. An innocuous resolution was adopted in favor of passing laws to punish attempts to bribe ball players, and, in an indirect jab at Ban Johnson, they congratulated and thanked Heydler for his continuing effort throughout 1920 to bring about a reorganization of professional ball. They then issued a stern ultimatum which gave the Loyal Five until November 1 to join in the new plan; otherwise, the three American League clubs would sunder themselves from the American League and unite with the eight National League clubs to form, with the addition of one new club, a twelve-club circuit. They would meet again November 8.

With a new baseball war in prospect, a good deal of maneuvering took place on each side during the ensuing three weeks, much of it behind the scenes. Recent material published by Bill Veeck, Jr., from the diary of Harry Grabiner, White Sox secretary, gives new information on what occurred and confirms much of what was already reported or surmised. The fight centered on the composition of the new tribunal, especially the chairmanship. Judge Landis had the inside track for the job. There were some, such as John Heydler and Bill Veeck, Sr., who wanted him from the first. By October 21 Alfred Austrian was able to advise Harry Grabiner that Veeck had told him six National League clubs were ready to vote for Landis as chairman and would accept a former sports editor and William H. McCarthy, president of the Pacific Coast League (to represent the minor leagues), as associate commissioners. The Brooklyn and Cincinnati clubs were still uncommitted, Veeck reported. So, counting the three maverick American League clubs, the score was nine out of eleven for Landis. In fact, Austrian told Grabiner that he had gone ahead and sounded out Landis about taking the job and that the judge wanted a few days to discuss it with his family. Austrian's impression was that the "salary will not satisfy him unless around $50,000."

While the Laskerite clubs were forming up behind Landis, Ban Johnson, at the head of his loyal quintet of owners, was apparently bent on the twofold purpose of maintaining his power and driving Comiskey out of baseball. He saw a chance to gain these objectives if the Lasker plan could be blocked by using the voting system whereby each major league voted as a unit. The result would be a deadlock, since Johnson was always assured of a 5-3 majority in the American

League. Failing this, the next best strategem was to dominate the new commission by landing his own man in the chairmanship.

Johnson's candidate was the judge presiding over the grand jury hearings, Charles MacDonald. In fact, a Chicago correspondent for the New York *Sun*, Leonard Edwardson, found himself indicted for libel for publishing a story in which he stated that Johnson had actually promised MacDonald the chairmanship of the commission. And one Soule, hired by Harry Grabiner to spy on Johnson, predicted on October 19 that the grand jury's report would be slanted toward praise of MacDonald and Johnson in order to boost the former for the chairmanship and to raise the latter's prestige to the point where he could exert enough influence to gain MacDonald's election.* This assessment fit in with Johnson's expressed desire to postpone consideration of reorganization until after the jury ended its hearings. Grabiner's agent also believed that Johnson would try to implicate McGraw and Kid Gleason, the White Sox manager, because of their "former connection with book making and gambling." On his part, Grabiner recorded in his diary that if any litigation arose out of Johnson's maneuvers, Heydler would "go the limit," since he had "enough against Johnson to sink a ship." Thus the two antagonistic bodies of major-league magnates were squaring off for a fight over who should control their industry. The outcome of the struggle would depend almost entirely on who would win the chairmanship of the new commission, and that issue was closely related to Ban Johnson's resolve to oust Comiskey from the White Sox franchise.

It was Johnson's move. Confronted with the November 1 deadline of the eleven-club alliance, he summoned the American League board of directors, composed of four of his five loyal owners, to meet in Chicago October 29. About this time a newspaper story revealed Johnson's plan to get rid of Comiskey. He had one card up his sleeve, the reporter said—the fact that just after the 1919 Series Redmon had told Comiskey, Grabiner, and Austrian that it had been framed. Therefore Comiskey had known of the fix but had not fired the guilty men. There was a section in the American League constitution that provided for the ouster of a club by a three-fourths vote if it failed to expel any player proved guilty of a conspiracy to throw a game, and Johnson, the story added, contended that three fourths meant three fourths of the clubs present at a meeting, not of the entire league membership.

After the meeting, the board of directors (in reality, Johnson)

* When the report did come out, its innocuous verbiage put the best possible face on the scandal and omitted any blast at Comiskey.

issued a statement rejecting the Lasker plan as "wholly ineffectual" for carrying out its intended purpose. The board disapproved of having baseball run by citizens without "experience in practical baseball affairs" and doubted that they should be allowed to manage "baseball properties in which large sums of money have been invested." What was needed, asserted the board, was a commission comprised of "practical baseball men" who understood the game "in all its details and knew intimately the history of all its players." What would stop gambling in baseball was the "certainty, speed, and severity" of punishment. The board also criticized the Lasker plan because it provided no representation for the minors. Nevertheless, the board recognized that there was a "strong feeling prevalent among the public in favor of some reorganization in baseball." Therefore it offered a counterproposal—that a nine-man committee be appointed, three men from each major league and three from the minor leagues, to work out a "feasible plan" for reorganization. Although Johnson had ignored the November 1 deadline, he had at least acknowledged that a change was inevitable. His hope was to shape and control it.

The New York *Times* attacked the counterproposal as a diversion to fend off reorganization and perpetuate the present baseball government. It scoffed at Johnson's sudden solicitude for the minors, which "caused many a smile" in baseball circles, since he could have put a minor-league representative on the National Commission long ago. Now, said the *Times*, he and the Loyal Five were using the minors to thwart the majority of the major-league club owners.

The Lasker faction intensified its courtship of the minors. At the outset it had deplored the lack of direct minor-league representation on the old Commission and had suggested McCarthy for membership on the new one. This wooing was pursued further by Heydler in a letter to the minors on October 22, inviting them to "propose" a candidate for the new tribunal. Few were fooled by this ploy. David Fultz, the one-time "agitator" of the Players' Fraternity, now respectably installed as president of the International League, saw through the flirtations of Heydler and the Laskerites. The plan, he submitted, was "excellent" for the major leagues but "illogical" for the minors, because it would put all baseball under control of the majors, since they would be the sole selectors of the three men on the commission. The minors could do no more than suggest; only the majors could vote. Thus "even our internal affairs," said Fultz prophetically, "will be governed by a group in whose election we have no voice."

Undeterred, Heydler renewed his solicitation of the minors, not only to offset the American League board's call for minor-league representation on a nine-man committee but to open the way for a peace settlement, even though the November 1 deadline had come and gone. In a letter to Johnson on November 3, Heydler again invited him and the Loyal Five to join the other eleven clubs at the coming November 8 meeting and to appoint a committee to meet with one from the minors for the purpose of working out a new organizational plan. Johnson again refused to attend a joint meeting, saying it would be sufficient for each major to appoint a three-man committee to meet with one from the minors.

The pro-Landis men awaited the approach of the crucial November 8 meeting with some apprehension. A new consideration had entered in: politics. Early on, Senator Warren Harding had asked Herrmann to cooperate with Lasker in pushing his plan. Then at a November 1 conference, Austrian told Grabiner, Veeck, and Lasker that Will Hays, chairman of the Republican National Committee, had exerted pressure on behalf of Judge MacDonald for chairman of the commission, on the flimsy pretext that he preferred that the Federal bench (Landis) not be tampered with. Apparently Johnson or one of his group had influence too.

Lasker was ready to make some concessions. He not only thought the minors should have representation on the commission but was even willing that the Loyal Five name one of the associates, provided Landis was chairman. Should Landis lose out, Lasker would not stand in the way of MacDonald. His main concern was to end the "domination of Johnson, who stood in the path of cleaning up the game."

Another cause for concern was fear that some Landis supporters might be getting cold feet, especially Ruppert, who had gone to Philadelphia to see one of the Loyal Five, Connie Mack, at the latter's invitation. Lasker thought that Ruppert was the "weakest" of their associates, that he was "money mad" and might not stand fast if it came to a baseball war. It was also at this time that Lasker found out from Stoneham that Johnson had tried to secure from him the Yankees' lease on the Polo Grounds in order to gain control of the franchise and drive Ruppert and Huston out; in exchange, Stoneham could pick the new Yankee owner and also name the third member of the new commission.* According to the Grabiner diary, Lasker planned to have Stoneham repeat this story to Ruppert before the November 8 meeting—undoubtedly for the purpose of holding Ruppert in line for Landis. Such jousting and intrigue continued up to the crucial November 8 meeting.

When the National and American League owners convened at the Congress Hotel, the "Hungry 5," as Grabiner called them, were also

* See above, chapter 13.

on the premises but in another room. They sent one of their group, Clark Griffith, into the meeting as their spokesman, but all he offered was the same nine-man committee proposal of Johnson's board of directors. The eleven clubs turned him down and made plain their determination to stick to the plan set forth in their October 18 meeting; the Loyal Five were welcome to join them, formally or informally, to discuss it—otherwise the eleven would proceed without them.

Further exchanges during the day failed to break the stalemate, so at four o'clock the eleven clubs reconvened and unanimously elected Judge Landis chairman of a new commission for a seven-year term at an annual salary of $50,000. The three anti-Johnson clubs withdrew from the American League, the old National League formally disbanded, and a twelve-club new National League was formed—the twelfth club to be the first to desert the Loyal Five or, if after a reasonable time none did, a new club would be set up in Detroit. Heydler was elected president and secretary-treasurer of the new circuit. The two other members of the new commission would be elected later, one of them by the minor leagues "if they desired." The new league adopted two measures obviously intended to restrain Johnson in the event he and his Loyal Five should decide to return: neither of the associate commissioners could be president of a league; and interleague questions were to be decided by a majority vote of all clubs in both major leagues rather than by vote of each league voting as a block. The combine then chose a six-man committee to call on Landis and proffer him the job. This committee comprised Veeck, Baker, Austrian, and—evidently to hitch them tighter to the Landis bandwagon—Herrmann and Ebbets, last of the National Leaguers to throw in for the judge, as well as Ruppert, whose steadfastness Lasker doubted. Landis told them he would consider the offer and reply in a few days. Upon this, the Loyal Five threatened to carry out plans, supposedly long contemplated, for putting new clubs into New York, Boston, and Chicago to compete with the three renegade clubs.

Each of the contending factions now attempted to shift the balance of power in its favor by face-to-face solicitation of minor-league support. Both the new National League and the decimated American League immediately sent committees to Kansas City, where the minors were holding their convention the next day, November 9. Most of the other owners and Ban Johnson also went along.

In a bellicose speech before the convention, Johnson called for war as "the best cleanser." What the game needed, he trumpeted, was "to be cleansed of undesirable club owners" who had "openly allowed gambling in their baseball parks." He attacked Lasker as "one who has not shed his swaddling clothes in baseball" and urged the minors to follow a neutral policy and refuse to join the new National League in the Lasker plan. He promised them equal representation on a new National Commission. Baseball, he declared, should remain in the hands of men who had given their lives to its development.

The New York *Times* reporter at the convention believed that the minors were impressed with the views of Johnson and his attorney, who followed him on the platform, but the paper's editorial expressed the opinion that the magnates were "incompetent to run their own business." Confidence in them, already shaken by the scandal, was further eroded when they appeared unable to run down rumors long in circulation. The obstacle to the needed revision, the *Times* went on, was Johnson, "once a brilliant and successful executive" who "now seems to think that baseball exists for his greater glory." The new twelve-club league was fighting for real reform, said the editorial; "the other side is fighting to protect the autocratic rights of a baseball Kaiser, who would rather ruin a business than lose his job."

The battle was practically over before it started. For all his fighting speech and vituperation, Johnson's game was ended. His loyal quintet crumpled in the face of what was almost certain to be a wasting and useless contest. Even as Johnson was speaking, Griffith was approaching Mrs. Ebbets to arrange a meeting with her husband. Intermittent conversations between different members of the discordant factions followed. The upshot was that the Loyal Five signified that they wanted peace and were prepared to conform to the new order established by the other eleven clubs at their November 8 session. News of peace came abruptly the next morning (oddly, the anniversary of the World War One armistice). As Garry Herrmann was addressing the convention, he was handed a note. He interrupted his speech to announce dramatically that the sixteen owners had agreed to meet by themselves in Chicago the next day, without the league presidents, lawyers, or stenographers.

The meeting of November 12 was a momentous one for Organized Baseball. There the owners framed for the industry the basic governmental structure that stands to this day. First they unanimously confirmed Landis's election. Even Phil Ball, faithful to Johnson to the end, grudgingly let Bob Quinn, his vice president, cast the vote of the St. Louis Browns. The new method of deciding interleague questions by a majority vote of the sixteen major-league owners was retained, with the additional proviso that, if there was no majority, then each major league would cast a single vote. If those two votes differed, the Commissioner, who was to preside at all joint meetings, would then cast the deciding vote. His decision was to be final. These arrangements were to be incorporated into a new or revised National Agreement drawn up by a six-man committee named by the major-league presidents. Each league would have three members on the committee, which would be assisted by a similar committee from the minors.

But what about the two associate commissioners, one of whom the minors were to be permitted to propose? The major-league owners agreed to forget about them and hand over the reins to Landis alone. After all the endearments so recently showered on them, the minor leagues were brushed aside like medieval rabble in the path of royalty.

Having made up, though perhaps not kissed, the major-league magnates, except for Phil Ball, hied themselves to the Federal Building to offer the crown to their chosen czar. As they filed into his courtroom, hats in hand, Landis looked up from the bench, bid the buzzing owners to be quiet, and directed them to his chambers. After letting them wait for nearly an hour, Landis entered and asked (as if he did not know) the purpose of the visit. Apprised of their errand, he professed reluctance to give up his judgeship. At the urging of the owners, he decided to retain it and requested them to subtract his $7500 judge's salary from the $50,000 they offered.° Finally, he demanded that the authority they granted him be absolute. The owners eagerly agreed.

Baseball men, fans, and the press greeted the appointment favorably. Pointing out that Landis combined a trained judicial mind with a keen interest in baseball, the *Times* called the choice "fortunate" and declared that "fans emitted a huge sigh of relief" at the news. If Landis received the cooperation of the owners, all would go well, but, the editorial cautioned, the test of their willingness to abide by the agreement would come when Landis decided a dispute over a valuable player.

The accession of Landis pleased John Heydler. He had favored change and was little affected by it; National League presidents never had much power anyway. True, he lost his position on the old National Commission, but he accepted that loss with relief. Ban Johnson's position was different. He was deeply wounded by the desertion of four of his five loyal owners, by his humiliating exclusion from the vital November 12 meeting, and by his reduction from the most prominent man in baseball to a schedule-maker and director of umpires. Nevertheless, for the time being he managed to say the proper words: "I am for Judge Landis, and I think these club owners have acted wisely." He also predicted there would be "no more fights."

He must have been jesting. Politicking in the American League re-

° There is evidence that he did not actually receive less than $50,000 because the $7500 was restored in the form of an expense account.

sumed almost immediately. In picking members for the committee charged with writing a new national agreement, Johnson passed over the insurrectionist owners and named Dunn, Shibe, and Navin. Next he saw to it that four "loyal" owners—Ball, Dunn, Griffith, and Shibe —were elected to his 1921 board of directors, thus breaking the eighteen-year-old American League precedent of selecting its board members in rotation, a precedent which, if followed, would have seated the three Insurrectionists.

These actions reopened the sniping within the American League. Colonel Huston accused Johnson of trying to perpetuate "old sores" and attacked him and his five "puppets" as an "unholy alliance." "The elimination of Johnson," declared the Colonel, "would automatically restore tranquility." Johnson fired back that he had always used the ballot whenever the rotation method would put "undesirable members" on the board, and at the meeting "it was the sentiment" that two owners should not be on it "as they had attempted to wreck" the American League. After reading this justification, Frazee joined the fray. In a letter to Johnson he said that if Johnson had been quoted correctly, he was "stating a deliberate falsehood." Johnson's words were, declared Frazee:

> one more evidence of your gross stupidity and incompetence. . . . I had hoped that you had learned something in the last two years. . . . I think it is about time for you to stop making threats and prove some of the many misleading statements and assertions you have made. . . . If you had any sense of justice or realization of the harm you have caused baseball, or one spark of manhood, or any regard for the game which has made you possible, you would tender your resignation.

The *Times* was critical too. It pictured Johnson as "reluctant to relinquish the power that was passing from his hands" and as still "bitter" over the Mays case because it "gave him his first real setback in baseball." His latest actions, said the *Times*, demonstrated that he and his "Willful Five" were dissenters from the new Landis regime, and "his show of acquiescence is the veriest hypocrisy."

In the meantime, Landis deferred taking up his new duties pending completion of the new National Agreement. In December he met with the duly-appointed twelve-man major-minor-league committee and with attorneys John Conway Toole, George Wharton Pepper, and James C. Jones at the Commodore Hotel in New York. Heydler (but not Ban Johnson) was also present. Using rough drafts prepared beforehand by Heydler and Toole as a basis for discussion, the group drew up an agreement which the major leagues approved at their meetings in New York December 10-12. Then Landis and the attorneys reviewed it and the major leagues ratified it at a special joint meeting in Chicago on January 12, 1921.* The agreement was to remain in effect for twenty-five years.

The new National Agreement provided for a Commissioner with the broadest investigative and punitive powers. He had complete authority "To investigate, either upon complaint or upon his own initiative, any act, transaction, or practice . . . suspected to be detrimental to the best interests of the national game of baseball" and the power to take punitive action, including fining or blacklisting, against leagues, clubs, officers, or players found guilty of such detrimental conduct. At the last minute Ban Johnson had tried to dilute the authority of the Commissioner by somehow getting the wording of this crucial clause changed to read that the Commissioner could merely "recommend" action, but Landis, having been alerted beforehand by Dreyfuss, was ready. He interrupted the reading of the document at the joint meeting and told the owners the clause must read to "take" action. He would retire from the room, he informed them, while they decided either to make the change or to find a new Commissioner. "You have told the world that my powers are to be absolute," he reminded them; "I wouldn't take this job for all the gold in the world unless I knew my hands were to be free." The owners complied.

The agreement also made the Commissioner final judge in all disputes involving leagues, clubs, and players. Finally, the owners snapped shut the lock on the chains they themselves forged by agreeing to be "bound by the decisions of the Commissioner" and "to the discipline imposed by him" and to waive their right of recourse to the courts. They further agreed to insert a similar provision into the contracts of their players and other employees and shortly issued a separate public statement pledging to abide by Landis's decisions "even when we believe them mistaken" and to refrain from public criticism of him or each other.

Under the new National Agreement the clubs retained the right to make all rules regulating the industry, although if the two major leagues disagreed, Landis had the deciding vote. As a sop to the major-league presidents, an Advisory Council was established, composed of them and Landis, and here too his vote was final whenever there was a difference of opinion. In effect, he rarely convened it while Johnson remained American League president.

The selection of Landis and his investment with autocratic authority had their paradoxical side. Landis, famed as a trust-busting judge who had not flinched from fining the Standard Oil Company, was

* The National Association signed a separate, though similar, agreement for the minors on January 10. See below, chapter 20.

consenting to preside over a monopoly whose legal status was still pending in the Federal courts; at the same time, he continued to sit on the Federal bench. The proud club owners, who had long writhed and complained under Ban Johnson's arbitrariness (in the thick of their fight over Carl Mays, the owners of the Yankees had cried out, "Czarism is unAmerican!") were now passing themselves abjectly and even eagerly under the yoke. In a fit of collective masochism they were making a panicky effort to expunge the stain of scandal and regain respectability. Only Phil Ball refused to join them; he alone declined to sign the agreement with Landis.

In creating a Commissioner to rule over them, the owners established the first "industry doctor" in America, a precedent soon followed by others, such as the motion-picture industry, which shortly named Will Hays "the Judge Landis of the movies" in order to stave off censorship bills threatening in thirty-six states. Eventually the idea of appointing a "czar" came under severe criticism as an easy way for a business engaged in questionable practices to give the appearance of cleaning house without having to face up to any public accounting. As John Gunther has written, the device inhibited external regulation and promoted hush-hush solutions. Hays, for example, succeeded only in adding hypocrisy to sex by giving motion pictures "moral" endings. Soon we shall see how the system operated in the baseball industry.

When Landis accepted the commissionership he promised an "untiring effort" to rid the business of gambling and to treat gamblers with "a firm hand." "If I catch any crook in baseball," he announced, "the rest of his life is going to be a hot one." He even asked fans to eliminate small wagers among themselves. The club owners expressed their support of his policy, and the new Advisory Council put $10,000 at his disposal to investigate crookedness. Late in November, after the Black Sox hearings but long before the trial, Landis made a statement that was to set the tone of his administration. Concerning the accused Chicago players, he said, "There is absolutely no chance for any of them to creep back into Organized Baseball. They will be and will remain outlaws. . . . It is sure that the guilt of some of them at least will be proved." Thus a Federal judge was condemning men to the blacklist before they had been tried in a court of law and whatever the outcome of their trial.

17

ACQUITTED BUT STILL CONDEMNED

THE NEW Commissioner of Organized Baseball displayed a strange aloofness toward the Black Sox case, despite his promises to root out gambling. In fact, when Ban Johnson asked him several months after he became Commissioner what he was doing about the case, Landis replied, "Nothing." Indeed, so many obstacles to its prosecution arose that there might not have been a trial at all had not Johnson pressed for one.

At the arraignment of the accused players in mid-February of 1921, the prosecution, now under the direction of the new administration, District Attorney Robert Crowe and his assistant, George Gorman, received a severe setback. Judge William Dever ruled the indictments faulty and granted a defense petition that a bill of particulars be presented. In order to gain time in which to comply, the prosecution requested a postponement of the trial because important evidence was missing from the records of the grand jury hearings. When the judge refused, Crowe charged "corruption of witnesses" and a "peculiar conspiracy." He revealed what for some time had been rumored, that "secrets" of the grand jury had been stolen from the files, and in this connection he called attention to the singular fact that three members of the former district attorney's office were now serving as attorneys for the defense.

Without a postponement Crowe entertained little hope of pursuing the case successfully. The players had filed affidavits repudiating their confessions, so the only substantial evidence left to the prosecution was Billy Maharg's, and he was a participant in the fix. Corroborating evidence was needed, and obtaining it required time—which the court declined to give. Crowe therefore offered a motion of *nolle prosequi*, figuring that by forgoing prosecution for the present he had a chance to collect additional evidence and witnesses, rebuild his case, then secure reindictments and bring the players to trial.

There were those who believed that halting prosecution of the case in this manner meant that the players would never be tried. In the face of this doubt, Landis declared that baseball could protect itself regardless of what happened in the courts, and he placed all eight accused players on his "ineligible" list. Up to this point Comiskey had retained them on his reserve list. Although he had suspended them after Maharg's disclosures, his notice of suspension was so worded as to leave a loophole for their possible return to his ball club. Now Landis's pronunciamento forced Comiskey's hand. He immediately sent a formal notice to the players releasing them from the club and terminating their contracts with it. Comiskey told the press that it had not been necessary for Landis to act, because the players were already on his own ineligible list.

In the meantime, Ban Johnson resuscitated the legal case against the players. Using American League funds and some of his own, he undertook to collect the legal ammunition needed by the district attorney. One of his trips was to Texas, where he tracked down Sleepy Bill Burns and persuaded him to turn state's evidence in exchange for the promise of immunity. Through Johnson's efforts, the five gamblers Zork, Franklin, Zelser, and the Levi brothers were added to the list of those indicted. Johnson also employed John "Ropes" O'Brien and ex-judge George Barrett as counsel, to counteract the apparent lethargy of Assistant District Attorney Gorman.

These exertions were instrumental in bringing about the trial that opened June 27, 1921, with Judge Hugo Friend presiding. Reindicted were seven Chicago players—Cicotte, Williams, Gandil, Risberg, Weaver, Jackson, and Felsch. Fred McMullin was omitted this time for lack of evidence. Ten gamblers were indicted, including Hal Chase.

All the players appeared, but the gamblers were less cooperative. Some, like Rachael Brown and Sport Sullivan, simply vanished. Chase was arrested in San Jose but released, and his $3000 bail money was returned because of a technicality. Abe Attell underwent the most remarkable metamorphosis since Jekyll and Hyde. With the help of William J. Fallon, he became another Attell. Arrested in New York, where he had returned after his Canadian trip, Attell swore he was not the same Attell as the one indicted and that he knew none of the ball players. The original complainant against Attell, Sam Pass, obligingly came to New York and testified that he had never seen this Attell before. Pass, a manufacturers' agent who had lost a reported $3000 betting on the White Sox in the Series, said he had volunteered to be a witness because he did not want to see an innocent man go to jail! There is little doubt that Fallon saw to it that Pass was reimbursed for his trouble, but Rothstein blandly denied that he had hired the "Great Mouthpiece" to protect the "Little Champ," or Sport Sullivan either.

Attorneys for two other gamblers, Carl Zork and Ben Franklin, made affidavit that their clients were too sick to appear. Mere mention of the affair upset Zork so badly, explained his attorney, that he "turns white, cries, and trembles." The state then produced an affidavit that the sufferer had very recently been seen on the street in St. Louis. When the court warned of contempt charges, Zork recovered in time for the trial.

The defendants were indicted on various counts of conspiracy: to defraud the public and the Chicago catcher, Ray Schalk; to commit a confidence game on Charles Nims, a Chicago fan who lost $250 betting on his heroes; and to commit a confidence game to injure the business of the American League and of Charles A. Comiskey.

Attorneys for the defense, reinforced by John "Ropes" O'Brien, who had suddenly switched to that side, moved immediately to quash the case on the ground that the indictments were illegal under Illinois law. The state's case was "lame," said attorney Ben Short; otherwise "You'd have the real leaders of the conspiracy here—the men who made millions—and not these ball players, who were reputed to be getting big salaries, but most of whom get practically nothing." The ensuing technical exchanges between the attorneys were impressive, at least to Shoeless Joe Jackson. "Those are certainly smart men, and that lawyer of mine is one lawyerin' bird," he said. "They better not get him riled up."

On July 5 the court denied the defense motion to dismiss the case, and the tedious process of impaneling the jury began. Curious spectators, mostly fans, crowded the hot courtroom daily to glimpse the stars in their new setting and to collect their autographs. Fans on hand on July 11 enjoyed an extra treat. A group of "Clean Sox," led by manager Kid Gleason, dropped in and, with handshakes, camaraderie, and what passes for badinage among players, fraternized with the "Black Sox." The Clean Sox even tickled ticklish Buck Weaver, who had been sitting apart each day from the others in the dock in order to accent his claim to innocence. "Hope you win the pennant, boys," Happy Felsch called out to the visitors, who replied, "Thanks, Happy. Good luck to you in your trial." Somehow this incident smudged the presumably clear distinction between good and evil, between innocent and accused. It certainly was at variance with the attitude previously professed by some of the Clean Sox at their dinner celebration after the confessions of Cicotte and Jackson.

At last, in mid-July, the court began hearing testimony. First, the opposing attorneys engaged in another exchange: "You won't get to first base with those confessions," shouted defense attorney Michael Ahearn. "We'll make a home run with them," answered Ben Short. Then Comiskey, the state's first witness, took the stand. He contributed little evidence but considerable excitement. In cross-examination, Short asked whether or not he had broken his contract and jumped from the American Association to the Players' League back in 1890. Comiskey, beside himself with rage, leaped up and shouted, "Don't you dare to say I ever jumped a contract. I never did that in my life. You can't belittle me!" He was finally quieted and sank back in his chair, "seemingly greatly fatigued." The fact was, of course, that as a player Comiskey did join the Brotherhood and violate the reserve clause in his contract by jumping from the St. Louis Browns to the Players' League.° The defense also tried to delve into Comiskey's financial policies but without much success, since the judge sustained objections. Later in the trial, however, the defense punctured the claim that Comiskey's business had been damaged by showing that after the alleged conspiracy his gate receipts had nearly doubled, climbing from $521,175.75 in 1919 to $910,206.59 in 1920.

At the close of the first day, George Gorman summed up for the prosecution. "We used our weakest lineup and shut them out. Wait until our real hitters get in." Thomas Nash replied in kind for the defense: "We took everything they sent over and didn't even burn our hands. We'll fan their heavy hitters."

The next day the state sent in its "heaviest hitter," Sleepy Bill Burns. Burns proved to be an effective witness, relating how Cicotte and Gandil had first approached him at the Ansonia with an offer to throw the Series for $100,000. Burns described various meetings he and Maharg had with Chase, Attell, Bennett (Zelser), and Rothstein to raise the bribe money, and he told of meetings at the Sinton with the accused players, Jackson excepted. He brought a laugh when he quoted Cicotte as saying, "I'll throw the first game if I have to throw the ball clear out of the Cincinnati ball park." In short, Burns elaborated on the Maharg story as reported by Isaminger. Under cross-examination he admitted that one reason he was testifying was that he was double-crossed by both Attell and the players. He and Maharg were supposed to have collected a "slice" of the payoff money from each, but they never received it. It had been on Gandil's assurance that the White Sox would lose the third game, as they had the first two, that Burns and Maharg had bet on Cincinnati and lost everything. Burns acknowledged that Ban Johnson had paid him $700 expense money to testify.

° See *Baseball: The Early Years*, page 233.

Billy Maharg recapitulated what he had told Isaminger and thus corroborated Burns's testimony. He, too, admitted that Johnson had paid his expenses, including wages lost while absent from his auto-plant job. Joe Gedeon, the Browns' infielder who had given information at the grand jury hearings, was present as a prosecution witness but was not called on to take the stand.

The trial took a startling turn on the third day when prosecuting attorney Gorman revealed that among the evidence missing from the grand jury files were the original confessions of the players and their waivers of immunity. Then Hartley Replogle, the former assistant district attorney, stated under oath that his boss, Maclay Hoyne, had taken papers from the files and that he, Replogle, had then informed Judge MacDonald, who presumably had impounded the grand jury records. When Gorman was asked where the confessions and waivers were, he replied, "Ask Arnold Rothstein—perhaps he can tell you." Ban Johnson added to the excitement by accusing Rothstein of paying $10,000 to obtain the confessions and other material from the prosecutor's office and, after making sure that the papers did not implicate him, turning them over to a newspaper friend who offered them for sale. Rothstein immediately issued denials and vowed to sue Johnson but never did.

What actually happened was that just before they left office, Hoyne and an assistant, Henry Berger, purloined the players' confessions and their waivers of immunity and also made sure there would be no evidence that might incriminate Rothstein. Behind the theft were William J. Fallon and Alfred Austrian, attorneys for Rothstein and Comiskey. When questioned by MacDonald, Hoyne had protested that he had a right to make copies of important papers for his own records. The incoming district attorney, Robert Crowe, had ordered an investigation, and Judge Landis had made a vague threat of "Federal action" if any evidence was found missing or to have been tampered with. But nothing was ever done about the stolen papers, and four years later, when Joe Jackson was suing for back pay, the confessions turned up in the possession of Comiskey's attorney; Comiskey could not explain how they got there. It is also interesting that when Bill Veeck, Jr., assumed control of the Chicago club in 1959, all the club's files were intact—except the ones for the crucial years 1918–19.

The revelation that the confessions were missing set off a complicated legal argument over whether unsigned carbon copies were admissible as evidence and whether the waivers of immunity had been signed voluntarily. The judge finally ruled that the copies were admissible, but each one would apply only to the individual player who had made it.

A puzzling development at the trial was the line of questioning directed at manager Kid Gleason and catcher Ray Schalk. During the Series no one had been more suspicious than those two that some of the players were giving less than their best. Yet a defense attorney was asking them, of all people, whether in their opinion the accused had played their best. Stranger still was the fact that the prosecution objected, although presumably it would have been advantageous to have the question answered.

In its summary the prosecution charged that "a swindle and a con game has been worked on the American people" and asked for five-year jail sentences and fines of $2000 for each of the accused. On its part the defense asserted that the state was "trying to make goats of underpaid ball players and penny-ante gamblers" and wanted to know why Rothstein, Chase, Brown, and Attell had been allowed to evade trial.

Judge Friend, in his instructions to the jury, pointed out that the state must show not only that the players had intended to throw games but that their purpose in doing so was to defraud the public and others. (Later, the New York *Times* said such "hair-splitting" was like asking if the defendant intended to commit murder or merely to cut his victim's head off.) The judge had already decided that there was so little evidence against Buck Weaver, Happy Felsch, and gambler Carl Zork that he would not allow a verdict against them to stand, and since the case against the Levi brothers had been dropped at the beginning of the trial, the only gambler left vulnerable was David Zelser.

After deliberating only a few hours on the evening of August 2, the jury acquitted Zelser, Zork, and all seven players. A scene of the "wildest confusion" erupted in the courtroom: spectators cheered, and hats and papers were tossed in the air; the jurors carried the players around on their shoulders. Chick Gandil bestowed a sailor's farewell on Ban Johnson: "Good-by, good luck, and to hell with you." The judge congratulated the jury on a "fair decision," and the players and jurymen then adjourned to a local restaurant, where they celebrated together late into the night. Soon District Attorney Crowe announced that the case was closed.

An overwhelming number of newspapers received the decision with disfavor. "Rather surprising," "baffles interpretation," "a petty and hollow triumph," and "a dangerous lesion in the American moral sense" were four typical comments from as many papers. The Black Sox had been "officially laundered," said the *Literary Digest*. Henry Ford's Dearborn *Independent* took off on a new tangent, pointing to a supposed preponderance of Jews in the bribery of ball players be-

fore, during, and perhaps after the World Series and blaming them
for having damaged sports in America, especially professional baseball. *Sporting News* answered this calumny with what was a fairly
enlightened point of view for those days. While it had mentioned at
times that men accused of bribing players were "largely Jews," said
Sporting News, it did not believe that just because a "bunch of
crooks" happened to be Jews that all Jews were necessarily crooked,
just as not all Irish were "grafters" or all Italians "hootch makers."

Despite Landis's having placed them on his ineligible list, the players hoped they might be restored to good standing because of their
acquittal by the jury. They were quickly disillusioned. On the very
next day after the trial, Landis handed down this decision:

> Regardless of the verdict of juries, no player that throws a ball game;
> no player that undertakes or promises to throw a ball game; no player
> that sits in a conference with a bunch of crooked players and gamblers
> where the ways and means of throwing games are planned and dis-
> cussed and does not promptly tell his club about it, will ever play
> professional baseball.

The ban included not only those players acquitted by the jury but
also Fred McMullin, who was not even indicted. In November Landis
added Joe Gedeon of the Browns to the list. Thus nine players were
permanently proscribed as a result of the scandal. The legend of Landis had begun.

Banished from Organized Baseball, the blackballed men tried to
play outside it. They received numerous offers to play from semi-pro-
fessional and "outlaw" clubs, particularly in the beginning, and for
some years often attracted good crowds. But after their expulsion Organized Baseball constantly harassed them in their efforts to play independent ball. Landis dangled his dread blacklist before any players
who dared participate in a game in which one of the ineligible players appeared. Teams began refusing to play them, and ball parks
were closed to them. Even before the trial the Chicago City Council
voted to recommend revoking the license of a park where five of the
accused men were playing.

To all petitions for reinstatement, whether from fans or from the
blacklisted players themselves, Landis remained impervious and un-
relenting. Buck Weaver, for example, petitioned time and time again,
both in person and in writing, in the following years. Time and time
again Landis refused to budge, on the ground that although Weaver
may not have participated in the actual throwing of games, he had
sat in on a meeting and therefore had "guilty knowledge," which he

had kept to himself.° Joe Jackson took the same bitter medicine. Years after being expelled, he applied for permission to manage the South Atlantic League's Greenville club in his home state of South Carolina. Landis denied his plea. Although throwing ball games was not a crime in Illinois, Landis said, Jackson's confession barred him even from the minors, because there could not be two standards of eligibility, one for the majors and one for the minor leagues.

Four of the Black Sox filed lawsuits. Felsch and Risberg failed to collect damages on a common-law conspiracy charge against the Chicago club in 1923, but Felsch did collect more than $1100 in back salary and interest in an out-of-court settlement of a breach of contract suit in 1925. Weaver and Jackson, both of whom had long-term contracts with Comiskey, sued for salary due under them. Weaver's case was dismissed. Jackson, after three weeks' testimony, actually won a jury verdict of $16,711.04 against the Chicago club, only to have Judge John J. Gregory set it aside and dismiss the case for the reason that the jury had not given proper attention to conflicting statements of witnesses. He also inferred that Jackson had perjured himself by contradicting the confession he had made during the grand jury hearings, the "lost" confession that Comiskey's attorney now produced. Both players, however, collected some money from Comiskey in an out-of-court settlement.

After their expulsion, the Black Sox gradually drifted into more prosaic occupations: plumber (Gandil), drug-store operator (Weaver), liquor-store owner (Jackson and Felsch), game warden (Cicotte), nurseryman (Williams), and dairy farmer (Risberg). They thus faded from public notice and kept silent over the years. Not until 1956 did Chick Gandil present in *Sports Illustrated* his version of the fateful events.

What deductions can be drawn about the Black Sox scandal? The task of judging the affair is doubly difficult even half a century afterwards because of the lack of source material and because countless journalistic accounts have encrusted the event in layers of preconceived assumptions and questionable opinions. By relying overmuch on Billy Maharg's story, the players' confessions, and the fact of Landis's blacklisting of the men, these accounts, with rare exceptions,°° conclude that the accused Chicago players (Weaver excepted) purposely lost the 1919 World Series to Cincinnati.

° Succeeding commissioners Chandler and Frick also refused to clear Weaver's name.
°° One is Victor Luhrs, *The Great Baseball Mystery* (New York: A. S. Barnes, 1966).

Unquestionably the accused men met with gamblers at various times to connive at throwing the Series. In fact, it was the players, not the gamblers, who initiated the scheme. The opinion of the grand jury foreman, Henry Brigham, that the players were "foolish, unsophisticated country boys who yielded to the temptations placed in their paths by the experienced gamblers" is not wholly correct. The Black Sox were foolish and some of them may have been unsophisticated, but along with many other ball players and club owners too, some of them were well-acquainted with gamblers and had no difficulty in approaching them. Chick Gandil, by his own admission long afterwards, was the one who went to Sport Sullivan with the proposition for throwing the Series. Another ringleader was Cicotte, who tried to recruit Buck Weaver as early as the team's second trip east, a fact which shows that some of the players were hatching a plan earlier than commonly believed and which lends credence to Charles Weeghman's assertion at the grand jury hearings that gambler Monte Tennes had alerted him to the fix in August.

Nor is there any doubt that some players accepted money, although it is not certain which ones received it and how much it amounted to. In any case, there is no disputing that some kind of plot existed.

But neither is there incontrovertible proof that the plot was carried out. Bungling characterized it from the beginning. It was kept about as quiet as a secret in a college-girls' dormitory. Rumors abounded before the Series started, and gamblers all over the country knew that something was afoot. Planning was so poor that the players stupidly entangled themselves with only the vaguest notion of how they would go about throwing the Series. Despite the various meetings, each player seemed to be uncertain of what he or the others would do once the games started.

Some of the players in some of the games undoubtedly tried to lose, but there is no certainty about which games they succeeded in deliberately losing, if any, and which games the White Sox won in spite of the efforts of some of them to lose. Lefty Williams in his confession said he was not sure whether the third game was supposed to be won or lost, whereas Jackson, in his, claimed that the accused did their best to lose it, but that Dickie Kerr won it anyway. Nor is there any way of knowing for certain which games the Cincinnati Reds won by their own efforts. After all, the opposing team must have had something to do with the results. Yet practically every account gives the impression that Chicago, like the hare in the fable, could defeat the Cincinnati tortoise any time it chose. The White Sox were undoubtedly superior, but the Reds, with some good pitchers and such outstanding players as Edd Roush, Heinie Groh, and Jake Daubert, were good enough to win the National League pennant and might very well have won the Series on their own.

The play-by-play descriptions and the box scores of the games offer no conclusive proof that games were thrown either. In fact, the Black Sox on the whole actually made a better showing in the games than the Clean Sox. A few examples will suffice. Joe Jackson led both teams with a .375 batting average, making twelve hits—still a record for an eight-game series, and Buck Weaver hit .324; whereas Eddie Collins, one of the Clean Sox, averaged only .226. Neither Weaver nor Jackson made an error in the field; Collins made two. In the third game, won by Chicago, Gandil drove in two of the Sox's three runs, and Risberg scored the other after hitting a triple. Fred McMullin made one hit in two tries as a pinch hitter; otherwise, he did not appear in the Series, so he could hardly have helped throw any games. To be sure, if one studies the play-by-play of the games with a view toward finding suspicious actions, he can find them; but if he tries to read the records without preconceptions, he is hard put to discover anything amiss.

The confessions of Cicotte, Jackson, Williams, and Felsch appear to be damning evidence, but the circumstances under which they were given—in the absence of counsel and with rights waived—must be taken into account. Accused persons under stress who are frightened and unaware of their rights, particularly the semi-literate or, like Joe Jackson, the illiterate, are apt to sign anything. Besides, Jackson and Felsch in their confessions almost seem to protest too much about their crookedness. Their claims could be construed as worried attempts to convince the gamblers that they had conscientiously tried to lose, as they were expected to.

And the so-called Clean Sox were not quite so pure as some have made them out to be. Surely they had some responsibility for protecting their profession. They knew that something was wrong, and more than once they admitted as much, but they did nothing about it. In a sense they were accessories to the fact. It may even be that some who were considered honest were implicated. I once asked Joe Jackson about the scandal, and he named one of the "honest" players and suggested I see him. For that matter, the entire team, as well as Comiskey and his manager, had participated in a highly dubious project in 1917 which some interpreted as bribery.[*]

The owners in general, and Comiskey in particular, must also share responsibility for what occurred in 1919. The folk expression "Outside hooey, inside fooey" is apropos of Comiskey's administrative policy. He made a favorable impression on the public through sportswriters,

[*] See below, chapter 19.

whom he wined and dined, and by contributing in various ways to civic causes; but with his players he was tight-fisted and penny-pinching. Considering their ability, his men were undoubtedly the worst paid in baseball. Embittered by financial ill-usage, they were in a receptive mood to listen to offers of easy money. Low salaries are not an excuse, but they are an explanation.

The only well-paid star on the team was Eddie Collins. He had had the foresight to demand a five-year contract at $15,000 when Comiskey bought him during the Federal League war. None of the others on the team came anywhere near making that much. Buck Weaver, the leading third baseman in baseball, was, next to Collins, the highest-paid man on the club in 1919, with $7250. Joe Jackson, one of the best players of the era, signed for $6000 in 1918 and 1919. In contrast, Edd Roush, the star outfielder of the Cincinnati Reds, made nearly twice as much. Eddie Cicotte, then a veteran of twelve years in the majors, received only $5000 in salary plus a "bonus" of $2000 after winning 28 games for the 1917 pennant-winners; for 1919 Cicotte's base pay remained about the same. The other accused pitcher, Claude Williams, was paid less than $3000 in 1919; he won 23 games that season. Utility infielder McMullin also earned less than $3000 that year, and Swede Risberg's salary was barely above it. Happy Felsch received about $4000, and Chick Gandil somewhat less. No wonder the defense counsel remarked that the players, whom the public believed to be making about $10,000, had nothing to show at the end of a season but a glove, a uniform, and a chew of tobacco.

When the public became aware of what Comiskey was really paying his players, he tried to counteract the growing impression of stinginess by giving the Clean Sox the well-publicized $1500 rewards for honesty. But Comiskey never really altered his short-sighted policy on player salaries. He offered Dickie Kerr, who had won two games in the 1919 World Series, only $4500 for 1920, and after Kerr won 21 games in 1920 he still was paid the same amount in 1921, although he had been offered $5000 to play with a semi-pro team in Chicago. Kerr rebelled in 1922, refused Comiskey's offer, and played independent ball in Texas. But because he played against some of the expelled Black Sox that year, Landis put him on the ineligible list for a season.

Whatever influence Comiskey's low salaries had on precipitating the scandal, his actions in dealing with it are open to criticism. Let us review them quickly in the light of additional evidence. He knew from the first that something sinister was going on. Monte Tennes had told Harry Grabiner as much after the first game, and manager Kid Gleason had expressed his doubts to Comiskey as well. Comiskey's initial reaction was to take steps against any dishonesty by alerting

Heydler during the Series and by evidently planning to fire any play-ers implicated. In fact, Hugh Fullerton revealed much later that when he predicted immediately after the Series that seven Chicago players would not be back on the team in 1920, he had really been quoting Comiskey. And, as previously shown, Comiskey temporarily held up the World Series checks of the suspected players.

But Comiskey soon had a change of heart. According to testimony reported in connection with Jackson's lawsuit in 1924, Shoeless Joe came to the White Sox office before leaving for home, showed Harry Grabiner $5000 in cash, and told him he had received it from other players who had thrown the Series. Grabiner advised him to go home and said that if anything was to be done about it, Comiskey would write to him. Grabiner told Comiskey about the incident, so both knew right after the Series that there had been crookedness and both admitted to it during the Jackson suit.

Apparently the temptation to protect his investment overcame any original desire Comiskey might have had to get to the bottom of the mess. He reverted to the habitual concealment tactics of the owners and denied rumors of crookedness. He obviously hoped the whole thing would blow over. Although he offered a $10,000 reward for evidence and took the precaution of launching an investigation, he had little fear of being taken up on the cash offer, and his investiga-tion scrutinized others besides his players, so that if the pot started calling the kettle black, the kettle would be able to retort in kind.

Joe Gedeon and Harry Redmon, "the St. Louis parties," did re-spond to the reward offer and come to Comiskey with information, but he dismissed their stories as hearsay. Furthermore, Cicotte's land-lady, the "mystery woman" of the grand jury hearings, was no mys-tery to Comiskey. She, too, had come to him after the Series and told of overhearing Cicotte's suspicious remark.

Knowing all this, Comiskey nevertheless went about signing the suspected players for the 1920 season. He not only proffered them contracts but in a number of cases violated his usual penurious policy and gave substantial raises. Cicotte's salary went from about $5000 to $10,000; Williams's from less than $3000 to $6000, plus bonuses that depended upon the number of games he won; Felsch's from about $4000 to $7000; and Jackson's from $6000 to $8000, with a three-year contract. Comiskey also handed out substantial bonuses after the 1919 Series: $3000 each to Cicotte and Felsch, and $875 to Williams.

At the time of Jackson's lawsuit news stories reported him as testi-fying that when Harry Grabiner came to Savannah to sign him to the new three-year contract, Jackson asked again what he should do about the $5000 given him by the other players, and that Grabiner had said the only sensible thing to do was to keep it; then Grabiner added that he knew who had thrown the Series. The editor of *Sporting News* pointed out, "Mr. Comiskey himself admits that he went about the business of re-signing the players involved in the sell-out of his club and his honor, knowing they had been accused of cheating, because of the necessary formality of 'protecting his club.'" Grabiner, too, said *Sporting News*, admitted that he knew Jackson was accused of cheating but nevertheless made the trip to Savannah to sign him for three years, for the same reason. Both acknowledged that their procedure was "unusual." *Sporting News* congratulated them on their "straightforwardness."

Even when the scandal came out into the open and he was forced to act, Comiskey left an opening in his suspension notices to the players to allow for their possible return. The contention that he had to keep his men reserved so that other clubs would not grab them has some merit, but it does not speak very well for the other owners. The pilferage of the players' confessions is further evidence of Comiskey's reluctance to part with his valuable property until the very end.

There are those who maintain that the reason nothing was done about the 1919 scandal for a full year was that Comiskey and Organized Baseball in general were helpless to take action because in the absence of sufficient proof they would have laid themselves open to libel suits. This argument is unconvincing. Comiskey may not have had conclusive proof, but he had enough to bring the scandal out into the open, and once he had done so, sufficient additional evidence would undoubtedly have been forthcoming, particularly since so many people were involved. As Harry Redmon remarked at the time of the hearings, the indictments finally brought against the players were based on no stronger evidence than that which he had given Comiskey nearly a year before. But at that time, said Redmon, the White Sox officials seemed more interested in the hundreds of thousands of dollars they stood to lose in player property than in cleaning up the situation. Even if one concedes the argument that there was not enough evidence, surely it was the duty of Comiskey and the other baseball people to spare no effort to obtain more.

The other baseball executives are also blameworthy. For too long they had looked the other way when something shady happened, or tried to conceal it. The most glaring product of their flabby policy was Hal Chase. Other players knew that for years he had instigated dishonest deals and gotten away with them. If he could, why not they? And, as already noted, some owners set a poor example by associating with people like Rothstein and Tennes or, as the trial brought out, by placing bets with gamblers or holding stakes for Abe

Attell, as did both John Seyes, secretary of the Chicago club, and
Clark Griffith, Washington owner.

Past experience should have alerted the owners and league presidents to be prepared to protect their industry at the slightest sign of
betrayal. Instead, they shrugged off or denied the ugly rumors about
the Series and then feigned disbelief and surprised shock when the
public learned the worst. As James Sinnott, correspondent for the
New York *Evening Mail,* observed in October 1920, newspapermen
who tried to "run down" the scandal "were handicapped by an apparent dislike of publicity on the part of organized baseball." To be sure,
Ban Johnson finally did make a genuine effort to dig out the facts, but
he did so for the wrong reasons—to destroy Comiskey and to out-
shine the new Commissioner. Johnson also crusaded under a banner
frayed by poor performance in the past, such as in the Cobb-Lajoie
batting-award fiasco of 1910 and in other incidents more appropri-
ately discussed later.

Then, too, the hearings and the trial itself are subject to skepti-
cism. Their declared purpose was to investigate gambling in professional baseball and presumably bring crooked practitioners to justice.
But none was ever punished, although there were numerous targets to
aim at.

The alleged fix apparently developed from two main directions:
Sport Sullivan and Brown (Nat Evans) formed one line of advance;
and Attell, Burns, and Maharg the other, with Arnold Rothstein
doing the manipulating from New York. Many regarded Rothstein as
the main fixer. Scott Fitzgerald mentioned him in *The Great Gatsby,*
thinly disguised as "Meyer Wolfsheim, the man who fixed the World's
Series in 1919." After Rothstein was shot, affidavits were found in his
files testifying to the fact that he had paid out $80,000 for the 1919
World Series fix.

Gamblers had also tried to work the other side of the street as well
—the Cincinnati team. Many years later Dan Daniel reported in the
New York *World-Telegram* that during the Series Edd Roush, having
been warned that gamblers had reached some Red players, convinced
manager Moran to hold a clubhouse meeting to clear the air. At the
meeting a Cincinnati pitcher described how he had angrily chased
away a stranger who had offered him $5000 to lose. The pitcher went
on to win his game.° The Reds, however, maintained that they saw
nothing suspicious in Chicago's play in the Series. Moran professed
"astonishment" that the Black Sox could have thrown the Series "and
us not know it," and Heinie Groh said Cicotte had a lot on the ball

° Roush later reiterated this story to Lawrence S. Ritter, who published it in
The Glory of Their Times.

when pitching to him. Dutch Ruether, who beat Cicotte in the opener, stated later that he thought he had been in a "tough game."

Despite the ubiquity of gamblers, the trial court steered away from them and concentrated on the ball players. As already noted, none of the important gamblers testified, and of the lot only Zelser was in the slightest jeopardy at the trial. Rothstein not only escaped indictment, he won hasty clearance from Hoyne and Austrian after his appearance at the hearings. Also ignored was Weeghman's clue that the Series fix had been planned as early as August 1919—a scent that might have been well worth following.

Other aspects of the trial raise doubts that it was bona fide: the unaccountable switch of four prosecuting attorneys over to the players' side and the question of who was paying their fees; the failure to interrogate Comiskey and his agent, John Hunter, about the findings of Comiskey's private investigation; the objection of the prosecution to questions that should have been to its advantage to have been answered; the unwillingness to inquire into the rifling of the grand jury files; and the alacrity with which the state prosecutor closed the case without any further effort to corral the absent gamblers.

Such omissions and obfuscations rendered the trial superficial at best, farcical at worst. No serious effort was made to uncover the full truth about the scandal or to really grapple with the gamblers. By containing the mess within limited perimeters and focusing primarily on the ball players, the trial served the interests of both the gamblers and the baseball industry. The gamblers eluded punishment, and the baseball industry emerged with the unpleasantness confined within its own lodge, from which Commissioner Landis, its new symbol of rectitude, expelled the players and in effect confirmed their guilt permanently in the eyes of journalists and the public.

In proscribing the players, Landis wielded not a sword of justice but an extra-legal scythe. He recognized no degrees of guilt but cut off from their livelihood seven ball players acquitted in a court of law and two others who were not even indicted. The same harsh penalty he gave to those assumed to have thrown the Series he meted out to a player who had appeared only briefly in it (McMullin), to another who probably had only "guilty knowledge" (Weaver), and even to one who was not on the team but who had sat in on a meeting with gamblers (Gedeon). Others, such as Rube Benton and Jean Dubuc, who also had "guilty knowledge," Landis left untouched. More astonishing, Landis not only overlooked Hal Chase, a prime fixer of the Series who had cheated for years, but even wrote him officially later that there was nothing against him. Comiskey, who, like some other baseball officials, could be said to have had "guilty knowledge," suffered only indirectly through the loss of his players.

One can argue plausibly that Landis's shock treatment was needed to restore public confidence in Organized Baseball, to demonstrate its determination to maintain its integrity, and to provide a stern example for other players; but the question of whether indiscriminate life sentences served justice is moot.

The end of the Black Sox scandal branded the nine expelled players as the villains who had betrayed the game; turned Comiskey into a martyr who had suffered financial loss and broken health; cast Johnson in the role of a crusader who had worked to cleanse the game; and glorified Landis as a savior whose stern penalties had restored Organized Baseball to purity. But the conclusion of the unfortunate affair of 1919 did not bring an end to scandal in baseball or to Landis-style justice.

PART FIVE

THE CZARIST REGIME

18

HALLMARKS OF A NEW ERA

IN THAT exuberant, roller-coaster decade between the close of the Great War and the onslaught of the Great Depression in 1929, professional baseball, along with the rest of American society, underwent marked change. These trends and developments, however novel and striking, flowed from the past. History is not a record of unrelated events. Rather it is like a great stream whose course is subject to sharp twistings and turnings and at times even violent gushes. And as the character and complexion of a civilization undergo transformation, its games and other forms of recreation reflect the change and also influence it. The interplay between baseball and American society in the 1920's was no exception.

A salient feature of the decade was its remarkable economic growth. The temporary postwar boom surrendered to a depression in 1921, but the economy recovered quickly and from 1923 until the 1929 crash the United States basked in seven prosperous years marred only by slight pauses in 1924 and 1927. It achieved a standard of living hitherto unequaled anywhere, as per capita income, which stood at $480 in 1900, bounded to $681 by 1929.

Professional baseball, too, attained new levels of prosperity in the 1920's, especially in the big leagues, where average club attendance rose fifty per cent over what it was in the decade before. The poorest figure of the period was still almost a million and a half higher than that of 1909, the peak year of the previous era. Attendance climbed above nine and a half million in 1924 and, except for a slight dip in 1928, held to that level for the next five years. Then in 1930 it rose well above ten million, excelling all previous attendance figures, even though the first year of depression had closed in upon the country. Although during the decade the population of the United States made its greatest absolute gain up to that time—seventeen million—major-league baseball attendance increased at an even faster pace.

343

Other demographic trends of the 1920's continued to be favorable to the box offices of Organized Baseball and, for that matter, to other commercialized amusements. Baseball's market was enlarged by the accelerated growth of the cities and small towns as Americans continued to desert the countryside. By 1930 fewer than 44 per cent of them dwelled in rural areas, as compared with 60 per cent in 1900. Although the continued rapid growth of California, Oregon, Texas, and Arizona presaged future major-league markets, it would take twenty-three more years before Organized Baseball bestirred itself from the territorial cocoon spun in 1903 and began to take advantage, albeit in haphazard fashion, of the shifts in American population.

Baseball income in the 'twenties remained geared almost exclusively to gate receipts. They were still the barometer of profit. In 1929 money taken at the gate represented 87.6 per cent of gross major-league income. Concession sales accounted for another 5.5 per cent. The rest came from miscellaneous sources like park rental and parking fees. Radio, and of course television, had not yet entered the ledgers, so the public was still paying practically the entire freight directly and, as shown by the attendance totals cited above, more generously than ever. How generously is indicated by the financial figures reported by major-league clubs. Each major league made a profit every single year from 1920 to 1930 inclusive, the American ranging from $119,195 to $1,459,352, and the National from $448,889 to $1,461,988. Fifteen out of the sixteen individual clubs turned a profit for the decade as a whole. The Boston Red Sox were the single exception. After their rape by the Yankees,* they suffered losses in five of the six years for which records are available. The Boston Nationals, showing losses in six of the eleven seasons, barely made it into the black ink. By far the biggest money-makers were the New York Yankees, who earned $3,516,588 during those eleven years. And these profit figures are probably conservative, accounting legerdemain being what it is. Nor do they reflect the salaries and expense allowances of club owners and executives, which are classified as expense. That is to say, an owner might be enjoying a comfortable salary and expense account while his books showed the club making a modest profit or even losing money.

The mainspring of economic growth in the 'twenties was the spectacular expansion of industry. Factory production nearly doubled between 1921 and 1929 as old industries burgeoned and new ones forged into the economy. One old one, the automobile, and a new one, radio, had a particular bearing on professional baseball. The auto industry had become a giant by 1929, when it turned out 4,-

* See below, chapter 22.

800,000 cars. More than 26,000,000 motor vehicles traversed the roads that year, and about one out of five Americans had a car, even if he did not own it outright.

Feelings were mixed regarding the impact of the automobile on professional ball. The new mobility of Americans, who were making gypsies look like stay-at-homes by comparison, enabled fans in suburban and rural areas to get to the games. On the other hand, owners, especially those in the minor leagues, were complaining that the male fan, who used to go to the ball game on Sunday afternoon, was now taking his wife and children for a family outing in the car instead. Factory workers were no longer asking for time off to attend a game. They needed money to pay for cars purchased "on time," because, like so many people in the 'twenties, they were caught up in the rash of installment buying that was corroding the old prewar doctrine that one should save up, buy only what he could afford, and pay cash. The parking problem was also becoming a headache for club owners. The postage-stamp-size lots adjacent to the parks which some owners provided were already wholly inadequate. In Brooklyn, for example, on a day when the ball park was filled, neighboring lots, private driveways and garages, and Flatbush streets were crammed with cars.

The broadcast of the 1920 presidential returns by station KDKA, Pittsburgh, signalled the genuine arrival of radio. Within two years people in three million homes were shushing each other as they strained their ears around scratchy crystal sets. Sales of radios and radio accessories leaped from $60,000,000 in 1922 to $842,000,000 in 1929, by which time there were more than six hundred broadcasting stations, inexorably breaking down provincialism, breaching cultural barriers, increasing sophistication, and creating national stereotypes.

Baseball magnates and sportswriters had serious misgivings over the possible effects the broadcasting of games might have on their gate receipts and jobs, and they strenuously opposed the new magic. A typical reaction was that of secretary Tierney of the Giants, who dismissed as "impossible and absurd" a proposal to broadcast the club's games because "it would cut into our attendance, besides hurting the newspapers. We want the fans following the game from the grandstand, not from their homes." The Baseball Writers' Association telegraphed Commissioner Landis and the major-league presidents to protest that, if the play-by-play details of games were broadcast directly from the parks, "it will kill circulation of afternoon papers and in the end will result in curtailment of baseball publicity." Phil Ball fought vigorously to get the American League to bar radio from the ball parks, and some National League owners did too, but the leagues decided to leave the question up to the individual clubs.

Just as electricity had overcome the bitter opposition of entrenched gas interests in the past, so did radio gradually prevail in baseball. While in the long run broadcasting stimulated interest in the game, there were complaints that in minor-league cities, particularly in the South, fans were avoiding the heat at the ball parks and listening to the games free in the coolness of their living rooms. A significant breakthrough came in 1921 when the Giants-Yankees World Series was broadcast by relay. Sandy Hunt, sports editor of the Newark *Sunday Call,* reported the games play by play from a telephone in a box seat at the Polo Grounds to Station WJZ's radio shack in Newark, where Tommy Cowan repeated the information over the air. Before long countless fans were able to listen to the "classic" in their homes or in the streets in front of stores that had rigged up amplifiers. The effusions of announcer Graham McNamee became familiar to millions. Whatever he lacked in knowledge and accuracy he made up for in personality. A second breakthrough came in 1925 when William Wrigley permitted his Chicago Cubs' games to be broadcast daily, despite protests of other Western clubs, especially St. Louis. Judging from the attendance figures, the club suffered no deleterious effects, but it would be years before all the other owners fell into line and allowed their games to be broadcast.

In the 1920's the real income of American workers increased at an astonishing rate, while at the same time the work week was shortened and paid vacations were lengthened. Ball players' salaries also continued to improve substantially, as they had done during the decade before. The Cincinnati club's 1929 payroll, for instance, was nearly four and a half times its 1910 total of $51,000. Salary expenditures of other major-league clubs also increased materially. The New York Yankees spent the most, $365,741 in 1929. The Chicago Cubs' $310,299 payroll was the highest in the National League in 1929. Pittsburgh's was the lowest, $140,422—even less than that of the defiled Boston Red Sox. The combined payrolls of all sixteen major-league clubs in 1929 came to $3,765,400.

How these lump sums were divided among individual players can be gathered from an analysis of two sample payrolls. Twenty-six men on the 1927 champion Yankees averaged nearly $10,000 each, but in this case an average is deceptive because of the gulf between Babe Ruth's $70,000 and the salaries of his teammates. A truer gauge is the median salary, $7000. The next highest-paid player after Ruth was pitcher Herb Pennock, who received $15,000. The two lowest-paid men on the team received $2500 each.

The Cincinnati Reds of 1924 divided $183,850 among twenty-three players, an average just short of $8000 apiece. The median figure was

$7500. Highest-paid was Edd Roush, with $19,000. The next highest salary was $12,000, paid to Eppa Rixey and Adolfo Luque. Jake Daubert got $11,000 and three others $10,000 each. These salaries may seem puny by contemporary standards, but in the 1960's a player would require nearly four times as many dollars to have purchasing power equivalent to that of a player in the 'twenties. To match Ruth's top pay of $80,000, for instance, a modern star would have to make at least a quarter of a million dollars.

Obviously, ball players of the 'twenties continued to be paid more than industrial workers and other wage earners outside the professions, particularly if one takes into account the maldistribution of wealth and the uneven prosperity of the so-called prosperous decade. According to the report of the conservative Brookings Institute, $2000 a year was the minimum family requirement to purchase the basic necessities, and 60 per cent of American families were below that figure in the crest year of 1929! Only 2.3 per cent of them received more than $10,000 and only 8 per cent had incomes over $5000. Judged by the Brookings yardstick, a major-league ball player was therefore rather handsomely rewarded.

But a comparison between the incomes of big-league ball players and those of other wage earners is like comparing dray horses with racers. The reader is reminded that, despite their relatively high salaries, players are actually exploited because of the owners' monopsony control over them through the reserve clause, which prevents them from commanding what they probably could in a free market. Even Babe Ruth, for all his fabulous salary, was underpaid in terms of his fantastic drawing power and the gate receipts he represented not only to the Yankees but to the league, and, as far as that goes, to baseball as a whole. A more glaring example has already been noted —Comiskey's niggardly pay scale for his White Sox stars, such as Joe Jackson and Eddie Cicotte. To argue, as former baseball commissioner Happy Chandler and others have done, that a big-leaguer may be a serf but he is certainly a highly paid one and that there are innumerable people who would gladly trade places with him is largely irrelevant. Of course there are many who would love to be in the enviable position of a big-league star. Certainly few will grieve over his plight. The point is that to condone a quasi-chattel system of labor, however high the remuneration, is to take a totalitarian point of view.

It is fruitless to try to list all the determinants of a professional player's salary. There are too many factors and intangibles involved. Most important are gate appeal and performance, but they are difficult to measure. Playing records, for all their detail, do not always measure true worth. A twenty-game winner with a strong batting team behind him may not be as good a pitcher as one who wins fewer games with weak support. Even his earned-run average may not tell the whole tale. A man with a high batting average may be worth less than one who hits with power or has the knack of driving in runs when they are needed. A high fielding average may indicate little more than inability to cover much ground. Nor do statistics list such imponderables as team play or the ability to inspire a team.

Naturally, with so much room for disagreement, salary disputes occur, but they differ in one respect from those in conventional business in that they are part of baseball's ritual, an off-season staple fed to the fans—more so in bygone days when there was less winter coverage of other sports in the newspapers. In fact, some salary duels were sham battles staged for publicity purposes. Over the years countless anecdotes about "holdouts" found their way into baseball lore. But if facts are stranger than fiction, they can also be more interesting; and to read some of the actual correspondence between players and owners conveys the truth and flavor of their salary negotiations as nothing else can.

An examination of these faded letters reveals, for instance, a difference in point of view over how rapidly merit should be reflected in the pay envelope. Players thoughtful enough to know their prime years were limited were anxious to make the most of them financially. "My stay up there [in the major leagues]," one wrote, "won't be as long as the owners. If the player does not get his money in good years then baseball is not a business to him and is not for me if I can make as much in cotton." And another observed: "Baseball is a player's livelihood and he must get value received for his best services. When he is at his best. He hasn't got a chance to get anything when he begins slipping." Owners, on the other hand, hesitated to pay a player what they considered too much too soon. If the man kept improving, he would keep expecting more, and the club would either be forced to go over its payroll budget or have a dissatisfied player on its hands. As Branch Rickey once expressed the idea, "it would be wrong . . . to exaggerate [a player's] expectations to the place where you could not meet them shortly"—in other words, pay him too much prematurely. So when a young man had a good season and argued that he was worth as much money as others on the team, the owners preferred to talk about "experience" and "seniority." "Sure you had a splendid year," a pitcher holding out for $14,000 was told in 1926, but "a four thousand dollar increase in one year is simply too ridiculous for consideration." The owner, who had offered an increase of two thousand dollars, held out the prospect of more money later by assuring the player that if he kept up the good work his "raises would continue in the future." To which the player tartly replied: "Never mind the future. It will take care of itself. A player should be paid on performance, not years."

Players sometimes drew comparisons between their salaries and those of better-paid men on other teams. Organized Baseball was and still is a highly secretive business, and salary figures, like other financial data, were as closely concealed as troop movements in wartime. Nevertheless, players somehow managed to have a fairly good idea of each other's pay and tried to put their information to use when they could. Thus one pitcher pointed out that "quite a few other pitchers" whose records were not as good as his got more money. Others employed the same argument. The stock answer of management was the one Branch Rickey once gave to a player: "What other clubs have paid or are paying to this or that player is not and cannot be our business."

However much owners might insist to their own players that what other clubs paid had nothing to do with their own salary offerings, in reality such comparisons were inescapable and were bound to influence the price of baseball labor. Rickey made them himself when they were to his advantage. For example, one of his negotiating strategems—and he had more of them than an old-time patent-medicine salesman—was to put off dissatisfied players with the claim that the club had the second-highest payroll in the league. Even assuming this was so, the argument was meaningless as far as the rank-and-file players were concerned, because the total was greatly inflated by the salary of Rogers Hornsby, the highest in the league. It is significant that in 1929, when Hornsby was no longer with the team, the St. Louis payroll ranked only sixth among the league's eight clubs, even though the Cardinals had won the pennant in 1928 and had had their best year to date financially. Furthermore, Rickey also told a Congressional committee many years later that one of the three factors that determined a man's pay was "comparative salaries paid to players of like age, experience, and ability." Once when Ebbets was negotiating a new contract with Wilbert Robinson, Robbie told him that another manager had just been given a big bonus and a two-year contract. Ebbets checked with the other manager's owner. He told him of Robbie's assertion and asked what his "salary arrangements" with his manager were, and in turn promised to keep the information "strictly confidential." The truth was that the owners knew a good deal about each other's finances—after all, they were partners. Only the press and the public were kept in the dark, or at best were given vague, often inflated estimates.

If owners did not know what their fellow magnates were spending, they could usually find out and take the information into account in gauging their own payrolls. Take the case of a man traded away from the Giants after they won the 1921 pennant and World Series. The chances were that they would finish at the top or near it the following season. But the player, having been traded from the club, had lost the prospect of making the extra money. Accordingly, he was demanding a big raise from his new club in compensation. His new owner wrote McGraw, the player's former manager, for advice. McGraw replied that, had the player remained with the Giants, they would have given him a $10,000 contract, "since world champs usually get an increase." "I believe," McGraw suggested, "that if you make a proposition to him to make good what money he would lose in case New York finishes one two three, that you will have no trouble in signing him."

Only a scarcely discernible line separated these cozy exchanges between owners from outright collusion. Barney Dreyfuss, replying to the pleas of a colleague who had so many holdouts one year that he suspected a "conspiracy," advised him to "sit tight and let them whistle." He would find, Dreyfuss assured him, that "very few hold out after it comes time to draw pay." Ebbets, who was having trouble signing his own players, also bucked up his beleaguered fellow magnate. After observing that newspaper reports "say you are going to the mat with your 'holdouts,'" the Brooklyn owner said that "if true and you need a 1st baseman I can let you have Mitchell or Schmadt [Schmandt]. I believe the time has come," he added, "when it will be to the interest of organized base ball to 'lock-out' one or more of these high priced 'holdups.'" Later on, when the season was about to begin, Ebbets wired: WE HAVE EXTRA OUTFIELDERS AND PITCHERS WILL HELP YOU OUT BY LOANING YOU AN OUTFIELDER AND A PITCHER IF YOU ARE IN BAD STRAITS. A few days later he sent another telegram congratulating the other owner on his firm stand against two stars still unsigned and declared: I WAS PREPARED HAD ANY OF OUR PLAYERS HELD OUT TO GO LIMIT AND WOULD NOT HAVE SOLD THEM FOR ANY AMOUNT. YOU ARE TAKING RIGHT STAND. IF I CAN HELP YOU WILL BE GLAD TO DO SO. BEST WISHES.

There was also an interesting case of collusion between an owner and one of his stars, in which they came to an agreement by resorting to an under-the-table method of payment. The owner bypassed his board of directors and secretly agreed to pay the player an additional $500 if the player would send "a straight telegram" accepting a two-year contract for $11,000 a year. The owner added: "[I will] personally . . . pay you five hundred extra myself each year on arrival but by all means treat latter absolutely confidential."

Salary was not necessarily the only subject of contention between owners and players. A promising pitcher wanted a clause inserted in his contract guaranteeing that if he were sent to the minors for more experience, he would receive his original salary. Another player with a home and business established in the city wished it to be understood that he would not be traded without his consent. A man traded "down the river" from a contending team to one with little chance of finishing in the money usually asked for a bonus and often got one, but one such player was told: "this is a fate that befalls ball players at times." Occasionally a player would try to have a club pay his wife's expenses to training camp. Such proposals were usually refused on the ground that a precedent would be set and others would demand the same.

An increasingly abrasive issue was the growing demand of players for part of the purchase price when they were sold. Players, aware of the big sums owners were receiving for some of them, wanted to share in their own appreciating market value. One sale that created quite a stir was that of pitcher Jack Bentley, who was sold by Baltimore to the Giants in 1923. Bentley was an outstanding minor-leaguer and could have played in the majors long since, except that Jack Dunn would not sell him until he finally got his price from New York, a reported $65,000 plus two players. But Bentley refused to sign a Giant contract unless he received a share of the purchase price. After a long holdout he finally accepted terms, but significantly the ball club refused to say whether or not he received a share of the sale price.

In 1925 this practice of selling livestock in spiked shoes came to the attention of Congressman Fiorello La Guardia, later one of New York City's most colorful mayors. He proposed a bill that would have imposed a 90 per cent Federal tax on the sale of player contracts involving $5000 or more unless the player himself received the entire purchase price. "Baseball is about the only profession or calling," La Guardia said, "where an individual in this country does not derive the benefits of his own efforts and proficiency." He brushed aside a cherished justification of baseball owners—to wit, that it is costly to develop a player and that they are therefore entitled to a return on their investment in him. La Guardia's reply was: "In my investigation, I failed to find that any great amount of expense is involved in the training of these young men, inasmuch as they play ball during the season and pay their way all the way through." As one student of baseball law has pointed out, if La Guardia's bill had gone through and cash sales of player contracts had been virtually halted, some of the abuses of the reserve rule would have been ended and its avowed purpose, to equalize competition, strengthened.

It is interesting to note some of the different approaches players took in bargaining for better contracts. One stated crisply, "I am asking for $8500, not more than I want but what I want." Another was more ingratiating; he hoped that a 33 per cent cut would be restored if he had a good season and placed his "faith in the fairness" of the owner. A third brought in his family: "You no doubt know I have a wife and two children and my expenses are far greater than the unmarried ball player and I cannot see my way clear for 4500 dollars." Sometimes players wrote their letters to the owners on business letterheads, in a not very subtle effort to give the impression that they were not wholly dependent on the club's largesse. A utility infielder on the 1927 Yankees promptly capitulated after receiving a letter from the general manager that said that if every player kept demanding the limit the club treasury would be empty. The infielder enclosed a facetious note with his signed contract stating that he was accepting terms immediately because he did not want to be pointed out as the man who broke Colonel Ruppert (a multimillionaire). Quick-tempered Adolfo Luque had Pepe Conte, the Cuban baseball factotum, act for him in salary negotiations. Apparently the owner had threatened to have Commissioner Landis place Luque on the blacklist for not signing, and Conte cleverly communicated Luque's rage to the owner while ostensibly deploring it: "I read your letter to him, and as he is the most illiterated [sic] man on [sic] captivity he raised cain and started to say at the top of his voice that you and Landis could go pllump [sic] to____ . Of course," Conte added blandly, "this is mere empty words pronounced by a man that has no education and that outside of his ability to pitch is a most perfect jack-ass."

Personality clashes are not to be overlooked in contract negotiations either. The owners, being human, allowed personal likes and dislikes to intrude at times, just as they permitted business considerations to subordinate those of "sport," in spite of their public protestations that they were working with single-minded purpose to construct a winning team. To cite only one example, in 1921 Ebbets tried to dispose of Zack Wheat, idol of Flatbush, "for personal reasons. . . . He has been too long in Brooklyn." In 1923 Ebbets had a long tussle with Wheat, ostensibly over a $500 increase. He offered the star the same contract as the year before, when Wheat had led the team in batting with a .335 average—$8300 plus the customary $500 for being team captain. "There are very few outfielders receiving more than you," Ebbets contended, and he made great to-do over the need for Wheat to show "loyalty to the Brooklyn club." A New York *Times* editorial apologized for a remark about the "parsimony" of Ebbets and asserted that many players had an "artistic" temperament and wanted to dictate to their employers. "Such attempts have to be met, as Mr. Ebbets met them, in the interest not only of good business and efficient organization, but of the game itself."

A certain dichotomy in the professional player's concept of himself obtruded upon the negotiating process. On the one hand he saw himself as a hero and an individualist. This view of himself and his position ran counter to collective action and was one of the reasons the ball player for the most part eschewed unionization. The ball player's hero image was reinforced by a somewhat immature approach to his occupation. It was, after all, a game, to which he could bring a boyish desire to play and a human desire for glory and acclaim. There is much significance in the tale of the old-time big-leaguer standing at a bar over a beer and laughing at the thought of having received money for what he would have done for nothing. "They paid me," he is supposed to have said, "not knowing that I would have paid my own way into the park for the opportunity to play ball." This side of the player's makeup was not lost upon owners. One man's former owner wrote his new owner that the player was "absolutely unreasonable" in salary demands but "he loves to play ball and [I] don't think you'll have trouble signing him."

On the other hand, the player also saw himself in the more prosaic role of a job-holder engaged in earning a living, a view that entailed laying aside his hero cap and donning that of a breadwinner who recognized that it took more than public adulation and press clippings to buy groceries. As one player in the midst of a salary squabble wrote his boss: "Please don't think that I am being stubborn . . . but I am sure you . . . will see that this is a business with me as well as with the club."

Two factors at least make it reasonable to believe that the players of the 'twenties were becoming more aware of the practical side of their lives. The decade was one of bare-faced materialism, exemplified in Calvin Coolidge's pithy phrase, "the business of the United States is business." It was also a decade of expanding educational opportunity. By 1930 a youngster's possibility of going to high school was five times greater than in 1900, and his chances of attending college were better than one in seven as against only one in thirty-three at the beginning of the century. Like almost everyone else, therefore, ball players as a group had more schooling than ever before. At the start of the 1927 season, according to one estimate, 107 men representing 79 colleges held one third of the regular positions on major-league teams. Conceivably they were more sophisticated and perhaps

more articulate when contract time rolled around than their predecessors had been. This being the case, the players would tend to
emphasize money more and more, but in doing so they would risk vi-
tiating their hero image and making it less believable. To attract fans,
professional baseball must stir their emotions through make-believe
and illusion. Its business nature must be muted, its non-pecuniary
features proclaimed. Its owners must assume the aspect of sportsmen
and its players that of heroes. These requirements and illusions have
become increasingly difficult to maintain in recent years.

But regardless of which image the player emphasized, that of a
hero or of an employee, he had no genuine bargaining strength. In
fact, the whole bargaining process had an unreal character. It was
more ritualistic than substantive, an exchange of gestures between
player and owner. The player could be stubborn or pliable, deferen-
tial or demanding. He could laboriously marshal the statistics of his
playing record and bombard the owner with them. All would avail
him little or nothing.

Take statistics, for example. Whatever figures the player presented
could always be neutralized by the owner with his own. To the arguments of one player who asked for an increase on the basis of his record, his owner answered with a deluge of data covering the player's
entire five years with the club, taking into account the number of
games the man played, his times at bat, runs scored, hits made, total
bases, stolen bases, and batting average, as well as the player's
monthly and seasonal salary. For one of the years the owner even
added the $600 he estimated the player had cost the club in expenses,
and on the basis of his figures concluded that the player had received
$581.65 for every run made, or $166.18 per base hit!

If negotiations reached an impasse, the owner's final response was
likely to be in the same vein as one made by Ebbets: "If you do not
show the proper spirit without delay, I shall be compelled to with-
draw contract offered, and assure you it will not be renewed." At
least one player understood his situation: "I realize as well as you do
that I am compelled to sign at your figures as are all other ball players." The players' position was well described by one of them:

> I didn't like being told what I was to get by an employer. . . . I
> liked it less when Rickey . . . issued an ultimatum . . . stating that if
> I did not report immediately he would cut down his already poor
> offer. What was I to do but report, which I did. I had no dough and
> had a baby only a little over a year old. . . . I had asked him several
> times, that I wanted to be traded to a spot where I could play regu-
> larly. . . . But he would not deal me off and I not only suffered in
> salary badly but deteriorated as a player.

Regardless of all the obstacles, including the players' own qualms, that have stood in the way of organizing, the idea had a strange vitality and was never quite abandoned. In 1922 the players made their fourth attempt to form a union, although as before they avoided using the term in their constitution. They named their organization the National Baseball Players Association of the United States, and they went through the usual routine of drawing up a constitution, electing officers, providing for an eleven-man executive board to serve one year, and setting dues at twenty dollars annually. To head the new organization they secured Ray Cannon of Milwaukee, who, like Fultz, was an attorney and former player, though not a big-leaguer, and who had represented some of the Black Sox in their salary suits. The basic objective of the association was the transformation of the players from "pawns of the club owners" into their equals. The owners of major-league clubs, declared the players, "have for a great number of years, been organized in a national body . . . and have acted unitedly in their dealings with baseball players. . . . Such body," they continued, "has constituted a virtual monopoly of the business end of baseball and no voice has ever been given to the ball players." Thus it was "necessary that the players shall deal with such owners and their organization as a unit." The players disclaimed any intention of striking but in their first resolution demanded to have a voting representative participate in the decision-making at the top.

The reaction of the baseball hierarchy to the union ran true to form. Ebbets vowed that he would not be "black-jacked into meeting unreasonable demands by my players. . . . If they go on strike next spring I will fight them with every means at my command." McGraw asserted that his players were "getting fabulous salaries" and that those who joined "are nothing less than ingrates." National League president Heydler saw no necessity for a union. Paternalism would do: "With Judge Landis at the head of organized baseball, every player knows he can always get a square deal. . . . Baseball today is conducted with proper regard for the rights of the players, the owners and the public"—the inference being that maybe such was not always the case. A New York *Times* editorial chose to revive an old saw: how many players could earn one fifth as much money in another calling?

The anxieties of the owners were premature. Although by the end of December the union was believed to have 225 members, it expired almost as soon as it was born. One reason for its demise was the lack of solidarity among the players, many of whom gave both public and private assurances that they were satisfied with conditions. A doubt-less apocryphal story printed later nevertheless contained a good deal of truth. It told of a player who was asked why it was that players had never formed an effective union such as actors had. "Hell!" he replied, "this ain't a coal mine; it's a ball yard. It would be a lot of satisfaction, now wouldn't it, to sit down and read over your union card after you'd struck out in the ninth with the bases full?"

Another project of the players, however, became a permanent success. In October 1924 they launched a purely charitable organization, the Association of Professional Ball Players, for the purpose of aiding sick and indigent players. This long-overdue and sorely needed agency originated on the West Coast, with headquarters in Los Angeles. The membership fee was only five dollars, and agents sent out to proselytize were very successful in enlisting a wide membership among major- and minor-league players, as well as former players and some umpires. Men convicted of a felony or blacklisted by Organized Baseball were barred. Within two years the Association claimed almost two thousand members. The owners themselves appropriated money to help the cause. Their willingness to contribute offers an interesting parallel to the prevailing policy of American business in the 1920's—staunch anti-unionism but advocacy of welfare capitalism as a backfire against the spread of organization among workers. In the years since the Association began, it has helped thousands of members from nineteen to ninety-five years of age who applied for assistance. According to a 1970 report, total assistance since the founding of the organization amounted to $1.6 million. In 1970, 4501 members paid $28,666 in dues and the Commissioner's office contributed $50,798. At any given time there are about fifty needy people receiving aid.

Hallmarks of the 'twenties treated thus far, such as economic and population trends and their relationship to baseball, are more susceptible to measurement than other characteristics of the period that are less tangible but nevertheless significant in revealing the spirit of the times. Such frenetic aberrations as flaming youth, bathtub gin, the flapper, jazz, and feverish new dances like the Charleston and Black Bottom are forever associated with that era. It was a time when hemlines rose nearly as high as the stock market and Clara Bow, the "It" girl, displaced girlishly innocent Mary Pickford as the female sex symbol on the movie screen. It was a time that venerated a host of athletic titans like Jack Dempsey (prize fighting), Bobby Jones (golf), Bill Tilden (tennis), Red Grange (college football), Gertrude Ederle (swimming), and of course Babe Ruth (baseball). It was a time when Americans were preoccupied with what Frederick Lewis Allen has called "tremendous trivia," when they were seized by "a contagion of delighted concern over things that were exciting but didn't matter profoundly."

Certain urges and inclinations, some relatively new, others long brewing, heaved beneath these surface vagaries of American society. An immediate reaction to the disillusionment of the hideous catastrophe of the Great War and the cynical self-seeking at Versailles was the rejection of traditional values, morals, and manners which, in a broad way, had formerly cemented the social order.

But it was not only the aftermath of war that created a climate in which accepted codes were challenged. Continued urbanization intensified the old rift between rural and urban America. City dwellers, especially the intellectuals and the sons of immigrants, felt that they had fewer ties with former values. Freudian psychology or, more correctly, its distortions, became the rage and encouraged people to cast off Victorian inhibitions and release their libidos. Life became faster paced, and the excitement generated by the war carried over. Experiencing a release from wartime pressures, people sought escape from serious problems. Surfeited by a diet of Wilsonian idealism and rhetoric, they welcomed the soothing homilies of Harding and the languid complacency of Coolidge. The press reflected the temper of the times. The tabloids and picture magazines were in the van, though not alone, in playing up crime, sex, and sports in preference to politics and foreign affairs.

Commercialized sports furnished a wide avenue for escape. They symbolized a return to "normalcy," to use Harding's barbarism, and provided an outlet especially for the growing urban masses who could indulge their appetite for exciting distraction as never before, thanks to prosperity and increased leisure. The press both mirrored and abetted the new emphasis on professional sports. Feature articles written in the purple prose of the gee-whiz style and the perfected arts of publicity created a remarkable array of heroes and a mania for breaking records. The unprecedented numbers of spectators moved social critics to warn of a new disease, "spectatoritis," and to write books on the "threat" and the "curse" of leisure. These books overlooked the fact that more people than ever before were also finding recreation in playing games themselves and in taking advantage of the national parks and open spaces which the automobile made accessible to them. In 1929 Americans spent an estimated four and a half billion dollars on all forms of recreation. As Harvey Wish has observed, sports and recreation were "too integral a part of the twenties to be considered incidental."

Baseball remained the supreme game for Americans, its emotional appeal possibly stronger than ever, fortified as it was by the magnetic spell of Babe Ruth and the new style of play that his prodigious batting feats compelled. But if this was a golden age for baseball, it also glittered for other sports, both amateur and commercialized. They came of age in the 'twenties and for the first time posed serious competition for the national game.

College football experienced phenomenal growth. The football tail wagged the campus dog more vigorously than ever as colleges and universities went all out for the professional entertainment business. They constructed costly stadiums, paid players with "scholarships" and fringe benefits, dressed up the product with bands and cheerleaders, and put on exciting spectacles for masses of people, most of whom had never seen a college, let alone attended one—the subway alumni, as they were called in New York City. These extravaganzas, to paraphrase Veblen, had about as much relevance to education as bullfighting to agriculture. But with the aid of high-powered publicity they became large-scale enterprises involving millions of dollars. Leading players, notably Notre Dame's celebrated backfield, the Four Horsemen, and Red Grange of Illinois, the Galloping Ghost, became national figures, as did such coaches as Notre Dame's Knute Rockne. Although in 1930 college football realized 21.5 millions of dollars in admissions, compared with professional baseball's 17 millions, baseball still maintained a wide margin over professional football as well as over other professional spectator sports such as hockey and racing.

Both golf and tennis emerged from their old leisure-class confines into the realm of popular sports. Public and private golf courses were built all over the country. In 1930 approximately two million golfers spent about twenty-nine million dollars to play, and golfing equipment accounted for more than a third of the value of all sporting goods manufactured. Owners were worried because many youngsters were swinging golf clubs instead of bats. Tennis also escaped from the classes to the masses, with more than 1,200,000 playing it annually on public courts alone.

Prize fighting led the way as far as big gates were concerned. Animated by the promotional talents of Tex Rickard, it enjoyed professional sport's first million-dollar gate in 1921, when Jack Dempsey defeated the Frenchman Georges Carpentier for the world's heavyweight championship. But the Dempsey-Gene Tunney bout in 1927 decisively shattered this mark by drawing $2,658,660 in gate receipts. Boxing's heavyweight title fights equalled or surpassed the World Series in public interest, and Dempsey, "the Manassa Mauler," was second to none in the galaxy of popular heroes.

Professional baseball's stiff competition from other commercialized

sports and from other forms of recreation was assuaged by its eventual victory in the fight to legalize Sunday ball. An increasingly secular, hedonistic society impatient of Puritan restraints put the churches
and old-line Sabbatarians on the defensive. Church members were
absenting themselves in growing numbers to play a round of golf or
take an automobile ride Sunday mornings. Many churches tried to
adjust to changing times by providing gymnasiums, game rooms, and
athletic fields, and by sponsoring baseball and basketball teams. A
contemporary study of twenty-seven Protestant churches in thirteen
cities revealed that twenty-four of them were sponsoring organized
teams. In the mid-'twenties I was able to persuade two other boys to
join me in attending a Sunday School in Flatbush, mainly because it
supplied complete baseball uniforms, the first we ever had, and an
opportunity to play on an organized baseball team Saturday afternoons and some evenings. Other members came out to watch, and we
received further recognition when the score was announced in Sunday School each week.

Although the issue of Sunday baseball came to a climax in the
'twenties, it was nearly as old as professional baseball,° and of course
Sunday blue-law legislation was much older still, dating from a Virginia statute of 1610. At the beginning of the twentieth century, only
the five major-league clubs operating in Chicago, St. Louis, and Cincinnati could legally play games on Sundays. Before the end of World
War One, three more—Detroit, Cleveland, and Washington—were
liberated, and thus half the major-league teams could play at home
on Sunday. Within fifteen years after World War One the major
leagues were completely victorious, the ban having been lifted in
their other four cities—New York, Boston, Philadelphia, and Pittsburgh. The relative speed with which the last resistance to Sunday
baseball disappeared was in itself a sign of the iconoclastic spirit of
the postwar era.

By the time Pennsylvania capitulated in November 1933, the country had come a long way in its attitude toward Sunday behavior. Not
so many years before, the well-to-do could go riding in the parks on
Sunday, but slum children could be arrested for playing ball there.
Three small boys were locked up in Boston in 1911 for playing ball,
and in 1913 four Brooklyn lads were arrested and made to stand for
twenty-four hours in a crowded jail cell for tossing a rubber ball
around in Prospect Park. *Sporting News* voiced indignation that a
certain New England preacher was not only free to drive his car on
Sundays but used it to check on whether ball playing was going on at
a local park, whereas working people's opportunity for Sunday

° See *Baseball: The Early Years, passim.*

amusement was practically nil because of blue laws. In 1912 another preacher summoned the local sheriff and tried to stop a Sunday game at New Britain, Connecticut. In the melee that followed, he was shoved down an embankment and his glasses were broken.

But more liberal voices were being heard, those of clergymen among them. In 1905 Bishop Hoban of Scranton's Catholic Diocese expressed the traditionally more lenient attitude of his Church regarding the Sabbath when he said that he favored letting men and boys play ball and engage in other harmless amusements on Sundays. Some years later it was reported that a small-town priest actually changed the hour of mass to accommodate parishioners who wanted to go to a game. In advocating Sunday ball in 1908, Rabbi Charles Fleischer of Boston pointed out that many had little to do and no place to go save the parks. "Let them have the open, let them enjoy the game of their hearts" was his message. The Reverend Mr. Paul Drake, pastor of President Taft's church at his summer residence in Beverly, Massachusetts, was quoted as saying in 1909:

> As for the minister, he does not need to play ball on Sunday; he has enough of it during the week if he chooses, but the laboring man has but Sunday to himself. As conditions are he does no wrong . . . to seek any legitimate mode of amusement and recreation on that day.

Two years later the Reverend Mr. Franklin Baker of the First Unitarian Church, Sacramento, California, recited "Casey at the Bat" and called the game "America's mental shower bath." Another who reflected the growing emphasis on the "social gospel" was a Long Island minister who actually organized a team to play on Sunday afternoons in 1919 but advised that he would probably preach a short sermon before the commencement of the game.

Sporting News and *Baseball Magazine* naturally were ardent for Sunday ball. After praising baseball's pure, elevated, and wholesome surroundings, *Sporting News* bit deep: Americans were not "slaves bound down by the narrow prejudices of a Puritanical psalm-singing minority but free people who work hard six days a week and have a right to spend . . . Sundays as [their] inclinations prompt." *Baseball Magazine* argued in 1911 that Sunday ball would spread the game in minor-league cities, increase its overall prosperity, and give the laboring class a chance to see games.

Some judges, mayors, and other public officials also began speaking out. William McAdoo, New York's police commissioner in 1904, saw no harm in Sunday games and said that people of the upstate rural areas had no right to deny the city boy the opportunity to get out of the tenement and enjoy the open air on Sundays. The well-known attorney George Wharton Pepper told in his autobiography of his fight for Sunday ball: "Everybody of the privileged class was enjoying golf or tennis or some other outdoor exercise on Sunday. It seemed to me a shame to deny similar opportunities to the underprivileged." To him, churches had no right to place legal restraints on the competition of other Sunday interests.

Such societies as the Sunshine League and the Personal Liberty League were formed to end blue laws and restore the Sabbath to the workers. In 1911, 25,000 Bostonians petitioned the governor to permit Sunday ball for the good of boys employed during the week—a sober reminder that many boys (about one out of every five between the ages of ten and fifteen) worked a six-day week in those days. Some women assented to Sunday ball as a counterattraction to more lurid enticements to their menfolk, such as dance halls and "vicious river excursions and degrading allurements" (leaving the nature of the latter to the imagination).

Opponents of Sunday ball defended their position doggedly. They denied that baseball offered relaxation, and as for getting fresh air, a good walk was better. They viewed the cursing and brawling that accompanied games as tending to lessen respect for the Sabbath. As one of them put it, a person "did not get a glimpse of God in a frenzied crowd." Sabbatarians also exerted constant pressure on officials to enforce laws against Sunday amusements. They tried to link baseball with the sale of liquor by claiming that Sunday games were mere feeders for saloons. The Ohio Anti-Saloon League's lobby, for instance, used the same argument. Others looked upon Sunday ball as a wedge for the opening of theaters, factories, and stores. Some even capitalized on the hysterical atmosphere of World War One. They charged that Sunday ball would lead to "the Germanization of the American Sunday," and after the defeat of the Kaiser's armies one opponent of Sunday ball saw the European Sabbath as the main cause of the demoralization of Germany! But there were two arguments put forward by the Sabbatarians that could not be gainsaid, namely, that Sunday ball offended many people and that it was against the law in many places.

Contrary to what one might expect, not every baseball man favored Sunday play, any more than every clergyman was against it. Barney Dreyfuss, for example, opposed it for fear of jeopardizing his weekday attendance and of alienating his regular clientele if he catered to a "cheaper element." A few players, like Branch Rickey, Christy Mathewson, and Frank Baker, objected to participating in Sunday games for personal reasons. Rickey was fired for refusing to play on Sundays, and Frank Baker was suspended in 1917 for the same reason. But as

Sporting News pointed out, they did not seem to object to having their salaries continued on Sundays, and some even went to the park to watch or to take tickets.

Meanwhile, the big-league clubs in those cities still under the ban were not idle. On the contrary, they employed a considerable variety of strategems in their effort to do business on the forbidden day. Since the law was sometimes interpreted as prohibiting merely the *business* of baseball on Sunday, to stay technically within the bounds the clubs allowed fans to enter free of charge, but once within the gates the customers had to buy scorecards at the regular admission price before they were seated. Another subterfuge was to give a "sacred concert," for which fans were ostensibly paying, and then play the ball game afterwards. Collection boxes were also distributed in lieu of selling tickets. In Brooklyn this dodge worked fairly well at first, and receipts were said to have totaled about the same, but Ebbets abandoned the idea when he began receiving too many buttons and other worthless items in the collection boxes. The Sunday-hungry clubs also tried playing games outside their city limits, either where baseball was legal or where the authorities were more lenient. Early in the century Detroit played its Sunday games in Burns Park, just beyond the city limits, where the enforcement officers were more benign.

The search for a Sunday sanctuary brought the New York Americans and the Brooklyn Nationals into conflict in 1904, at a time when the two major leagues were not on the friendliest terms anyhow. The Yankees wanted to transfer fourteen Sunday games to Ridgewood, Long Island, but Ebbets protested to the National Commission that his territorial rights were being violated. Ebbets reportedly had tried to secure the park for his own Sunday games but failed because he wanted too large a share of the gate receipts. The Commission ruled in favor of Brooklyn, but President Farrell's response was to openly defy the decision or skirt around it by assembling a squad from among his own regulars and some semi-pros, disguising it as the "All-Americans," and sending it to Ridgewood. He also vowed that if he could not play in Ridgewood on Sundays, he would prevent the Boston Nationals from using Weehawken, New Jersey, as a Sunday haven. A compromise was eventually reached when Ebbets agreed that the Yankees could play in Ridgewood when Brooklyn was on the road.

Major-league owners openly violated the Sunday laws or, perhaps more correctly, probed and tested them, since there was no clear-cut way of knowing how they were going to be interpreted at any given moment. For one thing, there was a hodge-podge of state and city laws, all with slightly different provisions. Take the year 1909, for example: New York City and Brooklyn banned Sunday ball, but the state law against it was not enforced in Albany, Troy, and Syracuse; it was allowed in Cincinnati and Toledo, but not in Cleveland; clubs in Wilkes-Barre and Scranton could play, but not those in Philadelphia and Pittsburgh. Yet in an industrial suburb of Pittsburgh, inhabited largely by immigrants who worked six days a week, Sunday games were played and were watched by thousands. Americans whose religion forbade such Sabbath activities protested in 1912 that these "aliens" should be taught "American ways." *Sporting News* responded vigorously that those "American ways" also included allowing little children to work six days a week in factories, and that the local Catholic prefect had no objection to the ball games since they took place after church was out.

There was also a wide variety of penalties for Sunday violation, some as severe as a $100 fine or six months in jail or both, some merely nominal. The conflicting rulings of judges, some of whom winked at the law, added to the confusion. For example, Judge Collins of the New York Court of Special Sessions discharged three men brought before him for throwing a ball on Sunday in 1914 with the following statement:

> To my mind Sunday ball playing is no crime, let the law be what it may. I would much rather have a son of mine go out and play ball on Sunday than go to a saloon. . . . While the police are bravely arresting boys for playing base ball they are not running quite as much risk as if they were tackling burglars or robbers.

On occasions when major-league clubs took their chances with the law the authorities usually limited themselves to the arrest of a few players and the imposition of token fines. During the war the Giants and the Reds played a Sunday game billed as a benefit for the 69th Regiment. The police, charging that it was a regularly scheduled game and a violation of the Sunday law, arrested McGraw and Mathewson, the two managers. However, Magistrate Francis X. McQuade, who later became part owner and treasurer of the Giants, discharged them with praise for contributing to a patriotic cause.

The ball clubs also lobbied and propagandized to further their cause. Ebbets and Ruppert wrote candidates for the state assembly in 1917 to ask their opinions on the question. Ebbets also sent a circular letter to all Brooklyn clergymen setting forth the point of view of the ball club. In Ohio four senators and eight representatives at the state capital requested season passes to the Cincinnati and Cleveland parks in exchange for their support in 1910. In 1911 the Ohio clubs' lobbyist had to promise state legislators twenty-five season passes. For one year total lobbying expenses in Ohio, probably shared by big-league teams as well as minor-league ones, came to $1500.

World War One and the weakening of traditional restraints that followed it hastened the transformation of Sunday into a more secularized day. Its religious character became increasingly watered down. The change was reflected in a statement in 1925 by Bishop William T. Manning, influential New York clergyman, in which he condoned golf and tennis on Sundays and asserted that "sports occupy just as important a place in our lives as prayers." However, he disapproved of commercialized athletics on that day. In 1927 an Episcopal clergyman in Boston endorsed Sunday ball with the remark, "I think Christ would be in favor of anything that would give the youth of the country honest recreation."

The last big push that was to bring Sunday ball to the major-league clubs still without it commenced in 1918. That year the need of war workers for Sunday amusement impelled the District of Columbia commissioners to legalize Sunday ball in Washington. New York's legislature climaxed the long struggle in that state by passing a local option law in 1919, sponsored by state Senator James J. Walker. The measure opened the way for the New York City Board of Aldermen to pass a Sunday ordinance permitting ball games after two o'clock in cases where admission was charged. Walker, who later became mayor of New York City, campaigned under the slogan "Walker Gave Us Sunday Baseball." A plaque inscribed "Friend and Fan, whose Sunday baseball law made it possible for millions of his fellow-citizens to enjoy the game" was installed in Walker's honor at the Polo Grounds. Minor-league cities in the state, like Syracuse, Rochester, and Buffalo, followed suit in approving Sunday ball, as did small towns like Warwick in upstate New York, which in 1922 after "the liveliest election held in the village in years" voted 533-345 in favor of legalizing baseball on Sundays.

In Brooklyn Ebbets pushed his fortune too far by scheduling his opening game on Easter Sunday in 1924, thus arousing a backlash among the local clergy, representatives of whom called on him to protest. Ebbets passed the buck to the league by saying it would have to approve cancellation of the game, but he promised not to play games on Easter in the future "if they can be avoided." "We are law-respecting and God-fearing people and won't do anything to offend the churches" (except play on Easter!).

Sunday ball was successful in Boston only after a protracted and acrimonious fight between officials of the Boston Braves and the city councilmen. In 1924 stories were circulated that members of the council had tried to extort $100,000 from Judge Emil Fuchs, president of the club, to pass a Sunday ordinance, and four years later Charles F. Adams, vice president of the club, openly charged that a councilman had asked the club for a bribe. Then at a public hearing before the Boston Finance Committee, Fuchs said he had been told by an intermediary that a member of the council had suggested a payment of $5000 to each of twelve councilmen in whose power it lay to block passage of the Sunday bill. Fuchs claimed he had dismissed the suggestion as "comical and ridiculous" and branded the group a "jitney chorus of Jesse James boys without horses."

The council hit back. In what the New York *Times* described as a "torrid" session, Fuchs was called a liar and Adams a narrow-minded hypocrite. They were vilified as "two financiers who have ruined both Boston baseball teams." If the council had not held up permission for the Braves to play on Sundays, said one councilman, Fuchs and Adams "would have a permit to rob the public by charging any price they desired." Fuchs was also questioned by the attorney general on the activities of the Outdoor Recreation League of Massachusetts, with which he was connected. The council then expressed willingness to release the Sunday ball ordinance, which it had tabled, to the mayor for signature, provided the club in its application for a permit to play agreed not to increase admission prices on Sundays. In addition, the two Boston clubs had to pay a license fee based on seating capacity, $2500 for the Braves and $1000 for the Red Sox. The mayor then finally signed the ordinance in January of 1929.

But the matter did not end there. The Braves were charged with violation of the Corrupt Practices Act, and checks amounting to $30,000, presumably used in connection with a campaign for Sunday sports, were produced as evidence. As a result, the club was fined $1000 for violation of the act, and Orrin Brusse, secretary-treasurer of the Outdoor Recreation League, was penalized $200 for filing false statements.

The last stronghold of Sunday laws that affected the major leagues was Pennsylvania, where as late as 1927 the state Supreme Court voted against Sunday ball 7-2, stating that "no one . . . would contend that professional baseball partakes in any way of the nature of holiness" and "We can not imagine . . . anything more worldly or unreligious in the way of employment than the playing of professional baseball as it is played today."

Connie Mack and the Shibes, stymied after repeated efforts to play on Sundays, turned in desperation to Camden, New Jersey, where they considered building a park and playing their Sunday games. But after the Athletics played a test game there one Sunday in 1926, the local court declared Sunday ball to be "worldly employment" in violation of the Sunday law. The club did not give up. The next year Shibe received assurances from "liberal leaders across the river" that they would arrange permission for the club to play in Camden permanently, including Sundays. On the strength of these promises, Shibe, in a plan that foreshadowed events of the 1950's, formed a syndicate with a view toward purchasing land, building a million-dollar park, and shifting the franchise to Camden. One month later, the Pennsylvania House of Representatives, faced with the possibility of losing the Athletics, passed an amendment to the blue law that would allow local option, but the matter languished for several more years, and it was not until 1934 that the two Philadelphia clubs and the Pittsburgh Pirates could play Sunday ball.

This series of victories, which at long last brought Sunday ball to all major-league cities and many minor-league ones, was an obvious factor in stimulating attendance and contributing to Organized Baseball's overall prosperity in the era marked by the administration of Judge Landis as the so-called czar of baseball, the development of the farm system under the astute hand of Branch Rickey, and the dramatics on the playing field generated by the home-run hitting of Babe Ruth.

19

RESIDUE OF SCANDAL

ORGANIZED BASEBALL entered upon the postwar era with a new form of government presided over by Judge Kenesaw Mountain Landis. Few baseball men have been accorded higher place in the industry's pantheon than that scowling, white-haired, hawk-visaged curmudgeon who affected battered hats, used salty language, chewed tobacco, and poked listeners in the ribs with a stiff right index finger. His quarter of a century as Commissioner has been transformed by baseball journalists and "historians" into a legend that still cloaks him. He and Babe Ruth are credited with rescuing professional baseball and restoring it to good repute after the Black Sox scandal: Ruth by extraordinary home-run hitting, Landis by fearless extirpation of wrongdoing. In speaking of his "dedication to justice," one writer said, "He was completely uncompromising in applying the letter of the law to wealthy club owners and second-string players alike." The legends about men live after them; their shortcomings are oft interred with their bones. The legend that covers Landis has proved lasting enough to serve as a gauge against which each of his successors has been measured. It also conceals much of Landis himself.

Landis was thirty-eight years old when President Theodore Roosevelt appointed him judge in the United States District Court for the Northern District of Illinois in 1905. His education and legal training for such a position were skimpy. After dropping out of high school at Logansport, Indiana, where he was reared, he taught himself shorthand and secured a job as a court reporter. He finished high school at night and enrolled in a YMCA law school at Cincinnati and then in the Union Law School of Chicago, where he received a law degree and admission to the bar in 1891. He never went to college. Two years later Judge Walter Q. Gresham, his father's commanding officer in the Civil War, went to Washington as Secretary of State under

Grover Cleveland and took Landis with him as his secretary. (Landis was named after Kennesaw Mountain—minus an *n*—where his father had been wounded while serving as a physician.) After Gresham's death two years later, Landis returned to Chicago to practice law and enter Republican politics. Frank Lowden, who was running for governor, put him in charge of his 1904 campaign. After Lowden lost the election he was offered a federal judgeship but declined it and recommended Landis for the post. Roosevelt appointed him.

Landis's meager scholastic background and limited legal training were nothing unusual in a day when academic requirements for the professions were much less stringent. But the combination of this lack and his authoritarian personality restricted his outlook and colored his decisions. Honest and fearless though he was, his spare frame housed a narrow, arbitrary, and vindictive nature. No lacklustre jurist was he. His consummate egotism and flare for showmanship caused a scholar to dub him "the grandstand judge" and Heywood Broun to remark, "His career typifies the heights to which dramatic talent may carry a man in America if only he has the foresight not to go on the stage."

Landis had a deep affection for baseball and looked upon the players more as heroes than as employees. He had a keen aversion to organized labor, liquor, and the New Deal. The rub was that he permitted his personal dislikes to warp his judicial objectivity. Visceral response and caprice often swayed his decisions. Even when lenient he was partial. He made what was probably his most important baseball decision before he became Commissioner, when he put off a verdict on the Federal League's suit. Afterwards he justified his action on other than legal grounds: "The court's expert knowledge of baseball obtained by more than 30 years of observation of the game as a spectator convinced me that if an order had been entered it would have been, if not destructive, at least vitally injurious to the game of baseball." Landis's career refutes the cliché that in America laws, not men, govern the land.

Rarely was Landis's courtroom dull. His procedure, said the New York *Times* in an understatement, was "unorthodox and shocking to sticklers for legal form." For one thing, Landis ordered people brought before him without subpoenas and held others without warrants. Henry F. Pringle stated that because Landis was a prohibitionist, he gave maximum terms to bootleggers, and in some cases he "blandly ignored the law in the interests of what he conceived to be justice." He indulged in prejudicial outbursts and harangues from the bench and later directed that they be stricken from the record; if an attorney objected, he would be threatened with contempt. Reporters, too, came under the judge's displeasure. Once he referred to the staff of *Sporting News* as "swine"; another time he subjected F. C. Lane of *Baseball Magazine* to such personal abuse in the presence of others that Lane wrote him an open letter protesting his treatment. A New York *Daily Mirror* reporter, Jack Lait, said, "His manner of handling witnesses, lawyers—and reporters—was more arbitrary than the behavior of any jurist I have ever seen."

Landis first achieved national prominence in 1907, two years after Roosevelt appointed him. It was the period of Roosevelt's trust-busting pyrotechnics and the Standard Oil Company's nadir of popularity. Landis, never one to miss a trend, imposed his famous $29,400,000 fine on Standard. The decision was overturned on appeal and the fine was never paid, but Landis won popular acclaim and a place on the front pages for days.

After his setback in the Standard Oil case, higher authority continued to overrule Landis with "startling frequency," notably in cases he adjudicated during and after World War One. When the United States entered the war, Landis not only jumped on the patriotic bandwagon, he helped to drive it along its jingoistic route. An illustration of the hysteria of the times was the declaration made by Elihu Root, Secretary of War under Taft and Roosevelt, at a Union League Club meeting in April 1917: "There are men walking about the streets of this city tonight who ought to be taken out at sunrise tomorrow and shot for treason." As this mood spread, the war to make the world safe for democracy nearly quenched freedom at home. Landis abetted the process. "Few men," wrote Pringle, "have been as zealous in the suppression of minorities, and his charges to juries were dangerously similar to patriotic addresses."

In 1918 more than a hundred members of the radical Industrial Workers of the World, including their leader Big Bill Haywood, were rounded up by agents of Attorney General A. Mitchell Palmer and tried en masse in Landis's court, some of them manacled and all watched over by a hundred guards. The air in the courtroom was reportedly "vibrant with the age-old struggle of the classes." The trial was characterized by H. C. Peterson, an authority on treatment of opponents of the war, as "a weird combination of justice and injustice." The defendants had already been tried in the press as "the Bolsheviki of America"; they were now arraigned on vaguely drawn charges of conspiracy to obstruct the war effort. Old I.W.W. literature, illegally seized, was placed in evidence, but little specific proof of individual unlawful acts was produced. It was soon apparent that what was really on trial was the I.W.W. as an organization.

On the whole, Landis conducted the trial with restraint, despite his

reputation as a foe of all radical groups. He also took a personal interest in the prisoners' comfort, even to the extent of ordering sixty
"metallic cuspidors" for their quarters. In his charge to the jury he
likewise appeared to be unbiased. But when, after an hour's delibera-
tion, the jury rendered a verdict of guilty, Landis reverted to form.
He imposed fines totaling $2,300,000 and maximum sentences varying
from one to twenty years in Chicago's Bridewell, where, he said, "the
work is much harder than in the Federal Prison." He also delivered a
tirade from the bench in which he took the view that the Bill of
Rights was a luxury that gave only fair-weather protection: "When
the country is at peace it is a legal right of free speech to oppose
going to war . . . but when once war is declared this right ceases."
Big Bill Haywood in his autobiography bitterly commented, "Pontius
Pilate or Bloody Jeffreys never enjoyed themselves better than did
Judge Landis when he was imposing these terrible sentences upon a
group of working men for whom he had no feeling of humanity, no
sense of justice." After the war other countries released political prisoners, but in America it was five years before President Coolidge
commuted the terms of the convicted I.W.W. members. When he did,
in 1923, Landis denounced him.

Landis, like Woodrow Wilson and Theodore Roosevelt, believed
that opponents of the war should pay the penalty even after the war
was over. The Reverend Mr. David Gerdes, a pacifist, came before
Landis after the war accused of having advised against buying Liberty Bonds because to do so was to kill Germans by proxy. "What
would you do if a Hun were to attack the honor of your daughter?"
Landis asked him and his brother, a member of the congregation.
When they answered that they would plead for her in the name of
God but would not endanger their souls by killing, Landis shouted,
"These men hold their measly little shriveled souls of more importance than the honor of their mother, wife, or daughter," and sen-
tenced Gerdes to ten years in Leavenworth, a sentence later commuted to a year and a day.

The famous postwar trial of Victor Berger and five other socialists
surfaced some of Landis's deepest antipathies. Not only were the accused members of a radical party, they were also anti-war, and in addition Berger was a German-Austrian emigré. Berger's attorney requested a change of venue and cited utterances by Landis to show
that the judge hated Germans and German-Americans and was personally biased against Berger and the others. For instance, Landis allegedly had said, "One must have a very judicial mind, indeed, not to
be prejudiced against the German-Americans in this country. Their
hearts are reeking with disloyalty."

Landis denied that he was unqualified and set aside the motion to assign another judge. Berger and the others were given twenty-year sentences for conspiracy. The United States Supreme Court reversed the decision, however, and disqualified Landis on account of his "prejudicial conduct before the trial." The government then abandoned further action. Later Landis himself showed that the Supreme Court was right. In a speech before the American Legion he said, "It was my great disappointment to give Berger only twenty years. . . . I believe the law should have enabled me to have had Berger lined up against a wall and shot." And a month before becoming baseball Commissioner he told a convention of schoolteachers that the opposition of the Socialist Party to the government during the war was "responsible for the fact that the bodies of thousands of American soldiers are now in France."

Landis's decision to retain his judgeship after becoming baseball Commissioner provoked heavy criticism from Congress, the American Bar Association, and the press. If Landis really despised money, as he pretended to do, wrote one critic, he would have turned down the "private sideline," or if his sole desire was to reinstate Organized Baseball to public favor, he could have done the job for nothing. In January 1921 T.J. Sutherland, a Chicago attorney, sent a petition to Congress and a letter to Chicago newspapers protesting Landis's "attempt to mulct the government" and his "example of vicious infidelity to public service." A month later Congressman B.F. Welty of Ohio introduced a resolution asking for an investigation of the legality of Landis's holding two offices. At the hearing that followed, Welty, calling for Landis's impeachment for "high crimes and misdemeanors," based his demand on five charges.

The most telling charge dealt with conflict of interest. Landis had contracted with Organized Baseball, Welty pointed out, at the very time litigation pertaining to the Black Sox and the Baltimore Federal League club was still pending, and when the latter case was at the stage in which Organized Baseball stood under a $240,000 fine for violation of the anti-trust laws. Welty submitted a letter from an owner, whose name he would not disclose, stating that "K.M. Landis, lawyer, means nothing to organized baseball, but K.M. Landis, judge of the Federal Court of the United States, was worth any price he might wish to ask." Welty considered this letter as evidence that the baseball magnates had in effect bribed Landis to become Commissioner. Welty also brought up the Federal League suit of 1915, which, he said, would have gone through the courts had not Landis arbitrated it. If Landis wished to maintain respect as a judge, declared Welty, he must "divorce himself from the fleshpots of illegal combinations."

The congressman further charged Landis with neglect of duty and cited a huge backlog of cases on his docket.

Nothing came of Welty's effort, however. The consensus in the House was that, while Landis had lowered the standards of the bench and of legal ethics, impeachment proceedings would not go far because no law was violated. This prediction proved correct, and the Judiciary Committee buried the matter. Landis himself professed to see nothing unethical in his dual employment. In an address before the Missouri Bar Association he said, "If there's an impropriety here I haven't seen it."

In the fall of 1921, the American Bar Association renewed the attack in a resolution expressing "unqualified condemnation" of Landis and describing his action as "derogatory to the dignity of the bench." Hampton L. Carson, former attorney general of Pennsylvania, who presented the resolution, stated that Landis was "soiling the ermine by yielding to the temptation of avarice and private gain." Senator N.B. Dial of South Carolina submitted the resolution to the Senate whence, after a hot debate, it was passed on to the Judiciary Committee, but again nothing was done.

Landis finally sent his resignation to President Harding in February 1922, to become effective March 1, after he had held the double job for more than fifteen months. Leslie O'Connor, the able young lawyer whom Landis appointed as his secretary, said much later that Landis would have resigned sooner but delayed until "one of those Washington storms blew over" so it would not appear that he had quit under fire.

As was to be expected in view of Landis's personality and background, he quickly made himself felt as Commissioner of Organized Baseball by proscribing the Black Sox players before their trial and reaffirming his decision after a court of law had acquitted them. But he soon found that the slate of scandal and gambling did not wipe clean so easily. Smudge marks from the past reappeared, and fresh ones were made during the first six years of his administration. Since these form a kind of epilogue to the Black Sox affair, it is convenient to discuss them separately from other aspects of his administration in the 1920's.

In March of 1921, less than two weeks after he banned the Black Sox, Landis added Eugene Paulette to his blacklist. While Paulette was playing for the St. Louis Cardinals in 1919, he had caused "gossip" on account of his association with St. Louis gamblers Carl Zork, soon to be a figure in the Black Sox scandal, and Elmer Farrar. The gamblers were said to have urged Paulette to cooperate with them by throwing games, and Paulette had received money from Farrar as a "loan," which he had not repaid. The player had also written Farrar to ask for more money, which he did not obtain, and allegedly offered to throw games. Paulette was traded to the Philadelphia Nationals during 1919. The club owners concerned knew about his associations but accepted his affidavit that he had done nothing crooked and let the matter go at that.

When Landis took office, however, President Baker of the Phillies decided to turn Paulette's incriminating letter over to him. Called before Landis, the player denied having thrown any games and insisted that during the 1920 season he had kept aloof from any "corrupting influences." The Commissioner ordered him to report again at a later date for further questioning, and when he failed to do so, Landis blacklisted him permanently. He asserted that Paulette had "offered to betray his team and that he put himself in the vicious power of Farrar and Zork." Landis was obviously trying to discourage associations between players and gamblers. In doing so, he banned Paulette for life not for throwing games but for allegedly offering to do so and for having, like many players and owners, hobnobbed with gamblers.

In June 1921 Landis banned pitcher Ray Fisher for life. Fisher had nothing to do with crookedness, gambling, or association with gamblers. He merely exercised his right to bargain with others outside Organized Baseball. Fisher had taken a cut of $1000 on his 1920 Cincinnati salary of $5500. Consequently, when he learned just before the season started that a coaching position was open at the University of Michigan, he obtained permission from manager Pat Moran to go to Ann Arbor for an interview. Having been offered the job, he returned to Cincinnati, met with Moran, Garry Herrmann, and other club officials, and asked to be released from his contract. The club now decided it needed Fisher and offered him a raise to stay. Fisher agreed to do so but, in view of his age (thirty-two), asked for the security of a two-year contract. When this was refused, he decided to accept the Michigan job. Garry Herrmann promised to put him on the voluntarily retired list, and the press so reported. But before long Fisher heard that he was to be placed on the blacklist, and when he chanced upon Landis in a Chicago hotel lobby he introduced himself and explained that he had received permission to go to Michigan. Landis was cordial but noncommittal.

Toward the close of the college season the "outlaw" Franklin club of Pennsylvania, believing Fisher would be blacklisted, began dickering with him. After the college season ended, Fisher wired Landis for a decision on his status. Landis put him off and added that he understood Fisher had agreed to sign with the Franklin club. Fisher told him he had not. Nevertheless he soon received a telegram from Landis saying that he was blacklisted. No explanation was given, no charges were made, no hearing was offered; nor did Fisher ever hear from the Cincinnati club or ask for a hearing or apply for reinstatement. He just signed with Franklin.

Thirty years later a document entitled "In Re Reinstatement Application of Player Ray L. Fisher" was found in Landis's files. In it Moran was quoted as saying he "positively refused to grant" Fisher permission to go to Michigan; that the Cincinnati club had offered a "large increase" in salary, but Fisher refused to carry out his contract; that Fisher applied for reinstatement after the college season and, pending consideration thereof, carried on negotiations with the Franklin team, which was composed largely of "contract violators," and had agreed to terms with them in case he was not reinstated. It concluded that "obviously" his application must be denied. Apparently Fisher's crime was his independent attitude in exercising a choice of employment outside Organized Baseball. Whatever the reason, Landis's permanent ban is incomprehensible.

Benny Kauff, outfielder for the New York Giants, was another player who came under the Landis frown of power in 1921. Unlike Paulette, whose alleged transgression at least pertained to baseball, Kauff was put on the "permanently ineligible" list because of an incident that had nothing to do with Organized Baseball.

The Giants had acquired Kauff for a reported $30,000 after the Federal League war, when players were auctioned off. After serving in the military, Kauff returned to the Giants and opened an automobile sales business on the side in partnership with his half brother. In February 1920 he was arrested and indicted for stealing a car and for receiving stolen cars. Released on bail, he played through the 1920 season, but it was his last. With the case still pending, Landis, declaring that Kauff's indictment showed he was probably guilty, ruled him ineligible just before the start of the 1921 season.

In May Kauff was acquitted in court and applied to the Commissioner for reinstatement, but Landis refused it. In September the player secured a temporary injunction directing the baseball authorities to show cause why they should not be restrained from interfering with Kauff's fulfillment of his contract with the Giants, pending the outcome of his suit for a permanent injunction. Judge Edward O. Whitaker of the New York Supreme Court said he was powerless to grant the injunction because Kauff's contract had expired. In reality, of course, the Giants were ready and willing to use Kauff; however, no New York club official would admit as much in the face of Landis's suspension of the player. Kauff appealed, but his case was dropped when his attorney Emil Fuchs (also attorney for Rothstein and later to become president of the Boston National League club) reached an agreement with Organized Baseball's attorneys John Conway Toole and George Wharton. Pepper.

Why was Kauff deprived of his livelihood and the New York club of his services, even though the court had acquitted him? Evidently because the outcome of his trial did not suit Landis. The Commissioner read the trial papers and wrote Kauff that the evidence they disclosed compromised his character and reputation so seriously that his presence in the New York lineup would "burden patrons of the game with grave apprehension as to its integrity." Later Landis took occasion to call Kauff's acquittal "one of the worst miscarriages of justice that ever came under my observation." Judge Whitaker, on the other hand, saw nothing wrong with Kauff's acquittal. On the contrary, even while denying Kauff a permanent injunction, he stated that "an apparent injustice has been done the plaintiff." Apart from the merits of Kauff's acquittal, the fact is that like the Black Sox he was put in double jeopardy. Exonerated under the law of the land, Kauff was still subject to the "law" of that government within a government which is Organized Baseball. Its "law" vested dictatorial power in the Commissioner, making him both judge and jury, and he chose to use that power against Kauff.

In 1922 Landis banished another Giant player, pitcher Phil Douglas, for "treachery." Douglas was a drunkard given to "the disappearing act" and to frequenting "resorts"; he was more a subject for pity than for punishment.° He had already knocked about with four major-league clubs before coming to the Giants in a 1919 trade. Manager McGraw, knowing Douglas's frailties, assigned a man to watch him.

Late in August Douglas eluded his latest "keeper," coach Jesse Burkett, an old-time star, and disappeared for several days. Burkett and some detectives finally found him in his room and took him to a sanatarium where he was kept incommunicado for five days while he dried out. After getting out, he was fined $100, suspended five days without pay, and charged with $224.30 for the sanatarium and for taxi fares. He also received one of McGraw's characteristic tongue-lashings.

At this time his club was virtually tied for first place with the St. Louis Cardinals. In a fit of pique Douglas wrote their outfielder, Leslie Mann:

> I want to leave here. I don't want to see this guy [McGraw] win the pennant. You know I can pitch, and I am afraid if I stay I will win the pennant for him.
>
> Talk this over with the boys,' and if it is all right send the goods to

° See above, chapter 6.

my house at night and I will go to fishing camp. Let me know if you
all will do this, and I will go home on the next train.

Whether Douglas was still suffering from the aftereffects of liquor or
drugs or was drunk again, he certainly was in a muddled frame of
mind. The last person to whom he should have sent such a message
was Leslie Mann, a tee-totaling YMCA enthusiast. Mann turned the
letter over to Branch Rickey, who forwarded it to the Commissioner.
When Douglas admitted writing it, Landis exiled him from Organized Baseball. It was "tragic and deplorable," Landis was quoted as
saying, "[but] there is no excuse to be offered for Douglas. He is the
victim of his own folly." McGraw denounced Douglas publicly as "the
dirtiest ball player I have ever seen." This was quite a superlative, in
view of his experience with men like Chase.

After his ouster Douglas engaged an attorney who wrote Landis to
ask for a hearing. Landis agreed to give one if the attorney had any
new evidence. But shortly Douglas was reported as having "another
breakdown," and there was no further mention of a lawsuit. About
ten years afterwards a sportswriter led an attempt to get him reinstated, but Landis was adamant, although he did send a check to the
player, who was badly off. When Douglas died in 1952 there was a
mortgage on his hillside cabin in Tennessee.

Douglas was not a dishonest player; he was an immature and sick
man. He threw no games, nor did he offer to throw any, and there is
no evidence of any collusion with gamblers. But in a distraught, be-
fuddled, and angry moment he wrote a foolish letter that brought him
a harsh punishment.

Landis made a complete turnabout in 1923 by ruling in favor of
none other than versatile Rube Benton, whose activities combined
pitching, boozing, wenching, and gambling, and who was accused of
perjury and possession of "guilty knowledge" of the 1919 World Series
plot. Although Benton had admitted knowing of the Black Sox fix beforehand, he had continued to play with the Giants until they
shipped him to the minor-league St. Paul team in the middle of 1921.
He was more or less persona non grata in the National League, and
in the American Ban Johnson made it clear that he was a "tainted"
player.

Benton did well with St. Paul, however, so Garry Herrmann decided to bring him back to Cincinnati, where he had begun his big-
league career. Heydler opposed the deal and in a guarded public
statement said he was confident Cincinnati would not go through
with it if the majority of National League clubs did not want Benton
back in the league; it was for them to decide, he said. Herrmann's ar-

gument was that if Benton was an "undesirable player" for the National League, he should have been equally unfit for the minors. At their February meeting a majority of National League owners backed Heydler—but they also voted to let Landis make the final decision.

Heydler had every reason to believe that the Commissioner would make short work of Benton. But to Heydler's amazement Landis ruled in favor of Benton and excoriated those who wanted to keep him out. Landis's decision was scrupulously fair to the player. The question, he said, was whether Benton was eligible to play anywhere: if he was ineligible to play with Cincinnati, then he was ineligible to play with St. Paul. He pointed out that it had never been contended that Benton was a dishonest player, and the National League had never taken disciplinary action against him. To the contrary, Landis noted—in a pointed thrust at the National League's concealment policy—Benton's "alleged irregularities" had been kept quiet and he was allowed to play with both New York and St. Paul. Certainly the time to bring accusations that could permanently deprive a man of his chief means of livelihood was at the time the alleged irregularities became known, "not at the objectors' discretion upwards of two years later." Landis concluded, "Player Benton is declared eligible."

At this unexpected decision, Heydler at first seemed ready to defy Landis: "It is our judgement that Benton is not the type of character of player we want and therefore I will not sanction his return to our organization." But after conferring privately with Landis, Heydler announced that Benton could play and that the matter was closed.

Landis's complaint against Heydler for waiting two years before trying to ban Benton from baseball might easily have been turned back upon him. As a *Sporting News* editorial pointed out, Landis, "knowing through the records or having read the public prints of the charges made against Rube Benton, himself is to some degree responsible for Benton being permitted to play ball in the seasons of 1921 and 1922, two full years." The editor could have added that Landis also was not bothered by any hobgoblin of consistency. He had banned Buck Weaver and Joe Gedeon for "guilty knowledge" but had kept Benton. He had also banned Paulette on *ex post facto* charges but objected to penalizing Benton for past transgressions. And if Benny Kauff was unfit to be associated with baseball because of his character, Benton was even less so. Landis's decision on Benton, wrote Francis C. Richter, ex-editor of the defunct *Sporting Life,* "did more to affect his dignity and prestige, and to undermine the magnates' faith in his judgment and his fitness for absolute power" than anything since the Black Sox.

These cases involving individual ball players were overshadowed by the O'Connell-Dolan affair, which erupted in 1924. This new scandal, coming as it did while memories of the Black Sox were still fresh, reawakened doubts about the integrity of Organized Baseball and raised questions about what really occurred that have been left unanswered to this day. It also centered upon the New York Giants in a way that curiously paralleled the 1908 episode involving them, the one that resulted in the never fully explained banishment of their team physician, Doc Creamer.

It was near the end of the season, and the Giants held a secure game-and-a-half lead over second-place Brooklyn. They had three games left to play, all with seventh-place Philadelphia, and Brooklyn had only two, with last-place Boston. Two New York victories would clinch the pennant regardless of what Brooklyn did. But, as J.G. Taylor Spink wrote later, there were "persons" who wanted to make the outcome of the pennant race a sure thing.

Before the first game Jimmy O'Connell, a young Giant outfielder, approached the Philadelphia shortstop Heinie Sand and offered him $500 if he would take it easy in the game. The Giants won the game and the pennant too, since Brooklyn lost that day; but meanwhile Sand had reported O'Connell's proposition to his manager, Art Fletcher, who informed John Heydler. Heydler relayed the information to Landis, who came to New York at once. After questioning Sand, Landis called in Charles Stoneham, the Giants' owner, and manager McGraw. McGraw expressed resentment that Heydler had not told him about it before calling Landis.

When Landis summoned O'Connell, the player readily admitted his guilt and said he had followed instructions from Cozy Dolan, a Giant coach variously called McGraw's "Man Friday," "body guard," "gumshoe," and "tale bearer." O'Connell also implicated three Giant stars, Frank Frisch, Ross Youngs, and George Kelly, who he said had inquired afterwards about Sand's response to his proposition. O'Connell gave the impression that others in the Giants' organization knew what was going on too. He later said, "I was working for the Giants and I thought the management wanted me to do it."

Landis next questioned Cozy Dolan, who exasperated him by persistently answering that he did not remember, and also Frisch, Youngs, and Kelly. He then announced that O'Connell and Dolan were permanently blacklisted, Dolan because his "testimony on his own behalf was of such a character as to be unacceptable." The Commissioner completely exonerated the other three players, whose testimony he characterized as "a clear refutation" of O'Connell's charges.

Why had Landis believed O'Connell's accusations against Dolan and not those against Frisch, Youngs, and Kelly? The reason, said a

Sporting News correspondent, was that Dolan's replies were "evasive" while those of the players were "straight-forward." Within a few months the public discovered just how straightforward the players' replies were. In January 1925 Landis issued the stenographic report of his hearings in order to allay the intimations of sportswriters that he was hiding something. According to the record, part of Youngs's statement was:

> I have heard talking around and such things mentioning it, but I don't remember who by. You hear fellows talking around that boys that are offering money and something like that. I never heard anything like this, offering money here. This is the first I heard of it.

Similarly, Frisch stated: "On a pennant contender, you always hear a lot of stuff like that, a lot of kidding and some other things. That is all I ever hear."

News that Landis had expelled O'Connell and Dolan broke just three days before the World Series. The Commissioner seemed to assume that his action ended the matter, and Heydler declared outright that the case was closed. But many were convinced there was more to it than met the eye. Ban Johnson and Barney Dreyfuss wanted Landis to call off the World Series, but he refused. Johnson, who still nursed his hatred of McGraw and his resentment of Landis, called for a federal investigation. This was tantamount to saying that Landis was unable or unwilling to get to the bottom of the affair. To the further vexation of the Commissioner, Congressman Sol Bloom of New York supported Johnson and called for a federal statute to regulate Organized Baseball as an interstate enterprise.

Johnson then underscored his displeasure with the handling of the case by peevishly absenting himself from the World Series. He also chose this moment, when the information would cause the most embarrassment to McGraw, to produce a hitherto secret affidavit given him in 1923 by Lou Criger, the old-time catcher of the Boston Red Sox, which disclosed an attempted fix of the 1903 World Series. According to Criger's sworn statement, one Anderson, a gambler, approached him at the Monongahela Hotel in Pittsburgh just before the Series and offered him $12,000 to see to it that Pittsburgh won. Criger had spurned the bribe and confided the incident only to his battery mate Cy Young. The story had been kept quiet for twenty years. In revealing the incident, Johnson took pains to point out that the affidavit stated that when Criger was first introduced to the gambler both Wilbert Robinson and John McGraw had been present.

Dreyfuss, whose Pittsburgh Pirates had finished a close third behind New York and Brooklyn, called for a thorough probe. Putting his finger on the crux, he declared it was insulting to the intelligence "to ask people to believe that two rather obscure members [of the Giants] would go and offer to pay somebody $500, solely of their own money, to have something crooked done that would benefit many other persons besides themselves." In addition, Dreyfuss made the cryptic remark: "The New York players change, but the manager remains the same." Dreyfuss followed up by going to Washington, where the Series was about to open, to seek out Landis and give him additional evidence. The Commissioner refused to talk to him and rudely left him and his manager standing in the hotel lobby.

There were reporters, too, who felt the same as Dreyfuss did. *Sporting News* editorialized:

> Who is behind this assault and other assaults on the integrity of the sport? . . . Surely no ball player of his own volition will do these things. When is the cleaning out, the general cleaning out, going to begin? That's what the fans want to know. Who inspired Dolan?

Reporter W.O. Phelan was caustic. All those who believed, he wrote, that "a green kid" and "a worn-out coach" devised the plot "without full directions from some crooked brain who neatly used them as a catspaw" should mobilize in the nearest telephone booth, where they would not be crowded. An unidentified New York writer was quoted as saying, "There have been a number of things happen in New York which deserved investigation, but everyone seems to be afraid of McGraw." A story in *Sporting News* claimed that even Landis recognized that the bribe money could not have come from O'Connell personally and therefore must have been contributed by the team or its management. Frank Richter criticized Landis severely and declared he "exhibited . . . an astonishing incapacity or unwillingness to probe the case to the bottom."

Some new developments helped to keep the murky episode before the public in the months after the World Series. One of them was Cozy Dolan's decision to sue Landis for defamation of character. His attorney was none other than William J. Fallon, counsel for Charles Stoneham and Arnold Rothstein. It was soon learned that McGraw was the one who had sent Dolan to see Fallon and the one who was paying him. Angered by this development, Landis conveyed his sentiments to the New York club's management in pungent language. Abruptly, before Fallon even filed papers, Dolan dropped the suit and left for his home in Oshkosh, Wisconsin.

Another bit of spice went into the stew the following January when it was discovered that George Kelly, one of the three named by O'Connell, and Sammy Bohne, a Cincinnati infielder, had become teammates of O'Connell's on a California basketball team. Heydler, expressing shock and disbelief, warned that Bohne and especially Kelly were jeopardizing their baseball standing, the inference being that association with an outcast contaminates. Garry Herrmann, while not agreeing with Heydler, took no chances on having Bohne blacklisted and ordered him not to play. In a little while, however, the basketball team saved Kelly and Bohne by the simple expedient of firing O'Connell.

Finally, New York District Attorney Joab H. Banton started an investigation and promised to prosecute if he found any violations of the criminal code. Landis sent him what evidence he had but admitted that he had no corroborating evidence against O'Connell. He did not even have O'Connell's original confession because at the time he questioned the player the stenographer was late in arriving, and when he did get there O'Connell was not asked to repeat what he had already told Landis—an oversight that was "puzzling to say the least," said *Sporting News*. After supplying the evidence he had, Landis left for Cuba. The assistant district attorney suggested dryly that the Commissioner might better have devoted less attention to golfing in the tropics and more to the baseball scandal in New York.

The investigation failed to uncover anything. Some ball players testified but not O'Connell, who refused to come east unless given immunity, which the district attorney was unwilling to grant. Neither were officials of the Giants called, nor Dreyfuss, Johnson, or Heydler. In his final report Banton stated that O'Connell "may" have been guilty and that Dolan, in his replies to Landis, "brought suspicion upon himself which has not been removed by my examination of Dolan." The district attorney found no legal evidence against Frisch, Youngs, and Kelly and declared that their "excellent reputations and manner of answering questions . . . points strongly to their innocence." Public opinion became sympathetic toward O'Connell as the unwitting "goat" of the piece, whereas fans booed Sand all over the National League circuit—in keeping with the American habit of venting displeasure more on those who expose wrongdoing than on the wrongdoers themselves.

Time has failed to remove the mystery veiling the O'Connell-Dolan scandal. The stock "explanations" boil down to three: gamblers who could not be reached were behind it; O'Connell, young, naive, or just plain stupid, allowed himself to become the "dupe" of unnamed others; a practical joke perpetrated by teammates hazing O'Connell ended in tragedy for him. But an editorial in *Sporting News* in January 1925 termed the Landis investigation "a screaming farce." And many years later that paper's editor, Taylor Spink, printed the intriguing statement: "Had 'Cozy Dolan,' backed by the Giants, gone through with it [the lawsuit], I believe the Commissioner would have ripped the game wide open."

Landis enjoyed a respite from scandals in 1925, and he almost got through 1926 without any—but not quite. Early in November came the stunning news that Detroit had granted Ty Cobb his unconditional release both as manager and player. Before fans recovered from that jolt they received a second one. A month later they learned that Tris Speaker was resigning as player-manager at Cleveland to enter private business. That these two pillars of the American League should just drop out of baseball was incredible. Although Cobb's managerial ability was debatable, he was still a valuable asset as a player. Speaker's departure was even more inexplicable. He had led the Indians to second place, only three games behind New York, and the club had made money accordingly. Yet all of a sudden, within the space of a month, the two renowned stars had quit. What lay back of it? Rumors spread, and sportswriters pestered baseball officials for more information.

A few days before Christmas it came. Landis made the breathtaking announcement that Cobb and Speaker had been "permitted to resign" in the face of accusations of fixing and betting on a game between Cleveland and Detroit on September 25, 1919. The chief evidence against them consisted of two letters, one written by Cobb and one by "Smokey" Joe Wood, to Hubert "Dutch" Leonard, a retired pitcher. Leonard had recently forwarded the letters to Ban Johnson, who had bought them for the American League. In 1919 Cobb and Leonard had both been on the Detroit team, and Speaker and Wood were with Cleveland. The Indians had already clinched second place, and Detroit had a chance to finish third by winning the game in question. According to Leonard, the four players met under the stands beforehand, and Speaker said something to the effect that Cobb and Leonard should not worry because "your club will win the game." (Detroit did win.) The four decided that since the game was to be a "set-up," they might as well make some money by betting on it.

Leonard's story was only partially substantiated by the letters. The one written by Wood, printed in the *Times,* read:

> Enclosed please find certified check for sixteen hundred and thirty dollars ($1,630.00).
> The only bet West ° could get down was $600 against $420 (10 to 7). Cobb did not get up a cent. He told us that and I believed him.

° Clubhouse man.

Could have put up some at 5 to 2 on Detroit, but did not, as that would make us put up $1000 to win $400.

We won the $420. I gave West $30, leaving $390, or $130 for each of us. Would not have cashed your check at all, but West thought he could get it up at 10 to 7, and I was going to put it all up at those odds. We would have won $1,750 for the $2,500 if we could have placed it.

If we ever have another chance like this we will know enough to try to get down early.

The pertinent passages in Cobb's letter were:

Wood and myself were considerably disappointed in our business proposition, as we had $2,000 to put into it and the other side quoted us $1,400, and when we finally secured that much money it was about 2 o'clock and they refused to deal with us, as they had men in Chicago to take up the matter with and they had no time, so we completely fell down and of course we felt badly over it.

Everything was open to Wood and he can tell you about it when we get together. It was quite a responsibility and I don't care for it again, I can assure you.

Although later in his ghosted book Cobb omitted mention of the incriminating letters and claimed he had never bet on an American League game, at the time of the scandal he admitted he had written the letter and acknowledged that there had been a betting proposition. He said he had always played to win, and that no game he had ever played in was to his knowledge fixed. He attributed Leonard's charges to resentment over his having sent Leonard to the minors and to Speaker's failure to claim him on waivers. Speaker denied all knowledge of the affair. He pointed out that there was no letter written by him and that he was not even mentioned in those written by Cobb and Wood.

In releasing the news, Landis dissimulated by telling reporters that it had not been made known earlier because "none of the men involved is now associated with baseball." (Cobb and Speaker had been released, and Wood, who was a coach at Yale, had been out of the major leagues since 1922; little attention was paid to him during the controversy.) In the next breath Landis said he would defer his decision on the accused until later in the winter. "Baseball is again on trial," said the *Times*," if for no other reason than the peculiar concealment of the Leonard charges."

If Landis was waiting to see which way the winds of public opinion would blow, he soon found out. By this time the public was probably satiated with scandals both in baseball and government. Besides, it was difficult for people to believe that strong competitors like Cobb and Speaker would lose intentionally. Fans and prominent public figures defended the players. If Cobb and Speaker had "been selling out all these years," said Will Rogers, "I would like to have seen them play when they wasn't selling." The Cleveland City Council adopted a resolution expressing confidence in Speaker. Both senators from Georgia, Cobb's home state, vowed to see that he received justice, and some Detroit citizens planned to petition American League owners to prefer charges of incompetence against Landis.

But before the issue was resolved, a new sensation diverted attention from the Cobb-Speaker affair. Swede Risberg, one of the exiled Black Sox, charged that a series of games had been thrown by Detroit in 1917. Manager Clarence "Pants" Rowland, Risberg claimed, had assured him beforehand that "Everything's all fixed," meaning that Detroit was going to "slough off" the two doubleheaders to Chicago on September 2 and 3 in order to put the White Sox at an advantage in their hot battle for first place against the Boston Red Sox. Chicago did win all four games. Later, said Risberg, each man on the Chicago team put up approximately $45 apiece towards a purse of $1100 as a reward for the Detroit pitchers. Players like Eddie Collins, Ray Schalk, and others who had been considered "clean" during the 1919 Series scandal had contributed to the bribe, and Comiskey himself knew about it. Risberg also claimed that two years later, in 1919, "some of our boys" decided to return Detroit's favor of 1917: "We ought to be good to Detroit. . . . So the last two games we had with Detroit we sloughed off." In addition, Risberg maintained that some players on the St. Louis Browns had taken it easy in certain games against Chicago in 1917 in exchange for "gifts." "They pushed Ty Cobb and Tris Speaker out on a piker bet. I think it's only fair that the 'white lilies' get the same treatment," stated Risberg. Chick Gandil, another of the Black Sox, then came out in support of Risberg's story and claimed he could tell even worse tales.

Landis brought Risberg from Minnesota to Chicago at Organized Baseball's expense and questioned him for two hours on New Year's Day. Landis was acting as though he had never heard of the accusations. Actually, back in 1922 Happy Felsch had made the same charges during his lawsuit against Comiskey, and at that time Landis had shrugged them off as not worth considering. Furthermore, an entry in Harry Grabiner's diary, dated February 16, 1921, shows that Ray Schalk had discussed the matter with Landis then. Another notation in the diary, dated October 10, 1919, stated that Ban Johnson had told District Attorney Hoyne he knew that Chicago players had bribed Detroit to throw games in 1917.

Landis invited some forty players connected with the 1917 White Sox and Tigers to hearings January 5 in Chicago, but before they convened, the defense position had already been staked out by the owners of the clubs involved: they admitted that the pool was collected, but not as a bribe for Detroit to lose to Chicago; they said it was a reward for beating the Boston Red Sox three times straight. Said Comiskey, "This matter was known to everybody. I am not condoning any one or any act." Eddie Collins, former captain of the Clean Sox, explained that the fund was raised more than a month after the series at issue—an implication that time converted a bribe into a gift. "In those days," Collins pointed out, "it was nothing out of the ordinary to give a player on another team some sort of a gift if he went out of the way to turn in a good performance against one of a team's leading rivals in the [pennant] race." Frank admission of this custom was somewhat disillusioning. It ran counter to the article of faith that the heroes were straining their hardest to win at all times.

Barney Dreyfuss then chimed in with a similar story. He charged that in 1921 the New York Giants had offered Brooklyn players money to beat Pittsburgh, the Giants' chief rival for the pennant. McGraw retorted that such a story was "too absurd to discuss," and Brooklyn manager Wilbert Robinson said, "I never heard of it. It is ridiculous." Phil Ball staunchly defended his Browns against having "taken it easy" against Chicago in 1917, although at the time he himself had accused them of not giving their best.*

More than thirty players, among them some of the most famous in the American League, and about fifty reporters crowded Landis's office for two days of hearings. In the presence of Risberg and Gandil they generally admitted that a pool had been formed and money had been given to Detroit, but they said that it was a reward for beating Boston, not for losing to Chicago. In a week or so Landis gave the accused blanket exoneration. Terming the pool a "gift fund," he declared the deed "an act of impropriety, reprehensible and censurable, but not an act of criminality."

By this time Landis had had his fill of old scandals. As he remarked off the record, "Won't these God damn things that happened before I came into baseball ever stop coming up?" He therefore decided to establish a five-year statute of limitations on baseball offenses. John Heydler called Landis's acquittal a common-sense view—by which he perhaps meant that the Commissioner could not very well blacklist more than thirty players. He attributed the incident to the "muddled" and "distressing" days when the United States was entering the World War. Ban Johnson was quoted as saying he had known of the

* See above, chapter 14.

fund raised for the Detroit players, but, he explained, "It was simply a reward for a player to use extra effort against a pennant rival. . . . Of course, it was wrong doing . . . yet it was not a criminal act."

In the meantime the fate of Cobb and Speaker remained in abeyance until January 27, when Landis rendered a verdict and a summary of the case. On the basis of this document and other information, it seems that Ban Johnson and the American League believed as far back as early September of 1926 that they possessed sufficient evidence to warrant getting rid of Cobb and Speaker. The two players had requested permission to resign without a hearing, because they believed that unless they could confront their accuser, Dutch Leonard—and he refused to come east from California for a hearing —even a mere announcement of his charges would damage them, experience having shown that "a vindication by baseball authority" based on lack of proof "has been labeled a 'whitewash.'" The American League had honored this request in order to save them and their families embarrassment. Ban Johnson had then turned the letters and other evidence over to Landis, not "to pass the buck," he said later, but as a courtesy. After talking with Cobb and Speaker, Landis acquiesced in their wish to bow out quietly, with the understanding that if the situation changed, a public announcement might be necessary.

As we have seen, the situation did change, to the extent that Landis felt constrained to release the story and the text of the letter just before Christmas. However, by reserving judgment on their guilt or innocence, he left Cobb and Speaker in limbo. Ban Johnson grasped the opportunity to criticize Landis openly and more waspishly than he had in the O'Connell-Dolan case. He was "amazed" that Landis had released the information sent him, which he had no right to do; the reason must have been "a desire for personal publicity." Johnson also proclaimed that Cobb and Speaker would never play in the American League again while he was president. With this attack on Landis, Johnson sounded his own knell in baseball.

When the real reason for their departure from baseball became known, Cobb and Speaker informed Landis of their wish to rescind their withdrawal from baseball and asked that their status be clarified. They also engaged attorneys. It was because of their request, said Landis, not as a result of Johnson's sending him the letters, that he was issuing his summary of the case and his decision. His verdict was practically a foregone conclusion in view of his disposition of the Risberg-Gandil charges and his declared statute of limitations. Landis ruled that the players "have not been, nor are they now, found guilty of fixing a ball game."

The two stars were returned to the reserve lists of Detroit and Cleveland, but since the respective owners, Frank Navin and Jim Dunn, no longer wanted them, they were made free agents. Landis made it plain, however, that they were to play only in the American League, not in the National, some of whose clubs indicated an interest in them. Cobb signed with Connie Mack's Philadelphia Athletics and Speaker with Washington, in spite of Johnson's vow to keep them out.

The entire affair must have been a bit mystifying to the customers, wrote W.O. McGeehan of the New York *Herald Tribune.* "First, they learn that two of the greatest synthetic heroes produced by the national pastime have been ousted for cause. Now they learn that there was no reason at all why they should have left the game excepting their personal differences with their owners." Cobb in his 1961 book attributed the affair to a "plot" hatched against him by Leonard, Navin, Johnson, and Landis: Leonard because of a thirst for "revenge"; Navin because of "acute desire to slide out from under" Cobb's $50,000 contract; Johnson because of "long hatred" of him and Speaker; and Landis because of his "phobia [mania] for projecting himself into the limelight."

In any event, the Commissioner's decision was a popular one and, as McGeehan remarked, "Landis made the best of an unfortunate situation," since the "charges were calculated to do great injury to professional baseball."

No other scandals came to public attention in the few remaining years of the 'twenties or in the 'thirties either. Landis kept some investigations "confidential," but this is not to say that they involved crookedness. New anti-fix rules and penalties recommended by Landis and adopted with slight modifications by the owners at the end of 1927 no doubt helped to keep the slate clean of villainy. Similar rules had existed in the National Agreement since 1903 but had not been enforced. The new rules barred a player for three years for offering or accepting a reward either for extra effort or for "going easy"; made permanently ineligible those players and club officials who bet on a game in which they were involved; suspended for one year those who bet on any other game; and banned for life a player who offered a gift to an umpire or an umpire who accepted one. Under the new National Agreement of 1921 Landis already had the broad power to blacklist a player for "the best interests of the game"; the additional regulations were simply more particularized and provided for the penalty of expulsion.

During his first several years Landis blacklisted some fifteen players permanently, including the eight Black Sox. Others were banned for varying periods for such offenses as participating in games in which ineligible players took part or playing with the outlaws. In 1924 there was a total of fifty-three players on the ineligible list. Landis also had a "secret police system," as the *Times* called it; he employed a detective whom nobody knew, and players discovered to have committed minor infractions were called in and warned.

The Black Sox scandal and those that followed also motivated a number of state legislatures to enact laws providing fines and imprisonment for throwing games and bribing ball players, and in some instances Landis encouraged lobbying for such measures. New York State's statutes, for example, provided for from one to five years in jail and a fine of $10,000 for such offenses and applied to "any professional or amateur game or sport." By 1960 at least thirty-two states had such statutes. They were rarely enforced, however, because of public complacency and the difficulty of discovering dishonesty.

The parent of fixed games, gambling, throve in the 1920's. Betting on the World Series was, as usual, especially heavy, and baseball lotteries and pools continued to flourish. One of the largest and most notorious pools was the Albany (New York) Pool, an outfit that dated back to 1905 and whose continued operation created a scandal because of the complicity of many politicians. In 1927 alone it grossed $4,066,401. Ban Johnson reported to Landis in 1922 that in Chicago pools were operating on a more extensive scale than in any other city, and they mulcted the public of fabulous sums yearly. In Ohio Governor Donahey issued a proclamation calling on mayors and sheriffs to enforce the law against pools and lotteries. "In every important urban center throughout the state," he said, there was gambling on baseball, and through no fault of its own the game had been made a vehicle for corrupting youth by means of punch boards, slot machines, and chances sold on games. "The perils of gambling have not been removed from baseball," Johnson warned, and "owners must take action if we are to escape another scandal." Landis himself declared that the "loathsome evil" of professional gamblers and pools menaced baseball. "The peril in the situation," he wrote one of the owners, "is that the public may not distinguish this species of gambling from the gambling that corrupts ball games."

To recognize the problem was one thing; to solve it was like trying to tunnel through a mountain with a chisel. Since 1903 the major-minor league agreement had contained a rule against gambling in ball parks which the owners were supposed to enforce. With the Black Sox vividly in mind, the owners now made a renewed bid to stop betting in their parks by employing detectives to evict, arrest, or bar gamblers from their parks altogether. In Brooklyn, for example, Ebbets got city policemen to work without pay on their off-duty days; in exchange, he contributed to the Police Department fund. The National League passed an innocuous resolution calling on state governors to sponsor legislation against gamblers and wagering on baseball. Landis asked newspapermen to stop printing weekly runs-scored tables, and in 1930 he ordered team managers not to announce their starting pitchers until "warmup" time.

Results were negligible. Dreyfuss, for instance, complained that Pittsburgh police did not take the matter seriously and that police magistrates discharged prisoners as fast as they were arrested. When he was told of this, Landis reputedly "roared" in the Schenley lobby, "Politics or no politics, we'll put a stop to gambling." Although betting inside the parks may have been reduced, in 1928 an article in *Outlook* claimed that baseball betting in general exceeded that on horse racing.

In his abhorrence of gambling Landis was driven into conflicts with baseball owners and players over race tracks, where he feared they might be corrupted by gamblers and fixers. His first encounter was with Charles A. Stoneham and John McGraw of the Giants. In 1919 they became owners of the Oriental Park and Jockey Club and the Casino Nacional in Havana. Stoneham was not the first nor would he be the last baseball owner to be involved with horses, but when Landis became Commissioner he informed Stoneham and McGraw that they must choose between racing and baseball, so they divested themselves of their Cuban property, although they continued to frequent the track.

Later that year (1921) Stoneham drew a severe reprimand when Landis learned that Arnold Rothstein had appeared as Stoneham's guest in his private box at the Polo Grounds. Landis extracted a promise from Stoneham not to invite Rothstein to his box again, but he did nothing about Stoneham's business relationship with him.

This relationship was multifaceted. Early on, Rothstein had acted as middleman when Stoneham, McGraw, and another Rothstein friend, Tammany magistrate Francis X. McQuade, bought the Giants. Judge McQuade once dismissed charges against twenty of twenty-one men arraigned after the shooting of three policemen in Rothstein's gambling establishment, the Partridge Club. An investigation of magistrates' courts by Judge Samuel Seabury in the early 1930's caused McQuade's resignation. Stoneham, the chief stockholder of the Giants, was a heavy gambler and, according to Bill Veeck, Jr., a "bookie and a ticket scalper." He was associated with Rothstein in a number of enterprises, including a rum-running deal. Rothstein had also been a partner in the short-lived Stoneham-McGraw race track venture. But it was the operation of Stoneham's brokerage business, in which Rothstein was his closest associate, which was shortly to embarrass the National League.

Stoneham conducted what was known as a bucket shop, an office where orders to buy or sell stock were taken but not executed; instead, the operator pocketed the customer's money and gambled on the possibility of buying the stock later at a lower price or selling it at a higher one. The bucketeer required little margin, operating a kind of cut-rate, bargain-basement securities supermarket, run on the installment plan. At that time there were no federal laws against bucketing, and local restrictions were avoided through political influence and payoffs. Both Stoneham and Rothstein had powerful connections with Tammany Hall, particularly through Boss Tom Foley. Rothstein handled the payoffs, and attorney William J. Fallon was available for legal assistance, including bribery of jurymen and the removal of records.

Stoneham, after making a fortune estimated at ten million dollars, closed his business and referred his customers to a number of other bucketeers, vouching for their moral and financial standing. All went bankrupt, most of them forced shut by the federal government, and their customers lost millions. Subsequent court action involving one of these companies, Fuller & McGee, revealed that Stoneham had continued to supply the firm with funds in the amount of $170,000. Fuller & McGee maintained that Stoneham had invested these funds in the company as a partner and hence was liable for its obligations, whereas Stoneham contended that the money was merely a loan made at the behest of Boss Foley. Stoneham was indicted for perjury and for using the mails to defraud.

The ensuing publicity, particularly the investigations of reporter Nat Ferber of Hearst's New York *American,* put the National League in an awkward position. President Heydler speculated, "Stoneham may feel eventually that for the good of baseball . . . his voluntary sale of the Giants . . . would be a wise move." But there was nothing the league could do, he said, since Stoneham had violated no baseball rule and in his four years in baseball had been an asset to the "sport." Besides, he added, indictment was not conviction.

Far from taking action against Stoneham, the league actually elected him to its board of directors while he was under indictment. Landis also failed to act against Stoneham—an omission that sportswriter Frank Menke pointed out was in sharp contrast with his peremptory dismissal of Benny Kauff. Menke remarked that when Kauff, "merely a ball player, and not possessed of money or power, as is Stoneham, was indicted on the charge of stealing an automobile, Landis became filled with righteous indignation." He "declared that there was no place in the game" for Kauff, and even after the player was acquitted, Landis refused to reinstate him. Stoneham gave no sign of wanting to leave baseball, and although neither the National League nor Landis moved against him, they doubtless were relieved when he was eventually acquitted.

Although Landis succeeded in getting Stoneham and McGraw to give up their race track, he came off second best in other brushes with baseball men over horses. Frank Navin, the Detroit club president, owned a stable and was a big bettor at the track. When Landis asked him to get rid of his racing property, he refused and threatened to take the Commissioner to court.

Rogers Hornsby, the batting star of the National League, was an inveterate bettor who gambled many thousands of dollars on horses. Questioned by Landis, the outspoken Hornsby held his ground. He told the Commissioner that what he did with his money was his own business and that at least he was not gambling other people's money in the stock market. The latter remark was probably a reference to Landis's loss of baseball funds through investments in Sam Insull's rickety utilities empire. However, Landis took a voluntary salary cut to make up for the loss.

When Landis on a visit to New York warned against betting on horses, he very likely had in mind the Yankee players, among whom betting was rampant. Players were checking racing results between innings, Colonel Huston complained. He wanted them to keep their minds on the game, not on a horse three thousand miles away.

Occupied though he was with scandals and related problems in the first years of his administration, Landis was able to take upon himself other issues, some of them of far-reaching importance to the future course of the business. The first noteworthy instance was his blockage of Heinie Groh's transfer from Cincinnati to New York in 1921. Groh, the leading third baseman of the National League, wanted a "little boost" ($2000) in his $10,000 pay of the previous season. Cincinnati refused him an increase, and a stubborn salary fight followed and persisted beyond the deadline for signing—ten days after the start of the season—after which a player automatically landed on Landis's ineligible list.

At length Groh indicated he no longer wanted to play for Cincinnati. He would stay only if he were paid $12,000 but would take $10,-000 if he were traded elsewhere. Herrmann explained the situation to the other National League owners and invited bids for Groh, but in order to teach the player an "object lesson," he made the condition that the club that got him would not give him a bonus or restore the back salary he had lost during his holdout.

The Giants made the best offer, $100,000 and three players. In the case of two of them Cincinnati had the choice of taking additional cash in lieu of either or both. Groh signed his contract with Cincinnati in the knowledge that he was going to be traded, and Herrmann then applied to Landis, whom he had kept informed, for the player's reinstatement.

But Landis, after further investigation, cancelled the trade and ordered Groh to play out the season with the Reds, on the ground that permitting him to dictate his terms would set a premium on "rebellious players." Groh objected strenuously, saying the Commissioner had no right to make a man play where he did not want to or to make him accept a salary that did not suit him. However, the owners concerned, Herrmann and Stoneham, resigned themselves to Landis's ruling—in sharp contrast with Ruppert and Huston, who had rebelled against Ban Johnson's interference when Carl Mays was traded under similar circumstances. Groh finished the season with the Reds and, although he did go to the Giants after it was over, the temporary cancellation of the trade served to discourage later dissatisfied players from pressuring a club into trading them. As the New York *Times* put it, the Landis decision was a warning to players that "deserting" a club for real or fancied grievances could not be rewarded by transfer to another club. It added that Landis should have ruled that in future such players would be suspended for a year.

After the 1921 season another big stir occurred over the old problem of post-season barnstorming, but this time it involved the ever famous Babe Ruth, who had already become the most dramatic player in the game. Players tended to consider barnstorming their privilege; however, to avoid the possibility of diminishing the prestige of the World Series, the owners had passed a rule forbidding those who participated in the Series from barnstorming right afterwards. Landis indicated that this rule would be upheld, but Ruth and two other Yankee players, Bob Meusel and Bill Piercy, brazenly defied him. Ruth's position, which had some justification, was that a player's productive period was short and he should not be deprived of an opportunity to make extra money while he could. Even the Yankee owners recognized that the rule seemed unjust in many respects. Nevertheless, they concurred with Landis that as long as it existed it should be enforced, although they maintained they were powerless to enforce it themselves.

When Ruth and the others went ahead, Landis put his back up, declaring that "this case resolves itself into a question of who is the biggest man in baseball, the Commissioner or the player who makes the most home runs." In any case, the tour was soon abandoned, primarily because of inclement weather, and Ruth switched to vaudeville at $3000 a week for twenty weeks.

December brought a tough announcement from Landis. He declared that Ruth, Meusel, and Piercy had "willfully and defiantly" violated the barnstorming rule in a "mutinous" act and decreed that the three players would not receive their World Series shares. Furthermore, they were suspended until May 20 of the following season, at which time they could apply for reinstatement.

Faced with the loss of Ruth, the biggest attraction in baseball, for such an extended period, Ruppert and Huston sent their attorney to see Landis to plead for an adjustment of the long suspension, since it would hurt them financially even though they were guiltless. Other owners, too, pleaded the losses they would suffer; and Ruth even went to Canossa, but Landis denied him an audience. Despite these and other efforts to have the Commissioner ease up, he held to the suspension, although eventually he did turn over the players' Series money. Ruth's late appearance in the lineup cost him the home-run leadership. His total fell to 35, four fewer than Ken Williams's, and his average dropped to .315.

The rule limiting barnstorming was soon modified. Players wishing to barnstorm could apply for permission from the league president and Landis. They could play through October, although the limit was shortly extended to November 10; any given barnstorming team was limited to three World Series players. But the significant outcome was that Landis had again successfully asserted his authority and made it clear to all that his fiat applied even to the greatest star.

In 1926 Landis interposed his dictum in connection with a player trade that forced Organized Baseball to take a clear-cut position on the problem of conflict of interest. That winter fans and writers were agog over news that the St. Louis Cardinals had swapped Rogers Hornsby to the New York Giants for Frank Frisch and Jimmy Ring. As player-manager, Hornsby had just led the Cardinals to the world championship. The New York *Times* guessed that for such a player as Hornsby the Giants must have thrown in at least $100,000 in cash, but Stoneham insisted that no money had changed hands. The St. Louis press flayed owner Sam Breadon for trading Hornsby away. His loss was "a terrible blow," moaned the St. Louis Chamber of Commerce. St. Louis fans threatened to boycott the team.

Why had Hornsby been traded at such an inopportune time? After all, the Cardinals had turned down a Giant offer of $250,000 for him several years before when they badly needed cash. Breadon's public explanation was that he was afraid Hornsby was on the downgrade as a player, and although he was willing to give Hornsby the $50,000 contract he wanted for one year, he could not risk the club's financial future by acquiescing in the player's demand for a three-year contract at such a figure.

The real reasons lay deeper. They stemmed in large measure from Hornsby's personality. Free-spoken and direct, utterly tactless and aloof—a "loner" among the players—Hornsby in his stiff-necked individualism butted his way through baseball. He quarrelled with a succession of owners and more than once stood up to Landis. Appropriate indeed was the title of his ghosted book: *My Fight with Baseball*.

Such was Hornsby's style on the Cardinals. He did not get along with his predecessor, manager Branch Rickey, and after succeeding Rickey he soon clashed with Sam Breadon. Hornsby had asked Breadon to cancel some late-season exhibition games because the Cardinals, with a genuine chance to win their first pennant, needed the time to rest. After a game Breadon came into the clubhouse, which is traditionally the manager's domain, and told Hornsby that the exhibition games would not be called off. Hornsby, with a volley of choice words, ordered the owner from the clubhouse. Breadon, "blushing and burning," made up his mind that such insults from an employee were intolerable and Hornsby would have to go; hence his transfer to the Giants that winter, despite his success in winning the pennant and the World Series.

But after the trade was completed an obstacle suddenly appeared —interlocking ownership. Hornsby owned 1167 shares of stock in the St. Louis club. How would it look to have the second largest stockholder in the Cardinals playing second base for the Giants? Landis ordered that Hornsby divest himself of his holdings before he could play for New York and more or less left it up to the parties concerned to work out a settlement.

It was not so easily done. Breadon offered to buy the stock from him but only at the price Hornsby had originally paid, about $43 a share. Hornsby had the stock appraised, however, and then demanded $105 a share, which would bring him a profit of something like $72,000. This demand infuriated Breadon, who had helped Hornsby buy the stock in the first place. With the new season approaching meanwhile, the tension grew. McGraw challenged John Heydler's (not Landis's) right to keep Hornsby from playing with the Giants and threatened legal action. "Heydler can't make new rules," he averred. Heydler repeated Landis's dictum that Hornsby could not play for New York unless he sold the stock: "the National League is against anything that smacks of syndicate baseball and will fight to maintain that stand."

Finally a compromise was reached when Hornsby lowered his price somewhat and the other National League club owners chipped in to help Breadon pay it. Figures vary somewhat, but according to the *Times* Hornsby was paid $100,000 plus $12,000 for legal fees—

Breadon putting in $86,000, seven National League clubs $2000 apiece, and New York $12,000. The controversy took on added significance when at the end of the year the major leagues passed a rule that no player could hold stock in one club after his transfer to another in the same league; if he did he would be ineligible to play for or manage his new team. In fact, he would not be permitted to own stock in a club to begin with unless the Advisory Council approved. The majors also put through a rule barring club officials from owning stock in other clubs or lending money to other clubs or players on them.

The year of the difficulty over Hornsby had its brighter side for the National League. In February 1926 it had celebrated its Golden Jubilee with a huge banquet at New York's Hotel Astor. Among the nearly one thousand guests were governors, mayors, authors, publishers, clerics, financiers, officers of the armed forces, and some old-time ball players. A message from President Coolidge read: "Not only because of the nation-wide devotion to this splendid game, but because of my own conviction that it has been a real moral and physical benefit to the nation, I send my congratulations for this occasion."

Landis, too, had his day of personal triumph, although for a time there was some doubt that it would come to pass. At their joint meeting on December 16, 1926, the major-league owners elected him for another seven-year term and raised his salary from $50,000 ° to $65,-000. The minor leagues also endorsed him. Yet the major-league owners had not been altogether enamored of him. After recovering from their panic during the Black Sox scandal, some of them began to grumble about his highhanded way of making decisions without their knowledge or without at least consulting them or working with the Advisory Board.

When Landis heard in 1923 that many of the magnates were grousing and wanted to pay him off, he took the offensive and offered to quit if they were dissatisfied, but the owners shied away from such a step. In 1926 the *Times* thought "ominous rumblings" from some quarters presaged a battle over Landis's reappointment. At this juncture John Heydler, long a Landis man, urged his re-election on the ground that his authority was necessary to Organized Baseball. If he "appears" to have "the powers of a Czar or dictator," explained Heydler, "it is because these prerogatives are forced upon him by the unusual nature of all the rivalries that come of keen sports competition."

Immediately after, the National League owners, who had been Landis's most ardent backers from the outset, expressed their continued confidence in him by voting to renew his contract for ten years.

° His pay had been restored to $50,000 after he resigned his judgeship.

The American Leaguers, however, were not quite so eager and it was not until the end of the year that they sent a three-man committee to see Landis. After assuring him of support, the committee discreetly asked for changes in his policy, in particular that he revive the moribund Advisory Board called for in his contract and that he allow Ban Johnson to return to this board, after having been kept off it for two years following his criticism of Landis over the O'Connell-Dolan case. Landis apparently indicated that he was not averse to this provided the owners saw to it that Johnson behaved. At any rate the American League—Comiskey excepted—then voted Johnson back on the board and joined the National League in electing Landis for a second term. Even Johnson gave him a reluctant acceptance: "Landis is all right," he said. "There are lots worse people than the Judge."

But Johnson could no more curb himself than could a hungry wolf in a sheepfold. Never a Landis enthusiast and galled by his appointment, Johnson had grooved his mind against the judge. He had criticized Landis's Standard Oil decision and his handling of the Federal League suit. Then, having failed to keep Landis from being made baseball Commissioner and thus superior in rank to him, Johnson proceeded to hector and embarrass him at every opportunity. Once Johnson even called a meeting of the American League in Chicago on the same date Landis had set for a joint meeting of the majors in New York. Landis, on his part, downgraded Johnson by ignoring the Advisory Board and taking over full control of the World Series. At the end of 1923 Landis presented to the American League owners a bill of particulars against Johnson and gave them to understand that they would have to control him.

The O'Connell-Dolan affair exacerbated the feud between them because of Landis's exclusion of Johnson from the case and Johnson's various expressions of disapproval of Landis's disposition of it. Johnson was even quoted in the press as having called Landis a "wild-eyed crazy nut." Johnson had also tried to usurp Landis's prerogative by taking it upon himself in 1924 to have detectives investigate gamblers who were supposedly tampering with Pacific Coast League players. He presented a report on the subject which aroused the minor leagues to protest and which the majors rejected as unsubstantiated.

The magnates pleaded for an end to the feud. As Ruppert said, two men who themselves had no investment in baseball were, by their inability to get along, threatening the investments of others. But Landis, thoroughly angry, was bent on a showdown. He told a committee that had come to patch up the quarrel that the American League owners must decide between himself and Johnson. The result was that the owners groveled before Landis and beseeched him to overlook Johnson's behavior. Seven of them signed and tendered to Landis an amazing document repudiating Johnson's actions:

> We recognize that conditions have arisen that are gravely harmful to Base Ball and that must be intolerable to you, and that these conditions have been created by the activities of the president of the American League.
>
> While you were dealing promptly and effectively with a most deplorable exception to Base Ball's honorable record [O'Connell-Dolan] our president sought to discredit your action and to cast suspicion upon the 1924 world series.
>
> One year ago you made known to us in his presence various of his activities, and it was our expectation and hope that the unanimous action then taken certainly would operate as a corrective, but in this expectation and hope we have been disappointed.
>
> We don't extenuate these things, nor question their effect on Base Ball. However, he has been president of our league since its inception, and we ask you to again overlook his conduct and accept from us these guarantees:
>
> 1. That his misconduct will cease or his immediate removal from office will follow.
>
> 2. That legislation will be adopted that will limit his activities to the internal affairs of the American League.
>
> 3. That any and all measures which you may deem advisable to secure the above will be adopted.

Phil Ball, the lone American Leaguer who did not sign the document so humiliating to Johnson, issued a pointed statement in his defense, calling Johnson "the biggest figure in the national game" and "a victim of the men whose gratitude has bowed to the dollar sign." Recalling the days of the Lasker plan, the editor of *Baseball Magazine*, F. C. Lane, maintained that Johnson had been right in opposing Landis's appointment, because no such power as Landis had should be given any man; it was absurd to hand over "the people's democratic game" to a dictator. Nevertheless, he conceded that Johnson went about things in the wrong way in 1924 by proposing cancellation of the World Series and calling for a federal investigation.

Perhaps to assuage Johnson's feelings, the owners raised his salary from $30,000 to $40,000 at the close of 1925 and extended his contract from 1930 to 1935. At their dinner that winter the Baseball Writers' Association lampooned the Landis-Johnson quarrel with this song:

> Ken Landis and Ban Johnson, they had a head-on clash.
> Ken Landis got the verdict but Johnson got the cash.

The magnates handed Ken the crown and raised a mighty cheer,
But they raised Ban Johnson's salary ten thousand bucks a year.

Johnson was seemingly pacified, and a semblance of harmony was reached when the American League restored him to the Advisory Board at the end of 1926. But within a week the Cobb-Speaker affair supervened, and Johnson outdid his previous performance in a renewed attack on Landis. Some of his outbursts were so wild and contradictory as to seem almost hysterical, perhaps owing in part to his failing health. This time Landis refused to take any more of Johnson's hectoring and carping. He summoned the American League magnates to a special meeting in Chicago to have it out. Said one reporter, the American League owners "tried a muzzle" on Johnson; this time they "may use a catapult."

He was right. The owners averted a direct confrontation between Landis and Johnson by assembling a day before Landis's meeting and relieving Johnson of his duties for an extended period, no doubt in the hope that the leave would become a permanent one. It was given out that the enforced vacation was for reasons of health, and Johnson's physician certified that he was indeed ill. Navin, vice president of the league, took over the duties of the presidency. The owners also formally repudiated all Johnson's words against Landis. The judge accepted this latest chastisement of Johnson and postponed the meeting he had called.

Although not expected back, Johnson fooled everybody by returning in time for the opening of the next season. He was soon grumbling about Landis again, and in an evident effort to assert his old authority he incensed Connie Mack by imposing unusually stiff penalties on two of his players, Ty Cobb and Al Simmons, after an altercation with an umpire.

The end for Johnson had come. At the request of the owners he called a special meeting for July 8. Johnson, however, shut himself in his hotel room and refused to preside at the meeting, and Frank Navin took charge. A three-man committee consisting of Ball, Griffith, and Ruppert was appointed to negotiate with Johnson—in reality, to persuade him to resign. After the committee's first visit, newsmen were admitted to Johnson's room and found him "wasted away a good deal," his face "drawn and peaked," but vehemently denying that he was going to resign. It took two more visits of the committee before Johnson decided to heed Ruppert's argument: "You can add years to your life by quitting." He wrote a brief statement tendering his resignation as of November 1 or earlier and stipulating that his salary was to stop immediately on his retirement.

It was an ignominious and pathetic end for the man who had for so long been the foremost executive in Organized Baseball. He had stayed too long. Hindsight suggests that he should have left when the American League owners bypassed him and joined with the National League in electing Landis. He could have stepped down then with more grace and dignity.

20

MINORS AND FARMERS

THE ATTENTION given the Black Sox scandal, the batting of Babe Ruth, and the election of Judge Landis largely obscured a phenomenon that was revolutionizing Organized Baseball—the farm system. It represented a form of vertical integration in which a major-league club owned or controlled a chain of minor-league clubs, with the object of assuring itself a steady supply of player talent. The idea of extending farming into a comprehensive system was developed by Branch Rickey of the St. Louis Cardinals, one of baseball's few genuine innovators.

Judge Landis opposed the farm system, but in his fight against it he found Rickey to be a more subtle and resourceful opponent than Ban Johnson ever was, and the farm system gradually but inexorably became a permanent part of Organized Baseball's structure, with individual major-league clubs controlling more and more minor-league clubs directly or indirectly. By 1952, for example, major-league clubs controlled 175 out of 319 minor-league clubs, about 55 per cent.

How was it possible for Rickey, and others who eventually aped him, to take over so many minor-league clubs? What impelled Rickey to undertake such purchases in the first place? And how was it that Landis was impotent to halt this trend? The answers lie in the character of the minors, the predicament of Rickey and the Cardinals, and the provisions of the new National Agreement of 1921.

The minor leagues had always been the source of most major-league talent, and as such had been the foundation of the professional structure. In some years there were as many as thirty or forty separate leagues employing thousands of young men. In 1909 *Spalding's Guide* estimated the value of minor-league properties at more than twenty million dollars. The minors' governing body, the National Association, was kept busier than the National Commission in promulgating contracts and trying to settle disputes. In 1912 its secretary

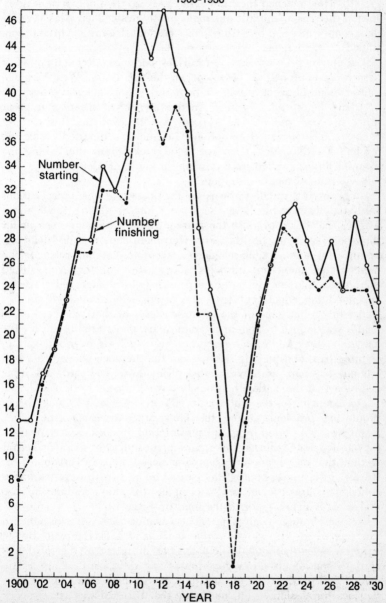

Number of Minor Leagues Starting and Finishing Each Year, 1900-1930

sent out 24,000 letters, an average of eighty each working day. Before the Federal League war the minors on the whole enjoyed increasing growth. They reached their low point in 1918 when only nine leagues started the season and just one managed to finish. Their peak year for the 1920's was 1923, but after that a gradual decline set in and continued for the balance of the decade.

The minors generally led a precarious existence, although not all of them were unprofitable. The owner of the Charleston, West Virginia, club claimed he went in with "a boot and a shoe" and came out with a "a bank book in five figures." Another owner said his average profit for a five-year period was $50,000, and he evaluated his club at $200,000. The Newark International League club reportedly was sold for half a million dollars in 1927, and Jack Dunn, after recovering from his financial plight in Baltimore during the Federal League war, left an estate of nearly a million.

Clubs in the smallest towns in the lowest league classifications were the least stable, and there were almost always some entire leagues that failed to finish the season. There were many reasons for their poor economic health. Garry Herrmann deplored the "dense ignorance" of minor-league magnates concerning baseball rules and lamented the "numerous mistakes" they made. *Sporting News* listed their small markets, scattered territories (which increased traveling expenses), inadequate publicity, lack of businesslike methods, and insufficient capital. One of the greatest causes of their poor economic health was failure to adhere to team salary limits established for the leagues. Other faults were extravagances such as overlong spring-training trips and playing seasons and the presence of syndicate ball —bogus baseball, as it was called. The unwieldy board and weak presidency of the National Association were also blamed.

The financing of the clubs, especially in the lowest leagues, was a perplexing problem. Before the farm system became established, teams were supported by group subscription, by local government, or by public-spirited businessmen. Group subscription was a makeshift method that merely served a temporary need. Fans in Paragould, Arkansas, for instance, bought the team's uniforms in 1910. Newark fans contributed $125,000 needed to complete the club's stadium in 1926 and actually oversubscribed the fund by $5920.

Support through local government was much less common. Often it was limited to propaganda urging citizens to back the team, but in 1917 the mayor of Buffalo actually was president of the local ball club. In Dubuque the city government spent $12,000 to equip a city-owned ball park for the use not only of its school teams but also for the local professionals, on the theory that baseball was as worthy of receiving public funds as YMCA's and other "uplifting" institutions. The manager of the team urged that millionaires, instead of endowing colleges and libraries, should endow minor leagues.

Frequently clubs were owned by local businessmen. As many as forty to sixty people might share ownership, but to have so large a number involved tended to impede administration of the club. Sam Breadon, the St. Louis owner, said that community ownership did not work because nobody really watched the investment. "What is anybody's property is nobody's property," he remarked. Even when clubs were owned by individuals as an investment, there were drawbacks. *Sporting News* claimed that many such owners were "baseball ignoramuses" who interfered with their team managers. Among them there were also magnates who at the end of every season threatened to quit unless local moneyed men made up their losses—or their pretended losses. Others were fly-by-night operators who absconded with club funds before the season was over and left behind bad debts and unpaid players. When this happened and a club fell apart, the onus was usually put on the territory rather than on the individual responsible. A lien was placed against the city or town for the amount of the club's indebtedness, and no club could operate in the locality until the lien was satisfied. Protection of the club's property rights in its players was also removed until their salaries were paid. By 1933 there was more than $400,000 in liened territory.

Financial irresponsibility could of course work a hardship on the players, as this sample letter written by one of them in 1911 illustrates:

> Gentlemen I done my duty as a ball player should. . . . Why should I be treated like this. This is the second time this happened to me in organized ball. I suppose Mr. Reed [president of the league] thinks the____ll with us boys see how they get their money. Gentlemen one third of the men in this league have money coming and it is a dirty shame the stuff they pull off in this circuit. I am a poor unfortunate ball player with nothing in the world so I hope you will make these people come to time.

One group of clubs sent out contracts in 1912 before it had even formed a league, inspiring a newspaper to headline the story "Married to a Corpse." The National Board of the minors often temporized on appeals from players—a habit that brought repeated criticism from Ban Johnson: "I am losing patience with the National Board for its dilatory manner in properly adjusting the claims of its players." Yet when players appealed from the board to the National Commission, chairman Garry Herrmann often told them their problem was an internal (minor-league) matter.

In 1912 Bob Quinn, secretary of the Columbus American Association club, having in mind that many owners were not meeting their financial obligations, suggested that they be required to deposit a certain sum with their league president as a guarantee for payment of players' salaries. Since baseball is a partnership, Quinn said, the partners should be responsible for the men to whom they award a franchise. Some leagues, like the Central and the Ohio State, adopted this plan. They required each of their clubs to post $1000 with the league president, who could pay a defaulting club's players and declare the franchise forfeit. Or the club could pay back gradually by having a share of its gate receipts withheld and sent to the league office for repayment to its sister clubs. The National Association itself, however, did not blanket all its minor leagues with such a requirement.

Both major and minor leagues were susceptible to fluctuating economic conditions, changes in consumer demand, and other external forces, but the lower leagues were more sensitive to them. The minors were practically wiped out by World War One. They suffered heavy losses during the Federal League war as well. Approximately fifty parks closed down in 1914, and in 1915 the number of leagues dropped from 40 to 29, of which only 22 completed their schedules. One hazard peculiar to the Southern League was yellow fever. An epidemic of it in 1905 brought strict quarantine in some of the Southern's cities, but league president Kavanaugh revamped the schedule and the clubs managed to complete their season. The impact of the automobile, radio, and movies on the minors was strong. Golf also hurt them, not so much because it kept attendance down, Sam Breadon thought, but because free spenders who used to put up money to keep the local ball team going were spending it "playing something themselves." Mike Sexton, president of the National Association, gloomily stated in 1926 that baseball had become a losing industry for the smaller leagues. Henceforth, owners were to dwell increasingly on the incursion of new competitors for the consumers' leisure dollar.

Another factor of supreme importance in the fortunes of the minors was their relations with the major leagues. Mutual interest that impelled them to cooperate lay at the root of the various major-minor league agreements. Just as the majors relied heavily on the minors as a seedbed for player talent, so the minors had to be assured that the majors would respect their property rights in players, since most of the minors depended on player sales in order to live. It was estimated in 1910 that only 40 per cent of the minors could survive on gate receipts alone. Substantial sums were realized from the traffic in players. In the period from 1909 to 1913 the majors spent $1,895,000 for players through direct purchase or draft, or about 9.2 per cent of their total receipts.

But there was another side to this coin of mutual interest. The majors naturally wanted access to minor-league talent on the cheapest possible basis, while the minors, like any sellers, wanted to get as much as they could for their personnel. Consequently the major-minor agreements were expedients that never wholly satisfied either party. Even after the signing of the 1903 agreement, friction continued, especially over the prices of drafted players and the number of players the majors could draft from the Class A minor leagues (lower leagues were subject to "universal" draft). Also in dispute was the number of men the majors could option out to the minors.

The minors also remained unrepresented on the National Commission, even though it had the authority to inflict fines and suspensions on them and had the final say in disagreements over ownership of minor-league players.° Nor have the minors ever had a voice in choosing the Commissioner of baseball, who rules over them.

Dissatisfaction crystallized in 1905 when hearings were held regarding an alleged "conspiracy" among the "silk-stocking" (Class A) leagues, which were suspected of plotting to break the National Agreement. Following this incident, the high minors wrung some concessions from the majors. It was then that the number of players the majors could draft from any Class A team each year was cut from two to one.°° The price of drafting them was also raised from $750 to $1000.

After further agitation and more rumors of a trade war, the high minors registered another gain in 1911 when the majors consented to a special AA classification for the American Association, the Pacific Coast League, and the International League. One of the reasons for placing these leagues "only a little lower than the angels" was the objection of other leagues, such as the Western Association and the Southern, to possible demotion to Class B when the 1910 census revealed that because of the low population of their territories they did not really qualify for the Class A status they held. So it was finally decided to advance the three aforementioned Class A leagues into a newly created AA class and let the others stay put,† in disregard of the minor leagues' own population requirement. A "liberal advance" in draft prices all along the line accompanied the new classification:

° In disputes between a major-league club and a minor-league club over a player, the secretary of the National Association and the president of the minor league whose player was involved were permitted to participate in the decision.

°° See chapter 9.

† The Pacific Coast League was incorrectly put in a high class to begin with, to induce it to leave outlawry and join Organized Baseball.

AA $2500, A $1500, B $1200, C $750, and D $500. Only one player could be selected from AA teams each season. Thus the trend toward rising draft prices and increasing exemptions continued apace.

With these measures the crisis between the majors and high minors subsided, but the hardships inflicted by the Federal League war and World War One led the minors again to threaten withdrawal from the National Agreement in protest against the majors' draft privileges and their farming of players under option agreements. Ban Johnson was not impressed. In what the *Times* called his "latest blast," he announced that after the war the National Commission was going to "abolish" the National Association, which "for years" had been "incapable of managing its own affairs," as evidenced by the fact that most of the problems that came before the National Commission were minor-league cases on appeal.

In a move to reach agreement, Johnson met with the presidents of three of the minor leagues, but without success. The minors issued an ultimatum setting 6 p.m. on January 17, 1919, as the deadline for answering their demands; however, the majors steadfastly refused to agree to end the draft or to grant the minors representation on the National Commission. As a result, the National Association withdrew from the National Agreement by "mutual consent," each side tacitly agreeing to respect property rights in players and territorial rights. Drafting was suspended.

Although some minor-leaguers were "elated" with the change, others recognized that such a fluid situation was "highly unsatisfactory," and efforts were soon made to write a new agreement. They came to naught. One reason was that the American League had its hands full with internal problems. In addition neither big league was anxious to enter into another pact formally tying the minors and themselves together while the Baltimore anti-monopoly suit was hanging over them. Thus it was that two years elapsed before the uncertainty in major-minor relations was remedied by the new agreement of January 1921 after Landis's election as Commissioner.

The new agreement represented a compromise. Draft prices were again increased and ranged from $1000 for Class D players to $4000 for Class A and $5000 for AA men; only one man could be selected from each AA and A club. The other classifications were, as before, subject to unrestricted draft of their players. Major-league clubs were permitted to option out eight men apiece for a maximum of two years, and the minors in turn could option men to lower leagues according to a sliding scale—AA clubs could "farm" six, A five, B four, and C three.

But the fulcrum of the pact was the provision granting any minor league the choice of exempting itself from the draft completely if it relinquished its own right to draft players from teams in lower classifications. Five minor leagues elected to do this: the three AA leagues (Pacific Coast and International Leagues and American Association), the Class A Western Association, and the Class B Three-I League. In other words, these five judged that they would be better off acquiring and disposing of men by purchase only, even though it meant surrendering their right to draft players from lower leagues. Finally, the minors accepted Landis as Commissioner but limited his investigatory power to cases in which the consideration was more than $300. A year later, however, they removed even this restriction.

The rise in the draft prices and the complete exemption from the draft of five minor leagues, particularly the three AA ones, further clogged the channels of advancement for players. In the exempt leagues the advancement of men capable of playing in the majors could be halted, or at least retarded, since they could move up only if their employers consented to the sale of their contracts. Not only that, those in lower leagues had a slimmer chance than before of advancing within the minors because the five exempt leagues, who heretofore might have been willing to buy them at the fixed draft price, would think twice before purchasing them at the higher prices of the open market.

But for the clubs in the draft-exempt leagues the new plan was a bonanza. They made "fantastic profits" selling players. The Pacific Coast League enjoyed one of the most prosperous periods ever while the new arrangement obtained. Baltimore of the International League realized nearly a million dollars in the 1920's from player sales. The *Times*, alluding to the fat profits that freedom from the draft brought club owner Jack Dunn, quipped that "At the slightest mention" of changing back to the draft, Dunn "runs away for two miles and then kicks in the side of a barn."

Landis was strongly opposed to draft exemption. He favored an unrestricted draft as a protection of the players' right to move up: "A situation where a group of ball players can be boxed into a minor league and can advance higher only at the whim of their employer, is intolerable and un-American. So long as I am on this job, I will fight for the full restoration of the draft." Minor-league officials denied that players were kept back. John Conway Toole, who had become president of the International League, repeated the old argument that no owner wanted to keep dissatisfied players, and if any were dissatisfied or even if a major-league club thought they were, their names should be submitted and he would guarantee that they would be traded for a "reasonable" figure. This sounded plausible enough, but the catch was that the minor-league club could decide what figure was reasonable.

Now that the draft-exempt leagues were riding high, it was the major leagues' turn to complain. They protested that they were being forced to pay exorbitant prices for new players. Ban Johnson privately castigated the draft-exempt leagues as the "Johnny Grab-alls" of the minors. Ebbets advocated a boycott: the majors would simply refuse to purchase players from the draft-exempt minors. *Sporting News* called this suggestion "a refusal to do business with people who refuse to do business with you—on your terms." The majors also made various proposals to increase draft prices if the minors would give up their exemption, but the three AA leagues voted down these offers.

After the 1922 season yet another attempt at compromise failed, and the bickering resumed. Heydler accused the minors of breaking the National Agreement, and the minor leagues made the same charge when the majors, without consulting the minors, increased their optional player list from 8 to 15 and announced that all players sent out after January 10, 1923, would be subject to the draft. Landis, maintaining that the action of the majors was justified, approved the increase, for he pointed out that at the time he took office there was no specific agreement as to the number of men that could be optioned out.

President McCarthy of the Pacific Coast League was thoroughly angered at the action of the major leagues and Landis's justification of it. He struck back fiercely. The minors had been "humbugged, deluded, deceived and cheated by the two major leagues . . . with the knowledge, consent and approval of the new Moses [Landis]." McCarthy said that at the minors' Louisville meeting they had cheered Landis's statement that, draft or no draft, the agreement would be lived up to; now the Commissioner had nullified it. The minors had been given "vacuum promises" and "Belasco poses," declared McCarthy, by the man whose proudest boast was his fine of Standard Oil, but who "was not big enough nor courageous enough to tell his over-fed and overprosperous employers" they must live up to a binding contract. It is "easy to exile" a ball player when he wants a salary increase, McCarthy sneered, but when the men who make the player a contract-jumper have their dollars threatened, "that's different." President Sexton of the National Association voiced disapproval of such "political expression." Landis did not respond.

The Pacific Coast League took a vote on McCarthy's idea of seceding altogether from the "autocratic rule of Landis," but they were split on the question. Other draft-exempt minors retaliated by voting not to accept any optioned players if they were subject to the draft. The majors refused to option players on such terms and were rumored to be considering the formation of a "Continental" or "Interallied" league as a developing ground for players. Heydler proposed a different idea, one thought by baseball people in the 1970's to be brand new—a training school where the majors could prepare their own recruits.

A new compromise known as the "modified draft" was reached in December of 1923. The majors agreed to send players on option and outright release to the draft-exempt leagues if the latter would permit certain players to be drafted. Four of the five exempt leagues shortly accepted this plan, in what amounted to a private agreement with the majors. The International League held out against it until the end of 1924.

But in the opinion of the majors, even under the modified draft the minors still had the advantage. In 1929 Ruppert complained at a major-league meeting that no ball club could afford to pay the prices the Yankees were paying for minor-leaguers. He said he believed he was "going to be forced into owning minor-league clubs, and so is every other major-league owner in this room." The majors therefore continued their efforts to get the minors to return to the unrestricted system by offering higher draft prices as bait. The minors refused.

Finally the majors decided to force the issue: the minors must either accept the universal draft or nothing. The AA leagues balked, but they left the way open to compromise by offering proposals of their own. Lengthy negotiations followed and resulted in a lasting agreement before the 1931 season, in which the minors surrendered their special privileges with respect to the draft. They also acceded to the majors' wish to option out 15 players instead of 8, and to increase the number of times any one player could be sent out on option from 2 to 3. The majors on their part granted a new, higher scale of draft prices: AA $7500, A $6000, B $4000, C $2500, D $2000. They further agreed not to draft a player from an AA club unless he had at least four years' experience in minor-league ball (three years for Class A) and to limit themselves to the selection of one player per club each year. Under this new agreement it was possible to hold a man in the minor leagues for seven years, even though he might be capable of playing major-league ball. He could be kept safe from the draft for four years and be sent down on option for three more by a major-league club, which need not ask other major-league teams to waive on him.

The tug of war between the majors and the minors in the 1920's was conducted within the context of the traditional relationship between them. Meanwhile, that relationship was quietly and gradually being revolutionized by Branch Rickey in his building of the St. Louis Cardinals' farm system.

Few individuals have made a greater imprint on Organized Baseball than Rickey. He was born of a poor and pious Ohio farm family. His character was formed by hard work, the little red schoolhouse, and a religious mother who punished his boyhood naughtiness by taking him to her bedroom and having him kneel and listen while she begged God's forgiveness for not having done her duty as a mother. "I felt as though I had hit her," he recalled later. When he started playing professional baseball Rickey vowed never to play on Sunday out of respect for his mother. He observed this pledge throughout his career and as a major-league manager always had a "Sunday manager" take his place. This personal scruple never dulled Rickey's sharpness in the marketplace, however. In June 1917, for example, he obtained the league's permission to advance a Monday game to the previous Sunday in order to create a Sunday doubleheader for his club. Not only that, when he heard about the "splendid crowd" that turned out and what a "good business proposition" it was, he requested that an August game be moved up in the same way and made part of another Sunday doubleheader.

Other manifestations of Rickey's Methodist upbringing were his evasion of direct profanity by habitually substituting "Judas Priest" for "Jesus Christ" and his abstinence from liquor. He was also a prohibitionist, but this personal persuasion did not prevent him from hiring drinkers if he thought they could help the organization, be they imaginative executives like Larry MacPhail, good players like Flint Rhem, or successful managers like Billy Southworth.

Nor did Rickey shrink from circumventing the rules. Like the other operators, he entered into gentlemen's agreements. He also slipped players out of the league to the minors by persuading other major-league club owners to waive claims to them, as in this wire: WE CANNOT LET ANY ONE OF THESE MEN GO TO YOUR CLUB THEREFORE APPRECIATE YOUR WITHDRAWING CLAIM—UNDER SAME CIRCUMSTANCES I AM SURE OUR CLUB WOULD BE GLAD TO FAVOR YOU.

Rickey also loved to talk and gained a reputation as an orator, frequently addressing YMCA's and church and civic groups. He was a master of circumlocution. Testifying before Congress, he produced this specimen: "You cannot have a basic trouble in which it is possible for you to meet in the marginal zone of wrong about a contract." Rickey's moralistic code combined with his pragmatic pursuit of profit repelled many, who saw him as a hypocritical mountebank.

The energy that Rickey exhibited all his life was early demonstrated in his zeal for an education, which enabled him to escape the

drudgery and limited horizons of farm life. Starting as a country
schoolteacher, he saved out of his $35-a-month salary and studied
to prepare for Ohio Wesleyan University, where he continued to earn
his way as athletic director and by playing baseball and football for
money on the side. After graduating in 1904 he signed as a catcher
with Dallas of the North Texas League. That August he joined Cincinnati but was soon released for refusing to play on Sundays. After
that he was like a rolling stone gathering polish. For the next eight
years or so he had a varied experience teaching and coaching in a
number of colleges and playing major-league ball for the St. Louis
Browns (1906) and the New York Highlanders (1907). His debut with
the Browns brought this comment from *Sporting News:* "He is a
high-strung youngster with ability and enthusiasm. . . . He earned
the plaudits of President Johnson, Umpires Sheridan and Klem, the
players of both teams and the spectators." While he was with the
Highlanders his arm went bad, and at the end of the season he announced his "retirement" from baseball to study law. Tuberculosis interrupted his plans in 1909, but after recovering at Saranac, he resumed his law training along with coaching at the University of
Michigan. Upon taking his degree in 1911, he began practice at
Boise, Idaho. His firm did so poorly that in a few months he left it to
his partners to look after and returned to coaching at Michigan.

As early as 1906 Rickey was already recommending college players
to professional teams. He continued to observe the collegians while
coaching at Michigan. Rickey was to have few equals in the rare skill
of sizing up young players and determining their potential as big-lea-
guers. He knew "how to put a dollar sign on a muscle" better than
anyone in baseball, as a later Commissioner, "Happy" Chandler, put
it. Rickey recommended some of the players he scouted to Robert
Hedges, president of the Browns. Evidently impressed, Hedges told
Rickey that he proposed purchasing the Kansas City club as a
Browns' farm and putting Branch in charge of it. Rickey declined, but
he did undertake a trip to the coast to scout the Pacific Coast League
for Hedges. In 1913 Hedges offered Rickey $7500 to be his assistant
and help build up the team. He could also retain his $1500 coaching
job at Michigan. This time Rickey accepted and thus began his long
administrative career in Organized Baseball.

Rickey used his many college contacts to help him in locating
young players and kept track of them in a little black book that was
to become famous. He then placed them on minor-league clubs with
which he had deals. Before the season was over he assumed the
added task of managing the Browns, replacing George Stovall.° Serious and industrious, Rickey banned poker playing, gave chalk talks

° See above, chapter 10.

to the team on baseball theory, and introduced other innovations that
drew a good deal of scoffing about "college methods" from the writers. A poem in *Sporting News* expressed their attitude:

> Branch Rickey is a funny cuss,
>   Though cussin he forbids;
> His rules have started quite a fuss
>   Among his Brownie kids.
> When Sunday comes he leaves his team
>   Completely in the lurch
> And Jimmy Austin rules supreme
>   While Branch hikes off to church.
>
> He's got a time clock on the field;
>   Don't let his Brownies smoke
> Those nasty cigarettes, or yield to
>   Poker and go "broke,"
> And when he wants to bawl them out
>   For some queer bone-head play
> He doesn't stage a swearin' bout
>   He does it high brow way.
>
> The ways McGraw and Tinker rule
>   Don't make a hit with Branch;
> The tongue is not a two edged tool
>   In Rickey's base ball ranch.
> But let him put the Browns across
>   An' we'll regard him highly;
> He's sure a puritanic boss—
>   He's base ball's Doctor Wiley.

Rickey, unperturbed by the sarcasm of critics over his "peculiari-
ties," continued to double as presidential assistant and field manager
in 1914 and 1915. Many believed that he was a poor manager, too
theoretical and over the heads of his players, but he did inject spirit
into the team and made it more interesting to watch. In 1915 he also
had on the club George Sisler, the college star whom he had "discovered" at Michigan.

Rickey's position changed when Phil Ball purchased the club at the
close of the Federal League war. Ball removed Rickey as field manager and likely would have let him go altogether except that Rickey
had already signed a contract for 1916. In an anomalous position,
with no title, and largely ignored, he continued his work anyway and
succeeded in getting another contract for 1917. His big opportunity
came when he was offered the presidency of the St. Louis Cardinals
at $15,000, double his salary. Mrs. Helene Britton, "the matron mag-

nate," had decided to sell the club for $350,000, an amount that would be raised by a public sale of stock. Rickey breached his contract with the Browns to accept the Cardinals' offer. He claimed that he had Ball's permission to leave but that Ball had withdrawn it after Rickey had already signed. Ball denied Rickey's claim and secured an injunction for breach of contract but was unsuccessful in stopping him.

Rickey's work with the Cardinals began in earnest when he returned from a short period of military service at the end of 1918. In addition to being president, Rickey also took on the job of team manager. In the meantime an automobile dealer named Sam Breadon, one of those who had bought a few shares of Cardinal stock at the time it was offered publicly, had gradually been buying up additional shares. By 1920 he had become president of the club, displacing Rickey, who was named vice president. Breadon, together with Rickey, continued to purchase more shares from among the hundreds of shareholders who had originally subscribed, until by 1922 Breadon had the controlling interest in the club. At the same time Rickey signed a new five-year contract as vice president and team manager at $25,000 a year plus 10 per cent of the profit. When the team slumped during the 1925 season, Breadon removed Rickey as manager and appointed Rogers Hornsby. Rickey was miffed and sold his stock to Breadon and Hornsby for $250,000; that was how Hornsby came to own the Cardinal stock that caused so much difficulty later. At the expiration of his contract in 1927 Rickey signed again for five years at $40,000 plus 10 per cent of the profit. But by this time the Cardinals were a far different organization both financially and artistically. When Rickey joined the club it was poverty-stricken and still owed Mrs. Britton $175,000 of the purchase price. Under the Breadon-Rickey combination, its condition improved markedly. Breadon cleared up the club's debts and raised working capital, and Rickey began to develop the farm system.

Rickey did not, of course, originate the idea of "farming out" promising young players as a future source of supply: major-league clubs had been doing it in one way or another for years, in spite of the rules against it.* What Rickey did was to carry the idea to its logical conclusion by linking together a whole chain of clubs comprised of teams in all minor-league classifications, from D to AA. This network made it possible to start youngsters at the bottom, sift out the best, and move them up, repeating the process at each level until the most highly skilled were ready for the majors or high minors.

Later Rickey explained that the farm system was "not a sudden

* See above, chapter 9.

stroke of somebody's originality or inceptional thinking." It was "occasioned by necessity." Impecunious clubs like St. Louis could not compete in the player market with wealthy ones like New York, Chicago, and Pittsburgh. St. Louis, a last-place team in 1918, was so impoverished that it used the same uniforms for two seasons, and Rickey said he went without salary for a time to help meet the payroll. Poor clubs suffered increased hardship while the draft was suspended from 1919 to 1921. Even after the 1921 National Agreement was signed, the only way majors could acquire players from the top minors was by purchase, because they were exempt from the draft. The rich clubs could pay the stiff player prices; but the poor ones, far from buying expensive men, had to sell the best of those they already had in order to remain solvent.°

To be sure, Rickey's many college friends apprised him of likely young players. Such prospects usually needed professional experience in the minors before they would qualify for major-league ball. Rickey could place them with a minor-league club with the understanding that he could retrieve them later, but there was nothing to prevent the minor-league owner from breaking the gentleman's agreement if he could get better terms from another major-league club. There was another problem that annoyed Rickey. When he or his scouts uncovered a good prospect and made an offer for him, the owner would call a rich club like the Giants and invite them to outbid Rickey—and usually they did. In effect, St. Louis scouts were flushing game for the hunters of other clubs.

Rickey, pondering over his problem, asked himself: "What can I do about it? I have no money. We owe $175,000." He believed that the power of wealth to create winning teams should be minimized and emphasis placed instead on work, planning, and good judgment. Good farmer that he was, Rickey decided to grow his own crop on his own land, as it were. He started by purchasing a half interest in the Fort Smith, Arkansas, club in 1919 for "a pittance." Very soon after, he bought 18 per cent of Houston of the Texas League, a higher-classification club where Fort Smith graduates could be assigned. Eventually the Cardinals acquired complete ownership of Houston. Before long St. Louis also purchased a half interest in Syracuse, its first AA farm team. A few years later the Cardinals bought the rest of the stock and in 1927 moved the franchise to Rochester in order to obtain a better market—an example, said Sporting News, of what can happen to a city's baseball when its club is operated by "alien ownership" under the "chain store plan."

Henceforward St. Louis continued to acquire ownership or control

° See below, chapter 22.

of minor-league clubs until it had built a baseball empire which, at its peak before World War Two, comprised thirty-two clubs containing six or seven hundred players and representing an investment of more than two million dollars. The satellite clubs were distributed according to classification as follows: AA, three; A, one; B, four; C, four; and D, twenty. (There was a Cardinal team in every one of the twenty Class D leagues.) The Cardinals owned fifteen of their clubs outright and controlled the rest through "working agreements."

The working agreement, another old device, had the advantage of a farm without the disadvantage that the minor-league club might become a burden, since the agreement could be renewed or terminated each year. A forerunner of this type of agreement was one suggested by the president of a minor-league club in 1911:

> . . . technically, legally and morally, Chattanooga would not be a farm for the Cincinnati Club, at the same time it would give you an opportunity to place all your promising players with a good 'A' club and good manager, with the assurance that if they develop you would not be held up for an exorbitant price, and it would enable you to get hold of a great many young players with the assurance that you would not lose money on them, and if they did develop . . . you could get them back.

In two cases St. Louis had a working agreement with the president of an entire league (Arkansas State and Nebraska State), the Cardinals to supply financial aid in exchange for the pick of all the players in the league.

The St. Louis system was a prompt and spectacular success. The "chain gang," as its detractors called it, produced a stream of young players—in fact, about three times the number needed by the parent club. St. Louis won its first National League championship in 1926 and in the next twenty years took eight more pennants and finished second six times.

The system also proved to be lucrative. Even though the Cardinals' paid attendance was much smaller than that of New York, Brooklyn, or Chicago, their profit was more than twice that of any other National League club between 1925 and 1950. Many of the high minor-league clubs in the Cardinal system made money themselves. St. Louis absorbed the losses of the lowest-classification clubs in its system, but if these became too great, the club was cut adrift.

The bulk of the Cardinals' profit came from the sale of surplus players. So extensively did St. Louis come to engross the player market that there were almost always fine young recruits ready to replace its major-league regulars. Therefore the Cardinals could sell off the established players and do so when they were at their peak or just passing it and would bring premium prices. The Cardinal system was so laden with players that some of its best minor-league prospects could also be sold to other major-league clubs. At one time there were no fewer than 65 players in the major leagues who at some time or other had been in the St. Louis organization. Besides, the Cardinals very rarely had to lay out large sums for players. Their acquisition of pitcher Jesse Haines in 1919 with a borrowed $10,000 was the last player-purchase the Cardinals made for more than twenty-five years. After that they acquired men cheap from their farm clubs and cheaper still—often for nothing—as free agents. And once they had these men, the club could keep their salaries relatively low. Eventually the Cardinals scoured the country for talent even more thoroughly by holding tryout camps, in which as many as four thousand boys were looked over and hundreds placed on "farms" for future harvesting.

Guiding and animating all was the genius of Rickey. Added to his unsurpassed ability to determine the possibilities of raw recruits was Rickey's capacity for building an efficient organization, hiring competent scouts, and appointing farm-team managers and coaches capable of teaching young players. He soon gained a reputation as a shrewd trader in the player market too. In addition, it was said that he was so adept at bargaining with players over salaries that they sometimes came away thanking him for a pay cut. Some attributed Rickey's tightness to the fact that he received a percentage of the club profits.

Not to be overlooked in the success of the Cardinals was Rickey's own thoroughness and unceasing labor. As a young man I once wrote to several major-league clubs, including St. Louis, to ask them to try out a young pitcher named Bill Lohrman, whom I had taught on the Brooklyn sandlots. I believed he had the makings of a big-leaguer. None of the clubs bothered to reply—except the Cardinals. Rickey wrote personally, directing the boy to present himself with the letter to the manager of the Rochester club. He did so and eventually reached the major leagues.

The question arises of how Rickey got away with constructing a farm system at all, flying in the face of baseball tradition as he was, and braving the hostility of Landis as well. There were several reasons. The no-farming rule of the 1903 National Agreement banned farming only in the sense of covering up through gentlemen's agreements; it did not specifically ban major-league ownership of minor-league clubs. Not until 1913 did the National Commission direct major-league clubs to dispose of any minor-league holdings, but the directive became a dead letter because of the Federal League war and the ensuing gradual breakdown of the National Commission. Under these circumstances the sprinkling of clubs that owned minor-league property held on to it. The gate was flung wide when the new National Agreement of 1921 omitted any ban on farming or minor-league ownership by the majors. Thus Rickey was able to stay within the letter of baseball rules, except perhaps in the case of his first few acquisitions, which were violations only insofar as they were contrary to the National Commission's bulletin.

As for Landis, he was early persuaded by Barney Dreyfuss and Frank Navin that a major-league club could not bear the expense of a string of minor-league teams. These experienced baseball men predicted that an edifice like Rickey's would collapse of its own weight, and on their advice Landis for a time did nothing. Besides, St. Louis had already established minor-league property rights that could not easily have been disturbed.

The striking success of Rickey's program soon reversed the position of St. Louis vis-à-vis the affluent clubs. Once the impoverished Cardinals could not compete with them; now they were hard put to compete with the Cardinals. The Rickey system affected the player market so potently that other major-league clubs began to copy it. In the words of Rickey: "I was removing a most favorable market when the St. Louis club was not required at the end of each season to sell its great players to the favorable competitors in its own league, and these people, then seeing the value of that thing, embraced it. 'First pity, then endure, then embrace,' says Pope."

By the end of 1928 major-league clubs had something like eighteen farms, still a small number, particularly since five of them belonged to the Cardinals. In some cases the minor-league club belonged to the major-league owner individually, instead of to his club. Nevertheless, the trend was unmistakable. The Cardinals already had two more purchases pending, and the Yankees, one of the five with no financial interest whatever in the minors as yet, stated that they expected to have such an interest shortly.

Landis's growing realization that the farm system was spreading rather than dying out, as he had been led to believe it would, did not change his opinion of it. His revulsion stemmed from his belief in local ownership of minor-league clubs and a free market in players to insure their advancement commensurate with their ability. Outside ownership, Landis maintained, imperiled local interest in the team and led "inevitably" to the assumption of the financial burden by the major-league club. This in turn created "unfair competition" for those clubs in the league that were independent and were struggling along on local resources. Eventually they too were driven to seek asylum, begging to be taken over by a major-league club. Outside control also hindered the progress of the players, Landis believed, because their advance depended upon the judgment and the interests of one club instead of upon several clubs through the free market and the draft.

Landis was well aware that the farm system was essentially a device for bypassing the rules. In 1921 he struck hard at gentlemen's agreements by freeing four players and fining the three major-league clubs that held them on minor-league teams by such agreements without having secured waivers or using options—the only "legal" exception to the no-farming rule. With the farm system the magnates were going the Commissioner one better and still staying within the rules limiting them to forty men. They no longer needed gentlemen's agreements to hide additional players. Ownership of a minor-league team gave them even more effective control of extra players; yet, technically, those on farm clubs had no major-league strings attached to them and therefore did not count in the forty-man limit.

Other opponents of the Rickey system, such as Ban Johnson and a minority of magnates, embellished Landis's arguments and supplied additional ones. They asserted that the farm system destroyed the independence of minor-league clubs as well as their free enterprise and initiative; then, if the major-league club decided to pull out, the minor was left debilitated, unfit to fend for itself, like a pampered household pet suddenly turned loose. Opponents thought farms harmed the players, who became puppets and had their path to advancement narrowed by abuse of the reserve clause through the vitiation of the waiver, draft, and player-limit rules.

Another objection was that the farm system added to the monopolistic character of baseball. Mike Kelly of the American Association likened major-league owners of farms to absentee landlords, "the curse of Ireland." Through their ownership the majors were able to dominate the minors at National Association meetings. As president Bonneau Peters of the Shreveport club said: ". . . our vote does not count very much. Those fellows [farm club presidents] are all instructed in all of our league meetings how to vote [on] certain matters in the league." One of the chief complaints of the minors themselves was that the parent club in need of reinforcements sometimes reached down in mid-season and plucked a minor-league favorite from the roster. Such raiding was particularly resented when the local team had a chance to win the championship of its league. Major-league clubs claimed that they tried to avoid this subversion of civic pride and interest, but, as one minor-league executive pointed out, the function of the minors was to develop men for the majors, not for local interest.

Rickey defended the farm system as a benefit rather than a bane to both the players and the minor leagues. Players received more attention, better instruction, and faster promotion, since it was to the interest of the parent club either to advance them or to sell them. Rickey, who could make a sophist tongue-tied with envy, asserted that ownership of farm clubs was really only the result of ownership of players: "We only own clubs because of our ownership or [correcting himself quickly] the production of free-agent players and no place to put them." The farm system was also a boon to the minors, according to Rickey. It gave them a stability that made them more attractive to local fans. In fact, Rickey went as far as to say that "the farm system was the savior of baseball, and without it today [1951] it is a problematical question whether you would have minor league baseball in the smallest minors at all."

More and more, baseball men came to agree with Rickey or at any rate to follow him. Even Barney Dreyfuss and Frank Navin became converts. Dreyfuss, mentioning players he had to let go because they were not quite ready for the Pirates and he had no place to store them, said that whether "you do believe in owning minor-league clubs or not . . . you have to have them yourself in order to put your ball players out on option." Likewise minor-league owners increasingly saw the advantage of major-league sponsorship and sought it out. As one of them said in trying to peddle a controlling interest in his club: "[I am] anxious to get a big league club to help me . . . I found out you can't get by without assistance from the majors." Even Landis had to admit that at Chattanooga in 1929 the hotel was "filled with minor-league people begging major-league clubs to take them over."

Yet there was little Landis could do about the farm system. It did not violate the existing rules, and he could not change the rules since he lacked power to legislate. He could, however, rail against the farm system and harass the magnates who had farms. At the joint major-league meeting of 1928 he called the roll and asked each club to disclose its minor-league holdings; when some of the owners reported losses on their minor-league operations, Landis told them he wished their losses were fourteen times greater.

But when Landis publicly attacked the farm system in 1929, Sam Breadon made a spirited defense and told Landis to his face at a joint meeting that he had "gone out of his way to hurt my business" and that his speeches gave the idea that "a foreign interest" went into towns and stole away the clubs from the people. The St. Louis owner quoted from a batch of lengthy communications from minor-league owners which pointed out the benefits they had gained from the sys-

tem and declared their gratitude. Upon this, Landis expressed cha-
grin that the minors were "almost unanimous on the proposition that
they wanted to be pulmotored" and "raped." He seemed particularly
astounded that some AA minor-league clubs had gained control of
still lower-classification clubs.

There was one other step Landis could take against the farm system. If he could not make the rules, he could interpret them, and
henceforward he was to watch closely for infractions and "illegal" disposition of players within a farm system. When he detected what he
considered ill-usage of players, he interceded to declare them free
agents, and often liberated them in wholesale lots.

But these measures turned out to be only rearguard actions. Landis
eventually went down in defeat on the principal issue of his twenty-
four-year administration, the farm system. That failure disproves the
myth of his omnipotence, just as his selective severity in disciplining
players and owners punctures the myth of his fearless, even-handed
disposition of justice. Even his reputation as "friend of the players"
needs modification, since it was based primarily on his liberation of
so many players from the "chain gangs" of farm systems.

Neither does the myth that Landis "saved" baseball and revived interest in it after the Black Sox scandal bear up under the facts. What
really saved baseball, legally at least, for the next half century was
the protective canopy spread over it by the United States Supreme
Court's decision in the Baltimore Federal League anti-trust suit
against Organized Baseball in 1922. In it Justice Holmes, speaking for
a unanimous court, ruled that the business of giving baseball exhibitions for profit was not "trade or commerce in the commonly-accepted
use of those words" because "personal effort, not related to production, is not a subject of commerce"; nor was it interstate, because the
movement of ball clubs across state lines was merely "incidental" to
the business. It should be noted that, contrary to what many believe,
Holmes did call baseball a business; time and again those who have
not troubled to read the text of the decision have claimed incorrectly
that the court said baseball was a sport and not a business.

Nor did Landis revive popular interest in Organized Baseball after
the Black Sox scandal, as is commonly believed. Attendance picked up
sharply as soon as the World War ended—before Landis entered the
picture—and it continued to climb. The fans were not turning out to
see Landis, colorful as he was. They were captivated by the batting
exploits of Babe Ruth, of whom more in the next chapter. It was
Ruth, as sportswriter W. O. McGeehan said, who shook the fans out
of their shock and bewilderment over the scandal and enabled the
baseball magnates "to take heart and to talk about the immortality of
the great American game" once more.

BASEBALL FORECAST: RAIN

by GERALD HOLLAND

Drawing by B. Wiseman first published in *Sports Illustrated*, interpreting the United States Supreme Court's decision in the Baltimore Federal League case.

But Landis did make a significant contribution to Organized Baseball. He kept the magnates in line to a greater extent than before—or since, for that matter. More important, he provided a symbol that reassured the public of baseball's honesty and integrity, so much so that, even after the magnates recovered from their fright over the Black Sox and began having second thoughts about Landis and the commissionership, they found it expedient to maintain the status quo while he lived, for to alter it would appear to be casting virtue into the street.

21

ENTER A SULTAN

THE 'TWENTIES ushered in changes in the fashion of playing baseball as radical as those in female attire and behavior. The pendulum of power swung decidedly toward the hitters. Batting averages went up, scoring increased, base stealing declined, and home runs, once as rare as a woman's drinking or smoking in public, became a regular feature of baseball. What caused this transformation?—the introduction of a livelier ball, the elimination of freak pitches, particularly the spitball, and the greater number of new baseballs used in each game.

Baseball officials and the ball manufacturers denied any deliberate intent to increase the resilience of the ball. They attributed the obvious spurt in batting to the use of better-quality yarn made of Australian wool, which was available after the war, and to tighter winding made possible by improved machinery. However, years later George Reach of the A. J. Reach Company admitted that his factory had enlivened the official ball from time to time and also deadened it when it got too lively.

Restrictions on pitching further aided batting. In February 1920 the joint rules committee of the major leagues made it illegal to tamper with the ball or apply any foreign substance to it, in effect banning such pitches as the emery ball, licorice ball, mud ball, and, most important, the spitball. No official explanation was given for outlawing the spitball, but for years a variety of objections had been made against it. Even the thought of pitchers expectorating on the ball was repulsive to some people. In fact, the American Association had already banned all freak pitches in 1918 on pain of a $25 fine for each offense. In the majors, however, the controversial "spitter" was not entirely proscribed, so that it took time for the full effect of the ban to be felt. Some pitchers were granted the right to continue using it. Upon the representations of "Spittin' Bill" Doak, seventeen active

pitchers who relied on the spitball for their effectiveness—and therefore their livelihood—were registered and exempted from the rule.
Some of them, notably Jack Quinn, Red Faber, and Burleigh Grimes,
the last to use it legally, pitched many more years and thus gave the
lie to the frequent contention that the pitch was hard on the arm.

The third innovation came after a pitched ball struck and killed
Ray Chapman in 1920. To reduce the danger of a batter's getting
"beaned," precaution was taken from then on to substitute a new ball
whenever the one in play became even slightly scuffed or soiled, because a pitched ball with a rough spot or scrape can swerve ("sail")
dangerously, since it is more affected by air currents than a smooth
one. But protecting the batter in this way added to the pitcher's woes.
Before, he often worked with a roughened, loose-covered, softened
ball; now he had to use a smooth, white, tight-covered new ball at all
times. It was harder to grip and to "put stuff on," it was more visible
and inviting to hit, and it also went faster and farther when it was
hit.

In 1925 a gesture was made toward redressing the balance. Pitchers
were allowed to use a resin bag for drying their fingers in order to
help them grip the ball better. This humane act on their behalf
caused a tiff that added to the tension between Landis and Johnson.
The National League readily agreed to the measure, but the American was against it for fear it would open the way to a return of freak
pitches. Consequently, the matter was referred to the joint rules committee, where a majority voted in favor of resin. Umpires were to
carry a small bag of it for pitchers to use if they requested it. But Ban
Johnson, declaring that the American League could nullify the committee's decision, forbade resin bags and served notice that he would
suspend anyone who used one. Johnson's announcement was interpreted as a slap at Landis, whose affirmative vote had been instrumental in carrying the measure through the rules committee.

It took considerable face-saving to overcome the seeming impasse.
Landis announced that the question was "not a matter for league contention" but "merely an aid to the pitcher as an individual." The
American League magnates met and passed a resolution calling for
compliance with Landis's directive that all umpires carry little mesh
bags of resin and produce them if asked. But they also resolved that
all team managers would be instructed "to request" their pitchers not
to ask for resin! Thus was the tempest over a resin bag settled. But
the American League's "artistic retreat," as a *Times* reporter called it,
put another chink in Johnson's waning power.

Another boon to the defense in general was the introduction in
1920 of the Bill Doak fielder's glove by Rawlings Sporting Goods

Company of St. Louis. In contrast with the earlier "pancake" style of glove, it had a natural pocket because of the longer, inward-curving thumb and the leather laces between the thumb and first finger. The laces could be adjusted to increase the size of the pocket. Later a small piece of flat leather was added, through which the laces ran; this innovation reduced the possibility of the player's grabbing one or both of the laces as he plucked the ball out of the glove to throw it. Fielding averages improved appreciably and the new-style mitt was popular among professionals and sandlot players for thirty years.

Denials, explanations, and "scientific" tests of the ball notwithstanding, baseball was a changed game, and it was the increased power of the offense that revolutionized it. The playing records were unmistakable proof. Combined major-league batting averages for 1920 were nearly 30 points higher than in 1915 and about 45 points higher by 1925. More batters became .300 hitters. In 1915 there were nine of them, but in 1927 there were thirty-five. The records show only four .400 batting averages between 1901 and 1920: those of Lajoie, Jackson, and Cobb (twice). But from 1920 through 1930 there were eight of them—twice as many in half the time: those of Cobb, Heilmann, Terry, Sisler (twice), and Hornsby (three times). With the heavier hitting went more scoring; by 1925 major-league teams were averaging two and a half more runs per game than in 1915.

Still, a person who was not convinced, or did not want to be, of the change in the ball could say that such figures indicated only that the pitchers were not as good as they once were. However, the amazing increase in home runs could not be thus explained away. Too many baseballs were bouncing off the fences or soaring over them. In 1915 major-leaguers hit 384 home runs. In 1920 they made 631. By 1925 the figure climbed to 1167, and in 1930 it jumped to 1565, quadruple that of 1915. Even the consumption of baseballs reflected what was happening. The National League alone used 22,095 of them in 1919, and the number increased each year so that by 1924 it reached 54,030. For the entire six years, 252,865 were used. Heydler attributed the increase to the longer spring exhibition-game schedules and to the greater number of balls used in the World Series. Ebbets thought another reason was that fewer balls were being returned from the stands. But the main cause was that more were being hit into the stands in the first place, not only during games but in batting practice.

As is now openly acknowledged, the ball was made even livelier in 1930. The "rabbit" in it really jumped that year. As one wag said, if you held a baseball close to your ear and listened intently you could hear the beat of the rabbit's heart. No fewer than twenty hitters batted .350 or better. Nine entire teams averaged .300 or more in hitting, and almost three and a half more runs per game were scored than in 1915.

As batting power increased, base stealing was on the way to becoming a lost art. Between 1921 and 1930 inclusive, there were 13,759 bases stolen, an average of 1.117 per game, which was only about half as many as in the previous decade when 26,734 were stolen, an average of 2.215 per game. In 1914 no fewer than thirty-four players stole twenty or more bases, but in 1923 the number shrank to eleven. Why try to steal a base and risk being put out when the chances of the batter's smashing the ball off the fence or over it were so much greater than they used to be?

The catalyst of change in the relationship between the offense and the defense in baseball was George Herman Ruth. In 1919 he startled the baseball world by hitting 29 home runs, breaking Ed Williamson's record of 27 made for the Chicago White Stockings back in 1884. The best that any twentieth-century player had done before Ruth was 24, made in 1915 by Cactus Cravath of the Phillies.

Ruth's bat was the medium. The club owners got its message and quickly translated it into a livelier ball. As Ring Lardner phrased it,

> . . . it ain't the old game which I have lost interest in it, but it is a game which the magnates has fixed up to please the public with their usual good judgment. . . . the master minds that controls baseball says to themselfs that if it is home runs that the public wants to see, why leave us give them home runs, so they fixed up a ball that if you don't miss it entirely it will clear the fence, and the result is that ball players which used to specialize in hump back liners to the pitcher is now amongst our leading sluggers.

In 1920 Ruth, then with New York, followed up with a stupendous total of 54 homers, and the Yankees doubled their attendance of 1919, setting a league record of 1,289,422, which stood until they themselves broke it in 1946. Ruth did even better in 1921. In what was probably his best season, he knocked out 59 home runs, drove in 170 runs and scored 177 himself, and made 204 hits totaling 457 bases for a batting average of .378. Ruth's highest home-run total for a season, 60 in 1927, was regarded as untouchable. It was not surpassed until 1961, when Roger Maris, another Yankee player, hit 61. Before retiring, Ruth amassed a grand total of 714 home runs, unsurpassed until 1974 by Henry Aaron.

Nevertheless, raw figures alone do not reveal the extent to which Ruth dominated his era. They do not show how he outdistanced his contemporaries. For example, his 60 home runs of 1927 represented 13.7 per cent of all the home runs hit in the whole American League.

He hit more homers that year than each of twelve entire major-league
teams. In his career Ruth hit a home run on the average of every 11.7
times at bat, a frequency percentage unequalled by other famed slug-
gers. In 1961 Branch Rickey estimated that a player would have to
hit about 180 home runs in a season to spread-eagle the field as Ruth
did, because overall home-run production by that time was more than
triple that of 1927. In addition, Ruth was one of the rare power hitters who also made a high percentage of safe hits. Only a handful of
players have surpassed his lifetime batting average of .342. He also
holds the lifetime record for bases on balls, 2056, many if not most of
them given intentionally, so feared was he as a home-run threat.

Because of his unequalled reputation as a home-run hitter, Ruth's
pitching skill is sometimes overlooked or slighted. But he was one of
the best of pitchers before Red Sox manager Ed Barrow switched him
to the outfield permanently in 1919 in order to have the advantage of
his batting power in every game. In 1915 his earned-run average,
1.75, was the best in the league. He never lost a World Series game,
and he pitched 29 consecutive scoreless innings in Series play, a record not broken until 1961 by Whitey Ford of the Yankees. Ruth even
won six out of nine pitching duels with the star Walter Johnson,
three of them by 1-0 scores. It should also be remembered that Ruth
was a fine outfielder—fast, a good judge of a fly ball, and a strong,
accurate thrower. He played first base, too, upon occasion!

Ruth was unmatched as a baseball gate attraction. Overnight he
became a national hero, idolized wherever he went. As early as September 1920 a Cincinnati businessman wrote: "Ruth is now known all
over the country if not the world. The opportunity to let the fans here
see him 'in action' would be a treat and incidentally a financial success." Thousands swarmed to the parks, many of them not so much to
see the game, a reporter said, as to watch Ruth "in a supreme moment." He attracted people who might be untutored in the subtleties
and refinements of inside baseball but who could understand and re-
spond to the clear, uncomplicated drama and beauty of one of his
towering drives, which had the directness and impact of one of Jack
Dempsey's knockout punches and which inspired the neologism
"Ruthian."

Towns on the Yankees' spring-training exhibition-game schedule
stipulated in their contracts with the Yankees that Ruth had to appear, and all along the exhibition route crowds came to see him. To
cite but one example: Lake Charles, Louisiana, declared a half-holiday "Babe Ruth Day" when he and the team came to town in March
1921. Banks and businesses closed, and most of the townsfolk jammed
the park and hung on trees and telegraph poles to see the game. A

Sporting News writer in 1920 snickered that Ruppert and Huston, "those excellent sportsmen," were willing to show Ruth in certain cities for only 85 per cent of the take and did not ask the mayor of each city to shine Ruth's shoes, nor did they demand the cotton crop for the privilege of their visit.

No athlete ever had greater renown. Details of his measurements and what purported to be his daily diet appeared in the newspapers. Many printed a syndicated box called "What Babe Ruth Did Today," showing his daily performance on the field. In 1920 he received $500 for sitting at a prominent table in Edelweiss Gardens, Chicago, for two evenings and making a speech, the gist of which was, "I haven't much to say and I hardly know how to say it, but I hope you all have a helluva good time." From time to time proposals were made in the United States Congress for a commemorative Babe Ruth stamp. He was not only "the Babe" but "the Bambino," "the Colossus of Clout," and "the Sultan of Swat." To other players he was "the big guy."

In terms of purchasing power, Ruth was the highest-paid player ever. His initial salary when he broke in with Baltimore was $600. He was getting $10,000 with the Red Sox when they shipped him to New York. There his Boston salary was doubled in 1920 and tripled in 1921. In 1922 he signed a five-year contract for $52,000 a year, an astronomical figure in those days, but the New York *Times* pointed out that he was "head and shoulders over the rest" and worth whatever he was paid. His value was shown by the fact that the ball club insured Ruth for $300,000 for nearly a decade. His annual salary for the years 1927 through 1929 was $70,000. He reached his peak income with $80,000 in the depression years of 1930 and 1931. There is a story that when he was holding out for more money in 1930, someone suggested that he should be more modest in his demands; after all, there was a depression, and he was asking for more money than President Hoover was getting. "What the hell has Hoover got to do with it?" Ruth supposedly replied. "Besides, I had a better year than he did." All told, Ruth made about a million dollars in salaries and ten World Series shares, and it is estimated that he made as much as another million from exhibition games, movies, radio, and endorsements.

The Yankees could well afford to pay him these huge salaries. New York was the largest baseball market, and Yankee Stadium, opened in 1923, was the biggest park in baseball. The stadium was made to order for Ruth. Since he was a left-handed "pull" hitter, most of his hits went toward right field. He could hit home runs anywhere, but the Yankee management made sure that he would get enough of them in New York by locating the right-field bleachers only 296 feet from home plate behind a low fence.

What manner of man was Ruth? To write about him, Arthur Daley of the *Times* once said, is like trying to paint a landscape on a postage stamp. With the passage of time, professional athletes become sportsmen in the way politicians become statesmen after they retire or die. Myths replace or dilute truth. So with Ruth. His escapades have often been euphemized as an outlet for healthy animal spirits and sweetened with saccharine stories of visits to sick boys in hospitals.

Ruth did genuinely like youngsters, but he scarcely qualified for Big Brothers of America. If he had, he would not have excited the perfervid acclaim that he did. The route to the common man's heart is paved with ribaldry and excess. What English king was more famous than Henry VIII? On the score of profligacy Ruth was well talented. He was a roisterer, hard-drinking and hard-swearing. He was always himself, natural, uninhibited, and undisciplined. No modern homogenized ball player was he. He was not even pasteurized. He was straight from the cow. Roger Kahn, one of the few who have portrayed him realistically, saw him as a man of "measureless lust, selfishness and appetites."

Ruth's bleak childhood explains much about him. He was not an orphan, though the myth that he was persists. His father, a Lutheran, was a Baltimore saloonkeeper. His mother, Kate Schamberger, was Catholic, and Ruth was one of two surviving children out of eight; she died when he was seventeen. His father, who had remarried, was killed in a street fight with his brother-in-law, but not until after Ruth was already in the major leagues. Ruth's childhood was not an enviable one. He was turned loose by neglectful parents on the tough streets of the neighborhood and among the hard characters of his father's saloon. That he became a juvenile delinquent is not surprising. "I was a bad kid," he said later.

At seven Ruth was placed in St. Mary's Industrial Home for Boys, an institution operated by the Brothers of the Xaverian Order for orphaned, wayward, incorrigible, and otherwise unfortunate lads. Ruth was in and out of St. Mary's five times, and during his twelve years of residence he learned the tailoring trade and played baseball. It was there in 1914, when Ruth was nineteen years old, that Jack Dunn signed him for trial with his Baltimore Orioles and assumed guardianship over him, since Ruth was still under age.

When he first came up, Ruth was a big, strong youth over six feet tall and weighed 195 pounds. He had not yet acquired the big belly that gluttony gradually grew for him. But he had the large head, blue-black hair, prominent, flat nose, massive shoulders, powerful biceps and wrists, incongruously slender, ballerina-like legs and ankles, and pigeon-toed walk so easily distinguishable and so familiar to fans. He needed no number on his uniform for identification. Off the field he dressed well, wore a camel's-hair coat and often a tan cap, and chewed a big cigar.

At bat he stood with the forward (right) foot closer to home plate than the left, his back turned somewhat toward the pitcher. In this "closed stance," as it is called, he gripped a heavy (47-ounce) bat at the end of the handle and moved it back and forth slowly and easily, the way a cat lashes its tail, as he peered over his shoulder awaiting the pitch. He swung the bat from his shoestrings, putting his whole body into a quick, rhythmic swing that followed a slightly upward arc, the better to lift the ball into the bleachers. When he hit one over the fence, he jogged around the bases with little, mincing steps, his arms bent, elbows close to the body, and tipped his cap as he crossed home plate. Home runs are no longer a novelty, but anyone who ever saw the Babe knows that no one ever hit them as stylishly and as dramatically as he did. He was awesome even in failure. When he swung and missed, as he often did, his follow-through propelled his body almost completely around and twisted his legs together like ropes. The crowd shuddered and buzzed: "What if he had connected?"

Inevitably, Ruth and Cobb were compared. They still are. But comparison of them as players is fruitless. The two great stars epitomized different eras and styles of play. One might as well try to compare a mastiff and a greyhound, or a grizzly and a tiger. But their personalities and temperaments can well be contrasted as representing different kinds of crowd appeal. Ruth was a "natural" ball player endowed with extraordinary gifts. He seemed to play ball almost by instinct. He did not, and there was no necessity for him to, pay attention to the "fine points" and tricks that Cobb employed and emphasized. Ruth took baseball, and indeed life, as it came. He was extroverted. Cobb was introverted. Ruth was bluff, hearty, and given to coarse humor. Cobb was cold and humorless. Ruth moved easily among people and had great rapport with crowds. Cobb was aloof, paranoid in his suspicions of people, and evoked their fear and respect rather than their affection. Ruth was profligate of his body and money. He squandered both in high living and dissipation until he was persuaded to establish a trust fund to enable him to live comfortably after he was through as a player. Cobb, on the other hand, husbanded his dollars and was more sparing of himself off the field.

Studies have shown that, if deprived children are suddenly exposed to plenty, they will grab frantically at everything offered them, whether they have use for it or not. Ruth fit this mold well. His mean, untutored youth ill fitted him for the sudden fortune and fame that fell to him. No doubt it accounts for much of his unrestrained pursuit of hedonistic pleasures. For him, money was for spending, and extravagance was his companion. "Ruth," wrote a reporter, "is just a great, big, overgrown boy. He loves a good time, and . . . there are always scores of idolizing admirers on hand to see that he does not suffer any pangs of ennui." By the time that statement was printed (1925) Ruth had owned nine of the most expensive automobiles available. Once in St. Louis during a hot spell he wore twenty-two silk shirts in three days and left them behind for the hotel chambermaid.

Just as money to Ruth was made for spending, so training rules were made to be broken. As sportswriter Tom Meany said, he kept the hours of a night watchman. Once Ping Bodie, who shared a room with Ruth on the road before Ruth began indulging in the extravagance of having his own private suite, was asked what it was like to room with the Babe. "I don't know," he is said to have answered. "I never see him. I room with his suitcase."

Of all the sobriquets given Ruth, that of "Sultan of Swat" is most appropriate, because "sultan" applied to him off the field as well. He dallied with women all over the circuit and also patronized the brothels. The clubhouse boy who sorted Ruth's pile of mail was under instructions to throw away all letters except "those with checks or from broads." His suite was always well stocked with prohibition liquor and beer. Two other Yankee players had standing invitations to his nightly revels. By midnight Ruth, having taken his pick from among the girls, bid the rest of the company good night and shooed them out the door. When the ball club left each town along the spring exhibition trail, a number of females always appeared at the station to see Ruth off. "So long, girls," Ruth would bellow as the train pulled out, "see you next spring." At one of their annual dinners the baseball writers included a song "I Wonder Where My Babe Ruth Is Tonight" in their show. The words went, "I know he's with a dame, I wonder what's her name," and so on. His dalliances sometimes proved costly. "There have been several cases, some of which have reached the newspapers," revealed a reporter for *Collier's Weekly*, "where the big, guileless Babe in the Wood has committed himself with women and been 'taken' for amounts ranging from a few hundred to thousands of dollars."

Ruth had trouble on the field too. We have already seen how he ran afoul of Landis for barnstorming. Once he jumped into the stands after a heckler, and he had several fracases with umpires. He punched one of them, Brick Owens, in 1917 and another time threw dirt in umpire Hildebrandt's face. Such umpire-baiting and his general disregard for authority brought Ruth a fine and a stern letter from Ban Johnson in June 1922, which read in part:

> I was keenly disappointed and amazed when I received Umpire Dineen's report recounting your shameful and abusive language to that official in the game . . . last Monday. . . . Your conduct . . . was reprehensible to a great degree—shocking to every American mother who permits her boy to go to a game. . . . It is a leading question as to whether it is permissible to allow a man of your influence and breeding to continue in the game. . . . A man of your stamp bodes no good in the profession.
>
> I have a thorough knowledge of your misconduct where you dragged your teammates to a violation of club rules absolutely at variance with discipline and loyalty. . . . It seems the period has arrived when you should allow some intelligence to creep into a mind that has plainly been warped.

Ruth's unbridled misbehavior laid him low in 1925. That spring he was stricken on the way north and finally had to be hospitalized at Asheville, North Carolina. The club put out a story that his collapse was caused by an attack of indigestion—"the stomach-ache that was heard round the world," as it was labeled. After being brought back to New York, he collapsed again on the way to St. Vincent's Hospital. There he underwent an operation, so the *Times* reported, for removal of an intestinal abscess. It was not his first illness. At least three times in as many years he was laid up, either by flu or by a throat infection, according to the newspapers, but never so seriously as in 1925. Not until June was he able to return to the lineup.

He was soon trying to pick up where he had left off in his outside activities. At last in August, Miller Huggins, the long-suffering little manager of the Yankees, forced a showdown in St. Louis after Ruth stayed out all night for several nights. Huggins imposed a $5000 fine (another Ruth record up until then) and suspended him for "misconduct." Asked if that meant drinking, Huggins answered, "Of course it means drinking, and it means a lot of other things besides." Highly indignant, Ruth called the fine "a joke": "They don't fine bootleggers $5,000, and men get out of murder charges for less." Then declaring that Huggins was "incompetent" and vowing that "either he quits or I quit," Ruth took off to see Colonel Ruppert. But the Colonel backed his manager. "Huggins is running the club, not Ruth," he said. After being closeted with the owner for half an hour, Ruth emerged to tell the waiting reporters that he was sorry and was going to apologize to

Huggins and behave himself. Huggins kept the suspension on for several days, and the fine stuck until after the manager's death in 1929, when general manager Ed Barrow returned the money. Ruth's batting average fell to .290 for the season, and he hit only 25 home runs.

But some of his best seasons lay ahead, and apparently his second marriage in 1929 tamed him down somewhat. His first one, entered into when he was only twenty, did not work out, and he and his wife were living apart when she died in a fire. His second wife was a widow with an eleven-year-old daughter, whom Ruth formally adopted, together with another girl, seven years old, who was a ward of Ruth and his first wife.

Ruth's life was that of a Horatio Alger hero insofar as it depicted the familiar climb from lowly boyhood state to adult success. But there the parallel ends. Unlike the Alger heroes, Ruth did not struggle upward laboriously by dint of hard work and patient penny-pinching, and his way of life was foreign to their stuffy, moralistic code. Indeed it may be that Ruth owed much of his tremendous popular appeal precisely to his flouting of the earlier code. Embodying as he did the more unrestrained spirit of the post-World War One era, in which Victorian conventions and precepts were breaking down, Ruth probably attracted masses of people who wished subconsciously that they were free and courageous enough to cast aside social restrictions the way he did. At the same time Ruth's warm, generous qualities helped people to overlook his foibles and transgressions. His liking for children, which was real despite all the treacle printed about it, was in accord with the hero *Gestalt*—sentiment and softness under a rough, uncouth exterior.

Whatever the judgments of his personality and character, they cannot efface his massive contribution to the baseball business or his name from the American scene. It may be trite to say his like will probably never appear again, but it is no less true. It was Ruth, as much as Judge Landis, who revived public interest in baseball on the muddy heels of the Black Sox scandal and who revolutionized the style of play in the process. By making the game more exciting, he enabled baseball to fend off competition from other spectator sports and to remain foremost in the 'twenties. His matchless drawing power created new fans and widened people's awareness of baseball, both at home and abroad. His gate appeal was also indirectly responsible for the construction of Yankee Stadium—"the house that Ruth built"—and for the general rise in the level of ball players' salaries. Finally, he very likely was the greatest all-round baseball player in history.

22

SOME OTHER NOTABLES

THE ADVENT of Babe Ruth and that by-product of his prowess, the lively ball, did nothing to correct the imbalance in major-league competition in the 'twenties. In the American League, New York won six of the ten championships. Washington and Philadelphia shared the other four, two apiece. In the National League, New York also won the most—four. St. Louis followed with three, Pittsburgh took two, and Chicago managed one. In other words, half of all the pennants went to the two New York clubs. Five other clubs divided the remaining ten, so that a nine-team majority was left empty-handed. Plainly, the reserve clause, vaunted as the indispensable guardian of competition, was even less effective in performing its function during the 'twenties than it had been in the two previous decades.

The six victories of the New York Americans signalled the founding of the so-called Yankee dynasty, a juggernaut that would sweep to twenty-nine pennants and twenty world championships in forty-four years. Various reasons have been advanced to account for the Yankees' success, including their able leadership, efficient organization, and expert scouting staff. All these they had, but it was money that was responsible for the initial leap forward that carried the club to its first three championships (1921–23) and thereby disproved the baseball axiom that pennants cannot be bought. Those victories were won by teams whose backbone consisted mostly of former Red Sox players masquerading in Yankee uniforms.

Ruppert's financial aid to Harry Frazee converted the once-powerful Red Sox into a Yankee fief. Frazee, who habitually invested in Broadway shows, was constantly short of money. To obtain cash he began selling his players. In the course of a few years he disposed of more than a dozen stars to the Yankees, and in the process changed the Red Sox into the "Dead Sox" and evoked widespread criticism of the "unholy alliance" between the two clubs. Commissioner Landis

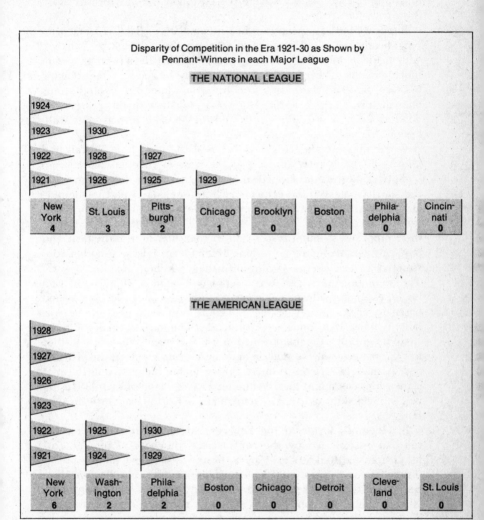

Disparity of Competition in the Era 1921-30 as Shown by
Pennant-Winners in each Major League

THE NATIONAL LEAGUE

New York 4	St. Louis 3	Pittsburgh 2	Chicago 1	Brooklyn 0	Boston 0	Philadelphia 0	Cincinnati 0
1924							
1923	1930						
1922	1928	1927					
1921	1926	1925	1929				

THE AMERICAN LEAGUE

New York 6	Washington 2	Philadelphia 2	Boston 0	Chicago 0	Detroit 0	Cleveland 0	St. Louis 0
1928							
1927							
1926							
1923							
1922	1925	1930					
1921	1924	1929					

could do nothing, since there was no rule to prevent such tie-ups until appropriate measures were passed following the Hornsby stock controversy of 1926.

Ruppert's initial expenditure had a cumulative effect. His first winning teams generated huge gate receipts, thus giving the Yankees, who made more money than any other club, the wealth to create more winners. They could keep the supply of good players flowing because they had the means to enlist able administrators and scouts who in turn could bait the best young talent with the prospect of good salaries, World Series cuts, and the glamour of becoming Yankees if they made the grade.

When Ruppert and Huston purchased the club from Farrell and Devery in the winter of 1914–15, it was, in baseball parlance, a humpty-dumpty team, lodged in seventh place. The improvement in the first few years of the colonels' regime was due in part to the purchase of first baseman Wally Pipp from Detroit and Home Run Baker from Philadelphia. Although Baker had left the Athletics, he was still their property, so the Yankees had to coax him from retirement and pay considerable money to Connie Mack for his release. Another constructive move was the signing of manager Miller Huggins in 1918. The "demi-tasse manager" was a scrawny little man with a reputation for baseball shrewdness, which he gained as a major-league second baseman and manager of the St. Louis Cardinals, the job he was holding when Ban Johnson recommended him to the Yankees. But the appointment of Huggins opened a rift between the colonels that left the manager in the middle and caused him much travail. Huston had pushed his friend Wilbert Robinson for the job, but Ruppert turned him down and then went ahead to sign Huggins while Huston was still on duty overseas. From then on Huston had little use for Huggins.

In Huggins's first year the Yankees finished fourth. They rose to third in 1919, aided by the controversial purchase of pitcher Carl Mays from the Red Sox for $40,000 in mid-season. But the big breakthrough came in 1920 with the acquisition of Ruth from Boston. Ruppert paid $125,000 for Ruth and advanced Frazee a loan of $350,000, taking a mortgage on Fenway Park as security. Frazee gradually liquidated the loan by periodically transferring more players to the Yankees. The Yankee team was further strengthened that year by the addition of Bob Meusel, who turned out to be a powerful hitter and the outfielder credited with the strongest throwing arm in baseball in his day. Nevertheless, the Yankees again finished third.

In October they made another key move. Because of the death of Harry Sparrow, they needed a new business manager. Again they found their man in the lush Boston oasis—the Red Sox field manager, Edward G. Barrow. At fifty-two Barrow had a proven baseball background based on a wealth of experience as player, newspaper reporter, major-league field manager, and minor-league president. In his quarter of a century as business manager for the Yankees, he was to build them into Organized Baseball's strongest organization, and he deserves, along with Ruppert's bankroll, much of the credit for the club's success.

Working in close concord with Huggins, Barrow wasted little time and less sentiment in continuing the piecemeal dismemberment of the Red Sox. In a four-for-four trade with them, New York got two pitchers, a catcher, and an infielder. Most important of these were Waite Hoyt and Wally Schang. Hoyt, who had attended the same Brooklyn schools as the author of this book, P.S. 92 and Erasmus Hall, and became known as "the Flatbush Schoolboy," was an outstanding right-hand pitcher for the Yankees in his eight years with them. Schang provided them a first-class catcher and good switch hitter for five seasons. The added strength was enough to bring the Yankees their first pennant.

Ruth was not the only playboy on the team, and Huggins at best would have been hard put to control his men. His task was magnified through lack of united support from the front office because of Huston's attitude toward him. Things got so out of hand at the New Orleans camp the spring following their first pennant that a reporter was constrained to write a story captioned "Yankees Training on Scotch." The transgressions continued into the season. Then one day Judge Landis appeared in the Yankee clubhouse armed with a detailed report of the players' outside activities, supplemented with an autographed picture. He proceeded to give them a severe tongue-lashing, much to their discomfiture. What had happened was that the club had employed a detective who, after ingratiating himself with the players, accompanied them on the road and on their evening rounds in each city. He kept a careful record of their misbehavior and even had them pose for a group picture—glassy-eyed, coats and ties off, brimming glasses raised—and then got them to autograph it!

According to conventional canons, the Yankees' conduct should have affected their playing, cost them the pennant, and taught them and the youth of America a lesson. It did none of these. They won again in 1922, helped, to be sure, by more Boston reinforcements: Everett Scott, considered the best shortstop in the league, and two more pitchers, Sad Sam Jones and Bullet Joe Bush. But with a strong St. Louis Browns team pressing them hard, the Yankees again dipped into Boston in July and came up with outfielder Elmer Smith and third baseman Jumping Joe Dugan, who took over from Home Run Baker, then beginning to slow down. Even at that they finished barely ahead of the Browns.

That fall the Yankees lost their second successive World Series to their unfriendly neighbors, the Giants, but for Huggins defeat proved a blessing in disguise. Huston wanted him fired forthwith, but Ruppert stuck with him. The discord was resolved when Huston sold out to Ruppert. Thus the Yankees were under single ownership for the first time and Huggins was left firmly entrenched. He responded with another pennant in 1923, which made the Yankees the only American League team until then to win three straight since the Detroit Tigers in 1907-9. To do it they reached out again—the reader can guess —to Boston for more pitchers, Herb Pennock and George Pipgras, a youngster who was to be very successful in the future. They now had a formidable pitching staff, the "Six-Star Final" sportswriters called it —Shawkey, Mays, Hoyt, Jones, Bush, and Pennock, all except Shawkey former Red Sox. In a fitting climax to the opening of their new stadium, the Yankees also went on to beat the Giants in the third successive "subway series" between the two New York teams and the first million-dollar World Series gate.

In 1924 a well-balanced, determined Washington team led by another "boy manager," Stanley Harris, beat the Yankees for the pennant. The leader of the pitching staff was Walter Johnson, still good enough to win 23 games in his eighteenth year with the same team. Relief pitcher Fred "Firpo" Marberry saved many a game with his blinding fast ball. Herold "Muddy" Ruel did the catching. He had been one of the Yankees' expendables traded off to Boston, but he quickly developed into an outstanding catcher. A strong infield, including manager Harris himself at second, and a capable outfield backed the pitchers. Sam Rice and Leon "Goose" Goslin, outfielders who later made the Hall of Fame, provided the main batting strength.

Washington's first pennant set off an emotional reaction in the capital and in much of the country that was memorable even for the 'twenties. "On the banks of the Potomac there is bedlam and madness," said the *Times.* "Thousands are tramping the streets in the wildest celebration ever seen in baseball." President Coolidge presented manager Harris with a silver cup and solemnly told the players that they had "made the national capital more truly the center of worthy and honorable national aspirations."

In the World Series Walter Johnson was the focus of the fans' sentiment. To them he was Sir Walter, the hero who had toiled so long and so patiently for so many arid seasons, finally to win his reward—

the opportunity to pitch in a World Series. All over the country people were rooting for him to win. The Giants, however, dampened
their hopes by beating Johnson in the two games he started. But he
had another chance in the seventh and deciding game, in which the
Giants were undone by some incredibly bad luck. They were two
runs ahead in the eighth inning when a ground ball hit by Bucky
Harris took an unexpected bounce past their third baseman, and the
tying run scored. Johnson was summoned from the bull pen to face
the Giants in the ninth. He held them at bay for four innings. Then in
Washington's half of the twelfth, fortune frowned on the Giants twice
more. First Hank Gowdy, the Giants' catcher, missed a pop fly that
would have been an easy out if his foot had not got caught in his
mask, which he had accidentally thrown in his own path as he started
after the ball. Thus given another chance, the batter, Muddy Ruel,
made a two-base hit. Johnson, the next batter, reached first base on a
Giant error. Again the ball was hit toward third base, this time by
Earl McNeely, Washington's center fielder, and again it took a crazy
bounce that enabled Ruel to score the winning run from second base.

Washington was again league champion in 1925 but lost to Pittsburgh in the World Series. The Senators took three of the first four
games, two of them with Johnson pitching, but the Pirates rallied to
win three in a row and beat Johnson in the deciding game. Although
Johnson was batted hard throughout, Harris kept him in the game
and was criticized by Ban Johnson afterwards for sacrificing a world
championship to "maudlin sentiment."

Beginning in 1926 the Yankees started their second cluster of three
straight championships. To do it they had to rebuild. The team had
reached its nadir in 1925, dropping all the way to seventh place. It
was the year of Ruth's illness and drastic fine. It was also the time
when several regulars, the worse for wear, had to be replaced. Whitey Witt gave way to Earle Combs as center fielder and leadoff batter. Shortstop Everett Scott was benched in May, ending his endurance record of 1,307 consecutive games. A month later Lou Gehrig
took over from Pipp at first base, where he was to stay for nearly
fourteen seasons and a record 2,130 consecutive games.

Gehrig was a home-grown product, having been born in New York
City and having played ball at Manhattan High School of Commerce
and at Columbia University. Plodding perseverence and a rugged
physique that seemed indestructable made him a great player. Although Gehrig was a competent fielder, it was his batting that made
him outstanding. He was a left-hand power hitter, and with him batting fourth behind Ruth the Yankees had the most devastating two-
man slugging combination in baseball. Excellent performer though he

was, Gehrig lacked flair and color. He was also fated to play in the
shadow of Ruth and, later, Joe Di Maggio. Consequently he never received quite a full measure of acclaim until after fatal illness ended
his career.

For 1926 Huggins gambled on a new second-base combination:
shortstop Mark Koenig, who had played in only a few games the
year before, and Tony Lazzeri, purchased from Salt Lake City, in
whose rarefied air he had hit 60 home runs. Lazzeri had never seen a
big-league game, let alone played in one, but he and Koenig came
through, and the Yankees made the steep climb back to first place,
where they remained for the next two years.

But the 1927 team is the one best remembered. In fact many sportswriters rate it the peerless team of baseball history. Its credentials are
impressive. It won 110 games, a record at the time, and finished 19
ahead of the runner-up Athletics. As a team the Yankees made 158
home runs, nearly three times as many as the Athletics' 56, the next-
highest club total. That was the year Ruth hit his 60; Gehrig had 47.
Between them they accounted for more than 24 per cent of the home
runs of the entire league (439). In runs batted in, Gehrig led the
league with 175. Ruth drove in 164. Besides hitting for distance, they
also hit for high average, .373 and .356 respectively. While Gehrig
and Ruth were the heaviest part of the attack, three other Yankee
regulars averaged better than .300—Combs, Meusel, and Lazzeri.
The last two joined Ruth and Gehrig in knocking in more than a
hundred runs each. Only four other players in the league accomplished that feat. The team also possessed strong pitching, led by
Hoyt, Pennock, Pipgras, and Urban Shocker, a spitball pitcher. Backing up these four was Wilcy Moore, the league's leading relief pitcher
that year with 19 victories.

Yet formidable as the 1927 Yankees were, it is doubtful that they
were the best team ever assembled. Obviously, they had tremendous
batting strength, but time has magnified it. They were not all home-
run hitters. The next highest total on the team after Gehrig's was Lazzeri's 18. That only five other players in the league hit more than ten
homers is testimony to the skill of Ruth and Gehrig (and Lazzeri as
well), but it is contradictory to the impression since given currency—
that all the Yankees were prolific home-run hitters. They did not all
have high batting averages either; several of the regulars hit below
.300.

A look at the Yankees' defense raises further doubts about their
being the nonpareils of baseball history. Although the pitching was
strong and the outfield excellent, the catching at best was only adequate, and there have been any number of better infields. A good ar-

gument can be made for the relative merits of half a dozen other teams, including some later Yankee combinations. However, trying to single out one team as the "all-time best" is an entertaining but futile pastime.

If one must indulge in this diversion, he can make a good case in support of the Philadelphia Athletics of 1929–31. Since 1922 Mack's club had gradually been moving upward after its seven seasons at the bottom following his wrecking of the 1914 team. In fact, the Athletics made a serious bid for the pennant in 1925 and in 1928 nearly nosed out the Yankees. In 1929 there was no stopping them. They swept to the pennant by an 18-game margin over the second-place Yankees.

It was a splendid team that Mack led to his last three championships. To assemble it he and the Shibes, entering the spirit of the prosperous 'twenties, went into the minor-league market and paid what were then big prices for likely players. Jack Dunn's Baltimore team was loaded with them. Players on International League teams were not subject to major-league draft, so Dunn could hold onto them until he was offered high prices. While he was waiting, his Baltimore club won seven International League pennants in succession. Dunn's prize commodity was pitcher Lefty Grove, for whom the Athletics paid $100,600 in ten annual installments. They also paid a big price to Dunn for another pitcher, George Earnshaw.

Those two became the aces of Mack's pitching staff. They were big, tall, rangy men who overpowered batters with blazing speed. Grove was possibly the best left-hander in history. Any time he pitched, the Athletics were almost a sure bet to win. In their three successive championship seasons, he accounted for 83 victories while losing only 15 games. He also ended his career in the select group of 300-game winners. Earnshaw did not last as long as Grove, but at his peak he was right behind him, for he won 67 games in the three pennant years while losing but 28. Three other important purchases from Baltimore were Rube Walberg, a big left-hand pitcher who won many games, second baseman Max Bishop, and shortstop Joe Boley, both highly competent fielders.

The Athletics' Portland, Oregon, farm club was the source of their first-string catcher Mickey Cochrane. It is doubtful if anyone ever played the position better than he did. Cochrane was full of fire and dash, and the fact that he batted third on a team with many good hitters is testimony to both his batting ability and speed of foot. Following Cochrane in the batting order were outfielder Al Simmons and first baseman Jimmy Foxx, who completed a row of hitters only a trifle less dreadful to pitchers than the Ruth-Gehrig-Meusel trio of the 1927 Yankees. Mack handed over several second-string players and a reported $40,000 to Milwaukee for Simmons. He was amply repaid. Simmons became a first-class outfielder and one of the best right-hand hitters that baseball ever produced. Like so many topflight batters, Simmons used an unorthodox style: he broke a cardinal rule of form by seemingly stepping away from the pitch instead of into it— "putting his foot in the bucket." But he could still hit pitches on the outside corner of the plate effectively because he used a long bat and gripped it at the end of the handle. Twice he won the batting championship of the league, and he finished his twenty-year major-league career with a lifetime average of .334.

Jimmy Foxx was only sixteen when Mack picked him up at the bargain counter upon the recommendation of his old third baseman Home Run Baker. Foxx, a stocky, powerfully built man called "The Beast," came up as a catcher. After experimenting with him at that position and at third base, Mack finally settled him at first. Although Simmons hit with great power (307 homers in his career), Foxx was the team's leading home-run hitter. One year he hit 58 of them. His career total of 534 made him one of the very few players who hit more than 500 home runs.

At third base Mack had a Philadelphia sandlot product, Jimmy Dykes, a good fielder and timely hitter, who had been with the club ever since 1918. Besides Simmons, the team had two other good outfielders who were hard hitters, Mule Haas and Bing Miller. In addition, the Athletics' bench was well supplied with reserve strength. Four members of the Athletics, Grove, Cochrane, Simmons, and Foxx, were eventually elected to the Hall of Fame, as against the Yankee quintet from the 1920's, Ruth, Gehrig, Hoyt, Pennock, and Combs. On balance, the 1927 Yankees had a stronger batting punch, but in other respects the Athletics were their equal or superior.

In the National League McGraw and his Giants reached their pinnacle by winning four straight times (1921–24), the first team to do so since Chris Von der Ahe's famed St. Louis Browns of the 1880's. Those four pennants brought McGraw's total to ten—a record for a manager equalled only by Casey Stengel, who, coincidentally, was an outfielder on the first three Giant winners of the 'twenties. McGraw's teams still played the earlier style of baseball. They featured speed, a versatile attack, and tight defense. It was only gradually that major-league batters tried to adopt the Ruth style of digging in firmly at the plate, gripping the bat down at the end, and swinging freely for distance.

One of the ingredients of the Giants' success was Charles Stoneham's cashbox. The Giants used it to acquire outstanding players from other clubs in the league and expensive recruits from the high minors. It was the "slum clubs" of the National League, Boston and Philadelphia, that were most susceptible to the lure of New York money. Nearly every season those two clubs battled each other to keep out of last place. They were caught in the vicious circle of having to sell their best players to make ends meet and then being stuck at the bottom of the league, where they could not make money because they had sold their best players. In return for giving up a key man, they usually received a second-string player or two, but hard cash provided the yeast. To help the fans swallow the concoction, they spread a frosting of flimflam over it: the club was "being strengthened" or it was "being rebuilt," and so on. In any event, Philadelphia and Boston fans could take consolation in knowing that they were always welcome to come out and watch their departed heroes when they returned in New York uniforms.

The Giants' habit of lifting a key player off the Philadelphia or Boston roster occurred with clocklike regularity. In August 1919 they secured Art Nehf, a first-class left-hand pitcher, from Boston. In June 1920 they acquired Dave Bancroft, the Phillies' star shortstop. In June of the following year, after Landis blocked them from getting Heinie Groh from Cincinnati, the Giants again shopped in Philadelphia, this time coming up with hard-hitting outfielder Emil "Irish" Meusel, brother of the Yankees' Bob. In July 1922 they obtained Hugh McQuillan, leading pitcher of their Boston satellite, to plug the hole created when Landis banished Phil Douglas. These four transactions formed a pattern. In each case the Giants were in a nip-and-tuck, mid-season fight for first place. In each case the addition of an outstanding player promised to tilt the balance in their favor. And each time a bundle of cash was the chief factor in consummating the deal.

These, of course, were not the only transactions the Giants made in the early 'twenties, nor were they the only ones in which cash figured prominently. Jimmy O'Connell, one of the "goats" of the 1924 scandal, had come to the Giants in 1923 from the Pacific Coast League, reputedly for $75,000. Mention has already been made of the Giants' $65,-000 purchase of Jack Bentley from Baltimore the same year. It is only right to add that the Giants did not secure all their players through large expenditures of cash. Some of McGraw's best acquisitions—men like Frank Frisch, Fred Lindstrom, Travis Jackson, and Bill Terry, all of whom played prominent roles in making four straight pennants possible—were recommended by his scouts, former players, or friends.

The mid- and late-season descents on the wretched Phillies and Boston in the midst of a tight race did not always succeed in nailing the pennant to New York's flagpole. The Giants finished second to

Cincinnati in 1919 in spite of the help from Nehf, the reinforcement from Boston, although probably nothing could have carried them to the pennant that year with the knavish Chase and Zimmerman in their line-up. Even with the aid of Bancroft, the ex-Philly, the Giants also finished next to Brooklyn in 1920. But the other Giant forays paid dividends. The timely acquisition of Meusel in 1921 and McQuillan in 1922 were vital in winning the pennants those years.

The purchase of McQuillan from the Boston Braves also led to a reform in the trading regulations. Coming as it did in July, with the Cardinals in the thick of the pennant race, the deal outraged St. Louisans, who were already seething over the Yankees' acquisition of Joe Dugan, a purchase that threatened to thwart the Browns' pennant hopes. Browns officials, players, fans, and civic groups had loudly denounced the Dugan deal and protested to Ban Johnson and Judge Landis. Now in the wake of it St. Louisans saw the other New York club resorting to the same tactics in an effort to snatch the pennant from their Cardinals. They saw their fond prospects of a double St. Louis victory being dissipated by the "unsporting" use of the New York clubs' financial power. F.W.A. Vesper, president of the St. Louis Chamber of Commerce, declared, "When a team hard-pushed in mid-season can conjure a neighboring city into selling its stars and to make sure-proof of their flag, baseball has reached a point where the pocketbook and not the club or players become the deciding factors." And all this was to say nothing of the plight of Boston fans, helpless before the two-pronged New York raid on their teams. The uproar impelled the magnates to pass a rule the following winter barring player transactions between major-league clubs after June 15 except at the waiver price.

Regardless of how they collected their players, the Giants of 1921–24 obviously had to be good to win four times in a row. It is difficult to choose the best of the four teams, but the 1922 edition serves as well as any of them as a basis of discussion. The strongest part of it was its infield, one of the best ever put together. At first base was tall, gangling George Kelly. Infielders had to be wide of the mark indeed for their throws to get past "High Pockets," so long was his reach. Kelly also had an exceptionally powerful throwing arm that enabled him to whip the ball across the diamond to third base with great speed, as the Yankees learned in the final game of the 1921 World Series. Kelly was also a dangerous distance hitter, always a threat to break up a game with a long drive.

Frank Frisch was the second baseman. He was not the smoothest of fielders but his ground-covering ability and spirited play more than compensated. He was a switch-hitter (one who bats right-handed against left-hand pitchers, and vice versa) and one of the relatively few really good ones. He was also an outstanding base stealer, and no one was faster going from home plate to second on a hit. Frisch's speed, which earned him his nickname "the Flash," his frequent head-first slides, and his penchant for losing his cap whenever he raced to get under a pop fly made him the most spectacular player on the Giants.

Bancroft was one of the best shortstops in baseball and the field leader of the Giants. He was given the responsibility of acting as the team's "cutoff" man. More than any other manager, McGraw stressed the cutoff play, a strategem that in effect doubled the chances of making a put-out. To execute it successfully the cutoff man had to size up the situation and make a split-second decision. When an outfielder throws to head off a runner trying either to score from second base or to advance from first to third base on a hit, the cutoff man must decide whether to intercept the throw. If he thinks the throw will beat the runner, he lets it go through; if not, he "cuts it off" in the hope of catching the batter, who may assume that the outfielder's throw is going all the way to home plate or third base and try to reach second on his hit. The quick-thinking Bancroft was especially good at making this play. In one World Series he cut down Yankee runners no fewer than three times. Rounding out the Giants' 1922 infield was Heinie Groh, then the premier third baseman in the league. When McGraw was frustrated in his attempt to get Groh in 1921, he arranged a trade with Philadelphia for second baseman Johnny Rawlings (plus outfielder Casey Stengel) and stationed Frisch at third. When he finally secured Groh for 1922, McGraw was able to move Frisch to second, where he belonged.

In Ross Youngs the Giants boasted a right fielder of exceptional gifts. He was a tough competitor who did everything well—hit, field, throw, and run. Stengel and Bill Cunningham alternated in center field, taking the place of George Burns, another fine outfielder, who had been sent to Cincinnati after the 1921 season together with catcher Mike Gonzalez and another one of Stoneham's checks, said to be for $100,000, for Groh. Irish Meusel completed the outfield. Behind the plate McGraw had no worries with two big brawny fellows, Frank Snyder and Earl Smith, doing the catching. Of the two, Snyder was the better receiver, but both swung potent bats. The pitching staff was competent but not outstanding, in fact not as good as that of the 1921 team.

The availability of good replacements played an essential part in keeping McGraw's pennant string unbroken in 1923 and 1924. Travis Jackson, an excellent fielder with a great throwing arm, took over as shortstop when Bancroft began to slip. When Groh developed a bad knee, Fred Lindstrom, only eighteen years old, filled the breach and developed into a fine fielder and hitter. And Bill Terry, a future member of the Hall of Fame and McGraw's successor as manager, was primed for first base, which he began sharing with Kelly by 1924.

Rejoice as McGraw might in his current champions, he nevertheless had reason for concern. He had watched the mounting popularity of Ruth and the Yankees with growing resentment. He and the Giants had long been the foremost names in baseball. They had reigned supreme among the actors and sporting crowd of Broadway. They had been the cynosure of New York's fans, who had paid relatively little attention to the Yankees until Ruth came along. Ironically, McGraw himself had helped lay the groundwork of Yankee rivalry. Knowing both Ruppert and Huston, he had introduced them to each other, and when he learned of their interest in purchasing a ball club, he had suggested that they buy the Yankees. He had also commended to the colonels Harry Sparrow, who became their first business manager. These Yankees were now elbowing him and the Giants from their accustomed position in the center of New York's baseball stage. Needless to say, the intrusion did not sit well with McGraw. He burned to thrash these upstarts in the World Series.

As indicated earlier in the chapter, he was partially successful. In the 1921 encounter the Giants came from behind and in a hard uphill fight won the final three contests to take the Series in eight games (that was the last series played according to the five-out-of-nine plan). Ruth missed the last three games, except for one appearance as a pinch hitter, because of an injury. The following year the Series between the two New York teams lasted only five games, and the best the Yankees could do was a tie in one of them. The tie occurred when umpire George Hildebrand called the game on account of darkness with the score 3 to 3 in the tenth inning, although there was still plenty of light left to play. The amazed fans concluded the stoppage was a put-up job to fatten the gate receipts by prolonging the Series. They had seen Hildebrand talking with Judge Landis in his box just before the game was stopped, so they assumed that it was Landis who had ordered the umpire to stop it. Angrily they milled around the judge, yelling "crook" and "robber" at him. "I may not be the smartest person in the United States," Landis is said to have exclaimed later, "but don't the damned fools think I know night from day?" Actually, Hildebrand had acted on advice from veteran umpire Bill Klem, who warned him that once another inning was started there might not be time to complete it before darkness set in. Landis acted immediately. Without consulting anyone, he took it upon himself to announce that the day's receipts, about $120,000, would be given to charity. His decision placated the public, but the owners, whose money he was disposing of, took a somewhat jaundiced view of it.

McGraw's elation at this second Series triumph over the Yankees was heightened by the impotence of their vaunted Ruth. The Giants' pitchers held him to only two hits and a miserable .118 average. But McGraw and the Giants had reached their high-water mark. As the reader will recall, they lost the next two World Series. The 1923 Yankee win over them spoiled McGraw's dream of being the first manager to capture three successive world championships. The defeat by Washington the next year was also hard to take, sealed as it was by the fluke plays in the final game.

It was Pittsburgh that toppled the Giants from the summit of the National League in 1925. An excellent infield leftside and outfield formed the hard core of the Pirates' team. Max Carey, center fielder and switch-hitting leadoff batter, had one of his best seasons, batting .343 and leading the league in stolen bases for the tenth time, a record. Flanking him was Clyde Barnhart in left and Kiki Cuyler in right field. Barnhart was a steady fielding, hard-hitting veteran. Cuyler was a sensational young player who had everything. His speed and strong arm ranked him among the leading outfielders. He could hit with the best of them, and it was his two-base hit off Walter Johnson with the bases full in the seventh game of that fall's World Series that finished Washington. In addition, Cuyler was an expert base stealer. With Cuyler, Carey, and George Grantham, their speedy first baseman, leading the way, the Pirates were a constant menace on the bases. And they were on the bases often. Practically all the regulars hit better than .300, and the team as a whole averaged .307.

The left side of the Pittsburgh infield remains unsurpassed. It is difficult to imagine anyone ever playing third base better than Pie Traynor did. The Pittsburgh star was tall, rangy, fast, and hard-throwing. He was especially adept at moving to his right, coming up with a hard ground smash hit over the third-base bag, and then rifling the ball across to first in time to get the runner. His ability to do this permitted him to play farther to his left away from the foul line than any other third baseman, so that he was able to intercept slow bounders hit to his left toward short. This ability of Traynor's in turn allowed Glenn Wright, the shortstop, to play deeper, thus giving him greater range in fielding balls hit hard to either side of him and, because of his powerful arm, still have time to throw the batter out. Wright and Traynor were both strong hitters as well. The Pirates had a good pitching staff but no standout. Their biggest winner was Lee "Specs"

Meadows, one of the first players to wear glasses, who won 19 games.

In 1926 the fruits of Branch Rickey's farm system ripened into the St. Louis Cardinals' first pennant and world championship. The most illustrious player on the team was Rogers Hornsby, manager and second baseman. Hornsby was a humorless baseball zealot. As the saying goes, he "ate, slept, and drank" the game. Betting on horses and playing the ladies' man were his only other interests. He neither drank nor smoked, and to preserve his batting eye he attended no movies and read nothing but newspaper headlines. Hornsby was not much of a second baseman, his well-known inability to handle pop flies being only the most glaring of his faults in the field. But at bat he was probably the best right-hand hitter in baseball history. His .358 lifetime batting average is second only to Cobb's .367, and he and Ty are the only twentieth-century players who averaged over .400 three times. In the five-year stretch from 1921 to 1925, Hornsby achieved an astounding .402 average. He won seven National League batting championships. Only Honus Wagner, with eight, did better. Nor do these figures fully reveal Hornsby's batting excellence. Not only did he hit often, he hit hard. He still leads the National League in slugging percentage (times at bat divided into total bases), and he made 302 home runs during his career.

Oddly, though, in the Cardinals' pennant-winning year Hornsby had what was for him a poor season: he averaged only .317. However, his teammate, first baseman Jim Bottomley, one of Rickey's first farm products, led the league in runs batted in, although his average also fell off to .298. Other ex-farmhands also helped. Young Tommy Thevenow performed brilliantly at short. He played in every game and led all league shortstops in chances accepted. Third baseman Lester Bell had his best season, hitting .325, the only time he was ever over the .300 mark. Fleet-footed Taylor Douthit gave the Cardinals first-class defense in center field. Another outfielder, Chick Hafey, was one of those talented players who gained recognition belatedly. He was a tall, broad-shouldered right-hand "pull" hitter. No one could smash the ball down the left-field foul line harder, and he had a throwing arm that matched that of Bob Meusel.

One of Branch Rickey's most advantageous trades was getting Bob O'Farrell from the Chicago Cubs the year before. O'Farrell was an excellent catcher. Although he was starting his thirteenth season in the majors, he proved to be one of the stalwarts of the team by catching 147 games and batting .293. Also helpful to the Cardinals was an early-season trade of outfielders, their Heinie Mueller for the Giants' Billy Southworth. This trade, initiated by McGraw, proved one of his worst. Southworth hit .320 and gave the Cardinals a very capable right-fielder, whereas Mueller failed with the Giants.

Another transaction that was crucial in winning the pennant was the acquisition of Grover Cleveland Alexander, the veteran right-hand pitching star. He was traded from the Cubs on waivers just before the deadline for the season. Although Alexander was past his prime, he was still a winning pitcher. He was also an alcoholic. But it was not so much his drinking that caused Joe McCarthy, the Cubs' new manager, to get rid of him. McCarthy had other heavy drinkers on the team. The problem was that Alexander was not always amenable to discipline. Adding to the difficulty was the fact that McCarthy had never managed or even played in the big league, and in the eyes of some of the players he was a "bush leaguer." McCarthy established his authority by getting rid of Alexander, the most prestigious member of the team. He sent him to the Cardinals, who had claimed him on waivers. Without the nine victories turned in by Alexander, the Cardinals could not have won the 1926 pennant. Other pitchers on whom the Cardinals relied were Flint Rhem, a young right-hander with a fast ball as fiery as his favorite beverage; Jesse Haines, an experienced knuckle-ball pitcher; and Bill Sherdel, a little left-hander whose specialty was a tantalizing slow ball.

An interesting member of the team was utility infielder George "Specs" Toporcer. No one today pays any attention to the sight of spectacles on a professional ball player, but in those days it was inconceivable that a person who wore glasses could hit and field in the major leagues. Toporcer was the first infielder to puncture this myth, and he did it before the development of shatterproof lenses. His natural position was second base, but with Hornsby a fixture at that position, Toporcer, who could have played regularly with a number of teams in the league, was relegated to the role of utility man and pinch hitter.

The Cardinals' first pennant, and the first for St. Louis since 1888, unleashed a wild celebration in the city that was comparable to the one with which Washington greeted its first pennant in 1924. A headline in the St. Louis *Globe-Democrat* read: "Armistice Day Recalled by Wild Orgy; Thousands Abandon Selves to Saturnalia of Celebration in Heavy Downpours of Rain." Fans carried signs reading "Hornsby for President; All the other Cardinals Cabinet Members." Two people were killed and thirty hurt in the celebrations.

The Cardinals then climaxed their successful year with a dramatic victory over the Yankees in the seventh game of the World Series. It is doubtful if any World Series story has been told more often. In the seventh inning, with the Cardinals leading 3 to 2, the Yankees had the bases filled with two out and the dangerous Tony Lazzeri coming to bat. In this tense situation manager Hornsby called the thirty-nine-year-old Alexander from the bull pen to pitch to Lazzeri. Alexander had already beaten the Yankees for the second time the day before. Now he struck out Lazzeri in the pinch. He then held the Yankees scoreless in the remaining two innings, and the Cardinals were world champions.

Pittsburgh returned to the top in 1927. They had finished only two games behind the Cardinals the year before and might have won but for dissension on the team. Fred Clarke, the Pirates' former player-manager and at that time a nominal vice president, irritated certain players by sitting on the bench and criticizing them. Team captain Max Carey and two others planned a meeting of the team with manager Bill McKechnie to discuss the situation. When McKechnie did not show up, they met anyway, but the players voted 18 to 6 in favor of Clarke. The news of the meeting got out, and the Pittsburgh owner cracked down on the three ringleaders: Carey was suspended without pay and then was sent to Brooklyn on waivers, and the other two, Carson Bigbee and Babe Adams, were released—despite the fact that they were the three senior members of the team. They appealed to Commissioner Landis, who referred them to league president Heydler. He exonerated the men of any wrongdoing but refused to interfere with the right of a club to suspend or release players.

The 1927 Pirates had essentially the same personnel as the team that had won two years before. Two outstanding exceptions were the remarkable Waner brothers. Lloyd, the younger, played center, and Paul right field. Both were slight men and very fast. Paul was one of the great hitters of baseball. His heavy drinking apparently relaxed him. It certainly did not interfere with his hitting. He finished with a lifetime average of .333 and was one of the handful of men who collected more than 3000 hits. Lloyd, who lacked Paul's power, was essentially a singles hitter and four times led the league in one-base hits. Both made the Hall of Fame. With Kiki Cuyler as the third outfielder, Pittsburgh possessed an outer defense rarely equalled. After winning the pennant by the narrow margin of a game and a half, they ran head on into the famous 1927 Yankee team in the World Series and were routed in four straight games.

In 1928 St. Louis was again the National League pennant winner. Several important changes had been made in the line-up since the Cardinals' 1926 victory. Playing second base was Frank Frisch, who had come to the club in the startling trade that had sent Hornsby to the Giants and caused the controversy over the sale of his stock in the

St. Louis club. Tommy Thevenow never fully recovered from a broken ankle he sustained in 1927, and the Cardinals had secured the veteran Rabbit Maranville, who played most of the year at shortstop. At third base little Andy High, who had a knack for getting hits when they counted, had replaced Lester Bell. The Cardinals also had a new catcher, Jimmy Wilson, obtained in a trade with the Phillies. Wilson went about his work unostentatiously, but he was a first-class catcher. In the World Series the Cardinals suffered the same fate as the Pirates the year before: the Yankees crushed them in four straight games.

While St. Louis and Pittsburgh were taking turns winning pennants, the Chicago Cubs were being rebuilt under the leadership of Joseph McCarthy, who later as leader of the Yankees was to become one of the most successful managers in baseball. McCarthy, who had assumed charge after the Cubs had finished last in 1925, had gradually pieced together a new team. His last and most important move was the addition of Rogers Hornsby. Chicago was Hornsby's fourth stopover on his travels from club to club in the National League. After St. Louis disposed of him to the Giants, he had another run-in with the front office and was traded off to Boston at the end of the 1927 season. He had been with the Braves only one year when they sent him to the Cubs in return for their usual trade goods—several mediocre players and $120,000 in cash. When the Cubs got Hornsby, W.O. McGeehan remarked that Phil Wrigley would probably have to raise the price of his chewing gum, or appeal to Chicagoans to chew more of it, to cover Hornsby's purchase price and salary. Hornsby played a significant part in bringing the 1929 pennant to Chicago by batting .380.

The Cubs' other power hitter was center fielder Hack Wilson, the most colorful member of the team. Wilson was a stumpy, square-shaped man with tiny feet but the barrel chest and biceps of a boilermaker. He always looked dirty on the field. No matter how neat and clean his uniform was at the start of a game, it became soiled as soon as the first pitch went past him, because of his habit of stepping out of the batter's box and bathing his sweaty hands and arms with dirt and then wiping them dry all over his uniform. Wilson loved to bat and preferred a high ball on the field—and a highball off it. Bill Veeck, Jr., tells of seeing Hack being sobered up in the clubhouse before a game by being doused in a tub of ice water. But Wilson never begged off from playing because of a hangover. In 1929 he had a fine year, averaging .345; however, his outstanding season was 1930 when he hit 56 home runs, a National League record, and batted in the stupendous total of 190 runs, a figure that has never been equalled.

In right field the club had none other than Kiki Cuyler, the ex-Pirate. Chicago was able to get him because he had clashed with his manager at Pittsburgh the year before. In 1929 he contributed a batting average of .360 to the Cubs' attack. The third regular outfielder, Riggs Stephenson, averaged a shade better, .362.

Like most pennant winners, Chicago had an effective pitching staff. It was headed by Charlie Root, who had a 19-and-6 record that made the best winning percentage in the league that year. However, Pat Malone, a big, red-faced fast-ball pitcher, was credited with more victories, 22, and Guy Bush, whose slight build belied his speed, accounted for 18.

Oddly enough, the Cubs were able to win the pennant by a wide margin despite the loss of their star catcher, Gabby Hartnett, who rates with the best catchers in baseball. He was a strapping fellow who liked to show off his splendid throwing arm by firing the ball around the infield during pre-game practice and after a put-out. He also liked to keep his pitchers alert by snapping the ball back to them after a pitch. Hartnett was a very good hitter who could drive the ball a long way. It was a sore arm that kept him out of the regular line-up, and the Cubs had to make a deal with Boston for Zack Taylor, an experienced man, to help out Mike Gonzales, the second-string catcher.

In the World Series that year Chicago lost to Connie Mack's Athletics in five games. This was the Series of the surprise pitcher and the ten-run inning. It appeared that Connie Mack's logical choice to pitch the opening game would be either one of his two stars, Lefty Grove or George Earnshaw, and everyone assumed that one of them would start. Instead he chose Howard Ehmke, a veteran who had pitched in only 11 games during the season. Ehmke not only won the game but set a new World Series record by striking out 13 Cubs. A myth has since grown up around this event, to the effect that Mack had selected Ehmke primarily for sentimental reasons—because Ehmke was approaching the end of his career and had never pitched in a World Series. But Mack's choice was based on sound strategy. He had every reason to believe that Ehmke, who was a right-hand sidearm pitcher with a good curve ball and good control, would be effective against the Cubs because their line-up was loaded with right-hand hitters (first baseman Charlie Grimm was their only left-hander) who were particularly potent against fast-ball pitching. Besides, Grove was bothered by a sore pitching hand, and Earnshaw was a fast-ball pitcher.

The ten-run inning burst upon the Cubs in the fourth game. The Athletics came to bat in the seventh with the score 8 to 0 against them and the game apparently lost, but in a remarkable display of batting power and aided by Hack Wilson's loss of two fly balls in the sun, they scored ten runs and won the game, 10 to 8.

The last National League pennant of the decade was taken by St. Louis after a sensational late-season winning streak in which they won 39 out of 49 games. Their pitching staff was strengthened by the emergence of Wild Bill Hallahan, another product of the Cardinals' farm system, into a first-rate pitcher. Hallahan was a short, compactly built left-hander who had had everything but control up to this time. Once he learned to get the ball over the plate, he became a star. The Cardinals also had help from the spitballer Burleigh Grimes, then thirty-eight years old, whom they got from Boston early in the season. Their excellent new shortstop was Charlie Gelbert, brought up from their Rochester farm the year before. However, the Cardinals lost their second World Series, this time succumbing to the Philadelphia Athletics in six games.

Of course all the outstanding players were not on pennant-winning teams. The first one who comes to mind is George Sisler. He was the sparkplug of the Browns in 1922, the year they might have won the pennant, instead of losing it by one game, had it not been for the late Yankee acquisition of Joe Dugan in the deal with the Boston Red Sox that caused such a hullabaloo in St. Louis. That year Sisler had as fine a season as any ball player could want. He not only batted a phenomenal .420 but hit safely in 41 consecutive games. He had already hit over .400 once before, in 1920.

Two Detroit outfielders, Harry Heilmann and Heinie Manush, between them accounted for half the league batting championships of the 'twenties. Heilmann won four of them, oddly in alternate years, and Manush the other. Heilmann attained the 1923 championship with a .403 average.

Although the Chicago White Sox did not recover for years from the decimation they suffered as the result of the scandal, they had some front-line players in the 'twenties, such as Red Faber, a spitball pitcher, and Ted Lyons, a polished performer who made pitching an art. Both pitched twenty years or more for the same club, both won more than 250 games, and both were elected to the Hall of Fame.

As some of the stars of the earlier era, like Cobb, Speaker, Collins, and Walter Johnson, faded from the scene during the 'twenties, a number of young players broke in who were to reach stardom in the future—men like Earl Averill, who became an outstanding slugger with the Cleveland Indians, Charlie Gehringer, who developed into one of the leading second basemen and hitters of baseball, and Mel Ott, who was to hit more than 500 home runs with the Giants.

The playing ranks were also enriched by the influx of men of Italian and Slavic extraction. The reader by now will recognize some of

these names: Tony Lazzeri, Babe Pinelli, Gus Mancuso, Mike Ga-
zella, Adam Comorosky, and John Grabowski. Like members of various other minorities, some anglicized their names: Frank Bodie
(Francesco Pezzolo), Peter Appleton (Peter Jablonowski), Joe Boley
(John Bolinsky), Al Simmons (Aloysius Szymanski), Lawton Witt
(Ladislaw Wittkowski), and Stanley Coveleski (Stanislaus Kowa-
lewski). The frequent appearance of similar names in major-league
box scores during the 'twenties and the increasing number of them in
later years reflected the so-called new immigration of the latter nineteenth and early twentieth centuries. Those were the years when people from southern and eastern Europe swarmed to the United States
by the million to work in the mines and factories or as unskilled laborers. Those of their offspring fortunate enough to make good in
professional baseball exemplified upward social mobility in much the
same way as the sons of Irish and German immigrants did in the
early years of baseball.

The 'twenties were also the heyday of those colorful incapables, the
Brooklyn Dodgers—or Robins, as they were then called. Baseball
lore is replete with oft-told anecdotes about the "Daffiness Boys," as
they are often referred to. What baseball devotee, for instance, has
not heard the one about the manager, Wilbert Robinson, "Robbie" or
"Uncle Wilbert," telling the team that he was forming a Bonehead
Club, to which a player would pay a fine every time he made a
"dumb" play—and then himself becoming the first member when he
gave the umpire an incorrect line-up. Or about Robbie's listing Dick
Cox on the line-up card because he could not spell the name of the
regular fielder, Oscar Roettger.

I well remember Robinson from the summer I spent on the bench
with him as the Brooklyn batboy. He was bumbling, very profane,
and very fat. Though outwardly gruff, he was generally popular with
Brooklyn fans and players. He was childishly superstitious, and when
things went wrong, as they often did, he blamed various jinxes. When
the team was in a losing streak, he would grumble, "We can't win in
this goddam park!" Robbie's warmth and simplicity made the fans
feel that they had a personal share in the fortunes of the team and in
helping him run it. He was always ready to argue strategy with them
under the stands or in the street, and he accepted taunts as personal
challenges. More than once I saw him step in front of the dugout to
shout back at some particularly loud-mouthed heckler.

Robbie handled the team with a light rein, leaving the players
largely on their own, off the field as well as on it. His rather slipshod
methods suited the kind of teams he had. Brooklyn in those years was
a way station for a good many players who had seen their best days
and were nearing the end of the road. Men like Dave Bancroft, Cot-

ton Tierney, Rube Bressler, Max Carey, Dutch Ruether, Spittin' Bill Doak, and Jughandle Johnny Morrison had been around the majors a long time. There was little that Robbie could have taught them even if he had had the inclination or the ability. But he did have a way of coaxing the most out of them. In 1924 the team finished second, only one and a half games behind the Giants, and in 1930, although the Robins ended up fourth, they were in close contention right up into September. But these facts are seldom allowed to detract from the team's reputation for zaniness.

Somehow Robbie always contrived to have some good, experienced pitchers around. He preferred them big and hard-throwing. None fitted his specifications better than Dazzy Vance, the star of the staff. Unlike men such as Alexander or Herb Pennock, Vance made pitching look as hard as it was. He exerted himself on every pitch, rearing back and firing the ball directly overhand. He had, as his nickname suggests, a dazzling fast ball. He also had a great curve ball—big, fast, and sharp-breaking—that made even the best hitters quail. "Big Daz," as Robbie called him, almost pitched the team to the pennant in 1924 when he won 28 games and lost only 6. That year he received the Most Valuable Player award over Hornsby, even though the latter hit .424. Vance led in strike-outs seven consecutive times, a National League record, and he finished up with a total of 197 victories, even though he was very late in finding himself because of wildness and arm trouble. He also won election to the Hall of Fame.

But the player most closely associated with the clownish antics of the Robins was Babe Herman. Brooklyn's Babe was one of the most cheered, booed, laughed-at, and loved players in Flatbush. He was the goat of most of the stories told about the Robins. He is remembered as a slightly crack-brained outfielder who got hit on the head with fly balls, slid into bases already occupied by teammates, carried smoldering cigar butts in his pocket, and told an encyclopedia salesman, "No, my kid can walk to school." His tall, lean frame and rather gawky movements somehow added to the impression of ineptitude.

But the real Babe Herman has become lost in the fables about him. He was a pleasant, decent man and far from stupid, especially at contract time. Contrary to the popular notion, he was not such a poor outfielder as he has been made out to be. His habit of wandering uncertainly under fly balls made him look ineffectual, but he usually ended up by catching them. One thing nobody could deny: Babe could hit. And like most players, he loved to swing the bat. One day I was kneeling in the "on-deck" circle next to him while he was waiting to bat. The man ahead of him walked, and the bunt sign was flashed to Herman. Babe took me into his confidence: "If Robbie thinks I'm gonna bunt, he's crazy. Watch this!" He stepped up to the plate, purposely bunted foul twice, then drove the next pitch off the right-field wall. "I shoulda known the Babe can't bunt," Robbie grunted contentedly. Herman's lifetime average came to .323, and in 1930 he hit .393 but missed the league batting title because Bill Terry chose that year to hit .401.

The ramshackle, off-beat character of the ball team was complemented by the disarray in the Brooklyn club's front office. Ebbets died in April 1925, on a day the Giants were scheduled to open a three-game series in Brooklyn. His partners, the McKeever brothers, and Robbie decided to play the game anyway. Said Robbie, "Charley wouldn't want anybody to miss a Giant-Brooklyn series just because he died." At the funeral Ed McKeever caught pneumonia and he died a week later. Steve McKeever, Robbie, and the club's directors then met and elected Robbie president, a choice that was the equivalent of selecting Falstaff to play Hamlet.

Robbie played it straight. He appointed Zack Wheat acting manager, left the bench, and began watching the games from a box seat like a proper president. But when the team did poorly he returned to the bench for extended intervals without ever relieving Wheat of his title. The result was that no one, least of all Wheat, knew who was running the team. Robbie finally ended up back in the dugout permanently, though still president, and Wheat's brief quasi-managerial career simply trickled away like water in desert sand.

The next year, 1926, a grievous quarrel erupted between Robbie and old Steve McKeever that stultified the administration of the club. The two ceased speaking to each other even to exchange insults, and the next several years were taken up chiefly with bitter in-fighting as the McKeever faction tried to force Robbie out and the Ebbets heirs strove to keep him in.

Meanwhile the team became notorious for the variety of bizarre ways in which it managed to lose ball games. The prize example was the time Babe Herman, after making a two-base hit with the bases full, wound up on third base with two other Brooklyn runners already there and gave Boston an easy double play and Robbie near apoplexy. Impossible? Not for the Daffiness Boys. This is how it happened. With one out, Herman drove the ball to the outfield. Hank De Berry lumbered home from third and scored. Dazzy Vance, after waiting on second to make sure the ball was not caught, plodded to third, started for home, and then, fearing he might be thrown out at the plate, decided to go back to third. Meanwhile, Chick Fewster, seeing the ball fall safe, dashed around from first base to third. Herman, trying to stretch his double into a three-base hit, also headed full speed for third, but when he arrived and found Vance and Fewster already in occupancy, he started back to second. Fewster, assuming that he was automatically out, stepped off the bag and was tagged by the Boston third baseman, who then threw to second to get the retreating Herman. Fans came to expect such lapses. The contagion even spread to the announcer, who called out one day, "Will the fans along the left field railing please remove their clothes?"

That Brooklyn fans continued to come out to Ebbets Field, if only for laughs, testified to their unshakable attachment to "their" team. Just as for children it is sufficient that candy be sweet, so for local fans the flavor of Brooklyn baseball satisfied, regardless of quality. Their craving for the game sprang from deep sources. No city had a longer baseball tradition, reaching back as it did to the amateur era of pre-Civil War days when Brooklyn was already gaining a reputation as the "city of baseball clubs." And there was always room to play ball in Brooklyn. Even as late as the 1920's many sections of the borough were still semi-rural in character, dotted with numerous vacant lots and fields where youngsters could choose up sides and play ball. In fact, some areas of Brooklyn, such as Flatlands, were still given over to truck farming.

But the ball-playing center was the Parade Grounds. That vast, rectangular open area in the heart of Flatbush was ringed by twenty-one baseball diamonds. On the Coney Island Avenue end of the grounds was a clubhouse equipped with locker rooms and showers. A host of independently organized amateur teams of all ages and qualities from all over Brooklyn played there weekends at two-hour intervals from 10 a.m. to 6 p.m. They "booked" their own games and usually played for anywhere from $5 to $25 and a ball. On Saturday afternoons the more stable teams played regularly scheduled games under the aegis of the Brooklyn Amateur League in either its junior or senior division. On certain weekday evenings strong industrial-league teams competed in twilight games. Still, there was never enough space to accommodate all the teams that sought permits for a diamond from the park department. Thousands of people turned out to watch and often to wager small amounts on the teams, and each of the outstanding ones among them was cheered by its own ardent following.

Besides the youngsters, there were older men who, unable to give up the game of their childhood, "worked out" afternoons, evenings, and weekends at the Parade Grounds. Among them was a sprinkling of former "professionals" who had "been away" for a trial with a professional club or, like Joe Wall, had played briefly in Organized Baseball. Some of them practically lived at the grounds, ever ready to talk baseball with boys or hit fungoes to them, sometimes even before the snow had melted. Brooklyn youth extracted additional baseball sustenance from the public schools, which sponsored elementary and high-school teams that played according to schedules and eligibility rules established by the P.S.A.L., the Public School Athletic League. Parochial and other private schools had their own teams as well.

Contact with baseball was therefore well-nigh inescapable for Brooklyn boys. They grew up in an environment pervaded by the game. Many opportunities to play it on sandlot and school teams beckoned them. Consequently generations of them became thoroughly imbued with baseball from earliest childhood. The game supplied a common interest that brought boys into a relationship that required them to judge one another primarily on merit and thereby helped them develop mutual respect despite cultural differences.

The cohesive value of baseball was particularly important in a polyglot city like Brooklyn. In my own neighborhood in Flatbush, for instance, there dwelled within the radius of a few blocks boys of English, Irish, Scottish, German, Italian, Austrian, Spanish, Swedish, and Chinese extraction, as well as Protestants, Catholics, and Jews. All of them played baseball side by side and against each other on the sandlots and in the schools.

Baseball was also a means of drawing boys out of Brooklyn's various ethnic neighborhoods in which the older people—Irish, Polish, Italian, and others—tended to huddle in familiar and secure proximity with their own kind. Their more venturesome offspring formed teams like the Celtics, the Polish Falcons, and the Lafayette Triangles (who were Italian-Americans) and sallied forth from their own areas to the Parade Grounds to play against boys of different backgrounds. All this is to say that a long tradition and grassroots experience of baseball helped forge the tribelike sentimental attachment of Brooklynites to the Brooklyn ball club.

This attachment was reinforced by the fans' sense of closeness to "Uncle" Robbie and the players, many of whom lived near Ebbets Field during the season. Robbie's wife, "Ma," and a good many of the players' wives were also known to the fans, and I still remember being taken into the park one day by Burleigh Grimes's wife and watching the game from an unaccustomed place, a reserved seat. Steve McKeever sipped his glass of milk every day at his seat in the last row of the lower tier behind home plate, where fans could easily approach (and reproach) him. His daughter Dearie was a popular, smiling favorite of countless youngsters who daily vied with each other for the privilege of opening the door of her garage across the street from Ebbets Field when she drove up, because they all knew that she would reward the lucky one with a pass to the game. Until he died in 1925 Ebbets could also be seen at the park, and Charles Ebbets, Jr., lived the year round on Sterling Street only a few blocks away. In short, the Brooklyn leaders were not remote from the fans.

Unlike modern baseball executives, they had no need to make studied efforts to create rapport. It was already there.

Ebbets Field itself contributed to the easy informality and intimacy between Brooklyn fans and their team. Ball parks were relatively small in those days, and Ebbets Field was cozier than most. The stands were close enough to the playing field for the players' facial expressions to be clearly seen. Their shouts could be heard distinctly, and they could hear those of the fans. As Zack Wheat jogged out to his position in left field at the start of each game, the fans in the bleachers opposite would shout, "How many today, Zack?" and he would always look over to them and hold up two fingers, signifying that he expected to get two hits. The bull pens at Ebbets Field were not hidden, as they usually are now; they were right in front of the left-field bleachers and the right-field stands, in full view of the fans, who could lean over the railing and banter with the pitchers and catchers assigned there. Whenever a threatening situation arose during the game and the manager signalled for a pitcher to start warming up, everyone could see him rise, remove his jacket, and begin throwing. To see a relief pitcher getting ready created an air of expectancy and excitement that added to the drama of baseball.

At Ebbets Field, in other words, fans had a feeling of "being in the game," as they still do at Boston's old Fenway Park. Modern parks are generally better appointed and much more comfortable than the old ones, but they have sacrificed intimacy for size. The players, seen from a distance, seem unreal and mechanical, more like puppets than flesh-and-blood athletes.

Cementing the bond between Brooklyn fans and the team was their detestation of the New York Giants. Nothing unites a tribe more effectively than a common foe, and the Giants served well to rally the various neighborhood clans of Brooklyn behind their team. Nowhere in baseball history can one find anything to equal the heartfelt antipathy between the two teams and their followers. Much of it grew out of a kind of provincial inferiority complex buried in Brooklyn breasts. In its way it was a miniature manifestation of the old metropolis-versus-hinterland antagonism that has threaded through American history ever since colonial times. Brooklyn had been a separate city until it was reluctantly amalgamated, along with the other boroughs, into a single New York City in 1898. But Manhattan continued to be equated with New York, even though Brooklyn's population was larger. Manhattan was Wall Street, Broadway, wealth, and urbanity. Brooklyn was an outland, more provincial and less sophisticated. "New Yorkers" spoke of "the wilds of Flatbush," and Brooklynites resented their pretensions.

The two ball clubs reflected these contrasts: the Giants were a rich, swaggering, winning team, kings of baseball, at least until Ruth and the Yankees came along; the Robins muddled along, occasionally winning, more often inept, and sometimes financially strapped. Zack Wheat told me that twice he loaned Ebbets money to meet his payroll. Even in 1889 the victory banquets of the two teams conveyed the difference in tone between them. The Giants attended their dinner in full dress, accompanied by a coterie of actors and other notables. The Brooklyn players attended theirs in business suits, and minus the celebrities.

Animosity between the clubs' management also played a part in their rivalry. The respective owners feuded publicly with each other in the local newspapers as far back as the 1890's. Later on, the lasting vendetta between McGraw and Robbie helped keep the temperature high between the teams and their adherents. Then, of course, competition was immeasurably sharpened because of the fact that New York was the only city boasting two teams in the same league. Comparisons were therefore not a matter of theory and conjecture. The two teams were measured each year in twenty-two hard-fought, sweaty encounters that were played before partisans of both sides, not just in front of a home audience, as was the case everywhere else in the league. In baseball's traditional seventh-inning stretch, the fans rise in the latter half of the seventh inning when the home team comes to bat. At Ebbets Field there was always a large contingent of Giant fans who, as the Giants came to bat at the start of the inning, stood up amidst cries in Brooklynese of "Sit down, yez bums yez!"

Brooklyn fans took the interborough rivalry more seriously than the "New Yorkers." Their team was usually the underdog. Their feeling of inferiority and probably subconscious envy of Manhattan made beating the Giants important and satisfying. So no matter how poorly the Robins did on the whole, if they trounced the "Jints," those "swellheads" from New York, with reasonable frequency, Brooklyn fans could put up with them.

The fans' feeling of close association and identification with the home team was not, however, peculiar to Brooklyn, although it may have been more intense there than elsewhere. In the early decades of this century, fans everywhere felt it. They took their local team and their baseball seriously. The pennant races were exciting and important even to the countless Americans who had never been to a big-league game, and the famous players were familiar and real even to those who had never laid eyes on them. Ultimately, it was this profound emotional grip on the public that gave the game genuine vitality in the era from 1903 to 1930 and made it a golden age for baseball.

APPENDIX

Sundries:

Awnings and flags
20 Curtains and pulleys
5 Desks
9 Cuspidors
Office safe and vault
Ticket-counting table
10 Ticket boxes
Copying-press and table
Printing press and type
Caps and badges for employees
Caps and uniforms for scorebook boys
Rubber stamps
Pictures of players and grounds
Hat-and-coat rack
1 dozen Office chairs
Tickets, account books, stationery, etc.
Stove and fixtures for office
Bed, bedding, etc., for groundkeeper in office
Bulletin board and fixtures for clubhouse
4 Player benches and awnings

Ground Tools and Implements:

Hand lawn mower
Horse lawn mower
Crosscut saw, 2 hand saws, 1 compass saw

461

Hatchet
Tape line
Brace, 4 bits
2 Spades, 10 shovels, 4 picks
Hammer, crossbar, level
4 Post-hole diggers
6 Brooms
Plane
Scythe, sickle
3 Rakes, hoe, weed-digger
2 Revolvers
1 Whitewashing machine
3 Wheelbarrows
Harness, wagon, horse
2 Watchman's clocks
Gong
Hand roller, four-horse roller
2 Wrenches, 3 chisels
2150 feet of Hose
18 Fire-plug reducers
Jack screw, saw clamp, saw setter
Bat bag, 3 base bags
Shears and wirecutter
25 Fire extinguishers
10 dozen Fire buckets
12 Ladders
2 Sprinkling cans
26 Water barrels

Bar Fixtures:

390 Beer mugs, 108 beer flips
92 Whiskey glasses
40 Ginger ale glasses
17 Claret glasses
25 Lemonade glasses
60 Water glasses
3 Scrub brushes, 3 feather dusters
2 Sugar buckets, 8 galvanized-iron buckets
Lemon squeezer, lemon knife, 2 lemon shakers
4 Ice scoops, ice shovel, large ice pick, 2 ice tongs
4 Paper buckets
6 Brass faucets
2 Mallets, 4 ice picks

2 Strainers, 7 corkscrews
6 Toddy spoons, 6 lemonade spoons
2 Glass straw holders, 2 packages straws
2 Glass brushes
3 Beer vents
Mirror, towel rack, comb and brush
50 Glass-drying towels, 8 roller towels, 20 counter towels
Hand truck
2 Ice coolers
2 Awnings
2 Mops, 3 brooms
19 Large wooden tubs

Ladies' Toilet Room:

Mirror and table
Lamp, chair, rug, folding screen

THE MOST important unpublished material used in research for this volume was the August Herrmann Papers in the Hall of Fame library at Cooperstown. This collection of more than seventy boxes containing thousands of letters, telegrams, memoranda, reports, and records pertaining to the years 1902–25, which was worked through systematically for the first time by anyone, is essential to any serious study of professional baseball during that era because of the many clues it provides to the day-by-day, behind-the-scenes operation of the business.

Other unpublished sources utilized were the Fiorello La Guardia Papers, stored in the Municipal Archives and Records Center, New York City, and the private correspondence of George Toporcer, former major-league player and executive, who also made available his scrapbooks and guidebooks, as did Lew Watts his collection of letters from professional ball players. The Alfred J. Scully baseball collection in the Chicago Historical Society includes letters, clippings on the Black Sox scandal, programs, announcements, Federal League score cards, and other memorabilia. In the New York Civil Liberties Union's file are clippings and pamphlets dealing with the I.W.W. trial before Judge Landis, and the New York Public Library's theatre collection has information about ball players' careers on the stage. The notebooks of Lee Allen, former historian at the Hall of Fame library, contain statistical data on ball players. Peter S. Craig, "Organized Baseball, An Industry Study of a Million Dollar Spectator Sport" (1950), an honors thesis written at Oberlin; Richard Armstrong, "The Unionization of Baseball" (1947), and Robert W. Smith, "The Business Side of Major League Baseball" (1948), unpublished senior theses written at Princeton, are all worth examination.

I have drawn much upon the work of New York Congressman Emanuel Celler's committee, Hearings Before the Subcommittee on Study of Monopoly Power, House of Representatives, 82nd Congress, 1st Session, Part 6, *Organized Baseball* (1952), and the committee's subsequent Report (1952). These 1875 pages of testimony, minutes of meetings, tables, charts, exhibits, and analysis are a storehouse of information about the operation and economic practices of the baseball industry. Further information of this kind is contained in the 3166 pages of Hearings Before the Antitrust Subcommittee, House of Representatives, 85th Congress, 1st Session, Parts 1–3, *Orga-*

nized Professional Team Sports (1957), and the 819 pages of Hearings Before the Subcommittee on Antitrust and Monopoly, United States Senate,
85th Congress, 2nd Session, *Organized Professional Team Sports* (1958).

The inquiry into Judge Landis's conduct is recorded in Hearings Before
the Judiciary Committee, House of Representatives, 66th Congress, 3rd Session, *Conduct of Judge Kenesaw Mountain Landis* (February 21, 1921),
and the subsequent report, *Impeachment Charges Against Judge Kenesaw
M. Landis* (March 2, 1921). The National Commission's Report for 1905–6
is in the Boston Public Library, and its Report covering 1906–8 is in the
New York Public Library, as are the minutes of the October 1901 New
York meeting of the National Association of Professional Baseball Leagues.
A copy of the first Constitution and By-Laws of the Association of Profes-
sional Ball Players (Los Angeles, 1926) is in the Herrmann Papers.

The weekly trade paper, *Sporting News*, with its comprehensive coverage
of baseball, is indispensable for research on the subject. Its files and those of
the New York *Times* from 1900 through 1930 were carefully combed.
Sporting Life, a leading early baseball paper, was used for the years
1900–1915. Files of other newspapers often cited in the text were examined
insofar as they were expected to supply additional details on particular
topics—for example, the Chicago *Tribune* and the Philadelphia *North
American* for the Black Sox scandal. More recent newspaper files and issues
of *Sporting News* often helped in relating the earlier period to the current
baseball scene.

Useful information was extracted from the *Spalding* and *Reach Official
Baseball Guides*, both of which continued to appear annually during the
years covered by this book. The *Baseball Blue Book*, also published yearly,
contains the various agreements and trade rules that comprise "baseball
law." For the playing records of individuals and teams I have relied upon
Hy Turkin and S. C. Thompson, *The Official Encyclopedia of Baseball*, 3rd
revised edition, and the *Little Red Book of Major League Baseball*, published annually by Elias Sports Bureau, Inc., whose general manager, Seymour Siwoff, supplied some special statistics requested.

For the legal aspects of professional baseball, articles were consulted in
the *Yale Law Journal, United States Law Review, New York Law Journal,
University of Chicago Law Review, University of Pennsylvania Law Review*, and *Columbia Legal Studies*. Among the leading articles, the best and
most comprehensive is Peter S. Craig, "Monopsony in Manpower: Organized Baseball Meets the Antitrust Laws," *Yale Law Journal* (March 1953).
L. A. Wilder, "Baseball and the Law," *Case and Comment* (August 1912),
surveys the laws pertaining to Sunday baseball. In "Baseball Law," *United
States Law Review* (May 1939), F. S. Johnson includes an interpretation of
the cases that resulted from the Federal League War. Harold Seymour,
"Ball, Bat and Bar," *Cleveland-Marshall Law Review* (September 1957),
outlines "baseball law" and its relation to civil law.

The text of court decisions in most of the law cases discussed in the book
were read and, whenever they were available, the briefs filed in connection
with them as well. These often revealed fresh information about professional

baseball apart from the legal questions at issue, much of it never published before. The most fruitful examples of such documents are the briefs and transcripts in the litigation between the Baltimore Federal League Club and Organized Baseball. This material contains: the stenographic minutes of the December 17, 1915, meeting of league representatives and the original memo outlining the terms of peace, which shed much light on the settlement of the Federal League War; the report of the Baltimore Federal League Club's directors to their stockholders, which supplies much factual data about the history and operation of the club and its controversy with Organized Baseball; information about the Federal League contract; the text of the 1914 Cincinnati Agreement with the Players' Fraternity; the entire correspondence and salient facts pertaining to the status of George Sisler and the controversy between the St. Louis and Pittsburgh clubs over him; and the revelation that Chief Justice Taft was approached to be Commissioner of Organized Baseball in 1918 and indicated he would accept but that the American League prevented his appointment.

Other examples of useful by-products derived from law cases are the original complaint of the Chicago White Sox against Hal Chase when he jumped to the Federal League, together with a copy of his contract and other documents, filed in the County Clerk's office, Buffalo, New York; the stenographic transcript of the testimony in the Lee Magee trial, which is in the Herrmann Papers and also reprinted in part in Lee Allen's *The National League Story* (New York, 1961); and the Brief for Appellees in Corbett and El Paso Baseball Club, Inc., *v.* Chandler, 6th Cir., Feb. 20, 1953, which has information on the contract between Organized Baseball and Western Union. The details of Bert Hageman's story are in B. B. P. Fraternity *v.* Boston Amer. L. B. B. Club 166, Appl. Div. 484, Affirmed 221, N. Y. 704 (1917). Some information is also available in the testimony heard in New York City in 1905 relating to Organized Baseball's own investigation of W. M. Kavanaugh's charges of a "conspiracy" in the American Association against Organized Baseball.

Countless books have been written about baseball, but prior to my projected three-volume series, the first volume of which, *Baseball: The Early Years*, appeared in 1960, there was no comprehensive, scholarly history of the subject. Meanwhile, baseball books continue to proliferate, practically all of them popularized works. Exceptions that were helpful in the research for this book were economist Ralph Andreano's *No Joy in Mudville* (Cambridge, Mass., 1965), a thoughtful little volume centered around a single theme, and Paul Gregory's *The Baseball Player: An Economic Study* (Washington, 1956), an analysis of the baseball player's occupation in terms of economics. A purportedly scholarly account that has come out in recent years merely retraces some of the ground first broken in *Baseball: The Early Years* and skims over the later period, undaunted by lack of adequate research. Many of the newest journalistic books that deal with particular aspects of baseball are of high quality—those by Leonard Koppett, Jim Brosnan, and Bill Veeck, Jr., to mention only a few.

The baseball books most worthwhile for the purposes of preparing this volume follow. Lee Allen's *The National League Story* (New York, 1961), and his *The American League Story* (New York, 1962), are lively surveys, though less critical than his earlier *100 Years of Baseball* (New York, 1950). Frederick Lieb's much more detailed *The Baseball Story* (New York, 1950) is the most serviceable general account. Older but still useful is Francis C. Richter, *Richter's History and Records of Baseball* (Philadelphia, 1914). Eliot Asinof, *Eight Men Out: The Black Sox and the 1919 World Series* (New York, 1963) is the best work on the subject, but for a stimulating, fresh interpretation of the scandal, Victor Luhrs, *The Great Baseball Mystery* (New York, 1966) should not be overlooked. Bill Veeck, *The Hustler's Handbook* (New York, 1965) is important especially for the chapter "Harry's Diary—1919," which reveals some new information about the scandal and the choice of Landis for commissioner.

Biographies and autobiographies (mostly ghostwritten) of players and other baseball figures abound. Few have much value but an exception is J. G. Taylor Spink's *Judge Landis and Twenty-Five Years of Baseball* (New York, 1947), a good summary of Landis's background and administration and one that does not whitewash him. Arthur Mann, *Branch Rickey, American in Action* (Boston, 1957) is a panegyric to Rickey but nevertheless includes much information about him. Rickey's own book, *The American Diamond: A Documentary of the Game of Baseball* (New York, 1965), is disappointing. Other biographies of merit are Edward Grant Barrow, *My Fifty Years of Baseball* (New York, 1951); Gustav Axelson, *"Commy": The Life Story of Charles A. Comiskey* (Chicago, 1919); and Tom Meany, *Babe Ruth* (New York, 1947). Ty Cobb (with Al Stump), *My Life in Baseball: The True Record* (New York, 1961) reveals more about Cobb than he intended.

Lawrence Ritter, *The Glory of Their Times* (New York, 1966) is a collection of player reminiscences that conveys much of the flavor of ball playing in the major leagues as it was in the early decades of the century. Charles Einstein, *Fireside Book of Baseball* (New York, 1956, 1958, 1968), 3 vols., is a rich anthology of baseball writings. Another fine collection is Bob Cook, *Wake up the Echoes* (New York, 1956), consisting of articles taken from the pages of the New York *Herald Tribune* and written by many leading sports writers including Heywood Broun, Red Smith, and John Kieran. Others of this type are Irving T. Marsh and Edward Ehre, *Best Sports Stories*, published annually; Peter Schwed and Herbert Warren Wind, *Great Stories from the World of Sport* (New York, 1958), 3 vols.; and Red Smith, *Red Smith's Sports Annual* (New York, 1961). Grantland Rice, *The Tumult and the Shouting: My Life in Sport* (New York, 1954) is also rewarding.

There is also a multitude of popularized major-league club histories by sports writers such as Shirley Povich, Harold Kaese, Franklin Lewis, Warren Brown, Frank Graham, Lee Allen, and particularly Fred Lieb, who has written a number of them as well as a biography of Connie Mack, all of which contain nuggets of information for the researcher.

For broader treatment of sports and leisure activities—their history and their place in American society—I used Foster Rhea Dulles, *America*

Learns to Play (Gloucester, Mass., 1963); Eric Larrabee and Rolf Meyersohn, eds., *Mass Leisure* (Glencoe, Ill., 1958); Robert Boyle, *Sport: Mirror of American Life* (Boston, 1963); Frederick W. Cozens and Florence S. Stempf, *Sports in American Life* (Chicago, 1953); and John R. Tunis, *The American Way in Sport* (New York, 1958).

Many books other than those devoted solely to baseball or sports also supplied grist for this volume. For the general background of the times essential for placing baseball in historical perspective, among the best are Federick Lewis Allen, *Only Yesterday* (New York, 1951) and his *The Big Change* (New York, 1952); Arthur S. Link, *American Epoch: A History of the United States Since the 1890's* (New York, 1958); Harvey Wish, *Contemporary America, The National Scene Since 1900* (New York, 1945); and William E. Leuchtenburg, *The Perils of Prosperity, 1914–32* (Chicago, 1958). Others in this category are Walter Lord, *The Good Years: From 1900 to the First World War* (New York, 1960); Alan Valentine, *1913: America Between Two Worlds* (New York, 1962); Samuel Rapport and Patricia Schartle, *America Remembers: Our Best-Loved Customs and Traditions* (Garden City, 1956); and William E. Bohn, *I Remember America* (New York, 1962).

Material on Landis's pre-baseball career was found in William T. Hutchinson, *Lowden of Illinois: The Life Story of Frank O. Lowden* (Chicago, 1957), Vol. I; Bill Haywood, *Bill Haywood's Book* (New York, 1929); H. C. Peterson and Gilbert Fite, *Opponents of War* (Madison, Wis., 1957); and Henry F. Pringle, "A Grand Stand Judge," in *Big Frogs* (New York, 1928).

Among the books on journalism used are Donald Elder, *Ring Lardner* (New York, 1956); Stanley Walker, *City Editor* (New York, 1934); and Stanley Woodward, *Sports Page* (New York, 1949). Also useful is Alvin F. Harlow, *Old Wires and New Waves: A History of the Telegraph, Telephone and Wireless* (New York, 1936).

Much important information came from Leo Katcher, *The Big Bankroll: The Life and Times of Arnold Rothstein* (New York, 1958), Gene Fowler, *The Great Mouthpiece; A Life of William J. Fallon* (New York, 1931), and Nat Ferber's exposé *I Found Out* (New York, 1939), with its detailed account of bucket shops. Lloyd Morris, *Incredible New York* (New York, 1951) and M. R. Werner, *Tammany Hall* (Westport, Conn., 1932) were also of assistance.

Other works that should be cited are Stanley B. Frank, *The Jew in Sports* (New York, 1936); George Wharton Pepper, *Philadelphia Lawyer, An Autobiography* (Philadelphia, 1944), and his *Men and Issues* (New York, 1924); Joe Laurie, Jr., *Vaudeville: From the Honky-Tonks to the Palace* (New York, 1953); John J. Riley, *A History of the American Soft Drink Industry* (Washington, D.C., 1958); Charles H. Candler, *Asa Griggs Candler* (Emory University, Atlanta, 1950); Nelson Algren, *Chicago: City on the Make* (Garden City, 1951); and Cleveland Amory and Frederic Bradlee, eds., *Vanity Fair: Selections from America's Most Memorable Magazine* (New York, 1960).

The periodical literature on baseball is voluminous. More than a thou-

sand articles were read in magazines and journals both contemporary and
current, both popular and scholarly. The most useful periodicals were *Baseball Magazine, Harper's Weekly, Literary Digest, Baseball Digest, Munsey's
Magazine, Independent, Collier's, Outlook, Nation's Business, Nation,
Newsweek, North American Review, Outing, Saturday Evening Post, Leslie's Magazine, New Republic, Life, American Magazine, Sports Illustrated,
McClure's Magazine, Everybody's Magazine, Esquire,* and *American Mercury.*

The most valuable scholarly articles were:

John R. Betts, "The Technological Revolution and the Rise of Sport," *Mississippi Valley Historical Review* (September 1953).

Harold C. Evans, "Baseball In Kansas, 1867–1940," *Kansas Historical Society Quarterly* (May 1940).

Joe Gerstein, "Anti-Semitism in Baseball," *Jewish Life* (July 1952).

"Inventions New and Interesting," *Scientific American* (September 1912).

H. S. Lehman, "Geographic Origin of Professional Baseball Players,"
Journal of Education Research (October 1940).

Walter Neale, "The Peculiar Economics of Professional Sports," *Quarterly
Journal of Economics* (February 1964).

Simon Rottenberg, "The Baseball Players' Labor Market," *Journal of Political Economy* (June 1956).

Harold Seymour, "Unions Fail in Organized Baseball," *Industrial Bulletin*,
New York State Department of Labor (April 1960).

Popular articles on baseball vary greatly in quality. Many of them are of
little or no value, and even the better ones must be used with caution, since
so many of them are biased and uncritical. The following sampling indicates
some of the more helpful selections from popular journals:

"The Baseball Business from the Inside," *Collier's* (March 1922).

"Big League Baseball," *Fortune* (August 1937).

H. Bradley, "McGraw," *American Mercury* (August 1932).

Hugh Fullerton, "Baseball on Trial," *New Republic* (October 20, 1920).

——, "Baseball the Business and the Sport," *Review of Reviews* (April
1921).

——, "How the Ball Players of the Big Leagues Live and Act When off
the Diamond," *American Magazine* (July 1911).

David Fultz, "President's Report," *Baseball Magazine* (February 1916).

Gerald Holland, "The Babe Ruth Papers," *Sports Illustrated* (December 21,
1959).

E. J. Kahn, "Profiles: The Story of Coca Cola," *New Yorker* (February and
March 1959).

Roger Kahn, "The Real Ruth," *Baseball Digest* (October–November 1959).

W. J. Klem with W. J. Slocum, "Umpire Bill Klem's Own Story," *Collier's*
(March and April 1951).

F. C. Lane, "The Sensational Evers Deal," *Baseball Magazine* (August
1914).

John Lardner, "That Was Baseball: The Crime of Shufflin Phil Douglas," *New Yorker* (May 12, 1956).

———, "Remember the Black Sox?" *Saturday Evening Post* (April 1938).

Marie O'Day, "They Reared Babe Ruth," *Catholic Digest* (September 1938).

Irving Sanborn, "The Slimy Trail of the Baseball Pool," *Baseball Magazine* (July 1925).

Robert Shaplen, "The Raid That Nearly Ruined Baseball," *Sports Illustrated* (August 1962).

C. D. Stewart, "United States of Base-Ball," *Century* (July 1907).

Al Stump, "Ty Cobb's Wild, 10-Month Fight to Live," *True Magazine* (December 1961).

C. S. Thompson, "15,000,000 a Year for Baseball," *Collier's* (July 1910).

Lewis Thompson and Charles Boswell, "Say It Ain't So, Joe!" *American Heritage* (June 1960).

F. Wallace, "College Men in the Big Leagues," *Scribner's* (October 1927).

E. F. Wolfe, "A Baseball Yarn Made Home Run Heroes," *Nation's Business* (April 1940).

E. M. Woolley, "Business Side of Baseball," *McClure's* (July 1912).

Victor S. Yarros, "The Chicago Social Trial," *Nation* (January 25, 1919).

Finally, a number of miscellaneous sources employed should be recorded. These include a pamphlet by Charles H. Genslinger, "Clark C. Griffith Ball and Bat Fund: Final Report" (Washington, D.C., 1919), in the New York Public Library; the National League's annual *Green Book* and National League press releases sent me regularly by Dave Grote, the league's director of public relations; letters and other material from officials of Rawlings Sporting Goods Company, A. G. Spalding and Bros., and the Coca Cola Company, containing information about their products as related to baseball; some information supplied by Western Union; and a television script by Roger Kahn, "Babe Ruth: A Look Behind the Legend" (n. d.). Firsthand information was also gained from conversations with various major leaguers who played during the period covered by this book, particularly George Toporcer, Ben De Mott, George Cunningham, Edd Roush, Joe Jackson, Zack Wheat, Sam Rice, and Charles Jamieson. I also drew upon my own boyhood experience at Ebbetts Field, especially my three summers as batboy, two of them for visiting National League teams and one for Brooklyn.